Frontiers in Social Dilemmas Research

Springer
Berlin
Heidelberg
New York
Barcelona
Budapest
Hong Kong
London
Milan
Paris
Santa Clara
Singapore
Tokyo

Wim B. G. Liebrand
David M. Messick (Eds.)

Frontiers in Social Dilemmas Research

With 67 Figures
and 41 Tables

Springer

Prof. Dr. Wim B. G. Liebrand
University of Groningen
Social Science Information Technology
Grote Rozenstraat 15
NL-9712 TG Groningen, The Netherlands

Prof. Dr. David M. Messick
Northwestern University
J. L. Kellogg Graduate School of Management
356 Leverone Hall
2001 Sheridan Road
Evanston, IL 60208-2001, USA

ISBN-13: 978-3-642-85263-3 e-ISBN-13: 978-3-642-85261-9
DOI: 10.1007/978-3-642-85261-9

Cataloging-in Publication Data applied for
Die Deutsche Bibliothek – CIP-Einheitsaufnahme
Frontiers in social dilemmas research: with 41 tables/Wim B. G. Liebrand; David M. Messick (ed.). – Berlin; Heidelberg; New York; Barcelona; Budapest; Hong Kong; London; Milan; Paris; Santa Clara; Singapore; Tokyo: Springer, 1996
NE: Liebrand, Wim B. G. [Hrsg.]

Softcover reprint of the hardcover 1st edition 1996

SPIN 10539344 42/2202-5 4 3 2 1 0 – Printed on acid-free paper

Preface

This book contains a selection of the contributions to the 6th International Conference on Social Dilemmas which was held in Wassenaar, The Netherlands, in June, 1995. The first of these conferences, held in 1984, had 17 participants, nearly all of whom were social psychologists. The current conference, in contrast, had more than 100 applications coming from many disciplines. This growth, in a mere 12 years, evidences the importance of the topic and the breadth of interest in it in the social and behavioral sciences.

This conference would not have happened without the support of the Netherlands Institute for Advanced Study in the Humanities and Social Sciences (NIAS). They provided a stimulating environment for the research group "Understanding Social Dilemmas" during the 1995/96 academic year. As the conclusion to this research year, NIAS and the Royal Dutch Academy of Sciences (KNAW) provided the opportunity and resources to organize this 6th Social Dilemma Conference. Although the size of the conference stretched NIAS's facilities, the conference went smoothly thanks largely to the skill and diplomacy of the NIAS staff. Without them the conference could not have been successful nor would this book exist. We are deeply grateful to NIAS, KNAW, and to the many NIAS people who made this conference a success.

Groningen , Evanston.
March, 1996

Wim Liebrand and David Messick

Contents

3 The Dynamic Perspective; Computer Simulations of Micro-macro Dynamics

Social Dilemmas: Individual, Collective, and Dynamic Perspectives

Wim B. G. Liebrand[1] and David M. Messick[2]

[1] SWI, University of Groningen, NL-9712 TG Groningen, NL
[2] Department of Organization Behavior, KGSM, Northwestern University, Evanston, IL 60201, USA

1 Introduction

Social dilemmas are complex situations in which we can choose what is in our own immediate best interest or what is in the best interest of our groups, which include ourselves as well as others. Finding solutions for social dilemmas constitutes one of the most important challenges for the social and behavioral sciences.

Social dilemmas are found everywhere; in both small and large social groups, in rural as well as urban settings, and in informal as well as formal organizations. A real-life example is the temptation to over-harvest fish and other renewable resources. Each additional ton of fish increases the fisherman's profits, but harms the collective fish stock, ultimately harming not only others but the fisherman himself. When all fishermen overharvest, the fishery may disappear as has happened with a number of species of fish. Everyone is worse off. Besides the overuse of vital resources, the underuse of behavior that would benefit the environment qualifies as another natural example. If we all walked more and drove less, we would all breathe better air. Other examples are: nonpaying riders on public transportation systems, arms reduction, overpopulation, and information hoarding.

Social dilemmas are interpersonal and intergroup situations that are characterized by an unfortunate pattern of incentives. The pattern is unfortunate because it tends to create highly unsatisfying outcomes for the participants--outcomes that are unsatisfying because all of the actors involved realize that each of them individually would have been much better off if everyone had behaved differently. The difficulty, however, is that the incentives to behave differently are not to be found in any short term perspective.

The interest in social dilemmas is widespread throughout the social and behavioral sciences. That interest arose because of a focus, beginning more or less with World War II, on the study of decision making. Early models of decision making were built on the concept of the "rational person" or "dollar maximizer" who projected the consequences of the various possible actions available, estimated the probabilities of events not directly under personal control, and then maximized personal gain.

Although the model of the rational person is intuitively compelling and in some sense "should" be valid, it was immediately apparent that this model was a poor description of the actual behavior of both lay persons and decision "experts." In other words, people generally do not conform to the elegant but simple predictions that these mathematically-derivedtheories of behavior made. Therefore, from the beginnings of the formal study of decision making, investigators - especially those from the social and behavioral sciences - have attempted to construct models that can better explain the actual behavior of decision makers.

The "discovery" of social dilemmas (in the sense that they could be formally described) was of major importance in research on decision making because it provided a formal demonstration of the inadequacy of the rational model to accompany the empirical demonstration. In a social dilemma, a collection of rational actors arrive at outcomes which are inferior to ones they could have received if they had each been "irrational".

Probably because of the combination of theoretical interest and real-world applicability, social dilemmas have come to be a major research area within the fields of experimental social psychology, sociology, political science, economics, management science, information science, and of course mathematics. More perhaps than most research fields, the study of social dilemmas always had an interdisciplinary flavor; conferences and edited volumes devoted to social dilemmas are characterized by contributions from many disciplines. This interdisciplinary field has been heavily dominated by game theory and the use of experimental games. By far the most renowned experimental game is the Prisoner's Dilemma Game, a prototypical social dilemma.

The Prisoner's Dilemma Game is illustrated in Luce and Raiffa (1957, p. 95) with the following anecdote.

> Two suspects are taken into custody and separated. The district attorney is certain that they are guilty of a specific crime, but he does not have adequate evidence to convict them at a trial. He points out to each prisoner, separately, that each of them has two alternatives: to confess to the crime the police are sure they have done, or not to confess. If they both do not confess, then the district attorney states he will book them on some very minor trumped-up charge such as petty larceny and illegal possession of a weapon, and they both will receive minor punishment; if they both confess they will be prosecuted, but he will recommend less than the most severe sentence; but if one confesses and the other does not, then the confessor will receive lenient treatment for turning state's evidence whereas the latter will get "the book" slapped at him. In terms of years in a penitentiary, the strategic problem might reduce to:

Table 1 The Prisoner's Dilemma.

		Prisoner B:	
Prisoner A:		Not Confess	Confess
	Not Confess	1 year each	10 years for A 1 month for B
	Confess	1 month for A 10 years for B	5 years each

For each prisoner it is obvious that confessing is better than not confessing, regardless of what the other prisoner does. Hence it is in their own interest to confess. The dilemma emerges now: confessing is better for both, thus the expected outcome is 5 years imprisonment for both, but they could have gotten one year only by not confessing.

The consequences associated with the four possible combination of choices are such that they result in the preference orderings depicted in Table 2. These preference orderings represent those of the standard Prisoner's Dilemma Game as used in much empirical research.

Table 2 Strict preference orderings for a Prisoner's Dilemma Game; (4) most preferred, (1) least preferred; the first number refers to the preference for you, the second one refers to the preferences of the other player.

	Other: C	Other: D
You: C	3 , 3	1 , 4
You: D	4 , 1	2 , 2

In this situation, C stands for 'cooperation' and D for 'defection'. The D choice, that is the selfish act, dominates the C choice, the choice in the collective interest. No matter what choice is made by the other person, the chooser is better off making the D choice to C. However, a mutual D choice results in the second worst outcome cell for both persons whereas each could have got a better outcome by choosing C.

Social dilemmas can be conceived as a generalization of the basic Prisoner Dilemma. Formal definitions have been provided among others by Dawes (1980) and Liebrand (1983). Dawes defines social dilemmas as Prisoner's Dilemmas for more than two people. In the broader definition by Liebrand, social dilemmas are defined as situations in which a self-interested choice yields the best payoff to the actor in at least one of the possible outcome configurations. Each of these self-interested choices, however, involves costs to the other people involved. When a large number of people make the self-interested choice, the costs accumulate, creating a situation in which everybody would have done better had they decided not to act in their own private interest.

2 The three key mechanisms in social dilemmas

Multi-person social dilemmas are significantly more complex than two person Prisoner Dilemmas. These complex situations involve three inter-related clusters of issues:

- at the level of individual actors, people decide whether or not they will act in their own direct interest;
- at the aggregate level we observe processes and characteristics which not necessarily can be explained by a simple generalization from the behavior of a single actor, and which in their turn may influence the actor's behavior at the micro level;
- through time, choices at the individual level influence that aggregate level and vice versa, creating dynamic processes which may (or may not) stabilize for longer or shorter periods.

Most of the research that social dilemma researchers, especially that of social psychologists, have done to date has been on the individual level. The reason for this emphasis is probably due to social psychologists' focus in the past several decades on individual cognitive processes. It is interesting to observe that the three key issues underlying social dilemmas relate to the 'level of analysis problem' identified in 1948 by Krech and Crutchfield who asked:

> Can social phenomena be fruitfully investigated on the level of individual behavior? Are there other, equally promising levels of social analysis? What are the appropriate units of analysis at each of these levels? What are the relations among these several levels of analysis?" (p. 14).

It is obvious that the individual perspective, the collective, and the dynamic perspective deal with different, but interrelated questions. They each have the potential to illuminate different aspects of social dilemmas. It should, however, also be obvious that in order to significantly improve our understanding of social dilemmas, we need all three levels of analysis. We have employed this trichotomy to organize the chapters in this book into three categories depending on the predominant level of analysis employed by the authors.

We begin the book with chapters that emphasize the collective or aggregate perspective. Vlek's paper reviews the importance of social dilemmas from the point of view of risk management at a societal and global standpoint. The contributions of Grzelak and Nejardt, on the one hand and Biel, Eek, and Gärling, on the other, describe public surveys, in Poland and Sweden, respectively, of attitudes toward issues of collective concern. Finally, the experimental contribution of Wilke, van Dijk, Morel, Monnikhof, & Zandvliet explores the role of coalitions in organizational social dilemmas.

At the level of individual choice, Kerr and Harris describe an experiment examining the role efficacy as the mechanism by means of which social motives influence individual cooperativeness. Van Dijk and Wilke probe the important role of fairness in social dilemmas while Foddy and Veronese ask if knowledge of the "rational" choice is sufficient to cause people to choose it. Wilke, Rutte, & Bornstein, as Vlek suggested, view environmental risk as a public good. Mlicki proposes the ancient custom of posting hostages can be a solution to social dilemmas while the last two papers in the section, those of Poppe & Zwikker and Snijders & Raub, explore two motivational influences on cooperation.

One of the features that distinguishes this book is the focus on dynamic processes. Computer simulation, of which we will say more presently, has provided a methodology for the exploration of the dynamic interplay of individual level processes and aggregate outcomes. Liebrand & Messick describe the global consequences of individual choice heuristics and Macy performs a similar analysis for neural networks and genetic algorithms. Conte offers a computational model for cooperative problem solving. Joireman, Shelley, Teta, Wilding, & Kuhlman explore the emergence of social motives through computer simulation and Takagi uses the same methodology to probe the foundations of generalized exchange (in contrast to the more common reciprocal exchange) for producing self-sacrificial altruism. Hegselmann examines how cellular automata, in one and two dimensions, can produce clusters of cooperation from simple processes, and Yamagishi & Hayashi demonstrate the importance of having a choice in whether or not one will interact with someone else. Stokman & Zeggelink show how friendship cliques can emerge within association networks, and Suleiman & Fisher show how intra-group policies, like the duration of a political term of office, can have a major impact on the course of inter-group conflict.

The papers in the third section of the book employ the relatively new methodology of computer simulation. It may be useful to say something more about this approach.

3 Computer Simulations

Computer simulations have been used in the social and behavioral sciences for many years, although their use has not been common. Their first applications, in line with the first usages of the digital computer, were with data analysis and statistics. The use of the computer for other than number crunching became possible when the first higher programming languages, like Fortran (1957) and Algol, LISP and COBOL (1960) became available. In fact, the first interactive computer game 'Spacewar' was developed in 1962 by Steve Russell, then a student at MIT. Another pioneer was ELIZA (Weizenbaum, 1966), a renowned program in which counseling sessions were simulated using natural language.

Among the early advocates of computer simulation were Newell, Shaw and Simon (1958) and Hovland (1960). They stressed the value of simulation for theory development about human problem solving. At that time the future developments of the computer seemed to be without any limits. Simon and Newell, for example, predicted in 1958 that within the next decade a digital computer would write music that had considerable aesthetic value, and that most theories in psychology would take the form of computer programs.

Progress, however, has been much, much slower than expected. With respect to computer simulation in the social and behavioral sciences, most applications were published after 1980 when the personal computer became more powerful and widely available. In a recent overview, Garson (1994) lists 168 social science computer simulation tools. He classifies them in terms of the underlying structural models: equation systems and probability, resource allocation and social process designs. Within the equation and probability models we find Forrester's Club of Rome world-resources models, and Feinberg and Johnson's (1988) model of a crowd and an outside agitator.

Among the Resource Allocation Models there are simulation tools for exploring The tragedy of the Commons (Ramsey, 1982), and tools with animation facilities like SimCity (1988) that allow students to develop and run a city. In the Social Process Models the users are allowed to "walk through" a set of historical (The Watergate Game, 1984) or realistic (The School Psychologist Simulation Program, 1992) simulations. Garson (1994, p. 69) concludes that better hardware facilities and new techniques like hypertext, interactive fiction, natural language, expert systems and pattern recognition, will make possible a new generation of social science simulation tools that will have a great impact on instruction, research and policy making.

Thus far, the impact of simulation on theory building, however, has been limited (cf. Ostrom, 1988; Troitzsch, in press). Fortunately, as this book on research in social dilemmas shows, times seem to be changing. Because of the increased availability of computers, more researchers are beginning to see application possibilities for them. The computer is not only a machine for highly complex calculations, it is, and it always was, a machine to manipulate symbols according to specified rules (algorithms). Symbols are part of a notational system, like computer language or our own natural language. Symbols therefore can represent anything, numbers, figures, or concepts. The same notational system that is used for symbols can represent algorithms. An algorithm contains intelligence because it 'knows' how to operate on the symbols in order to perform a specific task. The algorithm and the symbols constitute a computer program which can mimic or predict social behavior. To revise Simon and Newell's (1958) statement: computer programs have the form that behavioral and social theories should have.

A second reason that computer simulation is growing in popularity among social dilemma researchers is because of the highly complex social behavior that is involved. The late social psychologist, Thomas Ostrom (1988) identified five complexities which are can exceed the ability of theorists to hold all relevant postulates in mind and to accurately generate predictions. Each of these complexities is an intrinsic part of social dilemmas. They concern the multitude of latent and overt variables and all of their interactions, which are involved in the continuous action of all participants (1988, p. 385-390). Social dilemmas therefore provide a fertile research area for the use of computer simulation for theory construction and verification.

A computer model of social dilemmas may resemble mathematical models developed earlier. The models may be cellular automata, social networks, or neural networks. These models consist of nodes (automata, actors, neurons) and a specification of the relations between these nodes. The cellular automata paradigm, described by Wolfram (1986), is a well known computer model in physics, biology and population dynamics. Cellular automata consist of a number of cells (automata) arranged in a regular spacial pattern such as a checker board. Each automaton can adapt a finite ("cooperate" or "defect") number of states, depending upon the states of the automata in its neighborhood. The state of a system of cellular automata evolves over time because updating rules which change an automata state also change the environment of other automata.

In social networks a similar model is employed. Nodes represent individuals. The social relations among the individuals are characterized as directed connections (arrows) between the nodes (for an overview, see Wasserman & Faust, 1994). This type of model is a bit more flexible than cellular automata because it easily allows for different types of relationships between the actors. Basically, the structure of the connections between the actors depends upon the behavior of those actors.

The internal dynamics of neural networks is generally even more flexible than that of cellular automata and social networks. Neurons, are modeled as simple input-output elements, organized in several layers. Typically each neuron has several input and one output line. The parallel and directed information flow is modelled like the synaptic transmissions that occur between real neurons. On the basis of the differently weighted incoming signals, a transfer function determines whether or not there will be a signal on the output line. The network continuously adapts itself by changing internal parameters like weights, activation states and strength of connections. The parallel processing of information constitutes the most important difference with the cellular automata and social networks.

The computer simulations described in this book illustrate all three types of models. We propose that the depth and variety of the simulations that are described here testify to the power of this element of the frontier of social dilemma research.

References

Dawes, R. M. (1980). Social Dilemmas. *Annual Review of Psychology, 31*, 169-193.

Feinberg, W. E. & Johnson, N. R. (1988). Outside agitators and crowds: Results from a computer simulation model. *Social Forces, 67,* 398-423.

Garson, G. D. (1994). Social science computer simulation: Its history, design, and future. *Social Science Computer Review, 12,* 55-82.

Hovland, C.I. (1960). Computer simulation of thinking. *American Psychologist, 15*, 687-693.

Krech, D. & Crutchfield, R. S. (1948). *Theory and Problems of Social Psychology.* New York: McGraw-Hill.

Liebrand, W. B. G. (1983). A classification of social dilemma games. *Simulation and Games, 14,* 123-138.

Luce, R. D. & Raiffa, H. (1957). *Games and Decisions.* New York: Wiley.

Newell, A., Shaw, J.C., & Simon H.A. (1958). Elements of a theory of human problem solving. *Psychological Review, 65*, 151-166.

Ostrom, T.M. (1988). Computer simulation: The third symbol system. *Journal of Experimental Social Psychology, 24*, 381-392.

Simon, H.A. and Newell A. (1958) Heuristic problem solving: The next advance in operations research. *Operations Research*, January-February, 1-10.

Troizsch, K. G. (in press). Multilevel process modeling in the social sciences: Mathematical analysis and computer simulation. In W.B.G. Liebrand, R. Hegselmann, & A. Nowak (Eds.), *Computer modeling and the study of dynamic social processes*. Beverley Hills, CA: Sage

Wasserman, S., & Faust, K. (1994). *Social Network Analysis.* Cambridge: Cambridge University Press.

Weizenbaum, J. (1966) ELIZA - A computer program for the study of natural language communication between man and machine. *Communications of the ACM, vol 9*, 36-45.

Wolfram, S. (1986). *Theory and applications of cellular automata.* Singapore: World Scientific.

Collective Risk Generation and Risk Management: the Unexploited Potential of the Social Dilemmas Paradigm

Charles A.J. Vlek[1]

Department of Psychology, University of Groningen
Grote Kruisstraat 2/1, 9712 TS Groningen, The Netherlands

1 Introduction

A social dilemma is a situation where a collective cost or risk is incurred, taken or generated through the combined negative external effects of various individuals who act (relatively) independently from one another. Vivid present-day examples of collective risk generation via individual activities are: littering of public places by individuals spending some time in them; threats to the quality of public education through individuals' desires to increase private spending capacity; loss of natural open space through individual preferences for more spacious household premises; over-harvesting of ocean fish stocks for the survival of individual fishing organizations; local and regional air pollution from the use of numerous motor vehicles; and wholesale deforestation of tropical regions for the subsistence of local farmers and cattle-breeders. In many cases, collective risks also increase through the sheer growth in the number of separate actors such as inhabitants, households and commercial enterprises.

Social dilemmas are the subject of a fascinating area of scientific investigation. Reading or re-reading Hardin (1968), Platt (1973), Dawes, Delay and Chaplin (1974), Dawes (1980, 1991), Edney (1980), Stroebe and Frey (1982), Messick and Brewer (1983), Yamagishi (1986), Rapoport and Bornstein (1987), Liebrand, Messick and Wilke (1992*a*) and Komorita and Parks (1995), one gets taken by the disconcerting compellingness of socially damaging patterns of individual choices. One gets impressed by the decision-theoretic formalisms which indicate that social disaster may result from strictly rational, i.e., individually preferable economic behavior. And one gets convinced that 'cooperation for the common good' is the key towards resolving a social dilemma. If not imposed upon the relevant actors via certain structural measures - which in fact change the nature of the dilemma or

[1] The author is indebted to the editors and an anonimous reviewer for their wise suggestions regarding the improvement of an earlier version.

reduce individuals' freedom of choice, such cooperation would depend upon sufficient knowledge, morality and trust (Dawes, 1980).

Urgently needed innovative research, however, is held back by a professional inclination of investigators to stay close to the game-theoretic origins and formalisms of social dilemmas (e.g., Luce & Raiffa, 1957; Rapoport & Chammah, 1965), just like many studies of individual decision making have long suffered from their background in rational decision theory (see Beach, 1990). For too long, social dilemmas research has been based upon prespecified, well-defined social dilemma games, while largely ignoring relevant pre- and post-dilemma processes, and also ignoring the wider context and the oftentimes dynamic character of many a social dilemma situation. Hence, even after thirty years of social dilemmas research, behavioral scientists have not made available a comprehensive conceptual framework and operational methodology, by which practical social dilemma problems of varying type and scope may be sufficiently understood, and collective risks effectively controlled.

In this paper, the nature of social dilemmas (SDs) is described from the perspective of collective risk generation and risk management in real-life situations. The primary message is that the 'social dilemmas paradigm' (SD-paradigm, for short) is a systematic and comprehensive way of thinking about collective risk generation and risk management via the external effects of individual activities, and that it should (eventually) yield concepts, models, methods and procedures for diagnostic problem analysis, decision making on risk acceptance, risk control via individual behavior change, and computer simulations of dynamic social dilemma situations.

In Section 2 we will consider the occurrence of negative externalities, their varied sources, and the different conflicts that may arise when benefits have to be weighed against external costs and risks. A further description of social dilemmas is given in Section 3 which also provides an example and a distinction of three basic types. The broader conception provided enables us in Section 4 to distinguish three different actor perspectives, ranging from purely individual to entirely collective. Nine focal points of SD-analysis for researchers and policy makers will be indicated in Section 5. Against the background of relevant theory and research, these focal points of the SD-paradigm will be discussed one by one, in three subsections entitled 'problem diagnosis' (5.1), 'decision making' (5.2) and 'risk control' (5.3). The pivotal issue of strategies for behavior change to reduce collective risks will be separately treated in Section 6. Section 7 deals with a comprehensive risk management system known as tradeable exploitation rights, and with bond pledging or hostage posting. Inevitably, after all this, Section 8 offers a critical reconsideration of classic concepts in SDs research, such as selfishness, cooperation and rationality. To end the paper, Section 9 provides conclusions about the potential of the extended SD-paradigm for systematic diagnosis, decision making, risk control, and computer simulation of realistic social dilemma situations. Section 9 also draws attention to the inherent collective-risk generation nature of the economic free-market system, and to the 'democratic dilemma' in the establishment of institutions and procedures for collective-risk management.

2 Varieties of externalities

Life is full of negative externalities. We don't pay for such external consequences when we cause them to others, or to the environment. And we are not compensated for undergoing them, when others, or the environment, are causing them to us. Think, for example about occupying a place in a queue, carrying out a noisy do-it-yourself job at home, dumping waste in the woods, or accelerating your heavy motorcycle on a major city avenue. Sometimes the external effects of individual behavior are immediate and acute, and they may either be short-lived or have lasting impacts - such as from accidents. In other cases, behavioral externalities may go immediately unnoticed - such as exhaust gases from motorized transport, but they may have slowly developing impacts which manifest themselves only in the long run. Industrial installations may also cause significant public nuisance and environmental damage. Evidently, petrochemical refineries, municipal waste incinerators, bio-industrial pig-farms, and civilian airports all have their social and economic importance. But they are also sources of external nuisance, costs and risks to society and the environment.

The various examples indicate that there are *specific single* sources of externalities, such as amateur home-carpenters, disco-bar managers and electric power plant operators. But there are also *diffuse multiple* sources such as motorized traffic, park recreationists, households using their fossil-fueled heating systems, and industrial waste producers. Similarly, the receivers or (potential) victims of the negative externalities may be fairly well *concentrated* in a given location, but they may also be *wide-spread* and difficult to identify. Table 1 summarizes and illustrates the categorization following single versus multiple sources of externalities, and concentrated versus wide-spread receivers or victims of the external effects.

To be complete, Table 1 should contain a third, temporal dimension reflecting the fact that externalities may have immediate or delayed negative effects (or both). For example, the noisy motor-cycle on a city avenue embodies a short-term, transitory nuisance; but the ground-water pollution by excess pesticides on agricultural crops may constitute a long-term, gradually accumulating environmental problem.

Given that most activities having negative externalities are undertaken to achieve certain benefits for their initiator, the question is what there is to be weighed or traded off in a comparison of benefits versus (external) costs and risks. In the upper left cell of Table 1 specific single-actor benefits are to be weighed against concentrated nuisance, costs and/or risks to the local

Table 1. Different sources and receivers of externalities, with illustration of relevant activities.

		receivers/victims	
		concentrated	wide-spread
sources/ beneficiaries	single, specific	home-carpenters disco-bars small factories	waste incinerators electric power plants large airports
	diffuse, multiple	waste dumpers park vacationers car parkers (city)	passenger transport (cars) freight transport (trucks) household energy consumption

environment. In the upper right cell there seems to be a single specific initiator and source of externalities all right, but the benefits may be indirectly distributed across a larger population. However, the external nuisance, costs and risks also spread out, but relatively less so, thereby yielding a 'sacrificed' group of receivers (who may say 'NIMBY': "not in my back yard"; see Freudenburg and Pastor, 1992; Vlek, 1995*a*). The lower left cell of Table 1 offers a comparison between diffuse and limited multiple-actor benefits, and a local arena where nuisance, costs and risks are accumulated. And the lower right cell demands a balancing of diffuse multiple-actor benefits against wide-spread multiple-victim nuisance, costs and risks. It is here, especially, that the temporal dimension is significant; generally, many short-term individual benefits are to be weighed against long-term collective risks.

Conflicts of interest are involved to the extent that the beneficiaries at the sources of the externalities are other persons or organizations than the victims at the receiving side. There may be conflicts: (1) between limited single-source beneficiaries (e.g., the home-carpenter) and local, neighboring victims (annoyed by the noise); (2) between large single-source initiators (e.g., the airport manager) and a wide-spread population of victims (who suffer but can't deny the source's social importance); (3) between diffuse multiple beneficiaries (e.g., car parkers) and local victims (deploring the loss of space in their neighborhood); and (4) between a diffuse set of multiple beneficiaries (e.g., energy consumers) and a wide-spread collection of victims (who may suffer from air pollution).

The fourth case, the particular 'mixed motive' situation illustrated in the lower right cell of Table 1, is of special interest for the present chapter. Here, the two parties of (multiple) initiators/beneficiaries and (wide-spread) receivers/victims strongly overlap. Such a situation is usually characterized by direct individual benefits versus indirect collective costs and risks - which may significantly detract from the individual benefits, either on the short or on the long term. Here, reducing the collective cost and risk is dependent upon behavior change by all benefiting actors ("A better environment begins with yourself", says the Dutch Government - hopefully). There may, however, be an additional temptation to expect that such changes or restraint will be manifested by the other actors first, so that the individual may (but may not *need* to) join in when collective success is becoming apparent. Hence, the intrapersonal or intragroup dilemma, between acting either selfishly or cooperatively, may be strengthened by an interpersonal or intergroup conflict in which your own and others' interests collide.

It is the combined occurrence of the negative externalities of two or more individuals' actions, either immediate or delayed, which constitutes *a collective cost or risk, or cost/risk generation process*.[2] The problem of collective risk taking or risk generation through individually beneficial activities is conventionally referred to as a 'social dilemma'. The simplest situation in which this may be demonstrated is the two-person prisoners' dilemma in which the dominantly preferred choices of two actors combine to yield a jointly undesirable outcome. A specific example and two milder variants are given in Section 3.

3 What is a social dilemma?

A social dilemma is a situation of conflict between individual optimality and collective optimality of expected behavior consequences of two or more interdependent actors. The strength of this conflict largely depends upon the pattern of payoffs or utility values, the decision rule applied, and the number of actors involved. Typically, each individual's net (or ultimate) payoffs are contingent upon his/her own as well as others' behavior. A simple, schematized example is the following.

Suppose that the one half and the other half of the Amsterdam population are the two distinct actors in a social dilemma 'game'. Each actor, A and B in Table 2, has an independent choice between traveling (e.g., in going to work one morning) either by car or by bicycle. Before making their own choice, the one half of Amsterdam is not informed about the other half's preferences, and vice versa. Table 2 gives an imaginary pay-off matrix. The left entries in the four cells represent utility scores (on a 1-10 scale) for actor A whose options are ordered along the rows. The right cell entries are utility scores for actor B whose options are given along the columns. For example,

---

[2] Collectively combined externalities may be manifested either as sure costs, either immediate or delayed, or as uncertain costs, i.e., risks, again either on the short or on the long term, *or both*. For simplicity of exposition the terms risk and risk generation will henceforth be used instead of 'cost or risk', and 'cost/risk generation', respectively.

for actor B, going by car would be rather attractive (utility of 8) if actor A would go by bike, but it would be much less attractive (utility of 4) if A would also go by car. Alternatively, A's going by bike would be much less attractive (utility of 3) when B would go by car than when B would also take the bike (utility of 6). Note that when both actors (*all* Amsterdammers) would opt for going by bike, they would jointly end up in the upper left cell, with a utility score of 6 for each. This would be the collectively optimal solution. When, however, both A and B would choose the car, the end result would yield each a utility score of 4. This would be a collectively undesirable outcome.

The trap inherent in the payoff structure of Table 2 is that the option 'car' is *individually* more attractive than 'bike', whatever the other actor chooses to do. Decision-theoretically one would say that the socially undesirable or 'defective' behavior is individually dominant (strictly preferable) over the 'cooperative' behavior; the two actors find themselves in a *prisoners' dilemma*.[3]

Table 2. Payoff matrix for a simplified prisoners' dilemma situation (see text)

		actor B's options	
		bike	car
actor A's options	bike	6, 6	3, 8
	car	8, 3	4, 4

Note. Left cell entries are utility scores for actor A.
Right cell entries represent B's utilities.

Not all social dilemmas are as compelling as the prisoners' dilemma. The force and persistence of a social dilemma depend upon its payoff structure and upon the number of individuals involved. The former determines what decision principle or rule would induce people to 'defect' and forget about the collective interests, i.e., contribute to collective risk generation. Three basic types may be distinguished (Liebrand, 1983): the prisoners', chicken and trust social dilemmas, which differ in the basic structure of payoffs to

[3] If the options 'bike' and car' are replaced by YIMBY (Yes, In My Back Yard) and NIMBY (Not..), respectively, this prisoners' dilemma situation similarly applies to the example of two neighboring families (or municipalities) who need a common waste incinerator but contest its being sited in their own or in the other party's 'back yard'. Each party's dominating preference is *not* to have the facility on its premises (see Vlek, 1995*a*).

the different actors. The common property of all three types is the existence of individual incentives to promote self-interests (i.e., defect) rather than taking into account the collective interests (i.e., 'cooperate'). The *prisoners'* dilemma is the most powerful as each individual's preferred alternative is *dominating* the other option (see Table 2). Table 3 presents analogous payoff matrices characterizing the 'chicken dilemma' (3a) and the 'trust dilemma' (3b), respectively. These social dilemmas are based on rearrangements of the utility scores in Table 2. This implies that going by car or by bike is differently appreciated (than in Table 2) by each actor, given that the other actor would go either by car or by bike. The *chicken* social dilemma provokes defection under a *maximax* payoff rule[4] which implies strong optimism about the other person's cooperativeness ("let's assume the other goes by bike, then it's best for me to take the car"). The *trust* social dilemma makes defection attractive under a *maximin* payoff rule[5] implying pessimism about the other's cooperativeness ("I'm afraid the other will go by car; then it's best for me to also go by car").

Table 3. The 'chicken' (a) and 'trust' (b) social dilemma representations of two individual parties' utilities for city-traveling by bike or by car.

		B's options			B's options	
		bike	car		bike	car
actor A's options	bike	6, 6	4, 8	bike	8, 8	3, 6
	car	8, 4	3, 3	car	6, 3	4, 4
		(a) chicken dilemma			(b) trust dilemma	

Note. Left cell entries are utility scores for actor A. Right cell entries represent B's utilities.

[4] Under a maximax payoff rule a decision maker first looks for the maximum payoff possible under each choice alternative. He or she then selects the option having the maximum of those maximum payoffs. The maximax payoff rule, therefore, may be considered to be an 'optimistic' decision rule.

[5] Under a maximin payoff rule one first looks at the minimum possible payoff for each choice alternative; one then selects the option which has the maximum of those minimum payoffs. This may be considered to be a 'pessimistic' decision rule.

The special feature of both the 'chicken' and the 'trust' social dilemma is that the socially defective option (going by car) is not under *all* circumstances more attractive than the cooperative option (taking the bike). This means that actors' *a priori* beliefs in the other's cooperative tendencies may be influenced in order to bring about socially desirable choices. So: starting with a prisoners' dilemma (Table 2), if one would succeed in changing actors' utilities (their subjective evaluations) of possible decision outcomes such that their prisoners' dilemma is transformed into a chicken dilemma (Table 3a), or better still, into a trust dilemma (Table 3b), one would have additional possibilities to induce cooperative behavior among all actors.

The seriousness of a social dilemma generally increases with the number of actors involved, because this implies greater anonimity, lesser responsibility, lower perceived controllability, and a greater pessimism about cooperative behavior by others. Increasing the number of participants does not affect the payoff structure of the *prisoners'* dilemma: no matter how many persons would choose cooperatively, the defective choice alternative is always best for each individual. In a multi-person *chicken* dilemma, when more than a certain number of persons are expected to cooperate (i.e., go by bike), it is most attractive for the individual to defect (take the car); otherwise (s)he had better cooperate. The reverse goes for the *trust* dilemma: when more than a certain number are expected to 'cooperate', it is best for the individual to also cooperate; otherwise defection is better.

4 Actor perspectives on social dilemmas

Real-life social dilemma problems rarely allow for a simple distinction between individual actors and collective policy makers. Often there are several different types of actors involved, with various motivations and responsibilities regarding the externalities which accumulate into collective risk. Let us consider three different actor-perspectives, at the macro-, the micro- and the meso-level, respectively, of the collective (society) involved.

For a political decision maker at the macro-level, a social dilemma - if recognized as such - constitutes a permanent contrast between a (changing) collective risk and a social collection of (changing) individual benefits; minimization of the risk and maximization of the benefits are incompatible social goals between which a trade-off is to be made. If a social dilemma is not (yet) acknowledged as such, it may be brought to the policy maker's attention by groups of individual actors, particularly those who suffer from the collective cost or risk without deriving much benefit from contributors' activities. The policy maker's main task is a double one: to monitor and assess the collective risk, and to encourage individuals to change their behavior so as to keep, or make, the collective risk acceptably low.

In contrast, the individual actor's perspective at the micro-level is naturally focused on short-term benefits. For such individuals, a social dilemma may not appear as such: (a) because they are unaware of any collectively damaging externalities, (b) because they do not know about the seriousness of the social accumulation of externalities, (c) because they do not feel that the collective risk is appreciable (yet) in comparison to the (i.e., many people's) individual benefits, or (d) because they know that the collective risk is there but feel that nothing can be done about it (without endangering a reasonable quality of life to contributing actors), since it is the inevitable by-product of an 'autonomous' development of the collective. Individual actors may obviously differ amongst each other in their perception of a social dilemma. This complicates any approach towards managing the collective risk, as it forces policy makers to specifically address various types of dilemma perceivers and risk contributors.

At the meso-level of a large-scale social dilemma situation, one may find leaders or governing bodies of distinct groups or organizations of individual (micro-level) actors. These leading representatives may well play a double role. On the one hand they may - 'bottum up' - defend and promote their constituency's individual interests by protecting (often acquired) individual rights to shift off externalities to the collective, or even by demanding more room for this. On the other hand, group or organizational representatives may - 'top down' - aid macro-level policy makers in applying various strategies aimed at reducing collective risks via individual behavior change.

Social dilemmas basically have to do with common resources or common safety as an 'envelope' for individual survival and benefit-seeking. Therefore, a time-honored question is how a community of people could best be organized to maintain such common goods *without* unduly restricting individuals' freedom and responsibility to care for themselves and improve their own situation - which, in turn, may lead to over-exploitation of the commons. Historical answers to this question range from the State as a more or less benevolent dictator (Hobbes, 1651/1947) to self-supporting community organization (see Bullock and Baden, 1977; Ostrom, 1990; for examples), to 'bioregionalism' (Sale, 1985), the latter mainly characterized by regional self-sufficiency and a stationary, symbiotic economy.

In any social system for managing common resources and common safety, the mutual perception, allocation of responsibilities, and the either or not interactive decision processes of actors at the micro-, meso- and macro-level of society are crucial for determining the balance between individual enterprise and collective restraint. Here, there may be layered social dilemmas in which an overall common good is threatened not only by the competitive behavior of individuals within groups, but also by competition among relatively homogeneous groups ('meso-level actors') which defend their own interests against those of the collective (see Rapoport and Bornstein, 1987).

5 Nine focal points for research and policy attention

Given that a social dilemma by definition exceeds the physical, cognitive and motivational scope of ('boundedly rational') individual actors at the micro-level, the basic question is how the collective cost or risk can be validly assessed, effectively communicated and acceptably managed so as to stay within sustainable limits. Collective risk management is a matter of decision making about risk acceptance and the application of practical strategies for controlling the risk via individual behavior change. Collective risk management may be most effective if it links up with the diagnosis made about the social processes by which the risk is being generated or enhanced. And it needs monitoring and evaluation, so that its effects and side-effects may be fed back towards the contributing actors involved. Thus, understanding social dilemmas and managing collective risks as generated by individual actions revolves around nine foci of attention, as listed in Table 4.

Table 4. Nine foci of attention for dealing with social dilemmas

Problem diagnosis
1. Collective-risk analysis and assessment: description of the risk generation process in terms of actors, factors, mechanisms and effects
2. Risk perception and communication, social risk evaluation, recognition and acknowledgement of risk generation mechanism and structure
3. Analysis, assessment and communication of individual benefits: which, when, where, how important and to whom?
Decision making
4. Deciding about risk acceptance: weighing of collective risk against total individual benefits (diverse decision principles); decision about need for change
5. If 'risk unacceptable': specification of risk-reducing behavior alternatives
6. Setting of collective-risk reduction objectives, their translation into individual-behavior goals
Risk control
7. Design, deliberation and selection of policy strategies for behavior change: feasibility, acceptability and effectiveness
8. Programmatic application of various strategies and incentives for behavior change; targeting, timing, implementation and control
9. Monitoring, evaluation and feedback of effects of risk reduction measures and strategies

Table 4 is divided in three parts, to stress the fact that the nine points pertain to three basic tasks, viz. problem diagnosis, decision making and risk control. For the key problems in understanding and managing collective risks in social dilemma situations would seem to be: awareness and appreciation of the collective risk and the individual benefits (diagnosis), weighing of the collective risk against aggregate individual benefits (decision making), and individual behavior change or restraint, coupled with risk monitoring and feedback about changes in risk (risk control). These key topics will be discussed in the next subsections.

5.1 Problem diagnosis

Understanding collective risks and risk generation as a social process involves Foci 1, 2 and 3 of Table 4, which cover descriptive risk analysis, social risk perception and an appreciation of multi-actor benefits, respectively.

Focus 1: Collective-risk analysis, begins with a description of negative effects and their significance for the quality of life and environmental quality. In line with the examples used in Section 2, the collective risks may be expressed as city traffic noise, large amounts of waste, shortages of funds for public education, loss of natural open space, decline of ocean fish populations, large-scale air pollution, or wholesale deforestation. Risk analysis should also cover the individual sources of negative externalities and the major determinants of their behavior. It is particularly important to investigate the *motivations*, the *opportunities* and the *abilities* of individual actors to shift off some of their negative effects to the collective and/or to the environment. In this respect, Focus 1 overlaps with Focus 3 below, which deals with individual benefit-seeking.

Collective risk analysis should further clarify the relative contributions - direct and/or indirect - of micro-, meso- and macro-level actors in the collective as a whole (see Section 4). When the analysis covers the entire process of risk generation, which ranges from the causation and stimulation of individual actor behavior up to and including the collective effects and their negative feedback on individual actors, it will be easier (later) to design specific measures and strategies for behavior change to control or reduce collective risks. Thus conducted, a social risk generation analysis naturally covers two major sources of uncertainty in social dilemmas, viz. environmental uncertainty - about the availability, elasticity and recovery rate of collective goods, and social uncertainty, i.e., the probabilities associated to 'defective behavior' of (other) individual actors at the micro-, meso- and macro-level of the collective.[6]

Focus 2: Social risk perception and communication, deals with the vital issue of problem awareness among the actors facing the social dilemma. Only in the simplest situations is it impossible, or is it experimentally prohibited, for actors to exchange views and to learn about each other's preferences and intentions prior to manifesting their actual behavior. In most practical social dilemmas communication is possible in principle, and influences may be exerted on actors' behavioral intentions. In analogy to collective-risk analysis, problem awareness, too, may pertain to the entire process of collective risk generation, ranging from actors' behavior determinants via actual behaviors and the associated cost externalization, down to identifiable collective damage and risk, and its ultimate effects for human life and environmental quality.

However, there may be large differences in expertise between those who performed the collective-risk analysis under Focus 1, and the relevant actors who are actually generating and enhancing the collective risk, often without being much aware of it. Hence there may be serious problems of communication concerning the origin and the determinants of the risk, and - consequently - about the best ways to bring it under collective control. The minimal topics for collective-risk communication would seem to be: the nature and seriousness of the (current) risk itself, the behavioral sources (actors) and mechanisms of risk generation, and the boomerang character of the risk in relation to the expected quality of the immediate situation individual actors will (have to) be operating in. The latter aspect - expected boomeranging - is one of the psychologically most difficult issues. In many practical social dilemma situations the negative feedback from collective risks is delayed, indirect and rather uncertain, so that for a long time its boomerang effects are either unnoticeable or rather hard to believe.

The abundant literature on risk perception and communication (e.g., Covello, Von Winterfeldt & Slovic, 1986; Jungermann, Rohrmann & Wiedemann, 1990; Kasperson & Stallen, 1991) offers many useful ideas and conclusions about this important issue in risky decision making. In most studies on perceived risk and risk taking, 'risk' has somehow been defined in terms of probabilities and negative consequences projected at a certain time horizon. In social dilemma situations, however, risk generation (and risk

[6] See, e.g., Wit and Wilke (1995) who found that under conditions of high social uncertainty (about the extent of others' cooperativeness), increasing environmental uncertainty (about what would be needed to safeguard a common resource) led to diminished cooperation, compared to low environmental uncertainty under either high or low social uncertainty; see also Rapoport, Budescu, Suleiman and Weg (1992) on environmental uncertainty.

management) *as a process* would seem to be one additional topic of interest, next to the probabilities and seriousness of expected negative consequences for the collective. Thus current risk perception and communication research could significantly increase its scope and practical relevance when it would be extended to include social dilemma problems and social processes of collective risk generation; see also Vlek (1995*b*).

Focus 3: Assessment of benefits, is directed at the forces that pull individual actors towards behavioral choices and activities whose negative effects are, or may be, partly shifted off to the collective. The achievement of individual benefits, and the individual achievement of those benefits, by two or more interdependent actors, constitute the major driving force underlying collective risks. The greater the benefits, and the larger the individual freedom in choosing ways to achieve them, the stronger will be the discounting of risks and the temptation to externalize part of the costs and other negative effects. Achievable benefits may be sought under the influence of various personal and social *motivations*, but also under the invitation of *opportunities* created by others; and the benefit-seeking is, of course, dependent upon an actor's *ability* to carry out the relevant behavior. Thus benefit-seeking behavior determinants may be modeled in a Motivation-Opportunity-Ability-, or MOA-scheme (Batra & Ray, 1986; Ölander and Thøgerson, 1994; Jager, Van Asselt, Rotmans and Vlek, 1996 in press) which would enable one to address specific variables related to the likelihood of certain benefit-seeking behaviors.

Taken together, the various benefits sought by actors in a social dilemma situation may be seen as contributing, subjectively, to an actor's individual 'well-being'.[7] Presumably, this is also - partly - determined by the quality of certain collective and environmental goods. Therefore, one pertinent question is to what extent an actor's perceived well-being is based on his or her current set of immediate benefits, and in how far it depends on other, indirect types of benefit, which may occur elsewhere, later or to relevant others, and which the actor also enjoys or will enjoy, partly of course, as a member of the collective. This question implies: (a) that 'rationality', in the sense of outcome optimality, is a combination of direct and indirect (net) benefits, and (b) that the notion of individual well-being has a multi-attributive character involving some combination of present and future expected benefits of differing kinds. See Mentzel (1995), for a pertinent discussion in relation tot

---

[7] 'Well-being' is used rather loosely here. In fact it would involve an answer to the question of what individual actors, implicitly or explicitly, consider to be beneficial to themselves and what they would regard as nuisance, cost or damage. Making conceptions of well-being explicit and communicating about them seems useful and desirable in attempting to manage collective risks in social dilemma situations.

sustainable development, which suggests that 'managing the commons' necessitates revisions in popular conceptions of human well-being.

5.2 Decision making on risk management

The second general problem in handling social dilemmas is to decide whether the collective risk, as assessed and communicated under Foci 1 and 2 above, is or is not acceptable in view of the individual benefits as assessed under Focus 3. 'Unacceptable collective risk' would entail the necessity to do something about it, which requires an exploration of behavior alternatives and a specification of risk reduction goals and behavior objectives.

Focus 4: Deciding about risk acceptance, requires a weighing of the collective risk against the total collection of individual benefits, possibly occurring at various levels of the collective. Such weighing may be done directly, by making an explicit trade-off, but it may be more practical to do this indirectly, viz. by setting risk acceptance standards and testing a given collective-risk situation against them. The latter approach would amount to 'satisficing', i.e., deciding for an alternative which would be 'good enough' (or: 'not too bad'). Operational satisficing rules for deciding on collective risks involve *a priori* acceptance standards, whose values normally depend (also) upon the numerosity and importance of relevant actors' individual benefits. Trading-off collective risks against individual benefits may, of course, yield net payoff values associated to the behavioral options available to the various actors in the social dilemma. On the basis of these it may be determined if, when and to what extent a certain combination of individual behaviors, or rather: their externalities, results in a collective cost or risk which should be deemed unacceptable. But, however this is decided upon, 'unacceptable collective risk' always involves a trade-off between things that are good for the individual (directly) and things that are good for the collective as a whole (and thus indirectly for the individual).

The acceptability or unacceptability of collective risks may be decided by collective-policy makers, but it may also be perceived and communicated by individual and/or organizational actors at the micro- and/or the meso-level of the collective (see Section 4). To the extent that only macro-level actors find the collective risk unacceptable, there would be problems of communicating this - 'top down' - to lower-level actors in the collective, who might accuse macro-level decision makers of being 'dictatorial'. On the other hand, when micro-level actors find the collective risk *acceptable* and this view is represented effectively - 'bottum up' - at the meso- and especially the macro-level of the collective, it is unlikely that effective policies could be implemented for reducing the collective risk via individual behavior change. Hence the importance of social risk perception and communication (Focus 2 above) as a basis for collective-risk management.

Focus 5: Specification of risk-reducing behavior alternatives, is meant to open the perspectives for behavior change. If it has somehow been decided, in view of the total individual benefits involved, that the collective risk - as assessed and communicated - is intolerably high, it should be reduced. Since the risk is being generated through cost-shifting by individual actors, it is either the cost-shifting or the behavior itself, or both, that should be changed so as to diminish individuals' externalities. Specifying, designing, and providing feasible behavior alternatives that would have far fewer or even no external effects on the collective, is essential for accomplishing individual behavior change.

Processes of behavior change revolve around substituting current, collectively costly behavior by alternative, collectively benign behavior. Such a substitution process may be accomplished at the level of the current behavior, e.g., via cost internalization or via replacement by 'obvious' other behavior. But behavior substitution may well be performed at higher levels of an actor's goal hierarchy, e.g., via a change of customary goals or objectives such that the performance of cost-externalizing behaviors becomes altogether unneccesary. Higher-order behavior substitutions generally are more difficult to achieve and they may need more time than 'easy' substitutions, but their beneficial effects on the collective risk may be far more impressive. Designing and providing collectively benign behavior alternatives is the first general strategy for behavior change, as discussed under Focus 7 (and elaborated in Section 6) below. In this respect Foci 5 and 7 overlap.

Focus 6: Setting risk limits, translation into behavior objectives, is the last step on the way towards the application of one or more strategies for behavior change. If the collective risk is considered to be intolerable and if feasible behavior alternatives have been specified, then collective policy making further requires an indication of the dimensions along and the extent to which the collective risk is to be reduced. That is, collective-risk reduction goals need to be formulated. But, since risk reduction can only be achieved via individual behavior change, the risk reduction goals at the collective level need to be translated into behavior objectives at the individual level. Collective-risk management goals and individual-behavior objectives thus map onto the process of collective risk generation, and risk control is reflected back at the level of individual activities.

5.3 Collective-risk control

Actual control or reduction of collective risks covers the design and selection of strategies for behavior change, their programmatic application, and the monitoring and evaluation of their actual effects for collective qualities as well as for individuals' lives. Because of their central importance, strategies for behavior change will be briefly indicated here, under Focus 7, and further discussed in Sections 6 and 7 below. ·

Focus 7: Policy strategies for behavior change, is tuned towards the design, selection and specification of practical strategies for accomplishing behavior change at the levels of the collective where actors are contributing to the collective risk. The theoretical and empirical literature on social dilemmas reveals a wide range of proposed and/or tested 'solutions' which vary greatly in the way individual actors would be addressed (see, e.g., Dawes, 1980; Edney, 1980; Messick and Brewer, 1983; Wilke, 1989; see also Cook and Berrenberg, 1981; Sheth and Frazier, 1982; De Young, 1993). A customary distinction is made between structural strategies and psychological, or rather: cognitive-motivational strategies, which to a greater or lesser degree change the nature of the social dilemma and are more or less impinging upon the freedom of choice of individual actors. The large collection of specific 'solutions' to social dilemmas, i.e., ways to reduce individual contributions to collective risks, can be categorized into six-plus-one strategies for behavior change. Table 5 summarizes the seven strategies, and it indicates which specific 'solutions to social dilemmas' fall under which strategy. The strategies will be separately described and discussed in Section 6. Section 7 summarizes two comprehensive systems for collective-risk management.

Table 5. Strategies for collective-risk control in social dilemmas (see further Section 6)

1. Provision of physical alternatives & (re)arrangements (PhAA)
   [adding/deleting/changing behavior options, enhancing actors' efficacy]

2. Regulation-and-enforcement (RaE)
   [enacting laws, rules; setting/enforcing standards, explicit norms]

3. Financial-economic stimulation (FES)
   [rewards/fines, taxes, subsidies, posting bonds]

4. Provision of information, education, communication (IEC)
   [about risk generation, types and levels of risk, others' perceptions and intentions, risk reduction strategies]

5. Social modeling and support (SMS)
   [demonstrating cooperative behaviour, others' efficacy]

6. Organizational change (OCh)
   [resource privatization/territorialization, sanctioning system, leadership institution, organization for self-regulation]

7. Changing values and morality (CVM)
   [appeal to conscience, enhancing 'altruism' towards others and future generations]

Focus 8: Programmatic application of behavior-change strategies, deals with the actual implementation, timing and fine-tuning of strategies, as linked to specific substantive objectives for behavior change (see Focus 6). Important considerations here largely emerge from previous analysis (see the earlier foci of attention). They are: legitimation of policy measures, justification of behavior change, realistic prospects of personal and collective effects, foreseeable barriers and resistance to policy measures, possible positive and negative side-effects, and the promotion of trust in the cooperation of others and in the encouragement and eventual surveillance of cooperative behavior (see also Klandermans, 1992). Additional points of attention are the task distribution and timing of behavior-change measures and strategies by responsible policy makers, and the consistency of risk control policies across various kinds or domains of actor behavior. A general point to note is the availability of comprehensive theories of behavior. Examples are: instrumental and social learning theory (Skinner, 1953; Bandura, 1977), the theory of planned behavior (Ajzen, 1985, 1991), the theory of normative conduct (Cialdini, Kallgren & Reno, 1991), and social comparison theory (Masters & Smith, 1987). These and some other theories are highly relevant sources of ideas, findings and recommendations concerning the practical use of strategies for behavior change. Their actual utility, however, is dependent upon the behavioral mechanisms - reasoned or automatic, individual or social - underlying the social generation of collective risks.

Focus 9: Monitoring, evaluation and feedback, reflects the necessity of tracing the effects and side-effects of collective-risk control strategies on individuals' personal situation (their well-being or quality of life) and on the collective risk (broadly: environmental quality). Feedback concerning apparent reductions in collective-risk levels is essential for individual actors' (enduring) acceptance of changed behavior patterns that affect their own situation in terms of available options, freedom of choice and personal or organizational well-being. Feedback cannot be provided without monitoring and evaluation of what actually happens after the introduction of selected policy measures and strategies. Focus 9, therefore, is directed at collecting empirical data on the various points of interest for effective application of collective-risk control strategies, as discussed under Focus 7 and especially Focus 8. Again, key points here are target group definition, description of behavioral effects and side-effects (substitution processes), time course of effects, special barriers and kinds of resistance, net effects on the level of collective risk, and - of course - the degree of correspondence between expected or predicted effects and actually observed effects, both for individual actors and for the collective as a whole. Close monitoring and timely evaluation of effects not only allows one to evaluate and *a posteriori* justify the chosen program of risk control measures and strategies. It also enables one to change or adapt the course of the risk control program in view of observed insufficient results.

6 Strategies for behavior change to reduce collective risks

This section gives a further elaboration of Focus 7 above (see Table 5). Seven strategies for behavior change are described, and some remarks about their practical application are made. Two comprehensive risk management systems: 'tradeable exploitation rights' and bond pledging or hostage posting, are briefly discussed in Section 7. The seven strategies are the following.

1. *Provision of physical alternatives and (re)arrangements (PhAA)* may change the basic structure of a social dilemma through the addition of new or other behavior options for individual actors (see Focus 5 above). These may first of all increase or restore actors' freedom of choice. Secondly, through the application of other strategies (below) these options may gradually come to be preferred to current, collectively harmful options. New or other behavior options may involve purely technical changes in current activities, or they may imply more fundamental changes in behavior patterns, possibly associated with a change in behavior goals (see Focus 5 on 'substitution'). The underlying assumption for this strategy is that individual behavior is shaped in dependence upon technical facilities and in accordance with the physical environment in which it may take place.

2. *Regulation-and-enforcement (RaE)* generally serves to restrict individual actors' freedom of choice in a social dilemma situation. This sort of strategy is based on laws, regulations and standards issued by the leadership of the collective. Violations of them - if detected - are usually met with some kind of punishment, fine or disapproval. The underlying assumption is that official laws, regulations and standards are eventually internalized under the threat of punishment. The implication of such strategies is that there is an adequate organization for supervision, monitoring and enforcement.

3. *Financial-economic stimulation (FES)* typically alters the payoff structure of a given social dilemma and may thereby change its nature (see Section 3). Financial-economic strategies are designed to reward people (financially) for selecting certain behaviors having little or no external effect on the collective, or to punish them for behaving in a collectively burdening way. The relevant policy instruments are subsidies, discounts, levies, taxes, fines, tolls, and the like. The basic underlying assumption is that the behavior of individual actors is subject to the workings of the 'price mechanism' and that the demand-price elasticities involved are reasonably high.

4. *Information, education and communication (IEC)* is aimed at making relevant actors more aware of the collective costs and risks, and at persuading them towards (timely) 'cooperative' behavior. This kind of strategy may involve giving information, education, arguments, prompts and admonitions aimed at increasing actors' knowledge (e.g., of behavior alternatives), heightening their awareness (e.g., of environmental effects), affecting their attitudes, and strengthening their inclination and possibilities to adopt other, less harmful kinds of behavior. IEC is based on the assumption that the relevant

behavior is 'reasoned', and that influencing the cognitive processes underlying behavior choices will also affect those choices themselves.

5. *Social modeling and support (SMS)* would be focused on individual behavior change by introducing social influences which mediate social benefits and costs. SMS is based on the notion that collectively risky behavior (and the underlying cognitive structure) is strongly determined by social factors, such as social norms and customs, social comparison processes as occurring in status and power seeking, notions of privacy versus collectiveness, and the public examples set by prominent members of society. In SMS strategies these facts are exploited, e.g., by organizing family, company or community support in altering people's attitudes, preferences, and habits, by offering them behavior examples modeled by prominent countrymen, and by stimulating their trust in the cooperation of others to achieve collective goals.

6. *Organizational change (OCh)* is meant to work partly via physical changes in a social dilemma situation (which may as such even be eliminated), and partly through changes in the financial and/or social payoff structure. OCh strategies are aimed at modifying and adapting the structure and functioning of institutions, organizations, and 'lifestyles', so as to make these more amenable to alternative, more sustainable behavior systems, modes and practices. The basic assumption underlying OCh strategies is that individual behavior is embedded in, and significantly directed by the institutions, organizations, and generally adopted lifestyles characterizing the collective. Applying an OCh strategy should be inspired by the principal question of the optimal organization of maintaining common goods without undue restriction of individuals' freedom to act in their own interest. This point was already discussed in Section 4, on actor perspectives.

The research literature on resolving social dilemmas and particularly commons dilemmas (see Focus 7) leads up to a seventh strategy for behavior change, as follows.

7. *Changing values and morality (CVM).* This strategy involves appeals to the conscience of contributing actors, attempts to enhance their 'altruism' towards other actors and towards future generations, and measures to increase mutual trust among the actors in a social dilemma. The strategy may also entail a change in people's conceptions of quality-of-life, particularly in the relative importance they attach to collective and environmental qualities as components of their notion of human welfare and sustainable development. The basic assumption here is that people's values and morality form the roots of fundamental attitudes that guide and support lifestyles and specific behaviors. Also, the perceived morality of others appears to be a significant factor enhancing individual actors' willingness to cooperate for the common good (Van Lange, 1992).

Strategies 1 (PhAA), 2 (RaE) and 3 (FES), and certain (physical) forms of strategy 6 (OCh) would initiate so-called structural (or: hard) solutions to a social dilemma, whose basic nature or type would thereby be altered. Strategies 4 (IEC), 5 (SMS), certain other ('mental') forms of strategy 6 (OCh), and strategy 7 (CVM) would imply cognitive-motivational (or: soft) solutions. Through the latter, individual actors would be induced to behave in a cooperative (collectively optimal) manner, while the basic nature and payoff structure of the social dilemma would be maintained. Structural solution strategies are generally more effective, but they are often not available or not easily implemented. Specific cognitive-motivational solution strategies (IEC, SMS and some OCh) are more easy to design and apply, but their effectiveness is generally lower; in many cases, however, they are the only thing one could rely on. 'Changes in values and morality' (CVM) stands relatively by itself as a cultural solution on which much behavior change might come to rest. Here, the classical attitude-behavior question applies: Is CVM a prerequisite for 'cooperative' behavior change, or would such behavior change - originally induced otherwise - gradually lead to changes in values and morality?

Experienced social dilemmas researchers might propose, at this point, that there exists an eighth strategy for collective-risk control, viz. '*Wait and see*' (WaS). This would amount to doing nothing and awaiting the adaptive behavior of individual actors when 'the disease burns itself out'. From a social-scientific point of view this is an interesting possible way of responding to (rather than: managing) collective risks. But it cannot seriously be considered as an explicit (*a priori*) management strategy. However, to decide about any of the strategies summarized in Table 5, one may wish to assess beforehand how the balance of multiple individual benefits and collective risks would evolve when 'nothing' would be done to control the risks. Also, a strategy of WaS may eventually lead to the adoption of a genuine management strategy (Table 5), but - obviously - this would be 'too late'.

7 Tradeable exploitation rights

One special combination of strategies RaE (as central regulation), FES (as payment according to use), IEC (as information provision) and OCh (as privatization) may prove to be an effective as well as efficient approach toward managing collective risks and maintaining common goods. This is the management system known as 'tradeable emission permits', more generally to be labeled as *tradeable exploitation rights*. The idea here is that, for the collective as a whole, some central authority determines the maximum sustainable exploitation of some social or environmental resource (as to be consumed, enjoyed or polluted), and then distributes (equally, shall we say) among its constituents a collection of tickets each representing a fixed limited exploitation right. Tickets are tradeable, so that they may be purchased by those who need a greater-than-average resource use, from those whose demand is less than average. Ticket prices are established under the laws of demand and supply, but the total resource exploitation corresponding to the ownership of a certain number of tickets may not be exceeded. If necessary, the central authority may reduce the extent of exploitation per ticket. Or it may allow for increased exploitation, if the total resource regenerates more quickly than was originally estimated. See Koutstaal (1995) and Koutstaal and Nentjes (1995) for an economic and juridical analysis of the possibilities and limitations of 'tradeable emission permits'. The system contains several elements of the alternative commons dilemma games as discussed by Ostrom (1990, chapter 1).

Tradeable exploitation rights as a political-economic risk management system raises a number of fundamental questions. These are mainly concerned with the assessment of the maximum tolerable overall exploitation of a given resource, the initial distribution (or perhaps: 'auctioning out') of exploitation tickets, and the central authority's monitoring and control over actual resource exploitation and possible violations of individual purchased rights. Effective functioning of such a system obviously requires collective rules and a sanctioning system, efficient operation of demand-and-supply pricing mechanisms, and the provision of information and communication about exploitation rights, their availability and the monitoring-and-control over their actual utilization. If appropriately implemented, such a system would prohibit free riding, whilst the unfairness of a fixed exploitation charge to both small and large exploiters would be avoided (see the discussion of 'demand revelation' by Yamagishi, 1995, p. 313). How tradeable exploitation rights as a system actually works under variations in certain basic characteristics, is a matter of controlled experimentation and creative field study. Practical examples are the distribution of tradeable quota-rights for sea-fishing, dairy milk production and animal manure production, respectively, in the countries of the European Union.

Another interesting management system, involving a combination of strategies RaE, FES and IEC, is bond pledging or hostage posting for ensuring cooperative behavior. The basic idea is that individual actors 'promise' to be cooperative, and that they commit themselves by pledging a bond (which serves as a hostage). That is, the bond - or hostage - is lost when they defect and behave against the collective interest. Raub and Keren (1993) and Keren and Raub (1993) discuss the theoretical nature and implications of such a system, and they offer empirical evidence for its effectiveness. An interesting practical example from environmental policy is couched in a Swiss proposal to drastically increase the price of gasoline for motorcars, and then at the end of each year pay a bonus out of a national 'gasoline fund', to those who would prove to have driven less than a certain number of car-kilometers (VCS, 1990).

8 A reconsideration of classic SD-concepts

In view of the analysis followed in this chapter, various traditional SD-concepts seem to be getting a somewhat different meaning. The concept of *externality* has already been discussed in Section 2. Here it was stated that unpaid-for external effects may come from specific single sources or from diffuse multiple sources, and that the receivers or victims of externalities may be either spatially concentrated or wide-spread. *Dominating options* may be deliberately preferred behaviors - optimal under all circumstances, but in many cases they may be habitual behaviors to which the term 'preference' hardly applies; also there may be social norms and customs that make certain cost-shifting behaviors almost unavoidable.

Cooperation would be manifested by any actor whose external effects may be judged to be collectively acceptable, i.e., his or her contribution to the collective cost or risk is 'sustainable'. One problem here may be that an individual legally shifts off external costs. These, however, may appear to be intolerable contributions to a collective risk, in a situation where individual actors 'see no risk' or discount this in view of the direct individual benefits their behavior entails. So: how anyone could know whether he or she 'cooperates' or 'defects' is a question worth asking in any practical field study.

Knowledge, morality and *trust* (Dawes, 1980) seem to be focused on the collective-risk management side of an SD; however, crucial concepts for understanding the risk generation side seem to be actors' *motivation, opportunity* and *ability* to engage in certain collectively harmful behaviors. Ability, by the way, seems to be strongly related to *efficacy* in changing behavior and contributing to, or not detracting from the collective good.

The final concept to consider here is *rationality.* This turns out to be indicative of an optimal *balance* between direct individual benefits and indirect individual shares of collective goods; only if actors are unaware of, or assign no weight to, their share of the collective good (present and future), may they be called (single-mindedly) 'selfish'. Alternatively, those who would assign an exclusive weight to collective goods, may be called (single-mindedly) altruistic. It is important to note that the conflict between individual and collective interests often rests upon a convolution of two or more out of four different elementary dilemmas, which require a weighing of, respectively: (1) individual benefits against individual risks, (2) immediate versus delayed consequences, (3) consequences occurring 'here' versus those 'there', and (4) consequences for the individual versus consequences for others. Psychologically, the combination of these four 'survival dilemmas' offers a powerful temptation to 'defect' and act 'selfishly' (see Vlek and Keren, 1992). An interesting general observation is that, subjectively, any dilemma or combination of dilemmas may not exist at all, because the individual is maximally devoted to one side of it, with total disregard of the other side.

9 Conclusions on the extended SD-paradigm

This final section is devoted to some general issues of 'SD-thinking'. After a summary of the present extended SD-paradigm we wil successively consider the importance of computer simulation, the inherent collective-risk generation nature of the economic free-market system, and the 'democratic dilemma' in the establishment of institutions and procedures for collective-risk management.

To recapitulate: a social dilemma is a situation where a collective cost or risk (i.e., expected cost) is incurred, taken or generated through the combined negative externalities of various individuals who act (relatively) independently from one another. The *basic* problem is a conflict between (direct) individual interests and (more or less indirect) collective interests. This is nicely captured in well-defined social dilemma games such as discussed in Section 3. But the *general* problem is much wider in scope and may be described in terms of nine ordered foci of research and policy attention, summarized in Table 4 (Section 5). Thus formulated, the extended SD-paradigm is a systematic and comprehensive way of thinking about collective risk generation and risk management via the external effects of individual activities, which paradigm should (eventually) yield concepts, models, methods and procedures for: (1) diagnostic problem analysis, (2) decision making on risk acceptance, (3) risk control via individual behavior change, and (4) computer simulations of dynamic social dilemma situations. The first three of these main issues have been extensively dealt with above: collective-risk analysis (Section 5.1) is necessary for deciding on 'unacceptable risk' (5.2) which in turn should lead to risk control policies based on various strategies for behavior change of risk-contributing actors (5.3 and 6).

The fourth main issue, computer simulation of SD-situations, is of great future importance. There already are formal models of social (resource) dilemmas which lend themselves for computer programming; a classical derivation is given by Dawes et al. (1974). Also available are computer programs for simulating actors' decision strategies in repeated well-defined, limited social dilemma games, by which the 'outbreak of cooperation' may be demonstrated (Glance and Huberman, 1993, 1994), as well as the sustainability of cooperation (Messick and Liebrand, 1995). Summers (1996) has developed a computer program which nicely simulates collective resource use and the risk of resource depletion in a multi-actor situation with varying number of actors and varying resource needs and time horizon of actors.

Computer simulation of broadly-scoped SD-problems having various critical variables is necessary to the extent that such problems exceed the available formats, means and time for controlled experimentation, whilst theorization cannot (yet) be done convincingly enough. Computer simulation of SD-situations may cover several or all of the nine foci summarized in Table 4, and it would be directed at demonstrating the 'rise and fall' of collective risks as a function of individual (micro- but also meso-level) actors' behaviors, as fluctuating themselves under the influence of autonomous changes in motivations, opportunities and abilities (see Focus 3) and under the policy strategies applied with the aim to deliberately alter these.

The use of computer programs for improving our understanding of, and our communication about large-scale collective problems is also advocated in *State of the World 1994*, an annual report of the Worldwatch Institute in Washington D.C.: "Global thinking is a tall order: human beings are not naturally adept to it. To achieve it, we need tools that extend our senses and enhance our ability to comprehend the information they collect" (Young, 1994, p. 115). The extended SD-paradigm as unfolded in the present chapter might evolve to provide the conceptual and theoretical basis which is indispensable for designing adequate computer programs for simulating large-scale collective-risk generation and risk management.

The extended SD-paradigm may also be useful to comprehend what is currently happening to collective goods and qualities as a result of 'globalization' of economic processes under the philosophy of the free-market system. The essence here is that individual economic actors may extend their production and consumption patterns as efficiently as possible - thereby causing an 'eruption of externalities', with the purpose of optimally surviving themselves (on the short term). At the same time, governments step back and deregulate in the popular belief that 'the market' takes care of efficient resource use and the maintenance of collective goods. This development amounts to a decrease of actors' interdependency as regards individual *choices,* going along with an increase in interdependency as regards *outcomes*. Thus there seems to be a great need for restoring and enhancing government understanding and management of large-scale collective costs, risks and damage as emerging from the external effects of individual and organized economic actors in society. See Stern (1992), Corson (1994) and Goodland, Daly and Kellenberg (1994) for analyses and discussions of major driving forces underlying recent environmental over-exploitation. One slightly pessimistic conclusion from these analysis may be that 'cooperation' seems to be a rather limited term for describing the key toward resolving real-life social dilemmas.

Regarding collective-risk management we should realize that social dilemmas cannot be resolved. To live with them, as dilemmas, requires the striking and the maintenance of an optimal balance between a collective risk and a collection of individual benefits. Sections 6 and 7 deal with the question of how this could be accomplished. The central toolbox consists of six-plus-one general strategies for actors' behavior change (Focus 7). However, a crucial question concerning collective-risk management is: *who* is to evaluate the collective risk and decide about its intolerability, and who is to select and apply behavior-change strategies to achieve acceptable collective risk? A proper answer to this question necessitates the adoption of second-order risk management strategies. These are concerned with the institutions, legal frameworks and political procedures underlying collective-risk policy making (see Ostrom and Ostrom, 1977; Ostrom, 1990; Yamagishi, 1986, 1995). Electing a representative government which is willing and able to change individual citizens' behavior so as to restore or maintain important collective goods and environmental qualities, seems to be involving a *democratic dilemma* which again requires the striking of an optimal *balance* between government power and citizen power. Such a balance - once established - might be called democratically rational.

As already alluded to in the above, the extended SD-paradigm may yield a powerful conceptual framework and methodology for understanding collective risk generation and adequate risk management. Thus, we could eventually understand and know more about risk and uncertainty (social and environmental), structure and interpretation (as a function of 'framing'), and effective structural strategies for collective risk management, three issues put forward by Liebrand, Messick and Wilke (1992*b*) as the main 'current theoretical issues'.

It is often observed that manifestations of large-scale collective risks make individual people feel powerless about the possibility of effective risk control and its implications for their own behavior. They therefore tend to downplay or negate the collective problems they confront, whereby the latter may continue to exist or even further increase. A comprehensive model for understanding collective risk generation and a valid methodology for sustainable risk management may serve to improve our attitude toward, and our handling of some serious societal and environmental problems of the present time.

10 References

Ajzen, I. (1985). From intentions to actions: a theory of planned behavior. In J. Kuhl & J. Beckmann (Eds): *Action control: from cognition to behavior*. Heidelberg/New York: Springer.

Ajzen, I. (1991). The theory of planned behavior. *Organizational Behavior and Human Decision Processes*, 50, 179-211.

Bandura, A. (1977). *Social learning theory*. Englewood Cliffs (N.J.): Prentice-Hall.

Batra, R. & Ray, M.L. (1986). Situational effects of advertising repetition: the moderating effect of motivation, ability and opportunity to respond. *Journal of Consumer Research,* 12 (4), 432-445.

Beach, L.R. (1990). *Image theory: decision making in personal and organizational contexts.* Chichester (U.K.)/New York: Wiley.

Bullock, K. & Baden, J. (1977). Communes and the logic of the commons. In G. Hardin & J. Baden: *Managing the commons.* San Francisco: W.H. Freeman.

Cialdini, R.B., Kallgren, C.A. & Reno, R.R. (1991). A focus theory of normative conduct: a theoretical refinement and reevaluation of the role of norms in human behavior. In L. Berkowitz (Ed.): *Advances in experimental social psychology*. Volume 24, pp. 201-234.

Cook, S.W. & Berrenberg, J.L. (1981). Approaches to encouraging conservation behavior: a review and conceptual framework. *Journal of Social Issues*, 37 (2), 73-107.

Corson, W.H. (1994). Changing course: an outline of strategies for a sustainable future. *Futures* 26, 206-223.

Covello, V.T., Von Winterfeldt, D. & Slovic, P. (1986). Risk communication: a review of the literature. *Risk Abstracts*, 3, 171-182.

Dawes, R.M. (1980). Social dilemmas. *Annual Review of Psychology*, 31, 169-193.

Dawes, R.M. (1991). Social dilemmas, economic self interests, and evolutionary theory. In D.R. Brown & J.E. Keith Smith (Eds): *Frontiers in mathematical psychology: essays in honor of Clyde Coombs*. New York: Springer Verlag, 53-79.

Dawes, R.M., Delay, J. & Chaplin, W. (1974). The decision to pollute. *Environment and Planning*, 6, 3-10.

De Young, R. (1993). Changing behavior and making it stick. The conceptualization and management of conservation behavior. *Environment and Behavior*, 25 (4), 485-505.

Edney, J.J. (1980). The commons problem; alternative perspectives. *American Psychologist*, 35, 131-150.

Freudenburg, W.R. & Pastor, S.K. (1992). NIMBYs and LULUs: stalking the syndromes. *Journal of Social Issues*, 48 (4), 39-62.

Glance, N.S. & Huberman, B.A. (1993). The outbreak of cooperation. *Journal of Mathematical Sociology*, 17 (4), 281-302.

Glance, N.S. & Huberman, B.A. (1994). The dynamics of social dilemmas. *Scientific American*, 270 (March), 58-63.

Goodland, R., Daly, H. & Kellenberg, J. (1994). Burden sharing in the transition to environmental sustainability. *Futures* 26, 146-155.

Hardin, G. (1968). The tragedy of the commons. *Science*, 162, 1243-1248.

Hobbes.Th. (1851/1947). *Leviathan*. London/New York: Bobbs-Merrill.

Jager, W., Van Asselt, M., Costerman Boodt, P.M., Rotmans, J. & Vlek, C.A.J. (1996 in press). *Consumer behaviour: a modelling perspective in the context of integrated assessment of global change*. Groningen/Bilthoven (Neth.): University of Groningen and National Institute for Public Health and Environmental Protection. Globo Report Series.

Jungermann, H., Rohrmann, B. & Wiedemann, P.M. (Eds; 1990). *Risiko-konzepte, Risiko-konflikte, Risiko-kommunikation*. Jülich (Germ.): Forschungszentrum Jülich, Mongraphiën Band 3.

Kasperson, R.E. & Stallen, P.J. (Eds, 1991): *Communicating risks to the public*. Dordrecht/Boston: Kluwer Academic Publishers.

Keren, G.B. & Raub, W. (1993). Resolving social conflict through hostage posting: theoretical and empirical considerations. *Journal of Experimental Psychology: General*, 122 (4), 429-448.

Klandermans, B. (1992). Persuasive communication: measures to overcome real-life social dilemmas. In W. Liebrand, D. Messick & H. Wilke (Eds): *Social dilemmas. Theoretical issues and research findings*. Oxford/New York: Pergamon.

Komorita, S.S. & Parks, C.D. (1995). Mixed-motive interaction. *Annual Review of Psychology*, 46, 183-207.

Koutstaal, P.R. & Nentjes, A. (1995). Tradeable carbon permits in Europe; feasibility and comparison with taxes. *Journal of Common Market Studies*, 33 (2), 219-233.

Koutstaal, P.R. (1995). Tradeable permits for transito traffic through Austria. In F. Dietz et al. (Eds): *Environment, Incentives and the Common Market*. Dordrecht: Kluwer, 1995.

Liebrand, W.B.G. (1983). A classification of social dilemma games. *Simulation and Games*, 14, 123-138.

Liebrand, W., Messick, D. & Wilke, H. (1992*a*). *Social dilemmas. Theoretical issues and research findings*. Oxford/New York: Pergamon.

Liebrand, W., Messick, D. & Wilke, H. (1992*b*). Current theoretical issues. In W. Liebrand, D. Messick & H. Wilke (Eds): *Social dilemmas. Theoretical issues and research findings*. Oxford/New York: Pergamon.

Luce, R.D. & Raiffa, H. (1957). *Games and decisions; introduction and critical survey. New York: Wiley.*

Masters, J.C. & Smith, W.P. (Eds; 1987). *Social comparison, social justice and relative deprivation: theoretical and policy perspectives*. Volume 4. Hillsdale (N.J.): Erlbaum.

Mentzel, M. (1995). Welfare and its relation to the environmental question. In S. Zwerver, R. van Rompaey, M. Kok & M. Berk (Eds): *Climate change research: evaluation and policy implications*. Amsterdam: Elsevier Science Publishers, pp. 1255-1260.

Messick, D.M. & Brewer, M.B. (1983). Solving social dilemmas: a review. In L. Wheeler & P. Shaver (Eds): *Review of personality and social psychology. Volume 4*. Beverly Hills (Ca.): Sage.

Messick, D.M. & Liebrand, W.B.G. (1995). Individual heuristics and the dynamics of cooperation in large groups. *Psychological Review*, 102 (1), 131-145.

Ölander. F. & Thøgerson, J. (1994). *Understanding of consumer behaviour as a prerequisite for environmental protection*. Keynote address presented at 23rd International Congress of Applied Psychology. Aarhus (Dk): Aarhus School of Business, Haslegaardsvej 10, DK-8210 Aarhus V, Denmark.

Ostrom, E. (1990). *Governing the commons: the evolution of institutions for collective action*. Cambridge (UK)/New York: Cambridge University Press.

Ostrom, V. & Ostrom, E. (1977). A theory for institutional analysis of common pool problems. In G. Hardin & J. Baden: *Managing the commons*. San Francisco: W.H. Freeman, 157-172.

Platt, J. (1973). Social traps. *American Psychologist*, 28, 641-651.

Rapoport, A. & Chammah, A.M. (1965). *Prisoner's dilemma: a study in conflict and cooperation*. Ann Arbor (Mich.): Michigan University Press.

Rapoport, A., Budescu, D., Suleiman, R. & Weg, E. (1992). Social dilemmas with uniformly distributed resources. In W. Liebrand, D. Messick & H. Wilke (Eds): *Social dilemmas. Theoretical issues and research findings*. Oxford/New York: Pergamon.

Rapoport, A. & Bornstein, G. (1987). Intergroup competition for the provision of binary public goods. *Psychological Review*, 94, 291-299.

Raub, W. & Keren, G.B. (1993). Hostages as a commitment device: A game-theoretic model and an empirical test of some scenarios. *Journal of Economic Behavior and Organization*, 21, 43-68.

Sale, K. (1991). *Dwellers in the land* (orig. 1985). Philadelphia (Penn.): New Society Publications.

Sheth, J.N. & Frazier, G.L. (1982). A model of strategy mix, choice for planned social change. *Journal of Marketing*, 46, 15-26.

Skinner, B.F. (1953). *Science and human behavior*. New York: Macmillan.

Slovic, P. (1986). Informing and educating the people about risk. *Risk Analysis*, 6 (4), 403-416.

Stern, P.C. (1992). Psychological dimensions of global environmental change. *Annual Review of Psychology*, 43, 269-302.

Stroebe, W. & Frey, D. (1982). Self-interest and collective action: the economics and psychology of public goods. *British Journal of Social Psychology*, 21, 121-137.

Summers, C. (1996 in press). Multimedia environmental decision making simulations. *Behavioral Research Methods, Instruments and Computers.*

Van Lange, P.A.M. (1992). Rationality and morality in social dilemmas: the influence of social value orientations. In W. Liebrand, D. Messick & H. Wilke (Eds): *Social dilemmas. Theoretical issues and research findings*. Oxford/New York: Pergamon.

VCS: Verkehrs-Club der Schweiz (1990). *Oekobonus: ein durchführbarer Weg zur Reduktion des Strassenverkehrs* (Ecobonus: a feasible way toward the reduction of road traffic). Postfach, CH-3360 Herzogenbuchsee, Switzerland.

Vlek, C.A.J. (1995*a*). NIMBY als sociaal dilemma: een diagnose en wat therapie. (NIMBY as a social dillema: a diagnosis and some therapy). In B. van der Moolen & H. Voogd (Eds.): *Niet in mijn achtertuin, maar waar dan?* (Not in my back yard, but where then?). Alphen a/d Rijn: Samson Tjeenk Willink.

Vlek, C.A.J. (1995*b*). Understanding, accepting and controlling risks: a multistage framework for risk communication. *European Review of Applied Psychology, 45 (1), 49-54.*

Vlek, Ch. & G.B. Keren (1992): Behavioral decision theory and environmental risk management: assessment and resolution of four 'survival' dilemmas. *Acta Psychologica*, 80, 249-278.

Wilke, H. (1989). Promoting personal decisions supporting the achievement of risky public goods. In Ch. Vlek & G. Cvetkovich (Eds.): *Social decision methodology for technological projects*. Dordrecht/Boston: Kluwer.

Wit, A. & Wilke, H. (1995). Omgevings- en sociale onzekerheid in sociale dilemma's (Environmental and social uncertainty in social dilemmas). In N.K. De Vries, C.K.W. De Dreu, N. Ellemers & R. Vonk (Eds): *Fundamentele sociale psychologie* (Fundamental social psychology), Volume 9. Tilburg (Neth.): Tilburg University Press.

Yamagishi, T. (1986). The structural goal/expectation theory of cooperation in social dilemmas. In E.J. Lawler (Ed.): *Advances in group processes*. Volume 3, 51-87.

Yamagishi, T. (1995). Social dilemmas. In K.S. Cook, G.A. Fine & J.S. House (Eds): *Sociological perspectives on social psychology*. Boston: Allyn & Bacon.

Young, J.E. (1994). Using computers for the environment. In L.R. Brown et al. (Eds): *State of the World 1994.* New York/London: W.W. Norton.

Attitudes Toward Public Affairs In a Society in Transition[1]

Janusz Grzelak & Grazyna Nejtardt

Department of Psychology and Institute for Social Studies, University of Warsaw, Stawki 5/7, 00-183 Warsaw, Poland

Abstract. The chapter reports results of a panel study on citizens' attitudes toward sharing and contributing to public goods and services. The study was run in Poland, a nation in transition from a centrally planned to a free market economy, from a totalitarian to democratic political system. A collectivity that is experiencing change of this magnitude will seem quite peculiar unless one understands the psychological context in which the changes are taking place. Hence, the Results Section of the chapter begins with some background information about the current state of mind of the Polish people during the transition. The chapter as a whole, however, has two main purposes. First, we want to describe the attitudes of Poles toward public goods and services and to demonstrate how they depend upon demographic factors. Second, we would like to analyze certain methodological problems associated with measuring attitudes in surveys under conditions of rapid social change.

1 Introduction

A collection of individuals as well as the society as a whole can be viewed from social interdependence perspective, namely, in terms of number of actors, rules, types of control actors have over each other's outcomes, and the resulting distribution of outcomes. In this light the development of a market economy and political democracy in Eastern Europe denotes a fundamental change in social interdependence: new actors, new payoff matrices, and new rules of the game. To oversimplify, post-communist reforms have brought about civil society as evidenced by the rapid growth of independent political parties, units of local governments, voluntary associations, private resources. The new actors operate differently than pre-reform ones.

One of the more important social psychological changes associated with the reform concerns the relationship between self-interest and the public interest, whether that of the community, region, or state. In the past a public good was "nobody's" good. The commons was perceived as belonging to and controlled by the sole actor on political scene, the state (party) administration. And the state or party was, in a way,

[1] Preparation of this chapter was supported by grant 115/99203 from the Polish Committee for Scientific Research. We owe Grzegorz Krol our gratitude for his collaboration in writing the chapter. We also thank Eugene Burnstein for polishing our Polish English.

"untouchable" since its position was never dependent on election procedures.

For a vast majority of citizens, the relationship between how an individual behaved in respect to the commons and the way in which this public good was actually managed was virtually nil. For instance, citizens neither paid any income taxes nor were informed about the state or community budget and its allocation.

There were almost no occasions for average citizens to develop feeling of personal control over shared resources. On the other hand, the state seemed to provide some goods and services "for nothing", like education, Medicare, jobs, etc. In other words, the contingencies between how people contributed and how they benefitted were very unclear.

With the institutional changes needed to accommodate the market and democratic government came new opportunities for individual initiative. People were now free to organize, whatever their interests. Increasing awareness of their obligation as tax payers could manifest itself in changes in attitudes toward public goods and services.

At the same time, however, the transformations were often complex, rapid and "turbulent" and, hence, difficult to comprehend. The upshot was (as it is evidenced in the Results Section) that a large portion of society viewed their prospects for the future with feelings of social helplessness.

Let us elaborate a little on this aspect of interdependence. The phenomenon of social helplessness resembles that described in theories of learned helplessness: emotional, motivational, and cognitive deficits along with a decline in performance resulting from a severe loss of control (e.g., Seligman, 1975) However, psychological studies on learned helplessness are almost exclusively focused on individuals and most often ignore the social context. In other words, theories of learned helplessness say almost nothing about how helplessness is moderated by the group, community, or societal setting. Nor do they often take into account social factors as possible causes of helplessness either. Only a few exceptions can be found. For instance, Sinkin et al. (1983) showed that the same cognitive mechanisms, such as expectations of inefficacy, may underlay both individual and dyads and triads helplessness. Another example is Kerr's (Kerr, 1989; 1991) series of studies on expected group efficacy. Although the studies were not directly related to helplessness they showed that expectations about group efficacy are, among others, a function of group size.

In numerous situations individuals are not self-sufficient and they have to rely, at least in part, on other social actors -- other individuals, groups, organizations, offices, state institutions, etc. The effectiveness in gaining outcomes valued by an individual when control over them is mediated by another social actor depends upon at least two factors: (1) the other actor's competence, i.e. capability to supply the individual with outcomes he/she desires and (2) the structure of interdependence (Grzelak, 1988). Two interdependence parameters seem to be of special importance. The first parameter has to do with the correspondence of interests. For instance, if the actor's interests correspond to those of the individual, then the individual can afford to limit his/her control of their relationship to the cognitive level since the actions of the other are unlikely to require any intervention. The second parameter concerns the balance of control or power. Our interest is focused on situations in which there is a strong asymmetry between a powerful agent and powerless individuals (or groups).

A conjunction of four conditions, namely, (1) high dependence upon an external social actor for achieving desirable outcomes, (2) conflicts of interest between individual and actor, (3) powerlessness of the individual vis a vis the actor, and (4) absence of alternative ways of achieving these outcomes, are hypothesized to produce a feeling of helplessness and its cognitive-behavioral correlates (Grzelak, 1988, 1994).

In short, we think that combining the theoretical perspective of social interdependence and helplessness can provide a plausible explanation of the passivity and apathy that has characterized the vast majority of Poles in the pre-transition period when the party monopolized the management of resources.

It also appears that the Poles, and most likely citizens of other countries in this region of the world still experience a great deal of helplessness, although some of the sources of this feeling have changed. Now uncertainty produced by the rapidly changing economic and political environment accounts for helplessness to a much greater extent than in the past. The "old" was unjust, bad but rather predictable The "new" is supposed to be better but it is highly difficult to comprehend and to cope with.

Paradoxically, it was the communist elite, because of its experience in controlling "the commons", that was best prepared to take advantage of the transition. In all post-communist countries former party members appear to be pioneers in the new economic order. They knew how to manage resources and, hence, were not only the first but often the most successful entrepreneurs in the emerging free market environment. In other words, those who knew how to cope with the old know how to cope with the new, those helpless in the past remain, in large part, helpless now. It is congruent with the results of Wieczorkowska and Upmeyer's experimental studies (1991). Although it was shown that people are able to detect changes in contingency across experimental conditions, the individual differences in perception of control level remained stable.

It can be expected that people's cognitive representations of the new social reality develop as they engage more and more in public activities. Hence, adaptation may be simply a matter of experience. If so then it follows that as a precondition of adaptation individuals must attend to, encode, and elaborate upon those events that are significant to the society.

2 Research and Methodological Questions

Social interdependence approach seems to offer a plausible tool to analyze economic and social transformation at theoretical level. However, it is very difficult to investigate the complexity of interdependence structure in social psychological, empirical studies. In the study presented in this chapter we attempted to explore individual interdependence related attitudes rather than to examine the dynamics and structure of interdependence as a whole.

One of the main purposes of our study was to investigate the following questions:

* What distinguishes the people that have positive attitudes toward the public and the commons from those with negative attitudes?
* How have attitudes toward the public changed over time and what are the correlates of these changes?

The main part of the chapter concentrates on three attitude related variables:(1) readiness to contribute to the public by paying higher taxes, (2) involvement in public activities, (3) concern for overuse of the public goods and the commons. We examined how these attitudes are affected by a few selected demographic factors (age, gender, education, place of residence) and occupations. The chapter also deals with some methodological issues related to surveys as a method for studying attitudes toward social issues.

There are many ways to study people's behavior and attitudes in interdependence situations. All of them have, of course, some strengths as well as some shortcomings. Their value mainly depends on type of questions that a researcher wants to answer. The vast majority of studies done so far is based on the experimental paradigm. However, in empirical analyses of social dilemmas a variety of paradigms other than the experiment have been used. Various chapters of this book are the best evidence of diversity of methodological approaches, ranging from computer simulations through classical laboratory games, to field and survey studies. Interest in the latter increases as we become more and more concerned with a relationship between social reality and the way we conceptualize that reality.

Although conclusions drawn from surveys are in most cases not as strong in respect to causation as those derived from laboratory analogs of reality, we decided, nevertheless, to conduct a survey. There were at least three reasons for so doing.

Firstly, we were primarily interested in people's attitudes toward the public goods during the systemic changes in Poland. In other words, the purpose of this study was not only to test some theoretical relationships but also to monitor attitudes over time.

Secondly, we wanted to determine how and to what extent people's attitudes are related to social and economic status and to demographic factors. Socio-demographic variables are typically ignored or, if not, their role is regularly underestimated by social psychologists. Perhaps attention to demographic factors follows from the concentration on laboratory experiments in which it is useless to be concerned with variance associated with variables of this kind. It seemed obvious to us, however, that we could not neglect them in a study on people's attitudes toward real life issues, especially in the period of social change whose pace depends upon where respondents live, whether and what kind of job they have, etc. People's ability to cope with these changes may depend upon their age, marital status, and level of education.

Finally, to our knowledge there is no good psychological theory of macro-social phenomena that can be used to select a limited set of variables important in explaining reactions to social change. Hence, it seemed reasonable to us that a survey study would be a good way discovering such variables and, thereby, allow us to begin theory building. However, survey studies, as we noted, also rise many problems, several of which will be discussed at some length in the end of the chapter.

3 Method

Two survey studies were run[2], the first one in 1994 and the second one twelve months later, in 1995. A representative sample of adult Poles aging from 16 to 65 (totaling to 1660 Ss) was used in 1994 study. Selected occupational groups of the original sample

[2] A survey administered by the Social Opinion Research Center (CBOS).

(totaling to 618 Ss) were approached again in the second wave, in 1995. The two studies were based on questionnaires prepared by Grzelak and Giza-Poleszczuk in 1994[3] and by Grzelak and Wieczorkowska-Nejtardt in 1995. About 60% of questions were the same in both surveys. Interviews were conducted by professional interviewers. Most questions (including all analyzed in this chapter) were asked by interviewers, some parts of the questionnaire were to be filled out by respondents themselves (with interviewer's help only if necessary).

3.1 Assessment of Attitudes

The assessment of three main attitude variables was based on scales composed of a set of single questions.

* *Readiness to pay higher income taxes* was measured by a composite index of nine responses to the following items: Are you willing to pay slightly higher taxes given that they would be used to support: (1- no, 2 - yes) (A) Army, (B) Environment protection, © Unemployed in regions with structural unemployment, (D) Education and science, (E) Police, (F) Medicare personnel, (H) State plants being close to bankruptcy, (I) Agriculture, (G) Public works sector.

* *Involvement in social/public activities*. A question about everyday activities contained a list of 49 different activities ranging from 'looking through the window' to 'doing something useful in the union'. 12 of them related to public domain of life (involvement in a party, union, club, parish, etc.).Respondents were asked to estimate how often they are involved in each type of activities (3 = often, 2 = sometimes, 1 = very rarely or never). A mean value of 12 items was used as an index.

* *Concern for overuse of the commons*. The question or rather a set of questions was as follows: "Below you find a list of different behaviors. Some of them may concern you, some may concern other people. Which of the following behaviors are of personal concern to you and which are not? (1 - I do not care at all, ..., 4 - I do care a lot)

A) Someone pays lower taxes than he/she should by law.
B) A state clerk runs private errands during working hours.
C) Someone uses chemicals that pollute the environment.
D) Someone goes on a bus, train without buying a ticket.
E) Someone refuses to serve in the army.
F) Teenagers keep sitting outside the shop and behave noisily
G) Director of the school takes bribes for 'pushing' the child to the next grade
H) People throw rubbish, litter at random
I) Workers from the second-rate, public sector works attain next raise in wages
J) Somebody manages not to pay light bills

---

[3] The questionnaire was prepared in collaboration with Kwiatek and Kobylinski. The questionnaire was tested in several pilot studies before it was finally used by Social Opinion Research Center (CBOS).

K) Someone collects unemployment benefit for period longer than it is permitted by law
L) Someone drives his car much too fast
N) Someone does not pay a rent for his flat
O) Doctor admits to the hospital ward private patients for money
P) Councillor is not on duty when he should
R) Someone suffering from an infectious disease works with other people
S) Someone brings goods from abroad and does not pay customs duty

A summative scale was composed of all 17 items.

The first two variables deal with contribution to the public goods and services in a form of money and in a form of own public activity. The third variable is related to the use of the public but in an indirect way. A series of pilot studies showed that asking respondents directly about their own use (and/or overuse) was threatening and credibility of answers was highly questionable. Therefore, we decided to ask people about others' rather than about their own behavior.

4 Results

Although it seems self-evident, it is better to clarify at the very beginning that, like in any other survey studies, we did not measure attitudes as they manifest themselves in real life but respondents' self-reports about their attitudes. The latter may, for many reasons, deviate from actual attitudes. One of them is social desirability, or to put it in other words, respondents tendency to give answers that are socially acceptable. It is especially in the case of questions related to important social issues, like whether to contribute to the public pool or not. A short version of Marlow-Crown social approval scale[4] was used in our surveys. Subject location on the scale accounted for negligible portion of variance of declared attitudes.

The more questions are behavior related the more likely they reflect subjects' "true" attitude toward the issue (Wilson, Hodges,1992). For this reason we used questions about behaviors as well (activity). They correlate highly with other attitude manifestations like concern for overuse public goods. It is still safer to say that in our analyses we explained differences in ways in which people answer questions rather than differences in attitudes they really hold.

4.1 Poland '94: Social Mood, Feelings of Cognitive and Behavioral Control

As said earlier, the first part of the panel was a survey run in 1994 on a representative sample of Poles. The survey constituted a good basis to assess psychological condition of the Poles. Let us then start with a short characteristics of what the Poles were like in 1994.

The survey showed that a marked proportion of population revealed dissatisfaction with life and did not foresee any good prospects for the future. A low or rather low life

[4] A version used in many earlier surveys.

satisfaction was reported by 41.1% of respondents. Over 50% among them (21% of total population) considered their present (1994) state as the worst in their life. In general, life was judged as less satisfactory than it was in the past by 54.5% and as satisfactory as it was before only by 34.5%. Over 52.4 % did not expect anything good from the future. These results are consistent with results of other surveys on social mood run in Poland in years 1992-95 (CBOS, PGSS, Czapinski, 1993,1994).

Negative mood was accompanied by difficulties in foreseeing the course of future events at both macro-social and personal level. Almost two thirds of respondents (63%) reported that they understood less than before (meaning time before '89) when it came to "what was going on in Poland now". Over 82% said that they could not predict what could happen in their local community within the next months (90.3% within the next years). The figures were about the same when the state was in question. One third of respondents (32%) said that it was hard to predict what was going to happen in their personal life within the next months, and nearly 65% found it difficult to make predictions for the next two years.

Moreover, on average, Polish citizens did not feel they could exercise control over their social environment, although they desired to. They had feelings of lack of not only cognitive but also behavioral control over environment. For instance, 36.5% of population report a low (if any) control over own life, over 50% of that group have a feeling that they never experienced control lower than now. Fate, good or bad luck are considered by as many as 14% as factors deciding about one's life career, and by another 34.5% as playing very important role in determining life success.

When asked about the extent to which people can affect their closest environment, less than 10% of the respondents said that they could have a noticeable impact upon: what is being done for the unemployed (1.3%), accessibility of medical services (2.6%), decisions made by county representatives in local governments (3.7%), quality of teachers' work in local schools (6.3%), safety of neighborhood (9.2%), public transportation (4.6%).

Feelings about low impact upon the closest neighborhood could not result in control deprivation if people did not really aspire to control their social environment. It was not the case. The most frequent answer to a number of questions on who should affect various aspects of community life was that it should be inhabitants themselves: 37% to 75% answers, depending upon the type of decision.

A possible way to overcome difficulties in understanding reality and in exercising a sufficient control over outcomes is to delegate, to pass that control to others, the others being family members, friends, elected representatives, democratic institutions. A precondition for passing control to others is a belief that other people or institutions are more competent than we ourselves and that they will act in accordance with our interest. A trustworthy, cooperative and efficient other may be of greatest help for those who feel mentally lost, feel helpless, and insecure in the new world. Over 12% of respondents did not feel like trusting any of the local or state institution, any local leader, official, council member or alike when they had personal problems. As many as 10% of respondents did not have anybody among friends or family to rely on when they were in trouble.

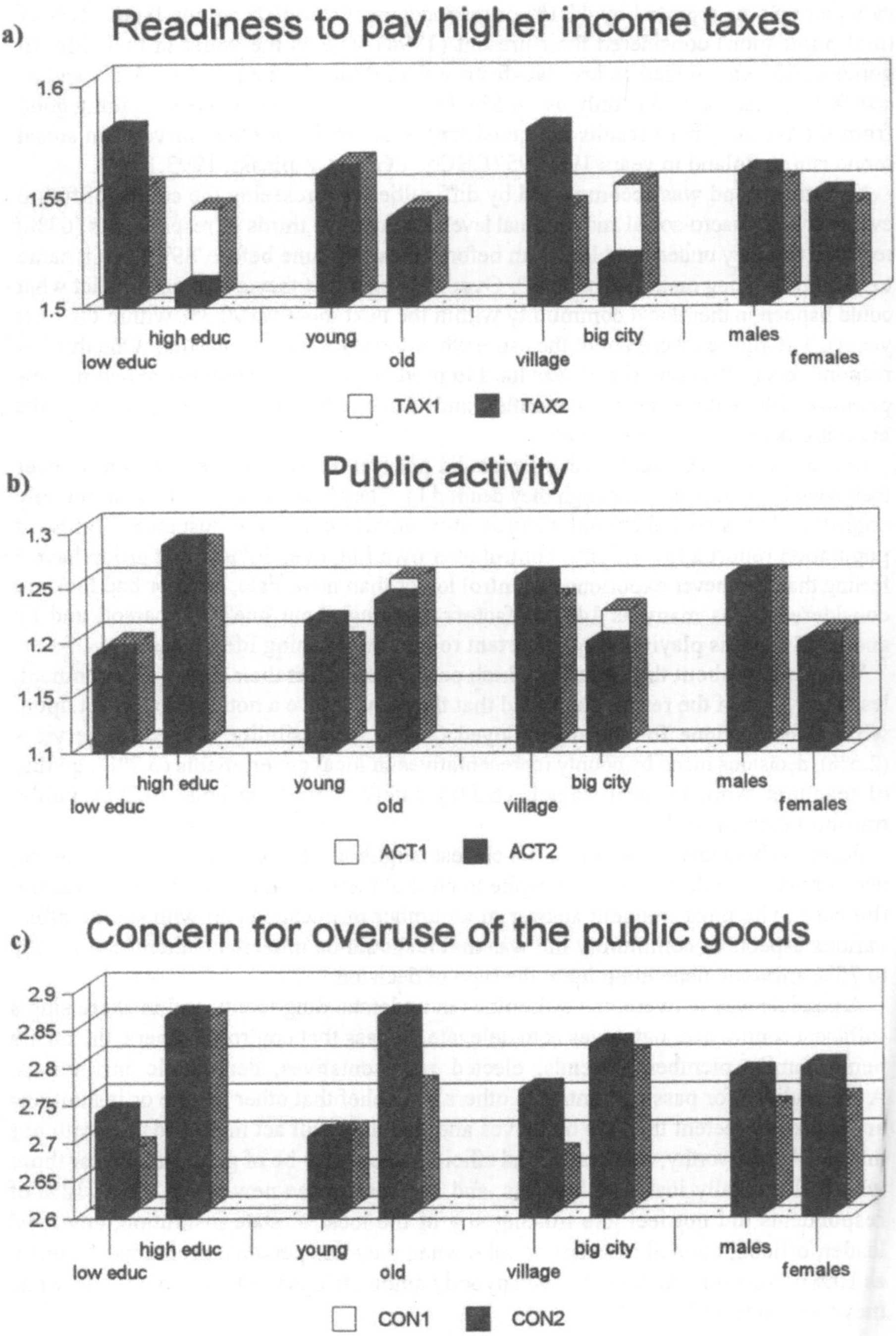

Fig. 1. Mean values for paying taxes (a), involvement in activity (b) and concern for overuse (c)

Are these numbers small or high? The answer depends, of course, upon a frame of reference, like relevant data from other countries. The results showed above form, however, a sufficient basis to say that quite a few Poles seem or at least seemed to be unhappy, powerless and lost in the new world although the systemic changes in our countries were supposed to make people happier and enjoying more control over own fate, close neighborhood or the state than they could enjoy in the past.

4.2 Attitudes Toward Social/public Affairs. Effects of Who You Are in Socio-demographic Terms

A series of analyses of variance were run with demographic variables (age, gender, education, place of residence) as four between subject factors, time (1994, 1995) as a within factor and attitudes as dependent measures. In all analyses a median split of demographic variables was used.

We failed in finding any main effect of time. Demographic factors turned out to explain large portions of attitude variance.

Individual's *involvement in social activities* was strongly affected by level of education ($F(1,607)=47.1, p<.001$), gender $F(1,607)=18.35, p<.005$), size of residence place ($F(1,607)=11.81, p<.001$). Mean values of activity measure are displayed in Figure 1. Involvement in social/public activity was associated with being man, older, better educated, and living in rural areas or in small towns rather than in big cities.

Age and education produced significant differences in *concern for overuse of the public*. Young respondents were less concerned than the older respondents ($F(1,612)=6.64$ $p<.01$). Less educated respondents showed lower concern than those with a higher level of education ($F(1,612)=14.76$ $P<.001$).

A significant effect of time by age interaction ($F(1,612)=3.92, p<.05$) was found. The effect can be attributed mainly to marked attitude change over time in those who are older. They became much more concerned for overuse in 1995 than in 1994 ($t=2.82, df=344, p<.005$).

Readiness to pay taxes was least affected by demographic factors. There were no main effects, and only interactions of time and place of residence ($F(1,597)=2.97$ $P<.09$) and time and education ($F(1,597)=2.91, p<.09$) were found as marginally significant. For instance, better educated respondents manifested lower readiness to pay taxes than those less educated in 1995, although the two groups did not differ at all in 1994.

As it was shown above, demographic factors affect attitudes to a high extent. We cannot analyze relationships between any other variables without taking into account variance produced by the demographic factors. Let us consider an example.

Activity and concern for overuse are correlated: $r=.22$. Both variables depend upon level of education, the higher education the higher they are. Partial correlation coefficient between activity and concern for controlled education equals .20. A coefficient for data standardized according to four demographic factors drops down to $r=.12$.

Concluding, some psychological effects become "visible" when psychological data are corrected, that is standardized according to demographic variables and the other way around. Taking demographic factors into analysis gave a chance to reveal relationships that could not be found otherwise and to find out that other relationship could be artifacts. In further analyses, in order to control for socio-demographic factors, we standardized all psychological data according to education, age, place of residence and run analyses for the standardized data.

Since education and place of residence are correlated with respondents occupation, we examined the effects of occupation as well. There were seven groups investigated in both '94 and '95 wave, that is students, unemployed, farmers, owners of small enterprises, employees of private enterprises, employees of state run industry, professionals in state services (education, Medicare, administration). Occupational groups did not differ significantly in involvement in public activity. They differed in their concern for overuse of the public ($F(1,152)=3.93$, $p<.05$). The mean values of demographically standardized variables are presented in Figure 2.

There were two groups of our special interest whose situation has changed within one year. They were farmers and state professionals. It occurred that the change in their objective situation has an impact on their attitudes. The significant interaction effect of occupational group by year ($F(1,152)=4.13$, $p<.05$) could be attributed to a marked decrease in concern among state professionals in 1995 as compared with 1994 ($t(66)=1.91$, $p<.06$). Also, a marginal effect of time and group interaction upon readiness to pay taxes was found ($F(1,149)=3.02$, $p<.08$). Of all groups only farmers showed a significant change in readiness to pay taxes: they were more willing to pay in 1995 than in 1994 ($t(83)=2.17$, $p<.03$).

4.3 Attitudes and Behavior

Having panel data from two years we could examine a causal relationship between attitudes and behavior. In this analysis we assumed that self-reports about one's own life activities are close to actual behavior and that both concern for overuse of goods and readiness to pay higher taxes are manifestations of motivational and evaluative elements of attitudes. It allowed us to test causal relationships between attitude and behavior. We tried to estimate the relative impact of attitude (like concern for overuse of goods and readiness to pay higher taxes) on activity.

We carried out analyses using so-called two-wave path model (Hendrickson & Jones,1987). Measurement errors for the observed measures of activity (ACT1 and ACT2 for years 1994 and 1995, respectively), readiness to pay taxes (TAX1 and TAX2), and concern for overuse (CONC1 and CONC2) were allowed to covary within the same year[5].

We failed to find any significant paths connecting concern for overuse of commons with activity and readiness to pay higher taxes. The data allowed us to test the hypothesis on causal relationships between TAX and ACT. Following the old discussion in the literature we test two mirror hypotheses:

(H1) Involvement in activity in 1994 (ACT1) leads to higher readiness to pay taxes in 1995 (TAX2), given paying taxes in 1994(TAX1).

[5] All analyses were based on correlation matrix.

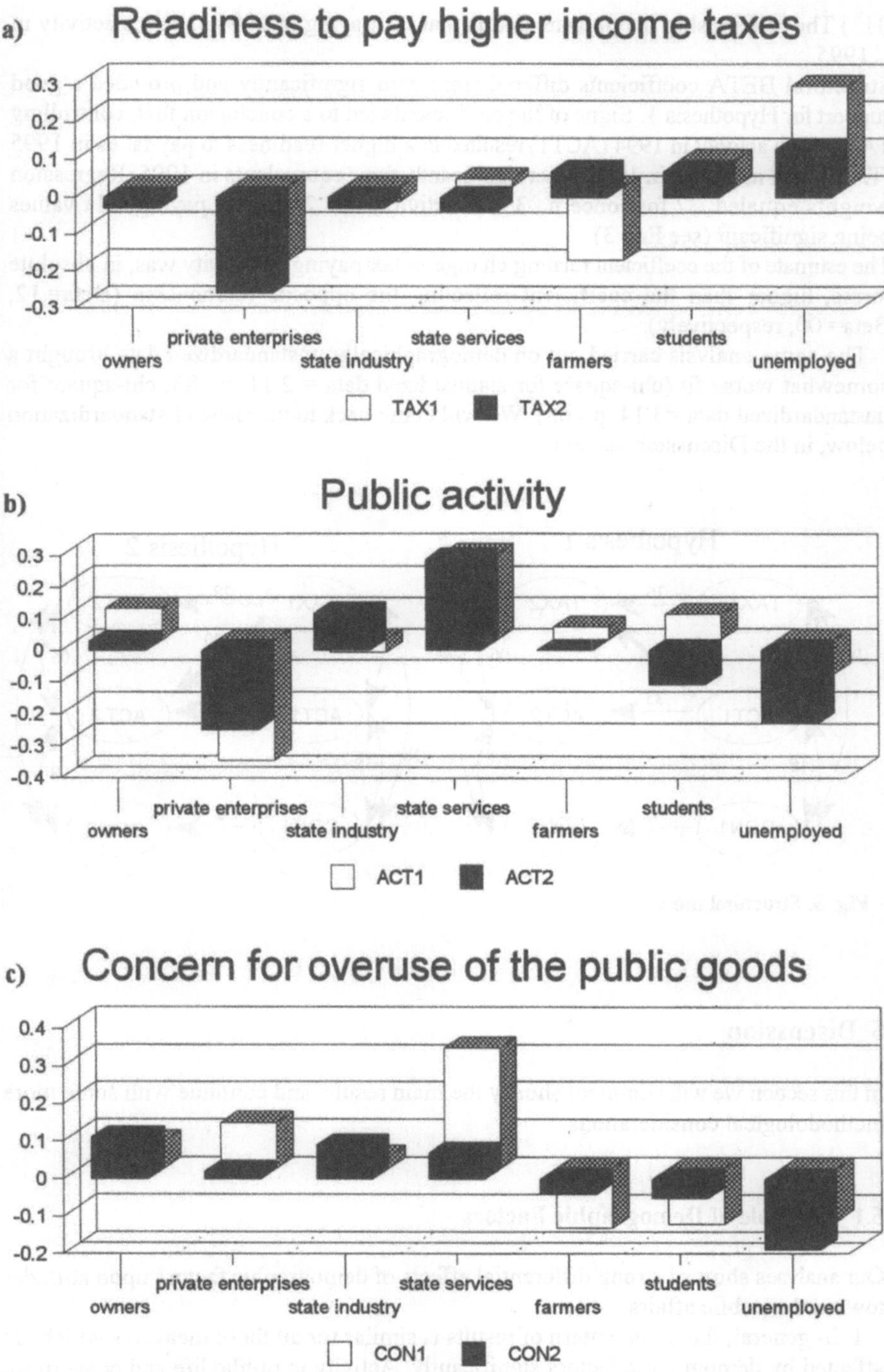

Fig. 2. Mean values for demographically standardized data (with respect to time and occupation)

(H2) The relationship is opposite, that is that tax paying in 1994 explains activity in 1995.

Structural BETA coefficients differed from zero significantly and provided a good support for Hypothesis 1. Signs of the coefficients led to a conclusion that, controlling TAX1, high activity in 1994 (ACT1) resulted in a higher readiness to pay taxes in 1995 (TAX2). All measures in 1994 affect significantly their equivalents in 1995. Regression weights equaled .32 for concern, .35 for activity, and .26 for tax paying, all t values being significant (see Fig. 3).

The estimate of the coefficient relating change in tax paying to activity was, in absolute terms, higher than the coefficient reflecting the opposite relationship (Beta=.12, Beta=.00, respectively).

The same analysis carried out on demographically unstandardized data brought a somewhat worse fit (chi-square for standardized data = 2.11, p<.83; chi-square for unstandardized data =3.14, p<.68). We will come back to the issue of standardization below, in the Discussion section.

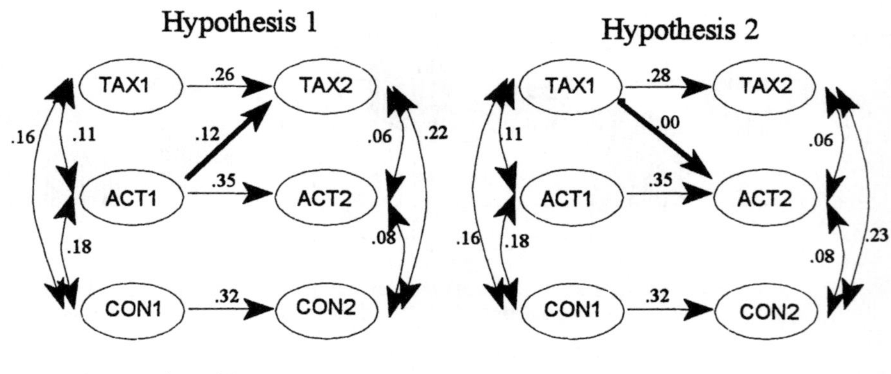

Fig. 3. Structural model

5 Discussion

In this section we will comment shortly the main results and continue with some more methodological considerations.

5.1 The Role of Demographic Factors

Our analyses showed strong differential effects of demographic factors upon attitudes toward the public affairs.

I. In general, the main pattern of results is similar for all those measures which are affected by demographic factors significantly. Activity in public life and concern for overuse of shared goods are associated with being older and better educated. In addition, activity is also associated with being a man and living in a smaller place of residence. A plausible and rather optimistic explanation is that 'pro-public' is, at least to some extent, a matter of learning. In other words it depends upon experience and competence. People who are educated are better qualified to grasp a rather complex individual-public contingencies. People who live longer and live in small communities have more opportunities to experience and learn these contingencies. The same refers to men as compared with women. Men in our culture have more opportunities to deal actively with the public than women.

It may not be surprising then that we observed an increase in concern for free-riding in older part of the sample. Again, the older may be better cognitively equipped, due to their experience. They learn that free-riding is at expense of those who pay, work, contribute. Does the fact that it is the educated people who manifest a much lower readiness to pay taxes only after a year work against our explanatory hypothesis?. Not necessarily. The educated are more and more concerned over time with free-riding, that is with being exploited, thus, not surprisingly, they may show lower and lower readiness to contribute. The "learning interpretation" should not be extended to interpersonal relationship. There is no evidence, whatsoever, that men, old or better educated people are more prosocial in interpersonal settings than female, young or less educated people. Complexity of the commons is much higher in macro-social settings than in dyadic or in small group ones. Another, not exclusive way of interpreting the results is that referring to occupation. A decreasing along the time concern for overuse of the public or free-riding among state professionals can be attributed to the fact that their jobs are secured by the state, are state protected, and therefore less exposed or less directly exposed to possible damages caused by overuse of the public. Farmers are also state protected but in a different way. They are highly subsidized by the state budget. They could experience this relationship especially in the period of last two years, and, in line, they show highest of all groups increase in readiness to pay higher taxes, that is to contribute to the budget. In sum, as we expected, the results demonstrated an important role that socio-demographic factors play in 'public' behavior. The role is often underestimated and quite often neglected in psychological studies. It seems worth mentioning, however, that at least some effects of demographic factors are likely to be mediated by psychological variables. In other words, demographic factors may have their own psychological meaning. For instance, a higher involvement in public activities in villages and small cities than in big cities can be attributed to the fact that such activity is more visible and, therefore, more likely to be rewarding in small communities than in large cities. The rewards could come from noticeability of own efficacy as well as from conforming to social norms to which an individual is much more exposed in small than in large communities.

II. Fast systemic changes ongoing in Central and Eastern European countries make monitoring attitude changes in time attractive. We succeeded in showing only some differences. In general, there were either no effects of time observed or, if any, then differences in a more prosocial or pro-public direction (except for paying taxes by better educated). It might be a manifestation of real attitude changes or manifestation of learning of what is good to say. It may be due to increase in social awareness of interdependence networks and pressure to conform to newly developed norms saying what is good to do and to say when the public issues are in question. We must admit that even the latter looks optimistic to us if we take into account that a few years ago very few people could understand what contribution and use of the public goods consists in. The most pronounced time effect is that showed by structural modeling. It is not against common sense that people involved in public activities learn to contribute more to the publicly shared pool. Again, it is surprising, however, that this causal relationship could be observed within a year.

III. We believe, and already expressed that belief in the introductory section of the chapter that individuals' attitudes toward public matters largely depend upon social interdependence structure. This includes both outcome allocation and power distribution properties of interdependence. We hope that further analyses of the panel data will show importance of these properties[6].

Analyses conducted so far made us think, however, that a relationship between individual's participation in social life, readiness to contribute to the public as well as sensitivity to various forms of free-riding on one side and demographic variables on the other may be not as simple as we thought. Groups of different demographic and, most likely, socio-economic status are exposed to different interdependence structures as well as they may perceive the same situations differently. As scientists studying interdependence we should then pay more attention to demographic factors by measuring their effects and/or controlling other effects for these factors. The last sentence leads us directly to methodological problems related to survey research.

5.2 Some Methodological Considerations

I. We paid a lot of attention to the effects of demographic factors in our study. However, demographic variables were also a source of noise whenever relationships between variables correlated with demographic factors were examined. In other words, we demographically standardized data to neutralize the effects demographic variables whenever the latter were not of our first interest. As we already showed in the Results Section, all statistical effects can be stronger when data are demographically standardized.

II. The second methodological point that we would like to make refers to the meaning of our data, more specifically, to sources of possible misinterpretations of how respondents respond to survey questions. It seems worth to repeat here what Strack and Martin (Strack & Martin, 1987) concluded on the basis of experiments conducted by cognitive psychologists. Every, even a very simple question initiates a series of cognitive processes in respondent's mind which include (1) question comprehension, (2) recollection of previous judgments on the same or similar issue, if any judgement has been ever made, (3) recollection of information relevant to the question, (4) judgment formation, (5) adjusting own judgment to response categories provided by the researcher, (6) phrasing the response. Each stage is a potential source for noncorrespondence between researcher's question and the response he/she gets as an answer. One of the main problem is what the respondents does when he/she faces difficulties in answering questions. He/she may conform to what perceives as socially

[6] The questionnaire contains a number of questions about individual control over, among others, public outcomes.

approved, or say he/she doesn't have an opinion ("I don't know", "hard to say") regardless whether it is true or not, or say that a given issue is out of his/her interest... Researcher can, at least to some extent, control some sources of "misleading" responses. Measuring need for social approval (as we did in our study with Marlowe-Crown scale) is one of ways. Another way is not to make easy answers that express indifference or lack of opinion. Providing an answer of "I don't know" type in explicit, overt way to the subjects increases frequency of such answers by 10-36% (Sulek, 1993). At least for some subject it is a way to avoid expressing any clear cut opinion even if they have one. In our study "don't know" answers were not easily available to respondents since they were not shown to them. Interviewers could, however, mark these answers in their questionnaire whenever they judged subject difficulties in answering questions as serious).

Still another way of getting a better insight into what respondents' answers really mean is asking a straight forward question about if respondents are interested in a given issue and, supposedly, have/had a good basis to form own judgement on the issue. While approaching subjects with questions in survey studies we usually assume that people have their opinions already formed. The assumptions is obviously not valid in case of people who have never thought of the issue in question. People vary in how often, if ever, they think of social matters.

Thinking about social issues may make these issues more important to respondents, and in consequence may make respondents more concerned with the public goods. We expected then that those who are "mentally" preoccupied with social affairs, as compared with those who are not, should manifest stronger prosocial attitudes.

We asked respondents how often they think about their own life and how often about social issues. The latter were asked as follows: How often do you think about (a scale from 1 =never to 5 = very often) (1) who is governing your district, (2) how your district should be managed, (3) what kind of people are now in power in Poland, (4) what kind of people should be in power in Poland. A summative scale of 4 items was a measure of variable that we named "Think".

The analysis revealed that "Think" is correlated with demographic factors. Men, educated, old and inhabitants of big cities think more than their respective counter groups. Students think of social matters least often (M=2.92), whereas farmers and private entrepreneurs think most often (3.47, 3.32, respectively). It was also found that, in general, there is a positive relationship between "Think" measure and attitudes: the more people think of social issues, the more active, concerned and ready to contribute to the public they are. It can be hypothesized that "think" leads to prosocial attitudes as well as the other way around. The causal direction cannot be examined in this study since measure was used only in 1994. "Think" variable modified, however, a number of effects.

An analysis based on a median split revealed differences in correlation coefficients between our main dependent variables. For instance, correlation coefficients between activity, readiness to pay taxes and concern for overuse were close to zero in the group scoring low (a median split was used) on the "think" scale whereas they were considerably high and significant in the group scoring high on the scale.

We expected that those who pay more attention to social affairs, think more about them have their attitudes better grounded, more crystallized. Therefore, various effects should appear stronger among those who think than among those who do not. To illustrate it we run structural modeling presented in Figure 3 once again in two groups separately: those who "think" and those who do not. The "think" filter strongly affected the results. A solution for those who think is better in terms of its fit, as well as coefficients. All paths are significant and show that the causal relationship is stronger than that those who do not think. In other words, high location on "Think" scale, that is a kind of cognitive interest in public affairs makes predictability of readiness to pay taxes and other variables higher then it is in the case of those who don't pay much attention to public matters.

* * *

Are all these comments relevant to what we do most often, that is to laboratory experiments? We do believe so. Laboratory experiments do not allow us to examine demographic effects. Being aware of importance of such effects may make us think of controlling the impact of demographic variables in experiments, for instance by selecting homogenous groups or counterbalancing factors in a systematic way.

The same may refer to the role of cognitive interest. Laboratory experiments are meant to be simplified analogs of real life situations. It is possible that interest in real public issues is also transferred to our lab and modifies behavior of subjects. It seems worth to examine whether subjects' thoughtfulness or their cognitive involvement in social/public issues affect experimental data as well.

* * *

We focused this chapter on selected methodological problems and on the impact of socio-demographic factors. We do not want, however, to leave the reader with an impression that strong, and possibly even overemphasized effects of these factors suppress other, more psychological variables. In other analyses, not reported in here, we have found that attitudes toward the public are also strongly influenced by psychological factors (for instance, by locus and desire for control).

References:

Bishop J. F., Oldendick R. W., Tuchfaber A. J., Benett, F.E. (1980). Pseudo-opinions on public affairs. *Public Opinion Quarterly*, 50, 240-250.

Czapinski, J.(1994). The anchorage of Polish soul. *Polish Psychological Bulletin,* 25,3.

Grzelak, J. (1991). Homo economicus. Should it be revisited? In M.Lerner & R.Vermunt (eds) *Social justice in human relations*. New York: Plenum Press.

Grzelak, J. (1993). Bezradnosc spoleczna. Szkic teoretyczny. (Social helplessness. A theoretical framework). In M. Kofta (ed.) *Psychologia aktywnosci* (Psychology of activity). Poznan: Nakom.

Kelley, H.H., Thibaut, .W. (1978). *Interpersonal relations. A theory of interdependence.* New York: Wiley.

Kerr, N.L. (1989). Illusions of efficacy. The effect of group size on perceived efficacy in social dilemmas. *Journal of Experimental Social Psychology*, 25, 287-313.

Kerr, N.L. (1991). Efficacy as a causal and moderating variable in social dilemmas. In W.Liebrand & D.Messick (eds.) *A social psychological approach to social dilemmas*. New York: Pergamon Press.

Hendrickson, L. & Jones, B. (1987). A study of longitudinal causal models comparing gain score analysis with structural equation approaches. In Cuttance P.Ecob, R.(ed.) *Structural Modeling by example.* New York: Cambridge Press.

Sinkin, D., Lederer, J., & Seligman, M. (1983). Learned helplessness in groups. *Behaviour Research and Therapy,* Vol. 21(6) 613-622.

Strack, F., Martin, L. L., (1987). Thinking, judging and communicating: A process account of context effects in attitude surveys. In H. J. Hippler, N. Schwarz, and S. Sudman (Eds.) *Social information processing and survey methodology,* pp.123-148, New York: Macmillan.

Sulek, A. (1993). Jak dziala filtr "nie wiem"? O perspektywie poznawczej w metodologii badan sondazowych (What does "don't know" filter do. A cognitive perspective in methodology of survey research). *Kultura i Spoleczenstwo,* 3, 31-44.

Wieczorkowska-Nejtardt G. (1995). Jak respondenci odpowiadaja na pytania sondazowe? (How do respondents answer survey questions?). *Nowiny Psychologiczne*, 2.

Wieczorkowska G., Upmeyer A.(1991). Judgment and Emotional Response to Different Response-Outcome relations: Role of individual differences in expectations of control. *Polish Psychological Bulletin*, 22,117-131.

Wilson, D. T, Hodges S D, (1992). Attitudes as temporary constructions. In L. L. Martin & A. Teffer (eds) *The construction of social judgements* (pp. 37 - 65). Hills Dale: Earlbaum.

Provision of Community Social Services: The Role of Distributive Fairness for Willingness to Pay[1]

Anders Biel, Daniel Eek, and Tommy Gärling

Department of Psychology, Göteborg University, Haraldsgatan 1, S-41314 Göteborg, Sweden

Abstract. In an attempt to generalize the GEF hypothesis (H. A. M. Wilke, 1991) to a real-life public-goods dilemma, the main question asked in three studies was whether perceived distributive fairness affects willingness to pay for community child care. In the first study, attitudes towards whether the quality of child care should be distributed equally to all children, according to the needs of the children, or proportional to how much the children's parents pay were surveyed in 1,840 Swedish parents living in five municipalities of different sizes. Preferences for different methods of payment were also measured. Although the results lent some support to the hypothesis that perceived distributive fairness plays a role, other factors were found to have a stronger effect on willingness to pay. The main survey results were replicated and extended in two additional studies employing a hypothetical society paradigm in which undergraduates were asked to respond to scenarios.

Key words. Community social services, child care, willingness to pay

1 Introduction

"Born free. Taxed to death." This message posted at the garage where one of the authors parks his car may reflect that unfairness is a prevailing circumstance in society. However, although most people some times regard taxes as a necessary evil, the provision of social services must be paid for by citizens in one way or another. Once the needed resources are provided they

---

[1]The studies reported in this chapter as well as its preparation were financially supported by grants from the Centre for Public Sector Research (CEFOS) at Göteborg University, Sweden. We thank Lennart Nilsson, Lars Strömberg, the editors and an anonymous reviewer for valuable suggestions, Sofia Flood and Vicki Johansson for assistance in collecting and processing the data.

can be distributed among members of the society. Does willingness to pay for community social services increase if this distribution is perceived as fair? If so, what is considered to be fair? In this chapter we first briefly review previous research which has addressed these questions, then we report three studies aimed at investigating the relationship between perceived distributive justice and willingness to pay for community child care.

Distributive-justice research focuses on how payoffs from joint efforts should be apportioned. According to Kinsey, Grasmick, and Smith (1991), research on people's evaluations of fairness of outcomes has been framed along two theoretical perspectives: an outcome-processing frame and a norm-processing frame. The former is represented by equity and exchange-based theories which basically assume that people believe that rewards should be in proportion to inputs (e.g., Adams, 1965; Homans, 1961). Thus, what an individual receives in terms of social services should match the inputs he or she provides. The latter perspective views fairness at a societal level and focuses on the question of whether the overall pattern of outcomes harmonizes with normative standards of what is fair (Folger, 1984, cited in Kinsey et al., 1991). According to Deutsch (1975) there are at least three discernible principles or standards of fair distribution of a common resource: (1) Equity, implying a distribution proportional to the recipients' contributions to the resource to be allocated; (2) Equality, implying that all receive the same; and (3) Need, implying that the most needy receive the most. Which of these principles will be applied may be related to collective goals. Thus, when economic production and efficiency are the goals, the principle of equity will be applied. Equality will be preferred in order to sustain mutual respect when social relations are in focus. Need will be the favoured principle when personal development and well-being are the primary goals.

Another line of research has investigated people's willingness to contribute to a public good such as a social service (Biel & Gärling, 1995; Dawes, 1980; Komorita & Parks, 1995). In a public-goods dilemma people are asked to contribute to a resource to which all have free access. Provided that a sufficient number contributes, everyone will benefit from the public good irrespective of whether they contribute or not. The dilemma exists since the individual "rational" choice is to not contribute. However, if everyone makes this choice everyone will end up worse off.

As Tyler and Dawes (1993) point out, although studies of social dilemmas and distributive justice share several features, contacts between the two fields have, with some exceptions (e.g., De Vries, 1991; Joireman,

Kuhlman, & Okuda, 1994; Van Dijk & Wilke, 1993), been rare. In earlier studies contributions and endowments have often been symmetrical (Van Lange, Liebrand, Messick, & Wilke, 1992). When the situation is symmetrical people tend to prefer equality (Rapoport, Budescu, Suleiman, & Weg, 1992; Rutte, Wilke, & Messick, 1987). This also seems to be the case when no information about wealth or benefits is given (Van Dijk & Grodzka, 1992). As suggested by Allison and Messick (1990), equality is then a natural principle or heuristic to apply. Support for this is found in a study by Harris and Joyce (1980). Although contributions were unequal in creating a resource, subjects nevertheless preferred to equalize outcomes.

The GEF hypothesis proposed by Wilke (1991; see also Samuelson, Messick, Wilke, & Rutte, 1986) explicitly introduces distributive fairness as a factor affecting cooperation in resource dilemmas. In essence the hypothesis states that greed (G) is constrained by a desire to use the resource efficiently (E) and a desire to realize fairness (F). Greed refers to the fact that individuals attempt to maximize their own benefits. However, if this leads to depletion of a resource, individuals will constrain their greed to preserve a resource efficiently. In addition, individuals generally attempt to ensure that the distribution of the benefits to themselves and others are fair. This is assumed to imply that benefits are equally distributed.

Support for the suggestion that people desire to obtain fairness was provided in studies by Van Dijk (1993). Concern for fairness was also shown to affect cooperation: Although some participants were able to extract more benefits from the resource than other participants, they only took about the same amount as the others.

However, an unequal distribution is sometimes considered fair. When participants are aware of an asymmetrical input, they may prefer equity (Messick & Schell, 1992; Van Dijk & Grodzka, 1992; Wilke, Liebrand, Lotgerink, & Buurma, 1986) if it is perceived to be justified (Messick & Schell, 1992; Van Dijk & Wilke, 1993). For instance, hard work to create a resource is a better reason than luck to switch from equality to equity. Also, in studies of asymmetric public-goods dilemmas with continuous contributions, participants with large resources or high profit rates contribute more than participants with small resources or low profit rates (Wit, Wilke, & Oppewal, 1992). Similarly, Rapoport (1988) and Rapoport and Suleiman (1993) reported that people with different endowments contributed the same proportion of their endowments.

The previous research highlights the role of perceived distributive fairness for cooperation in social dilemmas. However, without exception this research is laboratory-based. In a real-life public-goods dilemma, such as the provision of community social services, where knowledge of benefits and costs is incomplete, neither the collective interest of efficient resource management nor norms of distributive justice may be salient. Greed is perhaps then the dominant motive. In this chapter we report research which aims at extending previous laboratory results to the real-life public-good dilemma of payment for the provision of community child care. A test was conducted of the prediction derived from the GEF hypothesis (Wilke, 1991) that perceived distributive fairness increases willingness to pay. However, several other factors are also likely to affect cooperation. Below we will enumerate those which we believe are the most important ones reflecting or related to either fairness, greed, or efficiency. The general question posed was thus which weight perceived fairness of the distribution of quality of community child care has relative to these other factors. If it has, it would extend the generalizability of the GEF hypothesis to one class of real-life social dilemmas.

2 The Present Studies

In this section we report a survey of parents and two classroom experiments with undergraduates in which we investigated if people's willingness to pay for community child care is affected by how fair they perceive its quality to be distributed. The research was conducted in Sweden where child care is supplied by municipalities. Although fees and taxes for child care are based on income and degree of use rather than being equally distributed among parents of children who use child care, an official principle is that the *quality* of child care should be equal for all children. Whether this official equality principle is also perceived as fair or not was one specific question raised. Another specific question was whether those who endorse the principle are willing to pay for the service given that they believe that it is followed. In conflict with the official equality principle, some may believe that the quality of child care should be based on how much parents pay. We call this principle equity. A third possibility is that people believe that the quality of child care should be higher for young children whose needs are greater, irrespective of how much their parents pay. This is called the need principle. Although we assume that people may vary in how fair they consider the equality, equity, or need principles to be, willingness to pay for child care may still vary with the (absolute) difference between the degree to which the principle of distributing the quality of child care is perceived to be fair and the degree to which it is perceived to be followed. In addition to measuring willingness to pay for child care, in the survey we measured both how fair parents believed the equality, equity, and need principles were and the degree to which they believed these principles were followed in the municipalities where they lived. Employing a hypothetical society paradigm (Mitchell, Tetlock, Mellers, & Ordóñez, 1993), in the experiments we presented subjects with scenarios describing communities in which these three principles were followed. In addition to stating their willingness to pay, subjects rated the fairness of the indicated distribution.

A number of other factors are likely to also affect willingness to pay for community child care. First, as noted, parents may differ with respect to what they consider to be a fair distributive principle, and perhaps such differences depend on the degree they share the political ideology behind the official equality principle (Mitchell et al., 1993). Therefore, we expected an indirect effect of factors causing differences in perceived fairness. In the survey we accordingly predicted differences depending on political-party preferences.

Second, consistent with the GEF hypothesis (Wilke, 1991), some other factors may have a direct effect on willingness to pay, which are based on other fairness considerations than perceived distributive fairness. Such a factor is that people believe it is fair that payment is proportional to income (Rapoport, 1988; Rapoport & Suleiman, 1993; Van Dijk & Wilke, 1995; Wit, Wilke, & Oppewal, 1992). A positive relationship was therefore expected between income and willingness to pay. Furthermore, even though a majority do not want the quality of child care to depend on how much they pay, they may still believe it is fair that parents should pay according to how much they use the service. Accordingly, in the survey we expected willingness to pay to increase with a measure of degree of use. Similarly, in the experiments we expected willingness to pay to increase with income and need of child care, which were manipulated in the scenarios.

Interest in preserving the service may also be associated with willingness to pay (Marwell & Ames, 1979; Van Dijk & Wilke, 1995; Wit, Wilke, & Oppewal, 1992). For example, women may have a stronger interest than men in preserving child care services and thus are perhaps more willing to pay than are men. However, previous results concerning the effects of gender are ambiguous (Sell, Griffith, & Wilson, 1993). In the survey we also obtained measures of perceived quality and efficiency of the community child care. The higher quality and efficiency are perceived, the higher the interest may be in the resource. If so, we expected willingness to pay to increase with perceived quality and efficiency.

A recurrent research finding is that cooperation in social dilemmas increases when group size decreases (Hamburger, Guyer, & Fox, 1975; Komorita &

Lapworth, 1982; Messick & McClelland, 1983; Van Lange et al., 1992). An important reason may be that group identity increases (Tyler & Dawes, 1993). As a consequence, people feel more responsible. Similar difference may exist between large and small communities. In small communities people are more likely to know each other than they are in large communities (Milgram, 1970), and thus may more easily acquire a common group identity. The survey sampled parents from five different municipalities which varied in size. In the experiments municipality size was varied in the scenarios. Willingness to pay was expected to increase with decreasing size.

2.1 Survey

2.1.1 Method

Questionnaire. The questionnaire used in the survey was developed from a small number of face-to-face interviews and pilot questionnaires mailed to a sample of 50 respondents. Respondents answered questions about the perceived efficiency and quality of the service provided as well as background questions about gender, education, income, political-party preferences, and degree of use and payment for child care. As an index of perceived quality, respondents were asked to indicate on a 5-point scale how satisfied they were with the child care in their municipality. The measure of perceived efficiency was the degree (4-point scale) to which respondents agreed with the statement "The municipality resources for child care are used in an efficient way." Furthermore, respondents answered questions about what they considered to be a fair distribution of quality of child care in their municipality, how they believed it was actually distributed, and how willing they were to pay for the child care provided by the municipality. The three distributive principles of equality, need, and equity were presented in the form of three statements:

All children should have equally good care Younger children need better care and should have better care than older children If parents pay more, their children should have better care than if they pay less

An additional three questions leaving out "should" asked how quality of child care is actually distributed. Each statement for the two types of questions was rated on a 5-point scale ranging from "Should never be true/Is never true" to "Should always be true/Is always true". Willingness to pay was tapped by the following statements for each of three methods of payment, collective, fee, and a combined collective and fee:

I am prepared to pay for child care even if my own child does not use it
I am only prepared to pay for the child care my child uses
All should pay for child care, but I am prepared to pay more if my child uses it

The degree of agreement was indicated on a 5-point scale varying from "No, absolutely not" to "Yes, absolutely."

Procedure. The questionnaire, along with a cover letter and a stamped return envelope, was mailed to each member in the sample. After about two weeks all members in the sample were sent a combined reminder and gratitude letter. Approximately another four weeks later, the original package was mailed once again to those who had not responded by that time.

Respondents. 2,784 households with at least one child below school age were sampled from five municipalities of varying sizes (6,174, 23,854, 36,289, 68,924, and 433,811 residents, respectively). Usable questionnaires were obtained from 1,840 respondents, corresponding to an average response rate of 66.1%. Sixty-two percent of the respondents were women. The mean age was 34.8 years. About one-third had a university degree. Twenty-two percent had a monthly disposable household income above the national average for families with children (approximately $3,000).

2.1.2 Results

Fair Distributive Principle. Equality was by far considered to be the fairest principle of distributing the quality of community child care ($M = 4.75$). As many as 94.5% indicated that the principle should be true always or almost always (5 or 4 on the 5-point scale). Next most preferred was the need principle ($M = 2.91$). In this case 32.3% indicated a higher value than the midpoint on the scale, 30.3% a lower value. The equity principle was the least preferred ($M = 1.15$). Only 1.9% believed it should be true always or almost always.

Separate multiple regression analyses were performed with the ratings of fairness of each of the distributive principles as dependent variables. The independent variables were municipality size (effect coded), gender (dummy coded), disposable income (7-point scale), degree of use of community child care (3-point scale), degree of education (effect coded), perceived efficiency of community child care (4-point scale), perceived quality of community child care (4-point scale), and political-party preferences (effect coded). First, the analyses showed that the fairness ratings were reliably affected by political-party preferences. As compared to those who were politically indifferent, respondents preferring the social democrats rated the equality principle as fairer (beta = .114, $t_{1288} = 2.92$, $p < .01$) and the equity principle as less fair (beta = -.108, $t_{1280} = -2.69$, $p < .01$), those preferring the liberal party rated the need principle as fairer (beta = .134, $t_{1250} = 2.69$, $p < .01$), and those preferring the conservatives rated equality as less fair (beta = -.166, $t_{1288} = -3.86$, $p < .01$). Second, the analyses indicated that fairness of the need principle increased with income (beta = -.068, $t_{1250} = -2.31$, $p < .05$), and that fairness of the equality principle increased with degree of use of community child care (beta = .098, $t_{1288} = 3.27$, $p < .01$).

Willingness to Pay. Paying a fee was rated as the most preferred ($M = 3.93$, $SD = 1.44$), combined collective payment and fee the next most preferred ($M = 3.47$, $SD = 1.48$), and collective payment the least preferred method of payment ($M = 2.63$, $SD = 1.46$). Across all respondents, the ratings of collective and combined payment had a positive correlation ($r = .605$) and were both negatively correlated with the ratings of fee ($r = -.649$ and $r = -.462$, respectively).

A hierarchical regression analysis was performed with a willingness-to-pay index as dependent variable. In constructing this index, the ratings of collective and combined payments were summed and the ratings of fee subtracted from the sums. As Table 1 shows, in the first step of the regression analysis, the absolute difference between the ratings of how quality of child care should be distributed and how it was believed to be distributed was entered for each distributive principle. For all three principles the beta coefficients were significant, accounting however only for 1.8% of the variance in willingness to pay. Also, only for need the sign was the expected negative indicating that a larger difference decreased willingness to pay.

In the second step, the same independent variables as in the regression analyses on the ratings of fairness were entered. Several of these factors reliably affected willingness to pay. An increase in income and degree of use of community child care increased willingness to pay. With the exception of the next largest municipality, willingness to pay decreased with municipality size. Respondents with a university degree were more willing to pay compared to citizens with lower education levels. Conservative political party preferences decreased and socialist or liberal political party preferences increased willingness to pay.

Table 1. Summary of Hierarchical Regression Analysis of the Willingness-to-Pay Index (Survey).

Independent variable	M	SD	r	beta	t
Step 1					
Absolute difference equality	1.14	0.96	.066**	.089	3.35***
Absolute difference equity	0.76	0.97	.060*	.066	2.48*
Absolute difference need	0.94	0.93	-.057*	-.082	-3.08**
$\Delta R^2 = .018$, $F(3, 1191)=7.28$, $p<.001$					
Step 2					
Municipality size[1]					
A vs. E	0.05	0.56	.145***	.090	3.39***
B vs. E	-0.03	0.63	.135***	.158	5.93***
C vs. E	-0.03	0.63	.145***	.041	1.53
D vs. E	-0.06	0.66	-.013	-.098	-3.66***
Degree of municipality child care use	1.34	0.77	.157***	.149	5.59***
Perceived quality	3.94	0.96	.020	.004	0.15
Perceived efficiency	2.71	0.68	.036	.031	1.16
Disposable income	5.66	1.25	.130***	.108	4.06***
Gender (men vs. women)	0.63	0.48	-.076***	-.044	-1.65+
Degree of education vs. lower education					
High-school degree	0.41	0.70	.003	-.017	-0.65
University degree	0.21	0.65	.249***	.234	8.80***
Political party preference vs. no preference					
Left party	-0.10	0.45	.129***	.151	5.66***
Social democratic party	0.26	0.71	.021	-.006	-0.22
Center party	-0.11	0.43	.054*	.051	1.90+
Liberal party	-0.09	0.45	.119***	.128	4.83***
Conservative party	-0.04	0.52	.005	-.107	-4.02***
Christian democratic party	-0.13	0.40	.051*	-.097	-3.65***
Green party	-0.11	0.44	.115***	.137	5.14***
New democratic party	-0.13	0.40	.048+	-.022	-0.83
$\Delta R^2 = .153$, $F(20, 1174)=11.36$, $p<.001$					
$R^2_{adj} = .155$, $F(22, 1172)=10.97$, $p<.001$					

+ p<.10
* p<.05
** p<.01
*** p<.001

[1]A-E correspond to the order from the smallest to the largest municipality.

2.1.3 Discussion

In general agreement with much previous research (e.g., Allison & Messick, 1990), the results showed that equality was perceived as the fairest principle to distribute quality of community child care. However, on average the need principle was also rated as fair to some degree. Therefore, many people may be undecided about whether need or equality is fair. The results also verified that fairness of the equality and need principles was affected by political-party preferences. Specifically, as hypothesized, the degree to which the equality principle was rated to be fair depended on whether or not respondents preferred the social democrats, for whom equality is an important item on the political agenda. At the same time, the ratings of fairness of the different principles were unexpectedly influenced by income and degree of use of child care. These effects may reflect that people to some extent also take into account what they expect to receive themselves when expressing what they believe is a fair distributive principle. For instance, Shepelak and Alwin (1986) suggested that the need principle guides judgments of the fairness of ones own income but not judgments of the fairness of others' income.

Willingness to pay for community child care showed an expected increase with the difference between the ratings of fairness of the distributive principles and the degree to which respondents believed that they were true. However, the effect accounted for only a few percent of the variance in the ratings of willingness to pay. Furthermore, the direction of the effect was as expected only in the case of the need principle. Political-party preferences affected willingness to pay directly, not only indirectly through the ratings of fairness. Thus, in contrast to previous laboratory-based research on cooperation in social dilemmas supporting the GEF hypothesis (Wilke, 1991), the present results failed to provide unequivocal support. The weak support is not easily explained since several other factors (income, degree of use) were found to affect willingness to pay as predicted based on previous laboratory-based research. However, another unexpected finding was that willingness to pay increased rather than decreased with municipality size even though the regression analysis controlled for differences in political-party preferences, education, degree of use, and income. Perhaps residents of larger municipalities are more willing to pay for community child care because they have more need for it. Whether respondents had a university degree or not had the strongest relationship with willingness to pay. Additional hierarchical regression analyses suggested that this effect was unrelated to differences in political-party preferences, degree of use, income, or municipality size. Further studies are needed to find out the reason for this effect.

Finally, interest in preserving community child care was not related to willingness to pay, at least not with regard to gender, perceived quality and efficiency. These results are inconsistent with previous laboratory-based research showing that interest in the resource increases cooperation (Marwell & Ames, 1979; Van Dijk & Wilke, 1995; Wit, Wilke, & Oppewal, 1992).

2.2 Experiment 1

2.2.1 Problem and Method

The aim of the first experiment was to replicate the main results of the survey. A primary question asked was again whether fairness of the principles of equality, equity, and need in distributing the quality of community child care increases willingness to pay for the service. A hypothetical society paradigm (Mitchell et al., 1993) was used in which subjects were asked to imagine that they lived in one of several different municipalities. In these municipalities the quality of child care was distributed according to one of the above three principles. Thus, in contrast to the survey, subjects were told about the actual distributions. Subjects were also asked to imagine that they lived either in a small municipality with close contacts between people or in a large municipality where few knew each other, that their income was above or below average in that municipality, and that their need of child care was large because they had a young child or small because they had an older child. Thirty-two undergraduates (17 men with a mean age of 25.1 years and 15 women with a mean age of 25.3 years) rated fairness and willingness to pay exactly as these variables were rated in the survey. All subjects made each kind of rating once for each of the 24 scenarios. Subjects knew that the data collection procedure guaranteed their anonymity.

2.2.2 Results and Discussion

As in the survey, equality was on average rated as the most fair distributive principle (M = 4.2), followed by need (M = 3.9), and equity (M = 1.8). In separate multiple regression analyses based on the within-subject variance (21.0%, 15.5%, and 20.1% of the total variance of the ratings of fairness of equality, equity, and need, respectively), R^2_{adj}s for the dummy-coded independent variables income, need of child care, municipality size, and their interactions were .006 (equality), $F < 1$; .037 (need), $F(6, 186) = 1.19$, $p > .25$; and .133 (equity), $F(6, 186) = 4.75$, $p < .001$, respectively. Except for a significant effect of income on the ratings of fairness of the equity principle (beta = .157, t_{210} = 2.50, $p < .05$), no other effects reached significance. Equity was rated fairer when subjects imagined that their income was above average, possibly indicating that subjects were influenced by what they would receive themselves.

The willingness-to-pay index was constructed in the same way as in the survey. Means across subjects are given in Table 2. A multiple regression analysis based on the between-subjects variance yielded a R^2_{adj} of .043, $F(3, 252) = 4.80$, $p < .01$, with the ratings of fairness of the equality, equity, and need principles as independent variables. As in the survey, ratings of fairness of the need principle had a significant effect on willingness to pay (beta = .236, t_{210} = 3.63, $p < .001$). Again some weak support was thus obtained for the prediction derived from the GEF hypothesis that fairness of the distribution of quality of child care would affect willingness to pay for the service.

Table 2. Mean Ratings of Willingness to Pay Related to Income, Need, and Municipality Size (Experiment 1).

	Low income		High income	
	Low need	High need	Low need	High need
Small municipality	4.75	4.88	6.13	6.00
Large municipality	4.44	4.31	5.97	5.91

In a hierarchical regression analysis based on the within-subject variance (40.7% of the total variance of the willingness-to-pay index), the ratings of fairness entered in the first step yielded a R^2_{adj} of .109, $F(3, 252) = 5.68$, $p < .01$. The beta weights for the ratings of the need and equity principles were positive and reached significance (beta = .184, t_{210} = 5.27, $p < .001$, and beta = .114, t_{210} = 3.26, $p < .01$, respectively). That willingness to pay for child care is affected by the ratings of fairness was thus more clearly supported for the principles of equity and need.

In the next step of the regression analysis, the dummy coded within-subject factors income, need, municipality size, and their interactions were entered. R^2_{adj} reliably increased to .324, $F(7, 248) = 11.08$, $p < .001$, corresponding to the increase. Only income was significant (beta = .301, t_{210} = 8.65,

$p < .001$) due to more willingness to pay for a higher income. A nearly significant effect of municipality size (beta = -.059, $t_{210} = -1.70$, $p < .10$) suggested more willingness to pay in the smaller municipality. Need was not related to willingness to pay.

In summary, the results showed more clearly that willingness to pay for community child care is affected by fairness of the distribution of the quality of child care. Yet, as in the survey, the ratings of fairness did not account for more than a few percent of the variance across subjects in willingness to pay. In the experiment, substantially more of the within-subject variance was however accounted for. Furthermore, the finding that income influenced willingness to pay was replicated. When subjects imagined their income as being above average, they indicated more willingness to pay. However, need of child care did not affect willingness to pay, while in the survey the degree of utilization did. This inconsistency may be due to a weak manipulation of need. Finally, when subjects imagined that they lived in a smaller municipality, they showed more willingness to pay compared to when they imagined that they lived in a larger municipality. Although this effect was not significant, the trend was the expected opposite direction to that found in the survey.

2.3 Experiment 2

2.3.1 Problem and Method

Why did fairness of the distribution of the quality of community child care in both the preceding studies explain only a few percent of the variance in willingness to pay for the service? One possible reason is that fairness of the distribution of the quality was confounded with fairness of the method of payment. For instance, fairness according to the need principle may be important in the case of distributing the quality of community child care. However, such a preference may show no relationship to what is considered a fair method of payment. In the second experiment, rather than being asked to indicate willingness to pay for three different methods of payment which corresponded to either equality, equity, or a combination thereof, subjects were asked to show their interest in preserving the quality of child care by rating their willingness to pay a modest monthly fee. It was expected that these ratings more directly would reflect willingness to pay than the index used in the preceding studies, and therefore also show a stronger effect of the ratings of fairness of how the quality is distributed.

As in the preceding experiment, distributive principle, income, need of child care, and municipality size were manipulated in hypothetical municipalities where subjects were asked to imagine that they lived. However, income and need of child care were varied as between-subjects factors since it was suspected that subjects may have difficulty in changing their reference. Also, the manipulation of need was stronger in that subjects were either asked to imagine that they had younger children with large needs, or to imagine that they did not have any children.

Another sample of undergraduates (20 men and 28 women with a mean age of 27.0 and 27.8 years, respectively) participated as subjects. They were randomly assigned to four groups with the same distribution of men and women. Graphical scales were used for both the ratings of fairness of the distribution of the quality of child care in the municipalities and the ratings of willingness to pay a monthly fee to maintain this quality. In connection with the latter ratings, subjects were told that if 50% or more of all households paid, the municipality would be able to maintain the quality of child care which otherwise would be threatened. Subjects knew that the data collection procedure guaranteed their anonymity.

2.3.2 Results and Discussion

Once again equality was rated as the fairest principle of distribution (M = 83.9 on a scale from 0 to 100), followed by need (M = 61.6), and equity (M = 16.4). However, in contrast to the results of the preceding studies, multiple regression analyses did not yield any significant effects ($p > .25$). Thus, in this case subjects appeared to rate fairness without considering benefits to themselves.

The mean ratings of willingness to pay are given in Table 3. As may be seen, willingness to pay varies across the three distributive principles. Subjects were more willing to pay when the public good was distributed according to the equality principle (M = 69.6 on a scale from 0 to 100), somewhat less when it was distributed according to the need principle (M = 66.6), and least when it was distributed according to the equity principle (M = 57.6). A hierarchical multiple linear regression analyses based on the between-subjects variance (71% of the total variance) performed with the mean ratings of willingness to pay as dependent variable substantiated this observation. When the mean ratings of fairness were entered in the first step, a reliable R^2_{adj} of .013, $F(1, 286) = 3.76$, $p = .05$, was obtained. However, since the effect was not stronger than in the preceding two studies, its weakness in these studies can hardly be attributed to the measure of willingness to pay which was employed. In the next step, the dummy coded between-subjects factors income, need, and their interaction were entered. R^2_{adj} increased reliably to .334, $F(3, 284) = 47.6$, $p < .001$, corresponding to the increase. Income as well as need had significant effects (beta = .394, $t_{44} = 8.18$, $p < .001$, and .397, $t_{44} = 8.25$, $p < .001$, respectively) indicating more willingness to pay when income and need were high. Furthermore, their interaction also reached significance (beta = -.242, $t_{44} = -5.09$, $p < .001$). When both income and need were low, willingness to pay dropped substantially. This was particularly true for the scenarios where equity was the prevailing distributive principle.

Table 3. Mean Ratings of Willingness to Pay Related to Distributive Principle, Income, Need, and Municipality Size (Experiment 2).

	Distributive principle					
	Equality		Equity		Need	
	No need	Need	No need	Need	No need	Need
Low income						
Small municipality	59.3	74.0	19.8	67.7	48.1	73.9
Large municipality	48.5	64.5	15.7	63.0	48.2	67.3
High income						
Small municipality	76.0	86.8	62.8	85.4	75.1	80.7
Large municipality	67.5	80.3	62.6	84.1	65.4	73.9

Another hierarchical regression analysis based on the within-subject variance was performed with willingness to pay as dependent variable. R^2_{adj} for the ratings of fairness entered in the first step was in this case .214, $F(1, 287) = 78.14$, $p < .001$. With the dummy coded independent variable municipality size, the effect-coded distributive principles, their interactions, and the interactions with the between-subjects factors income and need entered in the last step, R^2_{adj} increased reliably to .814, $F(21, 266) = 55.43$, $p < .001$, corresponding to the increase. Significant effects due to the distributive principles were found over and above the effects mediated by the ratings of fairness (beta = .033, $t_{220} = 2.19$, $p < .05$, for equality vs. equity; beta = .184, $t_{220} = 12.34$, $p < .001$, for need vs. equity), indicating that subjects were more willing to pay when quality was distributed according to equality and need, respectively, as compared to when it was distributed according to equity. A significant beta weight for municipality size (beta = -.422, $t_{220} = -28.34$, $p < .001$) revealed more willingness to pay when subjects imagined that they lived in a small versus a large municipality. Some significant effects due to the interactions were also found but were not possible to interpret.

In summary, the results again showed that the ratings of fairness only accounted for a tiny portion of the variance across subjects of the ratings of willingness to pay, although substantially more variance was accounted for within subjects. Since the measure of willingness to pay was changed, some other factor than the method of measurement must be responsible. In addition to fairness, the distributive principles, income, need, and municipality size to some extent affected willingness to pay. It is particularly noteworthy that this applied to the distributive principles. Thus, there is no perfect agreement between these principles and the ratings of fairness. It is of course possible that the ratings not only reflect fairness but also, for instance, social desirability. Another possibility is that people not only take into account whether a principle is fair or not but also the consequences of applying it, and that these two judgments diverge. Expressed differently, people may perceive a distribution as fair in principle, but once applied they consider the consequences of its application for themselves.

3. General Discussion

A problem faced by many societies today is that individual households are becoming less and less able to contribute to social services and consequently the society must spend more money to maintain these services. Thus, it is important to gain knowledge about how to sustain willingness to pay for social services in times when such payments are becoming a burden for many households. Since the results of the present studies showed that willingness to pay is to some extent predicted from the GEF hypothesis (Wilke, 1991) which embraces a large number of results from laboratory-based social-dilemma studies (Komorita & Parks, 1995), it appears as if framing payment for social services as a public-goods or collective-goods dilemma may be a viable approach. At the same time, the results reinforced the generalizability of the GEF hypothesis to the class of real-life social dilemmas which the provision of community social services constitutes.

However, only weak support was obtained for the main implication of the GEF hypothesis that fairness of the distribution of quality of community child care would increase willingness to pay for the service. There are several possible reasons for this. Perhaps the most important one is that fairness did not vary much across individuals, either in the experiments with their rather homogeneous samples or in the survey with its more heterogeneous sample. Although some individual differences were observed to be related to different factors such as political-party preferences, income, and degree of use, almost all participants in the present studies believed that it is fair that quality of child care is distributed equally in the first place, and according to need in the second place. There was in fact strong objection against a distribution based on how much users pay. This is perhaps surprising since this principle is likely to be fair when applied to everyday economic transactions. It may also be fair if it is applied to the quantity of child care. Whether the endorsement of the equality (and need) principle pertaining to the quality of child care is only typical for the political system of Sweden is a question which must await further research. Nevertheless, that small individual differences in what is perceived to be fair may be an important reason for the weak support for the GEF hypothesis is suggested by the fact that fairness accounted for much more of the variance in willingness to pay across hypothetical municipalities in which the distributive principles varied.

It should be added that, in the survey, larger variation was observed in what respondents believed were the true distributions of the quality of child care in the different municipalities. The results suggested however that the perceived true distributions may be less important for willingness to pay. Nevertheless, it may be speculated that fairness influences willingness to pay when people experience that actual policy diverges greatly from their own conceptions of distributive justice. For instance, if the least fair principle of equity was implemented by authorities, willingness to pay for a social service might drastically decline.

It is also possible that other aspects of fairness influence cooperation in social dilemmas. In a recent field study (Tyler & Degoey, 1995), it was shown that people's willingness to restrict their water usage was related to behaviors of authorities and to procedural justice. Thus, people must feel that the system is fair if they are to cooperate with restrictive policies. However, which indicators of fairness that are of importance may vary from situation to situation. This is another problem that future research should address.

Finally, it is important to note that the main results of the present survey were successfully replicated in the experiments employing the hypothetical society paradigm (Mitchell et al., 1993). The advantage of having experimental control may thus be maintained while variations due to personal experiences are added. In future research these methods may serve complementary purposes.

4. References

Adams, J. S. (1965). Inequity in social exchange. In L. Berkowitz (Ed.), *Advances in experimental social psychology* (Vol. 2, pp. 267-299). New York: Academic Press.

Allison, S. T., & Messick, D. M. (1990). Social decision heuristics in the use of shared resources. *Journal of Behavioral Decision Making, 3*, 195-204.

Biel, A., & Gärling, T. (1995). The role of uncertainty in resource dilemmas. *Journal of Environmental Psychology*, 15, 221-233.

Dawes, R. M. (1980). Social dilemmas. *Annual Review of Psychology, 31*, 169-193.

Deutsch, M. (1975). Equity, equality, and need: What determines which value will be used as the basis for distributive justice? *Journal of Social Issues, 31*, 137-149.

De Vries, S. (1991). *Egoism, altruism, and social justice. Theory and experiments on cooperation in social dilemmas.* Unpublished doctoral dissertation, University of Groningen, the Netherlands.

Hamburger, H., Guyer, M., & Fox, J. (1975). Group size and cooperation. *Journal of Conflict Resolution, 19*, 503-531.

Harris, R. J., & Joyce, M. A. (1980). What's fair? It depends on how you phrase the question. *Journal of Personality and Social Psychology, 38*, 165-179.

Homans, G. C. (1974). *Social behavior: Its elementary forms.* Rev. ed. New York: Harcourt, Brace, & Jovanovich.

Joireman, J. A., Kuhlman, D. M., & Okuda, H. (1994). Fairness judgements in an asymmetric public goods dilemma. In U. Shulz, W. Albers, & U. Müller (Eds.), *Social dilemmas and cooperation* (pp. 99-116). Berlin: Springer.

Kinsey, K. A., Grasmick, H. G., & Smith, K. W. (1991). Framing justice: Taxpayer evaluations of personal tax burdens. *Law & Society Review, 25*, 845-873.

Komorita, S. S., & Lapworth, C. W. (1982). Cooperative choice among individuals versus groups in an *N*-person dilemma situation. *Journal of Personality and Social Psychology, 42*, 487-496.

Komorita, S. S., & Parks, C. D. (1995). Interpersonal relations: Mixed-motive interaction. *Annual Review of Psychology, 46*, 183-207.

Marwell, G., & Ames, R. E. (1979). Experiments on provision of public goods. I. Resources, interest, group size, and the free-rider problem. *American Journal of Sociology, 84*, 1335-1360.

Messick, D. M., & McClelland, C. L. (1983). Social traps and temporal traps. *Personality and Social Psychology Bulletin, 9*, 105-110.

Messick, D. M., & Schell, T. (1992). Evidence for an equality heuristic in social decision making. *Acta Psychologica, 80*, 311-323.

Milgram, S. (1970). The experience of living in cities. *Science, 167*, 1461-1468.

Mitchell, G., Tetlock, P. E., Mellers, B. A., & Ordóñez, L. D. (1993). Judgments of social justice: Compromises between equality and efficiency. *Journal of Personality and Social Psychology, 65*, 629-639.

Rapoport, A. (1988). Provision of step-level goods: Effects of inequality in resources. *Journal of Personality and Social Psychology, 54*, 432-440.

Rapoport, A., Budescu, D. V., Suleiman, R., & Weg, E. (1992). Social dilemmas with uniformly distributed resources. In W. B. G. Liebrand, D. M. Messick, & H. A. M. Wilke (Eds.), *Social dilemmas: Theoretical issues and research findings* (pp. 43-57). Oxford: Pergamon.

Rapoport, A., & Suleiman, R. (1993). Incremental contribution in step-level public goods games with asymmetric players. *Organizational Behavior and Human Decision Processes, 55*, 171-194.

Rutte, C. G., Wilke, H. A. M., & Messick, D. (1987). Scarcity or abundance caused by people or the environment as determinants of behavior in the resource dilemma. *Journal of Experimental Social Psychology, 23*, 208-216.

Samuelson, C. D., Messick, D. M., Wilke, H. A. M., & Rutte, C. G. (1986). Individual restraint and structural change as a solution to social dilemmas. In H. Wilke, D. Messick, & C. Rutte (Eds.), *Experimental social dilemmas* (pp. 29-53). New York: Lang.

Sell, J., Griffith, W. I., & Wilson, R. K. (1993). Are women more cooperative than men in social dilemmas? *Social Psychology Quarterly, 56*, 211-222.

Shepelak, N. J., & Alwin, D. F. (1986). Beliefs about inequality and perceptions of distributive justice. *American Sociological Review, 51*, 30-46.

Tyler, T., & Dawes, R. M. (1993). Fairness in groups: Comparing the self-interest and social identity perspectives. In B. A. Mellers, & J. Baron (Eds.), *Psychological perspectives on justice: Theory and applications* (pp. 87-108). New York: Cambridge University Press.

Tyler, T. R., & Degoey, P. (1995). Collective restraint in social dilemmas: Procedural justice and social identification effects on support for authorities. *Journal of Personality and Social Psychology, 69*, 482-497.

Van Dijk, E. (1993). *Coordination in asymmetric social dilemmas.* Unpublished doctoral dissertation, University of Leiden, the Netherlands.

Van Dijk, E., & Grodzka, M. (1992). The influence of endowments asymmetry and information level on the contribution to a public step good. *Journal of Economic Psychology, 13*, 329-342.

Van Dijk, E., & Wilke, H. A. M. (1993). Differential interests, equity, and public good provision. *Journal of Experimental Social Psychology, 29*, 1-16.

Van Dijk, E., & Wilke, H. A. M. (1995). Coordination rules in asymmetric social dilemmas: A comparison between public good dilemmas and resource dilemmas. *Journal of Experimental Social Psychology, 31*, 1-27.

Van Lange, P. A. M., Liebrand, W. B. G., Messick, D. M., & Wilke, H. A. M. (1992). Introduction and literature review. In W. Liebrand, D. M. Messick, & H. Wilke (Eds.), *Social dilemmas: Theoretical issues and research findings* (pp. 3-28). Oxford: Pergamon.

Wilke, H. A. M. (1991). Greed, efficiency and fairness in resource management situations. In W. Stroebe, & M. Hewstone (Eds.), *European Review of Social Psychology* (Vol 2, pp. 165-187). New York: Wiley.

Wilke, H. A. M., Liebrand, W. B. G., Lotgerink, B., & Buurma, B. (1986). Equity and individual preferences in a MDG. *European Journal of Social Psychology, 16*, 131-148.

Wit, A., Wilke, H. A. M., & Oppewal, H. (1992). Fairness in asymmetric social dilemmas. In W. B. G. Liebrand, D. M. Messick, & H. A. M. Wilke (Eds.), *Social dilemmas: Theoretical issues and research findings* (pp. 183-197). Oxford: Pergamon.

Concentration and Dispersion of Resources in Simulated Organizations Characterized by Equal or Unequal Power Relations

Henk Wilke, Eric van Dijk, Kaj Morel, Marjolein Olde Monnikhof, Marcel Zandvliet

Department of Social and Organizational Psychology, Leiden University, P.O. Box 9555, 2300 RB Leiden, The Netherlands

Abstract. In a recent review, Komorita and Parks (1995) suggest that the formation of coalitions and harvesting behavior in a social dilemma may be considered examples of a mixed-motive interdependency. In contrast, in the present study (see also Mannix, 1991; 1993) on a conceptual level coalition formation and social dilemmas are connected and applied to the problem of dispersion and concentration of resources in organizations. Thereafter, an experimental study is presented investigating negotiations about coalition formation and allocation of resources in social dilemmic organizations, which differ in two respects: the superordinate goal of the organization and the power of participants.

By means of a 2(superordinate goal: concentration, dispersion) x 2(power: symmetry, asymmetry) factorial design negotiation behaviors, formed coalitions and the allocation of outcomes are investigated. In symmetric and asymmetric power organizations, members are equal or unequal in power, respectively. In the dispersion and the concentration conditions over all rounds, the superordinate goal of the organization is best served by large or small coalitions, respectively. In all conditions within a round, each of the group members is best off by becoming a member of a winning coalition, and by obtaining a larger share of the outcomes of a coalition.

The major results of this study in which coalitions are embedded in a social dilemmatic organization are (1) coalitions are formed in agreement with the superordinate goal of organizations, and (2) as for the allocation of resources in equal power organizations Gamson's anti-competitive theory (Gamson, 1964), and for unequal power organizations Komorita's bargaining theory (Komorita & Chertkoff, 1973) is supported; (3) in unequal power organizations, members expressed to be more competitive and more proposals were necessary to form a coalition than in equal power organizations. The results are discussed in view of the social dilemma and coalition literature.

Keywords. Coalitions, distributive justice, power, concentration, dispersion

1 Introduction

In organizations quite often scarce resources are made available which through negotiation are assigned to specific departments. An example is a research organization in which the departments have to decide how extra funds or new technology should be divided. An important question is whether it is more efficient for the future of the total organization to assign these scarce resources to a small number of departments or to all departments.

An argument to assign scarce resources to a limited number of departments may be that each of the small number of departments being assigned more resources per department can make more progress or profit, and that this is collectively more efficient than when scarce resources are dispersed over a larger number of departments. However, also the opposite argument may be the case: an extra infusion in all departments concerned may collectively be more efficient, for example, because in that way a balanced development of departments within the organization may be facilitated.

The argument in favor of concentration implies that from the perspective of the organization small coalitions are beneficial, the argument in defense of dispersion suggests that it is more advantageous for the organization that large coalitions are formed. The 'concentration versus dispersion' problem is rather well-known in the organization literature. March & Simon (1958) and Mintzberg (1983) suggest that small coalitions are beneficial for the organization, while Mannix (1991, 1993; Mannix & White, 1992) advocates the position that large coalitions are in the future interest of the organization.

Apart from the superordinate interest of the organization the individual interests of the departments involved are of relevance. The individual interest of each department is best served when that department is member of a winning coalition and when a department succeeds in obtaining more of the benefits of this winning coalition. Coalition formation (Kelley & Thibaut, 1978) then refers to a mixed-motive situation. On the one hand there is competition between departments to become member of a coalition and to increase one's share of the outcomes of the coalition. On the other hand, coalescing and the division of the outcomes of a coalition is only possible when the involved parties cooperate.

As our previous discussion of effects of dispersion and concentration indicated, some coalitions may be harmful in view of the superordinate interest of the organization. Some coalitions may be in the individual interest of coalition partners in the short run, but may be detrimental for the organization in the future. In their recent review, Komorita and Parks (1995) characterize situations of coalition formation and social dilemmas separately as mixed-motive situations, because in each situation there exists a multi-level mixture of cooperation and competition. The foregoing analysis suggests that within organizations decision problems exist that carry features of coalition formation *and* social dilemmas. More precisely, organizations may face problems of coalition formation which are embedded within the structure of social dilemmas.

1.1 Coalition Formation Embedded in a Social Dilemmatic Organization

Mannix (1993; Mannix & White, 1992) characterizes an organization as a combination of departments which either can pursue their individual or their collective interest. In her experiments an organization was simulated in which five departments had to negotiate how to divide of R&D-money. Departments could divide an R&D-budget over 3, 4, or 5 departments. The experimental set-up resembled that of Resource dilemmas (cf. Messick et al., 1983) in which the division of the R&D budget in a particular round affected the amount of R&D-money for a subsequent round. If in a specific round a grand coalition was formed, the R&D-budget for the next trial increased with 3%. When in a specific round coalitions of three or four departments were formed, the R&D-budget for the next round, was reduced with 4% and 2%, respectively. Thus, it was in the common interest of all five departments to form the grand coalition (i.e., dispersion). It was in each department's interest to be part of a small coalition, however.

In the study of Mannix (1993), two types of organizations were introduced. In organizations characterized by equal power, the five departments had contributed equally in the past to the profit of their organization, i.e., 20% each. In the unequal power organizations the departments' contributions to the overall profit of their organization varied between 10% and 30%. The results indicated a general preference to form grand coalitions. The results also indicated, however, that unequal power organizations more often tended to form smaller coalitions (between three and four departments) than was the case in equal power organizations. Mannix concluded that power unequality has a negative effect on organizational goals, and that in unequal power organizations, departments are more competitive and more inclined to pursue their (short term) individual interests.

Mannix's research has provided valuable insights. It appeared that in organizations best served by dispersion of the R&D-budget over more departments mainly grand coalitions were formed. That departments predominantly furthered the organizational interests can be explained on the basis of social dilemma literature suggesting that group members are likely to reduce their consumption when this is collectively efficient (Messick, Wilke, Brewer, Kramer, Zemke, Lui, 1983; Samuelson, Rutte, Messick, Wilke, 1984; Rutte and Wilke, 1984), especially when they identify with the superordinate group (Brewer & Kramer, 1986; Wit & Wilke, 1992; see Tajfel & Turner, 1986; Turner, 1991).

More importantly, the results of Mannix (1993) indicated that unequal power relations enhanced competition about the composition of coalitions which was detrimental to the interest of the organization, suggesting that power inequality may hurt the collective interest. Thus, on the one hand Mannix's results are encouraging since it was shown that departments do act in the interest of the organization. On the other hand, her results suggest that power inequality may weaken the departments' concern for the superordinate interest.

The question may be raised whether Mannix's data are so unequivocal. Can one conclude on the basis of Mannix's data that departments (especially in equal power distributions) formed coalitions of five departments that departments were motivated to serve the collective interest (at the expense of their own short term interests)? An alternative explanation could be that in case of power equality departments had the desire not to exclude any department in the division of the

R&D-budget since they wanted to divide the final outcomes equally over all departments. As we will argue, the fact that power is distributed equally, may evoke a preference to divide final outcomes equally over all departments, i.e. departments may be motivated to divide final outcomes equally, and therefore turn to grand coalitions.

In order to decompose the influence of (a)symmetry and the long term interest of the organization, we manipulated the structure of the task the departments faced. It should be remembered that in her research set-up Mannix introduced an outcomes structure in which the general interest of the organization was best served by *dispersion* of the R&D-budget. As we noted before, *concentration* of resources can also be advantageous for organizations. When in situations of concentration departments would prefer to further the collective interest, they should form small coalitions. To investigate whether departments are truly motivated to pursue the collective interest, in the present study Mannix's dispersion condition in which the grand coalition is most advantageous for the organization, will be contrasted with a new condition in which the reverse is the case, the concentration condition. We reasoned that when departments would be led by the superordinate interest of their organization, they more often would tend to form large coalitions in the dispersion condition and small coalitions in the concentration condition.

As we will demonstrate, manipulating the structure of the social dilemma may also be helpful to gain more insight about the relation between the division of resources (the R&D-budget), and the formation of coalitions. For this purpose, in the following we first introduce some insights from the domain of the coalition formation.

1.2 Concentration and Dispersion, and the Division of Outcomes Within Coalitions

Coalition formation (for reviews, see Gamson, 1964; Komorita, 1984; Wilke, 1985) concerns the division of outcomes by actors who usually differ in power. Lacking a superordinate goal, they are assumed to be motivated to acquire as many outcomes as possible for themselves. Power (see Emmerson, 1964; French & Raven, 1969; Thibaut & Kelley, 1959; Lawler, 1975) refers to the bargaining strength of an actor during the negotiation process, which allows a stronger actor to acquire more outcomes than a weaker actor. Bargaining strength may be defined in a strategic and/or in a normative way (see Komorita & Hamilton, 1984; Komorita & Nagao, 1983; Komorita & Krawitz, 1983). Bargaining strength defined as strategic power (see e.g. Luce & Raiffa, 1957) may be operationalized as the number of times an actor may change a non-feasible coalition into a feasible or winning coalition. Strategic power may also be operationalized (see Van der Linden & Verbeek, 1985) as the additional value an actor can contribute to a coalition. For example, in quota-games an actor who is able to add a greater quotum to a coalition has greater strategic power than an actor who can contribute a smaller quotum. Besides strategic power differences, normative power may be at stake. Differential positions of actors may also have a normative function since coalition partners may take their positions into account when deciding what would be a fair distribution of the coalition outcomes. For example, when some actors have contributed more in the past, they may be entitled to more outcomes within a coalition (Adams, 1965; Messick & Cook, 1983; Mikula, 1980).

Departments having equal power, have no cues at their disposal to decide why one department should acquire more outcomes than another department, or why one department should be included into a coalition and another one excluded from a coalition. This reasoning is the core of Gamson's anti-competitive theory (Gamson, 1964). Gamson argues that when actors have no cues available to decide which subset of actors should form a coalition, they will tend to form a coalition with the least effort and conflict in a way that does justice to the equality of actors. Moreover, actors seeking conflict through competition, will be excluded from the coalition (for evidence, see Vinacke & Arkoff, 1957; Stryker & Psathas, 1960; Wilke et al., 1986). Accordingly, it may be argued that departments in symmetric or equal power organizations will be more motivated to form grand coalitions than departments in unequal power organizations. The symmetric distribution of power does not entitle one to exclude certain departments and/or to distribute coalition outcomes unequally.

Mannix (1993) established that in unequal power organizations actors experienced more competition than actors in equal power organizations. Her results suggested that in unequal power organizations, departments competed with regard to the composition of the coalitions (i.e., departments competed in the sense that they tried to exclude other departments by forming smaller coalitions), and with regard to the division of the coalition outcomes (i.e., there was more disagreement about the way to divide coalition outcomes). This final finding is in accordance with Komorita's bargaining theory of coalition formation (e.g., Komorita & Chertkoff, 1973; Komorita & Parks, 1995), stating that proposals of coalition partners proposed are biased by self-interest such that strong or more powerful actors depart from a proportional division and weak actors from an equal division. According to Komorita and Chertkoff, such highly competitive negotiations have as a result that coalition outcomes are finally divided in a way somewhere between equality and proportionality.

As we already noted, Mannix concluded that power inequality leads to competition, and that competition is detrimental for the collective interest. It should be remembered, however, that this conclusion pertains to the size of the coalition, i.e., the number of departments included in the coalition. Since she studied a situation in which dispersion was in the collective interest, competition about the composition of coalitions (leading to small coalitions) was indeed harmful to the organization. As we argued before, there are situations in which concentration is in the collective interest. A relevant question is then whether the increased competition in unequal power organizations is necessarily detrimental to the collective interest. Similarly, one may wonder whether competition should necessarily manifest itself in the size of coalition. As the present study will demonstrate, departments may also opt to compete with regard to the division of coalition outcomes without hurting the collective interest (cf., Komorita & Chertkoff, 1973; Komorita & Parks, 1995).

1.3 Research Questions

To investigate the formation of coalitions and its consequences for the concentration-dispersion problem, in the present study we replicated Mannix's set-up in which departments could divide the R&D-budget of their organization. Also in our study half of the organizations were characterized by equal power relations, the other half by unequal power relations. In addition to the dispersion condition of Mannix in which large coalitions were in the interest of the organization as a whole, we created a new condition in which concentration of resources in smaller coalitions was in the superordinate interest of the organization. Our primary attention concerned the process of negotiation. To investigate this, we recorded (a) the proposals of specific departments concerning the size of the coalition and the division of outcomes, and (b) the definite size of formed coalitions and the division of the R&D-budget. By means of additional measures, such as the motivation to compete, we tried to complement our understanding about the motivation of negotiators and the differences between situation of power equality and power inequality.

Our expectations were based on the social dilemma and the coalition formation literature. First, on the basis of the social dilemma literature (e.g., Brewer & Kramer, 1986) and a plausible interpretation of Mannix's results (Mannix, 1993), we expected that departments would be led by the collective interest. That is, we expected that the superordinate interest of the departments would lead to small coalitions in the concentration condition and to large coalitions in the dispersion condition. Second, because strategic considerations in unequal power organizations, we expected negotiating departments to be more competitive and we expected them to need more proposals to form a coalition as compared with negotiating departments in the equal power organizations. Third, based on Komorita's bargaining theory (Komorita, 1979), in the unequal power organizations we expected negotiating departments to make proposals which correspond with their strategic power positions. For the equal power organizations we expected the proposals to be based on equality (Gamson, 1964). Fourth, we expected final coalition outcomes to be divided more equally in equal power organizations than in unequal power organizations.

With regard to the consequences of the dynamic process of negotiation for the size of the definite coalitions we foresaw several possibilities. On the basis of Mannix's reasoning that competition will hurt the general interest of organizations, it may be expected that when the general interest is served by concentration the tendency to form large coalitions will be stronger in unequal power than in equal power organizations. Similarly, when the general interest is best served by dispersion of resources, small coalitions may more often be formed in unequal than in equal power organizations. On the basis of the reasoning of Mannix (1993) that competition leads to the formation of small coalitions (i.e., competition about the size of the coalition), it may be expected that power inequality may be beneficial for the organization in the concentration condition. Lastly, it is also possible that the absence of competition in organizations characterized by equal power relations, may enhance the formation of large coalitions (Gamson, 1964), and this may be beneficial in the dispersion condition, but harmful in the concentration condition.

2. Method

Subjects were 300 students at the University of Leiden (law, psychology and medicine). The subjects participated in groups of five, resulting in 60 groups. They were paid 10 Dutch guilders for their participation in the experiment which lasted about 1 hour. The subjects in each group were unknown to each other.

2.1 Experimental Design

The subjects were told that they were heads of one of five departments of the company Zephyr. The board of directors had reserved 1.000.000 guilders from profits made in former years, to be used for future R&D. The subjects were requested to divide this money. The goal of each head of a department was to gain as much money as possible for his or her department. The board of directors had determined that the R&D-budget would be allocated to a combination of three, four or five departments. The subjects were instructed that they would play 12 bargaining-rounds in which they could divide the R&D-budget. To minimize end-game effects, subjects actually played only 8 rounds.

Table 1. The 2x2 factorial design of the experiment

		Superordinate goal	
		Dispersion	Concentration
Power	Equal[1]	75 subjects 15 groups	75 subjects 15 groups
	Unequal[2]	75 subjects 15 groups	75 subjects 15 groups

[1] Equal: dept. 1, 2, 3, 4, 5; each have contributed 20%; [2] Unequal: dept. 1, 2, 3, 4, 5 have contributed 10%, 15%, 20%, 25%, 30% respectively.

We used a 2(power: equal/unequal) x 2(superordinate dependency: concentration/dispersion) factorial design. Departments in the equal power condition had contributed equally to the profits of Zephyr in the past, i.e., twenty percent. In the unequal power condition department one had contributed 10%, department two

15%, department three 20 %, department four 25% and department five 30% (see Table 1).

Superordinate dependency of a coalition mainly played a role in between the bargaining-rounds. Subjects in the dispersion condition were told that when they would allocate the R&D-budget to three of five departments, the budget would decrease by 7% in the following round. When the R&D-budget would be allocated to all five departments, the budget would increase by 7% in the following round. In the concentration condition this procedure was reversed. Allocating money to a coalition of three departments meant an increase of 7%, and allocation to a coalition of five departments meant a decrease of 7% of the R&D-budget for the following round. If subjects allocated the money to a coalition of four departments, the budget remained constant in the next round.

The above percentages differ from those introduced in the experiment Mannix (1993). In her experiment[1], the budget decreased with 3 and 2 percent when subjects formed a coalition of three or four members, respectively. The budget increased with 3 percent when they formed a coalition of five members. For two reasons, we decided not to let the budget increase or decrease when subjects formed a coalition of four members. First, we wanted to explore the effect of the status quo as a reference point for which the resource of the organization remained constant. Second, we thought that there was a certain disbalance in the design Mannix employed. In her study by forming a coalition of five members, the departments in her condition characterized by dispersion, had only one option to favorize the interest of the organization. By forming coalitions of three or four members the heads had two options to harm the interest of the organization. We did opt for +7% and -7%, since from results of a pilot study it appeared that -4% and +4% were not considered important enough to be taken into account as an indication of the superordinate interest of the organization.

Forming a specific coalition could mean that the R&D-budget increased or decreased in the following round. In the first round the budget always started with 1.000.000 Dutch guilders. In each round, after a coalition was formed, a fixed amount of 250.000 guilders was subtracted, because of 'research overhead costs'. The budget that finally was available for a combination was calculated as follows:

* In the dispersion condition: (1/2 * budget + 1/2 * budget * (sumtotal of percentages of profit generated)) - 250.000 Dfl;
* In the concentration condition: (budget * sumtotal of percentages of profit generated) - 250.000 Dfl.

To illustrate: In the first round (in which the budget was 1.000.000 Dfl. or guilders), subjects in the dispersion condition were facing the following outcomes: to divide 550.000 guilders between three departments (183.000 on the average) which had as a consequence that the budget decreased with 7% in the second round

---

1. We are indebted to Dr. Beta Mannix. On request she sent us an extensive description of the procedures of her experiment.

to 930.000 guilders, or to divide 750.000 guilders between five departments (150.000 on the average) which implied that the budget increased with 7% in the second round to 1.070.000.

During the experiment, these amounts were calculated per computer. The subjects knew how the amounts were computed and which options they had to consider, but they didn't have to do the calculating themselves.

2.2 Procedure

Upon arrival, subjects were seated behind five computers, which were interconnected. These computers were placed in the shape of a semi-circle and separated by wooden panels, so that the subjects couldn't see or communicate with each other, except by computer. Next to the computer was a written instruction, in which the experimental condition was explained, and a short summary, which repeated the main points of the instructions.

When the subjects were seated the experimenter introduced the experiment. It was explained that the subjects would negotiate by computer. This meant that group members sometimes would have to wait for each other and that communication was only allowed by computer. Next, the subjects started to read the written instructions. Subjects were randomly assigned to the experimental conditions.

2.3 Computer Procedure

In Mannix' (1993) set-up each group had a neutral group facilitator to assist group members in the decision making process. The facilitator managed the voting procedure and did all the computational work. During our experiment these tasks were performed by the central server and a personal computer for each department.

After reading the instructions, subjects started to work with the computer. First, they were told how to use the computer, especially how to make a proposal to the other departments. During the experiment, the department the subjects represented could be seen on top of their screen.

A proposal was made by answering three questions:

* How many departments do you want to be a member of the combination (three, four or five)?
* Which departments do you want to include in that combination? (When the subject chose a combination of five departments, all departments were automatically selected.) After answering this question, the computer calculated how much money could be divided between the members. This amount was presented together with the third question.
* How do you want to divide the money between the departments?

To allocate the money between the departments, it wasn't necessary for the subjects to compute amounts of money, they were allowed to type in proportions (for example: 1 for department one, 1 for department two, and 2 for department three). Next, the computer calculated the proportions and presented the amounts on the screen and asked if each of the assigned departments accepted the deal. The subjects were able to practice this procedure twice before the real bargaining started.

When the subjects had read the computer instructions, we asked a few questions about these instructions (manipulation-checks) to check whether the subjects understood the main characteristics of the experiment. After every response (correct or incorrect) the correct answer was displayed.
After all subjects had answered the questions the bargaining started. On the top of the monitor information was shown about the department the subject represented, the amount of money a department had gained during the previous rounds, which round was being played at that moment, and which proposals were being made in that round.

Next the bargaining started. One subject was given the possibility to make a proposal. The others had to wait until this proposal was completed. We told the subjects that the person given this possibility was randomly chosen. In reality, the assignment was arranged by means of a fixed list such that subjects had equal chances to make a proposal.

When a subject had made a proposal, this proposal was communicated to the other computer. On their monitor subjects could see which proposal had been made, the number of members in the coalition, which departments were part of that coalition and the allocation of the money between those departments. Only those departments which were selected as members of the coalition could vote for or against the proposal (by typing a yes (y) or a no (n)). If these departments voted unanimously in favor of that proposal, all subjects were shown on their screen that the proposal had been accepted. On the next screen all subjects were shown the consequences of the decision; how much money each department had gained and how much money was available for the following round. The information on top of the screen was updated. Next, another department was chosen to make a proposal during the following round. If all departments involved in a proposal did not agree with a proposal, this could again be seen on all screens, and another department was selected to make a proposal in the same round. If, during one round, there was no agreement after five proposals, the subjects were shown on screen that the departments had gained no R&D-money, that the budget for the following round was the same as in the current round and that the next round was started. (This procedure was already explained in the written instructions).

At the end of the eighth round, the negotiations were stopped. The subjects were shown how much money each department had gained. Several questions were posed about how one had experienced the bargaining (for example, how important competition had been). At the end, subjects were thoroughly debriefed and the purpose of the experiment was explained.

3. Results

Subjects' answers to the questions prior to the negotiations were analyzed with a 2(Power) x 2(Superordinate dependency) x 5(Department) ANOVA with Department as a within-subjects factor. For the data collected during the negotiations, the group is the unit of analysis. These data were mostly analyzed with a 2(Power) x 2(Superordinate dependency) ANOVA. Finally, we analyzed the answers to the questions that were asked after the negotiation rounds. Because the subjects had interacted during the bargaining, their responses were interdependent within their group. We analyzed these data with a completely randomized partially hierarchical design. This statistical method removes dependency of group members within groups, by the nesting groups under the two factors.

3.1 Manipulation Checks

To the question 'How much did your department contribute to the profit of the company, 10%,15%, 20%, 25% or 30%?', all subjects gave a correct answer. We also asked the subjects to choose the correct alternative:
1) if the money is allocated between three departments the research funding will decrease by 7%, but if the money is allocated between five departments, the research funding will increase by 7%. 2) if the money is allocated between three departments the research funding will increase by 7%, but if the money is allocated between five departments, the research funding will decrease by 7%.
All subjects chose the correct alternative which means that subjects in the dispersion condition chose alternative (1) and subjects in the concentration condition chose alternative (2). These results suggest that the manipulations of Power and' Superordinate dependency' were perceived as intended.

3.2 Group Data

3.2.1 Coalitions

A 2(Power) x 2(Superordinate dependency) x 8(Round) ANOVA with the size of the coalition as the dependent measure, revealed a significant effect for the factor Superordinate dependency ($F(1,56)=88.16$, $p<.001$). In the concentration condition the mean size of a coalition was smaller ($M=3.4$) than in the dispersion condition ($M=4.3$). Three separate ANOVA's, on the number of times coalitions of three, four or five departments were formed during 8 rounds, confirm the results of the previous analysis. Table 2 shows that subjects tended to form coalitions that were in the interest of the whole organization. Coalitions of three departments were more often formed in the Concentration condition ($M=5.4$) than in the Dispersion condition ($M=1.9$; $F(1,56)=59.9$;, $p<.01$). Coalitions of five departments were more often formed in the Dispersion condition (M=4.1) than in the Concentration condition (M=.9; F(1,56)=61.9, p<.01). Noteworthy are the results of the coalitions of four departments. Power had a significant effect (F(1,56)=7.96, p<.01). In the equal condition a coalition of four departments (neither individual gain nor the collective interest is served by this coalition) was formed more often than in the unequal power condition.

Table 2. Average number of times that a coalition of three, four and five departments has been formed

	Power equality		Power inequality	
	Concen-tration	Dispers-ion	Concen-tration	Dispers-ion
3	5.0	1.8	5.8	2.0
4	2.1	2.4	1.1	1.2
5	0.8	3.7	1.0	4.2

How many times did a department succeed in forming a coalition? To test whether the number of times a department became part of a coalition, was affected by Power and Superordinate dependency, we performed five 2 x 2 ANOVA'S (one ANOVA for each department). The results indicate that departments 1 and 2 (for their contributions, see Table 1) were included more often in the equal power condition than in the unequal power condition (F(1,56)=9.40, p<.01;F(1,56)=8.18, p<.01). Departments 1, 2 and 3 were more often included in a coalition in the dispersion condition than in the concentration condition (F(1,56)=11.21, p<.01; F(1,56)=19.54, p<.001; F(1,56)=15.92, p<.001, respectively).

3.2.2 Proposals

To investigate whether the factors Power and Superordinate dependency affected the number of rejected proposals, we performed a 2(Power) x 2(Superordinate dependency x 8(Round) ANOVA, with Round as within-subjects factor. We found a significant effect of the factor superordinate dependency ($F(1,56)=5.83$, $p<.05$): in the dispersion condition proposals were more often rejected (M=1.0) than in the concentration condition (M=0.71). This effect can possibly ascribed to the circumstance that small coalitions (meaning coalitions with fewer members) are formed more easily than large coalitions (Gamson, 1964). We also found the expected effect of the factor Power ($F(1,56)=8.62$, $p<.02$): in the unequal power condition proposals were more frequently rejected (M=1.01) than in the equal power condition (M=0.70).

3.2.3 Distribution Rules

We expected the allocation of the budget between the members of a coalition to be more unequal in the unequal power condition than in the equal power condition. To establish to what extent an allocation may be considered as equal, deviations from equality were computed.[2] To examine the effect of the factors Power and Superordinate dependency, we conducted a 2 x 2 ANOVA for the accepted proposals. Deviations from equality were significantly smaller in the equal power condition than in the unequal power condition (respectively: M=4860 and M=34092; $F(1,469)=310.56$, $p<.001$).

Thus, within the unequal power groups the budget was divided more unequally. We examined whether in the unequal power groups a specific distribution rule was employed. We made a distinction between the equality rule described above, the standard proportionality rule, and the compromise rule prescribing allocations half way between equality and the proportionality.[3]

---

[2] For each coalition we calculated what the outcomes for each department would be when actual outcomes would be allocated according to equality, i.e., outcomes of a coalition (O_c) divided by the size of that coalition (n). Next, we calculated the difference between the actual outcomes of a department (O_i), and its outcomes according to equality. These differences were totalled and divided by the size of the coalition. In formula:

$$(1) \quad \frac{\Sigma\, |(O_i - O_c/n)|}{n}$$

[3] For the equality rule, see footnote 2. For the proportionality and the compromise rule, O_c/n in the formula of footnote 2 has been replaced.

The proportionality rule prescribes that O_c should be divided in proportion to the contribution to the profit of the departments involved. Thus, consequently, for the proportionality rule O_c/n was replaced by $O_c * P_i/P_c$, where
P_i = contribution to the profit by department i from the coalition;
P_c = sum of contributions to the profit of all members of the coalition.
The compromise rule prescribes that the outcomes should be divided in between equality and

We examined whether departments that made proposals in the unequal power conditions would show strategic behavior, in that they employed the distribution rule that would benefit themselves (i.e., whether departments with an initial advantage in terms of greater profits would propose the proportionality rule, and departments with an initial disadvantage the equality rule). First we analyzed all proposals, and secondly we analyzed only those proposals that had been accepted. A 5(Departments) x 3(Rules) MANOVA's with Rule as a within-subjects factor indicated that for all proposals, as well as for accepted proposals, the least deviation from the compromise rule occurred (for accepted proposals, the mean deviations were M(equality)=34092; M(proportionality)=25188; M(compromise)=22622; $F(1,269)=28.01$; $p<.01$).[4]

Table 3. Deviations from the three distribution rules in unequal power organizations for departments 1 and 2 and for departments 4 and 5 (all proposals)

	Rule		
	Equality	Compromise	Proportionally
Dept. 1 & 2	35493	28524	29639
Dept. 4 & 5	40503	26283	23857

Over all proposals we found a significant effect of the specific department that made the proposals ($F(4,487)=3.46$, $p<.01$). Table 3 shows that departments with an initial disadvantage departed less from the equality rule than departments with an initial advantage. This effect was reversed with respect to the proportionality rule. The effect of the proposer did not appear in the accepted proposals, probably because departments had to agree on a compromise. These results corroborate the bargaining theory of Komorita and Chertkoff (1973).

3.2.4 *Questions after the Bargaining*

We asked subjects which considerations had affected (1 = not important; 7 = very

proportionality. Consequently, for the compromise rule O_c/n was replaced by: $\{O_c/n + (O_c/n * P_i/P_c)\}/2$.

[4] Degrees of freedom adapted with Huunh-Feldt Epsilon (.57796).

important) their bargaining behavior. Contributions made in the past to the profit of Zephyr were considered more important in the unequal power condition (M=4.5) than in the equal power condition (M=2.4; F(1,57)=7.01, p<.01). The consequences of the profit percentages for the allocation of outcomes were considered more important in the unequal power condition (M=4.8) than in the equal power condition (M=2.2; F(1,57)=4.57, p<.05). That all departments should receive an equal amount of money, was considered more important in the equal power condition (M=4.7) than in the unequal power condition (M=2.7; F(1,57)= 5.02, p<.05).

Table 4. Cooperation and competition, averages*

	Equal power		Unequal power	
	Concen-tration	Dis-persion	Concen-tration	Dis-persion
Together as much as possible	4.7	4.7	4.1	4.9
Competition through combination	3.1	3.3	3.7	3.1
Competition through division	2.9	3.1	3.7	3.3

* (1) = not important; (7) = very important

We posed one question about the importance of co-operation and two questions about the importance of competition (1 = very unimportant; 7 = very important). Responses were analyzed by means of 2 x 2 ANOVA'S., again with groups nested under the two factors.

Answers to the question about cooperation showed a significant effect of the factor Power (F(1,57)=4.72, p<.05) and an interaction-effect of Power with Superordinate dependency (F(1, 236)=4.72, p<.05). In the equal power condition cooperation was considered as more important than in the unequal power condition. The ANOVA'S on the two competition questions showed a significant interaction-effect of Power with Superordinate dependency (competition related to forming a combination: $F(1,236)=6.72$, $p<.05$; competition related to allocation: $F(1,236)=3.92$, $p<.05$). Table 4 shows that in the unequal power / concentration condition the importance of cooperation was considered *less* important, and that competition related to the forming of the coalition and to the division of outcomes was considered *more* important than in the other three conditions of the factorial design.

Table 4 suggests that in general competition was not considered to be of extreme importance. Moreover, our results concerning the experienced competition do not correspond with the results of Mannix (1993). In her experiment, in which only dispersion was introduced, she found that the subjects experienced more competition in the unequal power condition than in the equal power condition. We did not replicate these results. Instead, an effect for power did appear in our concentration condition, and not in the dispersion condition.

4. Discussion

By means of computer-controlled negotiations, heads of departments were to divide an R&D budget during eight rounds. Departments had equal or unequal power with regard to previous contributions to the profit of the organization. Moreover, dispersion or concentration of resources was relevant for the future interest of the organization. By checking these manipulations before and after negotiations, it was shown that these manipulations were successful.

For several reasons, the present study is of importance. First, computer-controlled negotiations make it possible to investigate the process of negotiations accurately, because negotiations are completely recorded. Second, since the present study concerns the intersection of coalition formation and social dilemmas, the present outcomes contribute to the social dilemma literature as well as to the literature on coalition formation. In experimental social dilemmas participants rarely have the opportunity to communicate about how much each participant, or combinations of participants will take from a common resource. However, in our study this was actually possible. In coalition studies, the consequences of coalition behavior are mostly restricted to one round. In the present study, coalition behavior actually had consequences for the future for the group at large. Third, because the present study is closely related to Mannix's study (Mannix, 1993), it is possible to view some of her conclusions in the light of the more extensive factorial design of the present study. In the following we will examine these points in somewhat greater detail.

Coalition formation in a social dilemma situation may be characterized as a multi-level 'mixed motive' situation (see e.g., Yamagishi, 1988; Bornstein, 1992). In the formation of coalitions there is an individual interest to gain as many outcomes as possible, but within a round this can only be achieved together with others. However, the formation of certain coalitions may be detrimental but also advantageous with regard to the interest of the organization as a whole in the future, that is, for the budget of the organization in the next round. The first conclusion is that concerning the formation of coalitions, the collective interest of the organization played a dominant role in the present study: in the concentration condition more often small coalitions were formed, whereas large coalitions were more often formed in the dispersion condition. This avoidance of defective coalitions is in accordance with findings from the social dilemma literature (see e.g., Schulz, Albers, & Mueller, 1994; Liebrand, Messick, & Wilke, 1992), in which it is shown that sharing a superordinate identity one is willing to make choices that are in the collective interest (see also Turner, 1991). This finding is of importance for our knowledge about coalition formation as until now coalition formation has only been investigated in view of the short-term interest of parties concerned.

That coalitions were mostly formed in the collective interest does not mean that the mixed-motive character of coalition formation has been totally absent within rounds. As for formation of coalitions per se there was some support for insights collected in the domain of coalition formation. In the present study power and unequal power groups were introduced. In unequal power groups, the negotiation strength of stronger departments was normatively as well as strategically stronger than the negotiation strength of weaker departments (see: Komorita & Hamilton, 1983), probably as a result of the dominant motivation to serve the collective interest. We did not find that in equal power groups larger coalitions were formed more often, as may be expected from the anti-competitive theory of Gamson (1964), nor that most frequently small coalitions were formed in unequal power groups (see Wilke, 1985). However, it was found that weaker departments were more often excluded from a coalition in the unequal power than departments 1 and 2 in the equal power condition, suggesting that negotiation strength did play a role as for coalition formation, be it not as strong as may expected according to theories of coalition formation (Komorita & Parks, 1995).

As for the allocation of outcomes, coalition-theoretical expectations were confirmed. In their proposals for the division of outcomes in unequal power organizations departments showed strategic behavior: strong departments departed more often from a proportional division, weak departments from an equal division. This strategic behavior was not observed in the definitively accepted proposals. The final division of outcomes in unequal power groups was a compromise between equality and proportionality. These results are in accordance with Komorita's point of view (Komorita & Chertkoff, 1973; Komorita, 1979; see also Levine & Moreland, 1990). For equal power groups, Gamson's anti-competitive theory (Gamson, 1964) predicts that outcomes are to be dividided in a way that the interpersonal conflict is kept at a minimum. Our analysis of the proposals indeed suggests that outcomes in equal power groups were divided in an equal way, at least more equally than in unequal power groups. Fewer proposals were also needed in equal power groups to form a coalition than in unequal power groups.

The present results on the division of outcomes in a social dilemma coalition-setting are of relevance to compare with the division of outcomes in pure social dilemma's. In pure social dilemma situations without communication, players can harvest from a common resource. In symmetric pure social dilemma situations behavior is tacitly coordinated by means of the equality rule, because this rule may be considered to be simple and fair (Allison & Messick, 1990; Allison, McQueen, & Schaerfl, 1991). In agreement herewith the results in the present study did show that after explicit bargaining the outcomes were predominantly divided equally in equal power groups.

In asymmetric pure social dilemmas it has frequently been observed (Wit, Wilke, & Oppewal, 1992; Marwell & Ames, 1979; Van Dijk & Wilke, 1993) that outcomes are divided proportionally, and that participants experience this to be fair. Van Dijk and Wilke (1993) established that in a pure social dilemma situation, the preference for the proportionality rule was not affected by strategic considerations, since weak *and* strong players, complied to the proportionality rule. Strategic behavior, however, was shown in the present study: weak players based their proposals on equality, while strong players based their proposals more often on proportionality. In their study, Van Dijk and Wilke (1993) explained the absence of strategic biasing in social dilemmas by suggesting that in studies where strategic behavior has been shown (Messick & Sentis, 1979, 1983; Komorita & Chertkoff, 1973), negotiation actually took place or was anticipated, and also that the absence of strategic behavior in pure social dilemmas may be attributed to the circumstance that choices are then made without negotiation. Well then, the results in the present study where negotiations took place and where strategic biasing definitely was found enhances the plausibility of this statement.

How do our results relate to those reported by Mannix? Mannix (1993) found in a situation characterized by dispersion that mainly large coalitions were formed. We replicated these results in the present study. Through the contrast with coalition formation in the concentration condition, in the present study it was shown that departments mainly formed coalitions that are in the interest of the organization. After all, it was shown that mainly small coalitions were formed in the concentration condition and large coalitions in the dispersion condition of the present study.

In her experiment where the collective interest was served by dispersion, Mannix (1993) found that small coalitions were more often formed in unequal power organizations than in equal power organizations. Her study suggests that unequal power may be disadvantageous for the collective interest. The results of the present study did not support this argument: as for the coalitions formed there was no effect for power, nor was a significant interaction of power x superordinate dependency observed. Perhaps the reported detrimental effect of power differences in Mannix' study may be attributed to the relatively weaker induction of the collective interest in her study. This was operationalized by a 3% increase of the budget by forming large coalitions. In the present study this was 7%. We propose that the relatively greater salience of the collective interest in our study may have weakened the tendency to form smaller coalitions in our unequal power conditions, and the tendency to form larger coalitions in our equal power conditions.

Proposals were more often rejected when unequal power than when equal power was involved. With Mannix (Mannix & White, 1992), we suggest that this result may be attributed to the smaller ambiguity with regard to the allocation of outcomes in the equal power condition. The allocation of outcomes in case of power equality is simple and easy, while in an unequal power condition, departments adopt a strategic attitude in order to arrive at a compromise as for the division of group outcomes.

For coalitions of four departments a power effect was found in our study. These coalitions were formed more often when power equality existed than when power inequality was involved. This result is not quite clear. Yet, it may be noted that in forming coalitions of four departments the collective interest was neither promoted nor damaged. Moreover, that coalitions of four departments were more often formed in the equal power conditions than in the unequal power conditions, may be attributed to more cooperation (Gamson, 1964) in conditions of equal power, as well as to more competition in unequal power conditions (Komorita & Chertkoff, 1973). That the difference between equal power and unequal power organizations did not appear from the formation of coalitions between three and five departments, may well be attributed to the relatively high saliency of the organizational interest in our study which might have suppressed the difference between equal and unequal power organizations.

Table 4 shows that competition in the unequal power/concentration condition was considered more important, while cooperation was considered as less important than in the other conditions. This result suggests that Mannix's presupposition that unequal power always leads to more competition about the composition of coalitions, should be further specified. When, as in the present study the superordinate interest is strongly dominant, the effect of power may be reduced when the large coalition is in the collective interest of the organization. However, when the small coalition is collectively efficient, competition may be stronger in unequal power than in equal power situations. This implies that when it is in the interest of organizations to form small coalitions, unequal power may stimulate competition more than equal power. Moreover, this enhanced competition may be beneficial in the concentration condition, since it enhances the formation of coalitions that are in the interest of the organization as a whole.

Will power have consequences for the dispersion or concentration of resources in organizations? It may be favorable for the future of an organization when scarce resources are divided over a small number of units (concentration), or when these scarce resources are divided over a large number of units (dispersion). March and Simon (1958) and Mintzberg (1983) suggest that concentration is in the interest of organizations, while Mannix (Mannix, 1993; Mannix & White, 1992) tacitly assume that dispersion is of greater interest to organizations. We did not investigate whether dispersion or concentration is more in the interest of organizations. Instead, the question was raised whether members of organizations are willing to consider the collective interest of the organization which was defined as future interest in dispersion or concentration, which was served by making large or small coalitions, respectively.

Results of the present study clearly showed that departments were willing to serve the collective interest, i.e., to form small coalitions when concentration, and to make large coalitions when dispersion was in the collective interest of the organization. In the specific circumstances of the present study, it appeared that power relations hardly had an effect on coalition formation. The specific circumstances in our study were that the superordinate interest was highly prominent in the eyes of the negotiators. However, this will not always be the case. When the superordinate interest is less prominent, for example, because one is not part of one and the same organization, but of different organizations (Brewer & Kramer, 1986), and/or when differences in rewards in serving the superordinate interest and the rewards in serving one's personal interest (Kelley & Grzelak, 1972) are smaller, power could be a decisive factor. Equality of power may induce dispersion when the personal interest of each of the departments in the scarce resources is prominent. This tendency to diffuse resources of the organization over all departments, may be advantageous to the organization when the organization as a whole is better off with dispersion, but disadvantageous when the organization is better off with concentration of resources. For power inequality this may be the other way around. Inequality may induce concentration of resources. This tendency to allocate resources to a small number of (powerful) departments, is favorable for an organization as a whole when the organization is better off with concentration, but harmful to an organization when an organization is served by dispersion.

References

Adams, J.S. (1965). Inequity in social exchange. In: L. Berkowitz (ed.), *Advances in experimental social psychology* (pp.267-299). (AP). New York.

Allison, S.T., McQueen, L.R., & Schaerfl, L.M. (1991). Social decision making processes and the equal partitionment of shared resources. *Journal of Experimental Social Psychology, 28*,23-42.

Allison, S.T., & Messick, D.M. (1990). Social decision heuristics in the use of shared resources. *Journal of Behavioral Decision Making, 3*, 195-204.

Bornstein, R.F. (1992). Sublimal mere exposure effects. In: R.F. Bornstein & T.S. Pittman (Eds.), *Perception without awareness: Cognitive, clinical and social perspectives* (pp.191-210). New York: Guildford.

Brewer, M.B., & Kramer, R.M. (1986). Choice behavior in social dilemmas: Effects of social identity, group size, and decision framing. *Journal of Personality and Social Psychology, 50*, 543-549.

Dawes, R.M. (1993). *Affirmative action programs: Discontinuities between thoughts about individuals and thoughts about groups.* Unpublished manuscript. Carnegie Mellon University.

Emerson, R.M. (1964). Power-depending relations: Two experiments. *Sociometry, 27*, 282-298.

French, J., & Raven, B. (1959). The basis of social power. In: D. Cartwright (ed.), *Studies in social power* (pp.150-167). Ann Arbor, MI: Institute for Social Research.

Gamson, W.A. (1964). Experimental studies of coalition formation. In: L. Berkowitz (ed.), *Advances in experimental psychology* (AP). New York.

Kelley, H.H., & Grzelak, J. (1972). Conflict between individual and common interest in an *N*-person relationship. *Journal of Personality and Social Psychology, 21*, 190-197.

Kelley, H.H., & Thibaut, J.W. (1978). *Interpersonal relations: A theory of interdependence.* New York: Wiley.

Komorita, S.S. (1979). An equal excess model of coalition formation. *Behavioral Science, 24*, 369-381.

Komorita, S.S. (1984). Coalition bargaining. In: L. Berkowitz (ed.), *Advances in experimental social psychology: Vol. 18*. New York: Academic Press.

Komorita, S.S., & Chertkoff, J.M. (1973). A bargaining theory of coaltion formation. *Psychological Review, 80*, 149-162.

Komorita, S.S., & Hamilton, T.P. (1984). Power and equity in coalition bargaining. In *Research in the sociology of organizations, Vol. 3*. Greenwich. CT: JAI Press.

Komorita, S.S., & Nagao, D. (1983). The functions of resources in coalition bargaining. *Journal of Personality and Social Psychology, 44*, 95-106.

Komorita, S.S., & Parks, C.D. (1995). Interpersonal relations: Mixed-motive interaction. *Annual Review of Psychology, 46*, 183-207.

Komorita, S.S., & Kravitz, D.A. (1983). Coalition formation: A social psychological approach. In: P.B. Paulus (ed.), *Basic group processes* (pp.145-151). Hillsdale, NJ: Erlbaum.

Lawler, E.J. (1975). The impact of status differences on coalition agreements: En experimental study. *Journal of Conflict Resolution, 19/2*, 271-285.

Levine, J.M., & Moreland, R.L. (1990). Progress in small group research. *Annual Review of Psychology, 41*, 585-634.

Liebrand, W.B.G., Messick, D.M., & Wilke, H.A.M. (1992). *Social dilemmas. Theoretical issues and research findings.* Oxford: Pergamon Press.

Luce, R.D., & Raiffa, H. (1957). *Games and decisions: Introduction and critical survey*. New York: Wiley.

Mannix, E.A. (1991). Resource dilemmas and discount rates in decision making groups. *Journal of Experimtal Social Psychology, 27*, 379-391.

Mannix, E.A. (1993). Organizations as resource dilemmas: The effects of power balance on coalition formation in small groups. *Organizational Behavior and Human Decision Processes, 55*, 1-22.

Mannix, E.A., & White, S. (1992). The impact of distributive uncertainty on coalition formation in organizations. *Organizational Behavior and Human Decision Processes, 51*, 198-219.

March, J.G., & Simon, H.A. (1958). *Organizations*. New York: Wiley.

Marwell, G., & Ames, R.E. (1979). Experiments on the provision of public goods, I: Resources, interest, group size, and the free-rider problem. *American Journal*

of Sociology, 84, 1335-1360.
Messick, D.M. (1995). Equality, fairness and social conflict. *Social Justice Research, 8/2*, 153-173.
Messick, D.M., & Cook, K.S. (1983). *Equity theory*. New York: Praeger.
Messick, D.M., & Sentis,K.P. (1979). Fairness and preference. *Journal of Experimental Social Psychology, 15*, 418-434.
Messick, D.M., & Sentis, K.P. (1983). Fairness, preference, and fairness biases. In: D.M. Messick & K.S. Cook (Eds.), *Equity theory* (pp.61-94). New York: Praeger.
Messick, D.M., Wilke, H., Brewer, M.B., Kramer, R.M., Zemke, P.E., & Lui, L. (1983). Individual adaptations and structural change as solutions to social dilemmas. *Journal of Personality and Social Psychology, 44*, 294-309.
Mikula, G. (1980). *Justice and social interaction*. New York: Springer-Verlag.
Mintzberg, H. (1983). *Power in and around organizations*. Englewood Cliffs, NJ: Prentice-Hall.
Samuelson, C.D., Messick, D.M., Rutte, C.G., & Wilke, H.A.M. (1984). Individual and structural solutions to resource dilemmas in two cultures. *Journal of Personality and Social Psychology, 47*, 91-104.
Schelling, T.C. (1978). *Micromotives and macrobehavior*. New York: Norton.
Schulz, U., Albers, W., & Mueller, U. (1994). *Social dilemmas and cooperation*. Berlin: Springer-Verlag.
Stryker, S., & Psathas, G. (1960). Research on coalitions in the triad: Findings, problems and strategy. *Sociometry, 23*, 217-230.
Tajfel, H., & Turner, J.C. (1986). The social identity theory of intergroup behavior. In: S. Worchel & W.G. Austin (Eds.), *Psychology of intergroup relations*, 2nd ed. (pp.7-24). Chicago, IL: Nelson-Hall.
Thibaut, J.W., & Kelley, H.H. (1959). *The social psychology of groups*. New York: Wiley.
Turner, J.C. (1991). *Social influence*. Pacific Grove, CA: Brooks/Cole.
Van de Kragt, A.J.C., Orbell, J.M., & Dawes, R.M. (1983). The minimal contribution set as a solution to public goods problems. *American Political Science Review, 77*, 112-122.
Van der Linden, W.J., & Verbeek, A. (1985). Coalition formation: A game-theoretic approach. In: H.A.M. Wilke (ed.), *Coalition formation* (pp.29-114). Amsterdam: Elsevier Science Publishers BV.
Van Dijk, E., & Wilke, H. (1993). Differential interests, equity, and public good provision. *Journal of Experimental Social Psychology, 29*, 1-16.
Vinacke, W.E., & Arkoff, A. (1957). An experimental study of coalitions in the triad. *American Sociologial Review, 22/1*, 406-414.
Wilke, H.A.M. (1985). *Coalition formation*. Amsterdam: North Holland Publishers.
Wilke, H.A.M., Liebrand, W.B.G., & Boer, K. de (1986). Standards of justice and quality of ower in a social dilemma situation. *British Journal of Social Psychology, 16*, 51-53.
Wit, A., Wilke, H.A.M., & Oppewal, H. (1992). Fairness in asymmetric social

dilemmas. In: W. Liebrand, D. Messick & H. Wilke (Eds.), *Social dilemmas: Theoretical issues and research findings* (pp.183-197). New York: Pergamon Press.

Yamagishi, T. (1988a). Seriousness of social dilemmas and the provision of a sanctioning system. *Psychology Quarterly, 51*, 32-42.

Yamagishi, T. (1988b). The provision of a sanctioning system in the United States and Japan. *Psychology Quarterly, 41*, 264-270.

Why Do Cooperators Cooperate?: Efficacy as a Moderator of Social Motive Effects[1]

Norbert L. Kerr[2] and Susan E. Harris[2]

Abstract. Two alternative explanations for the effect of social motives on cooperation in social dilemmas were identified. One explanation (a *transformation explanation*) suggests that those with more cooperative social motives attach greater weight to others' outcomes. The other explanation (a *moral explanation*) suggests that those with more cooperative social motives are generally more concerned with acting in a morally-prescribed fashion. The transformation explanation predicts that social motive effects should be moderated by the efficacy of cooperation; the moral explanation predicts no such moderating effect. An experiment that tested these competing predictions is reported. Its results supported a dual-process model--the transformation explanation holds under conditions where it is unclear whether or not cooperation is morally prescribed (e.g., when there had been no prior discussion of the dilemma), whereas the moral explanation holds under conditions where it is clearer that to cooperate is to 'do the right thing' (e.g. following group discussion of the dilemma).

Keywords: cooperation-contingent remedy, efficacy, public-good remedy, social dilemma, social motive, social orientations

1. Introduction

If any of us were facing a social dilemma--the commons grazing pasture of Garret Hardin, one of the public goods problems described by Mancur Olson, the

[1] The authors wish to thank Valerie Barry, Daniel Lawton, Brenda Murphy, Michelle Musser, Anne Pelarski, and Hajime Sugawara for their assistance as experimenters and data coders. Direct e-mail correspondence to kerr@pilot.msu.edu.

[2] Department of Psychology, Michigan State University, East Lansing, Michigan 48824-1117 USA.

prisoner's dilemma--I suspect that we each would have definite preferences about whom we would like the interdependent other(s) to be. We could probably bring certain individuals to mind who would almost certainly make a cooperative response under nearly any conditions, and others (hopefully fewer in number) who could be counted on to nearly always act competitively.

Although the literature is not terribly large (see Komorita & Parks, 1994), there is some good evidence of stable individual differences in social dilemma behavior. The most and best evidence concerns what have been variously termed social orientations, social values, or social motives (Messick & McClintock, 1968; Kuhlman, Camac, & Cunha, 1986). In principle, social motives reflect variation on a continuous individual difference variable, but in usual practice (although see Liebrand & McClintock, 1988, for an exception), distinctive types of social motives have been distinguished. 'Individualists' act as if the only person's welfare they are concerned with is their own (and hence, are sometimes [cf. Kuhlman, Brown, & Teta, 1992] labelled "O"s, for "own" benefit). Others, the so-called 'competitors,' act as if they were striving to maximize their outcomes relative to the other(s) (hence, their pseudonym of "R"s for "relative" benefit). And 'cooperators' act as if their goal was to maximize the group's or the joint outcome (hence, they are sometimes termed "J"s, for joint benefit). Although social motives have been linked to many interesting behavioral and perceptual differences in social dilemma contexts (see Komorita & Parks, 1994; van Lange, 1991; Liebrand, Messick, & Wilke, 1992, for reviews), the core finding with which we are most concerned is that, all else being equal, J's are more likely to act cooperatively than either O's or R's (e.g., Kramer et al., 1986; Kuhlman & Marshello, 1975; Liebrand & van Run, 1985; McClintock & Liebrand, 1988). The goal of the research reported in this chapter was to explore why this is true--why do 'cooperators' cooperate?

The present work grew out of a program of research (Kerr, in press) which has focused on the causes and consequences of a sense of efficacy in social dilemmas--the belief that one's cooperative acts will have some impact on the collective welfare. And one line of work within this program has focused on the *moderating* role of that sense of efficacy (Baron & Kenny, 1986)--whether and how other social dilemma effects depend upon and interact with the perceived efficacy of one's cooperative act. Elsewhere (Kerr, 1992; Kerr & Kaufman-Gilliland, 1994), we have argued that it is useful to distinguish between two types of social dilemma remedies (i.e., interventions or variables which can boost the rate of cooperation). One type is a *public-good* remedy. Public good remedies enhance cooperation by enhancing (in one way or another) the value that group members place on the collective's welfare. The efficacy of one's cooperative act should strongly moderate the effect of a public-good remedy. That is, *if* a variable affects cooperation precisely because it affects one's concern for the collective welfare, *then* the impact of that variable on cooperation should hinge on the degree to which one can actually enhance the collective's welfare through one's cooperative act (i.e., on the efficacy of cooperation). The impact of such a variable ought to be maximal when efficacy is maximal. Conversely, no matter how much more value one places on the collective welfare, one ought not to be any more likely to cooperate if one believes that one's cooperaion has absolutely no chance of affecting that collective welfare. This logic implies a diverging-fan moderation effect, like that pictured in the plot on the left of Figure 1. Such moderation effects have been observed; for example, Kerr, Sattler, & Kaufman-Gilliland (1994) found that the effect of a short (and apparently conflict laden) group interaction prior to considering a social dilemma was moderated in a diverging-fan manner by the experimentally manipulated efficacy of the cooperative act.

This is all relevant to our current focus on social motives *if* cooperative social motivation is a public-good remedy. And indeed, the original and still-dominant conception of social motives (Messick & McClintock, 1968; McClintock, 1978)

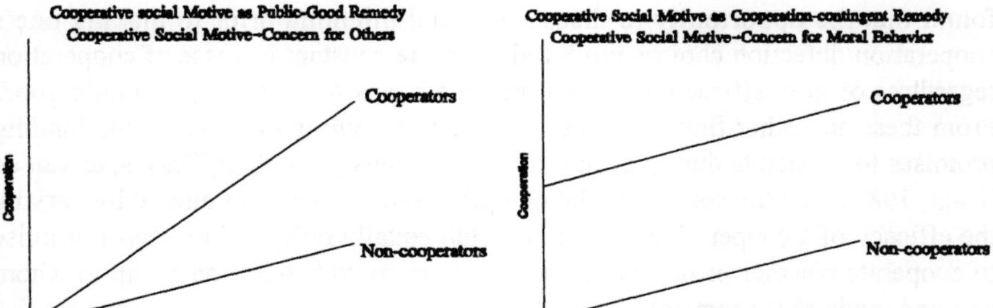

Figure 1. Efficacy moderation predictions for public-good and cooperation-contingent remedies

holds that cooperators chronically transform the social dilemma's given matrix by attaching some greater weight to the outcome of others, whereas individualists do not transform the given matrix and competitors actually attach a negative value to others' outcomes. If this *transformation explanation* is true, then social motive effects should be moderated with the diverging-fan pattern by a manipulation of the efficacy of a cooperative act--i.e., the differences in cooperativeness between J's and those with less cooperative social motives (i.e., O's and R's) ought to be directly proportional to the efficacy of the cooperative act.

There is another (non-exhaustive) type of social dilemma remedy which we have termed *cooperation-contingent* remedies. Such a remedy derives its effectiveness by making some salient incentive contingent on the cooperative act, per se, rather than by enhancing the value attached to cooperative welfare. Simple examples of cooperation-contingent remedies include the imposition of stiff penalties on the non-cooperative act of failing to pay taxes, or giving gifts to those who voluntarily contribute to keep their local public television station on the air. Such remedies should continue to provide their incentives for cooperation even if one's cooperative act turns out to be wholly inefficacious (i.e., to have absolutely no impact on) the collective welfare. For example, a national tax break for couples who limit their families to one child could have a restraining effect on birth rates even if other factors (e.g., unchecked immigration) meant that such family planning was ultimately inefficacious (i.e., would not defuse the nation's population bomb). A 'pure' cooperation-contingent remedy (i.e., one that both had no affect at all on one's concern for collective welfare and offered a fixed and constant incentive for a cooperative act, per se) should *not* be moderated by the efficacy[3] of one's cooperative act, producing a pattern of data like that in the plot on the right of Figure 1. Note that even though such a remedy does not affect one's concern for the collective welfare, whatever such concern exists independent of the remedying variable would make group members sensitive to the efficacy of cooperation--i.e., there should still be a clear efficacy simple effect within any level of the remedying variable.

Such patterns have also been observed. Kerr & Kaufman-Gilliland (1994) found that the opportunity to discuss a social dilemma prior to making one's cooperation/defection choices produced the same constant increase of cooperation regardless of how efficacious a cooperative act was for obtaining a public good. From these and other findings, they concluded that group members made binding promises to cooperate during such group discussions (cf. Orbell, Dawes, & van de Kragt, 1988), and the costs of violating such promises were not altered by varying the efficacy of a cooperative act (i.e., one felt equally obligated to keep a promise to cooperate whether or not that cooperative act could benefit the group to whom one had made that promise).

Liebrand, Jansen, Rijken, & Suhre's (1986) "might vs. morality" and related research (e.g., Sattler & Kerr, 1991; van Lange, 1992; van Lange & Kuhlman, 1994; van Lange & Liebrand, 1989) suggest that cooperative social motivation might likewise constitute a cooperation-contingent remedy. In that work, it has been repeatedly shown that those with cooperative social motives are relatively more sensitive to the moral implications of behavior in social dilemmas. For example, Liebrand et al. found that J's draw more extreme distinctions along a good-bad dimension between partners who always cooperate vs. always compete than do O's or R's. (The latter seem to be more sensitive to the implications of social dilemma behavior for power or dominance.) Thus, another reason why cooperative social motives may lead to more cooperation is that cooperation is perceived as better, more moral behavior in situations of social interdependence and that people with more cooperative social motives are more willing or eager to

---

[3] Note that we are focusing exclusively upon the efficacy of a cooperative act *for enhancing collective welfare or obtaining some public good.* A single act may simultaneously have very low efficacy in this sense (e.g., one's individual vote may have vanishingly small impact on providing the public good of a capable political leader) yet be highly efficacious for obtaining other, private goods (e.g., satisfying the requirements of an internalized "good citizen" role). See Kerr (1992; in press) for an extended discussion of such issues.

'do the right thing.' If this *moral explanation* of social motive effects is correct, the efficacy of one's cooperative act should *not* moderate such effects. That is, if the act of cooperation, per se, was viewed as more virtuous and virtue was more important to one, then no matter how efficacious one's act was (or wasn't) for enhancing the group's welfare, one could obtain virtue's rewards simply by acting more virtuously.[4]

Of course, it is also possible that both the transformation and the moral explanation are correct. In such a case, we could expect both (a) a significant simple main effect of social motive, even when the efficacy of cooperation is minimal (predicted by the moral explanation), and (b) a diverging-fan interaction between the efficacy of cooperation and social motive (predicted by the transformation explanation).

The primary objective of the research we describe below was to test these competing explanations. The base design called for blocking subjects on their social motives and then experimentally manipulating the efficacy of their cooperative acts. We also included another experimental manipulation. Half of our groups were given an opportunity to discuss the social dilemma prior to making their cooperate/defect choices, whereas the remainder could not discuss the dilemma. This treatment was included not only to replicate prior findings (e.g., Kerr & Kaufman-Gilliland, 1994; Kerr, Garst, Gerard, & Harris, 1995) on the effects of group discussion, but to see whether and how social motives might moderate these effects. For example, might the more morally-sensitive J's be more willing to make and keep promises to cooperate during group discussions than the more dominance-avoiding O's & R's?

2. Method

2.1 Experimental Social Dilemma Task

The task and procedure used in our experiment mirrored those employed by Kerr & Kaufman-Gilliland (1994). The experimental task was a variation (introduced by Kerr, 1992) on the basic step-level public good task (introduced by van de Kragt, Orbell, & Dawes, 1983). The experimental task is described as an investment game, played by a five-person group. Before each play of the game (i.e., trial), the experimenter ostensibly divides a 100-point pool among the five

[4] This logic assumes that the moral rewards of cooperation are not contingent on the effectiveness of one's actions. Other assumptions are possible, of course. For example, it may be seen as particularly virtuous to attempt to cooperate when there is little chance of aiding the group (and, indirectly, oneself). Or, it is possible that there is an 'inefficacy escape-clause' in the moral obligation to act cooperatively in contexts of social interdependence--i.e., you're obligated to act cooperatively *unless* there's just no way your cooperativeness can help others. The latter would produce a pattern more like that expected under the transformation explanation.

players. The number of points each player receives is called his/her "share." The only constraint on these shares is that no player's share can be greater than 50 points on any given play. Subjects are told that share size may differ from player to player and from play to play. Each player knows his/her own share size on each play but does not know the share size of any of the other players.

Before each play of the game, each group member is given $10 "start-up money". S/he then has to make a dichotomous choice in private--to "keep" the $10 (i.e., defect) or to "invest" (i.e., cooperate). To invest means that the endowment is irrevocably lost. The incentive for investment is that if enough members chose to invest, each person in the group (investors and non-investors alike) receive a $15 "bonus" (a public good). To earn this bonus, the sum of the share sizes for all group members who invest (termed the "point total") must exceed 50 points. If the point total was less than or equal to 50 points, then no bonus money is earned on that play. The efficacy of a cooperative choice for producing the public good is simply manipulated in this paradigm by varying a subject's share size.

Efficacy was manipulated within-subjects. All subjects played the game five times. The only task feature that varied across these trials was the subject's share size. Share sizes took on the following values: 1, 8, 15, 22, 29. Instructions suggested that the share sizes received on different trials were determined independently. The order in which a subject considered these five different versions of the task was randomized separately for each subject.

2.2 Social Motive Measure

Subjects' social motives were determined using a version of Messick and McClintock's (1968) decomposed game measure. For each of nine items, Ss are asked to select among three choices. Each choice allocates a certain number of points to oneself and to an anonymous other who ostensibly is making the same selection. One of the three choices should be preferred by someone with each of the three primary social motives. For example, in the following item,

	A	B	C
You get	480	540	480
Other gets	80	280	480

a R should prefer choice A because it maximizes the difference between own and other's outcome, a O should prefer choice B because it maximizes own outcome, and a J should prefer choice C, because it maximizes joint outcome. We required that a subject had to make more than two-thirds (i.e., at least 7 of 9) of his/her choices consistent with a social motive before s/he would be classified in that social motive group.

2.3 Subjects

The participants were 318 undergraduate students (150 males, 168 females) drawn from introductory psychology courses at Michigan State University. They received extra class credit for their participation. The social motives of 93 of these Ss could not be determined because they failed to meet the consistency criterion of the social motive measure. Thus, our analysis was based on the data for the remaining 218 subjects. There were 161 J's, 37 O's, and 27 R's; the latter two groups were combined to form a 'non-cooperators' condition to be contrasted with the cooperators (i.e., the J's).

2.4 Procedure

With minor exceptions, the experimental procedure was very similar to that followed in Kerr & Kaufman-Gilliland (1994). Subjects were scheduled in groups of five. Experimental sessions were randomly assigned to experimental conditions with the proviso that all five Ss had to show up in order to run a group-discussion condition. As subjects arrived at the lab, they were ushered into individual booths, each of which contained a microcomputer. In the no-discussion condition, if fewer than five subjects reported to the lab, the late arrival of the no-show subjects was simulated. Thus, in all conditions, subjects were led to believe that there were five participants at each experimental session.

Instructions were provided on the computer screen. Subjects first completed the social motive measure. Thereafter,[5] the public goods task was described. To check subjects' understanding of the game, a number of hypothetical game plays were described and subjects had to indicate the earnings of those who did and did not invest. In order to make subjects' invest choices consequential, a lottery procedure to convert game dollars into real dollars was then described. A randomly selected member of a randomly selected group would receive the amount jointly determined by his/her own and fellow group members' choices for one randomly chosen play. (A functionally equivalent Monte Carlo procedure was actually used later to identify and reward one subject.)

Subjects in the discussion condition were then fetched from their booths into a larger central room and given up to five minutes in which to conduct a face-to-face discussion of the investment game. The group could end the discussion before five minutes had elapsed if all five members agreed. Groups were allowed to discuss how they thought the game should be played and to plan any strategy not forbidden by the game's rules. Note that at this point group members did not know what their share sizes would be on any of the coming trials. Thus, group discussion could not assist in constructing a minimal contributing set (van de Kragt, et al.,

---

[5] After completing the social motive measure, there was also a manipulation of face-to-face discussion on an unrelated task (viz., a Winter Survival task; Johnson & Johnson, 1991, p. 227) in this experiment. However, unexpectedly (cf. Kerr, Sattler, & Kaufman-Gilliland, 1994) this experimental treatment did not affect cooperation. It was, of course, unconfounded with the social motive treatment of primary interest here. It will not be considered further in this report.

1983), nor could it thereby have simply reduced uncertainty about the dilemma (Budescu, Rapoport, & Suleiman, 1990; also see Kerr & Kaufman-Gilliland, 1994). They were also told that the discussions would be videotaped. Of course, Ss in the no-discussion condition simply proceeded on without any face-to-face discussion.

After being assured of the anonymity of their choices, the series of five trials then began. Afterwards,[6] subjects completed a short questionnaire and were then debriefed and excused.

3. Results

Previous research following very similar procedures (Kerr, 1992; Kerr & Kaufman-Gilliland, 1994; Kerr et al., 1994; Kerr, et al., 1995) had established a couple of useful points. First, that the share-size manipulation powerfully affects the perceived efficacy of a cooperative (i.e., invest) choice. In the light of this clear and consistent evidence, no explicit efficacy manipulation was included in the present study. Second, it had also been found in this paradigm that cooperation data are vulnerable to ceiling effects under certain conditions (viz., after group discussion and relatively large share sizes, e.g., share sizes > 22). To avoid the latter problem, we dropped the trial where share size = 29 from our analyses. And, to simplify the analyses, we dichotomized the efficacy manipulation by contrasting the trials in which share size (and, hence, efficacy) was lowest (viz. 1 and 8) with the trials where share size was larger (viz. 15 and 22). Thus, the final experimental design was a 2 (Social motive: Cooperators [J's] vs. Non-cooperators [O's & R's]) x 2 (Discussion) x 2 (Efficacy: Low vs. High) factorial with repeated measures on the last factor.

An analysis of variance on Ss' cooperative decisions[7] was conducted. Most of the results of this analysis were not of direct relevance to our current focus, but for completeness sake, might be quickly described. First, and unsurprisingly, there was a strong effect of efficacy, $F(1,221)=101.88$, $p<.001$; as share size increased, so did investment, low-efficacy=35.8% investing vs. high-efficacy=68.2% investing (see Figure 2). Second, there was a strong discussion main effect, $F(1,221)=13.07$, $p<.001$, replicating an oft-replicated effect (see Komorita & Parks, 1994, for a review). Overall, Ss chose to invest 58.4% of the time after group discussion versus 40.6% of the time without such discussion (again, see Fig. 2). Third, as Kerr & Kaufman-Gilliland (1994) found, the effect of discussion was *not* moderated by the efficacy of an invest choice, $F(1,221)<1$, ns (see Fig. 2). As

---

[6]There was also a second block of five game plays which was preceded by a manipulation of Ss' mindfulness (Langer, 1989). The purpose of this period of the study was unrelated to the present experimental objectives. These data are not considered in this report; they are described in Kerr et al. (1995; Experiment 2).

[7] Note that Lunney (1970) has found that analysis of variance is quite robust to the clear violation of the normality assumption which an ANOVA of dichotomous data entails.

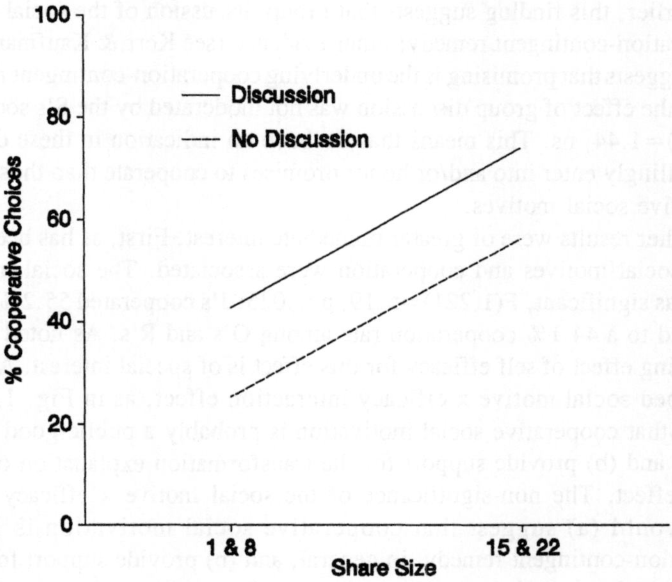

Figure 2. Effects of efficacy and discussion on cooperation

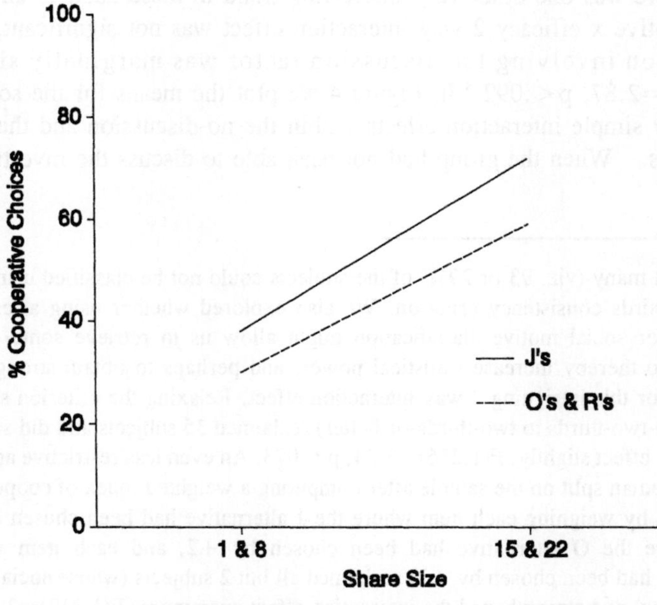

Figure 3. Effect of social motives on cooperation

noted earlier, this finding suggests that group discussion of the social dilemma is a cooperation-contingent remedy; other evidence (see Kerr & Kaufman-Gilliland, 1994) suggests that promising is the underlying cooperation-contingent mechanism. Fourth, the effect of group discussion was not moderated by the S's social motive, $F(1,221)=1.44$, ns. This means that we have no indication in these data that J's more willingly enter into and/or honor promises to cooperate than those with less-cooperative social motives.

Other results were of greater immediate interest. First, as has been routinely found, social motives and cooperation were associated. The social motive main effect was significant, $F(1,221)=5.19$, $p<.025$; J's cooperated 55.2% of the time compared to a 44.1% cooperation rate among O's and R's. As noted earlier, the moderating effect of self efficacy for this effect is of special interest. A significant fan-shaped social motive x efficacy interaction effect, as in Fig. 1, would (a) confirm that cooperative social motivation is probably a public-good remedy, in general, and (b) provide support for the transformation explanation of the social motive effect. The non-significance of the social motive x efficacy interaction effect would (a) suggest that cooperative social motivation is probably a cooperation-contingent remedy, in general, and (b) provide support for the moral explanation for the effect. As it turned out, efficacy did *not* directly moderate the social motive effect. The relevant means are plotted in Figure 3. Although visual inspection hints at a diverging-fan pattern, the social motive x efficacy interaction effect is clearly non-significant, $F(1,221)=.62$, ns.

There was one other very interesting trend in these data. Even though the social motive x efficacy 2-way interaction effect was not significant, the 3-way interaction involving the discussion factor was marginally significant, $F(1,221)=2.87$, $p<.092$.[8] In Figure 4 we plot the means for the social motive x efficacy simple interaction effects within the no-discussion and the discussion conditions. When the group had not been able to discuss the investment game,

---

[8] Recall that many (viz. 93 or 29%) of the subjects could not be classified using the better-than-two-thirds consistency criterion. We also explored whether using a less restrictive criterion for social motive classification might allow us to retrieve some of these lost subjects, to thereby increase statistical power, and perhaps to obtain stronger statistical evidence for this intriguing 3-way interaction effect. Relaxing the criterion slightly (from better-than-two-thirds to two-thirds-or-better) reclaimed 35 subjects and did strengthen the interaction effect slightly, $F(1,256)=3.24$, $p=.073$. An even less restrictive approach (viz. doing a median split on the sample after computing a weighted index of cooperative social motivation by weighing each item where the J alternative had been chosen by +3, each item where the O alternative had been chosen by +2, and each item where the R alternative had been chosen by +1) reclaimed all but 2 subjects (whose social motive data was missing) and strengthened the interaction effect even more, $F(1,312)=3.84$, $p=.051$. (Note that the pattern of other effects was not altered in these alternative analyses.) These analyses tended to increase our confidence that the joint moderation of social motive effects by both efficacy and discussion was a genuine effect.

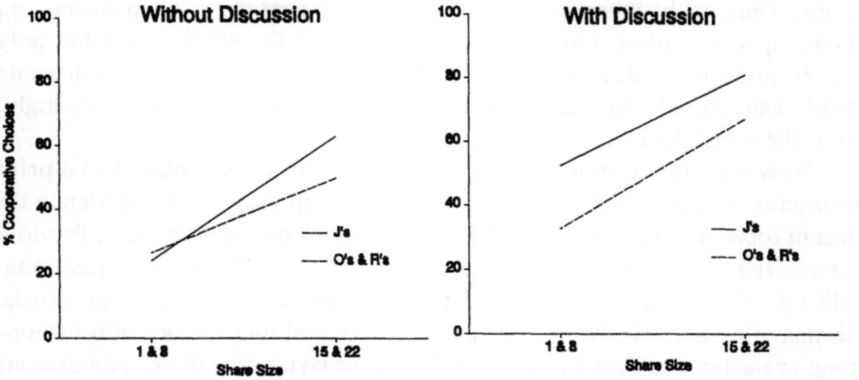

Figure 4. Decomposition of the discussion x efficacy x social motive interaction effect

efficacy appeared to moderate the effect of social motive in exactly the diverging-fan pattern expected under the transformation explanation, F(1,111)=3.48, p<.065.On the other hand, when the group had previously discussed the investment game, there was no indication of a significant diverging-fan (or any other) interaction effect, F(1,110)=.37, ns.

4. Discussion

The implications of these data for answering our question--why do 'cooperators' cooperate?--depend somewhat on how statistically conservative one wants to be. If one dismisses the marginally significant (p=.091) discussion x efficacy x social motive interaction effect, then one would have to conclude that the data are more consistent with the moral explanation for social motivation than the transformation explanation. Statistically, there was no evidence for moderation of social motivation effects by the efficacy of the invest choice--a clear prediction of the transformation explanation. Of course, null effects are always problematic (Greenwald, 1975), but there are a couple of good reasons to doubt that the present null efficacy x social motive interaction effect is simply a Type II error. First, the fact that both the efficacy and the social motive factors produced significant main effects on cooperation argues against restricted range on either variable. Second, the present sample size (218 Ss) provided good power for detecting such an effect--sufficient to detect what Cohen (1987) classifies as a medium interaction effect size with probability of .957.

If one is willing to seriously consider the marginal discussion x efficacy x social motive interaction effect, a somewhat more complex and more interesting picture emerges. The no-discussion condition is the more 'minimal' task situation. Here people have to rely largely on their personal intuitions about what behavior is 'right'--both morally and in terms of playing the game effectively. And in this situation, we did observe the diverging fan interaction signature of a public-good remedy. Thus, without any discussion of the investment game, cooperators (i.e., J's) did appear to place a higher value on obtaining the public good, but only invested more when there was a reasonable chance that such investment could actually help provide that public good (i.e., when efficacy was sufficiently high), just as the transformation explanation predicts.

However, this prediction was not confirmed when groups had a prior opportunity to discuss the investment game. Here, efficacy did not moderate the effect of social motive, the signature of a cooperation-contingent remedy. Previous research (e.g., Bonacich, 1972, 1976; Dawes et al., 1977; Kerr & Kaufman-Gilliland, 1994; Orbell et al., 1988) has shown that group discussion of a social dilemma often elicits active consideration of the moral implications of behavior--strong evaluations of cooperative vs. defecting behavior are voiced, promises are made, threats are expressed toward potential defectors, and language expressive of moral obligation is heard (e.g., "liar", "traitor", "cop out", "breaking one's word"). [Without a detailed analyses of the content of our group discussions, we cannot tell whether such language is more likely to be voiced by cooperators than by defectors. However, non-significance of the social motive x discussion interaction suggests that whatever is said and whoever says it, the impact of group discussion is comparable for more and less cooperative subjects.] Under such conditions, the cooperative choice may be generally recognized as the morally preferred course of action. And under such conditions, cooperators were more likely to cooperate than non-cooperators regardless of the efficacy of an invest choice, just as the moral explanation of social motivation predicts.

These results suggest a dual-process model of social motivation. When normative demands are unclear or not salient (e.g., our no-discussion condition), cooperators may indeed attach more value to others' welfare than non-cooperators. However, if normative demands requiring cooperative behavior become salient, cooperators become more concerned with 'doing the right thing' than non-cooperators, *but do not continue to be generally more concerned with others' welfare.* Had group discussion simply added a concern for doing the right thing among cooperators to a chronic, pre-existing concern for others, we would have expected to see the empirical signatures of *both* explanations in the discussion condition (viz. a fan shaped interaction effect for the transformation explanation *and* a simple social motive effect at minimal levels of efficacy for the moral explanation). But instead, group discussion appears to *change* the process underlying the social motive effect (from a prosocial transformation of outcomes to a heightened value on acting appropriately).

This is a relatively complex but not-implausible model of the basis of social motivation effects on cooperative behavior in social dilemmas. And, like most unanticipated models, it raises more questions than it resolves.

Can the key three-way interaction effect which here is only marginally significant be clearly replicated?

Can functional floor and ceiling effects (cf. Mlicki, 1992) be ruled out as alternative explanations of certain key findings in the present study (floor effects for the absence of social motive effects when efficacy is low without discussion; ceiling effects for the absence of a diverging-fan efficacy x social motive interaction with group discussion)?

Can complex differences between social motive groups in the impact of share size on perceived self efficacy be ruled out as another alternative explanation (Wilke, 1996)--e.g., the results in Figure 5 could follow if, compared to (Os & Rs), Js felt generally more self efficacious with group discussion and were more sensitive to share size without group discussion. A replication study which included direct assessments of perceived self efficacy could speak to this possibility.

What are the psychologically salient aspects of group discussion of a social dilemma which trigger the apparent shift in mediating process? What other situational treatments might likewise trigger such a shift?

Are there other individual difference or situational social dilemma remedies which look like public-good remedies under some conditions and cooperation-contingent remedies under others?

Such questions must await future research.

Although the present study did not conclusively answer the question, "why do 'cooperators' cooperate?," it did reillustrate the utility of one analytic tool--studying the moderating effects of the efficacy of cooperation. Such studies are useful for analyzing and understanding just why certain variables do affect cooperation. Moreover, by helping to identify cooperation-contingent social dilemma remedies, they can also be more practically useful. There are all too many real-world social dilemmas in which the efficacy of cooperation is manifestly low--very large, anonymous groups facing complex problems, sometimes with pernicious patterns of interdependence (e.g., requirements for close coordination). Under such conditions, cooperation-contingent remedies--like group discussion, like cooperative social motives following such group discussion--can continue to promote cooperation, despite the fact that one's cooperation cannot have much impact on collective welfare.

References

Baron, R. M., & Kenny, D. A. (1986). The moderator-mediator distinction in social psychological research: Conceptual, strategic, and statistical considerations. *Journal of Personality and Social Psychology, 51*, 1173-1182.

Bonacich, P. (1972). Norms and cohesion as adaptive responses to political conflict: An experimental study. *Sociometry, 35*, 357-375.

Bonacich, P. (1976). Secrecy and solidarity. *Sociometry, 39*, 200-208.

Budescu, D. V., Rapoport, A., & Suleiman, R. (1990). Resource dilemmas with environmental uncertainty and asymmetric players. *European Journal of Social Psychology*, **20**, 475-487.

Cohen, J. (1987). *Statistical power analysis for the behavioral sciences* (Revised Ed.). Hillsdale, NJ: L. Erlbaum.

Dawes, R. M., McTavish, J., & Shaklee, H. (1977). Behavior, communication, and assumptions about other people's behavior in a commons dilemma situation. *Journal of Personality and Social Psychology, 35*, 1-11.

Greenwald, A. (1975). Consequences of prejudice against the null hypothesis. *Psychological Bulletin, 82*, 1-20.

Johnson, D. W., & Johnson, F. P. (1991). *Joining together: Group theory and group skills*, 4th Ed. Englewood Cliffs, NJ: Prentice Hall.

Kerr, N. L. (1992). Efficacy as a causal and moderating variable in social dilemmas. In W. Liebrand, D. Messick, & H. Wilke, (Eds). *A social psychological approach to social dilemmas*. New York: Pergamon Press.

Kerr, N. L. (in press). "Does my contribution really matter?": Efficacy in social dilemmas. To appear in W. Stroebe & M. Hewstone (Eds.), *European Review of Social Psychology*, Vol. 7. Chichester: J. Wiley.

Kerr, N. L., Garst, J., Gerard, D. K., & Harris, S. (1995). That still, small voice: Commitment to cooperate as an internalized vs. a social norm. Unpublished paper (under editorial review), Michigan State University.

Kerr, N. L., & Kaufman-Gilliland, C. M. (1994). Communication, commitment, and cooperation in social dilemmas. *Journal of Personality and Social Psychology*, **66**, 513-529.

Kerr, N. L., Sattler, D. N., & Kaufman-Gilliland, C. (1994). Social identification and cooperation in social dilemmas. Presented at the Annual Convention of the Society of Experimental Social Psychology. October 14, 1994, Incline Village, NV, USA.

Komorita, S. S., & Parks, C. D. (1994). *Social dilemmas*. Madison, WS: Brown & Benchmark.

Kramer, R. M., McClintock, C. G., & Messick, D. M. (1986). Social values and cooperative response to a simulated resource conservation crisis. *Journal of Personality*, **54**, 576-592.

Kuhlman, D. M., Brown, C., & Teta, P. (1992). Judgments of cooperation and defection in social dilemmas: The moderating role of judge's social orientation. In Liebrand, W. B. G., Messick, D. M., & Wilke, H. A. M. (Eds.), *A social psychological approach to social dilemmas* (pp. 111-132). New York: Pergamon Press.

Kuhlman, D. M., Camac, C., & Cunha, D. A. (1986). Individual differences in social orientation. In H. Wilke, D. M. Messick, & C. G. Rutte (Eds.), *Experimental social dilemmas*. Frankfurt am Main: Verlag Peter Lang.

Kuhlman, D. M., & Marshello, A. (1975). Individual differences in game motivation as moderators of preprogrammed strategic effects in prisoner's dilemma. *Journal of Personality and Social Psychology, 32*, 992-931.

Langer, E. J. (1989). *Mindfulness*. Reading, MA: Addison-Wesley.

Liebrand, W.B.G., Jansen, R. Rijken, V., & Suhre, C. (1986). Might over morality: The interaction between social values and the interpretation of decision-making in experimental games. *Journal of Experimental Social Psychology, 22*, 203-215.

Liebrand, W. B. G., & McClintock, C. G. (1988). The ring measure of social values: A computerized procedure for assessing individual differences in information processing and social value orientation. *European Journal of Personality*, **2**, 217-230.

Liebrand, W. B. G., Messick, D. M., & Wilke, H. A. M. (Eds.) (1992). *A social psychological approach to social dilemmas*. New York: Pergamon Press.

Liebrand, W. B. G., & van Run, G. J. (1985). The effect of social motives across two cultures on behavior in social dilemmas. *Journal of Experimental Social Psychology*, **21**, 86-102.

Lunney, G. H. (1970). Using analysis of variance with a dichotomous dependent variable: An empirical study. *Journal of Educational Measurement, 7*, 263-269.

McClintock, C. G. (1978). Social values: Their definition, measurement, and development. *Journal of Research and Development in Education*, **12**, 121-137.

McClintock, C. G., & Liebrand, W. B. G. (1988). The role of interdependence structure, individual value orientation and other's strategy in social decision making: A transformational analysis. *Journal of Personality and Social Psychology*, **55**, 296-309.

Messick, D. M., & McClintock, C. G. (1968). Motivational basis of choice in experimental games. *Journal of Experimental Social Psychology, 4*, 1-25.

Mlicki, M. K. (1992). Rationality in social dilemmas: Steady cooperators, steady defectors and compromise seekers. Paper presented at the Fifth International Conference on Social Dilemmas, Bielefeld, Germany; July 11-15, 1992.

Orbell, J. M., Dawes, R. M., & van de Kragt, A. J. (1988). Explaining discussion induced cooperation. *Journal of Personality and Social Psychology, 54*, 811-819.

Sattler, D. N., & Kerr, N. L. (1991). Might versus morality explored: Motivational and cognitive bases for social motives. *Journal of Personality and Social Psychology*, **60**, 756-765.

van de Kragt, A., Orbell, J., & Dawes, R. M. (1983). The minimal contributing set as a solution to public goods problems. *American Political Science Review*, **77**, 112-122.

van Lange, P. A. M. (1991). *The rationality and morality of cooperation*. Groningen: Rijksuniversiteit Groningen.

van Lange, P. A. M. (1992). Rationality and morality in social dilemmas: The influence of social value orientations. In Liebrand, W. B. G., Messick, D. M., & Wilke, H. A. M. (Eds.), *A social psychological approach to social dilemmas* (pp. 133-146). New York: Pergamon Press.

van Lange, P. A. M., & Kuhlman, D. M. (1994). Social value orientations and impressions of partner's honesty and intelligence: A test of the might versus morality effect. *Journal of Personality and Social Psychology*, **67**, 126-141.

van Lange, P. A. M., & Liebrand, W. B. (1989). On perceiving morality and potency: Social values and the effects of person perception in a give-some dilemma. *European Journal of Personality*, **3**, 209-225.

Wilke, H. A. M. (1996). Personal communication. March 1, 1996.

Tacit Coordination and Fairness Judgments in Social Dilemmas

Eric van Dijk[1] and Henk Wilke[1]

[1] Department of Social and Organizational Psychology, Leiden University. P.O. Box 9555, 2300 RB Leiden, The Netherlands

Abstract. In this paper we argue that in social dilemma situations, group members often tacitly coordinate choice behavior on the basis of rules of fairness. Results are presented on the employment of coordination rules in asymmetric dilemmas. Three different research topics are covered, suggesting that tacit coordination of choice behavior is affected by the justification of asymmetries, the presentation of social dilemmas, and environmental uncertainty. On the basis of these research findings, general suggestions are formulated, as well as suggestions for future research on fairness and tacit coordination.

Keywords. Social dilemmas, fairness, tacit coordination

1 Introduction

In the typical social dilemma, group members make their decisions privately and anonymously. That is, in most research on social dilemmas group members face a situation of social uncertainty (cf. Messick, Allison & Samuelson, 1988). How do group members deal with social uncertainty in such complex situations? How do group members decide on their own choice behavior if they have no information about others' choice behavior?

As Schelling (1980) convincingly demonstrated, choice behavior can be coordinated even without communication. When group members realize they have a common interest, they might be willing to infer or reason 'what their fellow group members will decide', and to take this inference into account while making their own decision. That is, the fact that communication is prohibited does not prevent group members from expecting certain choice behavior of their fellow group members, and/or to have strict beliefs about what group members (including themselves) should decide.

Recent research on social dilemmas suggests that in situations of social uncertainty individual group members tacitly coordinate choice behavior by employing certain 'coordination rules.' The first research dealing with the employment of coordination rules in social dilemma situations focused on the employment of an 'equal division rule' in Resource dilemmas (Allison & Messick, 1990; Allison, McQueen, & Schaerfl, 1992; Samuelson & Allison, 1994). In these studies subjects could harvest points from a common resource. Being informed about the optimal group harvest, subjects appeared to anchor their choice behavior on the simple rule of all members harvesting an equal amount from this optimal group harvest.

What makes a rule attractive for implementation? In the early studies on the employment of the equal division rule, the emphasis was on the ease of implementation. The preference for the equal division rule was merely assumed to reflect a preference for simple decision heuristics. Even in these studies, however, it was acknowledged that there is a normative component in the sense that in order to be implemented, coordination rules must satisfy a norm of fairness. As Messick demonstrated, equality may often be assumed to satisfy a norm of fairness (see e.g., Messick, 1995).

That the equal division rule may satisfy a norm of fairness may be especially true in symmetric dilemmas. In symmetric dilemmas only one fairness norm seems appropriate: Since all members occupy identical positions, all members should display similar choice behavior. For example, in symmetric Public Good dilemmas all members should contribute an equal amount of endowments to the public good. In asymmetric dilemmas - dilemmas in which group members occupy different positions (e.g. in which some members possess more endowment than others) - other rules besides the equal division rule may become focal points for coordination. By studying asymmetric dilemmas we may increase our knowledge of the operation of coordination rules, and (its relation to) fairness considerations.

In a series of experiments we investigated preferences for coordination rules in asymmetric settings. In the following we will first review some of this research. On the basis of this research we will then elaborate on the function and nature of coordination rules.

2 Research on Coordination Rules

2.1 Coordination Rules in Asymmetric Dilemmas

As Schelling (1980) argued, in many mixed-motive situations people may feel they are in a position that requires coordination of choices. When communication is prohibited, and potential gains are at stake it may be worthwhile to predict others' choice behavior and to take this expected choice behavior into account when deciding on your own choice behavior. Schelling noted that fairness judgments may be effective focal points for coordination.

Fairness judgments may reduce uncertainty about how one (and others) should behave by defining what is considered to be appropriate behavior. In the words of Schelling: 'The moral force of fairness is greatly reinforced by the power of a 'fair' result to focus attention, if it fills the vacuum of indeterminacy that would otherwise exist.' (Schelling, 1980, p.73).

In this article we argue that group members anchor their actual choice behavior on these judgments of fairness. We will report results from a number of studies in which we examined fairness judgments and choice behavior. In these studies we first assessed to what extent the rules we distinguished accurately predicted fairness judgments. Since we hold the viewpoint that group members tacitly coordinate choice behavior on the basis of these rules of fairness, we referred to them as 'coordination rules.' On the basis of previous insights several coordination rules were distinguished. We assessed the discrepancy between what would be fair according to these rules, and what the subjects considered to be fair. In order to assess whether people anchored their actual choice behavior on fairness judgments we also assessed the correlations between fairness judgments and actual choice behavior. In all the studies reported in this article, high correlations between both measures were observed (correlations usually > .80).

The statement that choice behavior is governed by fairness norms is not new, and one does not need asymmetry to demonstrate that norms of fairness matter (see e.g. Kerr, in press). What asymmetry can offer, is the possibility to examine how different fairness considerations can influence choice behavior. In the following we will demonstrate the advantages of studying coordination rules in asymmetric dilemmas by presenting some of the results we obtained on three research topics: the justification of asymmetries, the presentation of social dilemmas, and environmental uncertainty.

2.2 Coordination Rules and the Justification of Asymmetries

We were not the first to investigate choice behavior in asymmetric dilemmas. In their influential article on public good provision, Marwell and Ames (1979) investigated, among other things, the effect of asymmetry of interests on the contributions to public step goods. In their experimental study, subjects could provide a public good (a bonus) that would be divided asymmetrically, some members would receive more of the bonus than others. The results indicated that High-Interest subjects contributed more than Low-Interest subjects. This finding was explained by suggesting that the subjects behaved in a way that they considered to be 'fair.' Apparently, investing a substantial part of the endowments was considered to be the fair thing to do. Another relevant study, conducted by Wit, Wilke, and Oppewal (1992), investigated the effect of asymmetry of interests in a linear public good setting. In four-person groups each individual contribution was said to be multiplied by two and to be divided among the group members. Two members would receive 33% while the other two would receive 17%. In line with the results of Marwell and Ames (1979) the results showed that High-Interest subjects contributed more endowments than Low-Interest subjects, a distribution that the subjects judged to be fair.

This discussion of previous research on asymmetric dilemmas is by no means exhaustive. The studies cited are important, however, since they indicate that choice behavior is related to fairness judgments. In particular, results of both studies indicated that actual contributions were in line with fairness judgments, and that people employ certain rules, other than equal division: both studies indicated that people preferred contributions to be distributed proportionally such that members having twice as much interest should contribute twice as much. It remained unclear, however, what caused decision makers to prefer a proportional distribution of contributions.

In a subsequent study (Van Dijk & Wilke, 1993), we related preferences for coordination rules in asymmetric dilemmas to equity theory (Adams, 1965; Walster, Walster, & Berscheid, 1978). We argued that preferences for coordination rules reflect a preference for a distribution of the final outcomes. We reasoned that the observed preference to contribute proportionally to the interest positions, was (at least partly) due to the circumstance that in previous research asymmetries were determined on the basis of a chance procedure. In terms of equity theory, one could say that interest positions were not justified by input differentials. In such situations, equity theory would predict that people would prefer the final outcomes to be distributed equally. Although a proportional distribution of contributions (people receiving twice as much of the public good should contribute twice as much) may not lead to a perfectly equal distribution of the final outcomes over the group members, it does keep differences moderate.

In the Van Dijk and Wilke (1993) study, in which we employed a linear public good setting, we manipulated the justification of the asymmetry of interests. Interest positions were either assigned on the basis of a chance procedure or on the basis of input differentials (members receiving twice as much from the public good supposedly had to participate twice as long in our experiment). We reasoned that the justification of the asymmetry would influence the preferred distribution of the final outcomes, and that the preferred distribution of final outcomes would determine which coordination rule people employed. In particular, we expected subjects to prefer a more equal distribution of the final outcomes if the asymmetry of interests was not justified by input differentials (i.e., if all members had equal inputs; interest positions were assigned on the basis of a chance procedure) than if it was justified by input differentials (members having twice as much interest in the public good had to participate twice as long). As for the preferences for coordination rules, we expected subjects to select a coordination rule that would be in accordance with their preferred distribution of final outcomes.

We distinguished two coordination rules: the *equal* contribution rule, and the *proportional* contribution rule. The equal contribution rule states that each group member should make an equal contribution. This rule is similar to the 'equal division rule' in Resource dilemmas, as defined by Allison and Messick (1990; cf. Allison et al., 1992; Samuelson & Allison, 1994). The proportional contribution rule prescribes that (in the case of asymmetric interests) the contribution should be proportional to the amount of interest that one has in the public good. In our experiment - with asymmetric interests - adherence to the equal contribution rule would result in an unequal distribution of the final outcomes. Differences in final outcomes would be smaller in the case of the proportional contribution rule.

The results of the study confirmed our reasoning that preferences for coordination rules are related to the preferred distribution of the final outcomes. Subjects preferred the final outcomes to be distributed more equally when the asymmetry of interests was not justified by input differentials than when it was justified by input differentials. Preferences for coordination rules were in accordance with the preferred distributions of the final outcomes: The proportional contribution rule was preferred more when the asymmetry was not justified than when it was justified. These results suggest that preferences for coordination rules are more than just a preference for simple decision rules. Under some conditions simple rules like equal division or equal contribution may suffice since they satisfy a norm of fairness. Under other conditions people may prefer to coordinate choice behavior on the basis of more complex rules (such as a proportionality rule). What rule people choose may be determined by the distribution of final outcomes they consider to be fair.

2.3 Coordination Rules and the Presentation of Social Dilemmas

Our study on the effect of justification suggested that different situations evoke different coordination rules. In the field of individual decision making it has repeatedly been demonstrated that one situation may be presented in different ways and that the problem presentation may affect people's decisions. For example, Kahneman and Tversky's (1979, 1984) Prospect theory states that people will evaluate outcomes differently when they are presented ('framed') as gains than if they are presented as losses.

Choice behavior in interpersonal settings such as social dilemmas may also be susceptible to presentation effects. An interesting possibility is that social dilemmas can either be presented as Public Good dilemmas or as Resource dilemmas. In the Public Good Dilemma, individuals can further the group interest by contributing endowments (in order to provide the public good) whereas their personal interests may induce them not to contribute. In the Resource Dilemma the individual faces a similar choice. Group members can harvest from a common resource. Whereas the group interest calls for moderate harvests, personal interests may induce the individual members to harvest excessively.

Do Public Good dilemmas evoke different choice behavior than Resource dilemmas? Research in which both dilemma types are compared has shown mixed results. Whereas some research demonstrated that group members are less cooperative in Public good dilemmas than in Resource dilemmas (e.g., Brewer & Kramer, 1986), other studies have shown no effect (e.g., Rutte, Wilke, & Messick, 1987; Messick et al., 1988) or even the reverse (e.g., Sonnemans, Schram, & Offermans, 1995).

In their interpretation of the effects of presentation of social dilemmas, most researchers turned to Kahneman and Tversky's (1979, 1984) Prospect theory. Prospect theory states that outcomes often are evaluated in terms of a reference point such that outcomes above the reference point are coded as gains and outcomes below the reference point are coded as losses. Prospect theory predicts that 'losses loom larger than gains', and (thus) that people are more risk-seeking in the domain of losses than in the domain of gains. Recently, however, Schwartz-Shea and Simmons (in press) argued that Prospect theory is an inappropriate model for analyzing choice behavior in social dilemmas. In *interpersonal* settings such as social dilemma situations it seems impossible to state beforehand what decisions should be regarded as gains and what decisions as losses. For example, contributing endowments in Public Good dilemmas may be regarded as (personal) loss, one could also interpret it as a (group) gain. In a similar way it appears impossible to identify beforehand risk-seeking and risk-avoiding behavior (see Rutte, Wilke, & Messick, 1987).

In a more recent study (Van Dijk & Wilke, 1995) we took a different approach by focusing on the employment of coordination rules in both dilemma types. Again, we focused on asymmetric dilemmas. For example, in one of these experiments (Van Dijk & Wilke, 1995, experiment 3), we compared a Public Good dilemma with a Resource dilemma in the case of asymmetry of interests. In the Public Good dilemma conditions a public step good was employed. Subjects were led to believe that they were a member of a four-person group, and that each member possessed *f*7.50 (*f*1 ≈ \$.60), which could be contributed to provide a monetary bonus of *f*30. The bonus - which would be provided if the group managed to contribute *f*12 - would be distributed asymmetrically: Two members would each receive *f*10, the other two would each receive *f*5. Subjects were either informed that they would receive *f*10 or that they would receive *f*5.

In the Resource dilemma conditions a one-trial Resource dilemma was employed in which group members could realize a monetary bonus. The payoff structure was identical to that of the Public Good dilemma conditions. Subjects learned they were a member of a four-person group, and that they controlled a common resource of *f*30. Each member could harvest up to *f*7.50. If the group managed to harvest less than *f*18 (i.e., if they would leave *f*12 or more), a bonus would be provided. As in the public Good conditions, the bonus of *f*30 would be distributed asymmetrically: Two members would each receive *f*10, the other two would each receive $f5$; subjects were either informed that they would receive $f10$ or that they would receive $f5$.

As mentioned, the main focus of the study was on the concept of coordination rules, and its relation to fairness considerations. How did the subjects coordinate their choice behavior? In agreement with previous research, subjects facing the Public Good dilemma appeared to employ the proportionality rule by contributing in proportion to their interest position (cf. Van Dijk & Wilke, 1993; Wit, Wilke, & Oppewal, 1992). Moreover, the results suggested that the provision point (of $f12$) functioned as a focal point for coordination: Fairness judgments and actual choice behavior indicated that subjects coordinated choice behavior on the proportionality rule, prescribing that 'low interest members' should contribute $f2$ and 'high interest members' should contribute $f4$ (with two low interest members and two high interest members this would mount up to $f12$).

Interestingly, the results indicated that choice behavior was coordinated differently in the Resource dilemma. Subjects in the Resource dilemma conditions appeared to employ what we termed the 'equal final outcomes rule', a rule prescribing that choice behavior should result in an equal distribution of the final outcomes: all members should end up with an equal amount of money. As in the Public Good dilemma conditions, the 'provision point' for the bonus appeared to function as a focal point. What should members in the Resource Dilemma decide when they harvest $f18$, and prefer all members to obtain equal final outcomes? Since high interest members received $f5$ more from the bonus than low interest members, equal final outcomes could only be obtained if high interest members would harvest $f5$ less than low interest members. Focusing on the provision point of $f18$ this would mean that the two high interest members should each harvest $f2$, and the low interest members should harvest $f7$. The results indeed indicated that this is what the subjects decided to do.

Apparently, the presentation of the social dilemmas affects the way choice behavior is (tacitly) coordinated. In our article, we suggested that this differential preference for coordination rules was the result of a differential saliency of the distribution of final outcomes in Public Good dilemmas and Resource dilemmas. In particular, we suggested that distributing outcomes fairly is more salient in Resource dilemmas than in Public Good dilemmas. Since subjects in Resource dilemmas have to divide the resource (i.e., to distribute outcomes over all group members) they may be more focused on determining what would be a fair distribution of the final outcomes. Indeed, the preference for the equal final outcomes rules seems more in accordance with predictions of equity theory than the preference for the proportionality rule in the Public Good dilemma. As we already reasoned, with equal inputs for all members, equity theory (Adams, 1965; Walster et al., 1978) predicts an equal distribution of the final outcomes.

The results of our study are also relevant for the question whether people are more cooperatively in Public Good dilemmas or in Resource dilemmas. In order to compare choice behavior in Public Good dilemmas and Resource dilemmas one should compare (as a measure of cooperativeness) the number of endowments contributed in the Public Good dilemma with the number of endowments left in the resource in the Resource dilemma. In our study, such a comparison indicated that low interest members were *more* cooperative in the Public Good Dilemma than in the Resource Dilemma. In contrast, high interest members were *less* cooperative in the Public Good Dilemma than in the Resource Dilemma. These differences were the consequence of the differential preference for coordination rules[1].

The Van Dijk and Wilke (1995, experiment 3) study was also relevant for the discussion whether preferences for coordination rules are more than a preference for simple heuristics. The fact that in our study on asymmetry of interests subjects preferred the more complex rule of equal final outcomes to more simple rules such as equal division (preferred in the studies on symmetric dilemmas by Allison and Messick, 1990; Allison et al., 1992; Samuelson & Allison, 1994) suggests that coordination rules are more than simple decision heuristics.

2.4 Coordination Rules and Environmental Uncertainty

The previous discussion on coordination rules suggests that when communication is prohibited, choice behavior may be tacitly coordinated by the use of coordination rules. That is, people may deal with social uncertainty by using coordination rules that are based on fairness considerations.

Research on symmetric dilemmas indicates that people employ the equal division rule, such that group members harvest an equal share. In order to implement such an equal division rule one requires information about the number of group members. The research on asymmetric dilemmas suggests that people coordinate choice behavior on the basis of (additional) information such as the interest positions of the group members. One could say then, that the previous research on coordination rules suggests that group members use information about the environmental characteristics of the dilemma (such as the number of participants, the interest positions etcetera) in order to decide on their individual choice behavior. Put differently, group members appear to use *environmental information* in order to reduce *social uncertainty*. In a recent

---

[1] In our study, strict adherence to the equal final outcomes in the Resource dilemma implied that high interest members should leave *f*5.50 in the resource whereas low interest members should leave *f*.50. Strict adherence to the proportionality rule in the Public Good dilemma implied that high interest members should contribute *f*4 and low interest members should contribute *f*2 (see for a more comprehensive discussion of the consequences of adherence to both rules Van Dijk & Wilke, 1995).

study (Van Dijk, Wilke, Wilke, & Metman, 1995), this observation was a starting point for our analysis of the effects of environmental uncertainty on choice behavior in social dilemmas.

Environmental uncertainty may be defined as uncertainty concerning the task environment (cf. Messick et al., 1988). In social dilemma situations, group members may be uncertain about numerous characteristics of the dilemma. For example, group members facing Resource dilemmas may be uncertain about the size of the resource, about the interest individual group members have in maintaining the resource, about the amount individual group members can harvest without damaging the collective's interest etcetera. Similarly, group members facing a Public Good dilemma may be uncertain about the individual wealth of all group members (how many endowments do all group members possess), the interest that individual group members have in providing the public good, about the provision point of the public good etcetera.

Until now, effects of environmental uncertainty were mainly investigated in Resource dilemmas, with environmental uncertainty being operationalized as uncertainty concerning the size of the common resource from which members could harvest (see Rapoport, Budescu, Suleiman & Weg, 1992; Budescu, Rapoport & Suleiman, 1992). In other words, previous research investigated the effect of uncertainty regarding the extent to which furthering the personal interests would damage the collective interest. The main conclusions from this research are that with increasing environmental uncertainty (regarding the size of the common resource) (a) group members overestimate the size of the common resource (b) group members harvest too much from the common resource and (c) group members display greater variability in their harvests.

In our recent study, we investigated how environmental uncertainty affected preferences for coordination rules. To predict effects of environmental uncertainty, we first analyzed what information subjects in the Van Dijk and Wilke study on asymmetry of interests (1995, experiment 3) needed to implement coordination rules. As mentioned, subjects in the Public Good dilemma conditions appeared to employ the proportionality rule whereas subjects in the Resource dilemma conditions appeared to employ the equal final outcomes rule.

What information did the subjects need to implement the proportionality rule in a Public Good dilemma? In this situation of asymmetric interests implementation of the proportionality rule required information about (a) the interest positions of all group members (how much did each group member receive from the bonus) and (b) the provision point (how much endowments should the group contribute in order to realize the bonus). In addition to this information, implementation of the equal final outcomes rule in the Resource dilemma required information about (c) the size of the bonus. After all, the subjects needed the information about the bonus size to determine how the final outcomes (after distribution of the bonus) would be distributed within the group.

This analysis thus suggested that information about the size of the bonus was crucial in the Resource dilemma (in order to implement the equal final outcomes rule), but not in the Public Good dilemma. In order to relate these differential informational requirements to the concept of environmental uncertainty, we turned to insights from the field of distributive justice.

In his behavioral theory of distributive justice, Güth (1994) classified justice standards on the basis of the amount of information needed to implement these rules. In this view standards are hierarchically ordered with 'superior' standards requiring more information than 'more basic' standards. One of the interesting aspects of the behavioral theory of distributive justice is the notion that the amount of information available may determine what standard will be used. In this respect Güth suggested that lack of information may lead people to prefer a more basic standard. For example, whereas people may prefer outcomes to be distributed according to individual inputs, lack of information about these inputs may lead members to opt for (the more basic) equality rule. Thus, whereas group members may prefer a certain standard once they have all information at their disposal, lack of information may lead them to employ more basic standards.

Güth referred to 'lack of information'. We extended these insights by hypothesizing that uncertainty about crucial information may lead people to prefer rules that do not require this uncertain information. In effect, we hypothesized that in social dilemma situations, people may want to avoid coordinating their decisions on the basis of uncertain or ambiguous information[2]. How can we translate these ideas to the context of social dilemmas? Since we reasoned that in an experimental setup like that of Van Dijk and Wilke (1995, experiment 3) with interests distributed asymmetrically, information about the bonus size was crucial in the Resource dilemma but not in the Public Good dilemma we manipulated information about the bonus size: The size of the bonus was either certain (i.e., the bonus was *f*30) or uncertain (anywhere between *f*19 and *f*41)[3]. Apart from this manipulation, the experimental setup was identical to that of Van Dijk and Wilke (1995).

Since our analysis of preferences for coordination rules indicated that information about the bonus was crucial in Resource dilemmas but not in Public Good dilemmas, we expected uncertainty about the bonus size to affect choice

---

[2] That people want to avoid situations of uncertainty and ambiguity has also been demonstrated in research on ambiguity (e.g., Frisch & Baron, 1988), indicating that issues of blame and responsibility are more salient in situations of ambiguity. It may be more difficult to defend to others (or to oneself) that one decided on the basis of uncertain information than it is to say that the decision was based on reliable and 'certain' information.

[3] This manipulation of the range resembles manipulations used in previous research on environmental uncertainty in social dilemmas (see for example, Rapoport et al., 1992)

behavior in Resource dilemmas but not in Public Good dilemmas. In particular, we expected a general preference for the proportionality rule in the Public Good dilemma (cf. Marwell & Ames, 1979; Van Dijk & Wilke, 1993; Wit et al., 1992). In the Resource dilemma we expected a preference for the equal final outcomes rule when the bonus size was certain (cf. Van Dijk & Wilke, 1995). When the bonus size was uncertain, we expected subjects to rely on alternative rules that did not require information about the bonus size. The results supported our theoretical analysis: subjects facing the Public Good dilemma appeared to employ the proportionality rule, regardless of the (un)certainty of the bonus size. Subjects facing the Resource dilemma appeared to employ the equal final outcomes rule when the bonus size was certain, but they predominantly turned to the what we termed 'inverse proportionality rule'. This rule did not require information about the bonus size; according to this rule members having twice as much interest in the bonus (which could be realized by restricting the harvests) should harvest twice as less.

The results of our study indicate that environmental uncertainty may lead to shifts in preferences for coordination rules. Previous research on environmental uncertainty did not acknowledge this possibility. This is understandable, however, since previous research concentrated on symmetric dilemmas. As we already stated, in symmetric dilemmas only one coordination rule seems appropriate, all members should display similar choice behavior (cf. Allison & Messick, 1990; Allison et al., 1992). In such situations, there is no reason to elaborate on shifts in preferences for coordination rules.

Whereas previous research suggested that environmental uncertainty promotes defection, the present study suggests that uncertainty may affect the coordination of choice behavior. In the present study, the effect of environmental uncertainty on cooperation and defection depended on the position group members occupied in the social dilemma: In the Resource dilemma conditions, low interest members harvested less under uncertainty than under certainty. In contrast, high interest members harvested more under uncertainty than under certainty. These effects did seem to be the direct consequence of a shift in preferences for coordination rules[4].

The general conclusion of our study on uncertainty is that people use environmental information to reduce social uncertainty. Moreover, the results of this study demonstrate that attention to the employment of coordination rules

---

[4] In the case of certainty, strict adherence to the equal final outcomes in the Resource dilemma implied that high interest members should leave *f*5.50 in the resource whereas low interest members should leave *f*.50. Adherence to the inverse proportionality rule implied that high interest members should leave *f*1.50 (they should harvest *f*6) and low interest members should contribute leave *f*4.50 (they should harvest *f*3) (see for a more comprehensive discussion of the consequences of adherence to both rules Van Dijk et al., 1995).

may increase our understanding of the way people deal with environmental uncertainty. Coordination rules then appear to be very useful tools to relate the concept of environmental uncertainty to social uncertainty. In his article on environmental and social uncertainty, Messick (Messick et al., 1988, p. 679) argued that 'The problem that is raised by the environmental uncertainty is the problem of optimality or efficiency, while the problem raised by social uncertainty is (...) coordination.' The present study suggests that both types of uncertainty may be interrelated in the sense that environmental uncertainty may affect the way people deal with social uncertainty.

3 General Conclusions and Suggestions

3.1 Coordination and Fairness

In several experiments we demonstrated the benefits of research on the employment of coordination rules. In his theorizing about tacit communication Schelling, argued that one of the functions of fairness considerations is that they may be used to coordinate choice behavior by functioning as a focal point. In agreement with this theorizing, we maintain that people use certain rules to determine what would be fair for each group member, and that they anchor their actual choice behavior on this fairness judgment.

In our experiments we emphasized the role of fairness considerations. When communication is prohibited, fairness judgments may function as focal points. There may be situations in which other focal points are more salient, however. One could argue, for example, that in business settings participants may be more inclined to base their expectations on strategic considerations than on considerations of fairness. In such situations, fairness judgments may not be crucial focal points for coordination. On the other hand, research in business settings does suggest that even market behavior of firms may be explained by fairness considerations (see for example Kahneman, Knetsch, and Thaler (1986) who explained economic behavior found in the labor market (e.g., wage negotiations) and consumer market (e.g., price setting) on the basis of fairness).

Thus, although we do not claim that fairness judgments will always be the main base for coordination, we do suggest that on many occasions fairness judgments may function as focal points for coordination. By relating choice behavior to preferences for coordination rules we may increase our understanding of the role of fairness in social dilemma situations. The results of our research suggest that fairness judgments affect choice behavior, and that what people consider to be fair is affected by the type of situation (e.g., by the justification of the asymmetry, the uncertainty of environmental information), and the presentation of the social dilemma.

3.2 Coordination Rules: more than Simple Heuristics

Whereas previous research on the employment of the equal division rule acknowledged that coordination rules may be based on fairness considerations, the general approach was that coordination rules reflect a preference for simple decisions. The results of our studies suggest that coordination rules are more than simple heuristics. Put differently, group members do not (necessarily) opt for the more simple rules, they appear to select the coordination rule that satisfies their preference for the distribution of the final outcomes.

In order to obtain a specific distribution of the final outcomes simple rules may often suffice. On other occasions, however, one may need more complex rules. In our introduction we already stated that in symmetric dilemmas the most simple rule (equal division) may suffice since it satisfies the preference for equal final outcomes. In asymmetric settings, however, equal division may not suffice. For example, when some members have more interest in the bonus than others, equal behavior will lead to an unequal distribution of the final outcomes (Van Dijk & Wilke, 1995, experiment 3). With equal inputs, group members may consider such an end result to be unfair. This is not to say that under situations of asymmetry the equal division rule will automatically result in unfair distributions of the final outcomes. For example, in a Resource dilemma with unequal access (i.e., some members may harvest more than others), equal division may be considered fair, since it does result in an equal distribution of the final outcomes (see Samuelson & Messick, 1986; Van Dijk & Wilke, 1995, experiment 1 and 2).

The question then becomes what group members consider to be a fair distribution of the final outcomes, and what coordination rules group members should employ to reach their preferred distribution of the final outcomes. In our research (see Van Dijk & Wilke, 1993) we related the preferred distribution of the final outcomes to insights derived from equity theory (Adams, 1965; Walster et al, 1978). We also suggested, however, that the presentation of a social dilemma may affect the salience of the distribution of the final outcomes (Van Dijk & Wilke, 1995). The distribution of the final outcomes appears to be more salient in Resource dilemmas than in Public Good dilemmas. This implies that future research on the employment of coordination rules should also incorporate notions about the salience of the final outcomes distribution.

3.3 Coordination Rules, Social Uncertainty, and Environmental Uncertainty

The results of our studies corroborate the general insight that even under situations of social uncertainty, choice behavior may be tacitly coordinated. One could say that by relying on coordination rules, people may reduce their sense of social uncertainty.

Our theoretical analysis of the information needed to implement coordination rules indicated that people use environmental information to deal with social uncertainty. The results of our research (Van Dijk et al., 1995) indicate that a theoretical analysis of the information needed to implement coordination rules may be helpful to formulate new hypotheses concerning the effect of environmental uncertainty in social dilemmas. In general terms, our results suggested that environmental uncertainty may affect the coordination of choice behavior, i.e., it may affect the way how group members deal with social uncertainty.

A focus on the type of information needed to implement coordination rules may help us to elaborate on various types of environmental uncertainty. In effect, we suggest that by analyzing what type of environmental information people actually use (i.e., what information people need to employ coordination rules) we may formulate new hypotheses about new types of environmental uncertainty. In our study on environmental uncertainty (Van Dijk et al., 1995), such an informational analysis indicated that information about the bonus size was crucial in Resource dilemmas but not in Public Good dilemmas. This analysis led us to investigate a new type of environmental uncertainty: Uncertainty about the bonus size. In general terms one could describe this type as uncertainty regarding the magnitude of the common interest. In a similar way it can be argued that in the case of asymmetry of interests uncertainty about interest positions will affect preferences for coordination rules (both in Public Good dilemmas and Resource dilemmas), and (thus) choice behavior.

In Van Dijk and Wilke (1995), we also compared asymmetry of access in a Resource dilemma (some members could harvest more than others) with asymmetry of endowments (some members possessed more endowments than others) in a Public Good dilemma. The results indicated that group members in the Resource dilemma employed the equal final outcomes rule: even though some members could harvest more than others, all members harvested equally from the common resource (since the bonus was divided equally, this resulted in an equal distribution of the final outcomes). Group members in the Public Good dilemma conditions employed the proportionality rule, prescribing that members should contribute in proportion to their endowments position (members possessing twice as many endowments should contribute twice as much; cf. van Dijk & Grodzka, 1992). An informational analysis suggests that information about the asymmetry was crucial in the Public Good dilemma, but not in the Resource dilemma. On the basis of our insights concerning effects of environmental uncertainty about crucial information, one could predict that - in an experimental setup similar to Van Dijk and Wilke (1995, experiment 1 and 2) - uncertainty about the endowments/access asymmetry will affect preferences for coordination rules an choice behavior in Public Good dilemmas, but not in Resource dilemmas.

These examples illustrate that our knowledge about preferences for coordination rules obtained in situations of 'environmental certainty' may guide our research about environmental uncertainty. If we know what coordination rules people prefer under certainty, we may determine what information is crucial, and thus what type of environmental uncertainty will affect choice behavior.

3.4 Social Dilemmas or Coordination Games?

Our results suggest that in social dilemma situations, people tacitly coordinate their choice behavior on the basis of environmental cues. Social dilemmas can be defined by two broad properties, (a) the personal interests of the individual group members do not coincide with the common interest of the group and (b) all group members would be better off if they all further the group interest than if they all pursue their individual interests.

The dilemma lies in the fact that whereas it may be beneficial for the group to cooperate, for individual group members it may be more beneficial not to cooperate. One might wonder, however, whether individual group members perceive the dilemma as such. It may be that group members perceive the dilemma as a coordination game, i.e., group members may *transform* the social dilemma structure into a coordination game (cf. Kelley & Thibaut, 1978) in which they are primarily concerned with figuring out how to coordinate choice behavior.

As we demonstrated, the tacit coordination process depends on the environmental information. In this respect, it is appropriate to note that fairness judgments may not always provide one unique focal point for coordination. In our studies on presentational effects of social dilemmas (Van Dijk & Wilke, 1995) and environmental uncertainty (Van Dijk et al., 1995) one focal point was the provision point for realization of the bonus. For example, subjects facing a Public Good dilemma knew how much they should contribute to provide the bonus. Our results indicated that subjects focused on this provision point in order to determine how much each member should contribute. On many occasions, however, such a provision point may be lacking. In the Van Dijk and Wilke (1993) study we employed a linear public good setting. Each individual contribution would be multiplied by a certain factor, and the outcomes would be divided among all members. It could be argued that in such a setting, with no provision point, members may be uncertain about the total contribution the group should make, and opportunities for tacit coordination may be limited. The general conclusion may be that when it is uncertain how much the group should give (in a Public Good dilemma) or take (in a Resource dilemma), opportunities for tacit coordination may be limited. Some indirect evidence for this proposition comes from research on uncertainty about the size of the common resource in symmetric dilemmas (e.g., Rapoport et al., 1992), suggesting that uncertainty about the resource size may induce group members to deviate from their 'fair share.'

Our research suggests that group members turn to normative 'cues' to coordinate their choice behavior. The coordinating potential of fairness considerations may lie in the fact that people expect others to depart from the same fairness principle as they do. One might wonder whether this will always be the case. As Messick recently noted 'in many situations, we know the appropriate way allocations should be made, regardless of who is making the decision. In unusual situations, however, there may be some ambiguity about which rule is appropriate' (Messick, 1995, p. 155). Will people coordinate their choice behavior on the basis of fairness considerations if they are uncertain about what their fellow group members think is fair? In our research we found great consistency in the fairness judgments. It may be worthwhile to investigate situations in which people are uncertain about what rule their fellow group members will employ. We suggest that under these conditions fairness considerations may 'loose' their coordinating potential, and actual choice behavior may be less based or anchored on fairness judgments.

For example, in our research we found that preferences for coordination rules were affected by the justification of asymmetries (Van Dijk & Wilke, 1993), and the presentation of social dilemmas (Van Dijk & Wilke, 1995). It may be worthwhile to extend this line of research by investigating preferences for coordination rules in situations in which people are uncertain how their fellow group members justify the asymmetries, or how their fellow group members perceive the dilemma. Since in such situations fairness may not 'fill the vacuum of indeterminacy', one could expect that people will be less likely to anchor their actual choice behavior on fairness judgments. Whether this will be 'good' or 'bad' for the collective will depend on what focal points people will turn to. Increasing our knowledge about the selection of 'alternative' focal points may be the next step toward a more comprehensive understanding of choice behavior in social dilemma situations.

Although obtained in experimental settings, the results discussed in the present paper may also be relevant for our understanding of behavior in real life settings. The concept of focal points essentially refers to the use of information. In order to understand behavior in real life setting then, one needs to assess what information people focus on when coordinating choice behavior. In this respect, it may be useful to assess how people perceive the dilemma they are facing, how they perceive inequalities (e.g., differential interests), and how certain they are about environmental characteristics of the dilemma. Since preferences for coordination rules appear to be dependent on the type of available information, such a course of action may also help us when deciding what type of information people should receive in order to promote cooperation.

References

Adams, J. S. (1965). Inequity in social exchange. In L. Berkowitz (Ed.), *Advances in Experimental Social Psychology* (Vol. 2, pp. 267-299). New

York: Academic Press.

Allison, S. T., McQueen, L. R., & Schaerfl, L. M. (1992). Social decision making processes and the equal partitionment of shared resources. *Journal of Experimental Social Psychology, 28*, 23-42.

Allison, S. T. & Messick, D. M. (1990). Social decision heuristics in the use of shared resources. *Journal of Behavioral Decision Making, 3*, 195-204.

Brewer, M. B. & Kramer, R. M. (1986). Choice behavior in social dilemmas: effects of social identity, group size, and decision framing. *Journal of Personality and Social Psychology, 50*, 543-549.

Budescu, D. V., Rapoport, A., & Suleiman, R. (1992). Simultaneous vs. sequential requests in resource dilemmas with incomplete information. *Acta Psychologica, 80*, 297-310.

Frisch, D. & Baron, J. (1988). Ambiguity and rationality. *Journal of Behavioral Decision Making, 1*, 149-157.

Güth, W. (1994). Distributive justice: A behavioral theory and empirical evidence. In H. Brandstätter & W. Güth (Eds.), *Essays on economic psychology* (pp. 153-176). Berlin: Springer Verlag.

Kahneman, D., Knetsch, J. L., & Thaler, R. H. (1986). Fairness as a constraint on profit seeking: Entitlements in the market. *American Economic Review, 76*, 728-741.

Kahneman, D. & Tversky, A. (1979). Prospect theory: an analysis of decision under risk. *Econometrica, 47*, 263-391.

Kahneman, D. & Tversky, A. (1984). Choices, values and frames. *American Psychologist, 39*, 341-350.

Kelley, H. H. & Thibaut, J. W. (1978). *Interpersonal relations: A theory of interdependence*. New York: Wiley.

Kerr, N. L. (in press). Norms in social dilemmas. In D. Schroeder (Ed.), *Social Dilemmas: Social Psychological Perspectives*. New York: Pergamon.

Marwell, G. & Ames, R. E. (1979). Experiments on the provision of public goods, I: Resources, interest, group size, and the free-rider problem. *American Journal of Sociology, 84*, 1335-1360.

Messick, D. M. (1995). Equality, fairness, and social conflict. *Social Justice Research, 8*, 153-173.

Messick, D. M., Allison, S. T., & Samuelson, C. D. (1988). Framing and communication effects on group members' responses to environmental and social uncertainty. In S. Maital (Ed.), *Applied Behavioural Economics* (Vol. 2, pp. 677-700). Brighton: Wheatsheaf.

Rapoport, A., Budescu, D. V., Suleiman, R., & Weg, E. (1992). Social dilemmas with uniformly distributed resources. In W. B. G. Liebrand, D. M. Messick, & H. A. M. Wilke (Eds.), *Social dilemmas: Theoretical issues and research findings* (pp. 43-57). Oxford: Pergamon Press.

Rutte, C. G., Wilke, H. A. M., & Messick, D. M. (1987). The effects of framing social dilemmas as give-some or take-some games. *British Journal of Social Psychology, 26*, 103-108.

Samuelson, C. D. & Allison, S. T. (1994). Cognitive factors affecting the use of social decision heuristics in resource-sharing tasks. *Organizational Behavior and Human Decision Processes, 58*, 1-27.

Samuelson, C. D. & Messick, D. M. (1986). Inequities in access to and use of shared resources in social dilemmas. *Journal of Personality and Social Psychology, 51*, 960-967.

Schelling, T. C. (1980). *The strategy of conflict*. Cambridge, Mass., Harvard University Press.

Schwartz-Shea, P. & Simmons, R. T. (in press). Social dilemmas and perceptions: experiments on framing and inconsequentiality. In: D. Schroeder (Ed.), *Social Dilemmas: Social Psychological Perspectives*. New York: Pergamon.

Sonnemans, J., Schram. A., & Offerman, T. (1995). *Public good provision and public bad prevention* (Report No. #TI-95-9). Amsterdam: Tinbergen Institute.

Van Dijk, E. & Grodzka, M. (1992). The influence of endowments asymmetry and information level on the contribution to a public step good. *Journal of Economic Psychology, 13*, 329-342.

Van Dijk, E. & Wilke, H. (1993). Differential interests, equity, and public good provision. *Journal of Experimental Social Psychology, 29*, 1-16.

Van Dijk, E. & Wilke, H. (1995). Coordination rules in asymmetric social dilemmas: A comparison between Public Good dilemmas and Resource dilemmas. *Journal of Experimental Social Psychology, 31*, 1-27.

Van Dijk, E., Wilke, H., Wilke, M., & Metman, L. (1995). *What information do we use in social dilemmas? Uncertainty and the employment of coordination rules*. Manuscript submitted for publication.

Walster, E., Walster, G. W. & Berscheid, E. (1978). *Equity: Theory and research*. Boston: Allyn & Bacon.

Wit, A. P., Wilke, H. A. M., & Oppewal, H. (1992). Fairness in asymmetric social dilemmas. In W. B. G. Liebrand, D. M. Messick, & H. A. M. Wilke (Eds.), *Social dilemmas: Theoretical issues and research findings* (pp. 183-197). New York: Pergamon Press.

Does Knowing the Jointly Rational Solution Make You Want to Pursue it? Motivational Orientation, Information, and Behavior in Two Social Dilemmas.[1]

Margaret Foddy and Daniel Veronese
School of Psychology, La Trobe University, Bundoora, Vic., Australia 3083.

Abstract

This paper reports two experiments which examined the impact of information about the collectively rational solution on the behaviour of individuals who differed in social value orientation. In the first, Rapoport's (1988) version of the 'largest number game' was given to subjects under minimal, and extended, information conditions. It was predicted that prosocial, or cooperative subjects would show higher levels of cooperation when given extended information, but that pro-self subjects would not, on the grounds that the latter are not motivated to maximize collective utility. Results supported the hypothesis, although absolute levels of cooperation remained low. The second study employed an investment dilemma game, in which subjects started with a fixed amount of money invested, and could withdraw all, part, or none of it. The rules of the game specified that the investment group would collapse if more than half of the funds were withdrawn. Cooperators and competitors were assigned to either a basic or extended information condition; in the latter, they were given additional information and examples about which behaviours were necessary to keep the investment account going to ensure that all would gain (joint maximisation), and which behaviours would be most likely to maximise individual gain /avoid loss, if others were not cooperative (individual maximising strategy). Extended information produced significantly higher rates of cooperation only for subjects with prosocial motives, as predicted. Across information conditions, competitors were significantly less cooperative than prosocial subjects. Expectations about others' investment behaviours were highly correlated with own investments. The pattern of results in the two studies is interpreted as consistent with the argument that information facilitates cooperation only in those who have a prosocial orientation.

---

[1] Thanks to Bernice Webster and Kelly Pratt for conducting the experimental sessions, to Wim Liebrand for supplying the computer program for the measure of social value orientations, and to Robyn Dawes for critical comments.

1 Introduction

In many real world dilemmas, people may lack an understanding of how their actions combine with those of others to produce group level outcomes. Many authors have suggested that this lack of "knowledge" (Dawes, 1980) or "understanding" (Kelley & Grzelak, 1972; Pruitt & Kimmel, 1977) may lead to less cooperative behavior. The definition of a "cooperative choice" takes different forms depending on the nature of the social dilemma[2], but in general refers to the choice of an alternative which, in contrast with the competitive choice, provides greater gain to others, while imposing some costs on self. In large scale social dilemmas, the impact of one individual's actions on others' outcomes is often small and invisible, while the higher individual gains from non-cooperation are salient. Presumably, anything which improves understanding of how non-cooperative choices combine to produce outcomes which are collectively deficient, should increase willingness to cooperate.

2 Knowledge: information about the structure of interdependence

One way that researchers have sought to study the effect of increased knowledge on behavior is to provide subjects with interpretive information which clearly delineates the effects of both cooperative and competitive actions on collective outcomes, in the short and long term. For example, Stern (1976) provided information about the long-term consequences of their actions to subjects playing a commons dilemma, and found that detailed information led to a higher rate of cooperative choices. However, the results of supplying such information have been mixed (e.g. Edney & Harper, 1978; Geller, Erickson & Buttram, 1983; Thompson & Stoutemyer, 1991).

Anatol Rapoport recently revived the question of "knowledge and understanding" (1988a, 1988b). He suggested that in some social dilemmas, there is a jointly rational solution, as well as a (deficient) individually rational solution, but that the former may be less salient because of the cultural emphasis on individual rationality. He conjectured that if subjects were given extended information about the nature of the social dilemma, and the collective advantage in choosing the collectively rational solution, then rates of cooperation would increase over those typically found in dilemmas where only minimal instructions were given (i.e., information describing the payoff matrix and rules of the game).

Rapoport reported effects of two levels of information, using a number of different social traps (Prisoner's Dilemma, weak Prisoner's Dilemma, Volunteer's

[2] Social dilemmas are defined, for purposes of this paper, as situations in which an individual receives a higher payoff for a socially defecting choice, than for a cooperative choice, but all individuals are better off if all cooperate than if all defect (Dawes, 1980, p. 169).

dilemma, and the Largest number game.[3] In full information conditions, the collectively rational strategy was described and emphasized. The impact of this information was surprisingly weak. Only in the Prisoner's Dilemma were rates of cooperation significantly higher in the full, compared with the minimal, instruction conditions. Rapoport used large anonymous samples, and obtained relatively little information about his subjects' characteristics or beliefs. There were no measures of levels of comprehension, and it is possible that subjects in the minimal information conditions may have understood the nature of their interdependence with others just as well as subjects in the maximal information groups.

Other researchers have examined the possibility that experience, or repeated play in dilemmas, might increase understanding of mutual dependence (e.g. Kelley and Grzelak, 1972), and improve resource management (Allison & Messick, 1985). Again, results have been mixed. Kelley & Grzelak (1972) observed that subjects with higher rate of cooperative responding seemed also to be those who had a better understanding of their interdependence. They raised the possibility that information gained through experience might have a selective effect, with prosocial individuals being more open to, and interested in, information about how the collective good might be advanced (see also Camac, 1992; Iedema & Poppe, 1994).

In this paper, we suggest that for interpretive information to effectively increase cooperation, it must be accompanied by valuing of collective versus individualistic or competitive outcomes. To attain cooperative outcomes, people need to both (a) know how to achieve them and (b)desire to achieve them. Thus, we concur with Dawes, and Pruitt & Kimmel, who claim that some level of "morality" or "motivation" must also be present. Toward this end, we study the moderating effect of social value orientation on the relationship between the provision of information and the incidence of cooperative behavior in two dilemma settings.

3 Social Motives

Researchers have identified individual differences in the utility gained from own and others' gain, which can be characterized as differences in social motives or social value orientations (the "morality" factor). On this account, culture and socialization teach people to place more or less value on the outcomes of others; they develop more or less stable preferences to see others do well, do worse, or to be indifferent to others' outcomes (Messick and McClintock, 1968; McClintock, 1972). As a single variable, motivational orientation (MO) shows up as a reasonably stable, reliable individual difference, which predicts behavior in games, preference for types of games, perceptions of others, and relative ease of learning or recognizing strategies used by others (Iedema & Poppe, 1994; Liebrand, 1984; Kramer & Goldman, 1995; Kuhlman, Camac & Cunha, 1986; van Lange, 1992).

---

[3] The largest number game will be described in detail later in this paper.

4 Information to facilitate goals

As argued above, one reason for the inconclusive results of "instructional programs" is that they do not recognize individual differences in goals. Information will be considered useful and worthy of attention to the extent that it helps the person identify the action most likely to realize his or her goal/social motivation.[4] Identification of an obvious strategy which would maximise joint gain and/or preserve the common resource, is not sufficient to ensure people will pursue it. Indeed, to the extent that full understanding of an interdependence structure also clarifies the strategies most appropriate for a person who would maximize relative, or individual gain, then one would predict a *decrease* in cooperative choices. This suggests that information serves to *facilitate* the pursuit of a person's goals.

This analysis is consistent with van Lange's suggestion that external forces which might be expected to increase or decrease cooperation can have a differential influence on people with different social value orientations (van Lange, 1992). Van Lange's examples include the variable effects of the strategy displayed by the other in matrix games, and the differential impact of external punishments for noncooperation on cooperators, competitors and individualists. Consistent with the argument made above about the impact of information, we suggest that people who do not possess a goal of maximising joint gain will not be influenced by factors which make it simpler or more attractive to do so; people who are not oriented solely to maximising individual utility will similarly be less moved by factors which enhance that goal. Thus, not only does "goal prescribe rationality" (van Lange and Liebrand, 1991), but goals moderate the influence of factors which may be designed to increase cooperation.

A related argument is made by Kramer and Goldman (1995), who provided evidence that a manipulation to enhance the identification of subjects with their groups in a dilemma setting, had a greater effect on levels of cooperation in cooperators than in competitors. These authors suggested that since cooperators already place a high value on collective outcomes, increasing the salience of group membership would be particularly effective, and produce a higher level of cooperative responses. In contrast, competitors seemed unresponsive to the manipulations to increase group identity.

The aim of the two experiments reported in this paper was to test the interaction of motives and information. There is, of course, a third "necessary" condition for

---

[4] In this paper, only "one-shot" or short term social dilemmas are considered, in which individual and competitive choices are clearly distinguishable from cooperative or jointly rational choices. In long term or repeated dilemmas, the relation between information and goals may be more complex, because the long term individually rational solution may overlap with the collectively rational solution, and may conflict with short term individual or competitive interests.

cooperation: trust, or belief in the cooperative intent of others (Dawes, 1980; Pruitt & Kimmel, 1977). If such trust is entirely lacking, it is unlikely that knowledge of cooperative solutions will elicit cooperation even among those motivated to maximize joint outcomes (e.g. Brann & Foddy, 1988; Yamagishi, 1986). Several researchers have suggested that expectations about others are correlated with one's own social values (e.g. Kelley & Stahelski, 1970; McClintock & Liebrand, 1988; Iedema & Poppe, 1994). However, it is not known whether interpretative information will have a differential effect on the expectations about others' behavior held by prosocial and proself individuals.

In the work reported in this paper, expectations about others were measured, but not systematically varied, except to the extent that the two different experimental dilemmas employed created rather different expectations for cooperation overall. The first study involved a dilemma in which low levels of trust were common.

5 Information effects in the Largest Number Game

The first study used the Largest Number Game, one of the dilemmas studied by Rapoport (1988a), and discussed at length by Hofstadter (1985). Rapoport used this dilemma because it has a well-defined, and unique jointly rational strategy, which is non-obvious to people when they first encounter the dilemma. The details of the game are best presented by way of the instructions used in the minimal information conditions of our experiment.

5.1 Largest number instructions

> The experimenter has $200 to give away. Every person in the study independently submits a whole number to the experimenter. The number can be any positive number greater than zero and smaller than infinity.
> If the highest number were, for example, 10, the prize would be $20.00. If two people submit the same highest number, they will split the prize. Similarly, if several people all tie on the same largest number, they will split the prize equally. Remember, the prize is the $200 divided by whatever the winning largest number turns out to.
>
> When all the numbers are in, the experimenter will work out the largest number, and determine the winner or winners. This will be in the next two weeks, when we have finished testing the 50 people in this study. The winning number will be announced in a letter to everyone who took part, but the name of the person(s) who submitted the largest number will not be given. Prize winners will be phoned and told how to pick up their prize money.

People who encounter this game first think it shows extraordinary naivete on the part of the experimenter, who will surely lose the $200 jackpot. Then the realization comes that it is a very competitive game indeed, and that one is almost forced to put in extremely high numbers, in order to "stay in the game". However, there is no unique individually rational strategy; any number greater than one may be beaten by an even higher number, and so one must think of higher and higher numbers if one wishes to be the sole winner of the game, and the prize for such a winner is likely to be very small. Thus, the individualistic or competitive strategy is the non-specific one of "choose a number that is higher than others are likely to choose".[5] There *is* a *unique* jointly rational strategy, and that is for everyone to submit the number "one", so that all will tie. Then the jackpot of $200 is divided by the number "one", and shared with everyone in the group.In the current experiment, the expected value to any individual of the jointly rational solution was about $4.00 ($200/50 participants); it was higher in Rapoport's experiments, where he had a jackpot of $1000 for 100 people (Rapoport, 1988a).

The Largest Number Game thus provides a setting in which the individually rational choice is more salient or available to subjects, and in which further information may reveal the counterintuitive jointly rational strategy of choosing the *smallest* number. Two information conditions were created: a basic, or minimal information condition, in which subjects were given the instructions outlined above; and an extended information condition, which gave further information, as follows:

> The idea for Largest Number game comes from a writer called Douglas Hofstadter, and you can read about it in his book called *Metamagical Themas*. Largest Number is one of many situations in which people are *socially interdependent*, in the sense that what happens to any one person depends partly on what other people do. In the Largest Number game, the first thing that comes to most people's minds is to find a number that is large enough to be larger than other people's numbers, but small enough that, when it is divided into the $200, there is a big enough result to make it worthwhile. However, everyone in this study is thinking the same thing--what can they put in that will be big enough, but not too big? The outcome of the game depends on your choice, but it depends on everyone else's as well, and that is why we say you are interdependent. You might come up with a good number, for example, 20, thinking you are pretty sure of getting $10.00 ($200/20), but others in the group of participants may also be thinking likewise, and someone may even think that 21 is an even better number, since 21 divided into $200 is almost as good as $10.00. However, this kind of reasoning leads to higher and higher numbers, with lower and lower prizes. There is another way of looking at the problem. If everyone in the group of people puts in 1 as their number, then the $200 is divided by 1, and shared among all the students

---

[5] Note that for the individualist, who wishes to maximize own gain, that putting in "one" is not an attractive alternative whatever s/he expects others to do; if they all put in "one", then it is best to put in "two"; if others do not put in "one", there is no reason for the individualist to do so. Rapoport would argue that it is *irrational* to choose other than "one", but the "goal prescribes rationality" principle leads prosocial individuals to choose >1.

in the study. So, if there are 50 students, each student would get $4 , so long as everyone had put in 1 as their number ($200/1=200, divided by 25 = $4). You have to be willing to share equally with all of the others for this to work. The major threat to this solution to the game is that, if any one person thinks that *everyone else* will put in 1 as their number, then it is pretty safe to put in 2 or 3, and get the prize for themselves. Not everyone likes to share, and some people prefer to get more than others, even if their own gains are not so high. The other problem is that, you can't be sure you can trust everyone to put in 1, especially since I am not letting you meet or communicate with each other.

The interaction hypothesis outlined above predicts that people with prosocial motives or goals will be more susceptible to information which identifies this strategy, while people who are individualistically or competitively motivated will not be influenced by it. Further, extended information about individually rational choices, should have an effect on people motivated by self interest, but not those with prosocial motives. In this study, we simply provided information, and made no attempt to persuade subjects to choose one course of action over another. However, we would argue that direct persuasive attempts would also have differential effects on individuals with different social motives.

5.2 Procedure

Subjects (15 male, 60 female) were undergraduate students in a range of disciplines at La Trobe University, Melbourne, who had volunteered to be in a subject pool.

Subjects were randomly assigned to the *basic* or *extended* information conditions of the largest number game; they were tested individually. The experiment was described to the subjects, and they then completed a computer-based measure of motivational orientation, (the Ring Measure of social values, (Liebrand, 1984)). This was followed by the Largest Number task (with brief or extended instructions), and a questionnaire which assessed their comprehension of aspects of the game. Subjects were debriefed, and paid $(AUS)5.00 for their participation. They were told they would be called in to receive the prize if they were the winner, and that the name of the winner would not be made public. Testing took between 30-40 minutes.

5.3 Measurement of social motives

The Ring program is a computerized version of a decomposed game, which allows subjects to indicate their preferred distribution of resources in an environment free of strategic considerations. The computer program presents a series of binary choices, in which the subject has to indicate a preference for one of two distributions of monetary outcomes to self and other. These choices sample an array of distributions of rewards to self and other, and the subject's pattern of choices provides an approximation of his/her social value orientation (Liebrand, 1984). While the scenario depicts a level of social interdependence (i.e indicating that the subject's outcomes will be affected by the choices of the other), the program gives no feedback about the other's choices. The program provides a summary of the total amount subjects gave to self and other, and thus an estimate of the weights subjects assign to own and other's payoffs. These weights in turn are used to estimate the angle of the subject's value vector extending from the origin of the own-other outcome plane (where own-outcomes are on the abscissa, and other-outcomes on the ordinate).

As in previous research with the Ring measure (e.g. Kuhlman, Camac, & Cunha, 1986; Liebrand, 1984; McClintock and Liebrand, 1988), subjects were classified according to their value vectors: 112.5 to 67.5 (altruistic); 67.5-22.5 (cooperative); 22.5-337.5 (individualistic); 337.5-292.5 (competitive). Since there were only 9 competitors, they were combined with the 31 individualists to make the *Pro-self* group (n=40); there were 34 cooperators who made up the *Pro-social* group. Thirteen subjects whose responses to the Ring Measure were inconsistent were excluded from the results. The experimenter who administered the Ring Measure and subsequent tasks was blind to the motivational orientation of the subjects.

Subjects were randomly assigned to the minimal (prosocial: n=17; proself: n=22) or extended (prosocial: n=17; proself: n=18) information condition. After subjects had read the relevant version of the instructions, they were given two minutes to consider the number they wished to submit, and then wrote their number on a slip of paper; the experimenter also asked subjects to predict what they thought would be the highest (largnum), and the most common number (avnum) submitted by others in the study. Subjects then completed a set of questions designed to assess their understanding of the rules of the game, and of the consequences of choosing the highest number, and of choosing "one", if everyone else chose "one".

Subjects read a debriefing sheet which explained the purpose of the experiment, and the experimenter answered their questions. They were then paid and dismissed. Since the largest number was too large to yield a payable prize ($200/largnum), the follow up letter to subjects advised them that no one had won the prize, and gave further information about the difficulty of obtaining cooperation in anonymous commons dilemmas.

5.4 Results

Numbers submitted. The range of numbers submitted by subjects was wide (from 1 to 500 X 10^{500}); for purposes of analysis, the log of the number is used.[6]

---

[6] Two subjects submitted extreme numbers (10^{24} and 500x10^{500}). Due to distortion of the results, the data from these subjects were not included in the analyses.

Figure 1 displays these results. A 2-way ANOVA[7] (motivational orientation X information condition) produced no main effects, but the predicted significant interaction between motivational orientation and information condition ($F(1, 70)$) = 6.025, $p<.02$). Simple main effects analysis showed that only the difference between pro-social subjects across the information conditions was significant, although the difference between the two MO groups in the extended information condition approached significance (p =.07). Analysis of covariance, using the subjects' expectations of the average number others would submit as the covariate, produced basically the same result: the interaction of information condition by MO was significant (F (1,70)=7.62, p <.01). The covariate also had a significant effect (F=18.07, p<.001), indicating that on average, subjects put in higher numbers when they thought others were doing the same.

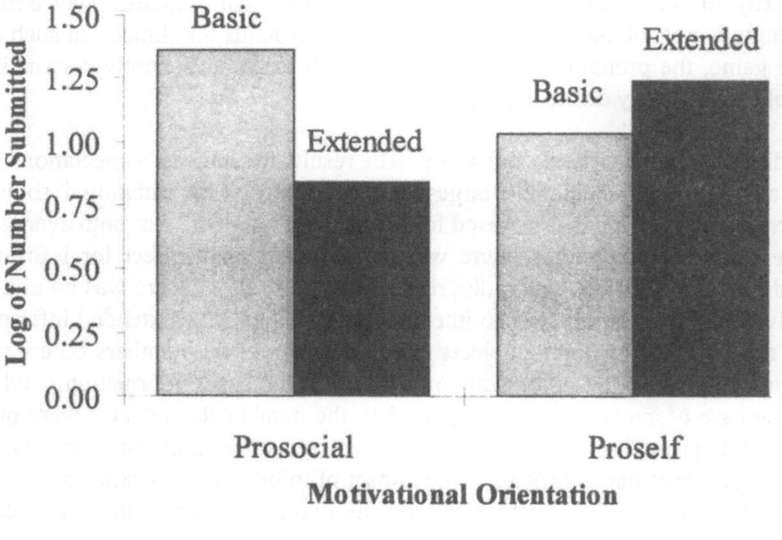

Figure 1. Means of log of numbers submitted by motivational orientation and information condition: Largest Number Game.

[7] Given the correlation of the three dependent variables (number submitted, average number predicted for others, largest number predicted), a multivariate analysis of variance might be considered more appropriate. Such an analysis was conducted, and produced virtually identical results. Three separate ANOVA's are reported in the text, plus a 2X2 analysis of covariance on number submitted, using "average number" as the covariate.

While the prosocial subjects in the basic information condition put in higher mean numbers than did the proself subjects, prosocial subjects given extended information put in significantly lower numbers than proself subjects in the corresponding condition. The frequency of subjects submitting the jointly rational number (1) was highest for cooperators in the extended information condition (n=5, or 29%). No cooperators submitted the number 1 in the basic information condition; and among the proself subjects, only one in each information condition submitted 1 as their number. In the extended information condition, subjects submitting low numbers gave reasons such as "I am willing to share the prize", and, "Any higher number would make the prize useless". In contrast, subjects who submitted very high numbers emphasized how this would guarantee that they would win. The person who submitted $500X10^{500}$ said it was the largest he could think of without getting ridiculously large. Generally no reasons were given for such choices, except for a comment from one subject: "I am a right bastard". A minority of subjects put in their favorite number. This suggests they think the dilemma is not solvable, and resort to irrational grounds for choice. In such a low trust game, the prominent unique joint solution is not sufficiently convincing to people, even if they desire joint gain.

Predictions about Other's Behavior. The results for subjects' expectations about the average number and the largest number likely to be submitted showed a different pattern from that reported for the subjects' number. For both average and largest number predictions, there was a significant main effect for information condition (F (1,70) =6.7 and 5.86, respectively, $p < .05$). There was no effect for motivational orientation, and no interaction (see Figure 2). Extended information had the effect of lowering subjects' predictions about the numbers others would submit, relative to the predictions of subjects in the basic information conditions (in the case of average number, lower than the number the subjects were putting in). While proself subjects made higher predictions than prosocial subjects, these differences were not significant. The impact of information on expectations about what others would do, was different for the two motivation groups. This can be seen in the pattern of numbers submitted by the subjects in the different conditions, but also in the relationship between number submitted, and expectations.

The correlation between the number submitted by a subject, and expectations about the average number was .40 overall; for cooperators, the correlation was .69 (p<.001), but for competitors, it was much smaller (.17, *n.s.*) That is, cooperators who submitted larger numbers also anticipated that others would do the same. The

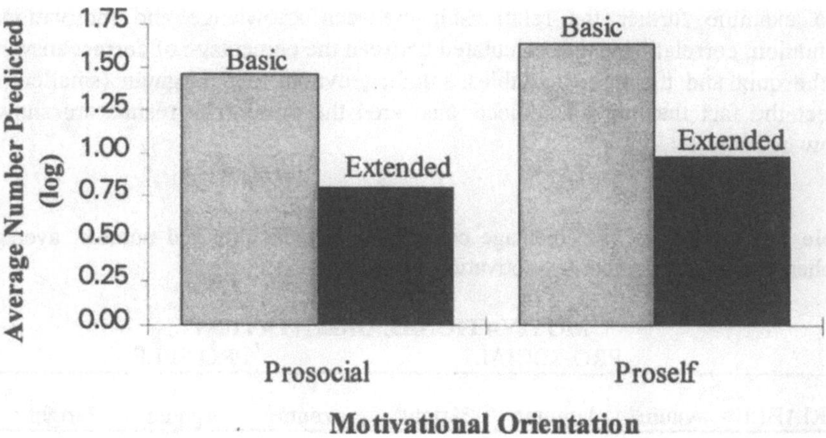

Figure 2. Means of logs of average number predicted by motivational orientation and information condition: Largest Number Game.

difference between cooperators and competitors was even greater for the largest number predicted: for cooperators, the correlation was positive and significant (.57; $p < .001$); in the case of competitors, it was negative (-.21, *n.s.*). In both information conditions, the difference between the number submitted by the subject, and his/her estimate of what the average person would submit, was negligible for prosocial subjects (-.10 in the basic condition, .03 in extended information). However, for pro-self subjects, the difference favoured self in the extended information condition (own-average number=.26), in contrast to the negative difference found in the basic information condition (-.61) These results suggest that prosocial subjects were "matching" their behavior to what they thought others might do, while pro-self subjects under extended information showed a tendency to take advantage of expected lower numbers from others, by putting in higher numbers.

Comprehension of strategies. Subjects were asked 6 questions to assess their understanding of the rules of the game, and of the consequences of choosing the number they had submitted; the number 1; and a number larger than that submitted by any other subject. The number of incorrect responses was lower in extended, compared with basic information conditions, but there were no differences across two MO groups. In particular, similar numbers of prosocial and proself S's correctly answered the question about the outcome if all subjects submitted the number 1: only 2 S's in each MO condition gave an incorrect answer when there was extended information, while twice as many were incorrect when only basic information was given. These results are somewhat attenuated, since subjects who could not answer more than two of the six questions correctly were excluded from the analysis, on the grounds that they had not comprehended the game.

To examine further the relationship between knowledge and motivational orientation, correlations were calculated between the percentage of correct answers on the quiz and the three variables, number, avnum, and largnum (smaller n's reflect the fact that not all subjects answered the quiz). The results are shown below in Table 1.

Table 1. Correlations of percentage correct answers on quiz and number, average number, and largest number by motivational orientation.

	MOTIVATIONAL ORIENTATION					
	PRO-SOCIAL			PRO-SELF		
VARIABLE	avnum	largnum	%right[a]	avnum	largnum	%right
number	.69**	.57**	-.38	.17	-.21	.23
avnum	-	.82**	-.32	-	.51**	-.34
largnum			-.46			-.26

[a] For %right answers on test, *n*=23 for pro-social, and *n*=30 for pro-self. For all other variables, *n*=34 for pro-social, and *n*=40 for pro-self.

Again, a different pattern was observed for the two motive groups: the more questions cooperators got right on the quiz, the *lower* the number they submitted; the reverse was true for pro-self subjects. While neither correlation is significantly different from zero, they are different from each other ($\underline{z}$=2.14, p<.02). This result suggests that the better pro-social subjects understood the game, and the nature of the interdependence, the more willing they were to cooperate; greater comprehension appeared to facilitate the goals of the competitive subjects as well, since they were more likely to submit higher numbers as their understanding of the structure of interdependence increased.

The results of the largest number study lend support to the hypothesis that information about jointly rational strategies will appeal only to those already disposed to collective interests. However, the dilemma is one in which very high levels of cooperation are required for a positive collective outcome, and a single defector can undermine the cooperative efforts of many. It is likely, therefore, that the facilitative effects of information may have been suppressed, despite the fact that the largest number game has a salient and unique collectively rational solution. In addition, any conclusions based on the lower numbers submitted by cooperators in the extended information condition must be tentative, since it is possible that subjects submitting a lower number, but not the number 1, were not acting with prosocial intent. The second experiment employed a social dilemma which was less extreme, and in which the choice of a prosocial alternative was unambiguous.

6. Information effects in an investment dilemma

The second experiment, with a different set of subjects, used an investment paradigm in which subjects could choose to take money and bonuses from an investment group immediately, or wait for the investment to grow, at which point more of the investors could benefit. It shared some features with the Volunteer's dilemma used by Rapoport (1988a) in his study of the effect of information on behaviour in social traps. Subjects started with a fixed amount of money invested, and could withdraw all, part, or none of it. The rules of the game specified that the investment group would collapse if more than half of the funds were withdrawn. In the *minimal information* condition, subjects were simply provided with details about how the investment account yielded dividends; in the *extended information* condition, further details and examples explained the behaviours necessary to maximize expected joint gain, and expected individual gain. Subjects indicated the amount they wished to withdraw, their expectations for others' behaviour, and answered questions to assess their understanding of aspects of the dilemma.

Each subject was told s/he was part of a 10 member investment group which had invested the sum of $6,000 in a high-yielding investment account--each member had invested $600. Given that difficult times might lie ahead for this investment institution, investors were informed that they could make a one-off mid-term withdrawal, ranging in $50 increments from $50 to $600. They were given an investment chart (see Table 2) which showed that different withdrawal amounts had associated with them different bonus payments, under certain conditions. The bonuses were attractive, and increased the more funds an investor withdrew. Money left in the account accumulated interest at a rate of 20%, so that at the end of the year, they would get 120% of what was in the account, over and above what they took out in withdrawal and bonuses on the first round.

However, bonuses were only paid if a critical amount remained in the investment account: the total amount withdrawn could not exceed half the initial $6000 invested (i.e. $3000). If this amount was not left, no bonuses were given, an no interest accrued to the remaining investment. The bank would then close down, and investors got only what they had withdrawn at mid-term. The bonus was greater when large amounts were withdrawn, and was calculated to meet the definition of a commons dilemma: D(efect) dominates C(ooperate), but all D produces a worse outcome than all C.

Thus, if a subject withdrew $600, and enough investors refrained from taking too much, the subject could gain $1,050. If not enough people refrained, s/he would just get the $600 withdrawn. The prominent *cooperative* solution to this game is for everyone to take $300 (with its additional $100 bonus), leaving half the funds in the account to gain interest; at the end, each subject would get another $360, for a total of $760 each, or a total for the group of $7600. This is more than the $6000 for the group, if the withdrawal limit is exceeded. It is also less than the $860 each subject would get if they all took only $50 at the start, and collected a $200 bonus, and left $550 to collect interest.[8] The prominent *non-cooperative* solution is to take $600 at the start, and hope to obtain the large bonus, if the bank did not close down.

Table 2. Payoff matrix for investment dilemma: possible bonuses and interest as a function of mid-term withdrawal choices.

Withdraw Now	+ Bonus	Mid-term Payoff	Deposit + Remaining	20% Interest + (Mid-term)	Final Payoff
$50	now + $150	= $200	$550	x 1.2 = $660 (+$200)	= $860
$100	now + $140	= $240	$500	x 1.2 = $600 (+$240)	=$840
$150	now + $130	= $280	$450	x 1.2 = $540 (+$280)	= $820
$200	now + $120	= $320	$400	x 1.2 = $480 (+$320)	= $800
$250	now + $110	= $360	$350	x 1.2 = $420 (+$360)	= $780
$300	now + $100	= $400	$300	x 1.2 = $360 (+$400)	= $760
Increased Mid-term Bonuses					
$350	now + $250	= $600	$250	x 1.2 =$300(+$600)	= $900
$400	now + $290	= $690	$200	x 1.2 =$240(+$690)	= $930
$450	now + $330	= $780	$150	x 1.2 =$180(+$780)	= $960
$500	now + $370	= $870	$100	x 1.2 =$120(+$870)	= $990
$550	now + $410	= $960	$50	x 1.2 = $ 60(+$960)	= $1020
$600	now + $450	= $1050	$0	is left to gain interest	= $1050

NOTE: No bonuses at mid term or final payoff unless midterm pool exceeded $3000 (50% of initial total).

Because the rules for investment and bonuses were complex, the dilemma lent itself to basic and extended information versions. Given only basic information, the temptation to "take the money and run" is salient. There is also a prominent, but not optimal collectively rational strategy (i.e. take $300 and leave $300). Additional information made this latter strategy more salient, clarified the advantages of taking only $50, but also emphasized the potential danger of being left the "sucker" if the bank collapsed. As in the largest number study, there was no attempt to persuade subjects to follow a particular strategy. It was assumed that competitors would not only attend more closely to the "greed and fear" features of the instructions, but would also be more influenced by them. Cooperators, by contrast, were expected to attend more to the information about the outcomes under mutual cooperation, and to find these superior to those which would ensue if all were to withdraw more than half their investments.

[8] Note that the optimal usage of this account is for four people to take $600, and the rest to take $50, but this is hard to coordinate without communication.

6.1 Procedure

Liebrand's Ring measure was used to identify cooperators and competitors; individualists were excluded from the study, because the contrast between cooperators and competitors allows for a clearer test of the goal facilitating effects of information. Forty-four females and 17 males (40 cooperators and 21 competitors) were assigned to one of two conditions: *basic information* (subjects were supplied with details of how the investment account worked); or *extended information* about cooperative and competitive strategies.

The cooperative strategy information stressed the importance of taking less than $300, so that everyone in the group would be able to gain. The competitive information identified the withdrawal of amounts over $300 as the behaviour which, while risking collective ruin, would give the greatest return to a few individuals, should enough members of the group refrain from taking a lot. In addition, it was stressed that even if the bank failed, those who took out $600 would end up best off in relative terms. Care was taken to give equal emphasis to the optimal strategy for mutual/group gain, and for the individual/relative gain objectives. No attempt was made to persuade the subjects, and they were told that there was no correct choice in the investment setting.

It was predicted that cooperators would orient to and remember the joint gain-maximizing information, and that their level of cooperation would be higher in the maximal information condition. Competitors were predicted to be unaffected by the information about the joint gain strategy, and to show lower levels of cooperation in the extended, compared with the basic, information condition.

At the end of the session, subjects answered two questions designed to assess their understanding of the rules of the investment game, and two questions each about the consequences of pursuing either the cooperative or the competitive strategy. They also indicated their expectations about what others in the group would do. They were paid $1 for every $100 they had taken from the pool.

6.2 Results

Results supported the predictions for cooperators, who took significantly less under maximal information (median of $50 vs $300). Competitors were slightly more competitive under the maximal, compared with minimal, information instructions, but there was a ceiling effect: competitors were very competitive under both sets of instructions (median of 600 in both cases, only one subject took less than $300). A two-way ANOVA (motivational orientation by information condition) produced a significant main effect for motivational orientation (F (1, 57) =140.76; p<.005), and for information (F (1, 57) = 24.04; p<.005). Differences between competitors and cooperators were large, supporting McClintock and Liebrand's (1988) argument for the importance of motivational orientation as a determinant of behaviour in social dilemmas (see Figure 3). These were modified by the predicted interaction effect (F (1, 57) =19.12;

p<.005). Simple main effects showed that information had its effect mainly on cooperators-- in the extended information condition, they withdrew an average of only \$95, compared with an average of \$280 in the basic information condition (below the \$300 per person needed to sustain the investment). Competitors, on the other hand, withdrew slightly *more* under the extended, compared with the basic information conditions (\$490 vs. \$464, respectively).

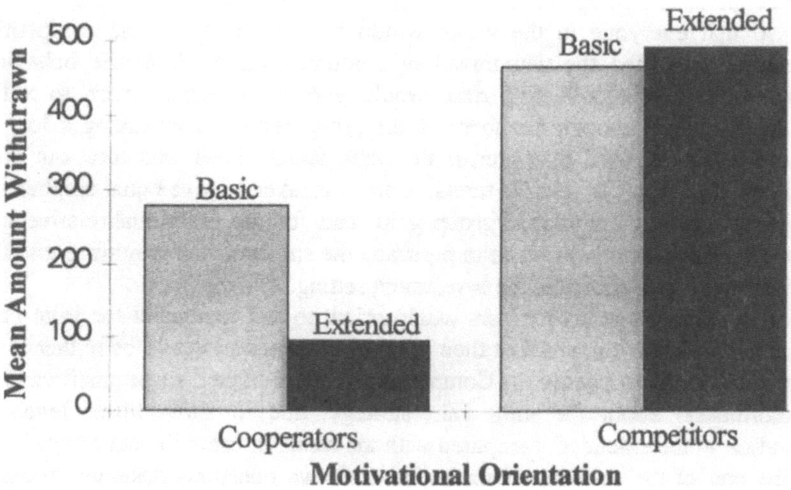

Figure 3. Mean withdrawals by motivational orientation and information conditions.

Expectations about other's behavior. Choice behaviour of cooperators and competitors appeared to be mediated by differential expectations about others' withdrawals; there was a positive correlation between subjects' predictions of what others would withdraw, and what they withdrew themselves. The correlation for cooperators was .68 in both information conditions; for competitors, the correlations were .83 and .70 in the basic, and extended information conditions respectively. These results contrast with the those for the largest number game, where competitors in the extended information condition seemed more likely to compete if they believed others were cooperating. In the investment game, cooperators almost unanimously expected other investors to withdraw less than or equal to \$300 each; cooperation for them is a safe course of action. Their lower level of withdrawals in the extended information conditions was also a subjectively "safe" choice, given that they expected others to stay under the \$300 safe limit. Competitors, by contrast, expected others to withdraw more than \$300, and this did not change in the extended information condition. For them, cooperation was not only undesirable, it was probably foolish.

Subjects also provided reasons for their expectations about others' likely investment decisions. These reasons were coded into four categories: 1) a belief that everyone would be concerned to ensure that everyone would be able to gain from the investment , and concern for joint gain; 2) belief that no-one should breach the 50% withdrawal limit which ensured the maintenance of the investment; 3) lack of trust in other investors; 4) a belief that others, as well as self, would want to maximize individual gain. Reasons in the first two categories were much more commonly given by cooperators (all but 4 had reasons in the first two categories); comments indicating the desirability of ensuring joint gain were highest in the maximal information conditions. Competitors' reasons mainly fell into categories three and four.

Comprehension of strategies. In the minimal information condition, cooperators and competitors understood the basic structure of the game equally well, as indicated in the mean percentage of correct answers to the two questions which tapped their understanding of the rules for investment and bonuses. The mean percentage correct was 85% for both groups on these questions. Thus, differences between the two motive groups in the basic information condition cannot be seen to result from differences in understanding. The MO groups were also similar under extended information, although the percentage of correct answers was higher. These results suggest that differences in behavior in the extended information condition were not due to differential comprehension of the individually and collectively rational strategies, but rather, to differences in reactions to the information by the two motive groups, and different expectations about the behavior of others.

From this study, it seemed reasonable to conclude that motivational orientation moderates the impact of information about jointly rational and about the competitive/individually rational strategies. It is not entirely clear whether it works through expectations about what others will do (assuming they will do what self will do), or by making salient the impact of one's behavior on others; the former suggests that competitors act in part to avoid being suckers; on the other hand, their expectations for others seems to be based on their analysis of what "anyone" would do in this situation. If information makes more salient how C and D affect the fate of others, one would expect it to facilitate cooperators' desire to act so as to ensure others can gain too; it should focus competitors on the choice which ensures the greatest chance of getting ahead.

7. Discussion

The results of the two experiments present a more positive view of the potential for increased knowledge to promote cooperation in social dilemmas than have previous studies (e.g. Edney and Harper, 1978; Rapoport, 1988a). Information which made more salient the collectively rational strategy significantly increased the prosocial choices of cooperators in the investment dilemma. Information about the unique jointly rational strategy in the largest number game led the prosocial subjects to submit lower numbers, and over a quarter of them chose the cooperative option of submitting "one". While the results for number submitted are difficult to interpret unambiguously as cooperation, the contrasting behavior of proself subjects (putting in higher numbers when given extended information), makes it plausible to do so. Thus, information which increases understanding may affect some of the people, some of the time. Recent analyses of large scale social dilemmas have shown that universal cooperation is not necessary for cooperation to be sustained, and that a small initial population of cooperators can lead to the establishment of mutually cooperative relationships over the long term (Axelrod, 1984; Macy, 1995; Messick and Liebrand, 1995). It is thus important to study conditions which facilitate the cooperative behavior of those who are already oriented to the collective good. In the research reported in this paper, there was some evidence that increased understanding also facilitated competitive goals. Further research is needed to establish this effect, because the experimental paradigms used did not leave as much room for increased competition, as for increased cooperation.

The impact of a subset of cooperators will vary across different kinds of dilemma settings. The Largest Number game presents an extreme dilemma, in which everyone must cooperate for the jointly rational solution to be reached. Additional understanding of this structure of interdependence may make the jointly rational strategy more salient, but it may also highlight the futility of cooperation, when a single defector can undermine cooperation. The low levels of cooperation in the Largest Number game are comprehensible, given the very low levels of trust expressed by subjects in their expectations about others' choices. The investment dilemma, on the other hand, can sustain a proportion of selfish choosers, so long as a critical mass of participants volunteer to act cooperatively. Caporael, Dawes, Orbell and van der Kragt (1989) reviewed studies of volunteer's dilemmas in which high levels of cooperation were achieved. In many of these, the key feature was the identification of a minimal contributing set. Such identification may be seen to be similar in many ways to the "knowledge" or "understanding" which has been the focus of this paper. The use of dilemma settings which have not been studied extensively has served to highlight the importance of paying close attention to the availability of individually and collectively rational strategies in any given dilemma structure, because they will define what can be learned through more extended information. Once the domain of dilemmas is expanded to include more than two choices (e.g. continuous response variables; multiple trial resource dilemmas), then the possibility arises that there will not be a unique strategy which is optimal for the pursuit of any given goal. Under such circumstances, knowledge of the structure of interdependence may not help the actor identify the means to maximize his or her goals. On the other hand, there are dilemmas in which the optimal strategy for at least some people is well-defined, and it is in these settings that we should expect information effects to be largest.

Different dilemmas may also produce different effects for expectations about others' behaviors, and this has implications for the interaction of expectations with social value orientations. There has been a great deal of interest in whether social value orientation *determines* expectations about others (e.g. Iedema & Poppe, 1995; van Lange & Liebrand, 1991). The relationship between motivational orientation, expectations and behavior was different in the two dilemmas used in the research reported here. In the investment dilemma, both cooperators and competitors tended to believe others would behave similarly to self, and these expectations seemed to underlie their choices. In the Largest Number game, proself subjects' predictions about others' behavior were similar to those made by prosocial players. Further, under extended information, these similar expectations led proself subjects to be even less cooperative than they expected others to be, while prosocials "matched" their choices to those expected of others. The greater consistency of expectations across social motive groups in the Largest Number game can probably be attributed to its highly competitive structure which induces low trust, and the attendant feelings of low efficacy (Kerr, 1989). The correlation between motive and expectation needs to be examined across a range of dilemmas, in order to decide whether there is a dispositional tendency to project one's motives onto others, or whether expectations derive much more from the parameters of the dilemma.

Our results suggest that researchers should pay closer attention to the three "jointly necessary" conditions for cooperation, posited by Dawes (1980), and by Pruitt & Kimmel (1977). The interaction effects obtained in both studies provide some support for the joint necessity argument, although we have suggested that more systematic study of expectations is also required. Although some previous research suggests that knowledge, trust, and morality may act *independently*, or additively, the studies reported in this paper are more consistent with an interaction hypothesis. More generally, we believe our approach indicates the utility of framing more complex hypotheses about the ways in which individual and environmental factors interact to produce cooperative and non-cooperative behavior in social dilemmas.

References

Allison, S.T. & Messick, D.M. (1985). Effects of experience on performance in a replenishable resource trap. *Journal of Personality and Social Psychology, 49*, 943-948.

Axelrod, R. (1984). *The evolution of cooperation*. New York: Basic Books.

Brann, P. & Foddy, M. (1988). Trust and the consumption of a deteriorating common resource .*Journal of conflict resolution, 31*, 615-630.

Caporael, L., Dawes, R., Orbell, J.& van de Kragt, A. (1989). Selfishness examined: Cooperation in the absence of egoistic incentives. *Behavioral and brain sciences, 12,* 683-99.

Camac, C. (1992). Information preferences in a two-person social dilemma. In:

W.B.G. Liebrand, D.M. Messick & H.A.M. Wilke, (Eds.), *Social dilemmas: Theoretical issues and research findings*. Oxford: Pergamon Press.

Dawes, R.M. (1980). Social dilemmas. *Annual review of psychology, 31*, 169-193.

Dawes, R. M.(1989). Statistical criteria for establishing a truly false consensus effect. *Journal of experimental social psychology, 25*, 1-17.

Edney, J.J. & Harper, C.S. (1978). The effects of information in a resource management problem: a social trap analog. *Human Ecology, 6:* 387-395.

Geller, E.S., Erickson, J.B., & Buttram, B.A. (1983). Attempts to promote residential water conservation with educational, behavioral, and engineering strategies. *Population and environment: Behavioral and social issues, 6*, 96-112.

Hofstadter, D. (1985). *Metamagical themas*. New York: Basic Books.

Iedema, J. & Poppe, M. (1994). Effects of social value orientation on expecting and learning others' orientations. *European journal of social psychology, 24*, 565-579.

Insko, C.A. and Schopler, J. (1987). Categorization, competition, and collectivity. In: C. Hendrick, (Ed.), *Review of personality and social psychology: Group processes, 8*, 213-251. New York: Sage.

Kelley, H.H. & Grezelak, J. (1972). Conflict between individual and common interest in an N-person relationship. *Journal of personality and social psychology, 21*, 190-197.

Kerr, N.L. (1989). Illusions of efficacy: The effects of group size on perceived efficacy in social dilemmas. *Journal of experimental social psychology, 25*, 287-313.

Kramer, R.M. & Goldman, L. (1995). Helping the group or helping yourself? Social motives and group identity in resource dilemmas. In: D. Schroeder, (Ed.), *Social dilemmas: Perspectives on individuals and groups*. Westport, Connecticut.: Praeger, 49-68.

Kuhlman, D.M., Camac, C.R., & Cunha, D.A. (1986). Individual differences in social orientation. In: Wilke, H.A.M., Messick, D.M., & Rutte, C. *Experimental social dilemmas*. Frankfurt: Verlag Peter Lang.

Liebrand, W.B.G. (1984). The effect of social motives, communication and group size on behavior in an N-person multi-stage mixed motive game. *European journal of social psychology, 14*, 239-264.

Macy, M.W. (1995). Pavlov and the evolution of cooperation: An experimental test. *Social psychology quarterly, 58*, 74-87.

McClintock, C.G. (1972). Social motivation - a set of propositions. *Behavioral Science, 17*, 438-454.

McClintock, C.G. & Liebrand, W.B.G. (1988). The role of interdependence structure, individual value orientation and other's strategy in social decision making: A transformational analysis. *Journal of personality and social psychology, 55*, 396-409.

Messick, D.M. & Liebrand, W.B.G. (1995). Individual heuristics and the dynamics of cooperation in large groups. *Psychological review, 102*, 131-145.

Messick, D.M. & McClintock, C.G. (1968). Motivational basis of choice in

experimental games. *Journal of experimental social psychology, 4*, 1-25.
Pruitt, D.G. & Kimmel, M.J. (1977). Twenty years of experimental gaming: Critique, synthesis, and suggestions for the future. *Annual review of psychology, 28*, 363-392.
Rapoport, A. (1988a). Experiments with N-person traps I: Prisoner's dilemma, weak prisoner's dilemma, and largest number. *Journal of conflict resolution, 32*, 457-472.
Rapoport, A. (1988b). Experiments with N-person traps II: Tragedy of the commons. *Journal of conflict resolution, 32*, 473-488.
Stern, P.C. (1976). Effects of incentives and education on resource conservation decisions in a simulated commons dilemma. *Journal of personality and social psychology, 34,* 1285-1292.
Thompson, S.C. & Stoutemyer, K. (1991). Water use as a commons dilemma: The effects of education that focuses on long-term consequences and individual action. *Environment and social behavior, 23*, 314-333.
Van Lange, P.A.M. (1992). Rationality and morality in social dilemmas: The influence of social value orientations. In: W.B.G. Liebrand, D.M. Messick & H.A.M. Wilke,(Eds.)*Social dilemmas: Theoretical issues and research findings.* Oxford: Pergamon Press.
Van Lange, P.A.M. & Liebrand, W.B.G. (1991). Social value orientation and intelligence:A test of the goal prescribes rationality principle. *European journal of social psychology, 21*, 273-292.
Yamagishi, T. (1986). The structural goal-expectation theory of cooperation in social dilemmas. In: E.J. Lawler (Ed.), *Advances in group processes, 3.* Greenwich, Connecticut: JAI press.

Reduction of Environmental Risk as a Public Good

Marieke Wilke[1], Christel G. Rutte[1] and Gary Bornstein[2]

[1] Department of Work and Organizational Psychology, University of Nijmegen, The Netherlands
[2] Department of Psychology, Hebrew University of Jerusalem, Israel

Abstract. When group members share their resources equally, regardless of their contribution to the collective group outcomes, equity norms may be violated. Some individuals may use the opportunity to take a free ride and as a result others will be put in the position of suckers. The equal division rule, however, has a clear advantage that has received little theoretical and empirical attention. Sharing with others reduces the risk associated with individual outcome in an uncertain environment and thus has the effect of insurance. We report an experiment in which we examined subjects' willingness to share with others as a function of environmental uncertainty and personal risk preferences. Specifically, each subject had to choose between an individual lottery and an equal share of a combined group lottery. We found that, when uncertain about their own outcome, risk-averse individuals prefer the less risky group option, whereas risk-seeking individuals prefer to take their own risk. Assuming that in real-life situations people are typically risk-averse, we conclude that the desire to reduce uncertainty concerning one's outcomes indeed motivates people to pool their risks with other group members.

1 Introduction

The anthropological literature is rich in examples of food-sharing practices among hunter-gatherer societies (Cashdan, 1985; Peterson, 1993). Sharing in these tribal societies is a generalized reciprocity norm which involves giving to others when they are in need without regard to the direct equality of balanced reciprocity (Sahlins, 1972). Anthropologists argue that the main function of this norm is to protect people from local scarcity and environmental variability. By its nature, the hunting and gathering life involves risk and uncertainty, particularly where there is no storage and provision is on a day-to-day basis, and "... were each hunter to produce only for his own domestic needs, everyone would eventually perish from hunger" (Ingold, 1983; p.145).

Sharing then is a form of insurance -- a social mechanism designed for buffering environmental and economic risks. In this form of risk management, a number of individuals join together, thereby making the individual payoffs collectively more predictable. By the law of large numbers, the larger the number of individuals (i. e., independent exposure units), the more closely the average outcome approaches the expected outcome. The benefit for the individual is the reduction of variability in outcome and the increased protection against the possibility of catastrophic loss. The cost is the obligation to help when someone else is in need. This payoff structure creates the familiar problem of free riding. While all members of a society are better off if they all share, each individual member has an incentive to free ride by declining to share his own resources with the others.

The "sharing" dilemma seems to be a particularly intriguing one. On the one hand, the higher the level of environmental uncertainty, the higher the need for reciprocity, or solidarity networks. On the other hand, higher levels of environmental variability render solutions to the free rider problem associated with such systems considerably more difficult. Cooperation in social dilemmas rests to a large extent on trust that others will do likewise (Messick & Brewer, 1983). Trust, in turn, is enhanced by confidence that noncooperators can be identified and sanctioned in some way (Yamagishi, 1988). When the resources available to group members are known with certainty, identifying free riders is relatively simple. When the resources are of a probabilistic nature, the ability to detect free riders is severely diminished. This is so because a failure to contribute one's fair share to the collective good may indicate bad luck as well as free riding. Clearly, a fluctuating environment makes it easier to get away with free riding. A particularly vivid example by Hiatt (1982) illustrates this point. Hiatt reported that a common practice among the Anbara (an Aboriginal tribe where sharing norms are strongly enforced) is eating during food collection so that the greater part of a person's produce is in advanced state of digestion by the time he or she returns to camp.

The issue of environmental uncertainty at the individual level, as opposed to the group level (Messick, Allison, & Samuelson, 1988; Suleiman & Rapoport, 1988), has received little attention in the social dilemma and public good literature. In the typical social dilemma study the resources available to the participants are fixed and their distribution is common knowledge. Our discussion above suggests that studying situations where individual resources are uncertain is interesting for two reasons. First, environmental uncertainty may be a primary reason why people are willing to form groups and share their resources with others. Second, environmental uncertainty increases social uncertainty which is detrimental to the stability and functioning of such groups.

The present study focused on the first issue, examining the factors that affect people's willingness to share their potential gains with others. We considered two such factors: the level of environmental uncertainty and personal attitudes toward risk. In our experimental task, each participant was faced with a binary decision between an individual lottery (e. g., winning f0, f5, or f10 with equal probabilities) and an aggregated group lottery (winning an equal share of n independent lotteries of this sort). Uncertainty was manipulated in two different ways; we manipulated the range of possible outcome (the larger the range the higher the level of uncertainty), and individual knowledge concerning the outcome of the gamble (the individual's decision was made either before or after she knew her own outcome).

The "sharing" game above is different from other public goods paradigms in an important sense. Whereas in a public-goods game contributions to the common pool are multiplied by a factor larger than one and divided equally among all participants, the decision to join the group in the sharing game does not increase the total amount of resources available. The net effect for the individual is to reduce the variance of the future outcome through replacing a gamble with large variance by one with smaller variance. Obviously, such substitution is attractive only to the extent that individuals are risk-aversive. Risk-neutral individuals are expected to be indifferent between the two gambles since both have the same expected value and risk-seeking individuals will in fact prefer the gamble with the higher variability. The assumption that people are risk-averse (especially in the domain of gains, see Tversky & Kahneman, 1986), is standard in most economic analysis. Nonetheless, since some participants might hold less conservative attitudes towards risk in a laboratory task involving relatively small amount of money, we measured the risk preferences of the participants and categorized them into risk-seeking and risk-averse types. Our predictions can be summarized as follows: Risk-averse subjects will tend to choose the less risky group option, and this tendency will be stronger the higher the level of environmental uncertainty. Risk-seeking subjects will exhibit the opposite pattern of behavior.

2 Method

Subjects and Design: The participants were 62 undergraduate students (25 men and 37 women) at the University of Nijmegen. They were recruited through campus advertisement promising monetary rewards for participation in a group decision-making task. Two manipulations of uncertainty were combined factorially. The first involved uncertainty concerning one's own outcome (present vs. absent), while the second involved the range of possible outcomes (large vs. small). In addition, for each participant we measured his or her risk preference and, based on median split, categorized them into risk-seeking vs. risk-averse types. This, then constitutes our third independent variable in the 2X2X2 design. Each participant had to choose between an individual lottery and an equal share in an aggregated (three-person) group lottery. This binary decision was our main dependent measure.

Procedure: Subjects reported to the laboratory in groups of three. Each subject was seated in a separate cubicle and handed written instructions. Subjects were told that their reward would be based on the color of a bead drawn randomly from an urn containing an equal number of white, blue, and red beads. Half the subjects chose their bead at the beginning of the experiment (no uncertainty condition) and were told that the particular color they happened to draw was worth f5. The other half of the subjects were told that they would make their choice at the end of the experiment. They were also told that a red bead was worth f5 and that the other two colors were worth f4 and f6 (in the small range condition) or f0 and f10 (in the large range condition). Subjects were then presented with the following choice: (I) a reward based on the outcome of their own lottery, or (G) a reward based on the outcome of the lotteries of all three group members. Specifically, each subject was told that if she chose option (I) her payoff would be determined by the color of the bead she herself drew. If she chose option (G) she would be joining two other participants who also drew beads from identical urns and her payoff would consist of one third of the total amounts earned by this three-person group. The instructions were followed by examples listing possible payoffs as a function of one's decision and the outcome of the lottery (or lotteries). After making their choices, subjects responded to a questionnaire in which they were asked the following questions concerning their risk preferences (Lenderink, 1994): a) Do you consider yourself a person who avoids or seeks risks in everyday life? (1=avoid risks often to 5=seek risks often), b) Do you consider yourself a person who takes many or few risks in everyday life? (1=few risks to 5=many risks), and c) Compared with other students of your age and gender, do you take fewer or more risks? (1=take fewer risks than others to 5=take more risks than others). Subjects were asked two additional questions concerning the manipulation of uncertainty. Finally, subjects in the no uncertainty conditions were paid f5 each, and subjects in the uncertainty conditions were paid according to their choice and the outcome of the lottery.

3 Results

Manipulation Check: The questions involving the manipulation were analyzed using a 2 (range of possible outcomes) X 2 (uncertainty) analysis of variance. As expected, subjects in the uncertainty conditions were less certain about the amount of money they would earn in the experiment (M=2.25) than subjects in the no uncertainty conditions (M=3.57), $F(1,58)=15.75$, $p<.0001$. Subjects in the large range of possible outcomes conditions perceived the low outcome as more negative (M=3.06) than subjects in the small range conditions (M=3.84), $F(1,58)=9.11$, $p<.004$.

Decisions: The answers on the three questions designed to measure risk preferences were averaged to form a risk preference index (Cronbach's alpha=.78). On the basis of a median split (Median=3.0), subjects were divided into risk-seeking and risk-averse groups.

Table 1. Proportions of Group Choices as a Function of Risk-type, Range of Outcomes and Uncertainty

	Uncertainty: *Yes*	*Uncertainty*: *No*	
Risk Seeking	Range: Large 4/9 (44.4%) Small 5/9 (55.6%) *Overall: 9/18 (50.0%)*	Range: Large 2/4 (50.0%) Small 6/8 (75.0%) *Overall: 8/12 (66.7%)*	*17/30 (56.7%)*
Risk Averse	Range: Large 7/7 (100 %) Small 6/7 (85.7%) *Overall: 13/14 (92.9%)*	Range: Large 5/11 (45.5%) Small 2/7 (28.6%) *Overall: 7/18 (38.9%)*	*20/32 (62.5%)*
	22/32 (67.75%)	*15/30 (50.0%)*	

Table 1 shows that 92.9% of the risk-averse subjects chose the group option in the uncertainty condition, as compared with only 38.9% in the no uncertainty condition. Risk-seeking subjects showed the opposite pattern of behavior; 50% of these subjects decided to join the group pool in the uncertainty condition, while 66.7% of them joined the group when there was no uncertainty. A 2X2X2 loglinear analysis (Haberman, 1978; Bishop, Feinberg & Holland, 1975) performed on the binary decision indicates that the interaction between uncertainty and risk preference is significant, Chi-square=9.49, df=1, p<.002. In addition, there is a significant main effect for uncertainty, Chi-square=4.85, df=1, p<.028. The main effect of range of possible outcomes was not significant, Chi-square=.58, df=1, n.s., while the interaction concerning range of possible outcomes and risk preference was only marginally significant, Chi-square=2.87, df=1, p=.09.

Since risk preferences were measured immediately after subjects made their decisions, it is possible that this measure was influenced by the actual decision made ("I must be a risk-taker since I just opted for the risky rather than the sure option"). As it turned out, however, the distribution of risk preferences was not dependent on the experimental condition to a significant degree. The difference between the number of risk-seekers in the no uncertainty condition (12 out of 30) and in the uncertainty condition (18 out of 30) is not significantly different from zero, Chi-square=1.65, df=1, p<.20. The same is true for the range of outcomes manipulation. 13 of the 31 subjects in the large range conditions were classified as risk seekers as compared with 17 out of 31 in the small range manipulation; this difference is not significant, Chi-square=1.04, df=1, p<.31.

4 Discussion

The results reported above generally confirm our predictions. Risk-averse individuals prefer the less risky group gamble when uncertain about their own outcome, while risk-seeking individuals prefer the more risky individual gamble under the same conditions. Assuming that in real life situations involving larger stakes most people are risk-averse, we can conclude that the desire to reduce uncertainty concerning one's outcomes indeed motivates people to pool their risks with other group members.

Our study included two manipulations of uncertainty, one involving subjects' knowledge about their own outcome, and the other involving the range of possible outcomes. Only the first manipulation had a significant effect on subjects' choice behavior. We are not sure at this point as to why the range of outcome manipulation failed. Future research will use larger payoffs and perhaps include the possibility of actually losing money in an attempt to shed more light on this issue.

People in Western societies use a great many means of coping with risk other than informal sharing and giving. Nevertheless, many of us are willing to help others similar to ourselves who are suffering from some misfortune (e. g., illness, natural disaster, etc.), and rely on receiving such help when we are in need. People's willingness to share their good luck with less fortunate others was demonstrated in a recent study by Selten & Ockenfels (1995). In their experiment subjects participated in a three-person game where each of the three players could independently win DM 10 with probability 2/3 and 0 with probability 1/3. Before the random draws were made each subject had to decide how much he or she would be willing to give to a loser (or losers) if there were any in the group, in case that subject was a winner. Most participants were willing to give a substantial portion of their winnings and expected the others to be equally generous.

The present study focused on the reduction of risk due to environmental uncertainty as a motivation for joining a group. Future research will examine the effect of outcome uncertainty in ongoing groups. In particular, we are interested in studying the interaction between environmental uncertainty and social uncertainty in dilemma-type situations. Incorporating environmental uncertainty into the standard social dilemma paradigms should be relatively simple. Rather than providing participants with fixed (commonly known) endowments, we will endow them on the basis of the outcome of a random process. The properties of the random distribution may (or may not) be common knowledge, but the information concerning the realization of the random process will be kept as private information. We believe that this modification will render the research paradigm a more realistic model of social dilemmas outside the laboratory.

References

Bishop, Y.M.M., Feinberg, S.E., & Holland, P.W. (1975). *Discrete multivariate analysis: Theory and practice*. Cambridge Mass.: MIT Press.

Cashdan, E. (1985). Coping with risk: Reciprocity among the Basarwa of Northern Botswana. *Man, 20*, 454-474.

Haberman, S.J. (1978). *Analysis of qualitative data Vol. 1*. London: Academic Press.

Hiatt, L. (1982). Traditional attitudes to land resources. In R. M. Berndt (Ed.) *Aboriginal sites: Rites and resource development*. Perth: University of Western Australia Press.

Ingold, T. (1983). The significance of storage in hunting societies. *Man, 18*, 553-517.

Lenderink, T.B., Meertens, R.M., & Vlek, C.A.J. (1995). Motieven voor persoonlijke en interpersoonlijke risiokeuzes. In: N.K. de Vries, C.K.W. de Dreu, N. Ellemers, & R. Vonk (Eds.) *Fundamentele Sociale Psychologie Deel 9* , pp. 209-220. Tilburg: Tilburg University Press.

Messick, D. M., & Brewer, M. B. (1983). Solving social dilemmas: A review. In L. Wheeler and P. Shaver (Eds.), *Review of personality and Social psychology Vol. 4*, pp. 11-44. Beverly Hills, CA: Sage.

Messick, D.M., Allison, S.T., & Samuelson, C.D. (1988). Framing and communication effects on group members' responses to environmental and social uncertainty. In: S. Maital (Ed.) *Applied Behavioural Economics Vol. 2*, pp. 677-700. New York: New York University Press.

Peterson, N. (1993). Demand Sharing: Reciprocity and the pressure for generosity among foragers. *American Anthropologist, 95*, 860-874.

Sahlins, M. (1972). *Stone Age economics*. Chicago: Aldine.

Selten, R., and Ockenfels, A. (1995). An experimental solidarity game. *Fourth Amsterdam Workshop on Experimental Economics*, 429-444.

Suleiman, R., & Rapoport, A. (1988). Environmental and social uncertainty in single-trial resource dilemmas. 11th Conference on: Subjective probability, utility and decision making. *Acta Psychologica*, *68*, 99-112.

Tversky A., and Kahneman D. (1986). Rational choice and the framing of decisions. *Journal of Business*, *59*, 251-278.

Yamagishi, T. (1988). Seriousness of social dilemmas and the provision of a sanctioning system. *Social Psychology Quarterly*, *51*, 32-42.

Hostage Posting as a Mechanism for Co-operation in the Prisoner's Dilemma Game[1]

Pawel P. Mlicki

Department of Sociology, Utrecht University, Heidelberglaan 1,
3584 CS Utrecht, The Netherlands

Abstract.

Investigates *hostage posting institution* as a mechanism of co-operation in the two-person Prisoner's Dilemma Game. Game-theoretic conditions are specified that are necessary to boost co-operative behaviour, and the role of transaction costs and bonuses (productive hostages) is discussed. An experiment is reported (N=216) that shows that games characterised by the Nash equilibrium or subgame-perfect equilibrium create conditions that are necessary but not sufficient to encourage actors to post a hostage, while games in which the maximin criterion is met ensure mutual hostage posting and co-operation. While transaction costs significantly discourage subjects from taking advantage of the hostage posting institution, productive hostages do not influence subjects' co-operative behaviour.

1 Introduction

In social dilemmas, the interests of participants are partly opposed but also partly convergent. In situations like these there exists a conflict between a tendency to maximize self-interest (a strategy labelled *defection*) and a tendency to maximize the interest of the collective (a strategy labelled *co-operation*; cf. Rapoport, 1974). Collectively rational behaviour, i.e. co-operation of all parties, leads to an outcome preferred by all when it is contrasted with an outcome of general defection. Defection, however, is a *dominant strategy* for an individual because, regardless of other parties' choices, it yields higher individual payoffs

[1] I am grateful to Werner Raub, Manuel Vree and Jeroen Weesie for their help at designing and conducting the experiment, and for their helpful comments in revising the manuscript. Financial support was provided by the Netherlands Organization for Scientific Research (NWO) under grant PGS 50-370.

than does co-operation. This clash between the individual and collective rationalities defines the existence of a social trap and the co-operation problem they must deal with (Hardin, 1968; Dawes 1980; Ostrom, 1990).

In our further theoretical consideration as well as in our empirical study, we restrict ourselves to just one experimental game, the well known Prisoner's Dilemma Game (PDG, see Table 1), which has frequently been used to model the whole range of social dilemmas (e.g. Nash, 1951; Luce & Raiffa, 1985 Ostrom, 1990; Binmore, 1994).

Table 1. The PDG. Numbers represent positive outcomes for both players. Letters between brackets refer to a general example of the PDG. The only strategy-combination that is in equilibrium is D1,D2

		Player 2	
		C2	D2
Player 1	C1	8,8 (R,R)	2,10 (S,T)
	D1	10,2 (T,S)	**4,4** (P,P)

For the analyses of players' behaviour in this game the following assumptions are made:

1) T > R > P > S,
2) both players are rational and assume that the other player is also rational,
3) players' utilities correspond with the numbers and, monotonically, the higher the number the higher the utility.

Both players have to choose, independently of each other, between C (co-operation) and D (defection). For both players strategy D is dominant. Therefore, rational players will always choose it and their payoffs will be 4 for each. Clearly, their individual strategies lead to a suboptimal result: there is a possibility to receive both 8 if they had both chosen C. Thus, an incentive-guided and individually rational strategy leads to an individually (and concurrently collectively) deficient outcome. This paradox constitutes the basic co-operation problem in social dilemmas.

Players can avoid the social trap if they both recognize that it ought to happen *before* they 'enter' the social dilemma. Any resolution to a conflict involves some change either in the actors, the alternatives, the payoffs, or the information structure (cf. Messick & Brewer, 1983). In our research, we concentrate on resolutions that refer to *the embeddedness of the interaction in a social dilemma within a broader social context* (Granovetter, 1985). Two types of embeddedness can be differentiated: *structural embeddedness* and *institutional embeddedness* (Raub & Weesie, 1992). The latter one denotes all kinds of social agreements, formal and informal that people voluntarily incur. We call them commitments. In the next paragraph we analyze the commitments as a co-operation mechanism at some length.

2 Credible Commitments: Hostages

Credible commitments are changes in the incentive structure that one may voluntarily incur to order to make his opportunistic behaviour unattractive. Each rational actor should want to participate in such an arrangement because otherwise a general defection with its aftermath can be expected. Hence, the person endorsing such an arrangement may want to restrict his own range of available behavioural alternatives because otherwise the costs of defection will exceed its benefits.

The notion of commitment and the fact that restricting ones own possibilities may be advantageous, are not new. Schelling (1960) identifies three characteristics a *credible commitment* should possess: it should be voluntarily incurred, it should be conspicuous for the other party, and should be binding for the one who has made it in this sense that he cannot reverse his obligation.

Such a commitment mechanism introduces an important change in the incentive structure of both actors, and consequently changes preferences concerning alternatives from which parties have to choose. It is important to stress that such commitments do not automatically force parties to particular choices; rather, they let them strategically adapt to the new situation (cf. Weesie and Raub, in press).

A systematic game theoretical analysis of the institution of hostage posting as a device for enhancing co-operation in the PDG has recently been provided by Weesie and Raub (in press). An empirical test of their analysis can be found in Raub and Keren (1993) and Keren and Raub (1993). In the present research we employed the paradigmatic framework developed by them, applying it to a group and computer assisted research setting rather than the individual one. In the following section the main items of their theory of hostage posting are presented.

3 Hostage Posting in the PDG with Complete Information

The hostage option is an additional move, built into the standard PDG procedure, which changes it into a two-step Prisoner's Dilemma Hostage Game (PDHG). It concerns a possibility to bet or post a certain amount of money called the 'hostage'. The size of the hostage must be more than T-R. Thus, both players have first to decide, independently of each other, whether or not to post a hostage. Four situations are possible: only Player 1 posts the hostage, only Player 2 does, they both post the hostage, neither of them does. Then, both are informed about each other's first move. The second move is a standard C or D choice (cf. Table 1), taken by both players independently of each other.

Keren and Raub (1993) analyze two types of strategies players can adopt in the one-trial PDHG: the inflexible strategy and the reactive strategy. The inflexible strategy prescribes not to post a hostage on the first move and to unconditionally defect on the second move. The reactive or flexible strategy dictates to post a hostage on the first move and to condition the second move on the other player's decision on the first move: to co-operate on the second move if the other player has also posted a hostage, and to defect if the other player has declined to post a hostage. Posting a hostage can be interpreted as an intention to co-operate in the subsequent move (signalling effect). To what degree hosting posting contains (1) a promise to co-operate on the second move, and (2) a threat to punish the other player with defection if he declines to post a hostage, depends on the rules that regulate the hostage institution. In the next paragraph these rules are analyzed at some length.

4 Rules of Hostage Institution

Different conditions can be created depending on the rules that pertain to the hostages (Keren & Raub, 1993; Raub & Keren, 1993). The first rule regulates whether hostages (a) must be posted bilaterally or, alternatively, (b) may be posted unilaterally. The second rule establishes when a hostage is forfeited: (c) if one unilaterally defects (which implies that the hostage is not forfeited when both players defect), or (d) when one defects regardless of what the other player does. The third rule determines the fate of the forfeited hostage: (e) it goes to the third mediating party, or (f) it goes to the other player.

The point is, given the values of T, R, P and S, and the value of the hostage H (H>T-R), to define the rules of the game such that the *Pareto*-optimal[2] outcome can be achieved as a result of individually rational behaviour of the players. In our study we obtained the following three equilibrium conditions by keeping the payoffs and the hostage value constant (H=4), while manipulating the rules of the hostage institution (for an advanced mathematical analysis of hostage games, see Weesie and Raub, in press):

---

[2] The outcome is *Pareto*-optimal if there does not exist an alternative outcome such that it is acceptable to all players and strictly preferred by some players.

4.1 Condition 1

Unilateral hostage posting is allowed; the hostage is lost when one defects; the hostage goes to a third mediating party:

			Player 2			
			H2-		H2+	
			C2	D2	C2	D2
Player 1	H1-	C1	8,8	2,10	8,8	2,6
		D1	10,2	***4,4***	**10,2**	4,0
	H1+	C1	8,8	**2,10**	**8,8**	2,6
		D1	6,2	0,4	6,2	0,0

Payoffs printed bold-face are associated with the strategy-combinations (C versus D choices) played by rational players, given the particular decisions concerning hostages. The payoffs printed bold-face *and* in italics are associated with the hostage decisions and C vs D strategy-combinations played by rational players.

In this condition, the player who posts a hostage 'makes a promise' to co-operate on the second move. His promise is credible in this sense that co-operation is then his best strategy if the other player co-operates (8>6). His decision to post a hostage forms, however, no threat to the other player if the other player had not posted a hostage, and who can be expected to defect, because co-operation is also then first player's best move (2>0). In other words, posting a hostage makes a player vulnerable. Thus, expecting the other player not to post a hostage (and to defect), a rational player should not do it either, and should, accordingly, defect on the second move. In game theoretical terms, we deal here with the equilibrium properties of reactive strategies.

The prediction in this 'promise credible' condition (PCC) is, therefore, that players will not post a hostage.

4.2 Condition 2

Unilateral hostage posting is allowed; the hostage is lost when one unilaterally defects (thus, the hostage is not forfeited when *both* players defect; the hostage goes to a third mediating party):

			Player 2			
			H2-		H2+	
			C2	D2	C2	D2
Player 1	H1-	C1	8,8	2,10	8,8	2,6
		D1	10,2	**4,4**	10,2	**4,4**
	H1+	C1	8,8	2,10	***8,8***	2,6
		D1	6,2	**4,4**	6,2	4,4

In this condition, as previously, the player who posts a hostage makes a credible promise to co-operate on the second move (8>6) if the other player also co-operates. This time, however, the decision to post a hostage makes threat credible as well: If the other player declines to post a hostage, and is expected to defect on the second move, the first player's best move is to defect as well (4>2). In other words, posting a hostage does not make a player vulnerable as was the case in condition 1. Thus, expecting the other player to post a hostage (and co-operate), a rational player should post a hostage and subsequently co-operate. In game theoretical terms, we deal here with subgame-perfectness of equilibria (cf. Selten, 1965).

The prediction in this 'promise and threat credible' condition (PTCC) is, therefore, that players will post a hostage.

It should be noted, nevertheless, that in this condition some vulnerability remains. Suppose that both players posted a hostage. If Player 1 co-operates on the second move and Player 2, for whatever reason, defects, the payoff for Player 1 is 2, which is less than 4 he would have received if he had not posted a hostage and defected. In this condition, therefore, the reactive strategy does not fulfil the maximin criterion because it does not maximize the worst outcome. In other words, the worst outcome that the reactive strategy can produce (i.e. 2) is worse than the worst outcome of the inflexible strategy (i.e. 4). This maximin criterion characterizes the next condition.

4.3 Condition 3

Only bilateral hostage posting is possible; the hostage is lost when one defects; the hostage goes to the partner:

			Player 2			
			H2-		H2+	
			C2	D2	C2	D2
Player 1	H1-	C1	8,8	2,10	8,8	2,10
		D1	10,2	**4,4**	10,2	**4,4**
	H1+	C1	8,8	2,10	***8,8***	6,6
		D1	10,2	**4,4**	6,6	4,4

Since the unilateral hostage posting is not allowed, payoffs in the H1+,H2- quadrant and in the H1-,H2+ quadrant are identical to the payoffs associated with the situation when neither of the players posts a hostage (H1-,H2-).

In this condition, in addition to the credible promise and threat, the maximin criterion of the flexible strategy is fulfilled. Indeed, even if Player 2 defects after having posted a hostage, the payoff for Player 1, who posted a hostage and co-operated, is 6, which is more than 4 that Player 1 would receive if they both played the inflexible strategy. In other words, co-operation is a dominant strategy and utilizing the reactive strategy coincides with the maximin criterion.

The prediction in this 'promise and threat credible, and maximin criterion met' condition (in short, maximin criterion condition or MCC) is that players will post a hostage.

5 Transaction Costs

The institution of hostages usually requires the involvement of mediators who endorse that the commitments the partners incur are credible. The participation of a mediator to monitor the course of the transaction, usually involves some costs. In our study we introduced, therefore, *transaction costs* (cf. Williamson, 1985, Chapter 2) players must pay if they post a hostage. Players bear these costs regardless of whether their hostage is subsequently returned or lost, and whether it is lost to the other player or to the third party. The transaction costs are always paid to the third party (the experimenter). In the experiment, subjects assigned to the PCC did not have the transaction costs manipulation; the reminder of subjects had this manipulation. The manipulation was discarded for the PCC because if transaction costs have any discouraging effect on subjects' use of the hostage posting mechanism, it should first of all manifest itself in the conditions in which favourable conditions prevail for hostage posting. As we predicted no hostage posting in the PCC, we would similarly predict no hostage posting if transaction costs had to be paid for the use of the hostage institution.

For subjects in the PTCC and MCC, half of them played the PDHG with the transaction costs, the other half, without. The cost of the hostage transaction was set to 1 guilder (approximately $ 0.60), the value that is low enough not to change the equilibria and, consequently, not to change predictions based on game theory. Therefore, we expect that subjects' tendency to post a hostage when the transaction costs are involved does not differ from their inclination to do so when it is free of charge.

6 Productive Hostages

An analogous concept to the transaction costs is an extra bonus both parties receive if they follow the flexible strategies, i.e. when they both post a hostage on the first move, and both co-operate on the second move. We call this bonus a *'productive hostage'* (Weesie & Raub, in press). In our research we utilized the idea of 'productive hostages'. Subjects assigned to the MCC did not have the productive hostages manipulation; the reminder of subjects had this manipulation. The manipulation was discarded for the MCC because if productive hostages have any promoting effect on subjects' use of the hostage posting mechanism, it should first of all manifest itself in the conditions in which less favourable conditions prevail for hostage posting. As we predicted that all subjects would post a hostage in the MCC, we would similarly predict that all subjects post a hostage in this condition if the mutual use of the hostage institution and the mutual co-operation are associated with a bonus[3]. For subjects in the PCC and PTCC, half of them were to receive a bonus (for both players) if they both followed the reactive strategy, while the second half did not receive this instruction. The value of the bonus was set to 1 guilder. Again, it is low enough not to change the predictions based on game theory. Therefore, we expect that subjects' tendency to post a hostage when the productive hostages are involved does not differ from their inclination to do so when the productive hostages are absent.

---

[3] According to the game theoretical predictions, rational players in the condition characterized by subgame-perfectness of equilibria should post a hostage. We decided, nevertheless, to utilize the productive hostages manipulation in this condition for two reasons: (1) as mentioned earlier, there exists some vulnerability of players who employ the reactive strategy under the rules prevailing in this condition because the maximin criterion is not met, and mutual expectations of rational behaviour are merely expectations and not knowledge; (2) the empirical findings by Keren and Raub (1993) strongly suggest that just these considerations are decisive for the adoption of the reactive strategies by players.

In our study we try to replicate the main results of the studies by Raub and Keren (1993, Experiment 1) and Keren and Raub (1993, Experiment 1). We use the same noncooperative game (PDG), and model it by introducing the institution of hostages. The same three equilibrium conditions are manipulated: the first condition being characterized by the equilibrium properties of reactive strategies (promise credible); the second condition possessing the quality of subgame-perfectness of equilibria (promise and threat credible); and the third condition in which additionally the maximin criterion is met. Further, we introduced transaction costs paid for the use of the hostage option, and a bonus (a productive hostage) for bilateral utilization of reactive strategies.

In our experiment we utilized computer assisted group sessions rather than the individual sessions utilized by Keren and Raub. In the discussion, possible consequences of these differences for the replication of their results are examined in detail.

7 Method

7.1 Subjects

In total, 216 Dutch students (62 male and 151 female) of the University of Utrecht participated in the study. They were volunteers promised at least 12 guilders for the participation. It was also indicated that depending on their performance subjects could earn more than 20 guilders.

7.2 Design

A 3 x 2 x 2 factorial design was utilized.
The first factor, **equilibrium properties**, included three conditions described in detail in the preceding section. The first was characterized by the equilibrium properties of reactive strategies (PCC); in the second condition the subgame-perfectness equilibrium existed (PTCC); the third condition met additionally the maximin criterion (MCC).

There were two conditions within the second factor, **transaction costs**, which were either present or absent. If present, subjects had to pay 1 guilder for posting a hostage.

Similarly, the third factor, **productive hostages**, had two levels: the productive hostages were either present or not. If present, subjects were paid out an additional bonus worth 1 guilder, if and only if they both first posted a hostage and subsequently both chose co-operation.

Of the twelve possible conditions, eight were actually run. There were two sessions per condition. In each of the 16 sessions between 10 and 16 subjects took part (mean=13.5).

7.3 Procedure

The experimental sessions were held in two rooms at the same time with an equal number of subjects in each group (between 5 and 8). First, all subjects gathered in one room. They were then randomly assigned to one of the two computer rooms, a procedure required for technical reasons. In each room there was one male experimenter. Throughout the experiment subjects were assured that, though in the two rooms, they were all considered as one group, all the treatments were identical for everyone, and that any future interaction between subjects might take place within one room as well as between the rooms.

The experimental games were played on pc's (each subject at one pc). The instructions were partly given on paper and partly displayed on the pc monitor. In addition to communicating their responses through the computer network, subjects were asked to indicate their answers on the forms.

Once seated at the pc's, subjects were requested not to talk with each other, and, in case of doubts, to raise their hands and ask the experimenter for assistance. The general procedure of the experiment was revealed. Subjects were informed that during the experiment they would communicate with another subject through the computer network but that they would not get to know with whom. Then, subjects were familiarized with the way the communication with another subject would go on. Each subject was informed that he or she would now be connected with a randomly selected subject. The connection was real but was not, in fact, established in a random way. In each session the same two computers located in two different rooms were connected to each other. Subjects could now exchange up to three messages. Each message could not be longer than 37 characters. This communication was meant to let subjects get used to this way of interacting with another subject and to believe that the connection was real. Then, subjects were instructed that a new connection would take place so that they would be paired with another subject randomly selected among all other participants. In fact, from now on they interacted with a preprogrammed computer. Visually both the real and bogus connections were identical so that subjects could not tell the difference.

During the session subjects encountered the following message several times: 'wait until the experimenter provides you with the password'. The 'passwords' were intended to let all subjects work at the same pace. The passwords were provided when all subjects (in both rooms) came to a particular place in the procedure. Both experimenters communicated with each other through the same computer network in order to synchronize the progress of the procedure in both rooms and, accordingly, for all subjects. During the session subjects could continually monitor their 'budgets', which were displayed on their pc screens, and which changed according to their decisions concerning hostages and co-operation vs. defection. Each subject started with the 6-guilder budget.

Then, subjects read the instructions that explained the rules of a simple PDG.

Subsequently, they played the PDG once. Each subject received the same feedback concerning the choice of the other player (in fact the preprogrammed computer): defection.

After having read the following instructions, which explained a PDG with a hostage posting option (and depending on the condition, transaction costs and productive hostages), subjects played this Prisoner's Dilemma Hostage Game. The simple PDG and the PDHG were ostensibly played with the same subject. The feedback from the other player (again, in fact the preprogrammed computer that played as a perfectly rational player) was identical for all subjects within one equilibrium condition. In the PCC, the other player utilized the inflexible strategy. In the two remaining equilibrium conditions, the other player utilized the reactive strategy.

Finally, subjects filled in a questionnaire and were paid the money they 'earned' in the games. Each session took about 1 hour.

For both versions, a simple one and with the hostage posting option, the same initial matrix was used (see Table 1). In the instructions to the two games, subjects were asked with emphasis to make such choices as to maximize their own outcomes.

8 Results

In the initial, simple PDG subjects had to make a choice between two colours representing a co-operative and a defective alternative. Collapsing across all the conditions, co-operation was chosen by 45% of subjects (97 individuals). Defection was chosen by 55% (119 subjects). Similar proportions were found in each condition, which shows that the randomization was successful.

In the PDG with a hostage posting option, subjects had first to decide whether or not to post a hostage. The main purpose was to replicate the results of Raub and Keren (1993), and Keren and Raub (1993), by means of the group-session and computer-assisted procedure. For comparison reasons, those subjects were selected for the analysis who did not have the manipulation of transaction costs and productive hostages (N=78). These results, and the results of the studies by Raub and Keren (1993), and Keren and Raub (1993), are summarized in Table 2.

Table 2. Percentage and number of subjects (between brackets) posting a hostage in Raub and Keren (1993, Experiment 1), Keren and Raub (1993, Experiment 1), and of the present experiment, separately for those subjects who defected in the simple PDG and for all subjects

equilibrium conditions	Raub & Keren (1993) Experiment 1 posting hostages	Keren & Raub (1993) Experiment 1 posting hostages	present study posting hostages
PCC			
from those defecting in simple PDG	17 (3)	11 (2)	31 (4)
from all subjects	17 (4)	7 (4)	46 (11)
PTCC			
from those defecting in simple PDG	50 (9)	28 (5)	63 (10)
from all subjects	50 (11)	33 (8)	65 (17)
MCC			
from those defecting in simple PDG	95 (18)	89 (16)	80 (12)
from all subjects	89 (25)	84 (21)	82 (23)

The main results of the research by Raub and Keren and Keren and Raub were replicated although the pattern of the present results is less articulated. The differences in proportions of subjects who posted a hostage under the different hostage rules support the predictions. Let us first consider these subjects who defected in the simple PDG. Fewer subjects posted a hostage in the PCC (31%) than in PTCC (63%) than in the MCC (80%; chi-square=7.10, df=2, $p < 0.03$). The same trend, however, is also significant for all subjects who defected and co-operated in the simple PDG, taken together (46%, 65% and 82%, respectively, chi-square=7.53, df=2, $p < 0.03$). The interaction between the choice in the simple PDG and the hostage posting decision in the PDHG is not significant (chi-square=1.77, df=1, p=0.18).

Among those subjects who defected in the simple PDG (44 individuals), two subjects chose defection in the PDHG after having posted a hostage, and one subject co-operated after having declined to post a hostage in this game. Thus, subjects' hostage posting decisions parallel closely their decisions taken on the second move of the PDHG. This allows to restrict our subsequent analysis to subjects' hostage decisions.

The effects of the transaction costs manipulation and the productive hostages manipulation on hostage posting decisions in the PDHG, are presented in Table 3.

Table 3. Percentage and number of subjects (between brackets) posting a hostage in the PDHG, as a function of transaction costs (TAC) and productive hostages (PH), separately for those subjects who defected in the simple PDG and for all subjects

	TAC		PH		
equilibrium conditions	no	yes	no	yes	All
PCC					
from those defecting in simple PDG	-	-	31 (4)	53 (9)	43 (13)
from all subjects	-	-	46 (11)	64 (18)	56 (29)
PTCC					
from those defecting in simple PDG	65 (17)	47 (17)	56 (19)	54 (15)	55 (34)
from all subjects	69 (36)	43 (24)	56 (30)	56 (30)	56 (60)
MCC					
from those defecting in simple PDG	80 (12)	50 (6)	-	-	67 (18)
from all subjects	82 (23)	46 (13)	-	-	64 (36)
All conditions (in which manipulation took place)					
from those defecting in simple PDG	71 (29)	48 (23)	49 (23)	53 (24)	55 (65)
from all subjects	74 (59)	44 (37)	53 (41)	59 (48)	58 (125)

The effects of the transaction costs manipulation on hostage posting behaviour can be examined for the PTCC and MCC only since it was not introduced in the 'promise credible' condition. The effect is significant for subjects who defected in the first PDG as well as for all subjects. For the former subjects, 71% of them posted a hostage when they did not have to pay the transaction cost for this operation, compared to 48% among those who had to pay for it (chi-square=4.74, df=1, p<0.03). For all subjects, the respective percentages amount to 74% and 44% (chi-square=11.17, df=1, p<0.01).

When the effects of the equilibrium properties factor are removed, the effect of transaction costs remain: the Mantel-Haenszel[4] chi-square=14.68, p<0.01, for subjects who defected in the first PDG; for all subjects the Mantel-Haenszel chi-square=4.21, p=0.04.

All these results indicate that the one-guilder expenditure attached to the transaction of hostage posting (a value that does not change the equilibrium properties of the game), significantly lowers the number of subjects taking advantage of the hostage posting mechanism, as compared to the situation in which this transaction was free of charge.

The effects of the productive hostages manipulation on hostage posting behaviour can be examined for PCC and PTCC only since it was not introduced in the MCC. The effects are not significant, either for these subjects who defected in the first PDG, or for all subjects. Similarly, when controlling for the equilibrium properties, the effects are absent. In other words, a bonus of one guilder (a value that does not change the equilibrium properties of the game) for the use of reactive strategies by both partners, does not encourage subjects to take advantage of the hostage posting option.

When the influence of the productive hostages is removed, the negative effect of transaction costs on the hostage posting decision remains (Mantel-Haenszel chi-square=7.46, p<0.01). When controlling for the influence of the transaction costs, the effect of productive hostages is still absent.

9 Discussion

In the present study, the main results of the research by Raub and Keren (1993) and Keren and Raub (1993) were replicated. In the Prisoner's Dilemma Hostage Game, the more favourable the conditions for posting a hostage, the more subjects do so. The choice between defection and co-operation taken in the simple PDG turned out not to moderate the subsequent hostage posting decisions. Regardless of their choice in the initial PDG, fewer subjects posted a hostage in the PCC than

---

[4] The Mantel-Haenszel statistic tests the association between two binary variables controlling for a stratification variable. In other words, it indicates a relation between A and B when effects of C are removed (cf. Wilkinson, 1990).

in the PTCC. Most subjects, more than 80%, posted a hostage in the MCC. It should be recalled that subjects had been confronted with the defection of the partner in the initial PDG. Therefore, if they played the second time again a simple PDG instead of a PDHG, the percentage of those defecting would be certainly higher than that in the first PDG (55%). This demonstrates the value of the hostage posting as a device to enhance co-operation in social dilemma situations (Schelling, 1960).

Our predictions based on game theory were that neither the transaction costs nor the productive hostages manipulation would have an effect on subjects' tendency to make use of the hostage posting option. The value of both the transaction costs and the bonus for the employment of the reactive strategies was set to 1 guilder, which is too low to change the equilibria. Thus, this manipulation should not affect choice behaviour of rational players. As predicted, the productive hostages manipulation had no effect on subjects' use of the hostage mechanism. Regardless the equilibrium condition and the initial choice in the PDG, an extra reward of one guilder resulting from the bilateral utilization of the reactive strategy did not stimulate subjects to mutual co-operation.

Contrary to our predictions, however, the manipulation of transaction costs proved to have a rather robust effect on subjects' use of the hostage posting mechanism. This effect shows in both equilibrium conditions in which this manipulation took place, *and does not interact with the productive hostages manipulation.* For both subjects who defected in the initial PDG and for all subjects, the 1 guilder expenditure paid to the experimenter for the use of the hostage option, pushed down the percentage of subjects posting a hostage from above 70 to below 50. Since the hostage option is designed to foster co-operation in social dilemmas and consequently to increase individual and collective outcomes, the counterproductive effect of transaction costs is also reflected in subjects earnings. Subjects earned on average about 10% more when the use of hostages was free of charge.

Two issues need consideration. First, why transaction costs significantly discourage people from using hostages even if these costs can be more than compensated by the profits ensuing from co-operation achieved and stabilized due to the hostage mechanism? Second, why transaction costs do discourage people from using hostages, and productive hostages do not stimulate people to take advantage of this mechanism? Regarding both problems, our data allow only to speculate in our endeavours to answer the questions. It is plausible that both effects (or rather, the unexpected effect of transaction costs and, in the context of this effect, the unexpected lack of effect of productive hostages) stem from subjects' attitude toward risk that plays a role in the decision making process (Lopes & Casey, 1994; Leon & Lopes, 1988). Subjects are confronted with uncertainty concerning the partner. Because partner's identity is unknown, equally unknown are his or her social value orientations, intelligence, utility functions, and the resulting behaviour in the games. Thus, even a rational player may under favourable conditions (like in the PTCC combined with the bonus for the mutual use of the reactive strategy) decline to post a hostage because the rationality of the partner can be doubted. The unpredictability of partner's behaviour makes this 1 guilder bonus very uncertain because it will be paid out only if *both* players follow a particular strategy.

Similarly, one guilder transaction costs is something *definitely* lost once a subject decides to post a hostage, and irrespectively of partner's behaviour. In our empirical test of transaction costs so far, these costs were interpreted as enforcement costs paid to the experimenter for monitoring the hostage arrangement; subjects were informed that 'Posting a hostage costs you *always* one guilder due to administration costs, regardless whether you will later get your hostage back or not'. Thus, transaction costs were paid independently not only of subjects' subsequent choice between co-operation and defection and, accordingly, the lot of their hostage (whether it was returned or forfeited), but also independently of the other player's behaviour concerning hostages. In other words, transaction costs were paid *unconditionally*, once a hostage was posted. The significant negative effect of transaction costs on subjects tendency to post a hostage may be due, therefore, to subjects' uncertainty concerning partner's rationality (cf. Deutsch, 1960, 1982; Colman, 1982). Thus, the hostage posting option that implies a certain loss of one guilder transaction costs, and an uncertain chance to get it (or even more) back, may not be regarded as an advantageous option.

Summing up, because of the unpredictability as to partner's behaviour, one guilder transaction costs paid for posting a hostage may be considered as a risky investment, while one guilder received as bonus for the reactive strategy displayed by *both* players may be regarded as a dubious reward.

9.1 Conclusions and Suggestions for further Research

In this paper the main issue addressed is how co-operation in social dilemmas can be achieved and stabilized. For this purpose we referred to the theory of hostage posting developed by Weesie and Raub (in press). Their game-theoretical model describes the conditions that should be fulfilled in order to cause hostage posting effectively enhance co-operation in social dilemmas. Because the empirical test of the hostage posting theory has been restricted so far to the two-person PDG, and the theory lays claim to be applicable to a broad scope of two- as well as *n*-person socials dilemmas, its further empirical test should include other social conflict situations studied in both laboratory and real life.

In a social dilemma in which players cannot discuss the choices they intend to make, voluntarily posting a hostage may play an important function as a means of communication. We call it a signalling effect of a hostage. In addition to the signalling effect itself, a hostage changes the incentive structure such that it binds the player who has posted a hostage to make a particular choice on the second move. For a rational player, the number of choice alternatives becomes thereby restricted. The change in the incentive structure as introduced by the hostage depends on the rules that regulate the hostage institution. Different rules, thus, affect the credibility of the commitment incurred by the act of hostage posting in different ways.

The present research supported the game theoretical prediction, and replicated the original findings by Raub and Keren (1993), and Keren and Raub (1993), that the more favourable the conditions for posting a hostage, the more subjects make use of this option, and consequently, the more co-operation is obtained. The general conclusion is, therefore, that a hostage posting option built into the structure of the Prisoner's Dilemma Game can significantly enhance co-operation. It should be remembered that the PDG is a social dilemma in which it is particularly difficult to establish co-operation because there are two stimuli that simultaneously encourage defection. The first stimulus is *fear* of being exploited by the other player. The second stimulus is *greed* to exploit the other player. Both incentives dictate defection in a one-shot PDG (cf. Bruins, Liebrand & Wilke, 1989; Van Lange, Liebrand & Kuhlman 1990).

Our speculations concerning the effects of transaction costs and their lack regarding productive hostages, need further research. Specifically, with all other elements of the experimental manipulation equal, two modifications can be introduced that affect the risk associated with the uncertainty concerning the decision of the other player. The productive hostages arrangement can be changed from being conditional to unconditional, and the transaction costs arrangement can be changed from unconditional to conditional. Both manipulations diminish the risks associated with the uncertainty concerning the other player and, consequently, make subjects' losses or gains more predictable.

References

Binmore, K. (1994). *Game Theory and the Social Contract (Vol. 1).* Cambridge: MIT Press.

Bruins, J.J., Liebrand, W.B.G. & Wilke, H.A.M. (1989). About the saliency of fear and greed in social dilemmas. *European Journal of Social Psychology, 19*, 155-161.

Colman, A.M. (1982). Game Theory and Experimental Games. Oxford: Pergamon Press.

Dawes, R.M. (1980). Social dilemmas. *Annual Review of Psychology, 31*, 169-193.

Deutsch, M. (1960). The effect of motivational orientation upon trust and suspicion. *Human Relations, 13*, 122-139.

Deutsch, M. (1982). Interdependence and psychological orientation. In V.J. Derlega & J. Grzelak (Eds), *Cooperation and Helping Behaviour*. New York: Academic Press.

Granovetter, M.S. (1985). Economic action and social structure: The problem of embeddedness. *American Journal of Sociology, 91*, 481-510.

Hardin, G. (1968). The tragedy of the commons. *Science, 162*, 1243-1248.

Keren, G. & Raub, W. (1993). Resolving social conflicts through hostage posting: Theoretical and empirical considerations. *Journal of Experimental Psychology, 122*, 429-448.

Leon, O.G. & Lopes, L.L. (1988). Risk preference and feedback. *Bulletin of the Psychonomic Society, 26*, 343-346.

Lopes, L.L & Casey, J.T. (1994). Tactical and strategic responsiveness in a competitive risk-taking game. *Acta Psychologica, 85*, 39-60.

Luce, R.D. & Raiffa, H. (1985). *Games and Decisions: Introduction and Critical Survey.* New York: Dover Publications.

Messick, D.M. & Brewer, M.B. (1983). Solving social dilemmas: A review. In I. Wheeler & P. Shaver (Eds.), *Review of Personality and Social Psychology (Vol. 4)* (pp. 11-44). Beverly Hills: Sage.

Nash, J. (1951). Non-cooperative games. *Annals of Mathematics, 54*, 289-295.

Ostrom, E. (1990). *Governing the Commons. The Evolution of Institutions for Collective Action.* Cambridge: Cambridge University Press.

Rapoport, A. (1974). Prisoner's Dilemma: Recollections and observations. In A. Rapoport (Ed.). *Game Theory as a Theory of Conflict Resolution.* Dordrecht: Reidel.

Raub, W. & Keren, G. (1993). Hostages as a commitment device: A game-theoretic model and an empirical test of some scenarios. *Journal of Economic Behavior and Organization, 21*, 43-67.

Raub, W. & Weesie, J. (1992). *The management of matches: Decentralized mechanisms for cooperative relations with applications to organizations and households.* Mimeo, Department of Sociology, Utrecht University, The Netherlands.

Schelling, T.C. (1960). *The Strategy of Conflict.* London: Oxford University Press.

Selten, R. (1965). Spieltheoretische Behandlung eines Ologopolmodells mit Nachfrageträgheit. *Zeitschrift für die gesamte Staatawissenschaft, 121,* 301-324.

Van Lange P.A.M., Liebrand W.B.G. & Kuhlman, D.M. (1990). Causal attribution of choice behaviour in three *N*-person prisoner's dilemma. *Journal of Experimental Social Psychology, 26,* 34-48.

Weesie, J. & Raub, W. (in press). *Private ordering: A comparative institutional analysis of hostage games.* Forthcoming in Journal of Mathematical Sociology.

Williamson, O.E. (1985). *The Economic Institutions of Capitalism.* New York: Free Press.

Wilkinson, L. (1990). *SYSTAT: The System for Statistics*, Evanston, IL: SYSTAT, Inc.

The Effect of Threshold Level on Greed, Fear, and Cooperation in Step-level Give-some and Take-some Dilemmas

Matthijs Poppe and Machteld Zwikker[1]

[1] Department of Psychology, Tilburg University,
P.O. Box 90153, 5000 LE Tilburg, the Netherlands

Abstract. An experiment is described in which 61 subjects made choices in nine trials of a give-some game as well as in nine trials of a take some game. Dependent on the trial 10 to 90 percent of the participants had to make a cooperative choice (contributing money in the give some game; not taking money in the take some game) in order to obtain a bonus for all participants. On the basis of the subjects' choices and their expectations about the choices of other participants subjects' greed, fear, solidarity and sense of duty were assessed. If a low percentage of the participants had to make a cooperative choice to obtain the bonus, subjects were more cooperative in the give some game than in the take some game while the opposite was the case if a high percentage of the participants had to make a cooperative choice. Whether the level of greed or fear was higher depended on the type of game and the percentage of cooperative choices required.

Keywords. Step-level dilemmas, give-some dilemmas, take-some dilemmas, threshold level, greed, fear.

1 Introduction

In many situations the decisions people make affect not only the decision maker's outcomes but also those of one or more other persons. An important category of such situations are social dilemmas. In the simplest form of a social dilemma, a person chooses between two alternatives. One alternative gives the decision maker higher outcomes than the other alternative. However, if many or all members of a group or organization or larger aggregate of people who are interdependent choose this alternative, the outcomes for everyone involved are low (Hardin, 1968; Dawes, 1980). Two types of social dilemmas can be distinguished (Dawes, 1980). In one type, the give-some dilemma or public good

---

[1] We thank the editors and an anonymous reviewer for valuable comments on an earlier version of this chapter.

dilemma, a minimum number of people have to contribute in order to obtain a public good for all (Olson, 1965). People who live in an area that is often threatened by floods, can protect themselves by building a dike. Not contributing to the construction costs each person less than contributing, but once the dike has been built everybody in the area is safe, including those who did not contribute. However, if not enough contributions to the construction of the dike are made, there will be no dike and all the people in the area will be in danger of losing their property and drowning. In the other type, the take-some dilemma or the commons dilemma (Hardin, 1968), there is a shared, often natural resource people can take from. Catching a lot of fish is more profitable than not catching them. However, if too many fishermen do so, the total number of fish in the ocean will decrease, and in the extreme may even become extinct.

Give-some and take-some dilemmas often have the structure of a step-level dilemma. Step-level dilemmas differ from linear dilemmas (Komorita & Parks, 1995). In a linear dilemma the value of the common good varies directly with the total amount the participants contribute or take. In a step-level dilemma there is an all-or-nothing relationship between the cooperation of the participants and the provision of a fixed bonus: only if enough participants are cooperative, a bonus is provided. Unlike the linear dilemma the step-level dilemma has an optimal level of contribution. In a step-level give-some dilemma (Frohlich & Oppenheimer, 1970; Van de Kragt, Orbell, & Dawes, 1983), at least a certain percentage of the group members have to contribute money (or at least a certain percentage of the money the group members started with, has to be contributed) to a common pool in order to obtain a bonus for all the group members, including those who did not contribute. In a step-level take-some dilemma (Rutte, Wilke, & Messick, 1987; Messick, Allison, & Samuelson, 1988), a certain percentage of the group members can take money from a common pool (or a certain percentage of the money in the pool can be taken) without forfeiting a bonus for all the group members, including those who took from the pool. The percentage of group members that have to be cooperative (to give money in a give-some dilemma or to refrain from taking money in a take-some dilemma) in order to get the bonus is called the threshold level.

At least three questions suggest themselves with regard to step-level give-some dilemmas and take-some dilemmas: (1) are people more cooperative at a low, an intermediate, or a high threshold level; (2) are people more cooperative in give-some or in take-some dilemmas; and (3) *why* people are (non)cooperative in give-some and take-some dilemmas.

1.1 Threshold level

The question of the threshold level at which people are more cooperative cannot be answered easily. Presumably, the expectation that enough people will cooperate declines as the threshold level increases. This sets up at least two conflicting forces: one realizes that there is an increasing need for more people to be cooperative, but one does not want to waste one's contribution or to have refrained from taking money in vain. Which of the two forces dominates can be examined only in experiments with two or more threshold levels. Dawes, Orbell, Simmons, and Van de Kragt (1986) found that 51.4 percent of the subjects contributed in a give-some dilemma if at least three out of seven group members (threshold level 43 percent) had to contribute in order to obtain a bonus and 64.3 percent if at least five group members (threshold level 71 percent) had to contribute. This difference is not significant ($p > .07$). In an experiment conducted by Suleiman and Rapoport (1992), the five subjects in a group had to contribute on an average at least 40, 60, or 80 percent of the endowments they had received in order to obtain a bonus. In these three conditions, the subjects contributed 53.0, 65.8, and 73.4 percent of their endowments, respectively. The authors did not report whether these differences were significant. In a series of five different experiments by Poppe (1988) subjects made six or nine choices. The threshold levels were at equal steps between 14 and 86 percent (for six choices) or 10 and 90 percent (for nine choices). In one experiment, no effect of threshold level on cooperation was found. In four experiments, there was a curvilinear relation of the percentage of subjects contributing and the threshold level, such that subjects were most cooperative at the threshold level of (about) 40 percent. The decrease in cooperation found in these experiments from a threshold level of (about) 40 percent to higher thresholds is in contrast to the increase found in the experiments of Dawes et al. (1986) and Suleiman and Rapoport (1992). In general, all these experiments involved give-some dilemmas, leaving open the question of the relation of cooperation and threshold levels in take-some dilemmas.

1.2 Give-some and take-some dilemmas

In order to determine whether people are more cooperative in give-some or in take-some dilemmas, Rutte et al. (1987) designed a give-some and a take-some step-level dilemma that were equivalent in payoff structure. The subjects participated in groups of six (or five, but then the amounts of money were adjusted). In the give-some dilemma, the subjects started with an endowment of 9 (Dutch) guilders. Each group member decided how much he or she contributed (between 0 and 9 guilders) to a common pool. If the group members together contributed at least 27 guilders, each of them could keep what was left of the endowment. If there were less than 27 guilders in the pool, all the subjects were fined and lost the entire amount of 9 guilders. In the take-some dilemma, the subjects were told that there were 27 guilders available for the six members of the group. Each member could take between 0 and 9 guilders. If the six group members together took more than 27 guilders, no member got anything. If the six group members took 27 guilders or less, each member could keep what he or she had taken. So, in both the give-some and the take-some dilemma, the threshold level was 50 percent. Messick et al. (1988) performed a similar experiment with groups of four subjects. In this experiment the threshold level was also 50 percent, both in the give-some and in the take-some dilemma. Neither in the experiment of Rutte et al. nor in the experiment of Messick et al. was a significant difference in cooperation found between the give-some and take-some dilemma.

Brewer and Kramer (1986), Komorita (1987), Komorita and Carnevale (1992) and McDaniel and Sistrunk (1991) also tried to answer the question whether people are more or less cooperative in give-some than in take-some dilemmas, but they did not use step-level dilemmas. In an experiment with a replenishable source, Brewer and Kramer (1986) found that, overall, subjects in the take-some dilemma were more cooperative than those in the give-some dilemma. However, this general conclusion was qualified by other variables. In the first of a series of experiments with N-person prisoner's dilemma games, Komorita (1987) found more cooperation in the give-some dilemma and, in a second experiment (Komorita & Carnevale, 1992), more cooperation in the take-some dilemma. In a third experiment (Komorita & Carnevale, 1992), it turned out that it was important whether the subjects trusted the others. If subjects had met the others (under the impression that they were the other group members) before they made their decisions, they were more cooperative in the give-some dilemma. McDaniel and Sistrunk (1991) conducted an experiment in which subjects could indicate on a six-point scale how willing they were to contribute in a give-some dilemma or to take in a take-some dilemma. In general, subjects were more willing to be cooperative in the give-some dilemma than in the take-some dilemma, especially if they had been informed that probably 50 or more percent of the participants would contribute. However, the interpretation of these results is hampered by the fact that the researchers had framed the two dilemmas differently: the give-some dilemma was presented as a scenario describing the formation of an agricultural cooperative and the take-some dilemma as a scenario about milk production. So, it is not clear to what extent the results were determined by the structure (give-some or take-some) or the content (agricultural cooperative or milk production) of the dilemma.

No clear conclusion can be drawn from the literature as to whether people are more cooperative in give-some or in take-some dilemma. The results of the experiments with dilemmas unlike step-level dilemmas are inconclusive. In the two experiments with step-level dilemmas, the level of cooperation in the give-some dilemma did not differ from that in the take-some dilemma. However, in both experiments only a threshold level was 50 percent was used. It is to be examined whether the conclusion is the same if one or more different threshold levels are used.

Table 1. Motives for (non)cooperation

	Expectation		
	Not enough others are cooperative	Enough -1 others are cooperative	Enough others are cooperative
Subject does not cooperate	*Fear*	*Irrationality*	*Greed*
Subject cooperates	*Sense of duty*	*Cruciality*	*Solidarity*

1.3 Greed and fear

The third question about social dilemmas concerns the reasons people may act (non)cooperatively. Usually, two reasons or motives for *defection* are distinguished: greed and fear (Dawes, 1980; Komorita & Parks, 1995). There is greed if one expects that enough others will be cooperative and there is no need to cooperate in order to create or to preserve the common good. Thus, it is possible to take a free ride. If one does not cooperate because of the expectation that not enough others will be cooperative there is fear of being gypped, being taken advantage of or wasting one's contribution[2].

It is also possible to focus on reasons or motives why people are *cooperative* in a social dilemma (Lynn & Oldenquist, 1986). Elster (1989) recognizes social norms which are conditional (like fairness) or nonconditional (like the Kantian norm) upon the cooperation of others. In this perspective, solidarity and a sense of duty can be distinguished (Poppe, 1988). There is solidarity if one expects that enough others will be cooperative so that the common good will be created or preserved, and one cooperates because one does not feel that only others should bear the costs or suffer the disadvantages. There is a sense of duty if one

---

[2] It should be noted that greed and fear are considered here as motives or reasons for noncooperation. In other studies (e.g. Coombs, 1973; Harris, 1969) greed and fear are considered as characteristics of the payoff structure.

expects that not enough others will be cooperative so the common good will not be created or preserved but one cooperates nonetheless because one is of the opinion that people must be cooperative in such a dilemma regardless of what others do. A third reason for cooperation is cruciality. There is cruciality if one expects that enough others save one will be cooperative and therefore by cooperating there will be just enough cooperators to create the public good or to preserve the common good. Not contributing in this case is irrational because everybody would obtain higher outcomes if one cooperated than if one did not cooperate. The three reasons for defection and the three reasons for cooperation are displayed in Table 1.

In several studies, researchers have tried to find out whether greed or fear is the more important reason for defection. In experiments with step-level dilemmas, give-some dilemmas were always used to answer this question. Most experiments consisted of a normal give-some dilemma and two half-dilemmas. Whether greed or fear was more important was determined by comparing the choices of a group of subjects in the normal give-some dilemma (the greed-fear dilemma) with the choices of two groups of subjects in two half-dilemmas. The structure of one half-dilemma (the no-greed dilemma) was such that there was no incentive for defection: subjects could waste their contributions but could not profit from others' contributions. In the other half-dilemma (the no-fear dilemma) there was no reason for fear: the subjects received a guarantee that they would get their money back if not enough others were cooperative. Dawes et al. (1986) found that greed was more important than fear. This was the case with threshold levels of 43 and 71 percent. Rapoport and Ested-Levy (1989), using a threshold level of 60 percent, found that both greed and fear were important, but greed more so than fear. In conditions in which the subjects received an endowment from the experimenter (as in the other experiments) Van Avermaet and Van Nieuwkerke (1989) found that both greed and fear were important. But in their experiment, in which the threshold level was 71 percent, fear was more important than greed. Further, Van Lange, Liebrand, Kiers and Zwaal (1989) using a threshold level of 80 percent found that fear was more important than greed. In five experiments conducted by Poppe (1988), greed and fear were assessed on the basis of the expectation and the choice, as described above. In these experiments, the threshold levels varied from (about) 10 percent to (about) 90 percent. If the threshold was lower than about 50 percent, greed was more important than fear, but if the threshold was higher than about 50 percent, fear was more important than greed.

In experiments in which dilemmas unlike step-level dilemmas were used, Bruins, Liebrand, and Wilke (1989) found that greed and fear were equally important. However, Komorita, Sweeney, and Kravitz (1980) and Poppe and Utens (1986) found that greed was more important than fear, while Yamagishi and Sato (1986) found the opposite.

In general, the results of experiments in which dilemmas unlike step-level dilemmas were used are quite confusing. With respect to the step-level dilemmas, it seems that greed is more important than fear if the threshold level is lower than 50 or 60 percent and that fear is more important than greed if the threshold level is higher than 50 or 60 percent. However, not all results fit into this pattern (e.g., the result of Dawes et al. (1986) at a threshold level of 71 percent). In any case, this conclusion is based on the results of experiments which are different in many respects, such as group size and endowment. But these experiments have one characteristic in common: all are about give-some dilemmas and not about take-some dilemmas. It would therefore be useful to perform an experiment using both a give-some and a take-some step-level dilemma with different threshold levels.

Consequently, there were three interrelated objectives in the present study. The first was to find out at which threshold level people are more cooperative in step-level give-some and take-some dilemmas. The second objective was to determine whether people are more cooperative in give-some or in take-some dilemmas and to find out whether the threshold level is of importance in this respect. The third objective was to study why people are (non)cooperative at different threshold levels of give-some and take-some dilemmas.

2 Method

2.1 Subjects

The materials for the experiment were sent to 78 students of Tilburg University who had not yet taken a course in social psychology and who had signed up to participate in an experiment on choice behavior. The students were told that they could earn a maximum of f 10 (about $ 6), but that the actual amount of money depended on their choices. Forms were returned by 14 male and 47 female students (age 19 to 27 years). At the end of the experiment, all subjects were paid f 10.

2.2 Design

The experiment had a 2 x 2 x (2 x 9) design. Besides gender of the subject, the order of presentation of the dilemmas was an independent between-subjects variable. Half of the students to whom the materials were sent were asked first to make choices in the give-some dilemma and then in the take-some dilemma. The other half were given the materials in the reverse order. The within-subjects variables were dilemma (give-some and take-some) and threshold level. In each of nine trials, a different percentage of participants had to make a cooperative choice (giving in the give-some dilemma or not-taking in the take-some dilemma) in order to obtain a bonus for all participants. The dependent variables were cooperation, expectation (whether enough others would be cooperative) and, derived from cooperation and expectation, the motives for making a (non)-cooperative choice: greed, irrationality, fear, solidarity, cruciality, and duty.

Table 2. Outcomes for (not) giving and (not) taking

Give-some dilemma

	Not enough others give	Enough others give
Subject gives	*f* 0	*f* 2
Subject does not give	*f* 1	*f* 3

Take-some dilemma

	Too many others take	Not too many others take
Subject does not take	*f* 0	*f* 2
Subject takes	*f* 1	*f* 3

2.3 Materials and procedure

The subjects received instructions for the give-some and for the take-some dilemma. The instructions for the first dilemma the subjects were presented with were as follows (instruction for the give-some game; between brackets instructions for the take-some game): 'In this part of the experiment you are going to make decisions in a number of trials. There are nine trials. Each trial can result in your getting money. After the experiment, one of the trials will be selected randomly. You will be paid the outcomes of that trial. About a hundred students at this university are participating in the experiment.

At the beginning of each trial you will get one guilder. The decision is:
- either you keep the guilder for yourself
- or you contribute the guilder to a common pool.
[- either you take one guilder from a common pool
- or you do not take one guilder from a common pool.]
In each trial a certain percentage (X %) of the participants [(Y %) of participants] will be announced. The payment rules are as follows:
If in a trial at least X % of all participants contribute a guilder to the pool, every participant (including those who did not contribute a guilder to the pool) will receive a bonus of two guilders. If in a trial less than X % of all participants contribute a guilder to the pool, nobody will receive a bonus (and those who contributed a guilder to the pool will lose their contribution). [If in a trial at most Y % of all participants take a guilder from the pool, every participant (including those who took a guilder from the pool) will receive a bonus of two guilders. If in a trial more than Y % of all participants take a guilder from the pool, nobody will receive a bonus (but those who took a guilder from the pool can keep it).]'

Then a schedule with the outcomes (see Table 2) was explained. In addition, an illustration of the possible consequences of the two alternatives was described. The instructions continued: 'Your decision to contribute or not [to take or not] in a certain trial should be made known on the following pages. You should also mention the percentage of the 100 participants that you expect to contribute [take] a guilder. We want to find out how well people can predict the choices others make. Therefore, we ask you to make your prediction as accurate as possible. The ten participants who make the most accurate predictions in this part of the experiment will each receive an additional bonus of f 5.'

The instructions for the second dilemma the subjects were presented with were almost identical. Only the phrasing of the first sentences was slightly adapted (e.g., '*Also* in this part of the experiment ..'). In the nine trials of the give-some, dilemma X was 40, 70, 10, 60, 90, 30, 50, 80, and 20 percent, respectively; in the nine trials of the take-some dilemma, Y was 30, 90, 60, 10, 70, 40, 20, 80 and 50, respectively. The order of the trials in the two dilemmas was almost, but not completely identical to prevent subjects from copying decisions. If 100 - Y = X, then the threshold levels in the take-some dilemma and the give-some dilemma are the same. In that case the two trials in the give-some dilemma and the take-some dilemma can be compared because in both dilemmas the same percentage of cooperative subjects is required to obtain the bonus.

Subjects were asked not to consult others before making their decisions. Further, they were requested to fill out the forms in the order indicated on the forms. Subjects were randomly assigned to the order condition. Subjects returned 30 forms of the give-some take-some order and 31 forms of the reverse order. At the same time, the subjects returned a form with their name, address, and bank account number in order to make payment possible. Some weeks after the experiment, a letter was sent to the subjects explaining more about the experiment and informing the subjects about some of the results.

3 Results

The first issue which will be dealt with is how cooperative the subjects were in the two dilemmas. This will be followed by a report on the percentage of the subjects who expected that enough others would behave cooperatively so that all participants could obtain a bonus. Lastly, the importance of greed, irrationality, fear, solidarity, cruciality, and duty as motives for (non)cooperation in the give-some and take-some dilemma will be described.

(M)ANOVA F-tests were used in the analysis of the dichotomous data. In several studies (e.g. Seeger & Gabrielson, 1968), no strong objections to this procedure were found. To be on the safe side, a second series of analyses was performed in which the nine trials were divided into three groups: low threshold trials (10, 20, or 30 percent cooperation required), medium threshold trials (40, 50, or 60 percent cooperation required) and high threshold trials (70, 80, or 90 percent cooperation required). The dependent variable was the number of cooperative decisions (from 0 to 3) in a group of trials. The results of the analyses of these scores did not lead to different conclusions. Therefore, only the results of the analyses on the dichotomous data will be presented.[3]

The analyses were preceded by analyses which included gender as an additional independent variable. Because the gender variable showed no significant main effects or interaction effects with dilemma or threshold level or both, this variable was excluded from further analyses.

3.1 Cooperation

The percentages of cooperative choices in each of the nine trials of the give-some and the take-some dilemma are shown in Figure 1A. An ANOVA was performed with order, dilemma and threshold level as independent variables and cooperation (contributing in the give-some dilemma or not-taking in the take-some dilemma) as the dependent variable. The ANOVA showed a significant effect of dilemma: in the give-some dilemma (M = 44.6 %), the subjects were more cooperative ($F(1,59) = 5.35$; $p < .01$) than in the take-some dilemma (M = 37.3 %). This effect of dilemma was qualified by a significant interaction effect ($F(1,59) = 8.48$; $p < .01$) of dilemma and order of presentation. In both dilemmas, the subjects were more cooperative if the give-some dilemma was presented first. No significant main effect of threshold level was found ($F(8,472) = 1.40$; $p > .15$), but there was a significant interaction effect ($F(8,472) = 14.26$;

[3] Both in the give-some and in the take-some dilemma, each triplet of successive trials consisted of one low threshold trial, one medium threshold trial, and one high threshold trial. Because the results of the analyses of the three groups of trials did not differ substantially from those of the nine separate trials, it can be concluded that the (small) differences in the order of trials in the give-some and the take-some did not matter.

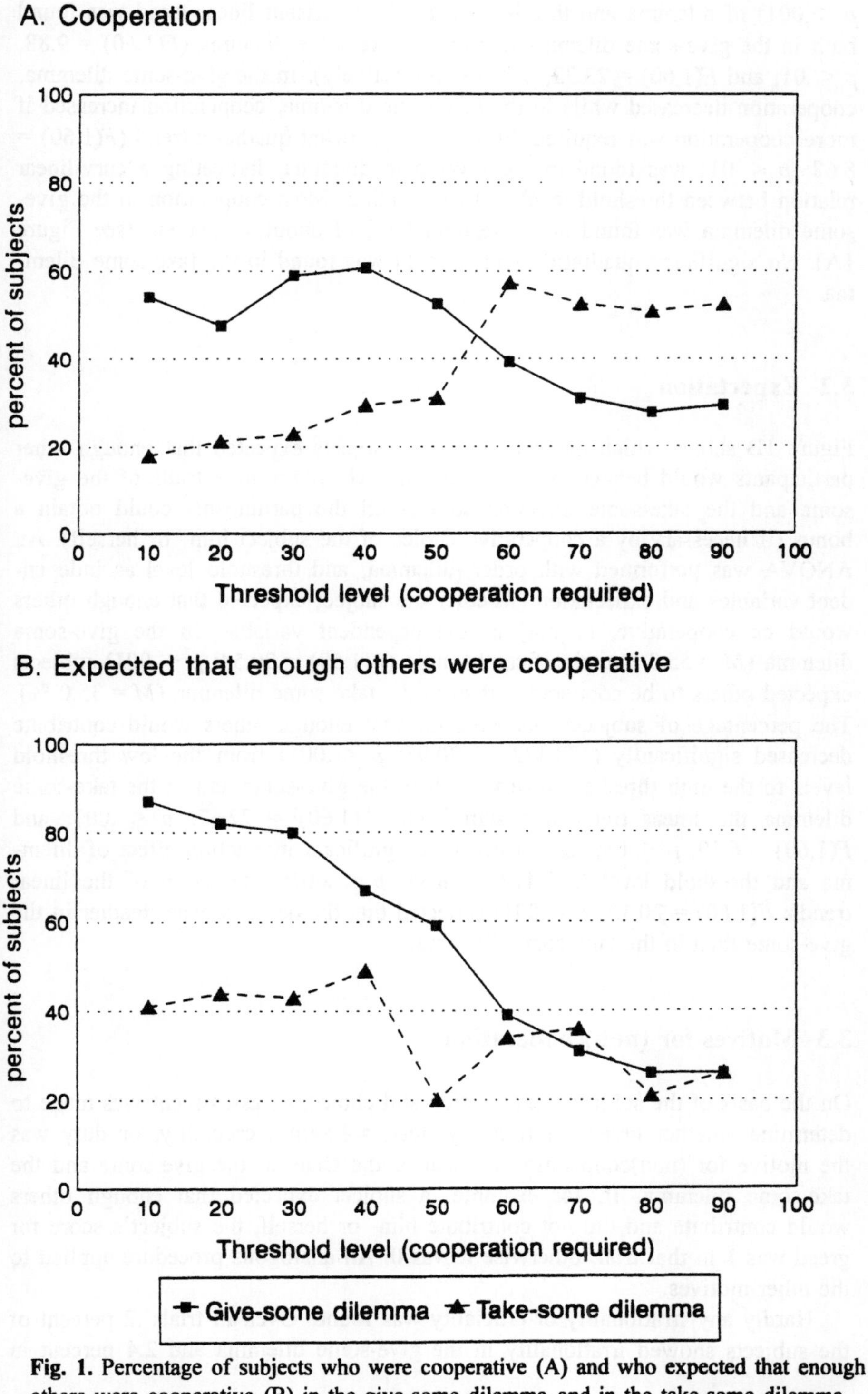

Fig. 1. Percentage of subjects who were cooperative (A) and who expected that enough others were cooperative (B) in the give-some dilemma and in the take-some dilemma.

$p < .001$) of dilemma and threshold level. A significant linear trend was found both in the give-some dilemma and in the take-some dilemma ($F(1,60) = 9.88$, $p < .01$; and $F(1,60) = 23.32$, $p < .01$, respectively). In the give-some dilemma, cooperation decreased while in the take-some dilemma, cooperation increased if more cooperation was required. Further, a significant quadratic trend ($F(1,60) = 8.68$; $p < .01$) was found in the give-some dilemma, indicating a curvilinear relation between threshold level and cooperation. Most cooperation in the give-some dilemma was found at a threshold level of about 40 percent (see Figure 1A). No significant quadratic trend ($F < 1$) was found in the take-some dilemma.

3.2 Expectation

Figure 1B shows which percentage of the subjects expected that enough other participants would behave cooperatively in each of the nine trials of the give-some and the take-some dilemma so that all the participants could obtain a bonus (if necessary by a cooperative choice of the subject him- or herself). An ANOVA was performed with order, dilemma, and threshold level as independent variables and expectation (whether the subject expected that enough others would be cooperative, or not) as the dependent variable. In the give-some dilemma ($M = 55.3$ %), significantly more ($F(1,59) = 30.54$; $p < .001$) subjects expected others to be cooperative than in the take-some dilemma ($M = 35.0$ %). The percentage of subjects that expected that enough others would contribute decreased significantly ($F(8,472) = 20.95$; $p < .001$) from the low threshold levels to the high threshold levels. Both in the give-some and in the take-some dilemma the linear trend was significant ($F(1,60) = 77.67$, $p < .001$; and $F(1,60) = 6.19$, $p < .05$, respectively). A significant interaction effect of dilemma and threshold level ($F(8,472) = 8.35$; $p < .001$; interaction of the linear trends: $F(1,60) = 20.15$; $p < .001$) reflected that the decrease was steadier in the give-some than in the take-some dilemma.

3.3 Motives for (non)cooperation

On the basis of the subject's expectation and choice, an assessment was made to determine whether greed, irrationality, fear, solidarity, cruciality, or duty was the motive for (non)cooperation in each of the trials of the give-some and the take-some dilemma. If, for example, a subject expected that enough others would contribute and did not contribute him- or herself, the subject's score for greed was 1 in that trial; otherwise it was 0. An analogous procedure applied to the other motives.

Hardly any irrationality or cruciality was found. Over all trials .2 percent of the subjects showed irrationality in the give-some dilemma and 2.4 percent in the take-some dilemma. The percentages of cruciality were .0 and 1.3, respectively. Because these percentages are very low, no further analyses were performed on cruciality and irrationality.

3.3.1 Greed and fear

One of the questions underlying this experiment is whether greed or fear is the more important reason for defection in give-some and take-some dilemmas. To answer that question, the greed and fear scores were analyzed in an ANOVA with motive (greed or fear), dilemma, order, and threshold level as independent variables. It should be noted that the sum of the greed and fear scores is the score of defection. So, effects not including motive have already been reported in the description of the (non)cooperation results.

A significant main effect of motive ($F(1,59) = 20.06$; $p < .001$), but no significant interaction effect of dilemma and motive ($F < 1$) were found. Averaged over all threshold levels, subjects showed more fear than greed, both in the give-some dilemma and in the take-some dilemma (see Figure 2). The main effect of motive was qualified by significant interaction effects of threshold level and motive ($F(8,472) = 19.68$; $p < .001$), dilemma, threshold level, and motive ($F(8,472) = 7.50$; $p < .001$) and dilemma, order, threshold level, and motive ($F(8,472) = 2.09$; $p < .05$). Because the latter two interaction effects imply that the effect of threshold level on greed and fear are different in the two dilemmas, ANOVAs with order, threshold level, and motive were performed for the give-some and take-some dilemma separately.

Give-some dilemma. In the give-some dilemma, the subjects generally showed more ($F(1,59) = 24.40$; $p < .001$) fear ($M = 38.8$ %) than greed ($M = 16.4$ %). However, a significant ($F(8,472) = 26.36$; $p < .001$) interaction effect of threshold level and motive indicated that the greed/fear ratio differs at different threshold levels. As can be seen in Figure 2A, greed decreased from the low to the medium and high threshold levels while fear increased substantially. These two tendencies were stronger when the subjects were presented with the take-some dilemma first and then with the give-some dilemma than when the order of presentation was the reverse (interaction effect of order, threshold level and motive: $F(8,472) = 3.00$; $p < .01$).

Take-some dilemma. In the take-some dilemma, the subjects also showed more ($F(1,59) = 7.70$; $p < .01$) fear ($M = 38.8$ %) than greed ($M = 20.8$ %). A significant interaction effect ($F(8,472) = 3.05$; $p < .01$) indicated that this difference was not the same at different threshold levels. As can be seen in Figure 2B, at the low threshold level, there was no difference between the importance of greed and fear, but at the medium and high threshold level, fear was more important than greed.

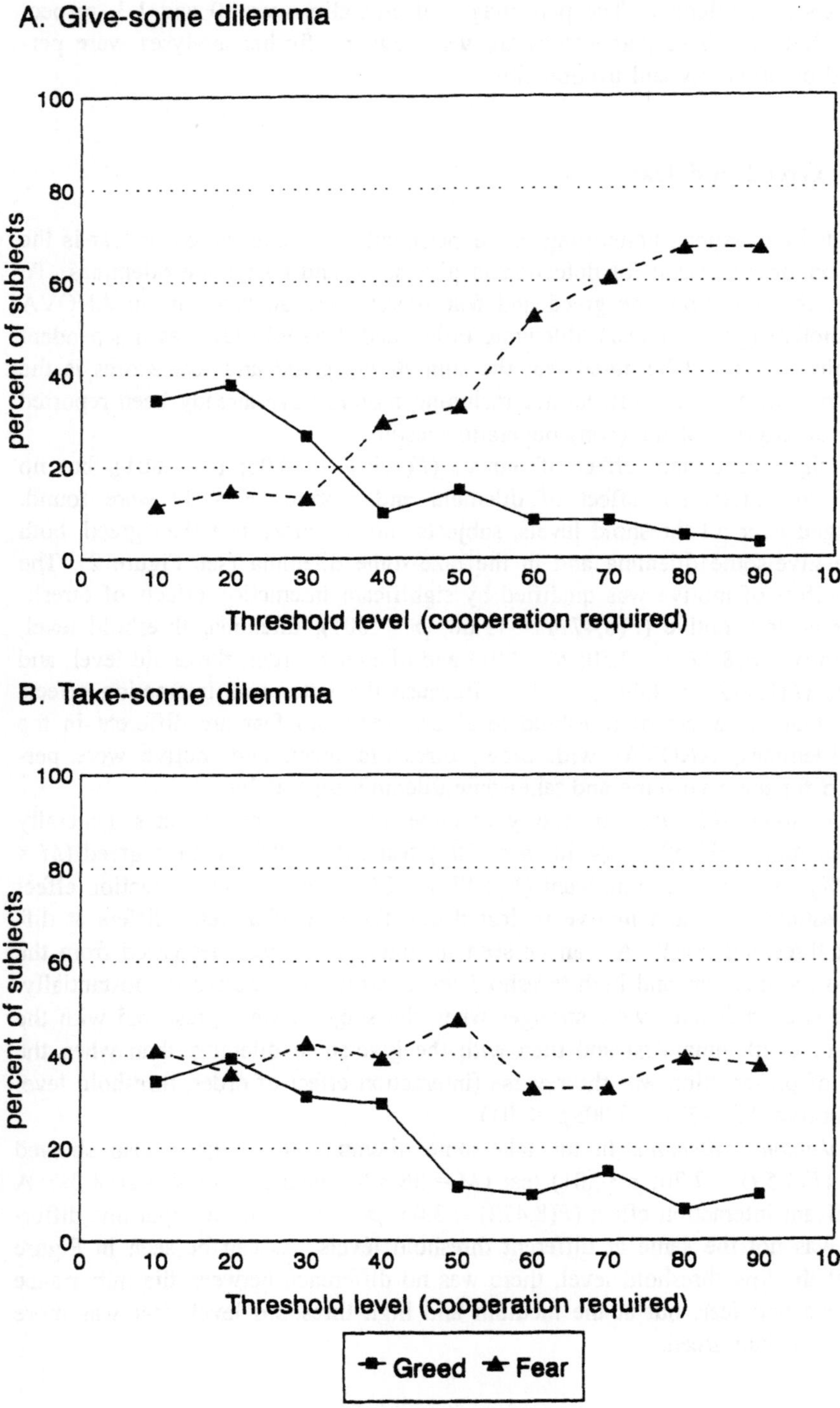

Fig. 2. Percentage of subjects who showed greed (A) and fear (B) in the give-some and in the take-some dilemma.

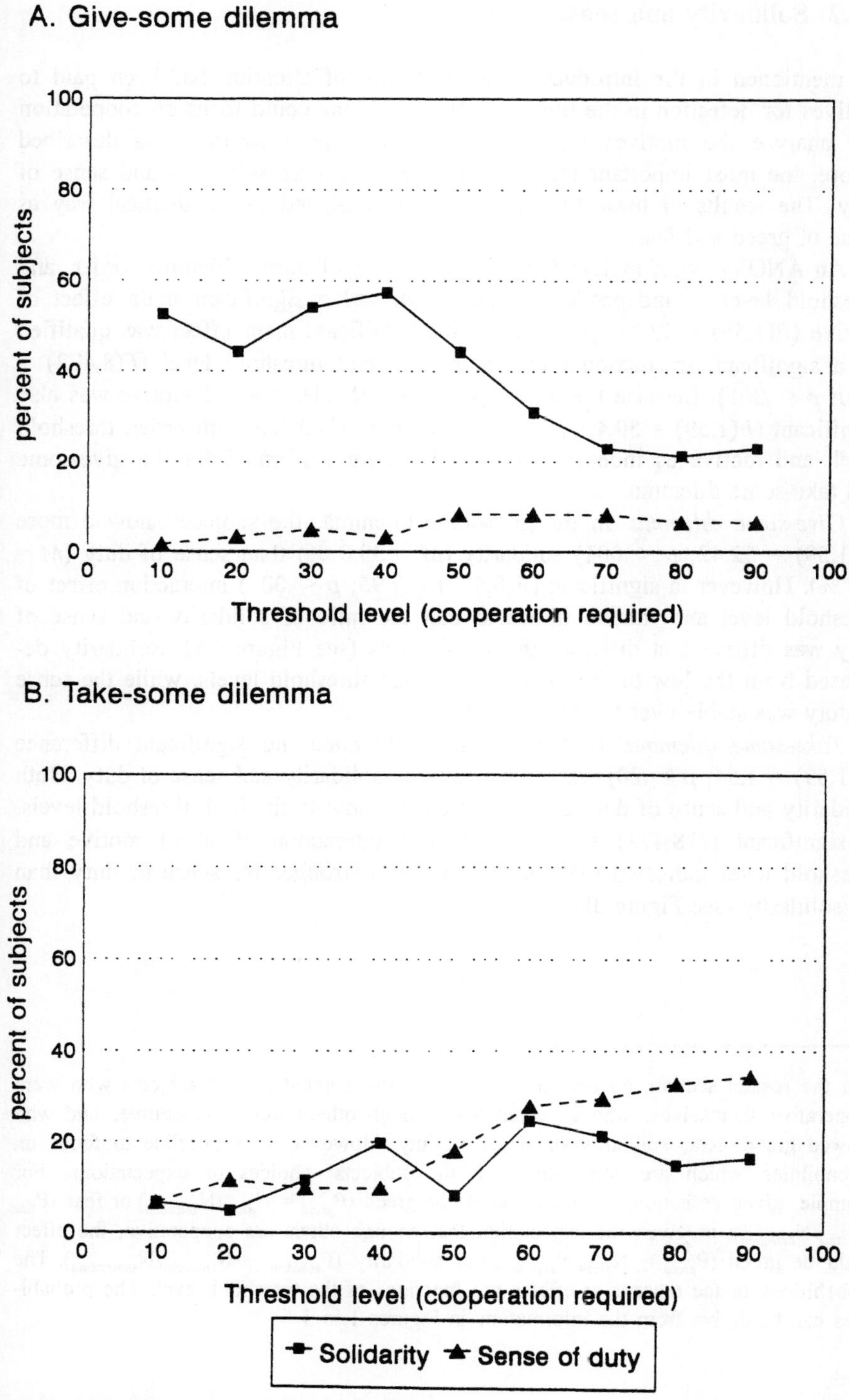

Fig. 3. Percentage of subjects who showed solidarity (A) and sense of duty (B) in the give-some and in the take-some dilemma.

3.3.2 Solidarity and sense of duty

As mentioned in the introduction, a great deal of attention has been paid to motives for defection in the literature. However, one could focus on cooperation and analyze the motives for cooperation in social dilemmas. As described before, the most important reasons for cooperation are solidarity and sense of duty. The results of these two motives were analyzed in an identical way as those of greed and fear.

An ANOVA with motive (solidarity or sense of duty), dilemma, order, and threshold level as independent variables showed a significant main effect of motive ($F(1,59) = 13.31$; $p < .001$). This significant main effect was qualified by a significant interaction effect of motive and threshold level ($F(8,472) = 7.70$; $p < .001$). Because the interaction effect of dilemma and motive was also significant ($F(1,59) = 50.49$; $p < .001$), separate ANOVAs with order, threshold level, and motive as independent variables were performed for the give-some and take-some dilemma.

Give-some dilemma. In the give-some dilemma, the subjects showed more ($F(1,59) = 52.42$; $p < .001$) solidarity ($M = 39.0$ %) than sense of duty ($M = 5.7$ %). However, a significant ($F(8,472) = 7.95$; $p < .001$) interaction effect of threshold level and motive indicated that the ratio of solidarity and sense of duty was different at different threshold levels (see Figure 3A). Solidarity decreased from the low to the medium and high threshold levels, while the sense of duty was stable over the threshold levels.

Take-some dilemma. In the take-some dilemma, no significant difference ($F(1,59) = 1.54$; $p > .20$) was found between solidarity and sense of duty. Both solidarity and sense of duty increased from the low to the high threshold levels. A significant ($F(8,472) = 2.22$; $p < .05$) interaction effect of motive and threshold level indicated that the increase was stronger for sense of duty than for solidarity (see Figure 3B)[4].

---

[4] In the results section, an account is given of the percentages of subjects who were cooperative themselves, who expected that enough others were cooperative, and who showed greed, fear, solidarity or sense of duty. However, it is possible to focus on probabilities which are conditioned on the subjects' choices or expectations. For example, given defection, the reason could be greed ($P_{greed} = N_{greed}/N_{defection}$) or fear ($P_{fear} = N_{fear}/N_{defection}$); or given the expectation that enough others are cooperative, the effect could be greed ($P_{greed} = N_{greed}/N_{expectation}$) or solidarity ($P_{solidarity} = N_{solidarity}/N_{expectation}$). The probabilities of the reasons or effects are functions of the threshold level. The probabilities can be derive from the information in Figures 1 to 3.

4 Discussion

Three interrelated questions were addressed in this experiment. One question was whether people are more cooperative in a give-some or in a take-some dilemma. If the data are averaged over all threshold levels, the results are quite clear: subjects were more cooperative in the give-some dilemma than in the take-some dilemma. However, if the threshold levels are taken into account, the conclusion is different. If the cooperation of 50 % or less of the participants was needed to secure the bonus, subjects were more cooperative in the give-some dilemma while they were more cooperative in the take-some dilemma if the cooperation of at least 60 percent of the participants was needed. So, the turning point is between the threshold levels of 50 and 60 percent. This is close to the threshold level of 50 percent which Rutte et al. (1987) and Messick et al. (1988) used in their experiments. This could explain why these researchers did not find a significant difference between the cooperation of the subjects in the give-some dilemma and the cooperation of those in the take-some dilemma.

Another question underlying this experiment was whether people are more cooperative at low, intermediate, or high threshold levels. If the give-some and take-some dilemmas are combined, the answer is that is does not matter what the threshold level is: cooperation did not vary significantly over trials. However, if the give-some dilemma and the take-some dilemma are considered separately, the answer is different. In the take-some dilemma, most cooperation was found at the threshold level of 60 percent. However, the curvilinear relation of threshold level and cooperation was not significant while the linear relation was: more cooperation at higher threshold levels. The cooperation in the give-some dilemma was almost the mirror image of that in the take-some dilemma. In the give-some dilemma, most cooperation was found at the threshold levels of 30 and 40 percent. In this dilemma, both the linear and the curvilinear relations were significant. Such a curvilinear relation between threshold level and cooperation in the give-some dilemma was also found in four experiments by Poppe (1988).

The third question underlying the experiment was why subjects were (non)cooperative. By relating the subjects' choices to their expectations, some more insight could be obtained into subjects' motives or reasons. At the low threshold levels of the give-some dilemma, subjects were not cooperative because of greed: they expected that enough others would contribute and did not contribute themselves. At the high threshold levels of this dilemma, subjects were not cooperative because of fear: they expected that not enough others would contribute and did not contribute themselves. This resulted in the most cooperation being at intermediate threshold levels. Many subjects contributed even though they expected that not enough others would contribute. Actually, the main reason for cooperation in the give-some dilemma was solidarity and not a sense of duty.

At the low threshold levels of the take-some dilemma, subjects were not cooperative because of both greed and fear. Greed decreased as the threshold level rose, while the level of fear did not change much. This resulted in the most cooperation being at higher threshold levels. Especially the sense of duty was more important at higher threshold levels of the take-some dilemma.

One of the most striking results is the difference between cooperation in the give-some dilemma and the take-some dilemma. In terms of an expected value approach, the two dilemmas are identical. Some researchers (e.g. Brewer & Kramer, 1986) reasoned that giving and taking in a social dilemma could be related to Kahneman and Tversky's (1984) ideas about preferences for risky or sure alternatives. However, others (e.g. Rutte e.a., 1987) noted that it is not clear which of the two choices in give-some and in take-some dilemmas constitutes a risky choice. Moreover, the results demonstrate that in addition to an individual's preference for risk taking, social motives such as solidarity and a sense of duty are also of importance.

The motives for cooperation and defection were assessed on the basis of the subjects' expectations and choices. One could wonder to what extent expectations and choices are independent. Actually, the subjects were asked for their expectations *after* they had made their choices. Therefore, the analysis of the expectation data was repeated but this time with the subject's cooperation as a covariate. None of the significant effects found in the ANOVA disappeared in the ANCOVA. The same procedure was followed with regard to cooperation. By considering expectation as a covariate in the analysis of cooperation, the main effect of dilemma was no longer significant. So, expectation had more effect on cooperation than the other way around. Because the motives were assessed on the basis of the subjects' choices and expectations, they do not really explain why the subjects cooperated: they are mainly descriptive. Nevertheless, the motives give useful additional information.

In the literature the three questions dealt with in this experiment have been considered separately. Certainly the most important outcome of this experiment is that it has been demonstrated that the three questions should be considered simultaneously. Therefore, whether people are more cooperative in give-some than in take-some dilemmas depends on the threshold level; whether people are more or less cooperative at one threshold level or another depends on the dilemma and whether greed or fear is a more important reason for defection, or solidarity or sense of duty a more important reason for cooperation, depends on the dilemma and the threshold level.

References

Brewer, M.B., & Kramer, R.M. (1986). Choice behavior in social dilemmas: effects of social identity, group size, and decision framing. *Journal of Personality and Social Psychology, 50*, 543-549.

Bruins, J.J., Liebrand, W.B.G., & Wilke, H.A.M. (1989). About the saliency of fear and greed in social dilemmas. *European Journal of Social Psychology, 19*, 155-161.

Coombs, C.H. (1973). A reparametrization of the prisoner's dilemma game. *Behavioral Science, 18*, 424-428.

Dawes, R.M. (1980). Social dilemmas. *Annual Review of Psychology, 31*, 169-193.

Dawes, R.M., Orbell, J.M., Simmons, R.T., & Van de Kragt, A.J.C. (1986). Organizing groups for collective action. *American Political Science Review, 80*, 1171-1185.

Elster, J. (1989). *The cement of society*. Cambridge: Cambridge University Press.

Frohlich, N., & Oppenheimer, J.A. (1970). I get by with a little help from my friends. *World Politics, 23*, 104-120.

Hardin, G. (1968). The tragedy of the commons. *Science, 162*, 1243-1248.

Harris, R.J. (1969). A geometric classification system for 2 x 2 interval symmetric games. *Behavioral Science, 14*, 133-146.

Kahneman, D., & Tversky, A. (1984). Choices, values, and frames. *American Psychologist, 39*, 341-350.

Komorita, S.S. (1987). Cooperative choice in decomposed social dilemmas. *Personality and Social Psychology Bulletin, 13*, 53-63.

Komorita, S.S., & Carnevale, P. (1992). Motivational arousal vs. decision framing in social dilemmas. In: W.B.G. Liebrand, D.M. Messick, & H.A.M. Wilke (Eds): *Social dilemmas*. Oxford: Pergamon Press, pp. 209-223.

Komorita, S.S., & Parks, C.D. (1995). Interpersonal relations: mixed-motive interaction. *Annual Review of Psychology, 46*, 183-207.

Komorita, S.S., Sweeney, J., & Kravitz, D.A. (1980). Cooperative choices in the n-person dilemma situations. *Journal of Personality and Social Psychology, 38*, 504-516.

Lynn, M. & Oldenquist, A. (1986). Egoistic and nonegoistic motives in social dilemma. *American Psychologist, 41*, 529-534.

McDaniel, W.C., & Sistrunk, F. (1991). Managment dilemmas and decisions. *Journal of Conflict Resolution, 35*, 21-42.

Messick, D.M., Allison, S.T., & Samuelson, C.D. (1988). Framing and communication effects on group members' responses to environmental and social uncertainty. In: S. Maital (Ed.): *Behavioral economics, Vol. II*. Brighton: Wheatsleaf Books, pp 677-700.

Olson, M. (1965). *The logic of collective action*. Cambridge MA: Harvard University Press.

Poppe, M. (1988). Greed and fear in step-level social dilemmas. Paper presented at the 3rd International Conference on Social Dilemmas, Groningen.

Poppe, M., & Utens, L. (1986). Effects of greed and fear of being gypped in a social dilemma situation with changing poolsize. *Journal of Economic Psychology*, *7*, 61-73.

Rapoport, A., & Ested-Levy, D. (1989). Provision of step-level public goods: effects of greed and fear of being gypped. *Organizational Behavior and Human Decision Processes*, *44*, 325-344.

Rutte, C.G., Wilke, H.A.M., & Messick, D.M. (1987). The effects of framing social dilemmas as give-some or take-some games. *British Journal of Social Psychology*, *26*, 103-108.

Seegers, P., & Gabrielson, A. (1968). Applicability of the Cochran *Q* test and the *F* test for statistical analysis of dichotomous data for dependent samples. *Psychological Bulletin*, *69*, 269-277.

Suleiman, R., & Rapoport, A. (1992). Provision of step-level public goods with contiuous contribution. *Journal of Behavioral Decision Making*, *5*, 133-153.

Van Avermaet, E., & Van Nieuwkerke, S. (1989). Bijdragen of niet bijdragen tot een gemeenschappelijk doel: de rol van hebzucht en vrees nader onderzocht [To contribute or not contribute to a common good: The role or greed and fear of being cheated]. *Nederlands Tijdschrift voor de Psychologie*, *44*, 217-224.

Van de Kragt, A.J.C, Orbell, J., & Dawes, R.M. (1983). The minimal contributing set as a solution to public goods problems. *American Political Science Review*, *77*, 112-122.

Van Lange, P.A.M., Liebrand, W.B.G., Kiers, H.A.L., & Zwaal, W. (1989). Redenen voor attributies van keuzegedrag in een N-personen prisoner's dilemma [Reasons for and attributions of choice behavior in an N-person prisoner's dilemma]. *Nederlands Tijdschrift voor de Psychologie*, *44*, 225-234.

Yamagishi, T., & Sato, K. (1986). Motivational basis of the public goods problem. *Journal of Personality and Social Psychology*, *50*, 67-73.

Does "The Motivating Power of Loss" Exist? An Experimental Test of the Effect of Losses on Cooperation*

Chris Snijders[1] and Werner Raub[2]

[1]Department of Sociology, Utrecht University, Heidelberglaan 1, 3584 CS Utrecht, The Netherlands. Email: snijders@fsw.ruu.nl

[2] Sozialwissenschaftliches Institut, Universität Erlangen-Nürnberg, Findelgasse 7-9, D-90402 Nürnberg, Germany. Email: raub@wsfg1.wiso.uni-erlangen.de

Abstract. We test the intuitively plausible suggestion that collective action is more easily achieved if cooperation is necessary to avoid losses compared to the situation where cooperation is necessary to increase gains. An experiment using different 2-person repeated Prisoner's Dilemmas as a simple example of a collective action situation was conducted and *refuted* this suggestion.

1. Cooperation in social dilemmas: gains versus losses

Much experimental research on the Prisoner's Dilemma (PD) and other "social dilemmas" has focused on effects of variations of the payoff structure on the frequency of cooperation and related dependent variables (see Rapoport, 1974; 26-7, Colman, 1982; 118-9, Van Lange, Liebrand, Messick & Wilke, 1992; 14-5 for overviews and further references). Surprisingly, however, there seems to be no systematic research that compares dilemmas where outcomes represent "gains" in terms of some underlying commodity like, e.g., money with dilemmas where outcomes represent "losses". Game-theoretic and experimental research on bargaining problems has recently investigated whether bargaining over gains differs from bargaining over losses (see Camerer, Johnson, Rymon & Sen, 1993). Such analyses are lacking for cooperation problems although it has been suggested

*The order of authorship is pseudo-randomized. Useful suggestions and comments by Norman Braun, Bernd Lahno, and Jeroen Weesie are gratefully acknowledged. Financial support was provided by the Netherlands Organization for Scientific Research (NWO) under grant PGS 50-370.

that they might be useful (see Van Lange, Liebrand, Messick & Wilke, 1992; 14-5, Murnighan & King, 1992; 168, 181, and Komorita & Carnevale, 1992: 210-1).[3]

An example of a social dilemma where outcomes represent gains is the case where the status quo for a set of actors is a situation without some valuable collective good. Production of a positive amount of the collective good is a gain relative to the status quo and requires cooperation of at least some of the actors. However, each actor has an individual incentive not to contribute to the production of the collective good and to free ride on the others' contributions. An example of a dilemma where outcomes represent losses is, conversely, the case where the actors can foresee that their current situation will deteriorate through the production of a collective bad. Cooperation of all actors reduces the amount of the collective bad and, hence, reduces losses compared to the situation where no cooperation is achieved. However, an actor minimizes his individual losses by abstaining from cooperation and free riding on the other actors' contributions for reducing the amount of the collective bad. We will refer to situations of the former type as situations where cooperation yields gains. Situations of the latter type will be referred to as situations where cooperation reduces losses. More concretely, consider labor disputes and compare the situation where cooperation of employees through collective action like, e.g., a spontaneous strike would yield higher wages or better working conditions with the situation where cooperation of employees would be necessary to confine wage reductions or a deterioration of working conditions.

A systematic comparison of social dilemmas where cooperation yields gains with social dilemmas where cooperation reduces losses seems useful because it has been forcefully argued that actors tend to evaluate outcomes in terms of changes in wealth or welfare relative to some initial position rather than in terms of final positions (see, e.g., Kahneman & Tversky, 1979; 277-80 for a well-known discussion and further references). Moreover, substantial empirical evidence has been accumulated which documents that actors tend to react differently to changes of similar size depending on whether the changes represent gains or losses (see Thaler, 1992; ch. 6 for a review). In the literature on collective action and social movements it has been recently stressed that collective action can be oriented toward gain for the participants as well as toward "the defense of existing rights or privileges that are under threat" (Walder, 1994; 2). While much theoretical

[3] We wish to compare conditions for cooperation in situations where cooperation is necessary to realize gains with conditions for cooperation in situations where cooperation is necessary to reduce losses. While this problem has been neglected in the literature, there has been some attention for another issue which should be clearly distinguished from our's, namely, "greed" versus "fear" as an instigator of defection in the PD (see Rapoport, Guyer & Gordon 1976; 104, 239, and Van Lange, Liebrand, Messick & Wilke, 1992; 15). "Greed" refers to an actor's incentive to defect in a PD in order to unilaterally exploit a cooperative partner. Conversely, "fear" refers to an actor's incentive to defect in a PD in order to avoid exploitation through a defecting partner.

work focuses on collective action for the provision of a collective good not currently enjoyed, Walder (1994) has argued from an empirical viewpoint that historically important social movements characteristically sought to avoid or reduce loss through the production of a collective bad. According to Walder (1994: 9), historical evidence suggests an "obvious" proposition: "that loss is a more powerful motivator than gain, or that groups threatened with loss will be more likely to protest than groups that seek proactively to achieve a gain".

The paper is organized as follows. The next section introduces the repeated 2-person Prisoner's Dilemma as a simple example of a problematic interdependent situation where cooperation could lead to increased gains or reduced losses. We then describe an experiment conducted to compare situations that yield gains with situations that reduce losses. A discussion concludes the paper.

2. Conditional cooperation in a repeated 2-person Prisoner's Dilemma

We consider the well known infinitely or indefinitely repeated symmetric 2-person Prisoner's Dilemma (2-PD) game (Γ) as a simple example of a cooperation problem. We assume complete information and common knowledge with respect to the structure of the game. Actors move simultaneously in the constituent game of Γ where each actor i has two pure strategies which we denote by C_i ("cooperation") and D_i ("defection"). We characterize i's outcomes M_i at the endnodes of Γ as changes in wealth for i, i.e., as differences in the amount of money i owns before and after the game has been played. Outcomes M_i depend on i's move X_i (either C_i or D_i) and on the move of the other player.

Since the game is symmetric, the payoffs are completely characterized by:

(1a) $M_1(C_1,D_2) = S$,

(1b) $M_1(D_1,D_2) = P$,

(1c) $M_1(C_1,C_2) = R$, and

(1d) $M_1(D_1,C_2) = T$,

with $S<P<R<T$.

According to (1a)--(1d), an actor gains more or loses less money if he chooses defection instead of cooperation (defection is a dominant strategy in the constituent game). Besides that, each actor gains more or loses less money if both actors choose C compared to the situation where both have chosen D.

Now consider the repeated game Γ. We assume that the 2-PD is infinitely or indefinitely repeated in rounds $t = 1, 2, ...$ In round t, all actors are informed on the behavior of all actors in all previous rounds $1, ... , t$-1. We assume exponential discounting of constituent game payoffs. Each actor is assumed to use the same discount parameter w ($0<w<1$). In the following, we interpret w as a continuation probability. Hence, we interpret Γ as an indefinitely repeated PD where w is the constant probability that round t+1 will be played after round t has been played, while 1-w is the probability that Γ is terminated after round t has been played.

We wish to compare cooperation rates in a 2-PD where outcomes represent gains ($S \geq 0$) with 2-PDs where outcomes represent losses ($T \leq 0$).

Let Γ^+ be a repeated 2-PD according to the characterization in this section with:

(2) $M_1(D_1,C_2) = T^+ > M_1(C_1,C_2) = R^+ > M_1(D_1,D_2) = P^+ > M_1(C_1,D_2) = S^+ \geq 0.$

Hence, Γ^+ is a repeated social dilemma where cooperation yields gains.

Now consider the game Γ^- which results from Γ^+ by subtracting *at least* an amount of T^+ from every payoff. Obviously, the highest possible payoff in Γ^- is then always smaller than or equal to zero. By comparing Γ^+ with Γ^-, we change the payoffs from gains to losses, while keeping the structure of the game intact. We test the alleged difference in cooperation for gains or against losses in an experiment by comparing cooperation rates for games Γ^+ with cooperation rates for corresponding games Γ^-.[4]

3. Method

All participants played an indefinitely repeated Prisoner's Dilemma with nonnegative payoffs (a *Gains Dilemma*), and an indefinitely repeated Prisoner's Dilemma with nonpositive payoffs (a *Losses Dilemma*). The payoff matrix for the *Losses Dilemma* was created by substracting a fixed amount of all possible payoffs in the *Gains Dilemma* as indicated in the previous section. Hence, the *Losses Dilemma* can be considered a kind of "shifted" *Gains Dilemma*. The probability to play a next round in a dilemma was set equal to 0.75.

[4]Note that Γ^+ and Γ^- are games with *different* outcomes. This distinguishes our approach from discussions on "give-some" and "take-some games" (see, e.g., Brewer & Kramer, 1986, and Komorita & Carnevale, 1992). The work on "give-some" and "take-some games" addresses the effects of "framing" essentially *identical* outcomes in different ways by manipulating the outcome that serves as a reference point.

3.1 Subjects

Participants were 190 male and female undergraduates. Part of them (44 out of 190) completed part of a course requirement by participating. The others reacted to an advertisement on a notice-board in the lobby of one of the buildings of Utrecht University that promised them a financial reward that could range between 6 and 36 Dutch guilders (6 Dutch guilders equals about 3.5 US dollars).

3.2 Design

We conducted eight sessions on three different days. The first two sessions (24 and 20 participants) were attended by participants that fulfilled course requirements by participating. The last six sessions (20, 26, 24, 24, 24, and 28 participants) were attended by participants that had reacted to the advertisement. All participants completed five different tasks. This paper only addresses tasks three and four: the *Gains Dilemma* and the *Losses Dilemma* (see Raub & Snijders, 1995 for a more extensive discussion of the experiment). In four sessions, participants completed the two tasks in that order. In the other four, these two tasks were completed in the reverse order. We used three different (sets of two) payoff matrices that only differed in the value of the payoff associated with unilateral cooperation. In all sessions, the values of P, R and T in the *Gains Dilemma* were equal to 4, 7, and 16 Dutch guilders respectively. In the first two sessions, S was equal to 1, in three further sessions, S was equal to 0 and in the three remaining sessions, S was equal to 2. The payoffs in the *Losses Dilemma* were equal to the payoffs for the *Gains Dilemma* minus 16 Dutch guilders.

3.3 Procedure

Per session, a maximum of 30 subjects could participate. Participants were evenly divided over two sides of a room, these two "semi-separated" sides being created by a screen of about 1.5 meter high across the middle of the room. Hence, participants were aware of the presence of a group of participants on the other side of the room, but could not see the participants in the other group during the session. Participants were instructed not to talk with each other, and they were told that the 20 Dutch guilders (about 12 US dollars) in front of them was for them, if they would take part in an experiment that could lead to a loss of a maximum of 16 Dutch guilders. After that, they were asked to read the instruction text. The instruction text explained the different tasks, one of which was the indefinitely repeated Prisoner's Dilemma, and the procedure at the end of the session: all participants were going to be paid or were going to lose money according to the choices they had made in one of the tasks they had completed. The task was determined randomly at the end of the session by picking a playing-card. If they would be payed or lose money according to their choices in either the *Gains* or the *Losses Dilemma*, they were told they would be payed or would lose money in accordance with the choices they had made *in the last round* of that particular dilemma.[5] The instruction text furthermore explained to them that they were connected to a random participant on the other side of the room while playing the *Gains Dilemma*, to another random participant while playing the *Losses Dilemma*, and that they would not find out which participants they were playing with. After all participants had made their choice for the first round of the first Prisoner's Dilemma all these choices were written down by the experimenter and passed on to the appropriate participants on the other side of the room. After all participants had received the choices of the other player, a roulette was spun to see which pairs of participants would go on to the next round of play in the dilemma. Each participant had received a card with his or her 27 "lucky slots" on the roulette wheel. If the ball fell in one of these 27 slots, the participant would have to play another round of the dilemma (with the same partner). It was made clear in the text that if the ball would fall in the "0" slot, the wheel would be spun again, which made the probability of continuing 0.75 (27 out of the 36 possible slots). The (pairs of) participants that went on to the next round then made their choices for that following round. This procedure was repeated until no (pairs of) participants were left playing that dilemma. After the completion of the first dilemma, participants were connected to a different participant on the other side of the room by switching the lucky slot cards and played the second dilemma in a similar way. After completion of all the tasks, participants were instructed to go individually to the counter in the corner of the room to determine the amount of money they had won or lost. The participants were not deceived in any way.

3.4 Results

Miscellaneous controls. Participants were quizzed (in writing) about the monetary consequences of the different choices they could make. Of the 90% (170 out of 190) that answered the control questions, 78% (132 out of 170) made no mistakes at all, 18% (30 out of 170) made one mistake, and 5% (8 out of 170) made two or more mistakes. About 10% (20 out of 190) did not fill out this part of the tasks at all because they were told that given the limited amount of time the experiment would continue with the next task before they had reached these control questions. Results on cooperation rates are displayed based on the choices of all participants. Restricting the results to the 132 participants that were able to complete the control questions without mistakes in the given amount of time leads to identical results.

---

[5]This procedure does not change the incentivestructure and was designed to eliminate possible wealth effects (see Raub & Snijders, 1995.

For all three different (sets of two) matrices we used, the monetary payoff for mutual defection plus the monetary payoff for unilateral cooperation is larger than twice the payoff for mutual cooperation. One could therefore argue that in such a Prisoner's Dilemma one should not try to get mutual cooperation started, but one should try to get an alternating pattern of unilateral cooperation and unilateral defection started. Though this is correct in principle, its empirical relevance is immediately refuted by a look at the data. The number of alternating patterns is very small, and does not increase with an increasing payoff for unilateral cooperation. The most frequently occuring pattern seems to be an initial period of "chaos", trying to figure out what the other player is doing, followed by mutual defection after a few rounds of play.

One of the tasks in the experiment was a (small) questionnaire. Participants were asked to write down their age, sex, highschool subjects, and some other characteristics. None of these lead to any difference that approached significance.

In the sessions where participants had to play the *Gains Dilemma* before the *Losses Dilemma*, results were not significantly different from the sessions where this order was reversed.

A final check concerned the participants' familiarity with game theory. Although some had experienced material on (Prisoner's Dilemma) games in classes, the results of the analyses did not significantly differ for experienced participants as compared to the others.

Cooperation rates. In table 1, the frequencies (percentages) of cooperative choices for both the *Gains Dilemma* and the *Losses Dilemma* are displayed:

Based on the first round only				
	***S* = 0** (n=70)	***S* = 1** (n=44)	***S* = 2** (n=76)	**Total** (n=190)
Gains Dilemma	15 (21.4)	25 (56.8)	19 (25.0)	59 (31.1)
Losses Dilemma	18 (25.7)	26 (59.1)	20 (26.3)	64 (33.7)
Based on the last round only				
	***S* = 0** (n=70)	***S* = 1** (n=44)	***S* = 2** (n=76)	**Total** (n=190)
Gains Dilemma	14 (20.0)	18 (40.9)	15 (19.7)	47 (24.7)
Losses Dilemma	16 (22.9)	22 (50.0)	15 (19.7)	53 (27.9)

Table 1. Frequencies (percentages) of cooperative choices for the *Gains Dilemma* and the *Losses Dilemma* based on the number of cooperators in the first round of the repeated game, and based on the last round of the repeated game.

Though the percentage of cooperation is somewhat larger in the *Losses Dilemma* than in the *Gains Dilemma*, it is obvious that none of these differences is significant.[6] It is striking that the percentage of cooperation in the S=1 condition is much larger than in the other two conditions. Since participants in the S=1 condition are the ones that fulfilled the course requirement, it seems reasonable to ascribe this higher level of cooperation to the fact that participants knew each other. However, for our purpose this does not pose a problem, since the relevant comparison is the within-subject comparison between the two different dilemmas.

4. Discussion

In this paper, we have compared social dilemmas where outcomes represent gains with dilemmas where outcomes represent losses. Though it has been suggested in the literature that cooperation will be achieved more easily (in the sense that actors are more willing to cooperate) to avoid losses than to increase gains, we found no evidence for a difference between these two conditions. One reason why we could not find a difference between the gains and the losses situation could be that we did not distinguish the different risk preferences of the participants in the analyses presented here. Scholars typically connect the supposed different kind of behavior in the case of losses to *risk-seekingness* of the actors. For example, Lindenberg seems to apply this argument in a discussion of "the motivating power of loss". He argues as follows:

> Following Kahneman and Tversky (1979) I assume that the gain/loss utility function is steeper for uncompensated losses than for gains. Linking this asymmetry to framing results in the following *loss hypothesis*, a hypothesis that may turn out to be of far-reaching consequences *a*) The avoidance of uncompensated loss (i.e., the prevention of imminent loss and the reduction of recent loss) is itself a good that frames certain decision situations; *b*) the likelihood that this frame dominates other possible frames in any given situation grows disproportionately with the size of the loss; c) the costs incurred in pursuing this goal may be higher than the value of the loss itself. For example, your wages have been cut (in your judgment) unfairly. The reduction of this loss may become a dominant goal, and you go out of your way to get even by working slower; by doing damage to factory property and by spending considerable time convincing others that some action should be taken. (Lindenberg, 1988; 52, all emphases in the original)

---

[6] A one-tailed Fisher's exact test comparing the respective frequencies for the *Gains* and the *Losses Dilemma* does not support the existence of significant differences for any p<0.34.

Lindenberg seems to suggest that wage reductions tend to induce a "definition of the situation" by the actors concerned such that the situation without wage reductions becomes their reference point. Moreover, he seems to envision a situation where spontaneous collective action is required to reduce or avoid the collective bad. Furthermore, he seemingly suggests that in such a situation actors are particularly prone to engage in active contributions for the reduction of the collective bad ("by spending considerable time convincing others that some action should be taken"), and that this is in accordance with Kahneman & Tversky (1979). We subscribe to the spirit of this argument to the extent that we believe that risk preferences have an influence on cooperation in a social dilemma. However, a game theoretical analysis in fact reveals a result that is *opposite* to what Lindenberg seems to suggest (Raub & Snijders, 1995). If we assume, following Kahneman & Tversky, that actors are risk-seeking for losses and risk-averse for gains (S-shaped utility), it can be shown that conditions for cooperation in repeated social dilemmas are *more* restrictive if outcomes represent losses than if outcomes represent gains. The reason is that risk aversion favorably affects the conditions for the existence of equilibria in conditionally cooperative strategies in the repeated social dilemma. In our experiment, we also assessed subjects' risk preferences for gains and losses (Raub & Snijders, 1995). We found, first, that - contrary to Kahneman and Tversky's conjecture - only 23% (43/190) of all participants chose in accordance with S-shaped utility, while 44% (83/190) are risk seeking for gains and losses, 22% (42/190) are risk averse for gains and losses, and 12% (22/190) are risk seeking for gains and risk averse for losses. We also found that risk preferences do affect cooperation as predicted by a game-theoretic model, i.e., there is evidence that risk aversion *favors* cooperation.

References

Brewer, M. B., & Kramer, R. M. (1986). Choice Behavior in Social Dilemmas: Effects of Social Identity, Group Size, and Decision Framing. *Journal of Personality and Social Psychology*, *50*, 3, 543-549.

Camerer, C. F., Johnson, E. J., Rymon, T. & Sen, S. (1993). Cognition and Framing in Sequential Bargaining for Gains and Losses. Pp. 27-47 in: *Frontiers of Game Theory*, edited by K. Binmore, A. Kirman & P. Tani. Cambridge, MA: MIT Press.

Colman, A. (1982). *Game Theory and Experimental Games*. Oxford: Pergamon Press.

Kahneman, D. & Tversky, A. (1979). Prospect Theory: An Analysis of Decision under Risk. *Econometrica*, 47, 263-291.

Komorita, S. S. & Carnevale, P. (1992). Motivational Arousal vs. Decision Framing in Social Dilemmas. Pp. 209-223 in: *Social Dilemmas: Theoretical Issues and Research Findings*, edited by W. B. G. Liebrand, D. M. Messick & H. A. Wilke. Oxford: Pergamon Press.

Lindenberg, S. (1988). Contractual Relations and Weak Solidarity: The Behavioral Basis of Restraints on Gain-maximization. *Journal of Institutional and Theoretical Economics*, 144, 39-58.

Murnighan, J. K. & King, T. R. (1992). The Effects of Leverage and Payoffs on Cooperative Behavior in Asymmetric Dilemmas. Pp. 163-182 in: *Social Dilemmas: Theoretical Issues and Research Findings*, edited by W. B. G. Liebrand, D. M. Messick & H. A. Wilke. Oxford: Pergamon Press.

Rapoport, A. (1974).Prisoner's Dilemma - Recollections and Observations. Pp. 17-34 in: *Game Theory as a Theory of Conflict Resolution*, edited by A. Rapoport. Dordrecht: Reidel.

Rapoport, A., Guyer, M. J. & Gordon, D. C. (1976). *The 2x2 Game*. Ann Arbor, Mich.: University of Michigan Press.

Raub, W. & Snijders, C. (1995). Gains, Losses, and Cooperation in Social Dilemmas: The Effects of Risk Preferences. *Mimeo*. Available from the authors.

Thaler, R. H. (1992). *The Winner's Curse. Paradoxes and Anomalies of Economic Life*. New York: Free Press.

van Lange, P. A. M., Liebrand, W. B. G., Messick, D. M. & Wilke, H. A. (1992) Introduction and Literature Review. Pp. 3-28 in: *Social Dilemmas: Theoretical Issues and Research Findings*, edited by W. B. G. Liebrand, D. M. Messick & H. A. Wilke. Oxford: Pergamon Press.

Walder, A. G. (1994) Implications of Loss Avoidance for Theories of Social Movements. *Mimeo*. Harvard University.

Computer Simulation of Cooperative Decision Making

Wim B. G. Liebrand[1] and David M. Messick[2]

[1] SWI, University of Groningen, NL-9712 TG Groningen, NL

[2] Department of Organization Behavior, KGSM, Northwestern University, Evanston, IL 60201, USA

1 Introduction

The focus of this chapter is on cooperative decision making in social dilemmas. We study the effect of some frequently used strategies or guidelines (heuristics) on making decisions in situations of uncertainty and conflict. There is uncertainty because we do not know how each of the others will behave, and there is conflict because our own interest is at odds with the collective interest.

The question of cooperation in situations of conflict, like social dilemmas, has a long history (Rushton, 1980). Prior research has identified many factors that affect our willingness to engage in self-sacrificial behavior (for a review see Liebrand, Messick & Wilke, 1992). These factors include the payoff structure, the perceived identifiability and efficacy of one's own behavior, others' expected behavior, individual differences, opportunities for communication and sanctioning, and the feeling of belonging to one of the groups involved.

The research field, however, is characterizedby an abundance of simple main and lower order interaction effects. What we lack is a theoretical model of the dynamics by which individual decision making shapes the characteristicsof a social group. We do not yet understand the mechanisms by which individuals decide to change their behavior and how these mechanisms affect the dynamics of the collective system.

The cellular automata paradigm (originally introduced by von Neumann and Ulam as "cellular spaces") is extremely well suited to studying these complex and dynamic systems (see also Sakado, 1971; Schelling, 1971; Wolfram, 1986). We therefore will use cellular automata to model individual decision making in a large population of actors, and study the processes of ongoing interactions where all of the actors are involved in a prototypical social dilemma relationship. First, however, we will describe and define social dilemmas and the decision strategies to be used in this study.

1.1 Social Dilemmas

Most of the studies of cooperation and competition use the well-know Prisoner's Dilemma as a prototypical social dilemma. In this study we use the Prisoner's Dilemma Game (PDG), displayed in Table 1. In this situation, C stands for 'cooperation' and D for 'defection.' The D choice, the selfish act, dominates the C choice, the choice in the collective interest. No matter what choice is made by the other person, the chooser is better off making the D choice to C. The C choice costs one unit in that the chooser gets one unit more by making the D choice, regardless of the other's action. The C choice provides two units to the other person, however. No matter what the other's choice, the other will get two units more if C is chosen. It is in each person's best interest to choose D, but it is in the best interest of the pair to choose C. Thus the group maximum is achieved when the individuals forego individual maximization. On a larger scale, groups with many individual maximizers (D choosers) will do more poorly than groups with few.

Table 1 Basic Prisoner's Dilemma

		Actor 2: C	Actor 2: D
Actor 1:	C	Actor 1: 2 units Actor 2: 2 units	Actor 1: 0 units Actor 2: 3 units
	D	Actor 1: 3 units Actor 2: 0 units	Actor 1: 1 unit Actor 2: 1 unit

The specific problem that we address in this chapter is to describe the global consequences of choice strategies in the social situation embodied by the Prisoners' Dilemma. In particular, we will examine what happens in large groups of individuals, all of whom use well-defined and adaptive decision heuristics for evaluating performance and generating choices in the PDG.

1.2. Decision Heuristics

In the following analysis, we distinguish two phases in the decision-making process. First, we enter a social dilemma with a specific propensity (p) to cooperate. We have acquired this propensity ($0 \leq p \leq 1$) in situations which had the same look or feeling to us. That is, we have learned how to behave in similar situations because our overt behavior was modified by reinforcement or extinction procedures. It is obvious that the sensitivity for the rewards and punishments received in the past, or those anticipated in the future, does differ from one individual to the other. We only assume that nobody is totally insensitive to those experiences and consequently will enter familiar situations with propensities based upon a generalization of past experiences.

The second phase consists of modifying behavior as a function of the outcomes of the behavior. As we know from social learning theory, any specific behavior in interdependency situations produces not only an external outcome, as given by the payoff structure, including any actual or anticipated rewards or punishments from others, it also starts an internal evaluation process. We evaluate the external outcome in terms of our own standards of conduct and subsequently respond in ways depending on the result of that evaluation process. That is, we subsequently adjust our propensities to cooperate in similar future situations. We focus on the process of changing behavior as a function of the quality of the outcomes (wins or losses) and of the standards by which the quality is judged (what is a win or loss).

The decision-making process described above can be nicely captured by two well-known decision heuristics. They are *Win-Stay, Lose-Change* (WSLC) and *Win-Cooperate, Lose-Defect* (WCLD). Both of these heuristics are based on mechanisms that have two components, an evaluation component and an action component. The evaluation procedure plays a crucial role in both WSLC and WCLD. What are the standards to which we compare our external outcomes in social interactions? A central element in this procedure is the location of the reference point or the comparison level (Thibaut & Kelley, 1959) that is used to evaluate the outcome. The same outcome can be evaluated as a win or a loss depending on whether it is above or below the relevant reference point. Moreover, it is well known that in social contexts the reference point will be strongly influenced by one's perception of the outcomes of similar others. Whether an outcome is "good" or "bad", whether it is a "win" or a "loss", will depend on the comparison one makes with the relevant reference group. In our study, therefore, we depart from ordinary game theoretical studies in which the magnitude of the payoffs is used. In our simulations, we want to embrace the realism that derives from assuming that outcomes are socially evaluated. As a result, "win" and "lose" are defined socially in terms of the payoffs of the neighbors. Specifically, "win" occurs when the payoff to the subject is equal to or greater than the average of the payoffs to the subject's neighbors. After the subject and its neighbor play the game, the payoff to the subject is compared to that social reference point. If the subject's payoff is at least as large as this average, the subject "wins." When the subject's payoff is smaller than this average of the neighbors, the subject "loses."

Both WSLC and WCLD use the same evaluation procedure but they differ with respect to the action component. After a "win", WSLC prescribes to *stay* with the behavior that "caused" the "win"; otherwise, it dictates a shift in the propensity to cooperate: *change* (Kelley, Thibaut, Radloff, & Mundy, 1962). Under the WCLD rule, it is assumed that winning will put the actor in a positive mood, which increases the propensity to cooperate (Krebs & Miller, 1985). In the same vein, after "losing", WCLD will generalize the bad feeling to a non-cooperative encounter with the next person.

1.3 Simulation Environment

In our study, we have a population in which all actors repeatedly interact with their neighbors under the 2 x 2 PDG contingencies shown in Table 1. Furthermore, all actors employ the same decision heuristic. What then will happen? Will we observe a stable proportion of the people cooperating? Will cooperation displace defection? Will there be swings in the proportion of cooperators?

To address these questions, we used a cellular automata approach in which we had a population of size n * n. All edges and corners were connected to each other, so we were dealing with a torus consisting of n^2 actors, or cellular automata. Each point in the two-dimensional population had eight neighbors (those comprising the 3 by 3 square). Thus a subject on the right-hand edge had a corresponding point on the left-hand edge as a neighbor, and subjects on the lower edge had corresponding points on the upper edge as neighbors, and vice versa. Initially, all actors randomly got assigned a probability of 0.5 of choosing C on the first play, while their decision heuristic (either WSLC or WCLD) determined what choice was made on subsequent trials. In addition, all payoff values of the basic Prisoner's Dilemma (Table 1) were distributed randomly among the actors, causing the expected payoff of any actor or neighborhood to be 1.5.

Actual decision making took place in the following framework. First, a subject and one of the eight surrounding neighbors were randomly chosen from the population. Subject and neighbor then played the PDG. The payoff to both the subject and the neighbor from the interaction was recorded. The payoff to the neighbor from that play was averaged together with the other seven neighbors' payoffs from the last time they were subjects. Then, the subject employed either WSLC or WCLD as the choice heuristic that determined what the subject's next choice was. This was one play. Another individual was then randomly selected and the process repeated itself. One "generation" was completed when a sample the size of the population had been selected to play. Sampling was done with replacement, however, so some individuals in the population may have played more than once and some may not have played at all. The simulation can be run for a fixed number of generations, or until some specified condition is met. One possible condition is that the population becomes either homogeneously cooperative or homogeneously defecting.

The choice that characterizeseach individual is the choice that the individual will use when the individual next plays, regardless of whether the play is as subject or neighbor. Only subjects recalculate the choice after an interaction, however; neighbors do not. (We have run some simulations in which this condition was changed and we observed few qualitative differences.)

The kinds of questions we want to answer with these simulations are the following: What happens to the frequency of cooperation in the population over time? If the population becomes homogeneous, if defection displaces cooperation or vice versa, how long (in generations) does it take to happen? If the population stays mixed, does it approach an equilibrium value and, if so, what is that value and how does it depend, if at all, on the parameters of the simulation?

2 Results

One of the first and most important things we noticed about the simulations is that cooperation does not disappear! The number of cooperators in each generation varies a bit around a more or less stable level for both WSLC and WCLD. Furthermore, the number of cooperators appeared to be consistently greater for the WCLD rule than for WSLC. Subsequent runs confirm this impression. WSLC yields about 40% cooperation and WCLD leads to roughly 55%.

A description solely in terms of the number of cooperators in the population would be an inadequate summary of the structure of cooperation in these groups. We can describe the populations in terms of how well the individuals did, whether there is a difference between cooperators and defectors in terms of their winnings, and we can ask whether there is a tendency for the population to become segregated so that cooperators tend to be close to other cooperators and likewise for defectors.

In our simulations, we characterize each individual in the population by the following features: (1) STATE: Is the individual a cooperator or a defector? (Will the individual choose C or D the next time the individual is sampled as subject or neighbor?); (2) LAST: What is the value of the last payoff the individual got when the individual was subject?; (3) WEALTH: What is the sum of the payoffs that the individual received as subject?; (4) COHESION: What is the relative fraction of the individual's neighbors who are like the subject with regard to cooperation and defection? From the cohesion measure, we will create an index that reflects the extent to which the spatial distribution of cooperation in the population is clustered.

An examination of LAST indicates that with WCLD strategies, cooperators have a higher last outcome than defectors. The reason for this is clear. Receiving a high outcome, either a 2 or a 3, tends to evoke a cooperative response in return because the high payoff is likely to be coded as a win. The association of high payoffs with cooperation occurs because individuals cooperate when they get good outcomes, not the other way around. With the WSLC rule, there is a tendency for the defectors to have somewhat higher LAST outcomes than cooperators. Notice in Table 1 that, following the highest paying DC outcome, MWSLC will always defect next because the three units won by the subject are always higher than the average of the eight neighbors (one neighbor got 0 units).

The WEALTH of the individuals becomes essentially identical over generations regardless of whether they are cooperators or defectors. This result seems to contradict the fact reported above pertaining to the LAST differences. But it is important to remember that our designation of an individual as a cooperator or defector pertains only to that individual's next choice. These categories do not refer to stable qualities of the individuals. An individual who is a cooperator one instant could be a defector the next. So the WEALTH of the cooperators and defectors does not differ.

Finally, we will devise an index that we call CLUSTER to measure the degree to which cooperators are found in the company of other cooperators and defectors are found in the presence of other defectors. For each individual, we count the proportion of neighbors that have the same cooperative feature as the individual. P(Coop|C) is the average proportion of cooperative neighbors that cooperators have and P(Def|D) is the average proportion of defectors in the neighborhood of the defectors. From these proportions, we subtract the overall proportions of the two types in the population to get D(C) = P(Coop|C)-P(C) and D(D) = P(Def|D) - P(D). On average, if the types tend to cluster, D(C) and D(D) should both be positive. There should be a higher probability of finding a cooperator in the neighborhood of another cooperator than the baseline likelihood and likewise for defectors. Our overall measure of clustering is simply CLUSTER = D(C) + D(D). If the types are randomly or evenly distributed throughout the population, this measure will be near zero. (Actually it will be slightly less than zero, but we will not go into the details of this here.)

Before turning to our major goal, the description of the prevalence and dynamics of cooperation in large groups, we must comment on some crucial differences we discovered between large groups and small ones.

2.1 Small Versus Large Groups

We take a group of nine to be the smallest group with which we will be concerned. This choice is based on the symmetry that, in a group of nine, each individual has eight neighbors and each individual is neighbor to every other individual. We have found important differences between groups of nine and larger groups.

The major finding with groups of nine is that such groups always become permanently homogeneous, either with cooperation or defection. WSLC becomes all-defect and WCLD becomes all-cooperate. For a group to become permanently homogeneous, it must be that once the group is in the state it will never leave, and there must be a positive probability that the group can enter the state. For WCLD, one can see that if the group entered the state in which all members were C so that they exchanged 2 points per play, they would receive outcomes that are coded as wins since they are equal to the outcomes of their neighbors, and they would continue to cooperate.

The dynamics under which WSLC turns into an all-D state are more subtle. First, it is not possible to go into an all-C state. The all-C state must be preceded by a eight-C and one-D state in which the D individual is subject. The D subject will always receive three points interacting with any neighbor and the three points will always be a win, causing the D to stay. It is possible for the group to become all-D, on the other hand. In an eight-D, one-C group, when the C is subject, the C will receive zero points which will always be coded as a loss, causing the cooperator to change to defection. The new all-D group will only be stable, however, if the mean of the payoffs is one or less, making the payoff for mutual defection (1 unit) coded a win.

The discussion above suggests that the processes by which small groups become homogeneous are different for the two heuristics. One manifestation of these differences is in the speed with which the groups become homogeneous. In a series of simulations, we observed that WCLD required significantly less generations to converge than the other heuristic. Although these effects are clearly significantly different, as in other cases where differences are obvious, we will not report statistical tests or significance levels.

The discovery that all of these rules converge in nine-person groups suggests two generalizations. First, there may be absorbing states for groups of all sizes and with enough generations; groups of any size will converge to one of the two homogeneous states. We cannot offer a formal proof of this suggestion, but it seems plausible that the principles that allow small groups to converge would also allow large groups to converge even though it might take very long to do so. For WCLD, which converged in an average of 11.3 generations when the population was 9, it took already close to 13,000 generations with a (small) group size of 36. The increase in generations for WSLC is even greater. For the nine-person group, it took 87.7 generations. But for the 36-person group, WSLC never reached the all-D state within more than 138,000 generations. For a 49-person group, neither WCLD nor WSLC reached absorbing states within 100.000 generations. It is obvious that, even over this small range, time to convergence is not linear in population size.

The first generalization is that there may, in principle, be absorbing states for all populations. The second is that, with large populations of 50 or 100 or more, the likelihood of convergence is so small that it can effectively be treated as zero. If time to convergence is essentially infinite, then the interesting questions have to do with the dynamics of cooperation in heterogeneous populations. Are there stable levels of cooperation supported by WSLC and WCLD? If so, what are those levels? Do they depend on factors like the size of the population or on the initial distribution of cooperators and defectors? And, more important, if we observe stable levels of cooperation, would we be able to predict their magnitude for each of the heuristics? It is to these issues that we now turn.

2.2 Cooperation in Large Groups

In this section we will summarize the results of scores of simulations that we have conducted. The results of these simulations have been described earlier in detail by Messick and Liebrand (1995) and were originally obtained by using a simulation package developed at the University of Warsaw (Gasik, 1990). All of the results, however, have been replicated by an independently developed computer program. We first outline some basic findings regarding the global consequences of WSLC and WCLD with different group sizes. Thereafter we describe some experiments that we have conducted using the basic population size of 100, in which the choice rules do not yield a homogeneous population.

We can summarize our basic group size findings by describing an experiment in which we manipulated the size of the population and the heuristic rule used to generate choices. In this experiment, we varied the population from 36 (6^2), 64 (8^2), 100 (10^2), 144 (12^2), to 196 (14^2). For each population size, each rule, following a random 50-50 initial assignment of cooperation and defection, was run for 50 generations. The status of the population at the end of the 50 generations was measured. Each rule was replicated 50 times for each population size, yielding a total of 500 simulations, each of which was 50 generations long. This experiment allows us to investigate the joint effects of population size and rule on the prevalence and distribution of cooperation, and it allows us to compare the efficiency of the rules in earning points.

In this, as in the other experiments, we will not list values of F-ratios nor present significance levels for most of the results we describe. We will discuss only effects that are large and significant. Our statistical tests are all extremely powerful because the noise levels are moderate at worst and because the experiments usually have a minimum of five hundred degrees of freedom for the error terms.

2.2.1 Group Size and Cooperation Levels

The only factor influencing the prevalence of cooperation was the rule. WSLC generated an average of 40.2% cooperation, while WCLD led to 55.4% cooperation. As with most of our simulations, population size does not influence the frequency of cooperation. As one would expect, however, as the population size increases, the standard deviation of the proportion of cooperators decreases with both rules.

2.2.2 Group Size and Clustering

Population size does have an influence on the distribution of cooperation and defection, however, although the influence is not as great as that of the rule. When we analyzed the CLUSTER variable, we found that WSLC tends not to be clustered, with a mean value of -.022, which is very close to the mean value of this statistic for the initial distributions which were randomly distributed. For WCLD, the mean of the cluster score is .116, giving evidence of moderate clustering. As the population sizes increase, moreover, the mean cluster score also tends to increase. With the smallest population used in this study, 36, WCLD had a mean cluster score of .069. The score was .136 for the largest population, 196. The variation of the cluster score as a function of population size was much larger for WCLD than for WSLC.

2.2.3 Group Size and Accumulated Payoffs

Next, we investigated the rules' earning ability. For each rule, we calculated the average WEALTH of the population. That is to say, we accumulated the payoffs, LAST, for each individual in the population for the 50 generations and then calculated the average of these totals. There was a large difference in favor of the WCLD rule (M = 77.51) over the WSLC rule (M = 70.25). (Complete cooperation would have gained 100 points per person and complete defection would have yielded 50 points per person. Purely random choosing would yield an average of 75 points per person, 1.5 points per generation on average.) The 77.51 points is significantly better than 75, and, of course, the 70.25 is significantly worse. Wealth was not influenced by the population size.

The WCLD rule earns more than the WSLC rule simply because it generates more cooperation. One can predict the average WEALTH accumulated by these rules from a knowledge of the stable levels of cooperation they support and the payoff units in the PDG matrix. Suppose the stable level of cooperation is *a*. That implies that the level of defection is *(1-a)*. Thus the probability that the CC outcome occurs is a^2, the DC and CD outcomes occur with probability *a(1-a)*, and the DD outcome occurs with probability $(1-a)^2$. Using the values in our payoff matrix, the average payoff per trial when the proportion of cooperation is *a*, E(P|a), can then be shown to be:

$$E(P|a) = 2a^2 + 3a(1-a) + (1-a)^2 = 1 + a \qquad (1)$$

When *a* = .4, the stable rate for WSLC, this leads to a per trial outcome of 1.4 units per trial or 70 units over 50 trials. When *a* = .55, as with WCLD, E(P|.55) = 1.55 per trial, yielding an expectation of 77.5 points over the 50 trials.

The difference between the average WEALTH of the cooperators and defectors, as expected, was very small. With the WSLC rule, cooperators earned 70 points on average and defectors earned 70.45. The difference was a little larger for the WCLD rule, under which cooperators won 78.42 points and defectors won 76.01. This latter difference reflects the fact that cooperators, under this rule, are cooperators because their last payoff was a "win" - it was "relatively" large. The appropriate causal description is that winners cooperate, not that cooperators win. This fact is apparent if we examine the average of the last payoffs received by the cooperators and defectors for WCLD. The former is 1.77 while the latter is 1.26. The same averages for WSLC are 1.07 and 1.62.

2.2.4 Initial Dependence

The prevalence of cooperation is stable over initial distributions of cooperators and defectors. In one experiment, we varied the initial relative density of cooperators from 1% to 90% in populations of 100, and we stopped the simulation after 25 generations. We ran 50 replications of each condition. The initial distributions had a very small but significant effect on the prevalence of cooperation, especially for the WCLD rule. The range of final rates of cooperation for WCLD was from about 54% to 59%, and that for WSLC was from 40% to about 42%. Other experiments have given similar results, indicating that the initial distribution has little or no effect on the prevalence of cooperation after as few as 15 generations. For present purposes, we conclude that the distribution of cooperation we observed in our basic experiment is not an artifact resulting from our use of 50-50 initial distributions of cooperators and defectors.

2.2.5 Speed of Achieving Stable Levels

One important issue that is not addressed by the group size study is the speed with which the population changes from its initial configuration. In one experiment, we varied the number of generations that the simulations ran before stopping. We varied the stopping time from 2 generations to 30. In all cases, the simulations began with random 50-50 distributions of the 100 cooperators and defectors. The results of this experiment are displayed in Figure 1. What is clear from this figure is that the proportion of cooperators rapidly settles in on the asymptotic values of about 40% for WSLC and 55% for WCLD. There is little change following trial number six. A similar pattern emerges with the analysis of the cluster variable. For WSLC, it rapidly reaches its base level of about -.017, showing no evidence of clustering. (We make this interpretation by comparing this mean with the clustering measure of the initial random distributions. The mean of the cluster measure for thousands of these initial distributions is -.01.) For the WCLD rule, the cluster measure rapidly grows to about .12. For the cluster index, an analysis of variance fails to detect a difference in the slopes for the two rules.

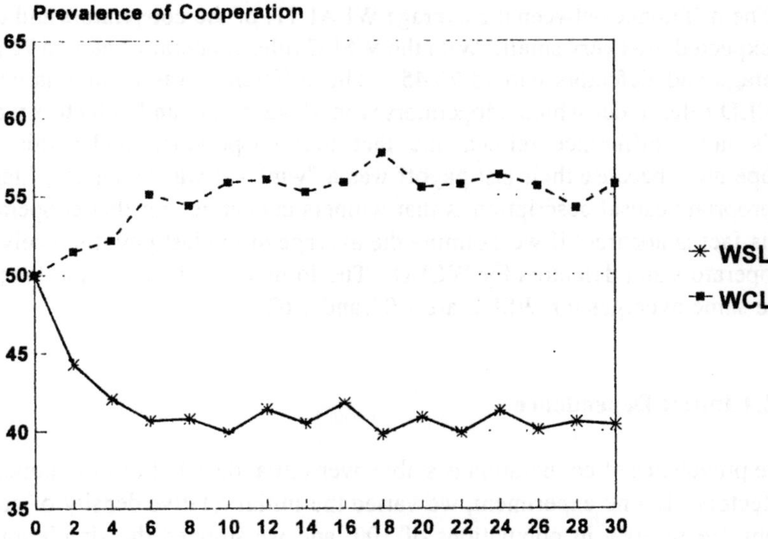

Fig. 1. Mean prevalence of cooperation for WSLC and WCLD as a function of generations. Each mean is based on 50 simulations.

3 Theoretical Model

After having observed stable levels of cooperation in large groups for both decision heuristics, we now turn to the question of whether we can predict the location of these equilibria. The problem predicting the overall level of cooperation for one choice rule actually consists of four parts. These correspond to the likelihoods that a subject will cooperate on the next trial, given the occurrence of each of the four outcome pairs of the preceding trial. Table 2 presents the next-choice consequences for both rules for each of the four outcome cells.

Table 2 Payoff and next-choice consequences for each of the four outcome cells of the PDG for two choice rules

S = Subject, N = Neighbor

Choice Pair (S,N)	C,C	C,D	D,C	D,D
Payoff to Subject	2	0	3	1
Next choice for WSLC	C¦win,D¦lose	D	D	D¦win,C¦lose
Next choice for WCLD	C¦win,D¦lose	D	C	C¦win,D¦lose

First, it is obvious that we are dealing with 'strong' decision heuristics because both WSLC and WCLD do not accept exploitation by the other: If the neighbor defects while the subject cooperates, then the subject will retaliate in the next move and defect as well. The reason, of course, is that the CD outcome will always be coded as a loss for the cooperator because it yields zero outcome units. The corresponding conditional probability that the subject will cooperate in the next game, therefore, is 0. These conditional probabilities are displayed in Table 3. After a DC outcome, it is also clear what the subject's next move will be: defect under WSLC and cooperate under WCLD.

Table 3 Unconditional probabilities of choice pairs and conditional probabilities of cooperation for WSLC and WCLD
The overall prevalence of cooperation is a, S = Subject, N = Neighbor

Choice Pair (S,N)	C,C	C,D	D,C	D,D
Probability of pair	a^2	a(1-a)	(1-a)a	$(1-a)^2$
P(C¦S,N) for WSLC	w_1	0	0	w_2
P(C¦S,N) for WCLD	w_1	0	1	w_3

For the diagonal outcome cells, things are more subtle. First, we will analyze the WSLC rule. For the CC outcome cell, we can expect another C-choice by the subject only if the last cooperative choice is coded as a win. The probability that this will happen is unknown, but we can denote that conditional probability as w_1. Similarly, after a DD-outcome, the subject will switch to a C-choice only if defection has been coded as a loss. The conditional probability of a cooperative choice under WSLC after a DD-outcome is w_2. The two conditional probabilities, w_1 and w_2 (Table 3), represent a fraction of the distribution of the payoffs in the local neighborhood. Cooperation is rewarded in case the average payoff of the neighbors is less or equal to two units. Defection is punished when the others on the average have more than one payoff unit.

Suppose both w_1 and w_2 would be equal to one (always play C in the next game). In that case, the overall level of cooperation for WSLC would be indicated by the relative occurrence of the CC and the DD outcome, because after CD and DC the subject will never cooperate on the next trial. We have seen before that these unconditional probabilities are a^2 (for CC) and $(1-a)^2$ (for DD), where we let the overall level of cooperation be denoted by a. In our hypothetical case, the overall level of cooperation for WSLC would be $a^2 + (1-a)^2$. We know, however, that both w_1 and w_2 normally would be less than 1, indicating that we have to multiply the unconditional probabilities with the corresponding conditional probabilities. Then the overall level of cooperation in the population for WSLC can be expressed as a sum of the products of conditional and unconditional probabilities for the diagonal cells:

$$a = w_1 a^2 \; + \; w_2(1-a)^2 \tag{2}$$

Using the conditional and unconditional probabilities shown in Table 3, we can also specify the equilibrium equation for WCLD. In this case, we do not have two as in WSLC, but three outcome pairs after which cooperation by the subject on the next move is possible. After a DC outcome, the subject will always cooperate. After CC or DD outcomes, the subject will cooperate if the outcomes 2 and 1, respectively, are coded as a win. The probability that the 2 is coded as a win is denoted by w_1, as with WSLC. After mutual defection, the subject will change to cooperation only if that defection is coded as a win. This conditional probability, in fact, is the complement of w_2 and will be denoted w_3 (Table 3). Taking the weighted sum of these three components yields the equilibrium equation for WCLD:

$$a = a^2 + a(1-a) + (1-a)^2 \, w_3 \tag{3}$$

3.1 Equi-Cooperation Contours

The two equilibrium equations specified above provide insight into the dynamic mechanisms responsible for the emergence of stable cooperation levels under WSLC and WCLD. To illustrate this, it is important to visualize the nature of the conditional probabilities w_1, w_2, and w_3. Figure 2 shows a hypothetical distribution of the neighbors' mean payoff. We can identify the conditional probabilities in this distribution. The probability w_1 is the area above and to the left of value 2 because that is the probability that cooperation is coded as a win. Similarly, w_2 is the area to the right of value 1 because that is the region in which 1 is coded as a loss. Finally, w_3 is (1- w_2), the probability that 1 is coded as a win.

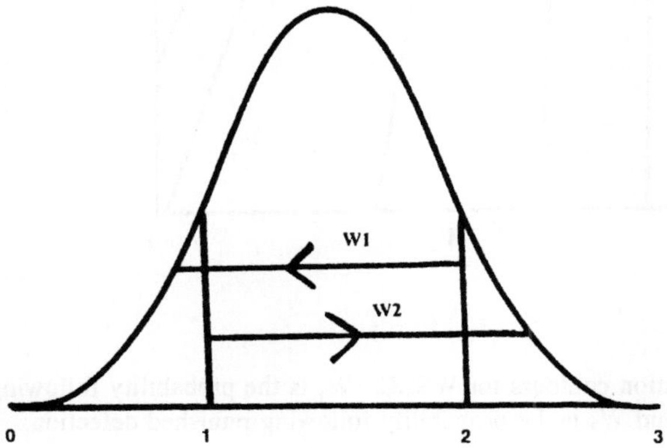

Fig. 2. Hypothetical distribution of neighbors' mean payoffs.

Both equilibrium equations can be specified in a slightly different way by solving them for w_1. For WSLC, this yields:

$$w_1 = a^{-1} - ((1 - a) / a)^2 w_2 \tag{4}$$

For WCLD, the corresponding equation is:

$$w_1 = 1 - ((1 - a) / a)^2 w_3 \tag{5}$$

Expressions (4) and (5) allow us to graphically display the interplay between the overall stable level of cooperation a, and the conditional probabilities. Figure 3 shows the equal cooperation contours for WSLC, and Figure 4 displays the corresponding ones for WCLD.

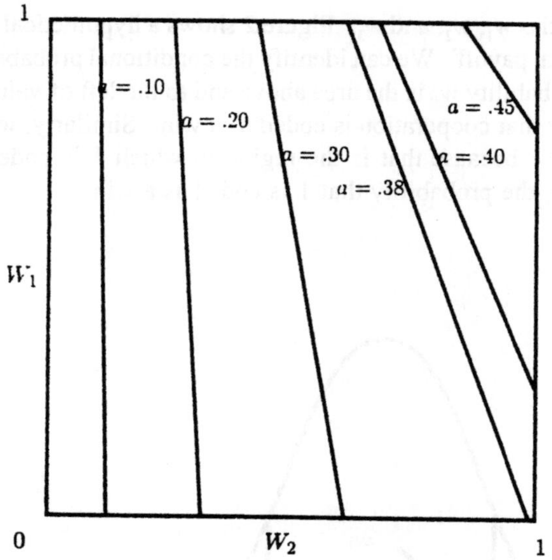

Fig. 3. Equal cooperation contours for WSLC. W_1 is the probability following rewarded mutual cooperation, and W_2 is the probability following punished defection.

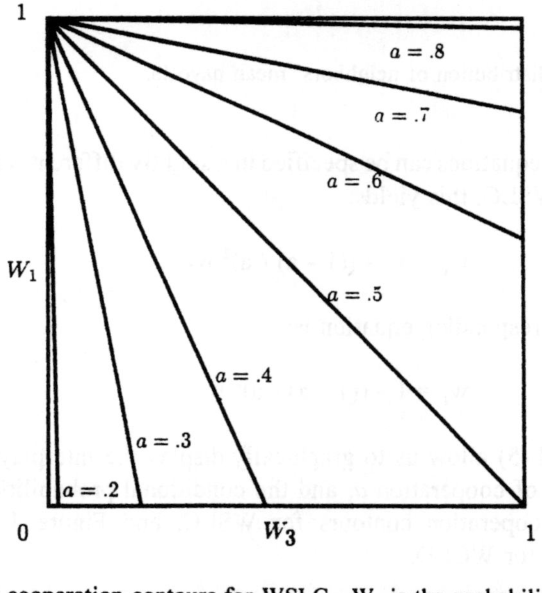

Fig. 4. Equal cooperation contours for WSLC. W_1 is the probability following rewarded mutual cooperation, and W_3 is the probability following punished defection.

Several things become obvious now. First of all, for both plots, we see that the two conditional probabilities are linearly and negatively related. For the same overall prevalence of cooperation, it holds that an increase of one conditional probability leads to a decrease of the value of the other. Next, it is surprising to see that WSLC will *never* generate more than 50% cooperation in the population. This upper limit can also be derived from Expression 4, since $0 \leq w_1, w_2 \geq 1$. In addition, for WSLC, we see that the overall prevalence of cooperation is more sensitive to changes in w_2 than to changes in w_1. In other words, changes related to the punishment of defection are likely to have more effect under WSLC than the manipulation of rewarded cooperation. For WCLD, the expected effects of changes in rewarded cooperation (w_1) and rewarded defection (w_3) are more similar (see Figure 4). Moreover, the overall level of cooperation can vary from 0 to 100%. As can be seen from expression (5), complete cooperation under WCLD can only be achieved if the probability of rewarded defection is zero.

4 A Theoretical Test

The above insights regarding the interplay of overall prevalence of cooperation and the conditional probabilities can be put to a test by manipulating the evaluation criterion of the two choice heuristics. The evaluation process employed in this study is the psychological heart of our simulations. This model proposes a social evaluation process that determines how outcomes are coded as wins or losses. By manipulating the evaluation criterion, we can indirectly manipulate the conditional probabilities, which, in turn, should yield predictable effects on cooperation levels.

The local social reference point separating winning from losing does not have to be exactly at the average of the neighbors. For instance, one might believe that one deserved more than the average neighbor or, alternatively, that one was happy with somewhat less than this benchmark. We explored the effects of shifting this boundary by systematically varying a bias parameter so that a win is coded when the outcome for the last game *plus* a (positive or negative) bias component is equal to or greater than the mean of the neighbors. When bias is positive, winning is more inclusive than when bias is negative. The larger the bias, therefore, the more frequent "stay" should be with WSLC and the more frequent "cooperate" should be with WCLD. A larger bias implies that the reference point in Figure 2 will be moved to the right, increasing w_1 and decreasing w_2. Because, for WSLC, w_2 is more important than w_1, we predict decreasing cooperation as bias increases (see Figure 3). The opposite prediction holds for WCLD because here a movement of the reference point to the right in Figure 2 increases both w_1 and w_3. For WCLD, an increase in bias would yield higher cooperation levels (see Figure 4).

The data that we will discuss result from varying the bias parameter from -.30 to .30 for both rules. We selected this range initially because it seemed small relative to the average value of the payoff units in our basic experiment. The effect of manipulating bias is displayed in Figure 5. Each of the means plotted here is the average of 50 simulations, each of which was 50 generations long with a population size of 100.

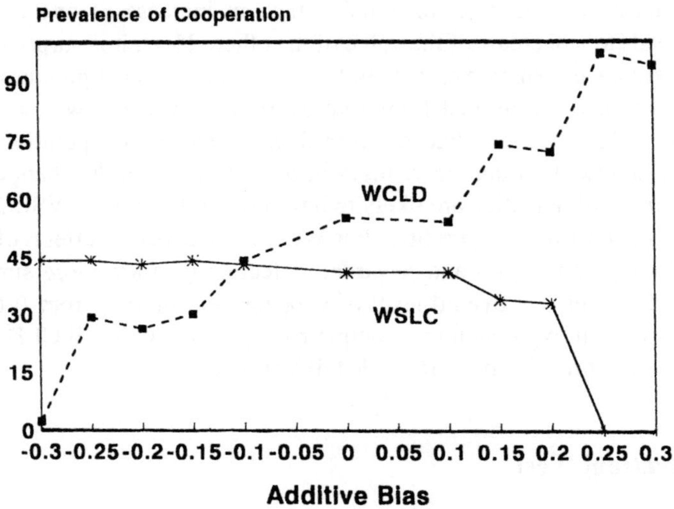

Fig. 5. Mean prevalence of cooperation for WSLC and WCLD as a function of additive bias. A win = subject's payoff + bias ≤ neighbors' mean payoff.

As predicted, as bias increased, cooperation increased for WCLD. It decreased, however, for WSLC. With a bias component of .30, we found homogeneous defection for WSLC and nearly homogeneous cooperation for WCLD. Furthermore, we also see that as bias decreased, the cooperation under WSLC did not exceed the theoretical maximum of 50%. For WCLD, cooperation varies from nearly 0 up to nearly 100%, as a function of relatively minor changes in the evaluation criterion.

The ways in which we implemented bias, by an additive element to the payoffs obtained from the last interaction, could represent subjective biasing processes as well as shifts in the criterion placement. For instance, for positive biases, additive biases that are greater than zero or proportional biases less than unity could be thought of as resulting from tendencies to belittle the outcomes of others and/or to exaggerate the value of one's own outcomes. Negative biases may represent the opposite tendencies: to demean one's own outcomes and to inflate the worth of others'. There is ample evidence for positive subjective bias in the experimental literature, and negative biases have often been associated with problems resulting from low self-esteem (Taylor, 1990). For present purposes, however, it is sufficient to conclude that the data from this study strongly support the predictions derived from the dynamic model.

5 Summary and Conclusions

In this chapter we have shown that new game theoretical approaches, combining more practical normative theories (Selten, 1991) with computer simulations, provide a powerful new research tool to study the dynamics of decision making in large groups. It appears that cooperation is sustainable in large groups where people interact under the highly competitive PD structure while using a competitive type of social comparison for the evaluation of their outcomes.

The two adaptive choice heuristics that we explored produced high, stable levels of cooperation in large groups. Thus far it has been observed by several scholars (Axelrod, 1984, Taylor, 1976, Friedman, 1971) that conditional cooperation should be possible in cases of iterated games where the players do not discount future outcomes too heavily. As has been pointed out by Bendor and Mookherjee (1987), however, these scholars all doubt that conditional cooperation will be feasible in very large populations (p. 131). In addition, Dawes (1980) observes that "all experimenters who have made explicit or implicit comparisons of dilemma games with varying numbers of players have concluded that subjects cooperate less in larger groups than in smaller ones."

In contrast, the research described here shows that there exists qualitative differences between small and large groups for WSLC and WCLD. After a critical group size, cooperation stabilizes for these choice heuristics. This finding demonstrates that Taylor's (1982) argument is inaccurate in the current context. According to Taylor (cited in Bendor & Mookherjee, 1987, p. 131):

> "voluntary cooperation is less likely to occur in large groups than in small ones, since a conditional cooperator must be able to monitor the behavior of others in the group so as to reassure himself that they are doing their parts and not taking advantage of him. Clearly, as the size of the group increases, this mutual monitoring becomes increasingly difficult and the "tacit contract" of conditional cooperation becomes increasingly fragile."

Mutual monitoring of all actors in very large groups is not only difficult, it is impossible. Fortunately, it is not a necessary condition for securing cooperation in iterated games. The competitive monitoring of some people to whom we are socially related is not only a more realistic option, but our theoretical approach shows that it also can be a sufficient condition for maintaining some level of cooperation.

The theoretical model allows us to predict changes in stable cooperation levels for two decision rules as a function of different payoff distributions in social neighborhoods. The model, therefore, adds to our knowledge of decision making under conflict, but its generality of course is limited. We assume, for instance, prisoner's dilemma contingencies, symmetrical interaction patterns, a fixed neighborhood, and homogeneous choice rules. In doing so, we deliberately deviated from evolutionary game theory and the proliferation of evolutionary contests among PDG strategies (Axelrod, 1984, Nielsen 1994). Our research interest is in the fate of cooperation if all people use the same strategy. In future work, we can explore the effects of heterogeneity in a variety of ways.

The second major theme of this research concerns the dynamic relationship between micro-level behavior and aggregate-level outcomes. In this study, we have seen that stable levels of cooperation "emerged", a phenomenon which cannot be fully understood if the level of analysis had been restricted to either the micro- or the macro-level. Recently, more researchers have been making the same point (e.g. Nowak, Szamrej, & Latané, 1990). Using methods from statistical thermodynamics, Glance and Huberman (1994) show that cooperation spontaneously can arise and stabilize in small groups in which all members initially were defecting. Nowak and May (1992) have shown that highly simplistic choice rules can generate "chaotically changing spatial patterns of extreme richness and beauty", patterns in which cooperators and defectors persist indefinitely. Hegselmann (in press) used the cellular automata approach to model social dynamics and to analyze the emergence of stable support networks in social dilemma situations. In a similar way, Nowak, Urbaniak, and Zienkowski (in press) have shown how the spread of economic changes in Poland could be made more understandable by successfully modelling them in computer simulations.

Computer simulations offer us the tools to analyze the dynamic relationship between individual behavior and the characteristics of the collective system. When we started this line of research, we were overwhelmed by the complexity and reactivity of our artificial world of decision makers. Gradually, we gained more control and are now able to outline some basic mechanisms. The theoretical model developed here, however, is still rudimentary. The next step will be to introduce more richness into our reconstruction of these social decision processes.

References

Axelrod, R. (1984). *The evolution of cooperation.* New York, NY: Basic Books.

Bendor, J., & Mookherjee, D. (1987). Institutional structure and the logic of ongoing collective action. *American Political Science Review, 81*, 129-154.

Dawes, R. (1980). Social dilemmas. *Annual Review of Psychology, 31*, 169-193.

Friedman, J. (1971). A non-cooperative equilibrium for supergames. *Review of Economic Studies, 38*, 1-12.

Gasik, S. (1990). *Definition of the warsaw simulation language.* Unpublished manuscript.

Glance, N. S., & Huberman, B. A. (1994). The dynamics of social dilemmas. *Scientific American, March*, 58-63.

Hegselmann, R. (in press). Modeling social dynamics by cellular automata. In W. B. G. Liebrand, A. Nowak, & R. Hegselmann (Eds.), *Computer modeling of social dynamics.*

Kelley, H. H., Thibaut, J. W., Radloff, R., & Mundy, D. (Eds.) (1962). The development of cooperation in the "minimal social situation" [Special issue]. *Psychological Monographs, 76*(19).

Krebs, D. L., & Miller, D. T. (1985). Altruism and aggression. In G. Lindzey, & E. Aronson (Eds.), *The handbook of social psychology, Vol. 1.* Hillsdale, NJ: Erlbaum.

Liebrand, W. B. G., Messick, D. M., & Wilke, H. A. M. (1992). *Social dilemmas: Theoretical issues and research findings.* Oxford, England: Pergamon Press.

Messick, D. M., & Liebrand, W. B. G. (1995). Individual heuristics and the dynamics of cooperation in large groups. *Psychological Review, 102*, 131-145.

Nielsen, F. (1994). Sociobiology and sociology. *Annual Review of Sociology, 20*, 267-303.

Nowak, M. A., & May, R. M. (1992). Evolutionary games and spatial chaos. *Nature, 359*, 826-829.

Nowak, A., Szamrej, J., & Latané, B. (1990). From private attitude to public opinion: A dynamic theory of social impact. *Psychological Review, 97*, 362-376.

Nowak, A., Urbaniak, J., & Zienkowski, L. (in press). Clustering processes in economic transition. In W. B. G. Liebrand, A. Nowak, & R. Hegselmann (Eds.), *Computer modeling of social dynamics.*

Rushton, J. P. (1980). *Altruism, socialization, and society.* Englewood Cliffs, NJ: Prentice Hall.

Sakado, J. M. (1971). The checkerboard model of social interaction. *Journal of Mathematical Sociology, 1*, 119-132.

Schelling, T. C. (1971). Dynamic models of segregation. *Journal of Mathematical Sociology, 1*, 143-186.

Selten, R. (1991). Evolution, learning, and economic behavior. *Games and Economic Behavior, 3*, 3-24.

Taylor, M. (1976). *Anarchy and cooperation.* New York, NY: Wiley.

Taylor, M. (1982). *Community, anarchy, and liberty.* Cambridge, England: Cambridge University Press.

Taylor, S. E. (1990). *Positive illusions.* New York, NY: Basic Books.

Thibaut, J. W., & Kelley, H. H. (1959). *The social psychology of groups.* New York, NY: Wiley.

Wolfram, S. (1986). *Theory and applications of cellular automata.* Singapore: World Scientific.

Natural Selection and Social Learning in Prisoner's Dilemma: Co-adaptation with Genetic Algorithms and Artificial Neural Networks*

Michael Macy[1]

Abstract. Evolutionary game theory has been used to study the viability of cooperation in a predatory world. While previous studies have helped to identify robust strategies, little is known about how success translates into the reproduction of cultural rules. Analogs of genetic replication may be deceptive if social learning and natural selection engender different population dynamics. I distinguished selection and learning based on whether rules are hardwired or softwired in the organisms that carry them. I then used genetic algorithms and artificial neural networks to operationalize the distinction. Applied for the first time to iterated Prisoner's Dilemma, neural network experiments showed that researchers may need to be much more cautious in using Darwinian analogs as templates for modeling the evolution of cultural rules.

Keywords. Prisoner's Dilemma, evolution of cooperation, genetic algorithm, neural network

Natural selection cannot select for behavior per se;
it can only select for mechanisms that produce behavior.

Cosmides and Tooby, 1987

1 Introduction

Evolutionary game theory has attracted the attention of sociologists interested in cooperation among self-interested free-agents (Lopreato 1990; Allison 1992; Kollock 1993; Nielsen 1994; Heckathorn forthcoming. For an overview, see

---

* Reprinted with permission of *Sociological Methods and Research*. This research was supported by a grant from the National Science Foundation, #SBR 95-11461.

1 Department of Sociology, Brandeis University, Waltham, MA 02254

Macy 1995). Axelrod's (1984) celebrated "computer tournament" led to the proliferation of evolutionary contests among strategies for playing iterated Prisoner's Dilemma. This game has two contestants, each with two choices, to “cooperate” or “defect.” The game is defined by the payoff inequality $T > R > P > S$, where T is the temptation to unilaterally defect, R is the reward when both cooperate, P is the punishment when both defect, and S is the payoff for suckers. In a single encounter, the best strategy is to defect, since $P > S$ (should the partner defect) and $T > R$ (should the partner cooperate). The dilemma is that the best choice for each means that both receive P, the worst possible collective outcome!

If the game is iterated, however, evolution might favor more enlightened solutions. Axelrod showed how a strategy of “Tit For Tat” (or TFT) might gain a foothold in a computational ecology infested with predators. TFT uses a simple protocol: "Cooperate on the first move and thereafter mimic your partner." The strategy is tough but fair. It never tries to exploit, is quick to forgive those who mend their ways, but never lets betrayals go unpunished. More aggressive strategies do better in a population of naive altruists, but by driving their prey to extinction, they dig their own graves. In contrast, TFT enjoys a decisive evolutionary edge: Unlike predators, it benefits from interacting with copies of itself.

Axelrod's work spawned numerous sociobiological offspring. Most of the subsequent research has focused on the identification of robust strategies (Schuessler 1989; Hirshleifer and Rasmusen 1989; Vanberg and Congleton 1992; Kollock 1993). Little attention has been directed to explaining how “fitness” translates into social influence, or how robust strategies might spread across a population. Analogs of natural selection may be a useful point of departure, but sociobiological models of cultural evolution may be overdue for a critical reconsideration. In evolutionary games, strategies like TFT are “hardwired”[2] in the contestants and can therefore only adapt as their hosts are replaced by organisms programmed with different protocols. Organisms are replaced when they lose out in the competitive struggle to survive and reproduce, hence the central importance of fitness in sociobiological models.

This is a reasonable assumption if rules are genetically inscribed as instinctual responses and selection pressures are tied to competition for survival. However, sociologists are often interested in extending evolutionary models to the spread of cultural rules, such as heuristic routines, conventions, rituals, moral sentiments, habits, and normative codes (Allison 1992; Kollock

---

2 Cognitive scientists use “hardwired” to refer to programming that minimizes the response time of an agent. Following Sigmund (1993, p. 177), I use the term to refer to programming that cannot be altered by the agent, with no implication of a faster response time. For example, reciprocity might be hardwired in an organism as a genetically encoded instinctual response, as distinguished from a culturally acquired norm of exchange.

1993; Heckathorn forthcoming). Unlike instinctual rules, cultural rules can be "softwired," that is, they can be modified and passed from one organism to another without the need to replace the host.

If agents are hardwired, adaptation can occur only at the level of the population; an organism can be replaced (through selection at the individual level), but cannot be modified. However, if rules are softwired, adaptation can proceed through reinforcement instead of reproduction. Reproduction alters the frequency distribution of strategies within a population of actors, while reinforcement alters the probability distribution of strategies within the repertoire of each individual. In simple reinforcement, the organism modifies its behavior in response to positive and negative feedback, as predicted by the "law of effect" (Thorndike 1911). Positive outcomes increase the probability that the associated behavior will be repeated, while negative outcomes reduce it. The process closely parallels the replication of hardwired rules, in which positive outcomes increase the rule's chances for survival and reproduction, while negative outcomes reduce it. However, with reinforcement, rules compete *within* the individuals that carry them, not *between* them.

If rules are softwired, two strategically interdependent individuals can evolve their relationship by learning how best to interact with someone who is trying to do the same, independently of the outcomes experienced by other elements of the population. The unit of co-adaptation is the set of actors directly influencing one another in response to the influence each receives. In a two-person interaction (or game), this unit is the dyad, in a three-person game, the triad, and so on. In contrast, if rules are hardwired, two interdependent players cannot adapt their protocols to one another's behavior. They cannot grow their relationship. In a two-person game, the unit of co-adaptation is not the dyad but the population of rule-carriers competing to reproduce.

Learning can also operate directly on the population distribution. For example, norms can jump from one organism to another by imitation (Dawkins 1976; Durham 1992; Boyd and Richerson 1985; Lopreato 1990). "Social learning" (Bandura 1977) refers to the combination of direct and vicarious reinforcement as the primary elements of human adaptation. Role-modeling can provide an efficient shortcut past the hard lessons of direct experience. If socially connected actors can learn from each other's experience, they can save themselves a good deal of time and grief.

Imitation is the principal rationale for modeling cultural evolution as an analog of natural selection (Boyd and Richerson 1985; Dawkins 1989). However, social influence differs decisively from sociobiological adaptation. Softwired rules can spread without replacement of their carriers, which means that reproductive fitness loses its privileged position as the criteria for replication. While "imitation of the fittest" is a reasonable specification of cultural selection pressures, it is clearly not the only possibility. For example, moral pressure against "free-riding" may be a function of the rate of compliance with the norm and the extent of social ties to deviants, as suggested by Latané's social impact theory (Nowak and Latané 1994) and simulated by Macy (1991b, 1993) and Gould (1993).

To sum up, sociobiology assumes that cooperation is grounded in instinctual rules that evolve in response to selection pressures that condition the chances for survival and reproduction. This hypothesis provided the point of departure for early efforts to model the cultural evolution of prosocial norms. The risk is that the replication of hardwired rules may be a misleading model for cultural evolution.

Social learning theory suggests an alternative model in which norms adapt to social feedback and then spread through imitation of significant others. If social learning converges with the evolutionary outcomes for hardwired actors, this will clearly increase the credibility of sociobiological approaches. If, on the other hand, the outcomes differ in interesting ways, then researchers will need to be much more cautious in using Darwinian analogs as templates for modeling the evolution of cultural rules.

This study tests the convergence of natural selection and social learning models when applied to the most widely studied problem in evolutionary game theory, the viability of cooperation in an iterated Prisoner's Dilemma. I modeled natural selection using genetic algorithms and social learning using artificial neural networks. Computer simulations showed how an emergent self-organizing system of interdependent co-adaptive agents might evolve very differently, depending on whether the protocols are hardwired.

2 The Evolution of Hardwired Strategies

The genetic algorithm was proposed by Holland (1975) as a problem-solving device, modeled after the recursive system in natural ecologies.[1] The algorithm provides a simple but elegant way to write a computer program that can improve through experience. The program consists of a string of symbols that carry machine instructions. The symbols are often binary digits called "bits" with values of 0 and 1. The string is analogous to a chromosome containing multiple genes. The analog of the gene is a bit or combination of bits that comprises a specific instruction. The values of the bits and bit-combinations are

---

1 Holland (1992) provides a straightforward explanation of the design and implementation of genetic algorithms. Nonspecialists interested in a delightfully playful introduction may also enjoy Prata's *Artificial Life Playhouse* (1993) or Sigmund's *Games of Life* (1993). Bainbridge (1995) is the best sociological introduction to artificial neural networks. For a more technical introduction, see Hinton (1992). Gallant's (1993) *Neural Network Learning* is a useful text. Bainbridge, Brent, Carley, Heise, Macy, Markovsky, and Skvoretz (1994) surveyed recent sociological applications of genetic algorithms, neural nets, and other models of what Bainbridge has appropriately termed "artificial social intelligence."

analogous to the alleles of the gene. A one-bit gene has two alleles (0 and 1), a two-bit gene has four alleles (00, 01, 10, and 11), and so on. The number of bits in a gene depends on the instruction. An instruction to cooperate or defect requires only a single bit. However, an instruction to cooperate, defect, or refuse to play requires two bits.

When the gene's instructions are followed, there is some performance evaluation that measures the program's reproductive fitness relative to other programs in a computational ecology. For example, it might be the payoff that is received in a round of Prisoner's Dilemma. Relative fitness determines the probability that each strategy will propagate. Propagation occurs when two mated programs recombine through processes like "crossover" and "inversion." In crossover, the mated programs (or strings) are randomly split and the "left" half of one string is combined with the "right" half of the other, and vice versa, creating two new strings. If two different protocols are each effective, but in different ways, crossover allows them to create an entirely new strategy that may combine the best abilities of each parent, making it superior to either. If so, then the new rule may go on to eventually displace both parent rules in the population of strategies. In addition, the new strings contain random copying errors. These mutations continually refresh the heterogeneity of the population, in the face of selection pressures that tend to reduce it.

To illustrate, consider the eight-bit string **10011010** mated with *11000101*. (The typefaces might represent gender, although the algorithm does not require sexual reproduction.) Each bit could be a specific gene, such as whether to cooperate under eight different conditions. In mating, the two parent strings are randomly broken, say after the third gene. The two offspring would then be **100***00101* and *110***11010**. However, a chance copying error on the last gene might make the second child a mutant, with *110***11011**.

2.1 Prisoner's Dilemma Experiments

Axelrod (1987) showed that genetic algorithms can be used to look for Prisoner's Dilemma strategies that do not evolve into a competitor that outperforms it. Axelrod used a genetic algorithm with a three-round memory. The chromosome contained 64 genes (four payoffs in each of three rounds, or 4 x 4 x 4), plus six more genes for what to do in the first three rounds. That yields 2^{70} possible strategies. "If a computer had examined these strategies at the rate of 100 per second since the beginning of the universe, less than one percent would have been checked by now" (Axelrod 1987, p. 34). However, by building on partial solutions, a genetic algorithm can chew through this problem in a few hours.

Axelrod used a population fixed at 20 players and allowed only 50 generations. He found that cooperation eventually flourished, "based upon an evolved ability to discriminate between those who will reciprocate cooperation and those who won't" (p. 38). However, his design used deterministic rules and no background noise. Protocols for reciprocity are known to be vulnerable to "echo effects" triggered by random miscues when interacting with other reciprocators (Axelrod and Dion 1988; Kollock 1993; Sigmund 1993). If either side should mistakenly defect, the result can be an indefinite series of recriminations, as noted by Sigmund. "Even the smallest background noise can come very costly to a Tit For Tat population...Mistakes cause feuds, and feuds do not pay" (1993, p. 192).

In a follow-up to Axelrod's research, Nowak and Sigmund (1993) relaxed the assumption of perfectly predictable behavior. They modeled iterated Prisoner's Dilemma as a Markov process among stochastic strategies consisting of four conditionally cooperative propensities, one for each of the four possible game outcomes. Their model had only one moment of memory and random cooperation on the first move. This model is equivalent to a genetic algorithm with a 4-gene chromosome but without crossover (which is not needed with very short strings) and "gray bits" instead of 0's and 1's. Unlike Axelrod, they allowed evolution to unfold for hundreds of thousands of generations.

Based on Axelrod's experiments, they had expected to see a "generous" variant of Tit For Tat flourish. This rule rewards cooperators by reciprocating but does not always retaliate against defectors. Instead, the clear evolutionary winner was "Win-Stay, Lose-Shift" (WSLS), a pragmatic rule based on the law of effect: repeat rewarded choices, otherwise switch. In Prisoner's Dilemma, a contestant is assumed to "win" if their partner cooperates and "lose" if their partner defects. TFT thus translates as "win-cooperate, lose-defect," or alternatively, "win-reward, lose-punish." TFT and WSLS have identical protocols for cooperation after *R* (a win) and defection after *S* (a loss). However, TFT cooperates after *T* (to reward the partner's cooperation), while WSLS defects (to repeat the rewarded behavior). Conversely, WSLS cooperates after *P* (to avoid further punishment), while TFT retaliates.

Conceptually, TFT and WSLS are complements: TFT teaches, WSLS learns. TFT rewards cooperation and punishes defection, as if trying to modify the partner's behavior. Conversely, WSLS modifies its own behavior by repeating choices that are rewarded and avoiding those that are punished. In effect, TFT promotes adaptation by teaching its partner a lesson, while WSLS contributes by getting the message.[4]

The conditions assumed by Nowak and Sigmund may have unduly favored WSLS over TFT. Nowak and Sigmund allowed only one moment of memory. A second memory register is required to implement more complex strategies that respond not to the partner's previous choice but to recent changes in the partner's behavior.

---

4 Curiously, TFT and WSLS do not get along as well as might be expected. If either side errantly defects, the result is an endless cycle of CD → DC → DD → CD.

Meanwhile, Axelrod limited evolution to only 50 generations and used deterministic rules that never made mistakes. As noted above, previous researches have shown that TFT is highly vulnerable to blood feuds triggered by random miscues, such as faulty memory, misperception, or Selten's (1975) "trembling hand" that occasionally pushes the wrong button (Kollock 1993; Bendor 1993). However, this problem can be easily solved by simply mutating a little higher threshold for retaliation. A more subtle threat to cooperation arises only in the *absence* of noise. Consider a world without error in which TFT is flourishing and predators have been driven to extinction. Universal cooperation creates a stable equilibrium where almost everyone cooperates after R. As long as their partners are cooperative, forgiving altruists cannot be distinguished from their streetwise and vengeful cousins, allowing the population to drift toward naive cooperation. Eventually, a mutant predator finds itself surrounded by suckers who have lowered their guard. The infection quickly spreads and social order collapses. As Sigmund put it, "The meek shall endanger the earth" (1993, p. 191).

Assuming that life has at least a trace of imperfection, with rare but inevitable miscues and faulty recollections, the problem of lowered immunity may not arise. WSLS can use errors to test whether a cooperative partner can be safely exploited, a trick that TFT cannot use. In short, Axelrod's failure to incorporate noise may have been unfair to WSLS, while Nowak and Sigmund's use of minimally complex strategies may have given it an unfair edge.

I therefore conducted an evolutionary experiment very similar to these precursors, but with an allowance for both perceptual and behavioral mistakes (that is, errors on both the input side and the output), and the ability to overlook occasional transgressions. I designed a genetic algorithm (called GENET[5]) that contained 21 genes. Each gene carried a specific instruction to cooperate or defect, for each of 21 conditions to which the device was capable of responding.

2.2 The Logic of GENET

Figure 1 diagrams the genetic code. The "trust gene" governs cooperation on the first move with a new partner (whose past behavior is unknown). Strategies that always cooperate on the first move are called "nice" (Axelrod 1984). Given the uncertainty with a partner whose past behavior is unknown, a nice strategy is one that is willing to trust a stranger. Trust gets the relationship off on the right foot and may be operationally defined as the propensity to cooperate in the absence of behavioral indicators.

---

5 All simulation models were programmed in Turbo Pascal 7.0. The source code is available from the author on request.

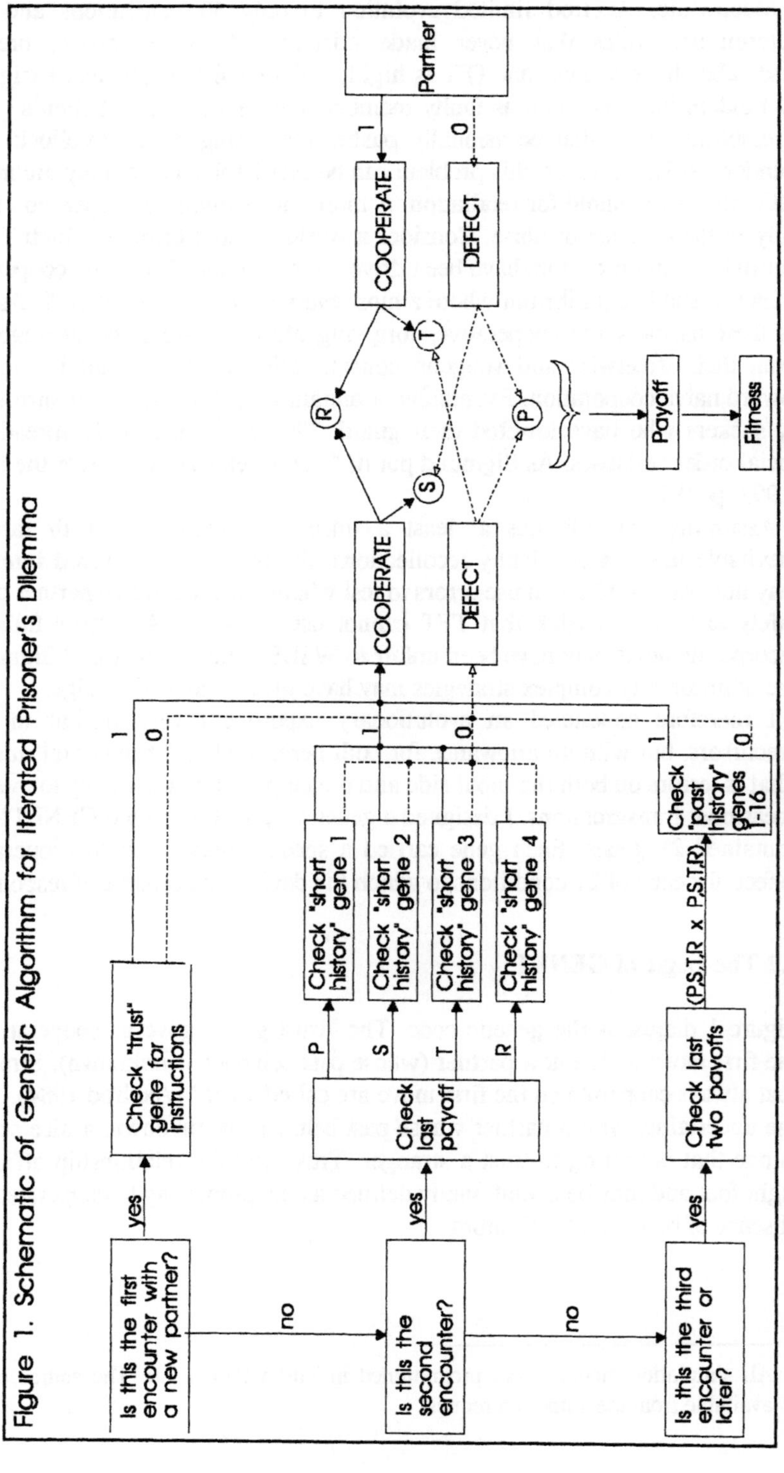

Figure 1. Schematic of Genetic Algorithm for Iterated Prisoner's Dilemma

On the second move, four "short-history" genes instruct the response to the four possible outcomes of the previous move. After that, sixteen "past-history" genes take over for the remainder of the relationship. The past-history genes respond to the payoffs from the two previous rounds. Two rounds are the minimum needed to see if "Tit For Two Tats" can evolve, a strategy that forgives an intermittent defection. The four payoffs in each of two rounds generate sixteen possibilities, each represented by a different gene. Overall, then, the algorithm assumes a chromosome with 21-genes, a single trust gene, four short-history genes, and 16 past-history genes. The chromosome governs the decision to cooperate, depending on whether there is no history, a history of one move, or a history of two moves.

To illustrate the design, consider the genes for playing Tit For Tat. The genes must instruct the organism to cooperate on the first move and thereafter mimic the partner's previous move. The trust gene for TFT must therefore contain a "1." There are four short-history genes, one for each of the four game payoffs in the first encounter with a new partner. A simple way to structure this is to use the decimal equivalents of the binary numbers corresponding to the four combinations of 1's and 0's representing cooperation and defection by each side in the previous round. Starting at the first of the four "short history" genes, if both players defected (00), the locator moves forward zero, that is, it remains on the first of the four genes. If the player is suckered (01), the locator moves forward one, to the second gene in the chain. In the opposite case (10), the locator moves forward two. And if both cooperated (11), the locator moves forward three. The protocol for TFT thus requires a "1" in genes 3 and 4 of the short-history string, corresponding to the two outcomes in which the partner cooperated.

The past-history genes work the same way, except here there are sixteen combinations, decimal 0 (or binary 0000) through decimal 15 (or binary 1111). The string must therefore contain 16 genes, each with two alleles, 0 (defect) or 1 (cooperate). For example, if both sides cooperated last time, and neither did the time before, the decimal input value is 3 (or binary 0011), which means "move forward three genes," to the fourth "past history" gene. If that gene contains a "1," the player will then cooperate.

Table 1 shows how the sixteen "past history" genes respond to four binary inputs for cooperation (1) and defection (0) by GENET and its partner at times *t*-2 and *t*-1, so as to implement the protocol to cooperate if your partner previously cooperated and defect if your partner previously defected. GENET starts at the first gene in the sequence and skips forward to the location designated by the four inputs. The table shows that genes 3, 4, 7, 8, 11, 12, 15, and 16 must contain a "1" and all others must be "0" in order for GENET to mimic its partner's previous move.

Overall, then, to play Tit For Tat, the chromosome must contain a 1 in the trust gene, and 1's in all short-history and past-history genes that correspond to all possible events in which the partner previously cooperated. It must also contain 0's in genes corresponding to all possible events in which the partner previously defected. The complete 21-gene chromosome for TFT is then 1,0011,0011001100110011 (the commas are used to designate the starting points for reading each of the three gene sequences).

Table 1: Genes for Reciprocity.

t-2		*t*-1		*t*		
Partner	Self	Partner	Self	Skip Forward	Gene	Allele
0	0	0	0	0	1	0
0	0	0	1	1	2	0
0	1	0	0	4	5	0
0	1	0	1	5	6	0
1	0	0	0	8	9	0
1	0	0	1	9	10	0
1	1	0	0	12	13	0
1	1	0	1	13	14	0
0	0	1	0	2	3	1
0	0	1	1	3	4	1
0	1	1	0	6	7	1
0	1	1	1	7	8	1
1	0	1	0	10	11	1
1	0	1	1	11	12	1
1	1	1	0	14	15	1
1	1	1	1	15	16	1

2.3 Mating Algorithm

The mating algorithm was based on stochastic sampling (Goldberg 1989). At the end of each generation, each individual's probability of mating was a linear function of relative performance during that generation:

$$P_{ij} = \frac{F_i}{\sum_{n=1}^{N} F_n} \qquad \text{for } j = 1 \text{ to } N,\ j \neq i \qquad (1)$$

where P_{ij} is the probability that j is mated with i, F_i is i's "fitness" (or cumulative payoff over all previous rounds in that generation), and N is the size of the population. If the best strategy had only a small performance edge over the worst, it had only a small edge in the race to reproduce. In contrast, Axelrod replaced all below-average strategies with offspring of above-average parents, even if the winners had only a small margin of victory. This may bias evolution against mutants that take small risks, such as those that "test the waters" by cooperating on the first move with a new partner.

With stochastic sampling, each individual, even the least fit, selected a mate from the fitness-weighted pool of eligibles. In each pairing, the two parents combined their chromosomes to create a single offspring that replaced the less-fit parent. The two chromosomes were combined through crossover. First they were split after a randomly chosen gene. The "left" half of one parent's chromosome was then combined with the "right" half of the other parent's to create a new chromosome of the same length as the parents' but with genetic material from each side. The amount contributed by each parent was random from 0 (all from 1 side) to 1 (all from the other). In addition, the strings were copied with an error rate of 0.02 (2 out of every 100 strings were copied with a single genetic mutation).

There were two additional sources of error, input and output. Input error means the partner's past move was perceived or remembered incorrectly. Output error means the gene's instructions were carried out incorrectly. However, GENET also had sufficient memory to overlook occasional transgressions, given the low probability of two consecutive errors.

2.4 Simulation Results

I applied GENET to an iterated Prisoner's Dilemma with the bilateral payoffs $R = 3$ for cooperation and $P = 1$ for defection, and the unilateral payoffs $S = 0$ for cooperation and $T = 5$ for defection (the payoffs used by Axelrod and by Nowak and Sigmund). I tested evolution from a random start (randomly programmed 21-bit strings), as well as from a "state of war" (all 21 genes were initialized at 0). The experiment then continued for 10^5 generations.

Each generation consisted of a 50-round game of iterated Prisoner's Dilemma, played with a single partner selected at random from a population of 100. (Multiple partners in a generation needlessly increases the search time.) Following Axelrod, as well as Nowak and Sigmund, I assumed zero population growth. Axelrod used 151 rounds, but 50 rounds were ample to afford conditionally cooperative rules the necessary "shadow of the future." Each generation began with a new partner, empty memory registers, and zero cumulative payoffs. Payoffs were then accumulated over the 50 rounds during each generation and represented the ability to compete in the race to reproduce.

Along with the phenotype of cooperation (based on observed behavior), the experiment also measured changes in genotypes for the "trust gene" and for four payoff responses, one for each of the four outcomes at t-1. I labeled these "conciliation," "forgiveness," "remorse," and "prudence," for the rules to cooperate after P, S, T, and R, respectively. Conciliation is the genotype for cooperation after repeated mutual defection (gene 1 in Table 1), the willingness to extend an olive branch after both sides have exchanged blows (but if the gesture is not reciprocated, there is no implication of appeasement or surrender). Its antithesis is resolve, the willingness to hold out, to persevere despite the costs. Forgiveness is the genotype for continued cooperation after being suckered; the antithesis is revenge (genes 2, 6, 10, and 14 in Table 1). Remorse is the complement of forgiveness, the genotype for switching to cooperation after making someone a sucker (genes 3, 7, 11, and 15). Finally, prudence is the response to repeated mutual cooperation, the willingness to resist the myopic temptation to score a quick hit (gene 16). Prudence was narrowly defined as a trait that, when echoed, sustains a stable local equilibrium at mutual cooperation. Hence, it was operationalized as the allele for a single gene. The same is true for resolve, which sustains mutual defection when echoed. In contrast, forgiveness and remorse were more broadly defined as traits that are applicable to unilateral outcomes that need not sustain a repeated pattern. Hence, forgiveness was operationalized as the aggregate of all four genes for cooperating after being suckered, and likewise for remorse.

Figure 2 chronicles the evolutionary history of cooperation over 10^5 generations, from a random start, with a two percent mutation rate and a two percent error rate evenly divided between input (perception or memory error) and output (response error). The results confirmed earlier findings by Nowak and Sigmund (1993).[6] A highly cooperative equilibrium was punctuated by very rapid evolutionary transitions and quick recovery of cooperation. The population dynamics resonate with Sigmund's summary of previous research on the evolution of cooperation in iterated Prisoner's Dilemma: "All these computer simulations carry the same, highly uplifting message. Cooperation evolves even in a totally selfish population. Envy and greed appear futile" (1993).

Moreover, as predicted by Nowak and Sigmund, the clear evolutionary winner was WSLS, not TFT. By definition, both TFT and WSLS are prudent but unforgiving. However, TFT is remorseful but resolute, while WSLS is conciliatory but without remorse. Looking at the first few generations following a random start, we see that TFT emerged immediately. Prudence, remorse, and trust spread quickly, while forgiveness and conciliation plummeted. However, TFT's initial success was short-lived. Within 8000 generations, conciliation and distrust of strangers had displaced remorse. From that point on, prudence

6 The term "confirm" may seem misplaced when referring to data from computer simulations. Despite their formality, these are nothing more than "thought experiments" that test only the internal validity of a theory and have no bearing on the external validity. Nevertheless, the experiments test hypotheses by manipulating variables under controlled conditions. I use terms like "confirm," "findings," and "results" to refer to the outcomes. Simulations also pose reliability problems. All experiments were repeated ten times to check reliability. Reported figures are representative illustrations.

and conciliation were highly robust and closely correlated with cooperation, while remorse flourished only in brief periods when cooperation had collapsed.

Figure 2. Evolution of Cooperation based on WSLS
(N = 100, e = 0.02)

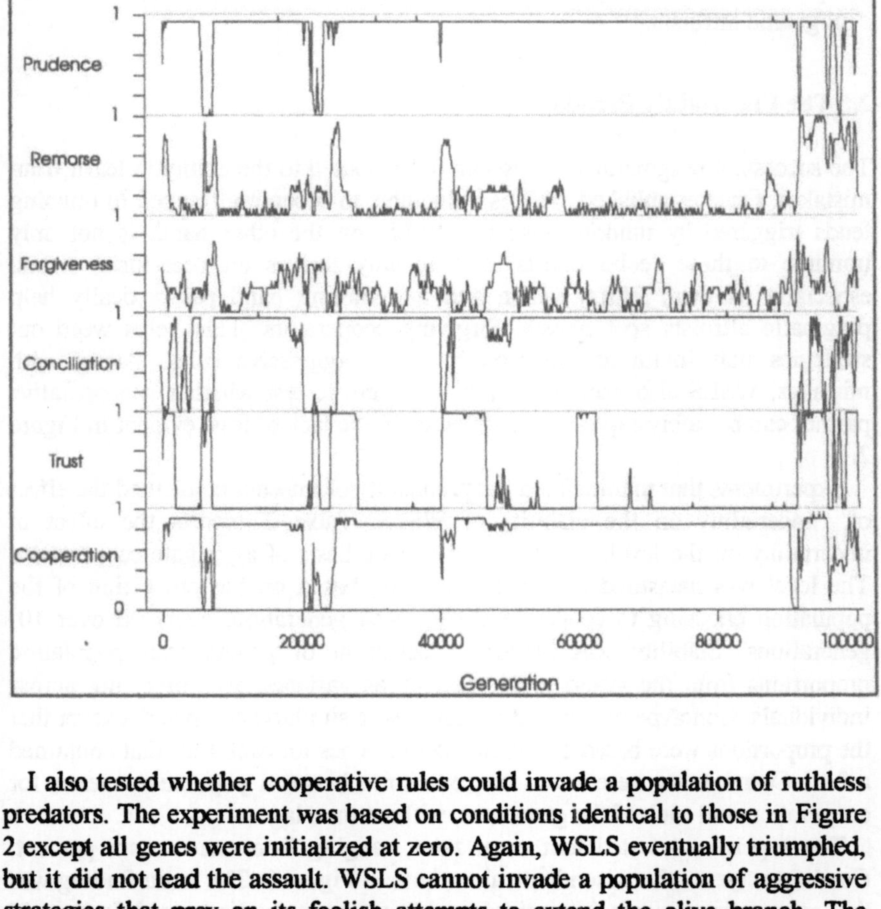

I also tested whether cooperative rules could invade a population of ruthless predators. The experiment was based on conditions identical to those in Figure 2 except all genes were initialized at zero. Again, WSLS eventually triumphed, but it did not lead the assault. WSLS cannot invade a population of aggressive strategies that prey on its foolish attempts to extend the olive branch. The eventual propagation of conciliation was a consequence, not a cause, of widespread cooperation. WSLS must rely on more resolute colleagues to give it the necessary foothold.

Over repeated simulations, the invasion of the predator population was usually led by a highly defensive reciprocator called Suspicious Tit For Tat, a protocol that rewards but never initiates cooperation. Its resolve (or unwillingness to offer conciliatory gestures) made it phenotypically indistinguishable from predators, allowing its genes for reciprocity to spread as dormant traits until there were sufficient copies to safely emerge from hiding. Eventually, a mutation produced a strain of prudent cooperators that used conciliatory gestures to search for benevolent partners. Paired with ample dormant reciprocators, the new rule (WSLS) easily outperformed the predators and quickly spread. The farther it spread, the better WSLS performed. Its performance suggests that the evolution of cooperation is based not on reciprocal altruism, as previously believed, but on its more adaptive cousin, "pragmatic altruism."

2.5 The Uncertainty Paradox

The success of pragmatic altruism can be attributed to the ability to learn from mistakes. Once established, TFT is vulnerable to becoming trapped in ongoing feuds triggered by random miscues. WSLS, on the other hand, is not only immune to these "echo effects" but actually thrives on occasional errors, especially its own. Blurry vision and a trembling hand paradoxically help pragmatic altruists spot naively forgiving cooperators. This helps weed out strategies that invite an invasion by more aggressive rules. Along with mistakes, WSLS also uses distrust of strangers to test whether a cooperative partner can be safely exploited, as reflected in the lack of trust evident in Figure 2.

Experiments that manipulated the probability of miscues confirmed the effect of uncertainty on the viability of WSLS. Table 2 reports the effect of uncertainty on the level, stability, and genetic basis of aggregate cooperation. The level was measured as the grand mean, based on the proportion of the population choosing to cooperate during each generation, averaged over 10^5 generations. Stability was based on deviation of generational population proportions from the grand mean, that is, as variance over time, not across individuals. Genotype means and variance were similarly computed, except that the proportions were based on the number of genes for each trait that contained a "1." Correlations were based on covariance between population means for cooperation and each of the genotypes, without time lag.

The experiment tested four error rates, ranging from zero to six percent. Conditions were otherwise identical to those in Figure 2. The main finding was that cooperation became increasingly stable as uncertainty increased. In a world without error, cooperation was much less stable and WSLS failed to secure a firm grip on the ecology.

This is a remarkable and counter-intuitive result. Adding a little noise at the individual level dramatically reduced uncertainty at the ecological level! With flawless information, a population of perfectly predictable individuals cooperated at about the rate that would be expected by random behavior (0.513), with random fluctuations between punctuated equilibria. However, as the behavior of the individuals became less certain, the behavior of the population became increasingly predictable, as indicated by the dramatic decline in the standard deviation, from 0.4 to 0.088.. With six percent error, WSLS quickly seized control and never lost its grip on the population. Aggregate cooperation barely wavered.

Table 2. Effect of Uncertainty on Level, Stability, and Sources of Cooperation.

	Mean[a]				Standard Deviation			
By Error Rate	0%	2%	4%	6%	0%	2%	4%	6%
Cooperation	.513	.807	.775	.678	.400	.215	.129	.088
Trust	.335	.246	.153	.090	.413	.415	.348	.259
Conciliation	.253	.783	.848	.909	.313	.316	.265	.146
Forgiveness	.363	.218	.118	.039	.193	.166	.130	.084
Remorse	.406	.179	.081	.040	.238	.256	.180	.128
Prudence	.621	.892	.928	.906	.399	.190	.101	.172

	Correlation with Cooperation			
By Error Rate	0%	2%	4%	6%
Trust	0.570*	-0.035	-0.264*	0.031
Conciliation	0.411*	0.695*	0.738*	0.788*
Forgiveness	-0.189*	-0.154*	-0.187*	-0.219*
Remorse	0.393*	-0.195*	-0.201*	-0.552*
Prudence	0.584*	0.609*	0.618*	0.789*

* Significant at the 0.01 level.
[a] All differences in means were significant at the 0.01 level.

Unfortunately, ecological stability was purchased at the expense of cooperation, as miscues took an ever greater toll on population welfare. Each accidental defection by WSLS triggers at least one retaliation before the echo dies out. Two percent uncertainty turned out to be close to the optimal tradeoff. Below two percent, WSLS could not get established, and cooperation suffered accordingly. Above two percent, WSLS approached evolutionary stability. By six percent, forgiveness and remorse were driven close to extinction (about 0.04), crowded out by conciliation and prudence (each over 0.9). However, the level of cooperation had declined, from 0.807 to 0.678.

The correlations revealed a similar pattern. As uncertainty increased, trust and remorse became less useful or even counter-productive, while conciliation and prudence became more closely associated with cooperation. In short, WSLS kept getting stronger as uncertainty increased, even though the effect on cooperation was non-monotonic.

To conclude, these experiments confirmed the evolutionary robustness of WSLS reported by Nowak and Sigmund. Reciprocators appeared to play a decisive role in the evolution of cooperation, securing a safe beachhead for more pragmatic altruists. In the long run, however, learning prevailed over teaching. Pragmatists rode reciprocators to power and then dispensed with them.

There is a strong temptation to draw out the moral implications of the demise of remorse and the triumph of conciliation. Beginning with Axelrod's evolutionary tournament over a decade ago, social scientists have used analogs of natural selection to explain the evolution of moral rules and cultural norms. For example, Darwinian logic informed Allison's (1992) model of the evolution of "beneficent norms" and Frank's (1988) explanation for "moral sentiments" grounded in emotion. More pointedly, the robustness of TFT (and its close cousins) has been used to explain diverse instances of reciprocity in social exchange, from tacit collusion in the Great War (Axelrod 1984) to loose reciprocity among the Inuit (Kollock 1993). The clear dominance of WSLS does not disprove the optimistic moral lessons previous theorists have drawn from TFT's success. Nice guys still finish first, they just turn out to be more conciliatory and less remorseful than previously believed.

However, the purpose of these experiments was not to challenge reciprocity as the basis of cooperation in social exchange. Quite the opposite. My chief concern is the tendency for social scientists to draw cultural lessons from the evolutionary robustness of any hardwired rule, TFT or WSLS. The problem is that cultural rules are softwired, procured through learning, not lineage. Cosmides and Tooby (1987, pp. 278-9) have warned researchers not "to apply evolutionary theory directly to the level of manifest behavior," but to use it "as a heuristic guide for the discovery of innate psychological mechanisms." Human biological adaptation has produced social organisms, not with an instinct to cooperate, but with an ability to *learn*. Once that faculty is flourishing, adaptation can proceed in an entirely new way. Hence, we need to study how cooperation might spread among organisms capable of rewiring their rules on the fly.

3 The Co-Adaptation of Softwired Strategies

As a genetically hardwired strategy, WSLS can change its behavior, based on associated outcomes, but it cannot change the rule that tells it to choose pragmatically. Simply put, while WSLS is guided by trial-and-error to cooperate or defect, it cannot learn to abandon a trial-and-error strategy in favor of reciprocity or some other protocol. The rule can only change when its carrier is crowded out by neighbors with better genes.

That is not the case, however, in the cultural evolution of cooperation. Cultural evolution can be modeled as an adaptive process among self-programmable devices capable of learning rules through interaction. This process differs from sociobiological evolution in that the rules are softwired, that is, the rules can be modified without replacing their carriers. If the logic of softwired adaptation differs in important ways, then previous studies, based on analogs of natural selection, should be restricted to the problem of instinctual cooperation and not generalized to the emergence of normative solidarity.

An artificial neural pathway is a simple type of self-programmable learning device based on parallel distributed processing (Rummelhart and McClelland 1988). Like genetic algorithms, neural nets have a biological analog, in this case, the nerve systems of living organisms. In elementary form, the device consists of a web of neuron-like units (or neurodes) that fire when triggered by impulses of sufficient strength, and in turn stimulate other units when fired. The magnitude of an impulse depends on the strength of the connection (or "synapses") between the two neurodes. The network learns by modifying these path coefficients in response to environmental feedback about its performance.

Neurodes consist of four types of units, as illustrated in Figure 3. The most straightforward are sensory and response units. Sensory units are triggered by input from the environment, such as the payoff from the previous round of an iterated Prisoner's Dilemma. In Figure 3, there are two sensory units. S1 has been activated by the environment (+1), while S2 has not (-1). For example, this might correspond to a condition in which the partner had cooperated on the previous play while the neural net had not. Response units, in turn, trigger action by the organism on the environment, such as the decision to cooperate or defect. In Figure 3, response unit R1 has been triggered, as indicated by the output value of +1.

The other two neurodes are less intuitive. Intermediate (or "hidden") units link sensory and response units so as to increase the combinations of multiple stimuli that can be differentiated. Figure 3 shows two hidden units, H1 and H2. Unlike sensory and response units, hidden units have no direct contact with the environment, hence their name. Finally, "bias" units are similar to hidden units but they have no inputs. Instead, they continuously fire, creating a predisposition toward excitation or inhibition in the units they stimulate, depending on the size and sign of the path coefficients. If the path weight is positive, the bias is toward excitation, and if the path is negative, the bias is toward inhibition.

A neurode fires when the sum of its weighted inputs exceeds zero. For example, in Figure 3, R1 fires because its total input is 0.1. Similarly, S1 fires because it is excited by a stimulus from the environment. When it fires, the neurode's output changes from -1 to 1, which means that its effect on later neurodes in the chain reverses. If the neurode was an inhibitor, it now becomes an excitor, and vice versa. In Figure 3, S1 excites both H1 and H2. The pathways that link the neurodes are weighted with values that determine the strength of the signals moving along the path. A low absolute value means that an input has little influence on the output. A large positive weight makes the input operate as an excitor. When it fires, the input excites an otherwise inhibited output. A large negative path weight makes the input operate as an inhibitor. When it fires, the input inhibits an otherwise excited output.

Figure 3. Schematic of Artificial Neural Network

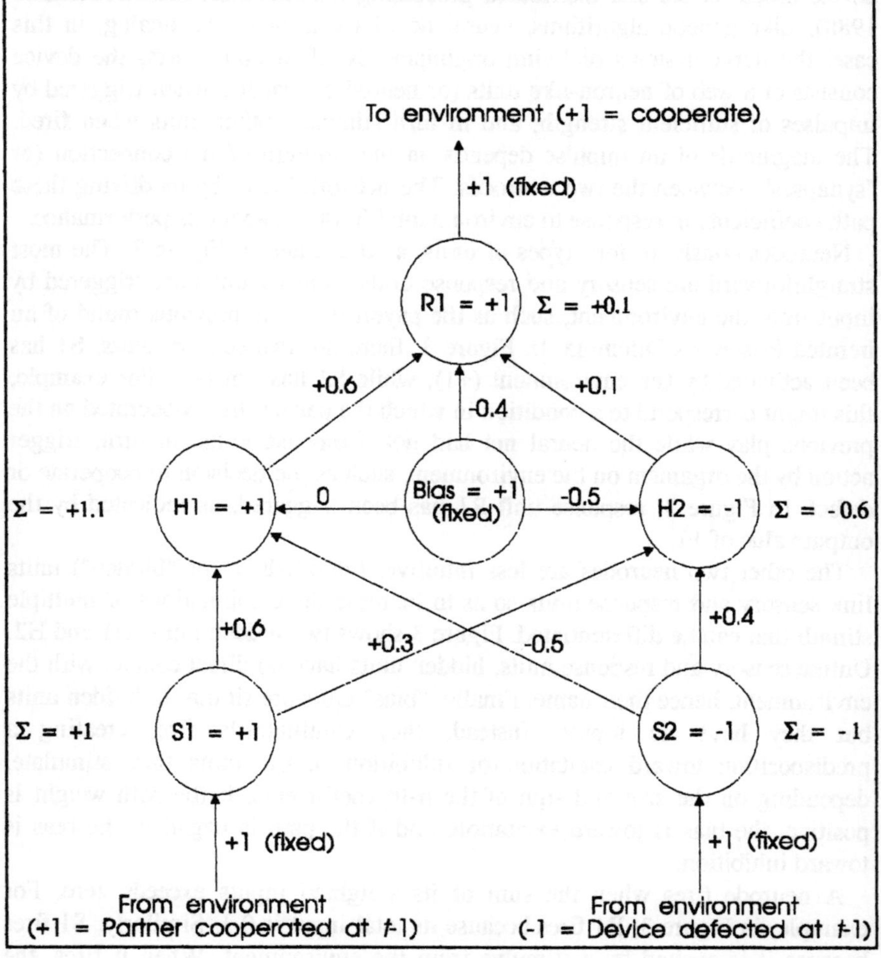

The neural device in Figure 3 has learned to play TFT. The device cooperates if S1 = 1 (partner cooperated last time) and S2 = -1 (device defected), as illustrated. The inputs to H1 are then 0.6*1, -0.5*-1, and 0, for a total of 1.1. Since 1.1>0, H1 fires, sending a value of 0.6 to R1. The inputs to H2 are 0.3 (from S1), -0.4 (from S2), and -0.5 (from bias), for a total of -0.6. Hence, H2 does not fire, sending a value of -0.1 to R1. R1 receives 0.6 (from H1), -0.1 (from H2), and -0.4 (from bias), for a total of 0.1, causing R1 to fire and the device to cooperate.

The device will also cooperate if S1 = S2 = 1. Now both H1 (total of 0.1) and H2 (total of 0.2) fire, causing R1 to fire (total of 0.3). However, the device will defect if S1 = S2 = -1 (both defect), or if S1 = -1 and S2 = 1 (the device is suckered).

The network learns by modifying the path weights linking its neurodes. Learning only occurs when the response to a given sensory input pattern is unsatisfactory. The paths are then adjusted so as to reduce the probability of repeating the mistake the next time this pattern is encountered.[7]

In many applications, neural nets are trained to recognize certain patterns or combinations of inputs. For example, suppose we want to train a neural net to predict stock prices from a set of market indicators. We first train the net to correctly "predict" known prices. The net begins with random path coefficients. These generate a prediction (or "wild guess"). The error is then used to adjust the coefficients in an iterative process that improves the predictions. These coefficients are analogous to those in a linear regression, and like a regression, the weights can then be applied to new data to predict the unknown. An important advantage of the net over least squares estimation is that it requires fewer assumptions about the functional form of the solution. On the other hand, this can also cause the net to over-fit the data. Hence, while neural nets can be very sharp prognosticators of the future, they can also generate badly convoluted interpretations of the past (Bainbridge et al. 1994, p. 428).

3.1 ANNET: A Prisoner's Dilemma Application

The Prisoner's Dilemma application in this study is a self-organizing community of co-adaptive devices that train one another on the fly, in response to the training they receive. Each individual consists of an artificial neural network, called ANNET, that is an elaboration of the Bush-Mosteller stochastic learning model I have used in several previous social dilemma simulation experiments (1990, 1991a, 1991b). The Bush-Mosteller model is equivalent to a neural net with only a single bias unit and an output, but with no sensory inputs or hidden units. Such a device is capable of learning *how often* to cooperate, but not *when* to cooperate, that is, it is incapable of learning conditional strategies. In contrast, ANNET can learn to differentiate

7 In principle, if a response unit fires at the wrong time, the weights that excited the unit would be reduced and the weights that inhibited the unit would be increased. In actuality, things are a bit more complicated; the effect of a weight also depends on the state of the neurode behind it, and so on back up the chain.

environmental cues and respond using more sophisticated protocols for contingent cooperation.

ANNET's predecessor is Bainbridge's MIND program (1995b), a neural network used to study the dynamics of social interaction.[8] It is a very simple device by the standards of the 1990's. ANNET has only 10 neurodes. The five sensory inputs are identical to the inputs to GENET (new partner, partner cooperated, ANNET cooperated, at times t-1 and t-2). When the partner is new, the first input value is 1 and the other four inputs are 0 (which means the input values are not known). If the partner has not changed since the previous interaction, the first input value is -1 and the other inputs are 1 for cooperation, -1 for defection, and 0 if unknown. (The t-2 inputs are still not known on the second interaction with a new partner.) There are also three hidden units, one bias, and one response unit.

ANNET functions the same way as the simple two-input device illustrated in Figure 3. All path coefficients were initially random and were then adjusted only if outcomes were unsatisfactory. The simulations assumed that the object of the game was to get one's partner to cooperate. Hence, an outcome was unsatisfactory if the partner defected. I implemented this assumption by subtracting a constant from the payoff matrix used with GENET, such that $T > R > 0 > P > S$. When the outcome was unsatisfactory, the paths were modified so as to reduce the probability of repeating the mistake. The correction was simply the product of the input, the output, and the negative payoff (either S or P). If an input and output both fired (+1) and the outcome was unsatisfactory, the correction was negatively signed and the path weight was reduced, thereby decreasing the excitation of the output. If the output fired but not the input, the weight was increased, so as to inhibit the output. If the input fired but not the output, the weight increased, so as to excite the output. And if neither fired, the weight was reduced (which decreased the inhibition). The more aversive the outcome (given that $S < P$), the stronger the correction. Finally, the adjustment included an error term that allowed for idiosyncrasy, and a constant that adjusted the learning rate. More formally,

$$W_{oi} = W_{oi} + s_i s_o \pi l e \qquad (2)$$

where W_{oi} is the coefficient for the path from i into o, s_i is the input stimulus to the path ($s_i = \pm 1$), s_o is the output stimulus ($s_o = \pm 1$), π is the payoff ($\pi \in$ [S,P], where $S < P < 0$), l is the learning rate ($0 < l < 1$), and e is an error term with a

8 Like Bainbridge's MIND (for "Minimally Intelligent Neural Device"), ANNET has only one layer of hidden units and does not require back propagation. MIND only modifies the path weights between input and hidden units. All other weights (between bias, hidden, and output units) are fixed. The key difference with MIND is that ANNET also modifies these weights, but only one set at a time, alternating between the sensory input side of the hidden layer and the response side (see note 7).

uniform distribution ($0 < e < 1$). ANNET's self-correcting logic keeps W_{oi} from wandering more than a few payoffs from zero.

3.2 The Unit of Co-Adaptation and the Destabilizing Effects of Uncertainty

Iterated Prisoner's Dilemma involves an ongoing relationship between two players. The dynamics of the relationship depend on whether their rules are softwired. Two hardwired interactants can influence each other's behavior, but they cannot change the rules that govern their behavior, in response to one another. The rules only change when their carriers are replaced, in response to competition not only from one another but from other rules in the ecology.

In contrast, two softwired interactants continually influence each other's rules. Here, the unit of co-adaptation is neither the rule nor the ecology but the dyad. In effect, two interacting neural nets become a single entity (the dyad) that searches through combinations of path coefficients until it finds a pair of strategies whose interaction yields two satisfactory outcomes (*R*). Although *T* is also satisfactory, it is paired with *S*, which is not, so the dyadic net keeps looking. Once *R* is found, learning stops and the mutually cooperative responses are repeated until a mistake is made or the relationship is terminated at the end of the game. The greater the uncertainty, the more mistakes and the more prolonged the search.

The easiest strategy pair for locking in cooperation is mutual prudence, the protocol to cooperate after *R*. Prudence can also be combined with mutual reconciliation, which induces self-sustaining joint cooperation after both sides have defected. With prudent reconciliation, non-remorse and vengefulness contribute to cooperation indirectly by inducing mutual defection, as a stepping stone to joint cooperation. These traits reduce to the protocol "defect after *T* and *S*; cooperate after *P* and *R*," or WSLS, the pragmatic strategy to keep doing what seems to work. The sequence moves from unilateral to bilateral defection and from there to a stable equilibrium at bilateral cooperation.

Other combinations are also possible. If one player is prudent, remorseful, and resolute (a strategy based on reciprocity), then the other needs to be prudent, forgiving, and conciliatory (a strategy that is naively cooperative). Now the sequence moves from bilateral to unilateral defection and then to bilateral cooperation. This shows that ANNET need not settle upon pragmatic altruism. ANNET is hardwired to change *rules* if the outcome is unsatisfactory, but because ANNET learns rules, not choices, ANNET can select a rule-pair based on reciprocity and naiveté rather than pragmatism.

Indeed, there is no guarantee that ANNET will find any of the possible cooperative solutions. The dyad must search through 21^2 possible rule-pairs, compared to only 2^2 choice-pairs when WSLS is hardwired. The coordination problem faced by the dyad may require more iterations than are available to the relationship. This suggests that in relationships of limited duration, the viability of cooperation will decrease with strategic complexity.

The search is also complicated by the possibility of mistakes. When WSLS is hardwired, it is trivially easy for a cooperative dyad to recover from occasional errors. The sequence is simply CC → DC → DD → CC. However, the search space for a stable rule pair is vastly larger, and this badly compromises recovery. Hence, the hypothesized effect of uncertainty is precisely the opposite of the effect observed with hardwired rules. With softwiring, rather than stabilizing the domination of WSLS at the ecological level, uncertainty may instead destabilize mutual cooperation at the dyadic level.

3.3 Simulation Results

The first experiment tested the hypothesized effects of uncertainty. Figure 4 reports ANNET's ability to find a cooperative solution to iterated Prisoner's Dilemma, from a random start, with and without the possibility of miscues. The graph traces the mean rate of cooperation at each iteration duration 100 games, each lasting 50 rounds, for a total of 5000 iterations. Learning occurred only when outcomes were unsatisfactory, that is, when the partner defected, with a learning rate[9] of 0.2. Otherwise, the experiment assumed conditions similar to those for GENET. Each game lasted for 50 rounds with a partner randomly chosen from a population of 100 contestants. The level of uncertainty was either 0 or 0.02, evenly divided between input and output errors (memory/perception and response, respectively).

Figure 4 shows that the effect of uncertainty on the evolution of cooperation was the opposite of the effect observed for hardwired rules: The equilibrium rate of cooperation was depressed by uncertainty. From a random start and no miscues, the population eventually attained near-universal cooperation, and averaged 0.89 over all 5000 iterations. In contrast, with an error rate of two percent, mean cooperation fell to 0.58. The change is the mirror image of what happened with hardwired rules: With no uncertainty, cooperation averaged about 0.51 but climbed to near-universal cooperation (and 0.81 overall) when the error rate was two percent (as indicated in Table 2).

This finding shows the danger in generalizing evolutionary logic from natural to social ecologies. If we assume uncertainty, natural selection badly overstates the prospects for the cultural evolution of cooperation. If we assume no uncertainty, natural selection badly understates the prospects. Either way, models of cultural evolution based on analogs of natural selection are likely to be misleading when applied to individuals capable of learning to cooperate.

---

9 This rate means that one-fifth of the payoff was applied to the alteration of the path coefficient The learning rate was optimized by testing ANNET's ability to recognize all possible combinations of sensory inputs. Like a fox chasing a clever rabbit, ANNET must balance raw speed against the risk of over-correction.

Figure 4. Effect of Uncertainty on Cooperation
(N = 100, 1 game = 50i)

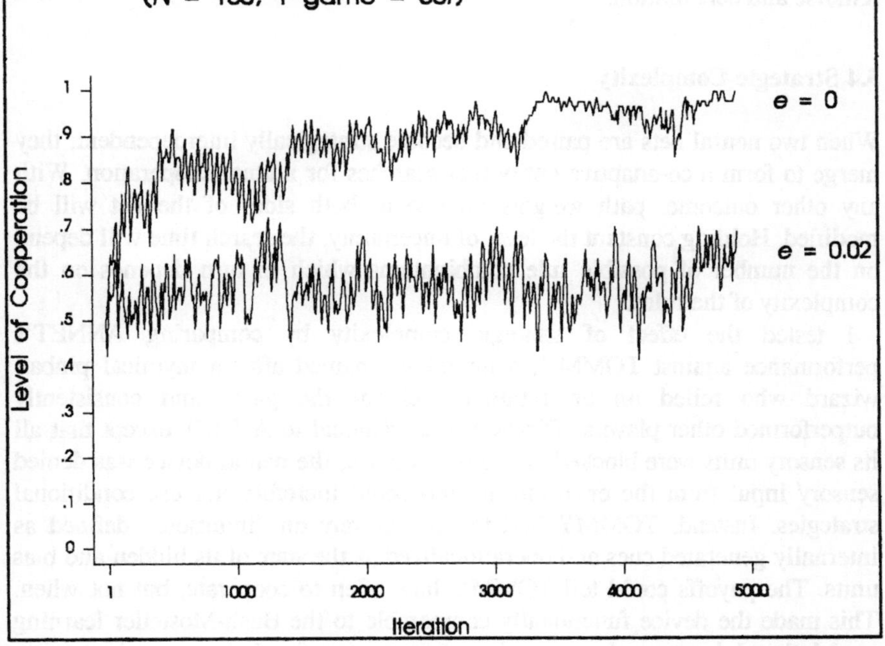

Comparison with Figure 2 reveals other differences between social learning and competitive selection. In Figure 4, there was no punctuated equilibrium. The disturbances were smaller and more frequent. Figure 4 also shows the main reason for disturbances: the level of trust lagged behind the level of cooperation. Note the cyclical drop in cooperation that occurred with the same period as each new partner. Each relationship started out with ambivalence about the new partner that was then overcome with experience. In the absence of mistakes, the population could eventually learn to trust strangers, but the process was clearly much more difficult than learning to trust a familiar face. Nevertheless, the overall level of trust was much higher than observed in Figure 2.

Inspection of the emergent rules at cooperative equilibrium reveals another difference with hardwired adaptation. At the end of the experiment, I forced latent rules to surface by inputting all possible combinations of stimulus events to each device and observing the response. Paradoxically, in a population of organisms that adapt through learning, WSLS did not emerge as the most viable strategy. Prudence and forgiveness were most prevalent, followed by remorse and conciliation.

3.4 Strategic Complexity

When two neural nets are paired and become strategically interdependent, they merge to form a co-adaptive entity that searches for mutual cooperation. With any other outcome, path weights on one or both sides of the net will be modified. Holding constant the level of uncertainty, the search time will depend on the number of possible rule combinations which in turn depends on the complexity of the rules.

I tested the effect of strategic complexity by comparing ANNET's performance against TOMMY, a neural net named after a mythical pinball wizard who relied on an intuitive feel for the game and consistently outperformed other players. TOMMY was identical to ANNET except that all its sensory units were blocked (set to 0). In effect, the neural device was denied sensory input from the environment and could therefore not use conditional strategies. Instead, TOMMY had to rely entirely on "intuition," defined as internally generated cues and operationalized as the state of its hidden and bias units. The payoffs could tell TOMMY how often to cooperate, but not when. This made the device functionally comparable to the Bush-Mosteller learning model that I have used in a series of computer simulation experiments on cooperation in social dilemmas.

One advantage of ignoring environmental cues is that one need not worry about making perceptual or memory errors, although response errors are still possible. I therefore gave TOMMY the same handicap as ANNET on the output side (a one percent error rate), but no input error. Figure 5 compares the performance of the two models over 100 iterations, which was all that TOMMY needed. The results are strikingly clear: Strategic complexity clearly compromised the search for a solution to Prisoner's Dilemma. Simply put, sensory deprivation prevented TOMMY from looking for social cues for when it was safe to cooperate. But when everyone overlooked the cues, the danger evaporated. TOMMY's success rested, quite literally, on blind faith.[10]

---

10 Kollock's (1993) study of reciprocity in iterated Prisoner's Dilemma quoted Ghandi's observation that "An eye for an eye leaves everyone blind." It now appears that blindness in Prisoner's Dilemma may not necessarily be a liability.

Figure 5. Effect of Strategic Complexity on Cooperation
(N = 100, e = 0.02, 1 game = 50i)

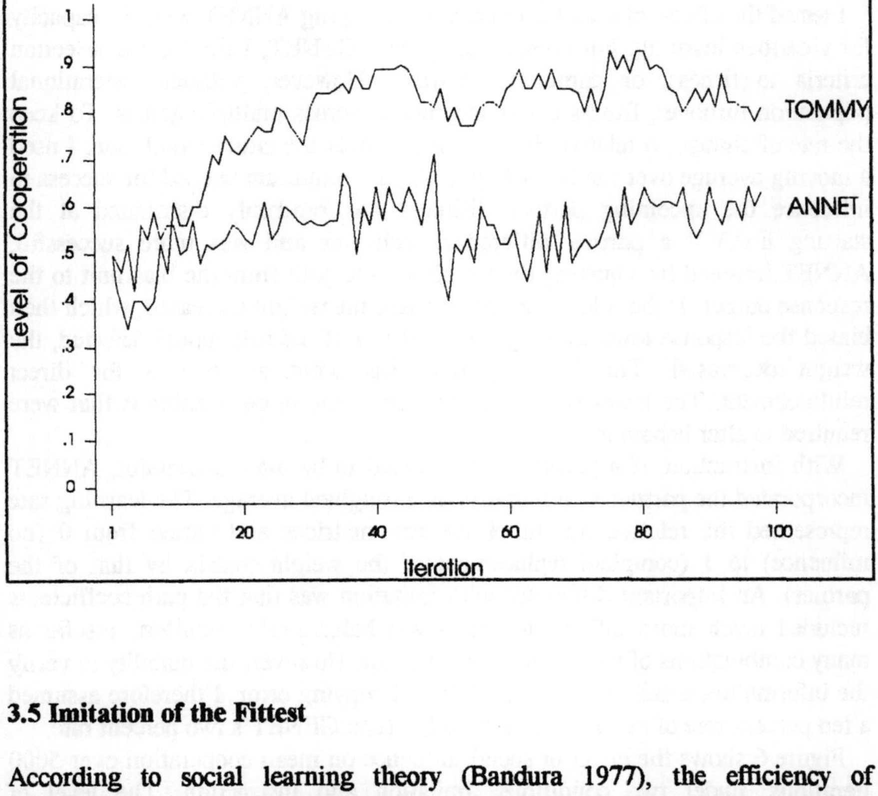

3.5 Imitation of the Fittest

According to social learning theory (Bandura 1977), the efficiency of adaptation can be enhanced through mimetic learning, or role modeling. "Imitation of the fittest" is the cultural analog of competitive selection pressures in natural ecologies. Imitating a more successful partner parallels the "mixing" of one's own genes with those of a fitter mate in the sociobiological specification. However, there is a decisive difference. Imitation operates only on rules that are behaviorally manifest. Hence, rules cannot spread unless they are directly observed. This precludes evolutionary drift--the spread of latent programs that would be snuffed out if they were immediately tested.

This limitation can be avoided if cultural transmission operates through instruction rather than imitation. An instructor can reveal protocols that apply to unobserved conditions. Instruction can provide access to latent rules but may also be distorted, by intentional deception or cognitive error (analogous to genetic mutation).

Both imitation and instruction differ from natural selection in two other ways. First, neither imitation nor instruction is necessarily triggered by a performance evaluation. The mimic may choose to copy those who are nice, nasty, widely imitated, or simply willing to share their secrets. Second, social influence does not involve replacement of the carrier of the displaced rule. This means that influential rules can spread without disrupting existing relationships.

I tested the effects of social influence by equipping ANNET with the capacity for vicarious learning. For comparability with GENET, I limited the selection criteria to fitness, or cumulative payoffs. However, without generational population turnover, fitness could accumulate across multiple games. To keep the rate of change in relative fitness constant over the entire simulation, I used a moving average over the last 100 payoffs, the minimum needed for success to influence the upcoming partner. (Fitness was randomly distributed at the starting line.) If a partner differed in behavior and was more successful, ANNET imitated by adjusting the weight on the path from the bias unit to the response output. If the role model cooperated, the weight increased, which then biased the response toward firing (cooperating). If the role model defected, the weight decreased. The learning rate was identical to that for direct reinforcement. The lower the rate of influence, the more repetitions that were required to alter behavior.

With instruction, if a partner was observed to be more successful, ANNET incorporated the partner's path matrix as a weighted average. The learning rate represented the relative weight of the two matrices and varied from 0 (no influence) to 1 (complete replacement of the weight matrix by that of the partner). An important difference with imitation was that the path coefficients included much more information than was behaviorally manifest, insofar as many combinations of stimuli may never occur. However, the inability to verify the information entails a high probability of copying error. I therefore assumed a ten percent rate of mutation, much higher than GENET's two percent rate.

Figure 6 shows the effect of social influence on mean cooperation over 5000 iterations, under two conditions, imitation and instruction. The level of influence ranged from zero to 1 in five steps. At 0.2, the rate of imitation was equal to the learning rate for direct reinforcement. At maximum influence, imitation had five times the impact of direct experience. For instruction, influence was measured as the weight of the mentor's path coefficients relative to the native values. At 0.5, the two rules were equally weighted. All other conditions were identical to those in Figure 4, with an error rate of 0.02, evenly divided between input and output errors.

The results show that social influence substantially increased the rate of cooperation. For instruction, the proportion of cooperative responses increased from 0.58 at no influence to 0.81 with a fully influential mentor. The effect of imitation was somewhat less pronounced, boosting cooperation to 0.72.

Figure 6. The Effect of Social Influence on Cooperation

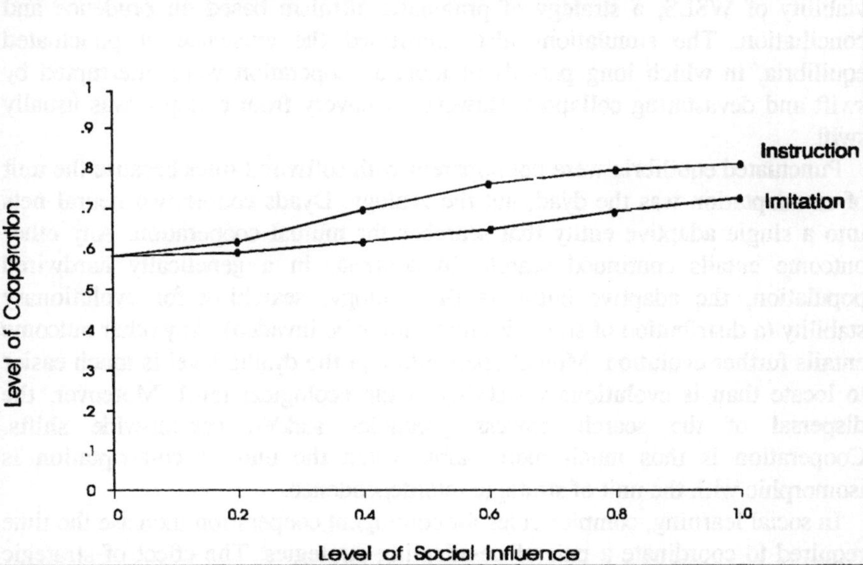

4 Conclusion

These simulation experiments tested the convergence of the sociobiological and social learning models when applied to the most widely studied problem in evolutionary game theory, the viability of cooperation in an iterated Prisoner's Dilemma. Natural selection and social learning can be differentiated based on whether rules are hardwired or softwired in the organisms that carry them. If rules are hardwired, adaptation can occur only at the ecological level; the individual organisms can be replaced but they cannot be modified. However, if rules are softwired, adaptation can proceed through reinforcement instead of reproduction. Reproduction alters the frequency distribution of strategies within a population of actors, while reinforcement alters the probability distribution of strategies within the repertoire of each individual.

I operationalized this distinction by modeling natural selection with a genetic algorithm and social learning with an artificial neural network. The models were applied to the problem of cooperation in an iterated Prisoner's Dilemma game in which the contestants knew the previous two moves and whether their partner was a stranger. Computer simulations showed how an emergent, self-organizing system of interdependent, co-adaptive agents might evolve very differently, depending on whether the rules were hardwired.

Findings based on a genetic algorithm corroborated the evolutionary viability of WSLS, a strategy of pragmatic altruism based on prudence and conciliation. The simulations also confirmed the existence of punctuated equilibria, in which long periods of mutual cooperation were interrupted by swift and devastating collapses. However, recovery from collapse was usually swift.

Punctuated equilibria were not apparent with softwired rules because the unit of co-adaptation was the dyad, not the ecology. Dyads couple two neural nets into a single adaptive entity that searches for mutual cooperation. Any other outcome entails continued search. In contrast, in a genetically hardwired population, the adaptive entity is the ecology, searching for evolutionary stability (a distribution of strategies that cannot be invaded). Any other outcome entails further evolution. Mutual cooperation at the dyadic level is much easier to locate than is evolutionary stability at the ecological level. Moreover, the dispersal of the search process precludes sudden system-wide shifts. Cooperation is thus much more stable when the unit of co-adaptation is isomorphic with the unit of strategic interdependence.

In social learning, complex rules for contingent cooperation increase the time required to coordinate a pair of co-adapting strategies. The effect of strategic complexity on learning contrasts markedly with the effect on natural selection. Complex hardwired rules create spaces where latent cooperative genes can be protected from selection pressures until the rules are sufficiently widespread that they can safely emerge.

The effect of uncertainty was also very different for social learning and natural selection. Mistakes badly complicated the dyadic coordination problem but helped hardwired pragmatists spot naive cooperators before they could lure in more aggressive rules.

As expected, social influence greatly improved the prospects for cooperation. Social learning allows new rules to spread through the population, through imitation and instruction. Influence provides an effective antidote to the effects of uncertainty by increasing the probability of bilateral choices relative to unilateral. This simplifies the coordination problem. The risk is that bilateral defectors will then trap one another in a hall of mirrors, with no escape. However, the costs of mutual defection bias imitation toward coordination of a mutually gratifying solution.

Further research is needed to test the generality of these results. These simulations assumed small, stable, and homogenous populations. The Prisoner's Dilemma game can also be extended to multilateral social dilemmas like "tragedy of the commons." Although this study did not include the formation of commitments, ANNET can be complicated with a second decision, whether to remain with the current partner or exit. A game with an option to exit would also challenge contestants to learn the benefits of commitment, and how to find a suitable mate. Future research should explore how co-adaptive agents might learn to build long-term relationships. (For a preliminary study, see Macy, Skvoretz, and Bainbridge 1995.)

Researchers might also want to test the effects of network structures as conduits for the spread of influence in social learning. Influence processes and cascade effects may be particularly important for understanding the viability of cooperation in multilateral games where synchronized cooperation is exponentially more difficult to attain.

In conclusion, the specific findings reported here should not be taken as definitive but as invitations to pursue a highly promising theory-building technology. Artificial neural networks have not been previously used to study social dilemmas. These experiments demonstrate the rich possibilities for promising sociological applications.

References

Allison, Paul (1992). "The Cultural Evolution of Beneficent Norms." Social Forces 71, 279-301

Axelrod, Robert (1984). The Evolution of Cooperation. New York: Basic.

____ (1987), "The Evolution of Strategies in the Iterated Prisoner's Dilemma." In L. Davis (Ed.) *Genetic Algorithms and Simulated Annealing.* London: Pitman.

Bainbridge, William (1995), "Neural Network Models of Religious Belief." *Sociological Perspectives.* In Press.

____ (1995), "Minimum Intelligent Neural Device: A Tool for Social Simulation." *Journal of Mathematical Sociology 19.*

Bainbridge, William, E Brent, K Carley, D Heise, M Macy, B Markovsky, and J Skvoretz (1994), "Artificial Social Intelligence." *Annual Review of Sociology 20*, 407-436.

Bandura, Albert (1977), *Social Learning Theory.* Englewood Cliffs, NJ: Prentice Hall.

Bendor, Jonathan (1993), "Uncertainty and the Evolution of Cooperation." *Journal of Conflict Resolution 37*, 709-734.

Boyd, Robert and Jeffrey Lorberbaum (1987), "No Pure Strategy is Evolutionarily Stable in the Repeated Prisoner's Dilemma Game." *Nature 327*, 58-59.

Boyd, Robert and Peter Richerson (1985), *Culture and the Evolutionary Process.* Chicago: University of Chicago Press.

Cosmides, Leda and John Tooby (1987). "From Evolution to Behavior: Evolutionary Psychology as the Missing Link?" In J. Dupré (Ed.) *The Latest on the Best.* Cambridge, MA: MIT Press.

Dawkins, Richard (1989), *The Selfish Gene*. Oxford: Oxford University Press.

Durham, W. (1992), "Applications of Evolutionary Culture Theory." *Annual Review of Anthropology 21*, 331-355.

Gallant, Stephen (1993), *Neural Network Learning.* Cambridge, MA: MIT Press.

Goldberg, David (1989), *Genetic Algorithms in Search, Optimization, and Machine Learning*. New York: Addison-Wesley.

Gould, Roger (1993), "Collective Action and Network Structure." *American Sociological Review 58*, 182-196.

Heckathorn, Douglas. Forthcoming. "The Dynamics and Dilemmas of Collective Action." *American Sociological Review*, April, 1996.

Hinton, Geoffrey (1992), "How Neural Networks Learn from Experience." *Scientific American 9*, 145-172.

Hirshleifer, David and Eric Rasmusen (1989), "Cooperation in a Repeated Prisoner's Dilemma with Ostracism." *Journal of Economic Behavior and Organization 12*, 87-106.

Holland, John (1975), *Adaptation in Natural and Artificial Systems.* Ann Arbor: University of Michigan Press.

_____ (1992), "Genetic Algorithms." *Scientific American 7*, 66-72.

Kollock, Peter (1993), "An Eye For an Eye Leaves Everyone Blind: Cooperation and Accounting Systems." *American Sociological Review 58*, 768-786

Lopreato, Joseph (1990), "From Social Evolutionism to Biocultural Evolutionism." *Sociological Forum 5*, 187-212.

Macy, Michael (1990), "Learning Theory and the Logic of Critical Mass." American Sociological Review 55, 809-826.

_____ (1991a), "Learning to Cooperate: Stochastic and Tacit Collusion in Social Exchange." American Journal *of Sociology 97*, 808-843.

_____ (1991b), "Chains of Cooperation: Threshold Effects in Collective Action." *American Sociological Review 56*, 730-747

_____ (1993). "Backward Looking Social Control." *American Sociological Review 58*, 819-36

Macy, Michael and Andreas Flache (1995), "Beyond Rationality in Theories of Choice." *Annual Review of Sociology 21*, 73-91.

Macy, Michael, John Skvoretz, and William Bainbridge (1995), "Telltale Signs: Learning to Cooperate with Strangers." Paper prepared for 1995 annual meeting, American Sociological Association, Washington DC.

Nielsen, François (1994), "Sociobiology and Sociology." *Annual Review of Sociology 20*, 267-303.

Nowak, Martin and Karl Sigmund (1993), "A Strategy of Win-Stay, Lose-Shift that Outperforms Tit-for-Tat in the Prisoner's Dilemma Game." *Nature 364*, 56-58.

Nowak, Andrzej and Bibb Latané (1994), "Simulating the Emergence of Social Order from Individual Behavior." In N. Gilbert and J. Doran (Eds.) *Simulating Societies.* London: UCL Press.

Prata, Stephen (1993), *Games of Life.* Corte Madera: Waite Group Press.

Rummelhart, David and James McClelland (1988), *Explorations in Parallel Distributed Processing: A Handbook of Models, Programs, and Exercises.* Cambridge, MA: MIT Press.

Schuessler, Rudolf (1989), "Exit Threats and Cooperation Under Anonymity. *Journal of Conflict Resolution 33*, 728-749.

Selten, Reinhard (1975), "Reexamination of the Perfectness Concept for Equilibrium Points in Extensive Games." *International Journal of Game Theory 4*, 25-55.

Sigmund, Karl (1993), *Games of Life*. Oxford: Oxford University Press.

Thorndike, Robert (1911), *Animal Intelligence: Experimental Studies.* New York: MacMillan.

Vanberg Viktor and Roger Congleton (1992), "Rationality, Morality, and Exit." American Political Science Review 86, 418-431.

Foundations of rational interaction in cognitive agents: a computational approach

Rosaria Conte

PSCS-Institute of Psychology, Cnr, V.le Marx 15, 00137 Rome, Italy

Abstract. In this paper, rational social action is grounded upon a cognitive agent architecture. The notion of cognitive agent here referred to is defined as: (a) an ideal-type construct -- not to be confused with the subjective, idiosyncratic individual as provided by the differential psychology; and (b) an AI-based notion, where the attention is drawn on the whole process that leads a system to acting, and on its internal makeup, i.e., the internal regulatory mechanisms and representations allowing a system to act adaptively in its environment.

Inter alia, the following features of a cognitive agent architecture will be examined:

- a cognitive, namely AI-, notion of goal -- as distinct from preference. Thanks to such a notion, motivations to action are not necessarily taken for granted, but can be derived and modified via some internal mechanism of goal-generation;
- while that of preference is a very static notion (modifiable, so to speak, only when the system is off-line), that of goal is a much more dynamic notion, since goals may be modified also when the system is on-line: goals may be abandoned, or transformed into intentions and put to execution, etc..
- the capacity to form representations of other agents, their goals, beliefs, etc. and act upon them, in order to influence them. Indeed, a cognitive agent's social action is seen as the capacity to act upon another agent's mind (modifying the currrent state of its beliefs, and then goals, or of its emotions). Unlike rational social action, cognitive social action is not only conceived of as one's attempt to get adjusted to other agents' moves; but also as one's attempt to get others to adjust themselves to one's own needs.

A computational instrument (DEPNET), calculating the network of dependence relations among agents in a common environment, and the formal theory of dependence upon which DEPNET is based, will be described. DEPNET will be shown to imply a very simple agent architecture, consisting of agents' goals, actions, and resources. However, such a basic architecture allows a complex structure of agents' interdependencies to emerge, and as a consequence, a variety of rational social (inter)actions to be predicted (influencing, exchange, and cooperation).

Keywords. Cognition, dependence networks, dynamics

1 Some features of rational agents

Formal theories of social agency basically share a notion of agent as essentially *rational* (cf. Moser 1990), and what this means is a set of specifications:

(a) *ideal-type*, as opposed to concrete;
(b) *self-interested*, as opposed to either benevolent or slavish: each agent aims at realising its own interests;
(c) *capitalising*, as opposed to hedonistic: rational agents are aimed at obtaining maximum benefits with minimum costs. Agents have a relative capacity for giving up current rewards in order to achieve future ones, if the former are lower than the latter.
(d) *socially competent*: rational agents may be endowed with different built-in social strategies (more or less cooperative, more or less retaliative, etc.; cf. Axelrod, 1984) and beliefs about the strategies played by others (cf. Bicchieri, 1990);
(e) *strategic*, as opposed to unbending; rational agents adjust their behaviours to the others' predictable moves. They will monitor their own actions by taking into account those potentially done by others.

Several criticisms of this notion have, of course, been forwarded. Some share the idea that it is too *idealistic*; for example, it does not take into account the *real* components of rewards (Pruitt, 1970; Komorita & Barth, 1985; Brewer & Kramer, 1986; Komorita & Ellis, 1995). More generally, the boundaries, the limits of natural agents' rationality (cf. Kahneman & Tversky, 1982) have been pointed out. Another line of criticism has to do with the notion of *self-interest*. According to many authors (Edney, 1980; Kramer & Brewer, 1986; Messick, 1974), agents are neither primarily nor necessarily concerned with egoistic motives (see also, Kramer & Goldman, 1995). Finally, many authors have shown that social experience enhances the agents' inclination to cooperate (Brewer, 1986).

Although quite serious, these criticisms do not seem to represent a real pain in the neck of rational thinkers. The rational theories are not meant to prescribe what types of motivations rational agents should have (whether altruistic or egoistic, self-oriented or group-oriented; cf. Harsanyi, 1990), but only a rational mechanisms for choosing the most rational course of action on the grounds of one's *subjective* preferences.

The criticisms moved so far, indeed, ask for some higher degree of mundane *realism*. The difference between the rational agent, as is designed by formal theories of social agency, and the natural agent, as modelled by the best-known critics of rationality is hierarchical. The natural agent is seen as a *sub-optimal* version of the rational agent, less efficient and more altruistic.

In this paper, we will designate both types of agents, the classical and the boundedly rational one, as rational, and will refer to the former as the strong model of rational agent, or strongly rational agent, and to the latter as the weak model of rational agent, or weakly rational.

Somewhat in contrast with either of the preceding views, in the present chapter, a view of *cognitive agent*, as proposed and employed within computational, namely AI, systems, will be suggested. But in order to do this, some further characteristics of the rational model must be examined first. These characteristics will be argued to carry important consequences for the extent to which such a model can handle the dynamics and emergence of social behaviour.

2 A want of dynamics in rational theories

Below, some further characteristics of the rational model of agency are pointed out.

2.1 The rational model of agency as a *descriptive* rather than a *constructive* model.

Rational theories aim to describe social life and test predictions derived from the assumptions of rationality (see above), rather than to construct (social) agents actually moving and behaving in their environment. The latter, which is an objective of research in multi-agent systems (for a comprehensive treatment, see Gasser, 1995), cannot be considered as an objective of rational theories. Indeed, even when these theories resort to computer simulation (cellular automata and the studies of the evolution of cooperation), they do not aim at running programs simulating separate, goal-oriented[1] agents, but rather to observe the spreading of some interactional strategies. The focus is on the minimal conditions for producing given collective effects (e.g. stable cooperation) rather than on programming separate agents and explore their interaction.

2.2 Rational agents as lacking internal architectures

This is a corollary of the preceding point. Since rational models are not intended to construct separate agents in interaction, agents modelled are not able to proceed all the way down from their built-in preferences to action execution. They are not provided with even the simplest tools for knowledge representation and management, problem solving and planning. At most, they are provided with some internal criteria for choice (preference rankings) and/or general rule(s) for decision-making. Moreover, they are not provided with an internal architecture that integrates these internal criteria and rules, allowing the agents to be initialised and to achieve their goals.

2.3 Rational agents as static

Rational agents are rather static for a variety of reasons.

---

[1] An agent is usually defined as any entity which is able to cause transitions among states (cf. Shoham and Tenneholz, 1992) of a given external world; in this sense, all simulation models can be said to simulate agencies. A separate, goal-oriented agent, instead, is one that operates transitions from states in such a way as to make a current world state to coincide with some internally represented state, which is its goal (cf. Conte & Castelfranchi, 1995). In this sense, a boiler is a goal-oriented agent. Now, not all simulation models deal with separate systems, each oriented to different goals or tasks. Unlike programs simulating the emergence of collective effects, multi-agent interaction is realised by letting separate goal-oriented systems interact in a common environment.

First, since rational agents are not provided with internal architectures, they do not actually achieve different and changing goals in a common environment. Their individual behaviours are far more predictable than what can be expected from atomic agents in multi-agent systems.

Secondly, and more interestingly, rational agents are not endowed with internal mechanisms for generating new "criteria" for choice, new goals. Their criteria, usually numerically ordered preferences, are built into the agents, and cannot be modified, abandoned or generated anew over the agents' lifetimes. As a consequence, agents are rather unmodifiable, rigid and nonemergent systems (for an analogous critique, see Axelrod, 1995). Their learning mechanisms are fairly confined within the limits of the spreading of interactional strategies.

Thirdly, the agents' responsiveness to social interaction is only limited to making a decision in the light of the others' moves. Within the rational framework, agents may have social influence on one another by mutually modifying their social beliefs and interactional strategies, rather than their motivations and preferences. On the contrary, as will be shown later on in this paper, a fundamental aspect of social life consists of acting *in order to* modify other agents' reasons for action, i.e. their goals, through modifying their beliefs. The bulk of social influence is to generate new goals in your fellows' minds. This feature of social agency has a strong impact in augmenting the dynamics of social systems.

2.4 *Pre-fabricated* as opposed to *emergent* sociality

Within the framework of rationality, sociality is essentially viewed as "pre-fabricated" strategies and/or structures. Therefore, it is not allowed to emerge from lower-level phenomena. As far as strategies, within the rational framework, interactional strategies are built into the agents. Even when agents are defined as altruistic, endowed with social values (Kuhlman & Marshello, 1975; McClinotock, 1978), social motives (Liebrand, 1984), collective hedonism (Williams et al., 1995), etc., these socially-oriented motivations are hypothesised as inherent components of human nature. Presumably, their emergence can be traced back to the evolutionary history of the species, or to individual learning. But it cannot be accounted for in terms of instrumental reasoning.

As far as social structures, they are also pre-established, embedded in the structure of the game considered[2]. Insufficient attention is paid to how to derive the structures of the games. The only effort in this direction concerns the properties of the resources (whether they are scarce, replenishable, etc.). But the quantity and quality of external, physical resources is not the only source for

[2]This feature is shared by the literature on social networks. The theory accounts for how power differentials arise from structural properties, e.g., exchange links (cfr. Marwell et al., 1988; Gould, 1993; Markovsky et al., 1993) existing among interrelated agents. However, in these theories, social structures are "given", rather than allowed to emerge from some lower-level phenomena. The agents' ties within a network are usually pre-established, rather than constructed. This does not only reduce the plausibility of the theory, but also, and moreover, its efficacy in accounting for the *emergence* of social structures.

social structures. Agents represent a special type of *resource* for one another, and not only a special type of *obstacle*.

In this paper, an emergent, dynamic view of both social structures and strategies is proposed in terms of the agents' internal *nonsocial* endowments.

3 Cognition as a dynamic version of rationality

In the present approach, a computational, AI model of cognitive agency[3] is presented. The cognitive agent here proposed is not intended as a bounded, but rather as a dynamic version of the rational agent. Cognition puts more dynamics into the agent thanks to several properties (cf. Castelfranchi & Conte, 1995).

First, a computational cognitive agent is conceived of as a rather complex architecture, integrating specialised tools for the management of the different tasks occurring between a goal being formed within an agent's mind and its execution. Over the course of this process, a cognitive agent may undergo a variety of changes, due to environmental events, of both a social and nonsocial nature.

Secondly, a cognitive agent is basically defined as a goal-oriented system. Cognition essentially is seated on two crucial pillars: beliefs and goals. However, the cognitive notion of *goal* is quite different from that of *preference* (for an analysis of goals and their dynamics, cf. Castelfranchi, 1994):

(a) while that of preference is an *idiosyncratic* notion, the cognitive notion of goal is an *ideal-type* one. The propositional content of goals is obviously idiosyncratic (I may want to buy a new car, while you happen to want to get a job), but their cognitive (read, symbolic and likely-to-be-mentally-manipulated) representation, their role within the agent and their relations to other mental attitudes (such as beliefs) is not.
(b) While the notion of a preference is a *quantitative* one, the notion of a goal is primarily a*qualitative* one. Goals are symbolic and modular representations that can be mentally manipulated. Their formal treatment, as well as the formal treatment of any other mental attitude, is basically binary (see Shoham & Cousins, 1994). In other words, a mental attitude is either held or not held by a given agent. Of course, goal values may be quantified; but the quantitative dimension is not prominent in the definition of goals. Goals are both qualitatively and quantitatively subject to change.
(c) Paradoxically, while the notion of preference is closer to the motivations of differential psychology, the cognitive notion of goal is closer to a planning notion (cf. Hobbs, 1990). While preferences are only quantitatively ordered, goals may be decomposed in hierarchical structures (plans). Therefore, that of preference is a more *static* notion, while goals are relatively more *dynamic* (see Castelfranchi, 1994):

(i) while preferences are built-into the agent, goals can be *generated* during and by means of planning;

---

[3]Usually, although not necessarily, an AI-agent is a cognitive agent, endowed with mental states and the capabilities to achieve its goals reasoning about its knowledge (for a definition, see Doran, in press).

(ii) goals may *change status* during the process from their being formed within an agent's mind and their pursuance. A goal status changes as a function of a number of tests, or queries: in some models (Cohen and Levesque, 1990), a goal that is not yet realised leads to an *achievement* goal; an achievement goal that is realisable leads to a *persistent* goal, and a persistent goal put to execution leads to an *intention* (see also Rao & Georgeff, 1992).

(iii) Finally, a *goal value varies* with the number of higher-level goals that goal achieves, as well as with the extent and probability to which it achieves them.

Finally, and as a consequence of the preceding features, unlike the rational model, the cognitive model is compatible with a dynamic approach to sociality; indeed, it allows for social goals and structures to emerge from the internal makeups of agents situated in a common environment. A cognitive model of agency provides two main grounds for sociality, (a) *agents' limited autonomy*: agents' internal makeups and their heterogeneity give rise to complex interdependencies, i.e., let dependence networks emerge, and (b) *agents' liability to influence one another*: a subset of goals, i.e. *social* goals (mentioning other agents in their internal representations), may be generated in the agents' minds thanks to the other agents' more or less direct influencing.

Below, a computational system for calculating special types of *social networks emerging* from the internal endowments of agents situated in a common world is presented. Thereafter, the role of such networks in the formation of some *new social goals* will be considered.

4 Implementing social networks into the agent architecture: the DEPNET system

Agents will be defined in terms of quite simple internal architectures, and the social networks are allowed to emerge from the dependence relationships existing among the agents.

4.1 The dependence Theory

Below, we will first describe a formal theory of dependence as presented in Sichman et al. (1994) on the basis of a pre-existing model developed by Castelfranchi et al. (1992; Conte & Castelfranchi, 1994). Next, we will illustrate a simulator, called DEPNET, that applies a dependence algorithm, based upon the previous formal model, to construct a dependence network among agents in a common environment (see also, Conte & Sichman, 1995).

4.1.1 Social dependence

We claim that social agents are plunged into a network of social relationships (Conte & Castelfranchi, 1994; 1995). The focus is on the agents' mental states, namely their goals. Social networks are here seen as patterns of relationships holding among the goals of a given set of agents.

The most fundamental relationship among agents' goals is *social dependence* (Castelfranchi et al., 1992), consisting of one agent needing the performance of another to achieve one of his/her goals. In the following section, a formal model of this notion and its properties will be presented and a system for calculating and using social dependence relations will be shown.

4.2 A formal theory of social dependence

The three basic notions of the social dependence theory are external description, dependence relations and dependence situations.

4.2.1 External description

We will call the system agency*external description*. It consists of a data structure composed of the set of *goals* each agent wants to achieve, the set of *actions* he[4] is able to perform, the set of *resources* he controls and the set of *plans* he has. A plan consists of a sequence of actions with its associated resources needed to accomplish them. However, an agent may have a plan whose actions or resources do not necessarily belong to his own set of actions or resources, and therefore he may *depend on others* in order to carry on a certain plan, and achieve a certain goal.

A description of a generic agent ag_i, meaning by generic, any agent whatsoever, (for a formal definition, see Appendix, eq.1) is composed of several entries, where the information about each agent ag_j that belongs to the agency is stored (Appendix, eq. 2). The external description is therefore a representation of the system agency from within an agent's mind. One could therefore ask, what relationship is there between the agents' beliefs and the real matters. As we intend to employ one and the same instrument for both types of representations (mental states and world states), we assume as an "objective" representation of the agency that which corresponds to the mental state of a specific agent, namely the observer. When referring to objective reality, therefore, we will actually refer to the mental state of the generic agent ag_i, assumed as observer. In those cases, to avoid confusion, subscripts referring to the generic agent will be dropped.

An entry corresponding to an agent ag_j has respectively the set of goals (eq. 3), actions (App., eq. 4), resources (App., eq. 5) and plans (App., eq. 6) ag_i believes ag_j has[5]. By, resources, we mean concrete objects that may be

---

[4]As a woman, I take the liberty to violate openly and deliberately the non-sexist convention prescribing scientists to employ "she" as much as or in place of "he" in impersonal reference. In the last two thousand years or so, with a few exceptions, men have been writing about women. Lets now have women writing about men.

[5]To be noted, our formal model employs a quite simplified formalism for representing plans. No reference is made to the vast and interesting AI literature on planning. Our plans are but mere lists of actions, deliberately ignoring the complexity of problems

required by performing actions. For the time being, we will conceive of resources as both non-consumable and re-usable (for example a pair of scissors is a resource for cutting a piece of cloth). In future development of the model, both constraints will actually be dropped. Finally, actions are costly. In this paper, however, and again for the sake of simplicity, action costs are assumed to be equal.

The beliefs a given agent, different from the observer, has regarding the others may be neither *necessarily true nor complete*. In order to illustrate the power of the proposed framework, we adopt the hypothesis of external description compatibility $(Ext^{entry}_{ag_i}(ag_j) = Ext^{entry}_{ag_j}(ag_j)) \wedge (Ext^{entry}_{ag_i}(ag_i) = Ext^{entry}_{ag_j}(ag_i))$ as a simplification. We denote as $P_{ag_i}(ag_j, g_k)$ the set of plans $p^l_{ag_i}(ag_j, g_k)$ that ag_i believes ag_j has in order to achieve the goal g_k (App., eq. 7). As the representation of plans are independent of the agents involved, we have simplified their notation. Each plan $p_l(g_k)$ (App., eq. 8) is composed of a goal g_k to be achieved, a (possibly empty) set of resources $R_{p_l(g_k)}$ used in this plan and a (possibly empty) sequence of instantiated actions $A^{inst}_{p_l(g_k)}$ used in this plan (App., eq. 9). Each instantiated action $a^{inst}_{m,p_l(g_k)}$(App., eq. 10) is composed of an action a_m and a (possibly empty) set of resources $R^{a_m}_{p_l(g_k)}$ used in this action, where $R^{a_m}_{p_l(g_k)} \subseteq R_{p_l(g_k)}$. Henceforth for simplicity of notation we will use P_{qk} and p_{lk} respectively instead of $P_{ag_i}(ag_q, g_k)$ and $p_l(g_k)$.We will also drop the subscript referring to the generic agent ag_i we are analysing (for instance, we will use $G(ag_j)$ instead of $G_{ag_i}(ag_j)$.)

4.2.2 Dependence relations

Using the external description defined above, we define the notions of autonomy and dependence as follows.

An agent ag_i is *a-autonomous* (action autonomous) for a given goal g_k, according to a set of plans P_{qk} (App., eq. 11) if there is a plan that achieves this goal in this set and every action appearing in this plan belongs to his own set of actions $A(ag_i)$. In other terms, an agent is a-autonomous if he is endowed with all the actions involved in at least one of the plans that achieves his goal: if his set of plans is non-empty, but none of those plans is exhausted by his actions, the agent is not a-autonomous. Analogously, we define the notion of *r*-

that this literature has addressed. Indeed, we did not mean to construct a planning tool. But, at least in principle, nothing prevents DEPNET from being used by a sophisticated planner either.

autonomy (resource autonomy) (App., eq. 12). Finally, an agent ag_i is *s-autonomous* (social autonomous) (App., eq. 13) if he is both a-autonomous and r-autonomous for this goal.

On the other hand, if an agent does not have all the actions (or resources) to achieve a given goal, according to a set of plans, he may depend on the others for this goal. An agent ag_i *a-depends* (action-depends) on another agent ag_j for a given goal g_k, according to a set of plans P_{qk} (App., eq. 14) if ag_i has g_k in his set of goals, he is not a-autonomous for g_k and there is a plan in P_{qk} that achieves g_k where at least one action used in this plan is in ag_j's set of actions $A(ag_j)$. In a similar way, we have defined the notion of *r-dependence* (resource-dependence) (App., eq. 15). Finally, an agent ag_i *s-depends* (social-depends) on another agent ag_j (App., eq. 16) if he either a-depends or r-depends on this latter.

4.2.3 Dependence situations

An agent who has constructed dependence networks can use this information when reasoning about others. For a given goal g_k, an agent ag_i can calculate for each other agent ag_j which is the *dependence situation* related to this goal.

We classify the dependence situations with regard to the *nature* of the dependence. Let us consider two agents ag_i and ag_j. Let us also suppose that agent ag_i has the goal g_k in his set of goals but he is not a-autonomous for it. According to the *nature* of the dependence, there are four different situations that may hold between these two agents, considering ag_i's reasoning mechanism:

(a) *Independence*: ag_i infers that he does not a-depend on ag_j for g_k (App., eq. 17);

(b) *Unilateral Dependence*: ag_i infers that he a-depends on ag_j for g_k, but this latter does not a-depend on him for any of his goals (App., eq.18); bilateral dependence takes two forms,

(c) *Mutual Dependence*: ag_i infers that he and ag_j a-depend on each other for the *same goal* g_k (App., eq. 19);

(d) *Reciprocal Dependence*: ag_i infers that he and ag_j a-depend on each other, but for *different goals* g_k and g_l (App., eq. 20).

Elsewhere (Sichman et al., 1994; Conte & Sichman, 1995), some detailed examples concerning these situations have been presented and their use has been discussed as a decision criterion when an agent has to choose his partners when trying to achieve a certain goal.

4.3 The DEPNET simulator

We have implemented a simulator, called DEPNET, which calculates both the dependence relations and situations between agents, and constructs the dependence networks of a given agent. According to the hypothesis of external description compatibility presented above, one single external description is shared by all agents. This simulator is composed of the following facilities:

(a)*agent edition module*: the user can dynamically create new agents and edit their goals, actions, resources, and plans, or modify the entry of an existing agent in the external description;
(b)*dependence network constructor:* this module constructs the various dependence networks of a given agent, either related to a specific goal or to all of his goals. It can construct both the action and the resource dependence networks for both cases;
(c)*dependence situation constructor*: this module calculates the dependence situations regarding a given agent and one of his goals. The user must specify a specific type of dependence situation he is interested in.

The DEPNET simulator was developed using the C++ programming language for UNIX platforms. The total number of lines of code is approximately 5800. Its interface is menu-driven, and the functions are closely related to the theoretical aspects described in the previous subsections.

4.3.1 How to calculate the degree of dependence

Dependence is a quantifiable relation. Ag_i can depend more or less on ag_j. The quantity of dependence derives primarily from the importance (or value) of the goal with regard to which ag_i is not autonomous. But of course, the quantity of dependence derives also from the number of goals with regard to which one is s-dependent. These two factors (value and number of goals) interact. If I depend on you to reach 2 goals of equal value, while you depend on me to reach a third goal whose value ecceeds the sum of the value of my goals, you depend on me to a higher degree.

4.4 The emergence of social networks

Thanks to DEPNET, and more generally to the model of dependence described earlier, social structures emerge out of the agents' properties and their sharing a common environment. In other words, it is sufficient to describe a bunch of agents in terms of different mental states and put them in a common environment (that is, in a world such that one's mental state and action may have a consequence on the fate of another; we will call this a *market*) in order for some social pattern of relationships among those agents to emerge. A dependence network (see Tables 4.4.1.1. and 4.4.1.2.) is but one such type of structure. We will show now both the emergent and dynamic properties of dependence structures.

4.4.1 The dynamics of social markets

Dependence structures are highly dynamic notions. This is so for two sets of reasons, respectively related to the agent architecture and the intrinsic nature of dependence structures.

Table 4.4.1.1. Market 1 and its dependence structure

	A	B	C	D
Goals:	Ga1	Gb1	Gc1	Gd1
	Ga2	Gb2	Gc2	Gd2
	Ga3	Gb3	Gc3	Gd3
Actions:	al	al	al	al
	aw	aj	ap	au
Plans:	Ga1:=al	Gb1:=al	Gc1:=al	Gd1:=al
	Ga2:=az	Gb2:=aw	Gc2:=aw	Gd2:=az
	Ga3:=au	Gb3:=az	Gc3:=az	Gd3:=ap

	Is A useful?	Is B useful?	Is C useful?	Is D useful?
A's goals	Ga1: Y	Ga1: Y	Ga1: Y	Ga1: Y
	Ga2: N	Ga2: N	Ga2: N	Ga2: N
	Ga3: N	Ga3: N	Ga3: N	Ga3: Y
B's goals	Gb1: Y	Gb1: Y	Gb1: Y	Gb1: Y
	Gb2: Y	Gb2: N	Gb2: N	Gb2: N
	Gb3: N	Gb3: N	Gb3: N	Gb3: N
C's goals	Gc1: Y	Gc1: Y	Gc1: Y	Gc1: Y
	Gc2: Y	Gc2: N	Gc2: N	Gc2: N
	Gc3: N	Gc3: N	Gc3: N	Gc3: N
D's goals	Gd1: Y	Gd1: Y	Gd1: Y	Gd1: Y
	Gd2: N	Gd2: N	Gd2: N	Gd2: N
	Gd3: N	Gd3: N	Gd3: N	Gd3: N

As for the former, in the model here presented, dependence is a social relationship holding between two (sets of) agents' mental states, and more specifically between their goals and competencies (here, exclusively represented by actrions). An agent's mental state, and especially its goals, is by definition a dynamic phenomenon. In an AI-based perspective, the agent's mental state is subject to change as a function of learning, interaction with the external environment, and planning. However, at present, DEPNET does not take advantage of this property of the mental states, and we will not examine it here in any further detail.

Table 4.4.1.2. : Market 2 and its dependence network

	A	B	C	D	E
Goals:	Ga1 Ga2 Ga3	Gb1 Gb2 Gb3	Gc1 Gc2 Gc3	Gd1 Gd2 Gd3	Ge1 Ge2 Ge3
Actions:	a1 aw	a1 aj	a1 ap	a1 au	az aw
Plans:	Ga1:=a1 Ga2:=az Ga3:=au	Gb1:=a1 Gb2:=aw Gb3:=az	Gc1:=a1 Gc2:=aw Gc3:=az	Gd1:=a1 Gd2:=az Gd3:=ap	Ge1:=a1 Ge2:=aw Ge3:=aj

	Is A useful?	Is B useful?	Is C useful?	Is D useful?	Is E useful?
A's goals	Ga1: Y	Ga1: Y	Ga1: Y	Ga1: Y	Ga1: N
	Ga2: **N**	Ga2: N	Ga2: N	Ga2: N	Ga2: N
	Ga3: N	Ga3: N	Ga3: N	Ga3: **Y**	Ga3: N
B's goals	Gb1: Y	Gb1: Y	Gb1: Y	Gb1: Y	Gb1: N
	Gb2: **Y**	Gb2: N	Gb2: N	Gb2: N	Gb2: **Y**
	Gb3: N	Gb3: N	Gb3: N	Gb3: N	Gb3: **Y**
C's goals	Gc1: Y	Gc1: Y	Gc1: Y	Gc1: Y	Gc1: N
	Gc2: **Y**	Gc2: N	Gc2: N	Gc2: N	Gc2: **Y**
	Gc3: N	Gc3: N	Gc3: N	Gc3: N	Gc3: **Y**
D's goals	Gd1: Y	Gd1: Y	Gd1: Y	Gd1: Y	Gd1: N
	Gd2: N	Gd2: N	Gd2: N	Gd2: N	Gd2: **Y**
	Gd3: N	Gd3: N	Gd3: N	Gd3: **N**	Gd3: N
E's goals	Ge1: **Y**	Ge1: **Y**	Ge1: **Y**	Ge1: **Y**	Ge1: N
	Ge2: Y	Ge2: N	Ge2: N	Ge2: N	Ge2: Y
	Ge3: N	Ge3: **Y**	Ge3: N	Ge3: N	Ge3: N

As for the intrinsic dynamic nature of dependence structures, they are subject to change as a function of the agents' social mobility[6]. By social mobility, it is meant the agents' entering or leaving any given social market, or their moving from one social market to another. The higher-level phenomenon -- a given market breaking into smaller separated units, or vice versa two or more markets uniting into a larger structure -- represents but a special example of the previous one, and will not be considered in detail. Let us consider how a given market is modified as a result of one new agent's entrance.

Consider Market 1 (see Table 4.4.1.1.). In this market, there are four agents, all endowed with the same number of goals and actions (here, resources have

[6]The temporal dimension has not yet been introduced into the system. The agency can be modified only by the user. However, some modifications are under implementation in order to increase the system dynamics. Different external descriptions will be allowed in the agents' representations, where each external description corresponds to a given social market. Furthermore, agents will be also endowed with a *migration* rule (f.i., if your overall dependence degree exceeds some threshold move randomly to another social markets among those available).

been dropped for simplicity) equally valued (therefore values have been also dropped). In the up row, agents' goals are listed (Ga1 being a goal of A, Gb2 a goal of b, etc.). Respectively in the middle and in the low row, agents' actions and plans are displayed. Looking at the dependence network in Table 4.4.1.1., in rows, you can read whether each agent is a-autonomous or not and with regard to which goal (e.g., A is a-autonomous (Y) with regard to his goal Ga1); if this is not the case, you can see whom he depends upon, be the latter another agent in the market (e.g., A depends on D (Y) with regard to his goal Ga3), or on an unavailable agent, (e.g., A depends on an unavailable agent with regard to his goal Ga2 (N)). In columns, you can read who is depending on the agent considered (e.g., A's actions are needed by both B and C; B and C depend on A, etc.)

When agent E enters the market, there is a dramatic re-structuration of dependence nets. As you can see in the lower side of Table 4.4.1.2., the dependence net of Market 2 is completely different from that of Market 1 as shown in Table 4.4.1.1.. In fact, networks are in a continue dynamics, since existing links disappear when some agent disappears, and new links can be established by introducing new agents. Look at agent A. After E entered the market, A is no more the only agent whom everybody else depends upon, because also E is able to perform a_w. In addition, B is now more socially useful because there is somebody who needs a_j.

5 When cooperation is more rational than defection

Three simple examples of DEPNET simulations will be provided in order to show how a particular dependence situation can lead to some specific social behaviour, such as influencing, cooperation and exchange (these examples are drawn from Conte & Sichman, 1995). For simplification, the examples proposed include only two agents, but simulations including a greater number of agents may be easily done. The blocks world will be used as a well-known and easy-to-be-modelled domain of analysis.

5.1 Three types of social action

The following types of social (inter)action may be distinguished:

(i) *influencing*: this occurs when an agent attempts to influence another agent to have a new goal (Castelfranchi, 1990; for a formal definition, see Conte & Castelfranchi, 1995, ch. 2);

(ii) *exchange*: this occurs when an agent complies with someone else's request in order to obtain reciprocation from the latter (again, for a formal definition, see Conte & Castelfranchi 1995, ch. 3);

(iii) *cooperation*: each agent agrees to accomplish a share of a multi-agent plan aimed to achieve a common goal (cf. Conte et al., 1991), that is, a goal with regard to which the agents need one another.

On the grounds of these notions, it is possible to show (cf. Conte & Castelfranchi, 1995, ch. 3) that while social exchange does not rule out cheating and deception, cooperation is instrinsically incompatible with them. In other words, while social exchange is not necessarily a pro-social action, cooperation is necessarily so. The reason lies in a planning-like account of these phenomena. Social exchange does not imply a unique multi-agent plan; rather, it arises at the intersection of two or more individual plans (as many as the number of exchanging agents). Therefore, exchanging agents are not really co-interested in the achievement of each other's goals. They are interested in the fates of each other's goals only as means for each to achieve their own goal[7]. On the contrary, in cooperation, there is no room for cheating since the goal is intrinsically a multi-agent goal: each agent is co-interested with everybody else in carrying out the common activity. Each is interested in all others doing their parts of the common job (see Balzer & Tuomela, 1995), and possibly each is willing to help others to do so.

As will be shown, this allows cooperation to be viewed, *under given dependence conditions and thanks to a notion of goal-oreinted dependence*, as more rational than defection even in a one-shot interaction.

5.2 Unilateral dependence and influencing

Fig. 5.2.1. Social dependence in the blocks world

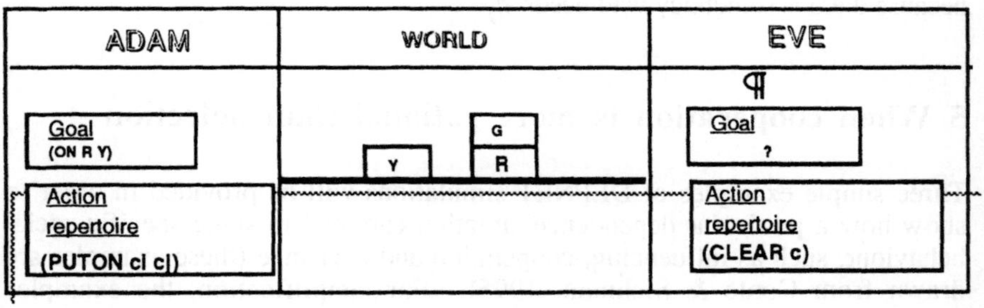

Let us consider two agents Adam and Eve, as presented in Figure 5.2.1. Adam 's goal is to put block R on block Y, and he has the action PUTON in his action set. Since in the blocks world, a block must be "cleartop" (should have no block on top) before being put on top of another, to reach his goal Adam needs to clear block Y, but he cannot perform this action. According to his external description, Eve has the action CLEAR in her action set, but does not have any current goal.

According to our algorithm, agent Adam infers that he is unilaterally dependent on agent Eve, and the simulation results are shown in Table 5.2.1..

[7]The notion of the dependence presented in this paper may remind many readers of the notion of Fate Control introduced by Kelley and Thibaut (1987) (I am grateful to the anonymous reviewer of an earlier version of this contribution for this suggestion). However, in my view, the similarity between these two notions is lesser than what appears to be the case. Unlike Fate Control (as I understand it), the present notion of dependence is a purely objective one. Therefore, it does not actually imply any real control on the side of the agent one is dependent upon.

Table 5.2.1. Unilateral dependence and influencing

	Is Adam useful?	Is Eve useful
Adam's goal: ON(R,Y) (10)	N	Y (5)
Eve's goal: CLEARTOP (Y)	N	Y

Adam is dependent on Eve for his goal ON(R,Y) valued 10. His degree of dependence is scored 5, since Eve can accomplish one of the two actions he needs. Eve, instead, is autonomus. As one can easily realise, from this situation, a new social goal of Adam's can be predicted: the goal that Eve has a new goal herself. This is what we have called a goal of influencing.

5.3 Reciprocal dependence and exchange

Let us now suppose that agent Adam has no longer the goal of putting R on top of Y, which has now become the goal of Eve. Adam, instead, has the goal that block G be right on the table, while agent Eve wants R to be on top of Y. According to our algorithm, agent Adam infers a reciprocal dependence regarding agent Eve for these two goals, and the simulation results are shown in Table 5.3.1..

Table 5.3.1. Reciprocal dependence and exchange

	Is Adam useful?	Is Eve useful?
Adam's goal: ONTABLE (G) (10)	N	Y (10)
Eve's goal: ON (R,Y) (10)	Y (5)	Y (5)

Agent Adam depends on Eve for his goal ONTABLE (G), and Eve, in turn, depends on Adam for her goal ON(R,Y). But Adam's degree of dependence is twice as higher than Eve's, since she can carry out the whole plan needed for Adam to achieve his goal, while he can only only execute one of the two actions she needs. This difference bears interesting and intuitive consequences in the agents' negotiation, which cannot be examined here. It can be formally shown (see Conte & Castelfranchi, 1995, ch 2), that reciprocal dependence leads to social exchange. Here, a proposal of exchange will be addressed if reciprocal dependence is mutually believed (in the present context, a mutual belief is equated with the agent's belief that a given information is shared with one or more other agents: no further level of belief nesting is implied). If this is not the case, that is, if reciprocal dependence is not mutually believed, a persuasive message ("Why don't you try to achieve your goal such-and-such? I bet you will fail"), and only afterwards, a proposal of exchange, will be sent out.

5.4 Mutual dependence and cooperation

Let us now suppose that Adam has no longer the goal of putting G on the table. Rather, both Adam and Eve want to put R on Y. Their action repertoire has not changed in the meantime. According to our algorithm, agent Adam infers that a mutual dependence occurs between himself and agent Eve. The results of the simulation are shown in Table 5.4.1..

Table 5.4.1. Mutual dependence and cooperation

	Is Adam useful?	Is Eve useful?
Adam's goal: ON(R,Y) (10)	Y (5)	Y (5)
Eve's goal: ON (R,Y) (10)	Y (5)	Y (5)

Here, both agents depend on each other for carrying out one of the two actions needed for achieveing one and the same goal. They depend on each other to the same extent (5). As in the previous case, it can be shown that mutual dependence leads to a proposal of cooperation (this has been shown in Conte & Castelfranchi, 1995, ch. 3), defined as the performance of a multi-agent plan for achieving one and the same goal. Indeed, if agents are mutually dependent with regard to a given goal, their cooperation will be necessary for them to achieve their common goal. Of course, actual cooperation implies mutual belief (Conte et al., 1991). Therefore, the agent will need to ascertain whether mutual dependence is mutually believed or not. A proposal for cooperation will be sent out only in the former case, while, in the latter, a persuasive communication will precede the proposal. In other words, the agent will attempt to make the other accept his/her own plan. An interesting sub-case of persuasion, likely to succeed, occurs when the other has no plan for the common goal. There is little doubt that a plan whatsoever will be accepted.

Now, it is quite evident that in a case of mutual dependence, cooperation is the most convenient solution for the agents involved. This is not a mere conceptual, or -worse- terminological, question. It entails a relevant empirical difference: while in conditions of mutual dependence, agents are willing, and interested, in helping one another to do their part of the job and achieve their common goal (see also Balzer & Tuomela, 1995), this is not so in, say, social exchange. On given conditions, i.e. mutual dependence, cooperation is a more convenient, that is, rational solution than less desirable social behaviors.

6 Conclusions

In this paper, a computational system, called DEPNET, for calculating dependence networks as emerging from quite simple agents architetcures has been described. This system is based upon a formal theory of social dependence first developed by Castelfranchi et al. (1992) and then implemented by Sichman et al. (1994). The agent architectures have been defined in terms of the agents' goals, resources, actions, and plans, as well as their beliefs about the other agents' mental states. DEPNET has been employed here to illustrate the potentialities of a computational model of cognitive agency for studying the emergence of social structures and strategies. Indeed, cognition has been here proposed as a way to conceptualise the (social) agent as essentially different from, although sharing some features with, rationality, both in its stronger, classical version and in its weaker, bounded one. Cognition is different in that it relies on a dynamic notion of goal, rather than on the static notion of preference; aims at designing and constructing complex, integrated architectures of agency, rather than merely describing and testing some assumptions about it; and, finally, allows for social strategies and structures to be derived from nonsocial phenomena and motivations, rather than simply postulated. In a word, cognition is viewed as a more dynamic version of rationality.

The dynamic potential of cognition are illustrated in two ways: (a) special types of social networks, i.e. dependence networks, are shown to emerge from the architectures of agents situated in a common enviromnment; (b) agents' new social goals and (inter)actions are allowed to emerge from their access to these dependence networks. In particular, in the context of special type of dependence relations, cooperative strategies are found to be more rational than less desirbale social behaviours (say, social exchange).

The dependence model implemented on DEPNET and DEPNET itself have proved so far quite fruitful instrumentssince they indicate a number of interesting research questions and directions for future research. Let us indicate some of them:

(a) *prediction of coalition formation in social markets*: thanks to further improvements in the formal model of dependence, DEPNET is now being augmented (see Veneziano et al., in preparation) by an algorithm (MICROdep) that calculates the social utility of each agent in the same market, and compares this results with the agents' actual partnerships. The hypothesis to be checked is whether the dependence network allows to predict the formation of real partnerships and the satisfaction agents obtain from them? Do the most useful agents form the most satisfactory partnerships?

(b) *Social migration*: what about the agents left out from partnerships? Further versions of DEPNET are intended to be augmented by an algorithm calculating the agents' migrations from one market to another. The dynamics of markets is expected to reflect upon the agents' fates. But what are the costs of migration from one market to another (for a simulation study tackling the question of agents' moving to a new neighbourhood, cf. Hegselmann, in preparation)? How do they interfere with the agents' choices?

(c) *Strategies of social choice*: agents may be endowed with different strategies for choosing their partners. Rationality scientists have explored very many types of strategies, grounded on payoff and/or risk matrix. In MICROdep, two heuristics have been implemented: goal-driven, which allows agents to choose partners under the pressure of the most motivating goal; utility-driven, which chooses partners allowing the highest utility. The latter may imply that the most motivating goal is dropped in favour of alternatives achieving a set of goals with a higher global value. These heuristics will be compared on a number of dimensions (e.g. the level of aggregation within a given market, agents' likelihood to migrate, etc).

References

Axelrod, R. (1984). The evolution of cooperation. New York: Basic.

Axelrod, R. (1995). The emergence of new political actors. In G.N. Gilbert § R. Conte (Eds.) Artificial Societies: the computer simulation of social life. London: UCL Press.

Balzer, W. & Tuomela, R. (1995). The structure and build-up of plan-based joint intentions. In J.L. Fiadeiro (Ed.) Proceedings of the 2nd Meeting of the ModelAge Group. Sesimbra, Lisbon: University of Portugal.

Bicchieri, C. (1990). Norms of cooperation. Ethics, 100, 838-861.

Brewer, M.B. (1986). The role of ethnocentrism in intergroup conflict. In S. Worchel & W. Austin (Eds.) Psychology of intergroup relations. Chicago: Nelson-Hall Publishers.

Brewer, M.B. & R.M. Kramer. 1986. Choice behavior in social dilemmas: Effects of social idnetity, group size and decision framing. Journal of Personality and Social Psychology, 8, 393-400.

Castelfranchi, C. (1994). Goal dynamics: How to change goals by changing beliefs. AIA '94, Second International Workshop on Abstract Intelligent Agent: Situation Assessment. Rome: ENEA.

Castelfranchi, C. & Conte, R. (1995). Agent exchange value. The emergence of organizational structures. Technical Report, TR-IP-PSCS, Rome: IP/CNR; submitted to Computational and Mathematical Organization Theory.

Castelfranchi, C. (1990). Social power: A missed point in DAI, MA and HCI. In Y. Demazeau & J.P. Mueller (Eds.) Decentralized AI. North-Holland: Elsevier.

Castelfranchi, C., Miceli, M. & Cesta, A. (1992). Dependence relations among autonomous agents. In Y. Demazeau & E. Werner (Eds.) Decentralized AI - 3. North-Holland: Elsevier.

Cohen, P.R. & Levesque, H.J. (1990). Intention is choice with commitment. Artificial Intelligence, 42, 213-261.

Conte, R. & Castelfranchi,C. (1995). Cognitive and social action. London: UCL Press.

Conte, R. & Castelfranchi, C. (1994). Mind is not enough. Precognitive bases of social action. In J. Doran & N. Gilbert (Eds.) Simulating societies: The computer simulation of social processes. London: UCL Press.

Conte, R. & Sichman, J.S. (1995). DEPNET: How to benefit from social dependence. Journal of Mathematical Sociology,2-3, 161-177.

Conte, R., Miceli, M. & C. Castelfranchi. (1991). Limits and levels of cooperation. Disentangling various types of prosocial interaction. In Y. Demazeau & J.P. Mueller (Eds.) Decentralized AI-2. North-Holland: Elsevier.

Doran, J. (1995). Simulating collective misbelief. Pre-proceedings of Simulating Societies '95, Boca Raton, FL, USA.

Edney, J.J. (1980). The commons problem: Alternative perspectives. American Psychologist, 35, 131-150.

Gasser, L. (Ed.) (1995). Proceedings of the 1st International Conference on Multi-Agent Systems, San Francisco: American Association of Artificial Intelligence.

Gould, R.V. (1993). Collective action and network structure. American Sociological Review, 58, 182-96.

Harsanyi, J.C. (1990). Advances in understanding rational behavior. In P.K. Moser (Ed.) Rationality in action. Contemporary approaches. New York: Cambridge University Press.

Hegselmann, R. Ultimatum game in Lineland, in preparation.

Hobbs, J.R. Artificial Intelligence and collective intentionality: Comments on Searle and on Grosz and Sidner. In P.R Cohen, J. Morgan & M.A. Pollack (Eds.) Intentions in Communication, Cambridge, MA: MIT Press.

Kahneman, D. & Tversky, A. (1982). The psychology of preferences. Scientific American, 246, 160-173.

Kelley, H.H. & Thibaut, J.W. (1978). Interpersonal relations: A theory of interdependence. New York: Wiley.

Komorita, S.S. & Barth, J.M. (1985). Components of reward in social dilemmas. Journal of Personality and Social Psychology, 48, 364-373.

Komorita, S.S & Ellis, A.L. (1995). Reward structure and cooperation in the n-person prisoner's dilemma. In D.A. Schroeder (Ed.) Social Dilemmas. Perspectives on individuals and groups. London: Praeger.

Kramer, R.M. & Brewer, M.B. (1986). Social group identity and the emergence of cooperation in resource conservation dilemmas. In H. Wilke, C. Rutte, D.M. Messick (Eds.) Experimental studies of social dilemmas. Frankfurt: Peter Lang Publishing Co.

Kramer, R.M. & Goldman, L. (1995). Helping the group or helping yourself? Social motives and group identity in resource dilemmas. In D.A. Schroeder (Ed.) Social Dilemmas. Perspectives on individuals and groups. London: Praeger.

Kuhlman, D.M. & Marshello, A. (1975). Individual differences in game motivation as moderators of preprogrammed strategic effects in prisoner's dilemma. Journal of Personality and Social Psychology, 32, 922-931.

Liebrand, W.B. (1984). The effect of social motives, communication, and group size on behavior in an n-person multi-stage mixed-motive game. European Journal of Social Psychology, 14, 239-264.

Markovsky, B., Skvoretz, J., Willer, D., Lovaglia, M.J., & Erger, J. (1993). The seeds of weak power: An extension of network exchange theory. American Sociological Review, 58, 197-209.

Marwell, G., Oliver, P., & Prahl, R. (1988). Social networks and collective action: A theory of the critical mass III. American Journal of Sociology, 94, 502-34.

McClinotock, C.G. (1978). Social values: Their definition, measurement, and development. Journal of Research and Development in Education, 12, 121-137.

Messick, D.M. (1974). When a little "group interest" goes a long way: Social motives and union joining. Organizational Behavior and Human Performance, 12, 331-334.

Moser, P.K. (Ed.) (1990). Rationality in action. Contemporary approaches. New York: Cambridge University Press.

Pruitt, D.G. (1970). Motivational processes in the decomposed prisoners' dilemma game. Journal of Personality and Social Psychology, 7, 21-27.

Rao, A.S. & Georgeff, M.P. (1991). Modelling rational agents within a BDI architecture. In J. Allen, R. Fikes, & Sandewall, E. (Eds.) Proceedings of the International Conference on Principles of Knowledge Representation and Reasoning. San Mateo, CA: Kaufmann.

Shoham, Y. & Cousins, S.B. (1994). Logics of mental attitudes in AI. In G. Lakemeyer & B. Nabel (Eds.) Foundations of knowledge representation and reasoning. Berlin: Springer-Verlag, LNAI.

Shoham, Y. & Tennenholtz, M. (1992a). On the syntehsis of useful social laws in artificial societies. Proceedings of the 10th National Conference on Artificial Intelliugence. San Mateo, CA: Kaufmann.

Sichman, J., Conte, R., Castelfranchi, C. & Demazeau., Y. (1994). A social reasoning mechanism based on dependence networks. Proceedings of the 11th European Conference on Artificial Intelligence, North-Holland: Elsevier.

Skvoretz, J. & Willer, D. (1993). Exclusion and power: a test of four theories of power in exchange networks. American Sociological Review, 58, 801-818.

Veneziano, V., Conte, R., Castelfranchi, C. MICROdep. The formation of partnerships, in preparation.

Williams, K.D., Jackson, J.M., & Karau, S.J. (1995). Collective hedonism: A social loafing analysis of social dilemmas. In D.A. Schroeder (Ed.) Social Dilemmas. Perspectives on individuals and groups. London: Praeger.

Appendix to the text

$$Ext_{ag_i} \stackrel{def}{\equiv} \bigcup_{j=1}^{n} Ext_{ag_i}^{entry}(ag_j) \tag{1}$$

$$Ext_{ag_i}^{entry}(ag_j) \stackrel{def}{\equiv} \left\{G_{ag_i}(ag_j), A_{ag_i}(ag_j), R_{ag_i}(ag_j), P_{ag_i}(ag_j)\right\} \tag{2}$$

$$G_{ag_i}(ag_j) \stackrel{def}{\equiv} \bigcup_{k=1}^{n_g} g_{ag_i}^{k}(ag_j) \tag{3}$$

$$A_{ag_i}(ag_j) \stackrel{def}{\equiv} \bigcup_{k=1}^{n_a} a_{ag_i}^{k}(ag_j) \tag{4}$$

$$R_{ag_i}\left(ag_j\right) \overset{def}{\equiv} \bigcup_{k=1}^{n_r} r_{ag_i}^k\left(ag_j\right) \tag{5}$$

$$P_{ag_i}\left(ag_j\right) \overset{def}{\equiv} \bigcup_{k=1}^{n_g} P_{ag_i}\left(ag_j, g_k\right) \tag{6}$$

$$P_{ag_i}\left(ag_j, g_k\right) \overset{def}{\equiv} \bigcup_{l=1}^{n_p} p_{ag_i}^l\left(ag_j, g_k\right) \tag{7}$$

$$p_l\left(g_k\right) \overset{def}{\equiv} \left\{g_k, R_{p_l(g_k)}, A_{p_l(g_k)}^{inst}\right\} \tag{8}$$

$$A_{p_l(g_k)}^{inst} \overset{def}{\equiv} \bigcup_{m=1}^{n_{ia}} a_{m,p_l(g_k)}^{inst} \tag{9}$$

$$a_{m,p_l(g_k)}^{inst} \overset{def}{\equiv} \left\{a_m, R_{p_l(g_k)}^{a_m}\right\} \tag{10}$$

$$a_{aut}(ag_i,g_k,P_{qk}) \overset{def}{\equiv} \exists g_k \in G(ag_i)\, \exists p_{lk} \in P_{qk}\, \forall a_{m,p_{lk}}^{inst} \in A_{p_{lk}}^{inst}\; a_m \in A(ag_i) \tag{11}$$

$$r_{aut}(ag_i,g_k,P_{qk}) \overset{def}{\equiv} \exists g_k \in G(ag_i)\, \exists p_{lk} \in P_{qk}\; \forall r_m \in R_{p_{lk}}\; r_m \in I \tag{12}$$

$$s_{aut}(ag_i,g_k,P_{qk}) \overset{def}{\equiv} a_{aut}(ag_i,g_k,P_{qk}) \wedge r_{aut}(ag_i,g_k,P_{qk}) \tag{13}$$

$$\begin{aligned} a_{dep}(ag_i,ag_j,g_k,P_{qk}) \overset{def}{\equiv} \; & \exists g_k \in G(ag_i)\, \neg a_{aut}(ag_i,g_k,P_{qk}) \wedge \\ & \exists p_{lk} \in P_{qk}\; \exists a_{m,p_{lk}}^{inst} \in A_{p_{lk}}^{inst}\; a_m \in A(ag \end{aligned} \tag{14}$$

$$\begin{aligned} r_{dep}(ag_i,ag_j,g_k,P_{qk}) \overset{def}{\equiv} \; & \exists g_k \in G(ag_i)\, \neg r_{aut}(ag_i,g_k,P_{qk}) \wedge \\ & \exists p_{lk} \in P_{qk}\; \exists r_m \in R_{p_{lk}}\; r_m \in R(ag_j) \end{aligned} \tag{15}$$

$$s_{dep}(ag_i,ag_j,g_k,P_{qk}) \overset{def}{\equiv} a_{dep}(ag_i,ag_j,g_k,P_{qk}) \vee r_{dep}(ag_i,ag_j,g_k,P_{qk}) \tag{16}$$

$$IND(ag_i,ag_j,g_k) \overset{def}{\equiv} \neg\, a_{dep}(ag_i,ag_j,g_k,P_{ik}) \tag{17}$$

$$UD(ag_i,ag_j,g_k) \stackrel{def}{\equiv} a_{dep}(ag_i,ag_j,g_k,P_{ik}) \wedge \neg\exists g_l \in G(ag_j)\, a_{dep}(ag_j,ag_i,g_l,P_{il}) \quad (18)$$

$$MD(ag_i,ag_j,g_k,P_{qk}) \stackrel{def}{\equiv} a_{dep}(ag_i,ag_j,g_k,P_{qk}) \wedge a_{dep}(ag_j,ag_i,g_k,P_{qk}) \quad (19)$$

$$RD(ag_i,ag_j,g_k,g_l,P_{qk},P_{ql}) \stackrel{def}{\equiv} a_{dep}(ag_i,ag_j,g_k,P_{qk}) \wedge \exists g_l \in G(ag_j)\, a_{dep}(ag_j,ag_i,g_l,P_{ql}) \quad (20)$$

Computer Simulation of Social Value Orientation: Vitality, Satisfaction, and Emergent Game Structures

Jeffrey A. Joireman[1], Gregory P. Shelley[1], Paul D. Teta[2], Jon Wilding[1], and D. Michael Kuhlman[1]

[1] Department of Psychology, University of Delaware, Newark, DE. 19711, USA
[2] Marketing Science Department, The M/A/R/C Group
7850 North Belt Line Road, Irving, TX. 75063, USA

Abstract. We examined dyadic interaction among eight archetypal social value orientations, or SVOs. (McClintock, 1978). These 8 SVOs differ in terms of two value systems: (1) concern with the well being of others and (2) concern with the well being of self (+,0 for *Altruism*; +,+ for *Cooperation*; 0,+ for *Individualism*; -,+ for *Competition*; -,0 for *Aggression*; -,- for *Sadomasochism*; 0,- for *Masochism*; and +,- for *Martyrdom*). All different pairs of SVOs (n=36) were formed, and each dyad played 60,000 2 x 2 games. For each game, the 2 payoffs in each cell of the matrix were generated randomly so that games had no particular structure (i.e., Prisoner's Dilemma, Chicken, etc), or symmetry. The decision process was based on Kelley and Thibaut's (1978) notion of transforming the *given* matrix into the *effective* matrix. That is, each SVO transformed the pair of given payoffs in each cell to a single number, or effective payoff (utility) based on its SVO (e.g., Cooperators took the sum of the payoffs to self and other; Altruists only considered the payoffs to the partner; Competitors subtracted the other's points from their own). Next, each SVO chose the row or column with the largest average utility. We examined the long term outcomes of each SVO in two ways: (1) accumulated *given* points referred to as *vitality*, and (2) accumulated *effective* points (utilities) referred to as *satisfaction*. **Vitality** was completely determined by two things: (1) player's concern with its own (given) outcomes, and (2) partner's concern with player's (given) outcomes. Although Individualism was the most vital SVO at the single person level, at the dyadic level, pairs of Cooperators were more vital than pairs of Individualists. For **Satisfaction**, no SVO did best overall. Satisfaction depended completely on the particular SVO pairing. The strongest mutual satisfaction was achieved by SVO pairs with identical *effective* matrices (e.g., Cooperator/Cooperator, Individualist/Altruist). **Emergent Games:** We also examined the long-term payoff matrices (the average of given points over 60,000 trials) produced by the pairings of different SVOs. A variety of such *Emergent Games* occurred, and the structure of each was tied perfectly to the SVO pair that formed it. Thus, the origins of structures are rooted in the social value systems of the involved parties. Notably, the Emergent Game produced by Cooperation versus Individualism is a classic Prisoner's Dilemma.

Authors Note: Thanks to Toshiaki Doi and Janusz Grzelak for their very helpful comments.
Please address correspondence to D.M. Kuhlman (email:kuhlman@strauss.udel.edu).

A substantial body of evidence indicates that behavior in interdependent settings is influenced by individual differences in social value orientation (SVO) typically defined in terms of the weight (positive, negative, neutral) an individual assigns to their own and another's interdependent outcomes (McClintock, 1978). Social value orientation has been shown to influence both choice behavior (Kramer, McClintock, & Messick, 1986; Kuhlman & Marshello, 1975; Liebrand & van Run, 1985; Liebrand, Wilke, Vogel, & Wolters, 1986; McClintock & Liebrand, 1988; Van Lange & Kuhlman, 1994) and expectations about others' choices (Kuhlman & Wimberley, 1976; Maki & McClintock, 1983) in a variety of social dilemmas. Evidence further suggests that SVO is a temporally stable disposition (Kuhlman, Camac, & Cunha, 1986) that extends in influence beyond the typical laboratory gaming paradigm (e.g., Eisenberger, Kuhlman, & Cotterell, 1992; McClintock & Allison, 1989; Van Vugt, Meertens, & Van Lange, 1995).

Most past research on SVO has tended to concentrate on four orientations, including *Altruism* (maximizing other's gain), *Cooperation* (maximizing joint gain), *Individualism* (maximizing own gain), and *Competition* (maximizing relative gain). While a focus on the "big four" orientations seems reasonable given their prevalence in the populations typically studied by social psychologists (i.e., college students), it nevertheless overlooks a number of interesting questions inherent in the broader range of theoretically-possible orientations (e.g., Griesinger & Livingston, 1973). In the present simulation, we examine the consequences of interaction among eight archetypal SVOs based on a two-dimensional space, the axes of which correspond to concern with own and concern with other's outcomes respectively (McClintock, 1978), as shown in Figure 1.

Figure 1. Eight Archetypal Social Value Orientations following McClintock (1978)

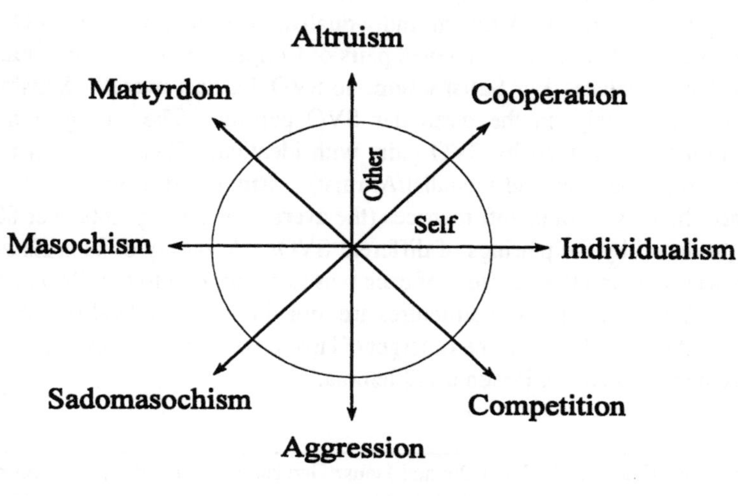

In the simulation, all possible dyads of SVOs are formed, with one being assigned the position of Row player and the other the position of Column player. Each SVO pair plays a series 60,000 2 x 2 games and outcomes for each player are accumulated . As described below, the choice made by each player on every trial is the rational expression of its concern with its own well-being and the well-being of its partner (i.e., its SVO). Over trials, no learning occurs in that behavior on trial *n* is not a function of any aspect of previous interaction. Choice is a simple expression of an enduring set of concerns for personal and social welfare. Thus, we are modeling a social system in which the individual decision makers act out of principle.

Given the focus of the present book, it might well be expected that the 60,000 2 x 2 games took one of the three forms of social dilemmas outlined by Liebrand (1983), including Prisoner's Dilemma, Chicken, or Trust. This however was not the case. Rather, on any given trial, the eight payoffs (four to the row player and four to the column player) were generated randomly. Why? Because in our view the specific payoff structures we encounter from moment to moment in our daily lives are numerous, highly variable, most likely not symmetric, and not necessarily dilemmas.

But, this moment to moment variability notwithstanding, it is ecologically valid to evaluate the consequences of any given approach to interaction in the very long term. To illustrate, consider that in any given hand of poker, a good player may win or lose. The telling index of her skill is her success over many games. Thus, our concern here is not on the specific trial by trial payoffs but rather on their average over many thousands of trials encompassing very different games with a variety of partners.

Our focus on the long term consequences of the eight archetypal orientations can be subdivided into two broad categories. First, we evaluate the effectiveness of the different SVOs by two different criteria, labelled *vitality* and *satisfaction*. Vitality corresponds to the outcomes associated with maintaining the physical well-being of the individual (e.g., money, food, etc.), whereas satisfaction represents the extent to which the goals of a particular SVO are being achieved with regard to the distribution of outcomes to self and others. From the theoretical perspective of Kelley and Thibaut (1978), vitality corresponds to the individual's outcomes in the "given" matrix of outcomes, while satisfaction is measured in terms of the transformed, or "effective" matrix of utilities. Within this context, we ask: Is there any single SVO which is overall most vital? Most satisfied? Are they different SVOs? And, on the basis of satisfaction, what patterns of attraction are likely to exist among the varying pairs of SVOs?

The second focus of the present chapter is more directly connected to the issue of social dilemmas. Here we examine the symmetric 2 x 2 payoff structures which "emerge" from the long term interactions of different SVO pairs. For example, consider two individuals who must commit to a long term SVO of either rigidly pursuing Altruism or rigidly pursuing Individualism. The set of four long term payoffs resulting from the combination of SVO choices (Altruist/ Altruist; Altruist/Individualist; Individualist/Altruist; Individualist/Individualist) constitutes what we refer to as an *emergent game*.

With respect to such emergent games, we ask two related questions: First, do any of these emergent games take the form of a social dilemma? Second, what relationship, if any, is there between the specific pairing of SVOs and the resulting structure of the emergent games? The identification of any subset of the emergent games as social dilemmas would provide a new perspective on one way such dilemmas might originate; not as the result of a world of finite resources populated by increasingly large numbers of egoists (e.g., Hardin, 1968), but rather, as a consequence of the rational expression of two individuals' concern for personal and social welfare (i.e., SVOs), in an environment free of resource depletion/scarcity problems. An answer to the second question regarding emergent games would point to a general mechanism accounting for their generation.

1 The Simulation

1.1 Generation of Interdependence Structures

In the simulation each SVO played 60,000 2 x 2 games with each of the eight SVOs. Thus, each SVO made a total of 480,000 (8 x 60,000) decisions, 60,000 with an Altruistic partner, 60,000 with a Cooperative partner and so on. On each trial, the specific 2 x 2 interdependence structure was generated by randomly assigning values to each of the eight payoffs within the matrix. Values were chosen from a uniform distribution in the interval of 0 to 1. This created a situation in which, from one trial to the next, the interdependence structures were highly variable, uncorrelated, asymmetric, and probably most often not dilemmas.

The variable interdependence structure represents one departure from traditional simulations which have typically employed the prisoner's dilemma structure (e.g., Axelrod, 1984; Messick & Liebrand, 1995). A second departure from these approaches involves the decision rule that was used. Whereas former simulations have tended to examine the influence of different decision strategies which involve or allow for learning (e.g., win-stay-lose-change or tit-for-tat), the present simulation makes choice based *solely* on the agent's SVO.

1.2 Decision Rule: Social Value Orientation and Expected Utility Maximization

For each SVO, choice was determined by a two-step process. First, each SVO transformed the payoffs in the randomly determined outcome matrix (i.e., the "given matrix," Kelley & Thibaut, 1978) into utilities based on the weight that SVO assigned to its own (w_1) and another's (w_2) outcomes. Adopting the general notation for the four payoffs in a 2 x 2 matrix,[1] the rows representing a choice between C and D, the columns, a choice between C' and D', the *row player's transformed outcomes* in each of the four cells can be expressed as follows:

---

1. Following Rapoport and Chammah (1965), we designate the *row player's* outcomes R (upper left), S (upper right), T (bottom left), P (bottom right). In the present paper, as the payoffs in the games are asymmetric, we introduce a separate notation for the *column player*: r (upper left), s (bottom left), t (top right), and p (bottom right).

Utility of cell CC' $\equiv CC'_u = w_1R + w_2r$ [1a]
Utility of cell CD' $\equiv CD'_u = w_1S + w_2t$ [1b]
Utility of cell DC' $\equiv DC'_u = w_1T + w_2s$ [1c]
Utility of cell DD' $\equiv DD'_u = w_1P + w_2p$ [1d]

Once the SVO transformed the given outcomes into the "effective matrix," its choice was the one that maximized expected utility within that matrix, where, from the *row player's* perspective, expected utility is defined as follows:

$$EU(C)=[p_C*CC'_u + p_{D'}*CD'_u] \quad [2a]$$
$$EU(D)=[p_C*DC'_u + p_{D'}*DD'_u] \quad [2b]$$

where p_C and $p_{D'}$ are subjective probabilities that the column player will choose C' and D' respectively. In keeping with past research (e.g., McClintock & Liebrand, 1988), it is assumed that both probabilities are equal to 0.5 Hence, the expected utility of any given row is simply the average of the cell utilities within that row. The transformation process and expected utility maximization for each of the eight archetypal SVOs faced with a prisoner's dilemma is illustrated in Table 1.

1.3 Vitality and Satisfaction

Once a SVO has chosen on the basis of Expected Utility Maximization, the success of that SVO can be evaluated in terms of its vitality and satisfaction, as noted earlier. Concretely, *vitality* refers to the average number of points gained over the block of 60,000 trials with a given partner. *Satisfaction* for a given SVO (conceptualized as the extent to which the goals of a particular SVO are being achieved) is that SVO's (transformed) outcome scaled by the range of possible (transformed) outcomes, as follows:

$$Satisfaction_{svo} = (Ot_{svo} - Lt_{svo})/(Ht_{svo} - Lt_{svo}) \quad [3]$$

where Ot = the actual transformed outcome, Lt = the lowest possible transformed outcome, Ht = the highest possible transformed outcome, and svo = the particular social value orientation of interest. For example, assuming the cooperator's transformed cell entries from Table 1, Rr = 84.84, St = 77.77, Ts = 77.77, and Pp = 42.42, the St outcome corresponds to a satisfaction level of .833 = (77.77-42.42)/(84.84-42.42).

2. Results

2.1 Vitality

Our first goal was to determine the effect of Own and Partner's Orientation on levels of vitality and satisfaction. Considering the effect of Own Orientation on vitality, an obvious expectation is that vitality should vary as a function of the weight one's Own Orientation applies to own outcomes, decreasing in a monotonic fashion from the individualistic SVO through the masochistic SVO (as shown in the

Table 1 Transformed Outcomes for Eight Archetypal Social Value Orientations, Expected Utility, and Predicted Row Choice in a Prisoner's Dilemma

Given Matrix:

	C'	D'
C	60 , 60	10 , 100
D	100 , 10	30 , 30

Effective Matrix:

Orientation	wS	wO	CC'	CD'	DC'	DD'	Row1	Row2	Rc
Alt	.00	1.00	60.00	100.00	10.00	30.00	80.00	20.00	1
Coo	.71	.71	84.84	77.77	77.77	42.42	81.31	60.10	1
Ind	1.00	.00	60.00	10.00	100.00	30.00	35.00	65.00	2
Com	.71	-.71	0.00	-63.63	63.63	0.00	-31.82	31.82	2
Agg	.00	-1.00	-60.00	-100.00	-10.00	-30.00	-80.00	-20.00	2
Sam	-.71	-.71	-84.84	-77.77	-77.77	-42.42	-81.31	-60.10	2
Mas	-1.00	.00	-60.00	-10.00	-100.00	-30.00	-35.00	-65.00	1
Mar	-.71	.71	0.00	63.63	-63.63	0.00	31.82	-31.82	1

Notes: Payoffs are from the row player's perspective; wS = weight to Self; wO = weight to Other; CC' corresponds to Row's choice of C and Column's choice of D; Row1 = utility of Row 1; Row2 = utility of Row 2; Rc = predicted row choice. Alt=Altruist; Coo=Cooperator; Ind=Individualist; Com=Competitor; Agg=Aggressor; Sam=Sadomasochist; Mas=Masochist; Mar=Martyr.

first column of Table 1). By contrast, vitality as a function of Partner's Orientation should vary systematically in terms of the weight the partner assigns to other's outcomes, decreasing in a monotonic fashion from the altruistic SVO through the aggressive SVO (as shown in the second column of Table 1). Further, it seems reasonable to expect that when identical SVOs interact, the highest vitality should be achieved by SVOs which have a positive concern with both own and other's outcomes (i.e., two Cooperators), while the lowest vitality should occur for the Sadomasochism pairing (i.e., a negative concern for both own and other's outcomes).

An examination of the mean vitality scores as a function of Own and Partner's Orientation (see Table 2) is wholly consistent with these expectations. The first thing to point out about Table 2 is that it is completely additive. That is, the value of any given cell in the table is completely determined by the sum of row effects (Partner's Orientation) and column effects (Own Orientation). Furthermore, each effect is equally important, accounting for 50% of the overall variability in the table. To rephrase, the set of vitality means in Table 2 is completely a function of reflexive control and fate control (Kelley & Thibaut, 1978). The additivity of this table allows for the use of marginal row and column means as indices of each orientation's impact on long-term vitality.

With regard to Own Orientation, and consistent with predictions, Table 2 shows that Individualism achieved the highest vitality (M = .616), followed by Competition and Cooperation (*M's* = .582), Aggression and Altruism (*M's* = .501 and .500, respectively), Sadomasochism and Martyrdom (*M's* = .418), and Masochism (M = .384). Turning to the Partner's contribution to vitality, the column marginal show that Altruism provided the highest vitality (M = .616), followed by Martyrdom and Cooperation (*M's* = .582), Masochism and Individualism (*M's* = .500), Sadomasochism and Competition (*M's* = .418), and Aggression (M = .383).

Furthermore, consistent with expectations, the highest vitality for pairs of identical SVOs (i.e., along the main diagonal) occurred for Cooperation (M = .663), while the lowest vitality achieved by identical pairs occurred for Sadomasochism (M = .335). Also of particular interest is the fact that universal Cooperation produces higher vitality than universal Individualism. Although the Individualistic SVO is "best" at the individual level, the Cooperative SVO is "best" at the group level. This result parallels one of the defining properties of a social dilemma (as we discuss below).

2.2 Satisfaction

In contrast to the results for vitality, the mean levels of satisfaction (Table 3) indicated that the effect of Own Orientation depended *completely* on the Partner's Orientation: the interaction (or, Behavior Control) component constituted 100% of the variance in the means. The structure of this interaction is quite sensible, considering the fact that satisfaction is based on achieving one's social goals. For example, the goal of the Individualist is to achieve the cell in which its own gain is the highest. And, of the eight possible partners, only one, the Altruist -- who places total and positive emphasis on the other's well being -- will attempt to

Table 2 Vitality as a Function of Own and Partner's Orientation

Partner's Orientation	Own Orientation								
	Alt	Coo	Ind	Com	Agg	Sam	Mas	Mar	*Mean*
Alt	0.617_R	0.699	0.733	0.697	0.618	0.534_T	0.500	0.534	0.616
Coo	0.583	0.663	0.699	0.664	0.582	0.500	0.465	0.501	0.582
Ind	0.500	0.581	0.616	0.582	0.501	0.417	0.384	0.419	0.500
Com	0.417	0.500	0.535	0.498	0.418	0.337	0.302	0.337	0.418
Agg	0.382	0.466	0.500	0.466	0.384	0.301	0.267	0.301	0.383
Sam	0.418_S	0.500	0.534	0.500	0.420	0.335_P	0.302	0.337	0.418
Mas	0.500	0.581	0.616	0.582	0.500	0.417	0.385	0.418	0.500
Mar	0.581	0.664	0.698	0.664	0.582	0.500	0.465	0.500	0.582
Mean	0.500	0.582	0.616	0.582	0.501	0.418	0.384	0.418	

Note: Alt=Altruist; Coo=Cooperator; Ind=Individualist; Com=Competitor; Agg=Aggressor; Sam=Sadomasochist; Mas=Masochist; Mar=Martyr. Subscripted vitality means designate outcomes for the Altruism-Sadomasochism emergent game presented in Table 4.

Table 3 Satisfaction as a Function of Own and Partner's Orientation

Partner's Orientation	Own Orientation								
	Alt	Coo	Ind	Com	Agg	Sam	Mas	Mar	*Mean*
Alt	0.694	0.817	**0.889**	0.817	0.696	0.570	0.501	0.570	0.694
Coo	0.822	**0.886**	0.821	0.695	0.566	0.500	0.568	0.693	0.694
Ind	**0.889**	0.817	0.694	0.569	0.500	0.571	0.693	0.816	0.694
Com	0.820	0.693	0.568	0.500	0.568	0.693	0.822	**0.887**	0.694
Agg	0.696	0.571	0.500	0.570	0.694	0.816	**0.889**	0.817	0.694
Sam	0.566	0.500	0.567	0.693	0.821	**0.888**	0.821	0.693	0.694
Mas	0.499	0.569	0.693	0.818	**0.889**	0.818	0.693	0.570	0.694
Mar	0.567	0.695	0.821	**0.887**	0.821	0.692	0.568	0.500	0.694
Mean	0.694	0.694	0.694	0.694	0.694	0.694	0.694	0.693	

Note: Alt=Altruist; Coo=Cooperator; Ind=Individualist; Com=Competitor; Agg=Aggressor; Sam=Sadomasochist; Mas=Masochist; Mar=Martyr. Bolded values represent likely partner pairings. **Bolded values represent the maximum satisfaction in the column.**

achieve the same cell. Thus, for the Altruist/Individualist dyad there will be a perfect correspondence of the utilities in the cells of the effective matrix. Examination of the satisfaction table shows that in every case satisfaction is maximal when the effective matrix for the row and column player are reciprocal.

Although it goes beyond the scope of the results presented in this paper, the satisfaction outcomes have important implications for levels of attraction between the orientations. Briefly, to examine likely partner pairings based on mutual satisfaction, we assume that attraction to (and pairing with) a partner will be more likely to the extent that (a) that partner provides the highest satisfaction, and (b) the partner reciprocates that attraction. As detailed above, we could expect strong mutual attraction between Individualists and Altruists, a dyad in which both partners are happy but only one is healthy. This is in strong contrast to the Cooperative/Cooperative dyad where both partners are strongly and mutually attracted, and in which both thrive.

2.3 The Structure(s) of Emergent Games

The second goal of our simulation was to examine the structure of the relationships that emerge for each of the pairs of (different) SVOs, focussing on two questions in particular: First, do any of the emergent games constitute social dilemmas? Second, is there a general mechanism which can account for the specific structure emerging from the pairing of any two SVOs? Prior to addressing either question, it will be helpful to illustrate more concretely our notion of an "emergent game," drawing on the vitality means presented in Table 2.

Assume for the moment that you and another person are each limited to a choice between two archetypal SVOs, say Altruism and Sadomasochism. The long-term payoff to each of you resulting from the four possible SVO combinations can be represented as a 2 x 2 symmetric game in normal form, as shown in the top of Table 4. For the purposes of comparison, the Cooperation-Individualism emergent game is also presented in this table.

Our first question asks, are either of these games social dilemmas? We will answer that question presently, but first consider why it's interesting and perhaps even important. It deals with the origins of dilemmas. Most of the theoretical work on social dilemmas has viewed their origin as essentially a matter of finite resources in a world populated by egoists (e.g., Hardin, 1968). But, at the risk of seeming cavalier, we will timidly suggest that the issue of finite resources is at least debatable (e.g., Tierney, 1990). Who knows what technological breakthroughs may solve problems of food production and distribution? We are not suggesting this as a coping strategy to deal with the stress induced by nightmares of an overpopulated, starving world. Rather, we are suggesting that it is at least possible that the problems of the world's carrying capacity and population growth might be solved via technology. In such a case, there would be little reason for people concerned with resource depletion in the real world to pay much attention to social dilemma research. Granting the assumption of inexhaustible resources, purely for the sake of argument, would social scientists of the sort reading this chapter have anything to study? The results of our simulation suggest

Table 4 Two Emergent Games in Normal Form

Altruism-Sadomasochism Emergent Game

	Altruism	Sadomasochism
Altruism	.617 , .617	.418 , .534
Sadomasochism	.534 , .418	.335 , .335

Cooperation-Individualism Emergent Game

	Cooperation	Individualism
Cooperation	.663 , .663	.581 , .699
Individualism	.699 , .581	.616 , .616

Note: Row player's outcomes shown to the left of the comma. Emergent Games based on the vitality means shown in Table 2, with outcomes for the Altruism-Sadomasochism game designated by subscripts in Table 2.

that the answer is yes; even when resources are infinite, as in the present simulation, *social dilemmas can emerge purely as a function of particular pairings of SVOs.*

Paraphrasing Liebrand's (1983) general definition, social dilemmas can be defined by three properties: (1) Each player has a preference for the strategy selection of the partner, the preferred strategy designated as C, the non-preferred (i.e., most threatening) strategy labelled D; (2) Each player has at least one of two reasons to select D, either *greed* (T>S) or *fear* (P>S) or both; and (3) If both players select D, the outcome (P) is inferior to that produced by mutual C (R). The three 2 x 2 symmetric games that satisfy these properties, include Prisoner's Dilemma (T > R > P > S), Chicken (T > R > S > P), and Trust (R > T > P > S).

Applying Liebrand's definition of a social dilemma to the emergent Altruism-Sadomasochism game in top portion of Table 4, it can be seen that this game is not a social dilemma: each player does hope the other chooses Altruism (i.e., C=Altruism, D=Sadomasochism), yet neither greed nor fear are present (R>T, S>P). By contrast, an examination of the Cooperation-Individualism emergent game in the bottom portion of Table 4 reveals a Prisoner's Dilemma structure, as T > R > P > S.

Given eight SVOs, there are 28 such emergent games. To generate each game, we first broadly labelled the strategy leading to the highest average outcome to the other as the *Altruistic Strategy* (AS) and the strategy leading to the lowest average outcome to the other as the *Non-Altruistic Strategy* (NAS). We subsequently ordered the payoffs {R, S, T, P} such that R = payoff given mutual selection of AS; S = payoff when one chooses AS and the other chooses NAS; T =when one chooses NAS and the other chooses AS; and P = payoff when both choose NAS. The full set of games appears in Table 5, with social dilemmas designated in bold. A number of additional parameters are presented in the table which are discussed in more detail in the next section.

As can be seen in Table 5, four of the emergent games correspond to a Prisoner's Dilemma. Perhaps the most salient of these emergent dilemmas is the Cooperation-Individualism game (# 4), as these two SVOs delineate the inherent conflict between individual and collective rationality embodied in the prisoner's dilemma (e.g., Kahan, 1974). While certainly interesting, of even more interest, possibly, is the fact that social dilemmas are not constrained to the pairing of Cooperative and Individualistic SVOs. Altruism and Competition generate a social dilemma, as do a number of other SVO pairings.

The preceding results give rise to a number of questions. For example, do such emergent social dilemmas have anything in common? Are certain SVOs, or combinations thereof, more likely to produce emergent social dilemmas than others? And, do the potential processes giving rise to emergent social dilemmas shed light on the origin of all (28) emergent games? The answer to each of these questions is yes, as we outline below.

3 Relationship between SVO Pairs and Emergent Games

3.1 A Common Metric

To relate any two SVOs to their corresponding emergent game, a common metric would be desirable. One possible system, proposed by Doi (1990) in his *Characteristic Space Theory*, allows for the classification of any symmetric 2 x 2 game along the same dimension which effectively defines SVO. In what follows, we present an adaption of Doi's theory which Teta (1994) has shown to be formally equivalent. This system is also consistent with Rapoport's (1967) k index, and Harris' (1969) taxonomic system.

We start by returning to the familiar two-dimensional model of SVO originally proposed by Griesinger and Livingston (1973) in which each orientation is represented as a vector in the self-other space (see Figure 1), with a corresponding angle (θ) defined with respect to the x-axis. This model describes differences between *people* in terms of the angle corresponding to their SVO (e.g., Altruists' θ = 90°, Individualists' θ = 0°, and so on).

Teta's adaption of Doi's model also allows for the representation of 2 x 2 *symmetric payoff structures* in terms of the *indifference angle* (θ'). The value of θ' for a given game corresponds to the SVO that would be indifferent between the game's alternatives. More specifically, θ' corresponds to the SVO for which the utility of Row 1 and Row 2 are the same. Teta shows that the tangent of θ' is a ratio of the payoffs in the game, as follows:

$$\tan \theta' = (S+P-R-T)/(R+S-T-P) \quad [4]$$

The indifference angle of a game, then, is a simple function of the generating vectors corresponding to the game's alternatives. As noted earlier, this common metric is completely consistent with earlier taxonomic systems presented by Rapoport (1967) and Harris (1969). For example, Rapoport's k index (originally given as (R-P)/(T-S)) is derivable from a game's indifference angle, as follows,

$$k = \text{tangent}\ (45° - \theta') \quad [5]$$

while Harris' (1969) taxonomic system for symmetric 2 x 2 games is based on two parameters, r_3 = (P-S)/(T-S) and r_4 = (T-R)/(T-S), which are subsumed under Rapoport's k index, such that,

$$k = 1 - (r_3 + r_4) \quad [6]$$

Equation [6] makes clear that differing combinations of r_3 and r_4 can lead to the same k value and hence the same indifference angle. This poses a problem if k (or the indifference angle) is to be used to designate the nature of any particular game. To illustrate, take two very different games, say a Chicken Dilemma (with r3=-.20, r4 = .50) and a Prisoner's Dilemma (with r3 = .10, r4 = .20). While these games are structurally very different, they yield the same k value (.70). Our point here is that in order to use k or the indifference angle as a unique marker for the emergent games, r_3 must equal r_4. As $r_3 = r_4$ in the present data[2], k or the indifference angle corresponds uniquely to a particular game.

3.2 Application to the Present Data

The preceding discussion was motivated by a desire to outline a metric which would describe both SVO and matrix games along a common dimension in order that we might examine the nature of the relationship between the eight archetypal SVOs used in our simulation, and the nature of the games which emerge from the 28 different pairings of these SVOs. Our question here asks if there is a systematic relationship between the particular pairing of SVOs and the structure of the game which emerges over the course of their long term interaction. Table 5 shows that the answer to both questions is yes.

The left portion of Table 5 shows the 28 SVO pairs with their respective vectors denoted as angles (θ, in columns 4-5). Column 6 displays the resultant angle between the two vectors, while column 7 indicates Rapoport's k value (from equation [5]). The right part of Table 5 displays the four parameters for each emergent game (based on the vitality means in Table 2), Harris' parameters (r_3, r_4), and Rapoport's k value. The latter k value is computed from the payoffs in the emergent game, while the former k value is based on the resultant of the two orientation angles that generated the game. A comparison of the k value generated a priori as a function of the SVO pairs (column 7), and the k value resulting from the emergent games (column 13) reveals a nearly perfect relationship between these indices (r = .999). The conclusion from these results is quite clear: When individuals interact over the long term, each driven blindly by a particular social motive, the structure of their long term relationship can be traced directly to the SVO choices available to the two parties.

4 Discussion

The present simulation examined two broad questions bearing on the long-term consequences of eight archetypal SVOs (McClintock, 1978). First, what is the long-term vitality (i.e., personal resources) and satisfaction (i.e., ability to achieve the goals of one's SVO) for each of the orientations over a wide variety of interdependence structures? Second, what is the nature of the relationship that "emerges" between various pairs of orientations? Which, if any, of these pairings result in social dilemmas? More generally, is there a relationship between the emergent games and the orientation pairs which generate them? Each of these questions is addressed in turn.

---

2. This is true in two respects. First, from a purely theoretical perspective, the generating vectors corresponding to the eight archetypal SVOs used in the present simulation are of equal length (see Table 1). Under these conditions, $r_3 = r_4$. Second, from an empirical perspective, as the means in Table 2 are completely additive, the emergent games they generate will always be such that $r_3 = r_4$.

Table 5 Emergent Games: Vitality

	SVOs		SVO Parameters			Emergent Game Parameters							
Game	AS	NAS	AS Angle	NAS Angle	Result Angle	Result K	R	S	T	P	r3	r4	K
1	*Alt*	*Ind*	*90*	*0*	*45.00*	*0.00*	*0.617*	*0.500*	*0.734*	*0.616*	*0.49*	*0.50*	*0.01*
2	**Alt**	**Com**	**90**	**315**	**22.50**	**0.41**	**0.617**	**0.417**	**0.697**	**0.498**	**0.29**	**0.29**	**0.42**
3	*Alt*	*Agg*	*90*	*270*	*0*	*1.00*	*0.617*	*0.382*	*0.618*	*0.384*	*0.01*	*0.00*	*0.99*
4	**Coo**	**Ind**	**45**	**0**	**22.50**	**0.41**	**0.664**	**0.581**	**0.699**	**0.616**	**0.29**	**0.30**	**0.41**
5	Mar	Ind	135	0	37.5	-0.41	0.500	0.419	0.698	0.616	0.70	0.71	-0.41
6	Alt	Sam	90	225	157.50	2.41	0.617	0.418	0.534	0.335	-0.71	-0.71	2.42
7	Alt	Mas	90	180	135.00	-Inf	0.617	0.500	0.500	0.385	363.89	366.97	-729.85
8	Alt	Mar	90	135	112.50	-2.41	0.617	0.581	0.534	0.500	1.73	1.75	-2.47
9	Coo	Com	45	315	0.00	1.00	0.664	0.500	0.664	0.498	-0.01	0.00	1.01
10	Coo	Agg	45	270	337.50	2.41	0.664	0.466	0.582	0.384	-0.71	-0.71	2.42
11	Coo	Sam	45	225	135.00	-Inf	0.665	0.500	0.500	0.335	666.27	664.80	-1330.07
12	Coo	Mas	45	180	112.50	-2.41	0.664	0.581	0.465	0.385	1.69	1.71	-2.39
13	Ind	Com	0	315	337.50	2.41	0.616	0.535	0.582	0.498	-0.78	-0.72	2.50
14	Ind	Agg	0	270	315.00	+Inf	0.616	0.500	0.601	0.384	-107.24	-106.13	214.37
15	Ind	Sam	0	225	292.50	-2.41	0.616	0.534	0.417	0.335	1.71	1.70	-2.41
16	Mar	Mas	135	180	157.50	2.41	0.500	0.418	0.465	0.385	-0.72	-0.74	2.46
17	Alt	Coo	90	45	67.50	-0.41	0.617	0.584	0.699	0.664	0.70	0.71	-0.41
18	Mas	Ind	180	0	90.00	-1.00	0.385	0.384	0.616	0.616	1.00	1.00	-1.00
19	Mar	Coo	135	45	90.00	-1.00	0.500	0.501	0.664	0.664	1.00	1.00	-1.00
20	Sam	Com	225	315	270.00	-1.00	0.335	0.337	0.500	0.498	0.99	1.01	-1.00

This table is continued on the next page

Table 5 (cont.)

	SVOs		SVO Parameters			Emergent Game Parameters							
Game	AS	NAS	AS Angle	NAS Angle	Result Angle	Result K	R	S	T	P	r3	r4	K
21	Mas	Com	180	315	247.50	-0.41	0.385	0.302	0.583	0.498	0.70	0.70	-0.40
22	*Mar*	*Com*	*135*	*315*	*225.00*	*0.00*	*0.500*	*0.337*	*0.664*	*0.498*	*0.49*	*0.50*	*0.01*
23	Sam	Agg	225	270	247.50	-0.41	0.335	0.301	0.420	0.384	0.70	0.71	-0.41
24	*Mas*	*Agg*	*180*	*270*	*225.00*	*0.00*	*0.385*	*0.267*	*0.500*	*0.384*	*0.50*	*0.49*	*0.00*
25	**Mar**	**Agg**	**135**	**270**	**202.50**	**0.41**	**0.500**	**0.301**	**0.583**	**0.384**	**0.29**	**0.30**	**0.41**
26	**Mas**	**Sam**	**180**	**225**	**202.50**	**0.41**	**0.385**	**0.303**	**0.417**	**0.335**	**0.28**	**0.29**	**0.43**
27	Com	Agg	315	270	292.50	-2.41	0.498	0.466	0.418	0.384	1.73	1.69	-2.42
28	Mar	Sam	135	225	180.00	1.00	0.500	0.337	0.500	0.335	-0.01	0.00	1.01

Note: AS=altruistic strategy; NAS=non altruistic strategy; AS Angle = angle (in degrees) for the most altruistic of the orientations in the pair; NAS Angle = angle for the least altruistic angle in the pair; Result Angle = the angle of the resultant vector produced by the AS and NAS angles; Result K = tangent(45-Result Angle); r3 = (P-S)/(T-S); r4 = (T-R)/(T-S); K = 1-(r3+r4). **Prisoner's Dilemmas appear in bold.** *Marginal Prisoner's Dilemmas, those with K values that lie on the border defining Prisoner's Dilemma Games (e.g., 0, and 1), appear in italics.*

Results for the long-term vitality of various SVOs were clear, and perhaps not too surprising. Vitality as a function of the player's own SVO was a perfect function of concern with own outcomes, with Individualism achieving the highest vitality, and Masochism the lowest. The simple correlation between the weight each orientation applies to its own well being with its vitality was 1.00. Vitality as a function of the partner's orientation was a perfect function of the partner's concern with others' outcomes, with Altruism providing the highest vitality, and Aggression providing the lowest vitality. The correlation between the partner orientations' weighting of the other's well-being with vitality was also 1.00. Restated, results revealed that own and partner's strategy were perfectly additive in determining vitality (i.e., completely determined by a combination of reflexive and fate control; Kelley & Thibaut, 1978).

In contrast to the findings for vitality, results indicated that satisfaction depended completely on the specific pairings of SVOs (i.e., behavior control; Kelley & Thibaut, 1978). A comparison of the results for vitality and satisfaction underscores the important point that two SVOs which may be attracted to one another on the basis of the other's ability to satisfy one's goals, may not necessarily constitute the most vital relationship. Taking this idea to the extreme, on the one hand, a strategy may be highly vital and very unsatisfied (e.g., Masochism with Altrusim), or, on the other hand, may be very weak but also very satisfied (e.g., Masochism with Aggression).[3]

Regarding the structure of emergent games, the most striking result in our opinion was the prisoner's dilemma produced by the orientation pair -- Individualism and Cooperation -- that captures the essence of the conflict between individual and collective rationality inherent in this game (Kahan, 1974). We think

---

3. The potential for an inverse relationship between vitality and satisfaction for various SVOs has interesting implications for the eventual distribution of SVOs in the population, a question we have addressed in subsequent simulations. Our preliminary work on movement in the simulated world has examined possible clustering of SVOs, as well as the eventual distribution of SVOs when they are allowed to reproduce in direct proportion to their vitality. In these simulations, movement is based on a number of factors. First, the strategy compares it's present satisfaction to some criterion value. If movement is to be attempted, the strategy attempts to move into one of the eight adjacent cells. In one simulation, the direction of movement is determined completely at random. In another, movement is directed toward the cell (i.e., partner) which would provide the highest satisfaction relative to the remaining seven surrounding cells, as well as the present satisfaction level. The success of attempted movement is determined in the same way, either randomly, or, on the basis of relative vitality of the invading and invaded cells. Results so far for both randomly determined movement and movement based on relative satisfaction show no indication of clustering, even after 10,000 trials. In addition to allowing movement in the simulated world, we have started exploring the potential distribution of orientations over time by allowing for reproduction of SVOs in direct proportion to their vitality. After as few as 10 trials, results reveal a population consisting entirely of Individualists.

there are important implications here for the real world. Specifically, as already stated, we assume that most of our moment to moment dyadic interactions are asymmetric, quite structureless, and ever-changing. Also, in many interactions, it is difficult if not impossible to apply contingent, reactive strategies such as tit-for-tat, win-stay-lose-change, etc. Still, the question of which policy (orientation) one should adopt as a general approach to interdependent relationships remains a meaningful question. Should one be Cooperative as a general principle? Individualistic? What advice shall we give our children and loved-ones whose long term interests are dear to our hearts? We tell them life's a dilemma. The introductory lectures we give our students on this game can be directly translated into a "life-lesson" on the rewards and costs of adopting either Cooperation or Individualism as a principle to live by.

Considering the structures of all 28 emergent games and their relation to the orientation pairs that generated them, the results are further evidence for the important theoretical point that both people *and* the games they play (at least symmetric ones) are describable in terms of SVO. Previous work (Doi, 1990) has focussed on this relationship in terms of choice behavior. Specifically, there are SVOs inside people, and there are games in the external environment. If we know the θ of a person and we know the θ' of the game, we can predict the person's choice. The present result shows that the long term structure of the relationships (θ') can grow out of the orientations of the involved parties (θ for row and θ for column). A very important point here is that the long term structure of a relationship can be modified by a change in one's general approach to it.

5 Concluding Comments

We close with some comments on computer simulation in the context of theory in social psychology. If social psychology is to be systematic then social psychologists must be as concerned with theory as they are with the details of their research procedures. Ideally, we strive for theories that are sufficiently well stated that their implications (whether right or wrong) are not a matter of individual interpretation and intuition, but in some sense, a *necessary* consequence of the theory itself. How else are we to know with any certainty if a set of observations is consistent or inconsistent with the theory? And, as we revise our theories in the harsh light of research findings, how else are we to know if the necessary consequences of the revised theory (which must also be well stated) are consistent with the result that forced the revision? In this context of theory construction, hypothesis testing, and theory revision, computer simulation is an important tool. It allows for the discovery of what one must predict in the next experiment given one's present theory, and of the way(s) in which that theory can be validly revised.

But computer simulation also allows for answering questions of the sort that simply aren't amenable to laboratory or field research; questions of the sort addressed in the present paper, having to do with the *necessary* long term consequences of a specific theoretical system. Such questions are important both in the sense of giving us a picture of the future and also in helping us to understand how the present world might have come about. Whether testing hypotheses or making long term projections, computer simulation requires the social psychologist to do something most of us find rather daunting: to be as precise and exact as possible about our theoretical ideas.

Adapting the generic textbook definition, let's remind ourselves that theories are (1) systems of variables, and (2) statements about the functional relationships between these variables. The variables can be roughly categorized into "antecedents" such as SVO, and the given and effective payoff structure, and into "consequents" such as vitality, satisfaction, and emergent games. Statements about the relationships between variables are also of two types. The first type concerns the functional relationships among the antecedent variables, such as the relationship between the given payoffs, SVO and the utilities of the effective matrix. The second type of statement concerns the relationship between antecedent and consequent variables, such as SVO and the structure of emergent games.

Statements regarding the functional relationships between antecedent variables are under the control of the theoretician. In computer simulations, it is necessary to define variables and functional relationships with sufficient precision that they can be faithfully translated to computer code, either by yourself or a programmer with whom you remain in constant and exhaustive communication. Once this is completed and the program is running, the researcher obtains information concerning the exact values of consequent variables (output) that necessarily flow from the input conditions. If, as is the case with most simulations, the theory involves one or more random components, the reliability of these exact consequent values is easily determined, either by (1) running a huge number of trials, (2) repeating the simulation run, or both.

On the basis of the simulation results, the researcher's task is to discover the second type of functional relationship, namely the one(s) between the antecedent (e.g., SVO) and consequent variables (e.g., vitality, satisfaction, and emergent games) in his/her theoretical system. At this point the task is to describe the relationship in as simple but complete a way as possible, and in terms of the theoretical system in which that relationship exists.

The very nature of simulation makes this task easier (not necessarily easy) because of the requirement that the theory be fully specified prior to the simulation run(s). Sometimes the relationships are pleasant confirmations of the researcher's intuitions, such as our results for vitality and satisfaction. Sometimes they come as a big surprise; the fact that the structure of emergent games is such a simple, beautiful, "compromise" of the SVO pairs that produce them was totally unanticipated.

Furthermore, the simulation approach provides the researcher with quantitative (numerical) information that allows him/her to attempt a description of results as mathematical formulae such as the one we observed between the emergent game's indifference angle (consequent) and the average of the SVO angles that generate the game (antecedents). One can achieve a sense of the robustness (generality) of these expressions by systematically changing features of the theory and observing their impact on the relationship between antecedent and consequent variables. If robustness is not observed the researcher has a very good idea of the antecedent conditions that moderate the relationship; he/she is the one that changed them.

Sooner or later, the theoretician may become concerned with the general validity of his/her formulae and so attempt a mathematical proof, either on their own or in collaboration with a mathematician. In either case, it is obvious that one needs to know what it is they are trying to prove before much can be done. And if earlier robustness simulations suggest moderator variables, this information is potentially of crucial importance to the mathematical work.

Here we have an instance of the bridge that computer simulation helps to build between social psychology and mathematics. Most of us are not mathematicians, but most of us are capable of spelling out the details of our theory (as uncomfortable as we might find doing so), generating a computer model and making descriptive sense of the results. That is, most of us are capable of providing mathematicians with the information they need to attempt proofs: (1) a statement of the relationship to be proven, and (2) a statement of the exact conditions under which the relationship is assumed generally true.

References

Axelrod, R. (1984). *The evolution of cooperation*. New York: Basic Books.

Doi, T. (1990). An experimental investigation of the validity of the characteristic space theory and the measurement of social motivation. *The Japanese Journal of Experimental Social Psychology, 29*, 15-24.

Eisenberger, R., Kuhlman, D. M., & Cotterell, N. (1992). Effects of social values, effort training, and goal structure on task persistence. *Journal of Research in Personality, 26*, 258-272.

Griesinger, D. W. & Livingston, J. W. (1973). Toward an interpersonal motivation in experimental games. *Behavioral Science, 18*, 173-188.

Hardin, G. (1968). The tragedy of the commons. *Science, 162*, 1243-1248.

Harris, R. J. (1969). A geometric classification system for 2 x 2 interval-symmetric games. *Behavioral Science, 14*, 138-146.

Kahan, J. P. (1974). Rationality, the prisoner's dilemma, and population. *Journal of Social Issues, 30*, 189-210.

Kelley, H. H., & Thibaut, J. W. (1978). *Interpersonal relations: A theory of interdependence*. New York: Wiley.

Kramer, R. M., McClintock, C. G., & Messick, D. M. (1986). Social values and cooperative response to a simulated resource conservation crisis. *Journal of Personality, 54*, 576-592.

Kuhlman, D. M., Camac, C. R., & Cunha, D. A. (1986). Individual differences in social orientation. In H. Wilke, D. Messick, and C. Rutte (Eds.), *Experimental social dilemmas* (p.151-176). New York: Verlag Peter Lang.

Kuhlman, D. M., & Marshello, A. F. J. (1975). Individual differences in game motivation as moderators of preprogrammed strategic effects in prisoner's dilemma. *Journal of Personality and Social Psychology, 32*, 922-931. (a)

Kuhlman, D. M., & Wimberley, D. L. (1976). Expectations of choice behavior held by cooperators, competitors, and individualists across four classes of experimental game. *Journal of Personality and Social Psychology, 34*, 69-81.

Liebrand, W. B. G. (1983). A classification of social dilemma games. *Simulation and Games, 14*, 123-138.

Liebrand, W. B. G. (1984). The effect of social motives, communication and group size on behavior in an N-person multi-stage mixed motive game. *European Journal of Social Psychology, 14*, 239-264.

Liebrand, W. B. G., & van Run, G. J. (1985). The effects of social motives on behavior in social dilemmas in two cultures. *Journal of Experimental Social Psychology, 21*, 86-102.

Liebrand, W. B. G., Wilke, H. A. M., Vogel, R., & Wolters, F. J. M. (1986). Value orientation and conformity. A study using three types of social dilemma games. *Journal of Conflict Resolution, 30*, 77-97.

Maki, J E., & McClintock, C. G. (1983). The accuracy of social value prediction: Actor and observer influences. *Journal of Personality and Social Psychology, 45*, 829-838.

McClintock, C. G. (1978). Social values: Their definition, measurement and development. *Journal of Research and Development in Education, 12*, 121-137.

McClintock, C. G., & Allison, S. T. (1989). Social value orientation and helping behavior. *Journal of Applied Social Psychology, 19*, 353-362.

McClintock, C. G., & Liebrand, W. B. G. (1988). Role of interdependence structure, individual value orientation, and another's strategy in social decision making: A transformational analysis. *Journal of Personality and Social Psychology, 55*, 396-409.

Messick, D. M., & Liebrand, W. B. G. (1995). Individual heuristics and the dynamics of cooperation in large groups. *Psychological Review, 102*, 131-145.

Rapoport, A. (1967). A note on the "index of cooperation" for prisoner's dilemma. *Journal of Conflict Resolution, 11*, 101-103.

Rapoport, A., & Chammah, A. M. (1965). *Prisoner's Dilemma.* Ann Arbor: University of Michigan Press.

Teta, P. D. (1994). *Structural and intrapersonal influences on decision making in 2 x 2 symmetric games.* Unpublished doctoral dissertation, University of Delaware.

Tierney, J. (1990). Betting on the Planet. *The New York Times Magazine, Dec. 2 (sec. 6)*, p. 52.

Van Lange, P. A. M., & Kuhlman, D. M. (1994). Social value orientations and impressions of partner's honesty and intelligence: A test of the might versus morality effect. *Journal of Personality and Social Psychology, 67*, 126-141.

Van Vugt, M., Meertens, R. M., & Van Lange, P. A. M. (1995). Car versus public transportation? The role of social value orientations in a real-life social dilemma. *Journal of Applied Social Psychology, 25*, 258-278.

The Generalized Exchange Perspective on the Evolution of Altruism

Eiji Takagi

Faculty of Liberal Arts, Saitama University, 255 Shimo-okubo, Urawa-shi, Saitama 338, Japan

Abstract. The purpose of this article is to demonstrate that altruism, conceived as "generalized exchange," can evolve within a society of egoists. I define the "evolutionary giving game," in which each player holds some resource as its budget and can give any portion of it to any player. This game enables us to analyze the emergence of various kinds of social exchange, including generalized exchange. The results of computer simulations based on this game show the following. Though an unconditional altruist strategy is quickly beaten by nonaltruistic one, a kind of conditional altruist strategy, "in-group altruist strategy," will robustly evolve. The in-group altruist strategy dictates that the player gives only to "in-group members." Here in-group members are those who contribute sufficiently. Those who contribute sufficiently, but give even to "out-group members" are also defined as out-group members. This strategy is consistent with in-group favoritism, observable in a variety of settings. The simulation results also show that the evolution of altruism based on this strategy is dependent on prospects of future contact, visibility, and risks.

Keywords. Altruism, generalized exchange, evolution, computer simulation.

1 Introduction

Every day, we observe a lot of human activities, among which we often find altruistic behaviors. As we usually focus our attention on individuals or their behaviors, it is natural that we view human altruistic behaviors as derived from individuals' motives and as influenced by situational factors. Social psychologists conceive altruistic behaviors in this way, and have successfully investigated the nature of altruistic motives (e.g., Batson, 1987), and the factors facilitating or hindering human altruism (e.g., Latane & Nida, 1981). The social psychological literature on altruism is now not only among the most important and well-researched areas in social psychology, but it also provides us with the most substantial information on *human* altruism.

If we move our attention away from individuals to society as a whole, however, we obtain a different picture. Here we find a system of altruistic behaviors, which I define as "generalized exchange." The instances of generalized exchange are not only observed locally, that is, observed in subgroups within the society such as families and peer groups, but also globally. An individual who is consciously or unconsciously involved in generalized exchange does favors for others, and receives help at a later date. An important characteristic of generalized exchange is that there is seemingly no definite connection between giving and receiving. Thus a society with generalized exchange is one where altruism prevails. And individual altruistic behavior can be seen as a part of the social phenomenon of generalized exchange.

I call the view that human altruism results from generalized exchange the "generalized exchange perspective" on altruism. I do not regard this perspective as applying to all forms of human altruistic behaviors, but do believe this perspective is a promising alternative explanation for altruism. The reason, I believe, we need such approach is that it may answer the most fundamental question in social psychology and the other social sciences: why does altruism exist in human societies?

1.1 Altruism Issue

The difficulty in establishing altruism is apparent if we realize that it works almost (not completely) as a public good. Every member of society is better off if altruism is provided, but he/she has incentives to "free ride." One may also well argue as follows. An altruism-dominant society is more likely to survive if the group selection process works properly. However, such group selection will work well only if very special conditions are met (e.g., Morgan, 1985), because an altruistic strategy (or gene) is easily invaded by noncooperative one (Nielsen, 1994). How then can we explain the fact that altruism has evolved in our societies, or at least, that altruism has not died out?

It was, of course, sociobiology that brought breakthroughs into the literature on altruism. Relevant here are the two concepts of kin selection and reciprocal altruism.

According to kin selection theory (Hamilton, 1964; Alexander, 1979), altruistic genes can be established in a population if the organisms carrying such genes benefit relatives who are also likely to be carrying the same genes. If an organism (P) is good to another organism (O) because of P's altruistic genes, O's fitness will increase while P's fitness decreases. However, P's *inclusive fitness* will be improved and P will obtain reproductive success if the following famous expression (Hamilton, 1964) holds:

$$B / C < 1 / r, \qquad (1)$$

where B and C denote O's benefit in fitness and P's cost respectively, and r is the coefficient of relatedness between P and O. The strength of the kin selection arguments resides in the fact that the kinship nepotism it predicts can be observed in a variety of species. Moreover, several hypotheses derived from such kin selection theory do not contradict data obtained in human populations. That is, a person is likely to be more altruistic toward his/her close kin than toward less related others (Essock-Vitale & McGuire, 1980, 1985; Simmons, 1991; cf. Segal, 1984). The Genetic Similarity Theory (Rushton, 1987, 1995), which is in the kin selection tradition, goes so far as to argue that a wide variety of in-group oriented altruism, including ethnic nepotism, can be explained genetically. I suspect that the ultimate status of kin selection arguments as models of *human* societies has not been established. Nevertheless, we cannot dispense with kin selection theory in understanding human societies, because without this perspective we cannot explain why most basic groups in all human societies are organized along kinship lines.

Reciprocal altruism (Trivers, 1971) is another sociobiological concept which has contributed to the understanding of altruism. If organisms are programmed to reciprocate favors, these organisms (or programs) are more likely to survive. Sociobiologists' interest in reciprocal altruism as opposed to kin selection seems to have declined, mainly, perhaps, because they have not been able to find so many instances of reciprocal altruism while observing non-human species (Taylor & McGuire, 1988; Koenig, 1988). However, instances among humans are so abundant that reciprocal altruism thinking came to be much more popular among social scientists, owing to the brilliant work of Axelrod (1984).

With some modifications, both kin selection and reciprocal altruism can be incorporated into non-biological models. Replace "genes" with "strategies" and "fitness" with "payoffs," and one obtains a game-theoretic, non-biological model of human behavior. Also promising is a cultural evolution theory based on the kin selection model (e.g., Allison, 1992), which uses a concept equivalent to "cultural relatedness" in place of biological relatedness.

Any attempt to construct a *social explanation* of altruism rather than a biological one should rely more heavily on the concept of reciprocal altruism than on that of kin selection. This is because a social explanation should accomplish its task using the logic of social interaction. Reciprocal altruism arguments, however, have a shortcoming in explaining altruism in human societies. Because of its pay-back nature, it is more appropriate to regard reciprocal altruism as cooperation, mutualism or social exchange than as altruism. Since we usually consider altruism to be different, we need a theory of generalized exchange.

1.2 Generalized Exchange

The term "generalized exchange" was originally suggested by Levi-Strauss (1949). Thereafter, social exchange theorists have regarded generalized exchange as a distinct type of social exchange (e.g., Ekeh, 1974). Generalized exchange is a well-defined concept, but has only been used to describe certain characteristic kinship structures. It was the anthropologist Sahlins (1965, 1972) who first substantiated the concept of *generalized reciprocity* (Befu, 1977). Sahlins characterized generalized reciprocity in terms of pure gifts with no obligation to repay. Thus the result of generalized reciprocity in a society is nothing but altruism. In this paper I use generalized exchange in the same sense as Sahlins' generalized reciprocity.

A well-known example of generalized exchange is the food sharing observable especially in hunter-gather societies (Tanaka, 1980; Woodburn, 1982). Even within market oriented modern societies, instances of generalized exchange can frequently be found in such groups as families, peer groups and communities.

Other things being equal, a society equipped with a system of generalized exchange is more efficient than others[1]. Some anthropologists showed food sharing to work as an insurance mechanism (e.g., Cashdan, 1985). Some computer simulations also predict that food sharing promotes the survival of societies (Winterhalder, 1986; cf. Morgan, 1985). Similarly, the generalized exchange practices we are ordinarily engaged in also promote our levels of welfare. However, such efficiency alone does not explain why generalized exchange has sometimes evolved. This is because the nonaltruistic (noncooperative) strategy may be *individually* more efficient, and because altruistic strategies may become extinct through individual selection processes.

The purpose of the present paper is to propose a social explanation of the evolution of altruism from the generalized exchange perspective. More specifically, I will argue the following. First I propose a computer simulation paradigm, which I call the "evolutionary giving game," in order to analyze the emergence of stable strategies in social systems. All the conclusions presented in this paper were drawn from the simulation results of this paradigm. The evolutionary giving game does not assume altruistic motives in the players, nor does it assume biological processes such as kin selection. The only assumption is

	Self	Other
give	0	2
not give	1	0

(a)

Player 1 \ Player 2	give	not give
give	2, 2	0, 3
not give	3, 0	1, 1

(b)

Matrix 1: **Payoffs**

[1] The long-term effects of food sharing may be detrimental to the development of a society. Complete food sharing, often called as "demand sharing," prevents able people from accumulating their wealth, and may hinder the emergence of more "advanced" economy (Kent, 1993; Peterson, 1993).

the players' learning. Secondly, I argue that a special kind of giving strategy, "in-group altruist strategy," will be selected in an egoists' world, and that it will lead to the establishment of generalized exchange. Other, more generous giving strategies will ultimately be beaten by the noncooperative (isolationist) strategy. Third, I will examine how some factors affect the evolution of generalized exchange and altruism, in order to understand the basic properties of generalized exchange.

2 Evolutionary Giving Game

In this section I will describe the evolutionary giving game (Takagi, 1994), whose concept is very simple. I contrived this game as a computer simulation paradigm for the purpose of analyzing a variety of social exchange situations.

2.1 Social Exchange Situations

The following example is useful for explaining my general idea on social exchange. Suppose you have 2 hours at your free disposal. If you spend your 2 hours listening to your favorite music, you obtain some pleasure (payoff), whose value is, say, 1. If instead you use your 2 hours to help one of your friends, who is in need of your advice or assistance, you may obtain nothing, but the friend will obtain a payoff of 2. Then you will find yourself in the situation described by **Matrix 1 (a)**. Suppose further that your friend also has some time available and you want a service that he/she can provide. You and your friend face the payoff matrix depicted by **Matrix 1 (b)**, which is just an instance of the 2-person Prisoners' Dilemma (2PD) game.

In a situation such as Matrix 1 (b), *exchange* takes place if both parties choose to give to each other. However, the two forms of exchange should be distinguished because the mechanisms leading to exchange are different. *Economic exchange* results if both parties make a contract or agreement on what and how they give to each other before they choose to give. The essential feature of economic exchange is such a contract, as implied in the concept of the "core" (a special set of agreeable solutions) in the market game (e.g., Debreu & Scarf, 1963). It is through contract that economic exchange is Pareto-optimal for the parties involved. In other words, economic exchange occurs as a cooperative game solution to giving dilemma situations like Matrix 1 (b). *Social exchange*, conversely, is characterized by the lack of such prior agreement. In the case of social exchange the parties give despite the fact that they did not agree how and what they will give to each other. Social exchange can thus be seen as a noncooperative game solution to giving dilemma situations. Due to the PD-like property of the situation, one cannot argue without qualification that mutual giving (i.e., social exchange) will always occur.

One may call the social exchange observable in Matrix 1 (b) a case of *restricted exchange*, since the parties are restricted to the two players. However, my present concern is with *generalized exchange*, which involves more than two parties. One may easily imagine a situation of generalized exchange by increasing the number of players. You have many candidates as recipients of your help. You decide to whom you should give and how much to each. The research paradigm I will present must make it possible that not only restricted exchange but also generalized exchange occurs.

The paradigm I call the evolutionary giving game assumes "social exchange situations," defined by the following conditions, as arenas in which social exchange can emerge.

(C1) There is more than one player.
(C2) Each player has its own resource. A player reserves some resource for itself, but can also give some to the other players. A player's *giving budget* is the part of the resource the player uses in giving to others.
(C3) A player obtains a higher level of payoffs by receiving a certain amount of resource from other players than by consuming the same amount of own resource.
(C4) Interaction between players must be "noncooperative" in the sense that they cannot coordinate mutual giving through communication with each other.

(C2) means that a player's giving is constrained by a budget limitation. Suppose that the resource is service measured in some unit of time, as is the case with the example above. You have only 24 hours to give in any day at the most. You cannot use 67 hours to help your friends every day. Thus your budget is always restricted. This condition also applies when the resource is material goods, because the material world is restricted, no matter how rich you are. Where the resource is information, the condition is not met, provided that there is no system of "intellectual property rights" or its equivalent. Another exception may be a "policy stance" by one player toward another. Imagine a case in which you declare "I will not be aggressive towards you." As long as non-aggression brings no costs to yourself, you can give such a declaration to as many persons as you like. Thus the budget constraint, if any, is negligible.

(C3) presupposes situations in which the resource a player owns is specialized in some way and the player has reserved some amount of its resource for its personal use. Since a player's own resource is already available, the other's resource is crucial for the player's payoffs. This condition is important, because exchange is meaningless without it and because it makes social exchange situations PD-like, as shown above. It should be also noted that this condition is not always necessary. As will be discussed later, social exchange is possible even if (C3) is not met, if the situation involves uncertainty and risks.

I introduced (C4) in order that the only available solution to the current problem will be social exchange. When (C1), (C2) and (C3) hold, the players will be induced to exchange. A market mechanism could solve the current problem perfectly and make all players satisfied. However, a market is a difficult institution to establish. A market secretary, who is able to aggregate the demands and supplies of participants, is necessary for the market mechanism to operate properly (Uzawa, 1960). Even bilateral economic exchange requires a mechanism to ensure that participants will not be exploited in transactions. (C4) means that the situations to be considered are "primitive" in nature, that mechanisms supporting economic exchange are not available, and that the players must be engaged in social exchange if they are to increase their respective payoffs.

2.2 Giving Game

The core part of the evolutionary giving game will be described here. A giving game with the following properties can apply to the social exchange situations described above.

(P1) Every player is conceived as a strategy-carrier. A player always acts as its strategy dictates.

(P2) A round of the game is composed of repeated trials.

(P3) Player i has its giving budget, B_i, for every trial.

(P4) Player i can freely divide B_i and give any portion of B_i to any player. When player i consumes some of the resource alone, that player can be said to give it to itself. The only requirement is that the player must dispose of B_i on the current trial. Player i's *giving level* is the part of B_i which player i gives to others.

(P5) Let x^i_m be the payoff which player i receives on the *m*th trial. The payoff player i gets throughout a round of the game, X_i, is as follows.

$$X_i = \sum_{m=1}^{\infty} x^i_m w^{m-1}, \qquad (2)$$

where w is a *discount factor* ($0<w<1.0$).

(P6) x^i_m is the weighted sum of the amounts of resource given by the players on the trial. That is, x^i_m = (the amount given by oneself) + r_v Σ(the amount given by the other player). r_v represents a ratio of the value of the other player's resource to that of the player's own resource. Since the value of the player's own resource is its magnitude of opportunity cost, r_v corresponds to the benefit/cost ratio (*B/C*) which appears in expression (1).

(P7) Players must play the game under a specified *information structure*. The default information structure is as follows: a player cannot know what the other player's strategy is, but does know the past exchange history of every player.

(P2) and (P5) show that the giving game is very similar to the supergame, or to the game used by Axelrod (1984). One can interpret the discount factor w in one of two ways. First, the discount factor means that future events are not heavily counted by the players, as economists usually assume. The second possibility is that *1-w* denotes the probability that the game terminates at the end of the trial.

The unique feature of the giving game comes from (P3) and (P4). A player can choose any other players as exchange partners and can give any amount of resource to them, subject to the budget constraint. A player has a high degree of freedom and can be engaged in restricted exchange or generalized exchange.

The information structure should also be explained. At first I conceived three levels of information structure. Under the *level 1* structure, a player can only be aware of its own exchange history. Although player A knows the exchange history between A and exchange partner B, A doesn't know how much B has given to a third party C. Under the *level 2* information structure, a player is assumed to know every player's exchange history. Player A knows not only the exchange history of A and B, but also between B and C, even if A has no contact with B or C at all. What a player cannot see under this level of structure is the strategy of the other player in novel situations. Under the *level 3* structure, a player is postulated as knowing everything, including how the other players' strategies will work.

(P7) indicates that the default information structure assumed in the giving game is the level 2. In other words, I stipulated a high level of information in this game. It seems to me that the level 2 structure is the prerequisite for the emergence of generalized exchange, and that level 1 is sufficient for restricted exchange. As the focus is placed upon generalized exchange in this paper, I choose the level 2 structure as the default here. Since the level of information necessary for generalized exchange will be of interest to everyone, I will discuss the effects of information (probability of observation) later.

2.3 Evolution of Strategies

The evolutionary giving game is a sequence of iterated rounds in the giving game. The game is evolutionary because the distribution of players' strategies will change during round iteration so that strategic evolution will take place. An advantage of the evolutionary giving game is that it enables us to see what kind of strategy will be stable in such an evolutionary process. The evolutionary aspect of the game is characterized by the following properties:

(P8) A *run* of the game is composed of iterated rounds.

(P9) The number of players is constant during the round-iteration. However, players' strategies may change as the iteration proceeds.

(P10) At the end of a round, *learning* of strategies occurs. That is, the strategies of the *m* players whose payoffs belong to the lowest *m* are replaced with the strategies of the *m* players whose payoffs are the upper *m*. The other players' strategies remain the same. Thus with every round, the strategies of *m* players change.

(P11) The game is terminated when the distribution of strategies has been *fixed*.

(P12) With a fixed probability, *mutation* of strategy will occur, and a player's strategy will change to another. The occurrence of mutation depends not on success or failure of a player's strategy but on chance.

In biological models, a change of strategy distribution is usually introduced through differential reproductive rates. However, since the evolutionary giving game is basically social, I have decided to assume here that strategic change occurs through a mechanism of observational learning or modeling. Every player in one generation will observe the achievements of the previous generation of players. In most cases a player of the next generation succeeds to the strategy of its social "ancestor" in the previous generation. However, the distribution of strategies will slowly change. Put simply, a player will abandon a poor strategy and will adopt a superior one. It might be assumed instead that the players of a game repeat a round again and again. During the repetition, the players observe the results of each round, and similar learning processes will take place.

Mutation is another source of change to strategy distribution. Evolutionary analyses (e.g., Axelrod, 1986) usually equip themselves with some mutation mechanisms. The reason why an evolutionary analysis needs the possibility of mutation comes from the fact that a strategy's performance may vary with the frequency distribution of strategies under which the strategy operates. A strategy may be superior under some frequency distributions and inferior under others. However, whether or not mutation is necessary depends on the case. Suppose a case where a strategy is so robust that it can flourish regardless of the distribution of strategies. In this case the introduction of a mutation mechanism will simply retard the fixation of the distribution of strategies[1]. The introduction of mutation is therefore almost meaningless. Conversely, suppose that a strategy was replaced under the initial distribution, but would flourish under a new distribution which had evolved. In the latter case, mutation is necessary for the strategy which is destined to win.

2.4 Specifications

I constructed computer simulation models based on the evolutionary giving game just outlined. I will describe below how I specified the parameters of the models. Specifications vary according to the analyses carried out, so the default values I assigned are described below.

The simulated society is composed of 100 players. A player is endowed with a resource whose amount is 10 on every trial (B_i = 10). The discount rate *w* is 0.95

---

[1] Mutation works as an error term in simulation models. In general, therefore, mutation will act in opposition to the tendencies produced through the simulated selection processes.

for all players. This value of w allows us to interpret the probability of the game stopping on the current trial as always 1/20, if we think of w as such probability rather than a simple discounting factor. The resource given by another player is twice as valuable as its own resource ($r\_v = 2.0$). The number of trials per round is 300. Because w is 0.95, the payoff calculated by the 300 times iteration is almost the same as in the case of infinite times iteration. Finally, the number of the players who change their strategies on every round is 5.

The game terminates when the frequency distribution of strategies has been fixed. The distribution of strategies is judged to be fixed if one of the following termination conditions is satisfied. (a) Only one strategy has survived. (b) Though more than one strategy has survived, all the strategies work in the same way under the current distribution of strategies. (c) The same distribution of strategies has continued for 3 consecutive rounds.

In the analyses below, I set the mutation mechanisms off. In preliminary simulations the introduction of mutation merely retarded the termination of the simulation.

2.5 Strategies

In principle, both generalized and restricted exchange strategies can work within the framework of the evolutionary giving game. A restricted exchange strategy is the strategy that requires the player to select exchange partners from other players, and to try to form a 2-party exchange relationship with each of them. A generalized exchange strategy is the one which requires the selection of some other players as the recipients of its resource according to a specific standard, and to give some resource to each of them. In the following sections, however, the strategies which enter the simulations are only generalized exchange variations.

For illustration, I will describe how the two most typical strategies operate in the game just mentioned. These strategies are the always-noncooperative strategy, NonCoop, and the Saint-like strategy, Altruist.

NonCoop is the strategy that always gives nothing. One may call NonCoop Isolationist, because it is never engaged in any kind of exchange. If all the players behave as NonCoop players, a NonCoop player will obtain the following payoff on a round under the conditions specified above.

$$X_i = 10\ (1-w^{300})/(1-w) \fallingdotseq 10\ (1-w^{\infty})/(1-w) = 10 / 0.05 = 200.$$

A society of NonCoops is evidently deficient. Under the assumption of $r\_v = 2.0$, players must engage in some form of exchange in order to increase their payoffs. The payoff value of 200 is one of the standard values, in the sense that at the worst even a NonCoop player can obtain this under the above conditions.

Altruist is a sucker strategy which requires the player to give everything to others unconditionally by choosing its recipients in a random fashion. The concept of Altruist is universal altruism (Hardin, 1982) or indiscriminate altruism.

Calculating similarly, an Altruist player obtains, on the average, a payoff of 400 in the all-Altruist society. A society of Altruists is therefore maximally efficient. The payoff of 400 is another standard value, in the sense that this value is the maximum mean payoff attainable.

Though highly efficient, the Altruists' society is fragile because selfish strategies can easily invade such a society. To be viable and stable, Altruist must be modified so that it can resist selfish invaders. Thus what kind of altruistic strategy can be stable and lead to an altruistic society? I will address myself to this question in the following sections.

3 How is Altruism Possible?

3.1 Universal Altruism Fails Absolutely

The initial step in my simulation analysis is the universal altruist strategy, Altruist. I programmed Altruist to work as follows. Altruist (a) sets the giving level at a maximum of 10, (b) selects 8 recipients randomly, and (c) gives 10/8 to each of the recipients.

To demonstrate how fragile the universal altruists' society is, I first conducted a simulation with an initial distribution of strategy of one NonCoop player and 99 Altruist players (**Simulation 1**). I replicated 10 runs. As everyone will suppose, NonCoop invaded Altruists at maximum speed, and Altruists died out quickly.

3.2 The Possibility of Conditional Altruism

I concluded that the drawback of Altruist lay in its noncontingent behavior. Altruist unconditionally gives even to absolute defectors. Therefore Altruist is very weak though ideally respectable. Then I considered the conditional altruist, C_Alt, which behaves as follows. C_Alt (a) sees only the other players who give their entire resource (10) on the previous trial as its "friends," (b) selects randomly *n* friends, if any (the maximum of *n* is 8), and (c) gives 10/*n* to each of the selected friends[1]. C_Alt is an n-person variant of tit-for-tat strategy. C_Alt will be nice to friends but not to "enemies." Due to its conditional nature, C_Alt might be able to beat NonCoop.

I conducted 10 simulation runs with C_Alt and NonCoop (**Simulation 2**). Initially, there were 5 C_Alt players and 95 NonCoop players. In every run, C_Alt beat NonCoop, whose players were completely extinguished. The result indicates that the conditional altruist is able, at least potentially, to evolve in egoistic environments.

---

[1] On the first trial, C_Alt selects 8 players at random, and gives 10/8 to each of them. This is also the case with C_Alt(x,y) and I_Alt(x,y), proposed later.

3.3 Generosity is Detrimental to the Evolution of Altruism

The success of C_Alt, however, is rather tricky. C_Alt is a package of two conditions. One is to see the players who sacrificed the entire resource as its friends. The other is to give its entire resource to friends. Let x denote the giving level of any player, and y the standard of giving level to identify friends. If we denote the conditional altruist strategy as C_Alt(x,y), C_Alt used in the previous simulation can be written as C_Alt(10,10). But there is no theoretical reason to assume that both x and y may be fixed at the maximum value, 10. Rather we should assume that players can select the values of x and y freely. What happens if we assume this?

I then tried the next simulation (**Simulation 3**). Each of the two variables x and y has five levels (0/2.5/5/7.5/10). Thus there are 25 (5x5) variations of C_Alt(x,y): C_Alt(5,5), C_(5,7.5), and so on. For example, C_Alt(7.5,2.5) is the strategy which dictates a player to see those who have contributed more than or equal to 2.5 as friends, and to give 7.5 resource away to friends as long as the player can find any friends. 10 runs were replicated. In the initial distribution of strategies, each of 25 C_Alt(x,y) was held by 2 players and NonCoop was held by 50 players. Since C_Alt(0,y) is the same as NonCoop, in sum there are 60 NonCoop players and 40 C_Alt(x,y) players in the initial state of the runs.

The results varied with the run. The distribution of strategies came to be fixed in 4 runs. A run was terminated if the number of rounds reached 150 without fixation. In all the 4 runs where the distribution became fixed, NonCoop dominated the societies completely. In 4 out of the 6 runs where fixation was not attained, C_Alt(10,y) tended to dominate but could not expel the other strategies. In the remaining 2 runs, C_Alt(x,y)s, whose values of x were intermediate levels, tended to flourish.

Fig. 1 (a) shows the process of the distribution change of the strategies in one of the 4 runs where fixation took place. The other 3 runs showed a similar pattern. Initially C_Alt(x,y) players with high levels of x increase, while NonCoop players (x=0) decrease. However, at a certain point, the situation changes dramatically.

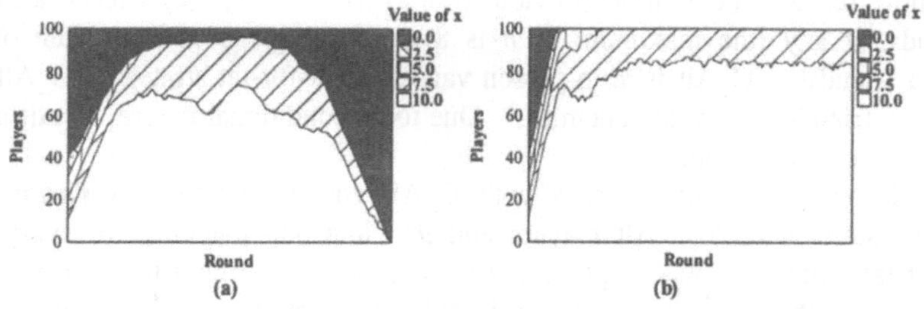

Fig. 1: Evolution Process (Simulation 3)

NonCoop begins to expel C_Alt(x,y) strategies and finally dominates the society. Why such a reversal occurs can be explained by the distribution of the values of y not displayed in Fig. 1. In the earlier phase of the simulation run, the players with C_Alt(10,y) increase, but their values of y tend to be low, mostly y=0. And when a lot of players have adopted C_Alt(10,0), NonCoop players begin to obtain high payoffs without sacrifice. Thereafter, NonCoop starts to fight back.

The process of **Fig. 1 (b)** is different from that of Fig. 1 (a) mainly because NonCoop strategy died in the former[1]. The remaining strategies are C_Alt(10,y) and C_Alt(7.5,y), with the former more dominant. Strange is the observation that y's values of C_Alt(10,y) tend to be low while those of C_Alt(7.5,y) are uniformly high[2], mostly y=10. Thus what can be observed in Fig. 1 (b) is the strange combination of the C_Alt(10,y) players, who give benefits even to C_Alt(7.5,y) players, and the C_Alt(7.5,y) players, who give mainly to C_Alt(10,y) players. C_Alt(10,y) and C_Alt(7.5,y) can be said to have co-evolved by benefiting each other. Of course, such co-evolution leads to a less efficient society in comparison with the cases in which only C_Alt(10,y) players have survived.

The results of simulation 3 suggest that C_Alt(x,y) whose value of y is low is most likely to flourish among the C_Alt(x,y) strategies, and that generosity of C_Alt(x,y) whose value of y is low has a detrimental effect on the evolution of altruism. I then conducted another simulation (**Simulation 4**), in which there are initially 95 NonCoop players and 5 C_Alt(10,y) players. The C_Alt(10,y) players have different values of y (0 - 10). I conducted 10 runs and found their results to be very similar to one another. **Fig. 2** shows the process of distribution change of strategies. The frequencies shown are the mean values of the 10 runs.

The pattern of Fig. 2 demonstrates more clearly the detrimental effect of the C_Alt(10,0) strategy. In the first phase of the simulation, the number of

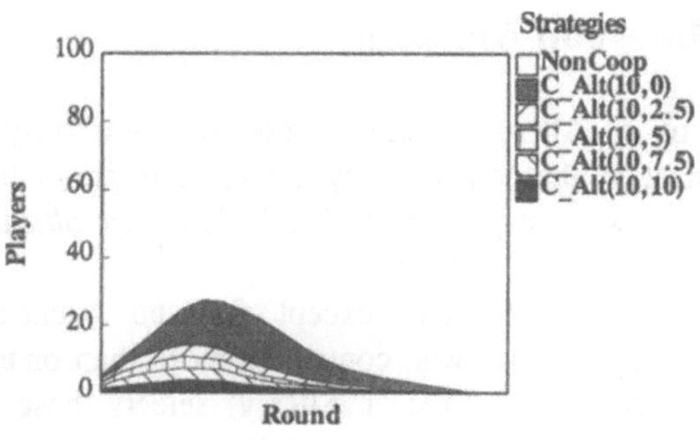

Fig. 2: Evolution Process (Simulation 4)

[1] I initially expected that all the simulation runs would conform to the process depicted in Fig. 1 (a) if mutation was introduced, because mutation would bring NonCoop back again. However, this expectation was not fulfilled.

[2] This is also true for the runs represented by Fig. 1 (a).

C_Alt(10,y) players increases up to about 30. However, the strategy which increases most is C_Alt(10,0). And when the proportion of C_Alt(10,0) players among C_Alt(10,y) players approaches 0.5, C_Alt(10,y)s begin to decline and finally die out[1].

It is easy to answer why C_Alt(x,y)s diminish when their values of y are low. As the value of y becomes low, C_Alt(x,y) becomes more similar to Altruist, which is easily exploited by NonCoop. But why is C_Alt(x,y) with a low value of y more likely to thrive than C_Alt(x,y) with a high value of y?

The following simplified example illustrates the reason. Suppose that there are two C_Alt players, one being C_Alt(10,10) and the other C_Alt(10,0), among NonCoop players. The C_Alt(10,10) player gives only to the C_Alt(10,0) player, because the latter player is the sole player who meets the former player's standard, y=10. The C_Alt(10,0) player, therefore, obtains the entire resource of the C_Alt(10,10) player. However, the C_Alt(10,0) player gives even to NonCoop players. So the C_Alt(10,10) player's chances of getting benefits from the C_Alt(10,0) player are very low. Evidently, C_Alt(10,0) tends to prosper and C_Alt(10,10) becomes extinct.

The above considerations imply the following. The conditional altruist strategy, C_Alt(x,y), is potentially a viable strategy and can be stable under some circumstances[2]. However, C_Alt(x,y) is far from perfect. C_Alt(x,y) tends to be generous (values of y become low). And if the size of the C_Alt(x,y) with a low value of y comes to be sufficiently large, C_Alt(x,y) cannot be stable and tends to be displaced by NonCoop. Paradoxically, therefore, increased generosity is detrimental to the evolution of altruism. Although generosity may be a moral virtue, a generous player is just a prodigal son or daughter who tends to destroy societal welfare.

3.4 Robustness of In-group Altruism

If the incompleteness of C_Alt(x,y) comes from its generosity-facilitating tendency, a conditional strategy that is generosity-hindering might be more viable. I therefore introduced a new strategy which I call *in-group altruist strategy*, expressed as I_Alt(x,y).

I_Alt(x,y) is the same as C_Alt(x,y) except for the friends-identifying mechanism. C_Alt(x,y) regards those who contribute more than or equal to y as friends. I_Alt(x,y) demands more. First, I_Alt(x,y) selects those giving more than or equal to y. But secondly, I_Alt(x,y) calculates the total amount of resource a selected player has given to the other selected players. If the total amount thus calculated is less than y, I_Alt(x,y) redefines the selected player as an

---

[1] The results are almost the same, if the simulation starts from an initial state of one C_Alt(10,0) player, 4 C_Alt(10,10) players and 95 NonCoop players.

[2] The other simulation results shows that C_Alt(10,y) dominates if there are more C_Alt(x,y) players initially.

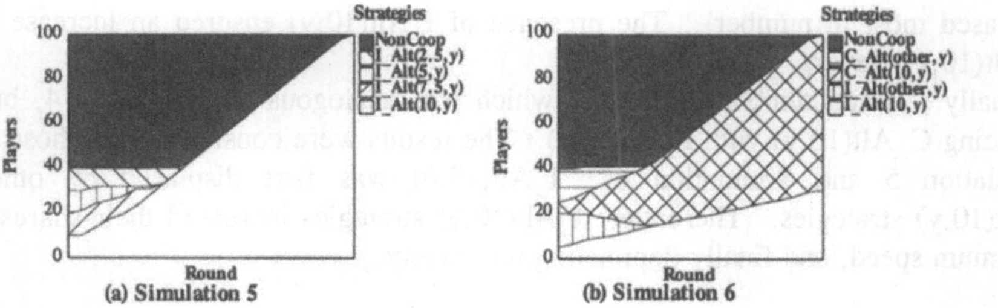

(a) Simulation 5 (b) Simulation 6

Fig. 3: Evolution of I_Alt Strategies

enemy. Otherwise, I_Alt(x,y) accepts the selected player as a true friend. I_Alt(x,y) seems to have overcome the shortcoming of C_Alt(x,y), since I_Alt(x,y) avoids benefiting generous players.

One might restate the essence of I_Alt(x,y) as follows. I_Alt(x,y) compels its carrier to set a group boundary within which is the in-group and beyond which is the out-group. In-group members are good citizens, while out-group members are bad deviants or evil heretics. I_Alt(x,y) also requires its carrier to be good only to in-group members, who are also required to be nice only to in-group members. I call I_Alt(x,y) an in-group altruist strategy, because it is essentially in-group oriented and discriminating against out-groups.

The following simulation (**Simulation 5**) is the same as Simulation 3 except that C_Alt(x,y) is replaced with I_Alt(x,y). Since the results of the 10 runs replicated were almost identical, the results were averaged and exhibited as **Fig. 3 (a)**. The frequency distribution of strategies became fixed in all the 10 simulation runs. In the early period of the run, I_Alt(x,y)s whose values of x are lower than 10 were displaced by I_Alt(10,y) strategies. Only I_Alt(10,10) gained carrier. Then I_Alt(10,y) began to invade the NonCoop territory. Finally only I_Alt(10,y) strategies remained, and the run terminated because the termination condition (b) was met. The results show that I_Alt(x,y) lacks the shortcoming from which C_Alt(x,y) suffered.

In **Simulation 6**, the number of NonCoop players in the initial state is 60, as in Simulation 5, but this time I_Alt(x,y) strategies and C_Alt(x,y) strategies were equally distributed. The number of I_Alt(10,10) carriers in the starting round was just one. Again, the simulation results were almost identical for the 10 runs. Fixation judged by condition (b) was attained in every case. **Fig. 3 (b)** shows the average process of evolution. In the early phase, C_Alt(x,y) and I_Alt(x,y) strategies whose values of x were lower than 10 died out. Then C_Alt(10,y) and I_Alt(10,y) began to invade the NonCoop group, finally expelling all the NonCoops. In this simulation, it is not I_Alt(10,y) but C_Alt(10,y) which increased most in number[1]. The presence of I_Alt(10,y) ensured an increase of C_Alt(10,y) players.

Finally I conducted **Simulation** 7, which was analogous to Simulation 4, but replacing C_Alt(10,y) with I_Alt(10,y). The results were consistent with those of Simulation 5 and Simulation 6. I_Alt(10,0) was first displaced by other I_Alt(10,y) strategies. Thereafter, I_Alt(10,y) strategies increased their shares at maximum speed, and finally dominating the society.

3.5 Discussion

The results described above demonstrate that the in-group altruist strategy is robust and can be stable under a variety of circumstances. These results are quite consistent with Messick's (1991) intriguing analysis, which showed a fitness advantage of "group-based altruists" (those who are altruistic toward altruists) over "nonaltruists" and "universal altruists." However, in-group altruists behave in a more complicated way than the group-based altruists or simple conditional altruists. They give only to those who give only to full altruists. In this sense, the strategy is doubly in-group oriented.

The implication of the above results is clear. The in-group altruist strategy requires the carrier to do favors only to in-group oriented in-group members (good citizens) and to discriminate against out-group members (deviants and their confederates). Hardin's (1982) argument that discrimination is a necessary part of altruism can be understood in the light of this strategy. Moreover, this strategy is congruent with the well-known psychological tendency called "in-group favoritism" (Brewer & Kramer, 1985; Tajfel, 1982; Messick & Mackie, 1989). In-group favoritism is supportive of discriminate altruism (Messick, 1991). My speculation is that in-group favoritism is universal because the survival of a society is dependent on the evolution of altruism, and because altruism is also dependent on the in-group altruist strategy[2].

---

[1] This is explained as follows. C_Alt(10,y) players will benefit others who do not satisfy the standard of I_Alt(10,y) without violating the same standard themselves. Since any player's budget is limited, an I_Alt(10,y) player benefits a C_Alt(10,y) player more, on the average, than the latter benefits the former. Thus C_Alt(10,y) is a little more advantageous than I_Alt(10,y) as long as strategies whose value of y is lower than y exist. However, C_Alt(10,y) does not displace I_Alt(10,y).

[2] It should be noted that the meaning of discriminating altruism or in-group favoritism is more than what is implied by the in-group altruist strategy. This strategy simply splits the world into two groups: the in-group which is composed of altruists and the out-group which is composed of deviant nonaltruists and their confederates. On the other hand, the concept of discriminating altruism provides us with a view that the society is divided into more than one sub-group (e.g., ethnic groups), within each of which in-group oriented altruism is maintained. The in-group altruist strategy per se does not explain the existence of such "group-centric altruism." However, additional simulation analysis shows that an

The above simulation results should also be discussed from the viewpoint of social dilemma research. Altruism can be seen as a public good, since every player is better off if altruism is established in the society and since a simple altruist is easily exploited. In general, a public good is hard to establish without additional incentives. Such reasoning might lead us to expect that establishing altruism would be also difficult. However, the simulation results showed that a strategy like I_Alt(x,y) can establish altruism without introducing incentives such as penalties. How, then, is altruism possible? The answer lies in the difference between typical social dilemma situations and the social exchange situations assumed in the above simulations. In social exchange situations, a player can exclude nonaltruistic players from altruistic benefits simply by choosing not to give to them. In this sense, altruism may be a public good, but not a pure public good. Rather, altruism can be considered a *club good* which is available only to club members.

4 Factors Affecting Altruism Evolution

The previous section dealt with what kind of generalized exchange strategy is likely to promote the evolution of altruism. The tentative conclusion was that a strategy with some in-group favoritism can be viable. However, whether or not any viable strategy leads to the establishment of altruism may depend on external factors. In this section, I will examine the effects of the following factors on the evolution of altruism: the prospect of future contact, visibility, and risks.

4.1 The Prospect of Future Contact

In terms of the supergame analysis, the probability that the game will continue must be high for cooperation to be an equilibrium (e.g., Friedman, 1986; cf. Axelrod, 1984). Thus in the evolutionary giving game, the players' expectation that the game will last must be maintained at a high level in order for altruism to evolve.

In the giving game, such prospects are represented by the discount factor *w*. I therefore conducted a simulation analysis manipulating the value of *w* (**Simulation 8**). In the initial state in every run, there are 20 NonCoop players, 40 C_Alt(x,y) players and 40 I_Alt(x,y) players. For either of C_Alt(x,y) and I_Alt(x,y), x has 4 levels (2.5/5/7.5/10) and y has 5 levels (0 - 10). The manipulated factor *w* has 4 levels (0.7/0.6/0.5/0.4). For each level of *w*, I replicated 10 runs. The strategy distributions became fixed in these 40 runs.

(continued) in-group altruist strategy which identifies group markers can bring about group-centric altruism (Takagi, 1995).

The results shows that the critical value of *w* is between 0.6 and 0.5. In the cases where *w* is equal to 0.7 or 0.6, the frequencies of the strategies other than C_Alt(10,y) or I_Alt(10,y) are very small. On the other hand, when *w* is equal to 0.5 or 0.4, NonCoop players dominated. It seems that when the value of *w* goes down beyond a critical value, generalized exchange breaks down in a catastrophic way. Assuming that *w* is 0.6, simple calculation leads to 2.5 as an expectation of the final trial number.

4.2 Visibility

So far, I have assumed the level 2 structure of information mentioned above. This information structure assures perfect visibility among the players. Each player is able to detect the other player's deviance. Here deviance means failure to meet other players' friend-standard. Below I relax the conditions and will examine the effects of visibility.

I denote the strategies used here as I_Alt(x,y; *p*), or simply I_Alt(*p*). I always assign 10 to x and y. As y is 10 for all players, the norm of the society dictates every player to contribute 10. The variable *p* is the probability that the carrier player conforms to the norm (contributes all) on a given trial. Then I_Alt(*p*) player deviates (contributes nothing) with probability *1-p*. I_Alt(0) is identical to NonCoop. The factor of *p* has five levels (0.0/0.25/0.5/0.75/1.0).

In the following three simulation analyses, I manipulate the probability that a player observes another player's behavior (conformity or deviation). The initial distribution of strategies is always the same, 20 players for each of the five *p* levels.

In the first analysis (**Simulation 9**), the players are assumed to judge generously. If player A has a chance to observe player B and discovers B's deviance, A will decide not to give to B on the next trial. However, when A has observed B's conformity, or has no chance to observe B, A assumes B's conformity, even if A has observed B's deviance many times previously. The

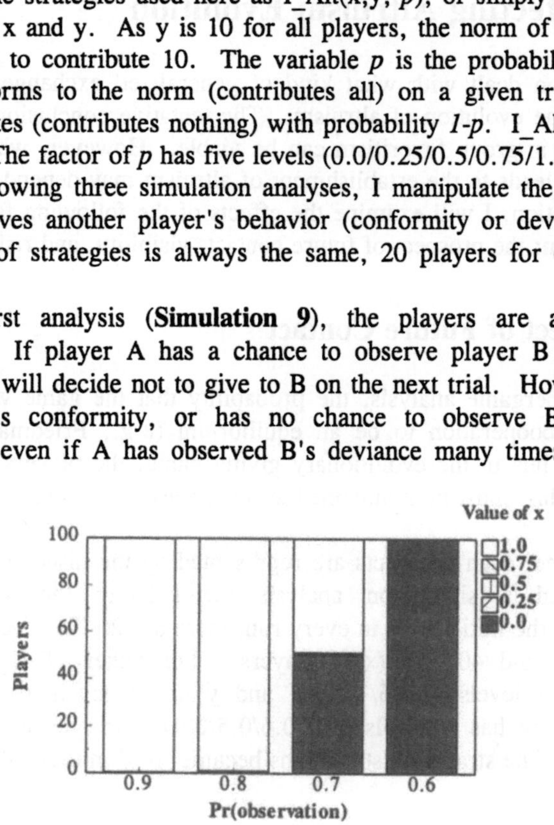

Fig. 4: Effect of Observation Probability (Simulation 9)

probability of observation, Pdetect, has 4 levels (0.9/0.8/0.7/0.6). I replicated 10 runs for each level.

In all the runs the distribution of strategies attained fixation. The distributions of the mean frequencies are shown in **Fig. 4**. In the case where Pdetect is 0.9 or 0.8, almost all the players finally adopted I_Alt(1.0), so that altruism was firmly established. In contrast, when Pdetect is as low as 0.6, every player uniformly came to adopt I_Alt(0.0), which is identical to NonCoop, in every run. Mixed results were obtained in case of Pdetect 0.7, where 5 runs ended in I_Alt(1.0) dominance and the other 5 runs in I_Alt(0.0) dominance. It seems that the critical value of Pdetect lies around 0.7, and more importantly that a high level of visibility is a prerequisite for the evolution of altruism.

The results of Simulation 9 might not seem entirely convincing, because the results are based on the premise that a player consistently assumes another player's conformity. It would be more reasonable to postulate that judgment of others' conformity as well as judgment of deviation depends on observation.

Thus in the next analysis (**Simulation 10**), I assumed that if player A observes player B's deviance on some trial, A will continue to assume that B is deviating until A observes B's conformity. Likewise, if A observes B's conformity, A goes on assuming B's conformity until A observes B's deviation. The other conditions of Simulation 10 are the same as in Simulation 9.

Of interest is the speculation that the probability of observation, Pdetect, may have the opposite effects under current assumptions. On the one hand, the low level of Pdetect may urge players to deviate because their violation of the norm is invisible. On the other hand, the low level of Pdetect may suppress deviation. Once a player's deviant act is observed, the player may continue to be regarded as a deviant even after the player has become a conformist. Thus the cost of being a deviant is higher in the case of low Pdetect, and therefore a player may be more likely to conform.

Initially, I set four levels of Pdetect (0.4/0.3/0.2/0.1) and carried out 10 simulation runs for each level. The results are summarized on the left side of **Fig. 5**. Surprisingly, almost perfect altruism resulted even when Pdetect was as low as

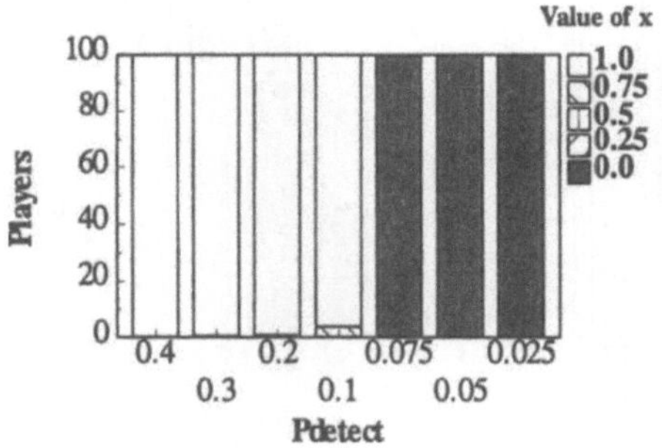

Fig. 5: Effect of Observation Probability (Simulation 10)

0.1. It seems that the deviance-suppressing effect of low Pdetect value dominated. I added three further levels of Pdetect (from 0.075 to 0.025) and also conducted 10 runs for each. Only a completely deviant strategy I_Alt(0.0) survived in these conditions, as one can see on the right side of Fig. 5. The critical value of Pdetect in this case seems to be located at a little less than 0.1.

The results of Simulation 10 contain one interesting implication. When the player's judgment of another player's conformity/deviance is completely observation-dependent as assumed in Simulation 10, altruism will be maintained even when the probability of observation is substantially low. If it is the case, altruism may persist even under low visibility.

Some may think the assumption in Simulation 10 implausible. In the analysis above, probability of observation refers simultaneously to detecting deviance and detecting conformity. However, it may well be argued that people will conspicuously exhibit evidence of their conformity, but will conceal their deviant acts. This is the very reason why coercive power is so often deficient (Ring & Kelley, 1963). In other words, the probability of detecting conformity should be higher than that of detecting deviance.

In **Simulation 11**, therefore, I fixed the value of the probability of detecting conformity at 0.9, and varied only the value of the probability of detecting deviance (denoted as Pdetect). Thus in this analysis, players' conformity is very likely to be observed, but their deviant acts are less likely to be detected. Pdetect has eight levels from 0.8 down to 0.05. I conducted 10 runs for each of the Pdetect levels. The other conditions were the same as those in Simulations 9 and 10.

The results are summarized in **Fig. 6**. In all the runs the distributions of strategies came to be fixed by satisfying condition (a) or (c). As can be seen, the perfect altruist strategy I_Alt(1.0) flourished when Pdetect was in the range between 0.7 and 0.5. But as Pdetect was lowered, the strategies of lower levels of

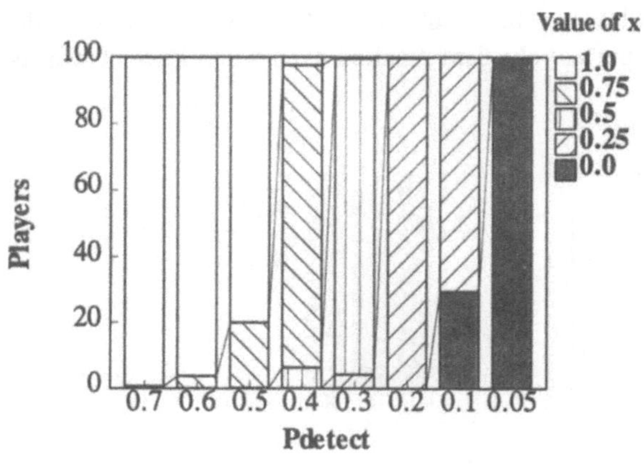

Fig. 6: Effect of Observation Probability (Simulation 11)

altruism tended to be selected. When Pdetect was as low as 0.1, some players became absolute deviants. When Pdetect was the lowest, altruism completely disappeared. These results demonstrate that a low level of probability in detecting deviance has a detrimental effect on altruism. Conversely, a comparison between Fig. 6 and Fig. 5 illustrates that a low level of probability in detecting conformity contributes to the evolution of altruism. However, the results shown in Fig. 6 suggest that an intermediate level of the probability in detecting deviance (e.g., Pdetect = 0.5) is enough for altruism to be maintained, even when the probability of conformity observation is very high. Even when Pdetect is rather low, some but not complete level of altruism can exist.

4.3 Generalized Exchange as an Insurance Mechanism

Generalized exchange will work as an insurance mechanism. Where generalized exchange exists, a player's payoff is less dependent on the player's own resource because the player can obtain from others. The most impressive example of generalized exchange is the food sharing practices observed in hunter-gatherer societies, or more precisely in "egalitarian" foraging societies (e.g., Tanaka, 1980; Woodburn, 1982). In the opinion of some anthropologists, sharing is a mean of buffering fluctuation in resources and of coping with risk (e.g., Cashdan, 1980, 1985). The results of computer simulations also indicate that sharing reduces risk and promotes group survival (Winterhalder, 1986; cf. Morgan, 1985). When obtaining resource income is uncertain and other mechanisms such as storage are not available, people seem actually to engage in generalized exchange (Cashdan, 1980, 1985; Hames, 1990; Kaplan, Hill & Hurtado, 1990; Smith, 1988; Wiessner, 1982). Although in modern societies the storage of material goods and money is available, storage of service is almost impossible. Thus generalized exchange of services will be established even in modern societies.

The insurance view of generalized exchange is important for the following reason. If generalized exchange is a mean of buffering the resource fluctuation, the assumption that the other's resource is more valuable than the player's own resource is unnecessary, since there may be a risk premium. Assuming that the value of the other player's resource and of one's own are equal, and that there is no risk, no generalized exchange strategy can expel NonCoop, because on the average the payoffs are the same. However, if there is a risk and every player has a motive to avoid it (i.e., the utility function of players is risk-aversive), players will bring about generalized exchange even if the value of the other player's resource is equal to, or even a little less than, the value of one's own resource.

To demonstrate this reasoning, I conducted the following analysis (**Simulation 12**), introducing uncertainty as follows. A player will be either rich (B_i = 18) or poor (B_i = 2), with a probability of 1/2 on every trial. To make players risk-aversive, payoffs are log-transformed. The new payoff value is $\log(1.0 + X_i)$. C_Alt(x,y), I_Alt(x,y) and NonCoop are distributed in the same way as in

Simulation 8 in the initial state. However, in this case, x and y are not the absolute values of resource but the proportion of the resource a player contributes out of its budget. Factor x has four levels (1.0,/0.75/0.5/0.25), and factor y has five levels (1.0/0.75/0.5/0.25/0.0). For example, C_Alt(0.5, 0.75) player gives 50% of its budget and regards players who give 75% of their resource as friends. 10 runs were replicated.

The results are consistent with the expectation. In every run the distribution of strategies became fixed. **Fig. 7** indicates the change in mean frequencies of strategies. The only strategy which survived is I_Alt(1.0,1.0). This strategy invaded all the other I_Alt(x,y) strategies and C_Alt(x,y) strategies, and finally displaced NonCoop.

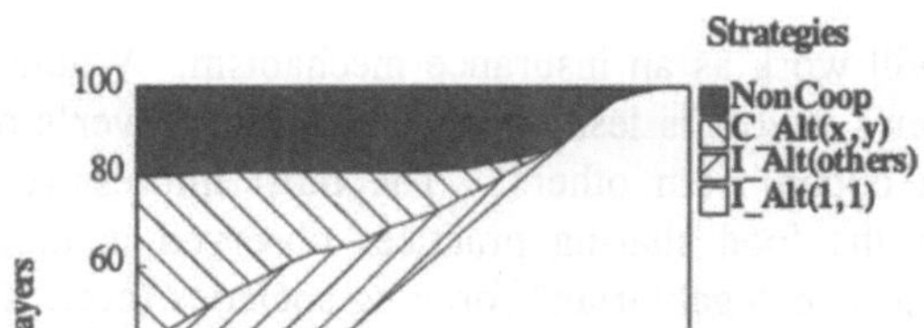

Fig. 7: Evolution under Risk (Simulation 12)

4.4 Discussion

In this section I identified three factors affecting the evolution of altruism, that is, the prospect of future contact, visibility, and risks. Through simulations, these factors were found to have effects that accorded with our common sense. Low prospects of future contact and a low probability of observation tend to destroy generalized exchange. Uncertainty of income resource tends to facilitate the emergence of altruism. However, some results are a little surprising. Generalized exchange may evolve even when the prospect of future contact is not very high and the probability of detecting deviance rather low. In any situation containing risks, the in-group altruist strategy is more likely to survive than the simple conditional altruist strategy. This last result suggests that in-group favoritism might be more accentuated in situations with risks.

5 Concluding Remarks

In this paper I have outlined the generalized exchange perspective on altruism. Using computer simulations based on the evolutionary giving game, I have demonstrated the possibility that altruism, or generalized exchange, evolves from social interaction. I have also indicated the factors that will affect the evolution of altruism. These results are, of course, not so general, because the parameter values and the situations assumed in these simulations are very special. Additional efforts in model building and empirical examination are needed in order to improve the generalizability of the results.

The perspective presented here has another large task. It should be remembered that the ultimate goal of the social exchange perspective was to explain not processes of social exchange but the emergence of various forms of social order, or "social facts" (Durkheim, 1950), using the concept of exchange (e.g., Blau, 1964; Emerson, 1972ab, 1976; Homans, 1961, 1967, 1974). This is also the case with my generalized exchange perspective. I believe that the generalized exchange perspective will offer considerable insight into the emergence of the following social facts: group-centrism, justice rules such as equity and equality, support systems for the incapacitated, and stratification. This line of analysis is the next task for this perspective to carry out.

References

Alexander, R. D. (1979). Natural selection and social exchange. In R.L. Burgess & T.L. Huston (Eds.) *Social Exchange in Developing Relationships*. N.Y.: Academic Press.

Allison, P. D. (1992). The cultural evolution of beneficent norms. *Social Forces*, *71*, 279-301.

Austin, W., Walster, E. & Utne, M. K. (1976). Equity and the law. *Advances in Experimental Social Psychology*, *9*, 163-190.

Axelrod, R. (1984). *The Evolution of Cooperation*. New York: Basic Books.

Axelrod, R. (1986). An evolutionary approach to norms. *American Political Science Review*, *80*, 1095-1111.

Batson, C. D. (1987). Prosocial motivation: Is it ever truly altruistic? *Advances of Experimental Social Psychology*, *20*, 65-122.

Befu, H. (1977). Social exchange. *Annual Review of Anthropology*, *6*, 255-281.

Blau, P. M. (1964). *Exchange and Power in Social Life*. New York: Wiley.

Brewer, M. B. & Kramer, R. M. (1985). The psychology of intergroup attitudes and behavior. *Annual Review of Psychology*, *36*, 219-243.

Cashdan, E. A. (1980). Egalitarianism among hunters and gatherers. *American Anthropologists*, *82*, 116-120.

Cashdan, E. A. (1985). Coping with risk: Reciprocity among the Basarwa of Northern Botswana. *Man (N.S.)*, *20*, 454-474.

Debreu, G. & Scarf, H. (1963). A limit theorem on the core of an economy. *International Economic Review*, *4*, 235-246.

Durkheim, E. (1950). *Les regles de la methode sociologique*. Paris: Press Universitaires de France.

Ekeh, P. P. (1974). *Social Exchange Theory*. Cambridge, MA: Harvard Univ. Press.

Emerson, R. M. (1972a). Exchange theory, Part I. In J. Berger, M. Zelditch, Jr. & B. Anderson (Eds.) *Sociological Theories in Progress*. Boston: Houghton Mifflin, Pp.38- 57.

Emerson, R.M. (1972b). Exchange theory, Part II. In J.Berger, M.Zelditch, Jr. & B. Anderson (Eds.) *Sociological Theories in Progress*. Boston: Houghton Mifflin.

Emerson, R. M. (1976). Social Exchange theory. *Annual Review of Sociology*, *2*, 335-362.

Essock-Vitale, S. M. & McGuire, M. T. (1980). Predictions derived from the theories of kin selection and reciprocation assessed by anthropological data. *Ethology and Sociobiology*, *1*, 233-243.

Essock-Vitale, S. M. & McGuire, M. T. (1985). Women's lives viewed from an evolutionary perspective.II. Patterns of helping. *Ethology and Sociobiology*, *5*, 155-173.

Friedman, J. W. (1986). *Game Theory with Applications to Economics*. Oxford: Oxford Univ. Press.

Hames, R. (1990). Sharing among the Yanomamo: Part I, The effect of risk. In E. A. Cashdan (Ed.) *Risk and Uncertainty in Tribal and Peasant Economies*. Boulder: Westview.

Hamilton, W. D. (1964). The genetic theory of social behavior. I and II. *Journal of Theoretical Biology*, *7*, 1-52.

Hardin, G. (1982). Discriminating altruisms. *Zygon*, *17*, 163-186.

Homans, G. C. (1961). *Social Behavior*. New York: Harcourt-Brace.

Homans, G. C. (1967). Fundamental social processes. In N. J. Smelser (Ed.) *Sociology: An Introduction*. New York: Wiley.

Homans, G. C. (1974). *Social Behavior (Revised Edition)*. New York: Harcourt-Brace.

Kaplan, H., Hill, K. & Hurtado, A. M. (1990). Risk, foraging and food sharing among the Ache. In E. A.Cashdan (Ed.) *Risk and Uncertainty in Tribal and Peasant Economies*. Boulder: Westview.

Kent, S. (1993). Sharing in an egalitarian Kalahari community. *Man (N.S.)*, *28*, 479-514.

Koenig, W.D. (1988). Reciprocal altruism in birds: A critical review. *Ethology and Sociobiology*, *9*, 73-84.

Latane, B. & Nida, S. (1981). Ten years of research on group size and helping. *Psychological Bulletin*, *89*, 308-324.

Levi-Strauss, C. (1949). *Les Structures Elementaire de la Parente*. Paris: Press Universitaires de France.

Messick, D. M. (1991). On the evolution of group-based altruism. In R. Selten (Ed.) *Evolution and Game Dynamics*. New York: Springer-Verlag.

Messick, D. M. & Mackie, D. M. (1991). Intergroup relations. *Annual Review of Psychology*, *40*, 45-81.

Morgan, C. J. (1985). Natural selection for altruism in structured populations. *Ethology and Sociobiology*, *6*, 211-218.

Nielsen, F. (1994). Sociobiology and sociology. *Annual Review of Sociology*, *20*, 267-303.

Peterson, N. (1993). Demand sharing: Reciprocity and the pressure for generosity among foragers. *American Anthropologist*, *95*, 860-874.

Ring, K. & Kelley, H. H. (1963). A comparison of augmentation and reduction as modes of influence. *Journal of Abnormal and Social Psychology*, *66*, 95-102.

Rushton, J. P. (1987). Evolution, altruism and genetic similarity theory. *Mankind Quarterly*, *27*, 379-396.

Rushton, J. P. (1995). *Race, Evolution, and Behavior.* New Brunswick, NJ: Transaction.

Segal, N. L. (1984). Cooperation, competition, and altruism within twin sets: A reappraisal. *Ethology and Sociobiology*, *5*, 163-177.

Sahlins, M. D. (1965). On the sociology of primitive exchange. In M. Banton (Ed.) *The Relevance of Models for Social Anthropology*. New York: Praeger.

Sahlins, M. D. (1972). *Stone Age Economics*. Chicago: Aldine.

Simmons, R. G. (1991). Presidential address on Altruism and Sociology. *Sociological Quarterly*, *32*, 1-22.

Smith, E.A. (1988). Risk and uncertainty in the 'original affluent society': Evolutionary ecology of resource-sharing and land tenure. In T. Ingold, D. Riches & J. Woodburn. (Eds.) *Hunters and Gatherers: History, Evolution, and Social Change.* Oxford: Berg.

Tajfel, H. (1982). Social psychology of intergroup relations. *Annual Review of Psychology*, *33*, 1-39.

Takagi, E. (1994). The evolutionary giving game: A computer simulation paradigm for the study of social exchange (in Japanese). *Reports of Saitama University*, *30*, 23-55.

Takagi, E. (1995). The group-centrism puzzle (in Japanese). *Reports of Saitama University, 31, 17-40.*

Tanaka, J. (1980). *The San, Hunter-gatherers of the Kalahari: A Study in Ecological Anthropology*. Tokyo: Univ. of Tokyo Press.

Taylor, C. E. & McGuire, M. T. (1988). Reciprocal altruism: 15 years later. *Ethology and Sociobiology*, *9*, 67-72.

Trivers, R. L. (1971). The evolution of reciprocal altruism. *Quarterly Review of Biology*, *46*, 35-57.

Uzawa, H. (1960). 'Walras' tatonnement in the theory of exchange. *Review of Economic Studies*, *27*, 182-194.

Winterhalder, B. (1986). Diet choice, risk, and food sharing in a stochastic environment. *Journal of Anthropological Archaeology*, *5*, 369-392.

Wiessner, P. (1982). Risk, reciprocity and social influences on !Kung San economics. In E. Leacock & R. Lee (Eds.) *Politics and History in Band Societies*. Cambridge: Cambridge Univ. Press.
Woodburn, J. (1982). Egalitarian societies. *Man (N.S.)*, *17*, 431-451.

Acknowledgment. I wish to thank an anonymous reviewer and the editors for their helpful comments on an earlier version of this article. I would also like to express my gratitude to the following colleagues who have been supportive of this study: Ken'ichi Nishiyama, Toshiharu Abe, and Atsushi Miura.

Social Dilemmas in Lineland and Flatland[1]

Rainer Hegselmann

Institut für Philosophie, Universität Bayreuth, Postfach, D-95444 Bayreuth

1. Cellular Automata Based Modeling

Understanding social processes in which numerous agents are involved in iterated interactions is a difficult task. In the following I want to demonstrate that models based on rigorous simplifications are a promising approach for understanding complex social dynamics. The simplifications will go as far as to assume that individuals are living on a line interacting with neighbors to the left and to the right (Lineland). Another rigorous simplification will be that individuals are living on a checkerboard, interacting with their neighbors in the north, south, east and west (Flatland).

The idealizations which constitute Lineland and Flatland are typical for a type of modeling which is based on what is called *cellular automata* (CA). From a general point of view basic features of a CA are:[2]

- There is a D-*dimensionsal* lattice.
- Time is advancing in *discrete* steps.
- There is a *finite* number of states. At each site of the lattice we have a cell, which is in one of the possible states. (To put it in another way: *Finite automata* are residing in all sites of the D-dimensional lattice.)
- The cells change their states according to *local* rules. Locality is both locality in space and time. So the state of a cell in a next period depends upon the states of neighboring cells in the last t periods. Usually only the last period affects the future. By definition each cell is part of its neighborhood.
- The transition rules usually used are *deterministic;* but *indeterministic* rules are allowed, too.
- The system is *homogeneous* in the sense that the set of possible states is the same for each cell and the same transition rule applies to each cell.
- The updating procedure may consist of applying the transition rule *simultaneously*. Another updating method may be to select cells *randomly*.[3]

---

[1] The title is inspired by Edwin. A. Abbot's novel *Flatland - A Romance of Many Dimensions.*

[2] A short and easy to read introduction to CA is Casti (1992; vol.1, chapter 3).

[3] Originally CA was introduced by John von Neumann and Stanislaw Ulam at the end of the forties (Neumann, 1966) mainly to give a reductionist model of life and self-reproduction. Usually CA based models ask for a lot of iterated computations. As computers became more available, many new CA based models have been developed in science and engineering, and nowadays are used extensively. The applications range from crystal growth, soil erosion, diffusion and fluid dynamics to pattern growth and clashes of galaxies (Burks, 1970; Demongeot, Goles & Tchuente, 1985; Wolfram, 1986; Toffoli & Mar-

In what follows I hope to show that *modeling based on low dimensional CA is a promising approach to analyze social dynamics*. There are at least three more general claims I want to support by giving two examples of CA based models, both regarding the dynamics of social dilemmas with numerous people involved.

- CA and a lot of social dynamics have some basic features in common: Over the periods of time numerous people are interacting, interactions and information are local, there are overlapping neighborhoods. Given we have a social process which has those abstract properties it is an obvious and quite natural idea to model that process in a CA framework, because then *CA cover some basic features of a real world process*. The very essence of those models can be described as being *multi agent systems, based on locality, and an overlapping interaction structure*. Under a lot of circumstances the two last assumptions are much more plausible then claiming that between all actors interactions have the same probability to take place or that all actors have (good or bad) informations about all parts of the world.
- *Within* the world of CA based models quantitative explanations and quantitative predictions will often be possible. But one can learn about the *"real" world* also. The lessons to be taken away in that respect may be called *qualitative understanding,* which then allows for qualitative explanations and predictions with regard to real world phenomena. In short: *CA based modeling may provide a qualitative understanding of real world phenomena, where at least for the time being we can not accomplish more.*
- CA based models make it quite clear how certain *macro effects* are dynamic results of decisions and mechanisms operating on a *micro level* only. Order, structure, clustering and segregation can be generated by local rules of a micro level. The basic features of CA (interacting cells, overlapping neighborhoods, locality, and a discrete time) make it almost impossible not to focus on the evolution of macro structures and emerging macro properties. As it seems there is no simpler modeling framework allowing for that. Under this perspective *CA based modeling contributes to a better understanding of micro/macro relations.*

The two models I will present are not the first ones one can find in the social sciences. Earlier examples are Sakoda (1949, 1971), Schelling (1969, 1971), A. Nowak, Szamrej & Latane (1990) and Keenan & OBrien (1993). Examples for CA based modeling with regard to social dilemmas are Axelrod (1984; 158ff.), M. Nowak & May (1992; 1993), Bruch (1993), Hegselmann (1994), Kirchkamp

---

golus, 1987; Gutowitz, 1991). Moreover, CA can be regarded as parallel processing computers and are therefore interesting for computer scientists. Some steps toward classifications of CA have been made (Wolfram, 1984), but the analytical understanding of CA has remained poor. Hence simulations play an important role.

(1994) and Messick & Liebrand (1995).[4] The next two sections will give in detail examples for modeling the dynamics of social dilemmas by using CA of low dimensions.

2. Social Dilemmas in Lineland

In the section to follow I will analyze the dynamics of *N-person-prisoner's dilemmas in Lineland, i.e. in a one-dimensional world. Figure 1* gives lattices for one-dimensional CA. To the left we have a world with 12 cells. Cells at the right or left end of that world do not have neighbors to the right or to the left, respectively. To the right of *figure 1* the ends of a one-dimensional world are pasted. As a consequence *each* cell has adjacent cells to the right and to the left.

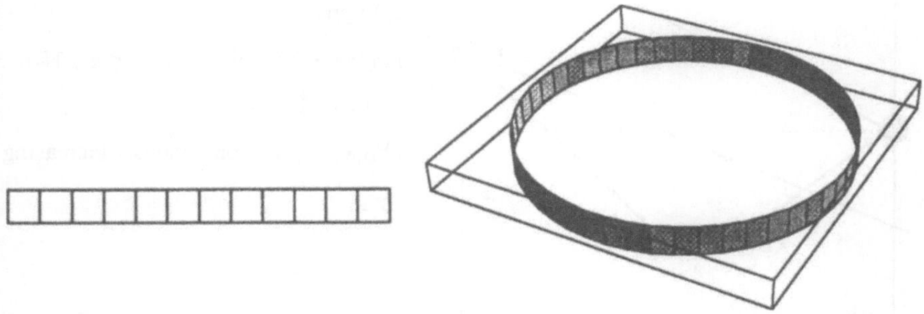

Figure 1: *One-dimensional CA. Left: Without pasting ends. Right: With pasted ends.*

With regard to *spatial locality* there are different ways to define neighborhoods. *Figure 2* shows two different neighborhoods for a one-dimensional CA. To the left, only the next cell to the right and the next cell to the left are neighbors of the (dark) center cell. To the right of *figure 2* a wider definition of neighborhood is used. Now the next two cells to the left and to the right define the neighborhood. One can easily define even wider neighborhoods analogously.

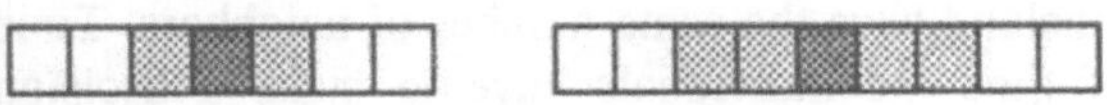

Figure 2: *Different neighborhood templates in one-dimensional CA.*

To characterize the payoffs of the N-person prisoner's dilemma that is played by the inhabitants of lineland one can follow Schelling's (1973) idea. Doing that we characterize the payoffs by two functions as in *figure 3*. The functions characterize the payoff for a defecting choice or a cooperative choice, respectively, each

[4] In the social sciences those models did not see the light of the day under the name of or with reference to CA. They were baptized "checkerboard models". For a short history of CA based modeling in the social sciences cf. Hegselmann (1996).

of them depending on the number of cooperating *others (!)*.As a consequence of the conditions laid upon the functions, each individual is better off by a defecting choice *independent of how many others may cooperate*. For all x it holds that $P_D(x) > P_C(x)$. So defection is a dominant strategy and rational players will use it. But if all actors defect they get the payoff $P_D(0)$ and that is less then the payoff $P_C(N-1)$, i.e. the payoff they obtain by everyone cooperating.

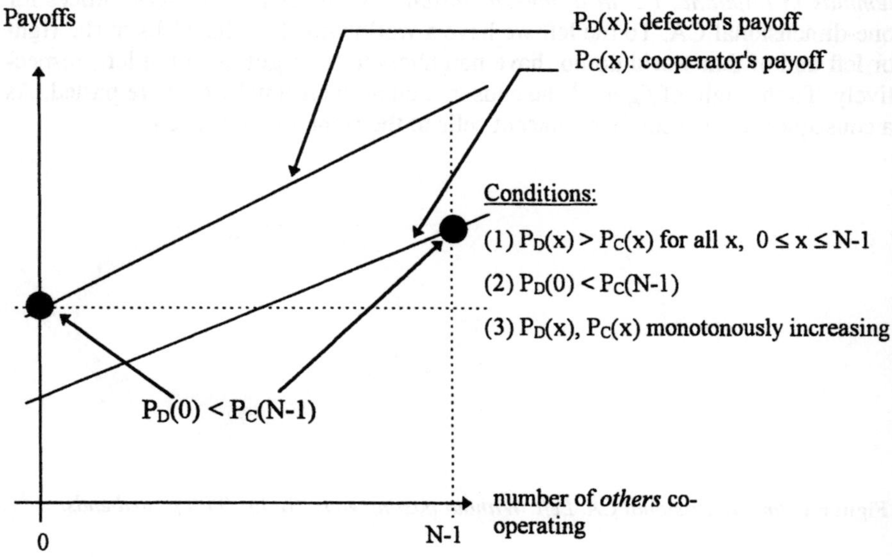

Figure 3: *N-person prisoner's dilemma*

In Lineland all cells are occupied by individuals. So there are no empty cells. The line which constitutes Lineland is pasted as in *figure 1* to the left. They *simultaneously* play PDs with all individuals in their *neighborhood*, which is defined as the next 3 cells both to the right and to the left. Because the line is pasted at its ends all inhabitants of Lineland have the same number of neighbors. Time is discrete. In each period of time the individuals have to make a decision whether to cooperate or defect in the games they play with all their neighbors. As a consequence the individuals play PDs again and again. The fact that the games are iterated instead of being played just once allows for new types of behavior. One may start to make the decision whether to cooperate or to defect depending on what the neighbors have done in the past. For example, one might apply principles which ask for cooperation as long as a certain number of neighbors is cooperating. In the following model the individuals apply a much simpler rule, they *imitate average success*. They simply find out whether, on the average, cooperative or defecting choices yield higher payoffs during the last period in their neighborhood. Then they choose the best strategy. In the case that defecting and cooperative choices yield the same average payoff, an individual will stick to the strategy it used in the last period.

So we can regard our individuals as equipped with some elementary intellectual capacities: They have a memory of one period; they are able to observe the strategies their neighbors applied in the last period, to detect and to sum up their payoffs, to identify the best strategy, and to commit themselves to that strategy.

One can run Lineland with different assumptions about payoffs, neighborhoods, initial cluster size or frequency of cooperation. It is, for instance, easy to find constellations which immediately lead to the ceasing of cooperation. Other constellations result in almost everyone becoming a cooperator after some periods. In the following experiments I will use a parameter constellation which leads to more interesting dynamics, especially to dramatic fluctuations in the frequencies of cooperation and defection.

Cooperation in Lineland

World:
We have a one-dimensional world of cells arranged as a circle. All cells are occupied by individuals.

Neighborhood:
The neighborhood within which an individual is interacting consists of three cells to the left and three cells to the right.

Game:
Each cell plays an N-person PD with all neighbors (therefore N=7).

Payoffs:
(a) defectors: $P_D(x) = 9x + 6$
(b) cooperators: $P_C(x) = 8x$
x is the number of *others* cooperating.

Decision principle:
Individuals use in the next period that strategy which yields the highest average payoff in the present period in their neighborhood, i.e. three cells to the left and three cells to the right. If that payoff is the same for cooperation and defection, than individuals stick to their present strategy. A strategy that does not occur within a neighborhood is supposed to yield a payoff of zero.

Figure 4: *Basic structures of Lineland*

Figure 5 shows the dynamics of cooperation in the one-dimensional world described above. White cells are defectors, dark cells are cooperators. The dynamics start with a cluster of five cooperating individuals in the middle of the first line, i.e. the first period. The length of the world is 80 cells. *Figure 5* shows the first 60 periods.

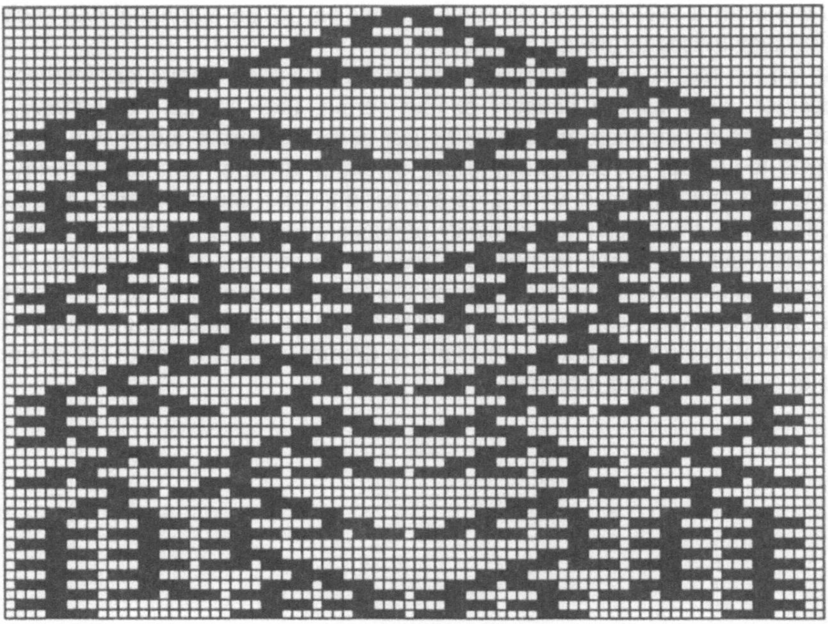

Figure 5: *Dynamics of cooperation in a one-dimensional world starting with a cluster of 5 cooperators. Length of the world 80 cells.*

For an understanding of what is going on *figure 6* provides some necessary information. It describes the first four periods. Since the emerging pattern is symmetric, only the individual in the middle of the five cooperators and those to the right of that are taken into account. Grey cells are occupied by cooperators, white cells are defecting. The cells contain four entries. The *first* one regards the number of cooperating *others* that the individual has in its neighborhood. For the cell in the center of the cluster of five cooperators in the first period the number is four, for cells at the left or right end of that cluster this number is three. The *second* entry in each cell gives the payoff that individual gets. Those payoffs depend on the number of cooperating others and whether or not an individual is cooperating. The payoffs can easily be calculated according to the two payoff functions defined in *Figure 3*. The *third* and *fourth* entry in a cell regard average payoffs for cooperation and defection that an individual observes in his neighborhood. In cases in which there are no cooperators or defectors those values are zero.

	1	2	3	4	5	6	7	8	9	10	11	12	13	14	15
x	4	4	3	3	2	1	0	0	0	0	0	0	0,0	0,0	0,0
own	32,0	32,0	24,0	33,0	24,0	15,0	6,0	6,0	6,0	6,0	6,0	6,0	6,0	6,0	6,0
ØC	28,8	28,8	30,0	29,3	28,0	24,0	0,0	0,0	0,0	0,0	0,0	0,0	0,0	0,0	0,0
ØD	33,0	28,5	24,0	19,5	16,8	15,0	13,7	9,9	7,3	6,0	6,0	6,0	6,0	6,0	6,0
x	6	5	5	4	4	3	3	2	1	0	0	0	0	0,0	0,0
own	60,0	40,0	40,0	32,0	32,0	24,0	33,0	24,0	15,0	6,0	6,0	6,0	6,0	6,0	6,0
ØC	37,3	37,3	34,6	33,6	32,0	32,0	29,3	28,0	24,0	0,0	0,0	0,0	0,0	0,0	0,0
ØD	60,0	60,0	60,0	46,5	28,5	24,0	19,5	16,8	15,0	13,7	9,9	7,3	6,0	6,0	6,0
x	0	1	2	3	3	4	4	4	3	3	2	1	0	0	0
own	6	15,0	24,0	33,0	24,0	32,0	32,0	32,0	24,0	33,0	24,0	15,0	6,0	6,0	6,0
ØC	0,0	24,0	28,0	29,3	30,0	28,8	28,8	28,8	30,0	29,3	28,0	24,0	0,0	0,0	0,0
ØD	21,4	19,5	18,6	19,5	24,0	28,5	33,0	28,5	24,0	19,5	16,8	15,0	13,7	9,9	7,3
x	6	5	5	4	5	5	6	5	5	4	4	3	3	2	1
own	60,0	40,0	40,0	32,0	40,0	40,0	60,0	40,0	40,0	32,0	32,0	24,0	33,0	24,0	15,0
ØC	37,3	38,7	38,7	38,4	38,7	38,7	37,3	37,3	34,6	33,6	33,6	32	29,3	28	24
ØD	60,o	60,0	60,0	60,0	60,0	60,0	60,0	60,0	6,0	46,5	28,5	24	19,5	16,8	15

Figure 6: The first 4 periods

Inspecting of *figure 6*, it becomes obvious that the initial cluster of cooperators can grow in a special way. The two outer cells at the right end of the cluster have neighborhoods in which the average success of cooperation is greater than the average success of defection, and the same is true for the three defectors in columns 4 to 6. Defectors living more to the right do not observe cooperation at all. The individual in the middle of the starting cluster of cooperators observes two successful defectors, those next to the right and the left end of the cluster. By having three cooperating neighbors they each obtain the payoff of 33, the highest payoff anybody gets in the first period. Since those two defectors are the only ones the cooperator in the center of the cluster is able to observe, that individual will switch to defection in the second period. By doing that, this individual gets into the most attractive situation possible: In period 2 the individual in column 1 is surrounded by three cooperating neighbors to the right and (in *figure 6* not visible) to the left. As a consequence that individual gets the highest payoff possible. For the cooperators in columns 2 to 4, the average payoff for defection is higher than the average payoff for cooperation. So they will turn to defection in period 3. At the same time the three former defectors in columns 7 to 9 switch to cooperation in period 3. Therefore in period 3 there is a cluster of five cooperators in columns 5 to 9. In period 4 this evolves to two clusters of five cooperators each. But the former cooperator in the middle of the cluster of period 3 changes over to defection. Mirroring the right half of period 4 to the left (or simply looking at period 4 in *figure 5*) we get four clusters each with five cooperators, separated from each other by three single defectors. Again, those three defectors get the highest possible payoff in that world. For all individuals in columns 1 to 10 and the corresponding individuals in the left half, the average payoff for defection is higher than the average payoff for cooperation, bringing all to defect in period 5. But as it happened before in period 3, there are two clusters of five cooperators remaining, one cluster in the right half, one in the left. More generally:

- Individuals in the center of a cluster of five cooperators will always switch to defection in the next period. That is because the average payoff for defections he or she observes is always greater than the average payoff for cooperation - even under the worst conditions for the two visible defectors, i.e. having only three cooperating neighbors.
- Clusters of cooperators can release clusters of cooperators. They have the same length as the original cluster, namely five cells. The two outer cells of the initial cluster stick to cooperation and three adjacent defectors (to the left or to the right) switch to cooperation.
- The process of releasing clusters gets into trouble if two clusters of cooperators are coming too close together. In the case that there is a *single* defector left in between two clusters of cooperators all cooperators which can observe that single defector will switch to defection.

These dynamics lead to quite complicated patterns. As it can be seen in *figure 5* we have a process by which we get a growing number of cooperators for some periods. But again and again we are faced with dramatic break downs of cooperation, caused by the fact, that clusters of cooperators came too close to each other. In *figure 5* that effect starts at period 2. In the following period all cooperators which can observe the single defector between the clusters turn to defection. In period 4 we have again a structure with three *single* defectors in between cooperating clusters and as a result only two remaining clusters of cooperators in the next period. Then again period 8 has exactly that structure which precedes a catastrophy, now based on 7 single defectors in between cooperating clusters. In larger or even infinite worlds this regularity would work longer or even for ever. But the world depicted in *figure 5* has a length of 80 cells only. As a consequence with period 13 the cooperating clusters growing to the left and those growing to the right have the same defecting neighbors. In this way new and complicated patterns evolve.

Figure 7 illustrates a world that differs from that in *figure 5* only in that the length now is 640 cells. The first 480 periods are calculated.

Figure 7: *Dynamics of cooperation in a one-dimensional world starting with a cluster of 5 cooperators. Length of the world 640 cells.*

Figure 7 makes it quite clear that repeatedly, be it on a more local or be it on a more global scale, cooperation is almost non existent. But some and sometimes only two cooperating clusters survive - enough to start again. Presumebly the cyclic behavior persists for ever.

A quite complicated behavior ensues if we start with a *random distribution* of cooperation and defection as in *figure 8*. The payoff structure and the number of neighbors are kept constant.

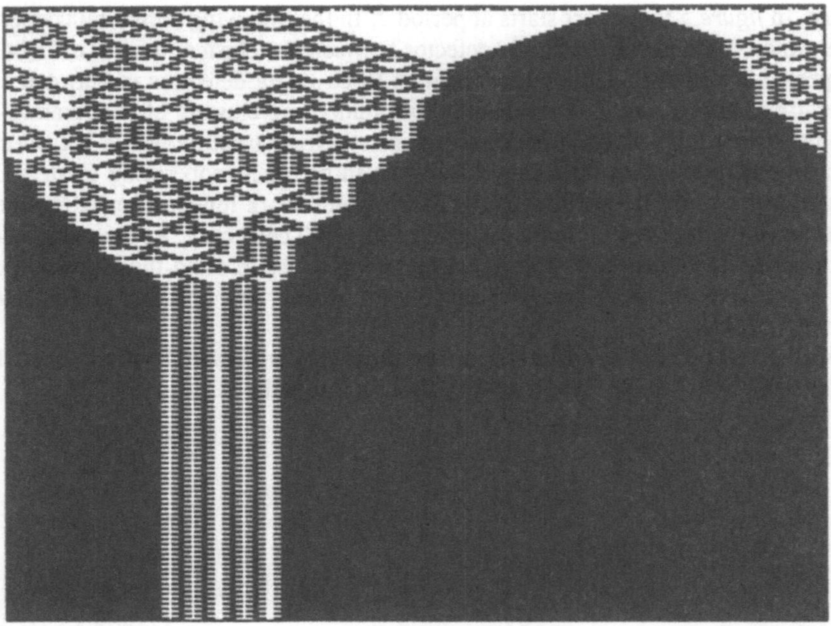

Figure 8: Dynamics of cooperation in a one-dimensional world starting with 240 randomly distributed cooperators. Total number of individuals is 320 (=length of the world).

To understand in detail what is going on in *figure 8* we would have to analyze many more constellations than are computed in *figure 6*. For the present purpose a detailed understanding of the dynamics in *figure 8* is not necessary because the points of major importance are the following:

- The assumptions and decision rules which constitute and govern Lineland are quite *simple*, but the dynamics of Lineland is *complex*. To put it the other way round: if the task is to understand complex dynamics, it may be a good idea to consider simple mechanisms and rules generating that complexity.
- The one-dimensional CA that Lineland is provides a framework for understanding the growth of clusters as well as their breaking down and recovering. It becomes quite clear that processes going on at the border between cooperators and defectors are crucial for the future development. Understanding growing and shrinking of clusters is important from a theoretical and a practical point of view.

Those insights are important because despite some decades of intensive theoretical and experimental research on social dilemmas it is more or less only now that we have started to analyze one of the most important aspects of the problems of cooperation, namely their *dynamics*. It is exactly that aspect to which even one-dimensional CA based models can contribute substantially.

3. Support Networks in Flatland[5]

In the section to follow we will deal with a special two-dimensional CA called *Flatland. Figure 9* gives examples of lattices of a two-dimensional CA. To the left we have a finite 9×9 grid. To the right all edges of a finite grid are pasted. Therefore we can regard that two-dimensional world as the *surface* of a certain 3-dimensional solid, a torus.

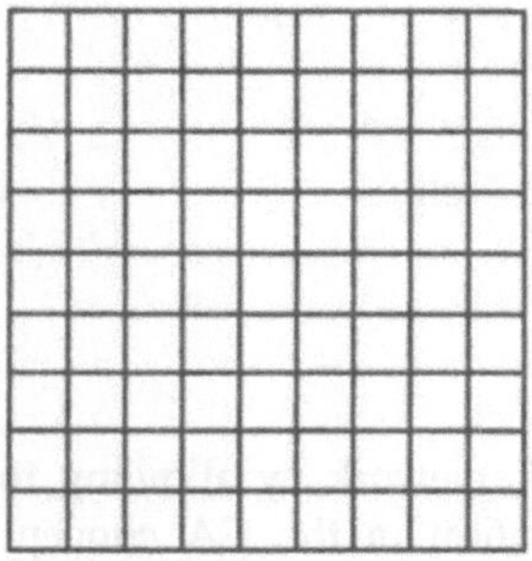

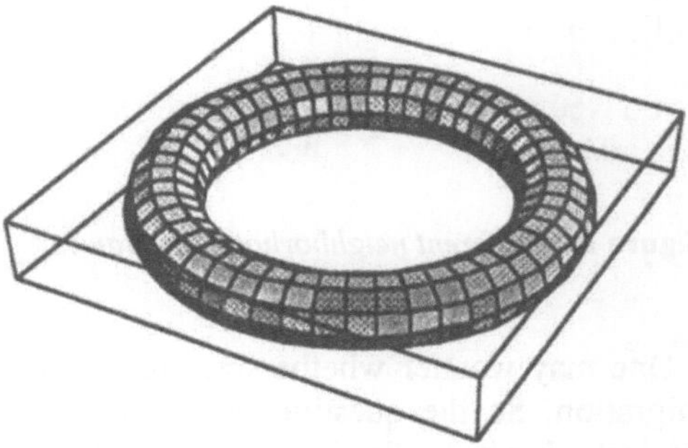

Figure 9: *Two-dimensional CA. Left: without pasting edges. Right: with pasting edges.*

Figure 10 shows three different neighborhoods in two-dimensional lattices. In *figure 10a* we have the so-called *von Neumann-neighborhood.* For this type of neighborhood, the neighbors of the dark center cell are the cells in the north, south, east, and west. Since the center cell is part of its neighborhood by definition, the center cell has 5 neighbors. In *Figure 10b* and *10c*, *Moore-neighborhoods* of a different size are given. Moore neighborhoods include cells in diagonal directions as well and always form a square pattern. Obviously Moore-neighborhoods of all sizes (but restricted by the length of a given cellular world) are possible, but neighborhoods may have quite a different structure, being, for example, hexagonal rather than rectangular.

The central question approached within this two-dimensional structure is how networks of mutual support evolve in a world

- which is exclusively inhabited by *rational egoists*
- who for one become needy with *different* probabilities
- who secondly can and must *choose* their partners *themselves,*
- and lastly who will choose their partners in *opportunistic ways*?

The general idea is to model support relationships according to a *two person support game*, in which players play simultaneously and independently from each

---

[5] The model was originally developed in Hegselmann (1994, 1994a).

other with all their neighbors in their neighborhood. From time to time players have the *chance to migrate* within their two-dimensional checkerboard world.

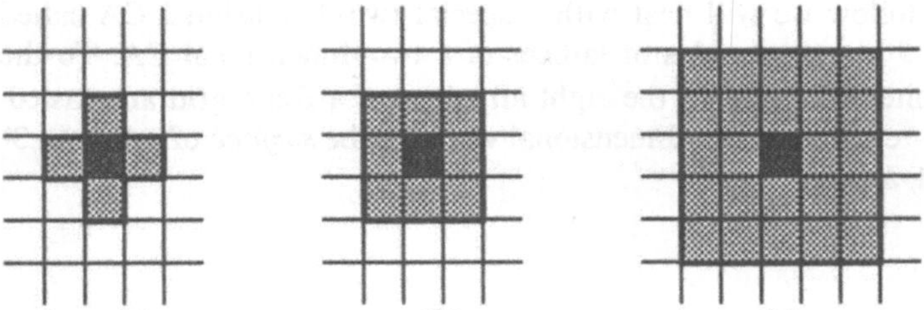

Figure 10: *Different neighborhood templates.*

One may wonder whether we are leaving the CA framework by allowing for migration. So the question is how to integrate migration in the CA concept? Basically having cells changing their state is sufficient to include migrations: one makes a distinction between two kinds of states, that of being empty and that of being occupied by an actor. All cells are thus either empty or occupied. The state of being occupied can be realized in different ways. For instance, it can be occupied by an individual of this or that class. Moving of an actor to an empty cell in his neighborhood can then be described as an application of a (complicated) rule by which an occupied center cell and an empty neighboring one exchange states. Thus including migration indeed does *not* imply an extension of the CA concept. Migration is a matter of *interpretation* of states or choosing the right set of states. It is in this sense that models with migration are CA based models.
More in detail the central components of Flatland are:

(a) Support game
The basic game is specified in *figure 11*. It is a fundamental characteristic of the game that both players will become dependent on help with a certain probability, p_1 or p_2. The probabilities remain constant throughout the game. $(1-p_1)$ and $(1-p_2)$ are the probabilities that player 1 and player 2, respectively will not become needy. The first move of the game is chosen by *nature*: According to the probabilities p_1 and p_2, it is by chance that both, none, or only player 1 or only player 2 will be in need of help. So it is possible that *neither of them* is in need of help or that *both* are at the same time. In the first case neither needs help, while in the second neither is able to help. Whoever is in need of help cannot help the other. On the other hand a player *not* in need of help has to decide whether he or she wants to help or not. The decision, to help or not to help, is a move of the game. Players who are not able to help cannot make a move. Thus, depending on nature's chance moves, either player 1 or player 2 or neither can make a move.

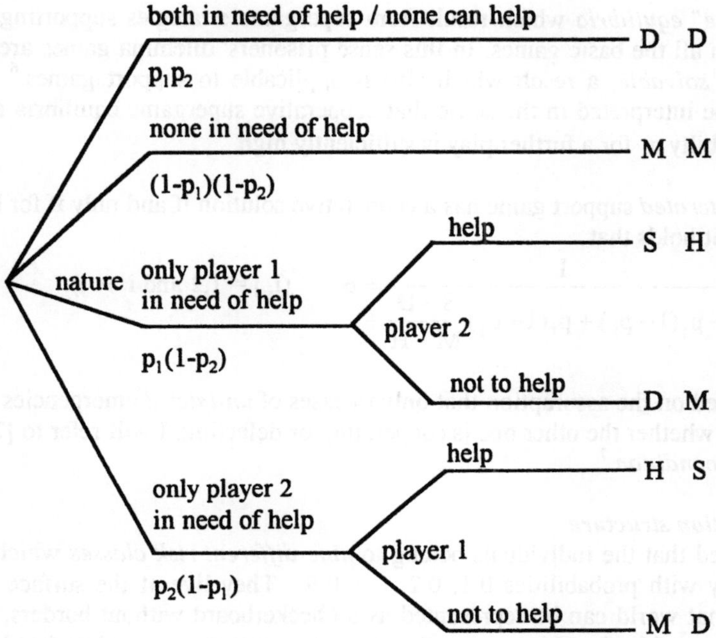

S : Saved D: Drowned $S > D$
M: Move on H: Help $M > H$
p_1 : probability that player 1 will become needy
p_2: probability that player 2 will become needy
$0 < p_1, p_2 < 1$

Figure 11: *Support game*

Because M > H, neither player 1 nor player 2 will give support to the other player at their decision node. So, *not* to help at all is a *dominant* strategy. That remains true even if the *expected* payoff of mutual support is greater than the *expected* payoff for not giving support to each other, i.e. if for both players it holds that

[1] $p_i(1-p_j)(S-D) > p_j(1-p_i)(M-H)$ $(i,j = 1,2 \text{ and } i \neq j)$.

Provided that the condition in [1] is fulfilled, mutual support is profitable for both players. Therefore [1] describes a condition under which the support game turns into a 2-person prisoners' dilemma with an inefficient solution. I will refer to [1] as the *PD-condition*.

It is a well-known fact (cf. Taylor 1976, 1987; Axelrod 1984; Friedman 1986) that prisoners' dilemma games, if the basic game is *iterated*, can have *"cooperative" equilibria* which result from supergame strategies supporting cooperation in all the basic games. In this sense prisoners' dilemma games are *cooperatively solvable*, a result which also is applicable to support games.[6] The result can be interpreted in the sense that cooperative supergame equilibria exist if the probabilty α for a further play is sufficiently high.

[2] An *iterated* support game has a cooperative solution if and only if for both players it holds that

$$\alpha_i \geq \frac{1}{1-p_j(1-p_i)+p_i(1-p_j)\frac{S-D}{M-H}} = \alpha_i^+ \quad (i, j = 1,2 \text{ and } i \neq j).$$

[2] is based on the assumption that only in cases of *unilateral* emergencies is it *observable* whether the other one is cooperating or defecting. I will refer to [2] as the *COOP-condition.*[7]

(b) Interaction structure

It is assumed that the individuals belong to *nine different risk classes* which become needy with probabilities 0.1, 0.2, ... , 0.9. They live at the surface of a *torus.* So that world can be represented as a checkerboard without borders. The *interaction neighborhood* is supposed to be a von Neumann neighborhood. An initial distribution of individuals and empty cells is *created by chance*.

(c) Migration options

In each period a random generator allocates migration options with an *exogenously set probability*. Such options can be used, but it is not a must. Migration is possible within a certain *migration window*, but *only to vacant destination cells.* The options are evaluated and/or used in a *sequential* order according to the results of a lottery. After that a new period starts. The migration window, a square of an odd size with the individual which has an option in the center, has the same size, for instance 11×11, for all individuals.

(d) Generally accessible information and intelligence

Each individual instantly *knows the risk class of all his (real or potential) neighbors* and is informed about the payoffs of the support game. The probability of getting migration options is common knowledge and is used to calculate a pessimistic proxy for being neighbors and therefore having a further round of play with the next period. "Pessimistic" means the individuals assume that every option will be used to leave. With q as the probability for getting a migration option we therefore have a probability of stability $\alpha = (1-q)(1-q)$. Using all this information, everyone decides whether conditions [1] and [2] are fullfilled. If both condi-

---

[6] But notice that there are many other equilibria also.

[7] The proof of [2] only exists as a manuscript.

tions are met, two neighbors will support each other.[8] Otherwise, both of the neighboring players will defect.

(e) Partners of different attractiveness

Everyone knows that partners of different risk classes may be of different attractivness. All individuals know that -relative to their own risk class- they are in a *best social position* when they are surrounded by four individuals which are members of the best risk class willing to engage in support relationships with them. On the other hand, there are worst *social positions*: being surrounded by empty cells only or by only those individuals with whom support relations are not possible. An individual will be satisfied with a position which offers *a certain fraction of the difference between the payoff at the best and the worst social position*. This fraction is called *minimum level*. *Satisfied individuals* will migrate only if they can get a position which is at least as good as the position they have. *Dissatisfied individuals* will seize every migration option and accept even worse new locations in order to find a better position by future moves which are accessible from that new location.

In the following I will describe *three experiments*. For the initial conditions look at *figure 12)*. They differ with regard to the probabilities with which the individuals get migration options. One should notice that the possibility of functioning support relations between members of different risk classes is affected by that probability. All other parameters are kept constant.

Figures 13 to 15 show the evolved structures of societies after 1000 periods. They all started with a primordial soup. For interpretation of the figures one should know:

- White cells are empty cells.
- Round cells are dissatisfied (i.e. get less than the assumed minimum level of 50%) *or* they are cells which under the given condition do not have any chance of finding partner for mutual support. Filled squares are satisfied.
- Short white lines connecting two individuals indicate functioning support relations between them.
- Different patterns and grey levels represent different risk classes according to the legend at the bottom of the figures. Risk class 1 becomes needy with probability p = 0.1, risk class 2 with p = 0.2, etc.

---

[8] This implies to assume that an equilibrium selection problem is solved.

Support Networks in Flatland

Basics:

interaction window: von Neumann neighborhood
migration window: 11×11 with the given position in the center.
world: 21×21 (torus)

Class structure:

individuals per risk class: 35 ⇒ a total of 315 individuals / 136 empty sites

Payoffs and minimum level:

Saved = 5 Drowned = 1 Move on = 7 Help = 6

$$\Rightarrow \frac{\text{profit}}{\text{cost}} = 4$$

minimul level = 50 %

Probabilities for getting migration options:

0.05 ⇒ $\alpha = 0.903$ (*first* experiment)
0.10 ⇒ $\alpha = 0.810$ (*second* experiment)
0.15 ⇒ $\alpha = 0.723$ (*third* experiment)

Use of migration options:

a) dissatisfied individuals decide for a best *alternative* location.
b) satisfied individuals move only if the alternative location is *at least as good as* the given one.
c) individuals knowing that they can not find partners at all *move randomly*.

Figure 12: *Initial conditions*

Even from a *superficial* inspection it is obvious that a *well-ordered support network* emerged out of an initial chaos. So one can state that support networks can evolve even in a world of rational egoists who are differently endowed by nature and who choose their partners opportunistically. By closer inspection one will find more interesting details.

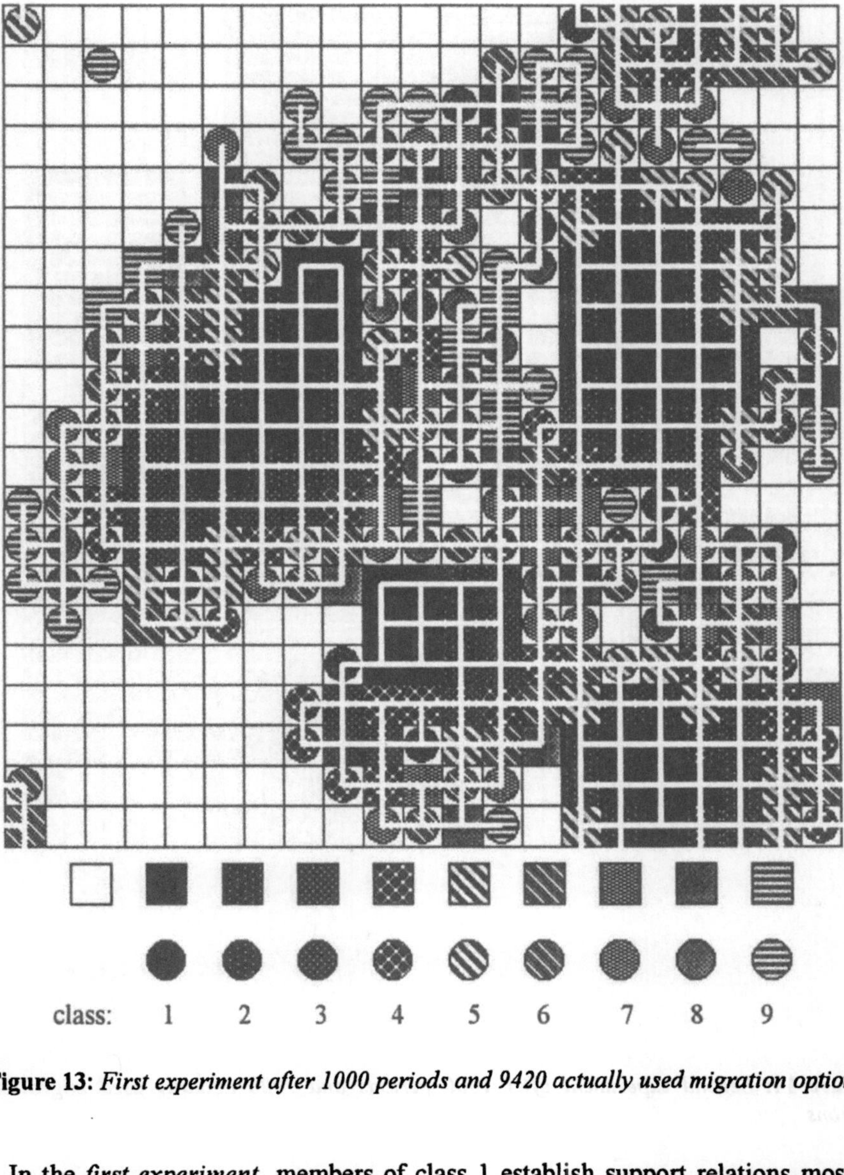

Figure 13: *First experiment after 1000 periods and 9420 actually used migration options*

In the *first experiment,* members of class 1 establish support relations mostly among themselves. However, support relations with members of class 2 exist also. This latter class is living around the areas occupied by class 1. Quite often we find members of class 3 just behind those of class 2, behind them members of classes 4 and 5. Class 9 could find partners only in class 8 and 9. The members of those classes are living more or less on the egde of the networks. Segregation is less strongly developed by those in the middle of the risk classes than those in the extremes.

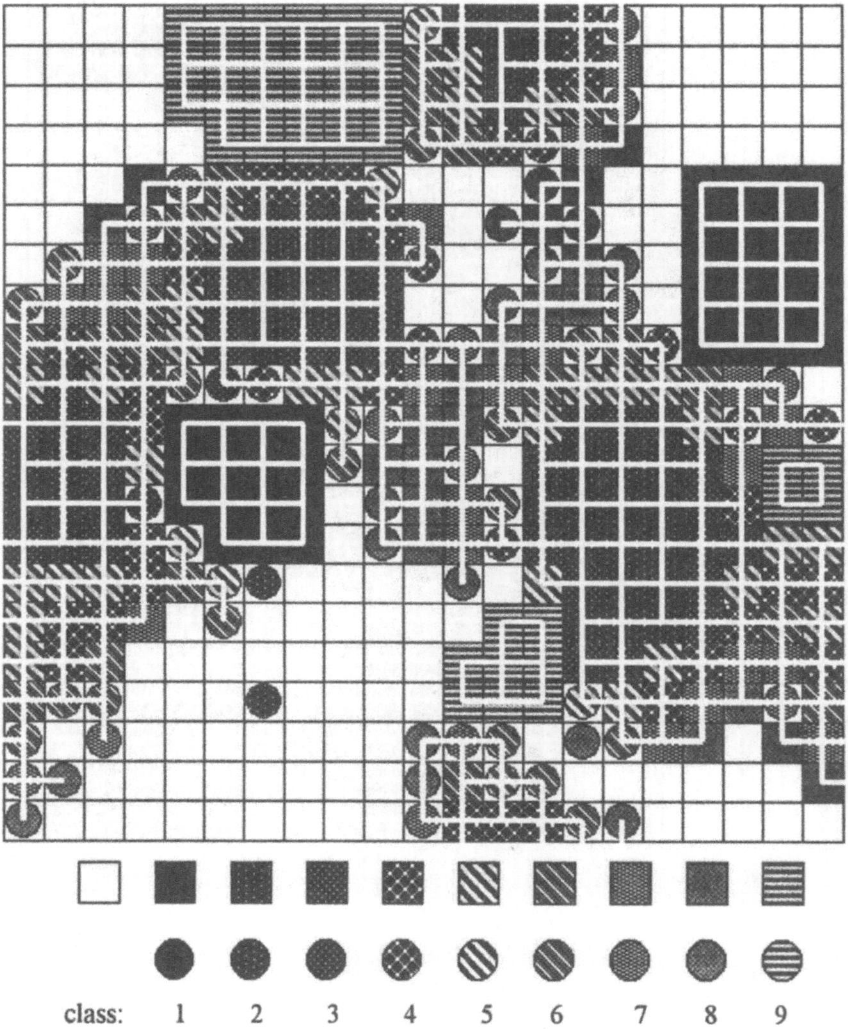

Figure 14: *Second experiment after 1000 periods and 7020 actually used migration options*

In the *second experiment* the members of the best and the worst risk class establish support relations only among themselves. In different areas we find closed networks of members of those classes. Members of class 2 seem to be cores of networks often surrounded by members of class 3. Around them we find members of classes 4 and 5. It is now class 6 and 7 which is living on the edges of the networks. And it is again in the middle of the risk classes where segregation is less dramatic.

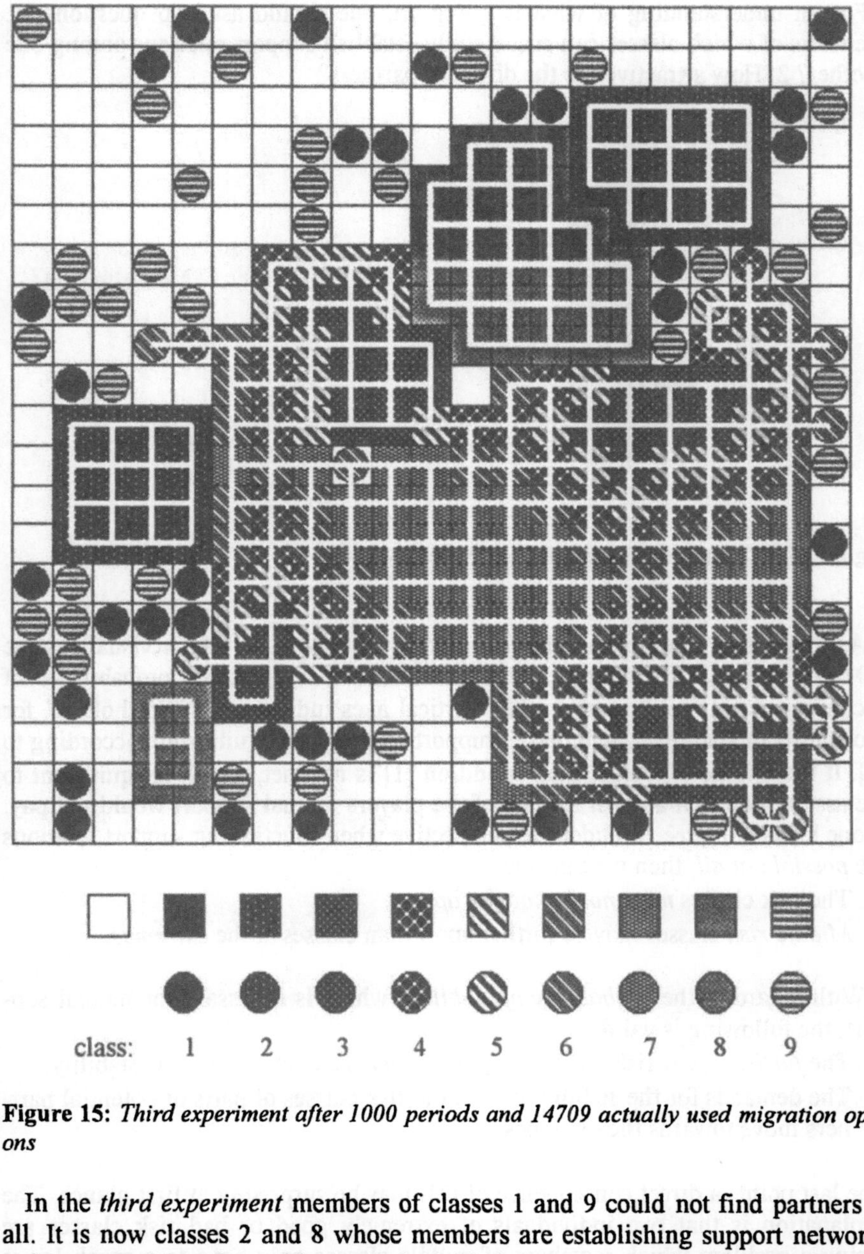

Figure 15: ***Third experiment after 1000 periods and 14709 actually used migration options***

In the *third experiment* members of classes 1 and 9 could not find partners at all. It is now classes 2 and 8 whose members are establishing support networks only among themselves. Often members of class 3 are a nucleus for networks in which they are surrounded by members of class 4, around them class 5, then 6. The members of class 7 are strongly separated, living partly as neighbors of class 6, and partly within their own class.

For an understanding of what is going on, one should ask two questions: 1. Members of which classes can successfully establish support relations among one another? 2. How attractive are the different partners?

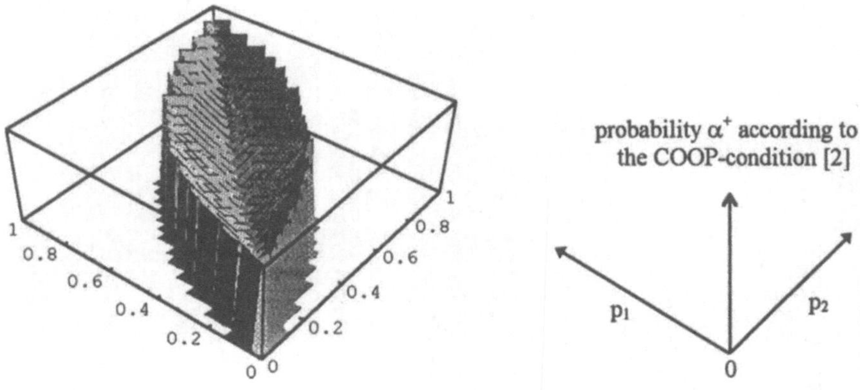

Figure 16: PD- and COOP-condition for (S-D)/(M-H) = 4.

As to the first question an answer is given by *figure 16*, which visualizes the PD- and the COOP-condition. The horizontal axis represents probabilities of becoming needy, i.e. p_1 and p_2. The vertical axes indicates the threshold α^+ for probability of stability which makes support relations an equilibrium according to [2]. If there is no α^+-value, then condition [1] is not met, which is equivalent to the assumption that at least for one of the players mutual support would not pay. If one looks at *figure 16* under the perspective when functioning support relations are *possible at all*, then we can state:

- The risk classes *must not be too far apart.*
- *Middle risk* classes may be further apart than classes at the *extremes*.

With regard to the *probability of stability*, which is necessary for mutual support, the following is valid:

- The *further apart* risk classes are, the *higher* the demands for the stability.
- The demands for the stability *rise* as the risk classes of pairs of potential partners move towards the extremes.

The last point -a direct consequence of [2]- may be surprising at first glance. The explanation is that two individuals of extremely good or bad risk classes are facing a problem which members of middle classes only have to a much lower degree: It is very likely that members of two extremely *good* risk classes will do not need help. Members of two extremely *bad* risk classes will probably be in need of help simultaneously and thus neither of them will be able to help. In *both* cases the situation of unilateral emergency will rarely occur. Therefore the expected utility of mutual support decreases at the extremes. At the same time it becomes more difficult to find out whether the other one is cooperating or defecting. Thus a probability of stability making support relations for middle risk classes viable might not be sufficient for pairs of extreme risk classes.

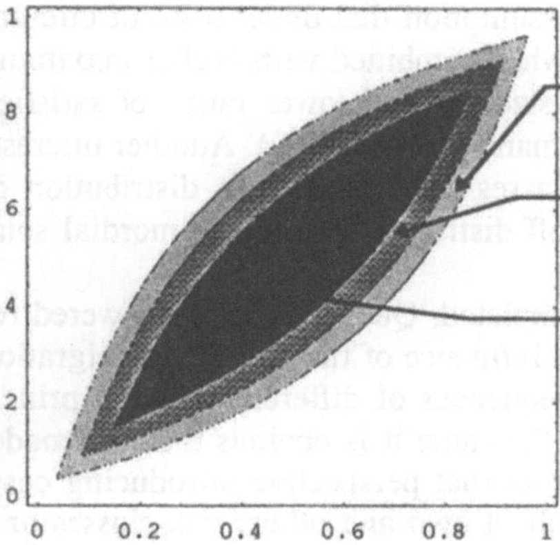

Figure 17: *The lense like areas contain those pairings of risks for which in the three experiments the COOP-condition [2] is fullfilled.*

With regard to our three experiments now one can state: With an *increasing* probability of getting migration options the pessimistic proxy for the probability of stability *decreases*. Therefore the lense-like area of pairs for which mutual support is a feasable solution is *shrinking*. *Figure 17* gives an overview. So, in the first experiment we had functioning support relations even among members of classes 1 *and* 2 and, furthermore, between classes 8 *and* 9. In the second experiment, based on a lower probability of stability, those classes were too far apart to make mutual support a solution. In the third experiment classes 8 and 9 fall victim to the effect that an again decreased stability destroyed the possibility of mutual support for the extreme classes.

To understand the often-onion like structures of the evolved networks one must not concentrate alone on pairings which could support each other in principle. One has to concentrate on problems and consequences of different attractivness also. The different degrees to which partners are attractive can be characterized as follows:

[3] $\Gamma_i = p_i(1-p_j)(S-D) - p_j(1-p_i)(M-H)$

By an inspection of the support game as given in *Figure 11* it can easily be verified that Γ_i is the difference between what i can expect with and without mutual support in an interaction with j. One might refer to Γ_i as the *support surplus*. That surplus depends on p_j; i.e., the others' probability of becoming needy. Γ_i can be maximized by finding a partner belonging to the lowest risk class with which condition [1] and [2] are met: i.e. with which mutual support is possible at all. Consequently, worse classes try to become neighbors of better classes which are looking for better partners as well. Worse classes are satisfied with neighboring better classes, but it is just that which makes those better classes willing to move. Closer statistical analysis of those dynamics has yet to be done. But the simulations done up till now support the assumption that under a lot of circumstances wider possiblities of pairing, even when combined with higher maximum surplus for all classes, may result in less stability and lower ratios of satisfied individuals in at least some classes (Hegselmann 1994a; 380 f.). Another interesting result is that strong segregation of classes may result in a distribution of payoffs which is more equal than the payoff distribution in the primordial soup (Hegselmann 1994a; 383f.).

The analysis of the model is yet to be completed. Questions to be answered regard degrees of clustering and segregation, influence of the size of the migration window, different class distributions, consequences of different decision principles for how to use migration options. At the same it is obvious that the model itself should be improved and extended: from that perspective introducing costs for migration, entrance barriers, learning about own and others risk classes or a dynamic of the probability to become needy have to be considered.

4. Why CA Based Modeling and Simulations?

The foregoing examples of low dimension CA based models were intended to support the assumption that this type of modeling is a fruitful approach to understanding the dynamics of social dynamics. Based on the fact that locality, overlapping, and iteration are properties of a significant part of social dynamics, CA cover some basic features of a real world process. Given we have a social process which has those abstract properties CA based models, i.e. rigorously simplified worlds like Lineland and Flatland, can provide a qualitative understanding of real world phenomena. They contribute especially to a better understanding of micro/macro relations.But there is more to be mentioned:

- Macro effects of CA based models are often good examples and sometimes even paradigmatic cases for *unintended consequences* of social actions. In Schelling's segregation models (Schelling 1969, 1971) individuals do not intend to live in same color areas. Nevertheless, it is there where they end up. In the support network model described above, the individuals are interested in maximizing their utilities and not in segregation (or increasing overall equality). But it is exactly that which they produce by their maximizing behavior. More general, *CA based modeling contributes to better understanding of the phenomenon of unintended consequences.*
- CA based modeling does not exclude centralized institutions in the model. For instance, one might have an institution providing some common knowledge about what is going on in the world. But what is much more important is that the very essence of CA can be described as being a *mult- agent system, based on locality, and an overlapping interaction structure*. Since CA based modeling is flexible enough to allow for narrow or wide definitions of local-

ity, it provides a *natural framework for studying social self-organization* and its political relative, i.e. the *invisible hand paradigm*. According to that paradigm individuals acting in a more or less self-interested way will nevertheless produce desirable collective results on a macro level. Since that hope is not an a priori truth *CA based modeling is a promising framework to do basic research on a fundamental question about societal organization.*

- What is an unintended consequence for an individual may for a researcher be a surprising and, before that, unknown consequence of his theoretical assumptions. More general: our deductive capabilities are not that good. That becomes a crucial fact if it comes to understanding processes in which numerous agents are repeatedly interacting. Since generating these dynamics requires highly complex calculations, simulations are a useful deductive method to explore the consequences of our theories. Simulation results can be related to empirical knowledge, they can stimulate new empiricial studies and they me even stimulate ideas of theorems which may be successfully proven by analytical means. Therefore *modeling and simulating are tools to explore theoretical assumptions and to develop theories - and that holds for CA based modeling and simulating also.*[9]
- In CA based models one finds an (almost) inherent *"spirit of simplicity" in approaching complexity*. With regard to social applications, the subject of analysis is *single elementary* social interactions and mechanisms, for example, looking for attractive partners, influencing each other, deciding to cooperate or to defect, finding a neighborhood which meets certain requirements, etc. Models of that type are *totally different from climate models*, where numerous different mechanisms and modules interfere. "Thick models" (Kliemt 1996) like that make sense only if all the components are sufficiently well understood and therefore those models are resident in more mature sciences, but usually not in the social sciences. CA based modeling allows for focusing on the dynamics of elementary social interactions. *Given the modest state of the art in the social sciences CA based modeling seems to be an appropriate approach.*

What above has been said in favor of CA based modeling does not mean that there are not any restrictions. In Hegselmann (1996) it is shown that there are even severe dangers in using the CA approach, for example the danger of creating artefacts caused by badly designed *updating procedures*. Other problems are due to restrictions on possible interaction structures, caused by the *geometry* of neighborhoods. One should know those problems, dangers and restrictions. Therefore with CA based modeling it is as it is with all frameworks: one has to make sensible use of it.

---

[9] For a systematization of different types and functions of simulations cf. Hartmann (1996), Kliemt (1996), Troitzsch (1996).

References

Axelrod, R. (1984). *The evolution of cooperation.* New York: Basic Books.

Bruch, E. (1993). *The evolution of cooperation in neighbourhood structures.* Bonn University: manuscript.

Burks, A.W. (1970). *Essays on cellular automata.* Urbana (Il.): University of Illinois Press.

Casti, J.L. (1992). *Reality rules - Picturing the world in mathematics* (Vol.I: The fundamentals; Vol.II: The frontier). New York: Wiley & Sons.

Demongeot, J., Goles, E. & Tchuente, M. (Eds.) (1985). *Dynamical systems and cellular automata.* London: Academic Press.

Friedman, J.W. (1986). *Game theory with applications to economics* (2nd ed. 1991). Oxford: Oxford UP.

Gutowitz, H. (Ed.) (1991). *Cellular automata - theory and experiment.* Cambridge (MA): MIT Press.

Hartmann, St. (1996). The world as a process - Simulations in the natural and social sciences. In R.Hegselmann, U. Mueller & K.G. Troitzsch (Eds.) *Modeling and simulation in the social sciences from a philosophy of science point of view* [Theory and Decision Library]. Dordrecht: Kluver (in press).

Hegselmann, R. (1994). Zur Selbstorganisation von Solidarnetzwerken unter Ungleichen - Ein Simulationsmodell. In K. Homann (Hg.) *Wirtschaftsethische Perspektiven I - Theorie, Ordnungsfragen, Internationale Institutuionen.* Berlin: Duncker & Humblot.

-/- (1994a). Solidarität in einer egoistischen Welt - Eine Simulation. In J.Nida-Rümelin (Hg) *Praktische Rationalität - Grundlagen und ethische Anwendungen des rational choice-Paradigmas.* Berlin: de Gruyter.

-/- (1996). Cellular automata in the social sciences - Perspectivs, restrictions and artefacts. In R.Hegselmann, U. Mueller & K.G. Troitzsch (Eds.) *Modeling and simulation in the social sciences from a philosophy of science point of view* [Theory and Decision Library]. Dordrecht: Kluver (in press).

Kirchkamp, O. (1994). *Spatial evolution of automata in the prisoners' dilemma.* Bonn university: manuscript.

Kliemt, H. (1996), Simulation and rational practice. In R.Hegselmann, U. Mueller & K.G. Troitzsch (Eds.) *Modeling and simulation in the social sciences from a philosophy of science point of view* [Theory and Decision Library]. Dordrecht: Kluver (in press).

Messick, D.M. & Liebrand, W.B.G. (1995). Individual heuristics and the dynamics of cooperation in large groups. *Psychological Review, 102,* 131-145.

Lehman, R.S. (1977). *Computer simulation and modeling - An introduction.* Hillsdale: Lawrence Erlbaum Associations.

Liebrand, W. , Messick, D. & Wilke, H. (Eds.) (1992). *Social dilemmas - Theoretical issues and resarch findings.* Oxford: Pergamon.

Neumann, J.v. (1966). *Theory of self-reproducing automata* (edited and completed by Arthur W.Burks). Urbana: University of Illinois Press.

Nowak, A., Szamrej, J. & Latane, B. (1990). From private attitude to public opinion - Dynamic theory of social impact. *Psychological Review, 97,* 362-376.

Nowak, M.A. & R.M.May (1992). Evolutionary games and spatial chaos. *Nature, 359,* 826-829.

- /- (1993). The spatial dilemmas of evolution. *International Journal of Bifurcation and Chaos, 3,* 35-78.

Sakoda, J.M. (1949). *Minidoka - An analysis of changing patterns of social interaction.* Berkeley: University of California, doctoral dissertation.

-/- (1971). The checkerboard model of social interaction. *Journal of Mathematical Sociology, 1,* 119-132.

Schelling, Th. (1969). Models of segregation. *American Economic Review, 59,* 488-493.

-/- (1971). Dynamic models of segregation. *Journal of Mathematical sociology,* 1, 143-186.

Schulz, U., Albers, W. & Mueller, U. (Eds.) (1994). *Social dilemmas and cooperation.* Berlin: Springer.

Taylor, M. (1987). *The possibility of cooperation* (revised edition of: Anarchy and cooperation, 1976). London: Wiley & Sons.

Toffoli, T. & Margolus, N. (1987). *Cellular automata machines - A new viroment for modeling.* Cambridge (MA): MIT Press.

Troitzsch, K.G. (1996). Multilevel modeling in the social sciences - Mathematical analysis and computer simulation. In W.B.G. Liebrand, R. Hegselmann & A. Nowak (Eds.) *Computer modeling and the study of dynamic social processes.* Thousand Oaks: Sage (in press).

Wolfram, St. (1984). Universality and complexity in cellular automata. *Physica D, 10,* 1-35.

-/- (Ed.) (1986), *Theory and applications of cellular automata.* Singapore: World Scientific.

Selective Play: Social Embeddedness of Social Dilemmas

Toshio Yamagishi[1] and Nahoko Hayashi[2]

[1] Department of Behavioral Science, Faculty of Letters, Hokkaido University, Sapporo 060, Japan

[2] Department of Behavioral Science, Faculty of Letters, Hokkaido University, Sapporo 060, Japan

1 Introduction

Research on social dilemmas and related problems are currently witnessing new, encompassing developments in theory and methods. In this paper, we will focus on one specific aspect of those developments—i.e., development of the "selective play" paradigm. The attention of social dilemma researchers has traditionally been focused on isolated dyads or groups, and the wider context in which dyads or groups are embedded has traditionally been ignored. In this traditional research paradigm, players are implicitly assumed to be locked in a particular dyad or a group, having no chance of moving out and joining another dyad or group. This traditional research paradigm may be called the "forced play" paradigm (Hayashi, 1995a) in the sense that players are "forced" to interact with particular partners. Some of the interdependent relations we observe in the real world may be of this kind. A good example is the US-USSR relation before the collapsing of the Soviet Union. The two partners (the US and the USSR) are "forced" to interact with each other no matter how strongly either party wanted to avoid interaction. However, many of the interdependent relations in the real world are not of this kind. Actually, only very few types of relationship (such as one between a parent and a child or between two siblings) are forced ones in this sense. Most personal as well as formal relationships we deal with in everyday life come with the possibility of exit. In our life, we typically choose to interact with our partners, and each has at least a partial freedom to leave the relation. Even the most long-lasting relationships such as marriage and friendship in the most contemporary societies entail possibilities of termination by voluntary moves of the people involved. People often form relations and leave them looking for better alternatives. Although the exit option was included in some of earlier studies of social dilemmas (e.g., Marwell & Schumitt, 1975; Orbell, Schwartz-Shea & Simmons,1984) it was in the late 80's that social dilemma researchers, though small in number yet, started systematic research efforts to explore theoretical implications of the option for leaving the current relationship and choosing a new partner. Resulting research paradigm may be called the "selective play" paradigm (Orbell & Dawes,1991; Hayashi,1995a). The purpose of this chapter is to explore theoretical implications of this emerging new paradigm. An additional purpose of this chapter is to provide a chance for the English speaking reader to be exposed to a literature on selective play published or reported in Japanese.

2 From Forced Play to Non-forced Play

Schuessler's computer simulation study (1989) is among the earliest attempts to move social dilemma research out of the constraint of "forced play." "Players" in his simulation had an "exit option," or a choice of staying in or leaving the current relation. The one who stayed played a prisoner's dilemma game with the same partner. The one who decided to leave was randomly matched with another player who similarly had left the current relation. Based on his simulation results, Schuessler concluded that a strategy he called CONCO performed very well in this situation. The strategy starts with cooperation and keeps cooperating with the same partner until the partner defects. Once the partner defects, CONCO exits the relation. Another computer simulation study in which the exit option was introduced is one conducted by Vanberg & Congleton (1992). The situation used in their simulation, however, was different from Schuessler's (1989) in that players who exited in Vanberg & Congleton's simulation did not have a chance to find an alternative partner. In contrast, players who exited in Schuessler's simulation were randomly matched with another player who similarly exited. Despite this difference, however, the best performing strategy in Vanberg and Congleton's simulation, "Prudent Moral Strategy," was basically the same as the best performer, CONCO, in Schuessler's simulation.

These two studies set up the first step toward moving from the forced-play paradigm to the selective play paradigm. Players in the above simulations had an option for leaving a PD relation if they were not satisfied with the current partner. They were not forced to play with a particular partner as in the ordinary iterated prisoner's dilemma. On the other hand, those players were not given a choice of partners. Players in Vanberg & Congleton's simulation were left alone without anyone to turn to once they deserted the initially assigned partner. Players in Schuessler's simulation were randomly matched with another partner as they left the current relation. Although introduction of the exit option freed players from the confinement of the forced relationship, they were not conceived as actors who voluntarily seek and form relationships. Thus, the paradigm used in Schuessler's (1989) or Vanberg & Congleton's (1992) simulations was the "non-forced play" paradigm, but it was not the fully-fledged "selective play paradigm" yet.

3 From Non-forced Play to Selective Play

The fully-fledged selective play paradigm was inaugurated with the introduction of the option for choosing partners (in addition to the option for exiting the current relationship) in a series of experimental and simulation studies of *prisoner's di-*

lemma networks by Hayashi, Yamagishi and their collaborators (Hayashi,1993, 1995b; Hayashi, Jin & Yamagishi,1993; Jin, Hayashi, Shinotsuka,1993; Yamagishi, Hayashi & Jin,1994). Players in those studies voluntarily formed relations in addition to voluntarily terminating relations. As an initial step in examining the similarities and differences between forced play and selective play situations, Hayashi et al. (1993; also reported in Yamagishi et al.,1994 in English) examined whether or not the *tit-for-tat* (TFT) strategy, which had proven to be the best performer in Axelrod's (1984) computer tournament involving isolated dyads, was also as effective in the selective play situation. For this purpose, they conducted a computer simulation of a prisoner's dilemma network (PD network). Each player in this simulation had two types of strategies, *selection strategy* and *action strategy*. Selection strategies were used to select partners whom the player wished to interact with. A PD game for the particular trial was played between two players who wished to interact with each other. Players selected partners based on their selection strategies at the beginning of each trial, and a different set of pairs played PD games in each trial. Whether to cooperate or defect with the mutually selected partner was decided based on the player's action strategy.

Results of this initial study of PD networks (Hayashi et al.,1993) indicated that the effect of the selection strategy was several times as large as the effect of the action strategy—i.e., how to choose a partner was much more important than how to act toward the chosen partner—pointing to the need for further research on the selection strategy. However, since there had been practically no systematic studies of selection strategies, we did not even know what selection strategies were possible and what were often used. As a means to find out what kinds of selection strategy can be used in PD network situations, we decided to hold a computer tournament of the "prisoner's dilemma network," a tournament similar to the famous one organized by Axelrod (1984). In the original computer tournament sponsored by Axelrod, the *tit-for-tat* (TFT) strategy submitted by Anatol Rapoport was the overall winner. Strategies that were far more complicated than the simple TFT, many of which were designed to outsmart the partner, could not perform better than TFT. The superior overall performance of TFT was attributed by Axelrod (1984) to the following four characteristics: (1) TFT is nice. It never is the first to defect. Therefore, it does not initiate a vicious circle of mutual defection. (2) TFT immediately retaliates when the partner defects, and thus the partner can easily understand the consequence of attempting free riding. (3) TFT is forgiving. It forgives the formerly defected partner as soon as he/she cooperates again. (4) TFT is clear, simple, and thus predictable.

The computer tournament we organized involved a more complicated decision environment. The PD game in this tournament was played not in isolated dyads as in the Axelrod's tournament. Instead, the *dyadic PD relations were embedded in a larger network structure*. "Players" (actually, computer programs representing submitted strategies) in this computer tournament were allowed to choose partners to play a PD game with, and the choice of the partner took place in each trial. Results of this computer tournament that took place in the fall of 1991 and the winter of 1992 are reported in Hayashi (1993; also a summary is reported in Yamagishi et al., 1994, in English), and thus we are not going to present the results in details. In a word, the result consistently pointed to the effectiveness of the *out-for-tat* (OFT) strategy. "Out-for-tat" is the name given by Hayashi (1993) to the strategy originally called PURGE by Tatsuya Kameda, the author of the strategy. The OFT player (1) always cooperates (i.e., the action strategy is the unconditional cooperation), (2) sticks with the current partner insofar as the partner cooperates, and (3) deserts the partner as soon as the partner defects. OFT keeps choosing the same partner and keeps cooperating insofar as the partner cooperates, but deserts the partner and turn to someone else. All top four performers in the tournament had these three features of the OFT strategy. The best overall performer, PURGE, had an additional feature of forgiveness. Additional computer simulations reported in Hayashi (1993) and Yamagishi et al. (1994) demonstrated that it was actually the feature of forgiveness that put PURGE above the other strategies sharing the other features of OFT.

The best was simple in this PD network simulation as in Axelrod's (1984) dyadic PD simulation. Actually, the excellent performance of OFT points to the same set of conclusions as the ones proposed by Axelrod (1984) about the success of strategies in isolated dyadic relations. Axelrod (1984) lists aforementioned four features of the TFT strategy, the winner of his computer tournament: "niceness," retaliation, forgiveness, and clarity. Parallelism of these features and the four features of OFT presented above is clear. (1) Both TFT and OFT are nice. TFT never is the first to defect. OFT never defects. (2) Both TFT and OFT are retaliatory. TFT retaliates a partner's defection with defection. OFT retaliates a partner's defection with desertion of the relationship. (3) Both TFT and OFT are forgiving. TFT responds partner's cooperation with cooperation no matter how uncooperative the partner used to be. OFT gives a second chance to the one who defected before. The best performers in the previous simulations, CONCO in Schuessler's (1989) simulation and PMS in Vanberg & Congleton's (1992) simulation, had three of the four features of OFT; the only feature unique to OFT was forgiveness. Forgiveness was unique to OFT since players in the previous two simulations did not choose their partners. Whether players forgive previous betrayers is relevant only when they choose with whom they interact.

Two laboratory experiments have been conducted so far in the selective play context. First is a four-person group experiment in which subjects had a choice of partners to play a PD game with (Jin et al.,1993; also a brief summary of this experiment is reported in Yamagishi et al.,1994 in English). The second is a 6- and 8-person group experiment in which subjects decided whether to stay in the current relationship or desert the current partner and take a chance in interacting with a stranger (Hayashi & Yamagishi,1995).[1] In both of these experiments, subjects did show a tendency to use the OFT strategy. First, the overall cooperation rates in these experiments were quite high. Second, subjects kept interacting with the same

[1] More details of this experiment will be presented later.

partner insofar as the partner continued cooperating, but as soon as the partner failed to cooperate subjects tended to quickly desert the relation. In sum, subjects in those experiments showed a tendency not to respond in kind (defection for defection) but to respond by deserting "unfaithful" partners.

4 Selection of Partners versus Selection of Matrices

The basic principles of the OFT strategy may be applied even in the forced play situation in which two partners have no alternative partners to turn to. In an experiment of iterated dyadic prisoner's dilemma, Yamagishi and Kakiuchi constructed a situation in which subjects could select the size of their own outcomes in the payoff matrix.[2] Subjects started with a matrix shown in Figure 1a, in which their own payoffs were negative when the partner defected. At the beginning of each of the following trials, each subject was given a chance to alter their own (not the partner's) payoffs by adding or subtracting the original payoffs from the current ones. For example, if A decided to increase the size of her payoffs at the beginning of the second trial, she would play the matrix shown in Figure 1b. If she continued to increase her payoffs in the third trial, the matrix would become the one shown in Figure 1c. If she decides to decrease the size in the fourth trial, the matrix turns back to Figure 1b. The subject could increase or decrease her payoffs only by one step at a time. As the subject increased the payoffs, potential rewards became greater. At the same time, potential losses became larger, too. Thus, increasing the size of own payoffs meant big gains with a risk of big losses. The question marks in Figures 1b and 1c indicate that the subject did not know the size of the partner's payoffs that might have been changed by the partner.[3]

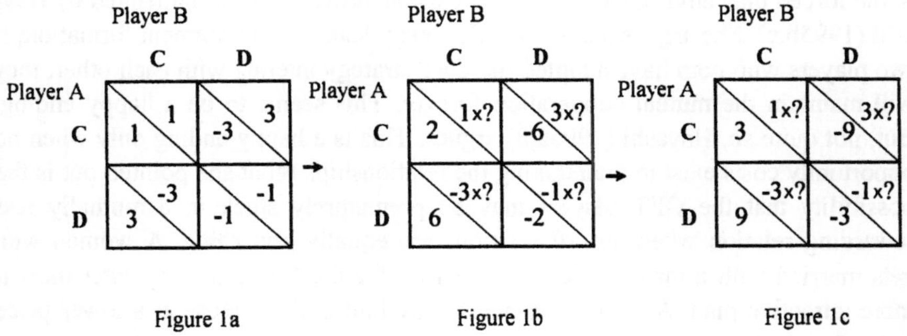

Figure 1 Choice of payoff size in Yamagishi & Kakiuchi's experiment

[2] This experiment has just been completed, and thus has not been written up for publication or presentation.
[3] We are currently designing another experiment in which the partner's payoff sizes are also displayed.

In this experiment, two subjects were forced to play with each other. Nonetheless, they were able to partially disengage themselves from the relationship by reducing the size of the payoffs (i.e., small gains with a risk of small losses), or they were able to get involved more strongly in the relationship by increasing the size of the payoffs. Instead of the binary choice of playing or not playing with a particular partner, subjects in this experiment had a choice of the degree of playing. The original purpose of this experiment was to test a hypothesis that high-trusters would increase the size of the payoffs and thus would be able to build personalized trust more quickly than low-trusters. This hypothesis was confirmed by the experimental results. What is more interesting in the current context concerns the differential use of OFT versus TFT by high- and low-trusters.[4] High-trusters tended to use the OFT strategy. They kept cooperating no matter what the choice of the partner was. Facing the defection choice by the partner, however, they tended to reduce the size of the payoffs instead of responding in kind (i.e., by defecting themselves). In contrast, low-trusters tended to use the TFT strategy, responding to defection by the partner by own defection. It was not uncommon for low-trusters facing defection by the partner to increase the size of the payoffs and then defect; it seemed that they wanted to get even by exploiting the partner more severely. The preliminary analysis of this experiment suggests that OFT is a more efficient strategy than TFT when a non-forced aspect is introduced into a forced, dyadic PD situation.[5]

5 When Neighbor's Green Is in Fact Greener

The computer simulations and laboratory experiments briefly described above consistently point out the advantage of the OFT strategy. The OFT strategy seems to be as powerful and robust in the selective play environment as is the TFT strategy in the forced play environment. This conclusion, however, was challenged by Hayashi (1995b,c). She argues that the OFT strategy leads to commitment formation; if two players who both have adopted the OFT strategy interact with each other, they will maintain the mutual cooperation forever. This seems to be a happy ending. But, not quite so, Hayashi (1995a,b) argues. This is a happy ending only when no opportunity costs exist in maintaining the relationship. What she pointed out is the possibility that the OFT players may be prematurely stuck in a mutually less rewarding relation when not all relations are equally rewarding. A woman who gets married with a man she fell in love with for the first time may later meet a more attractive man. A buyer of a house may find a nicer house at a lower price only after she has closed the deal.

Realizing the importance of the opportunity costs in evaluating the advantage of the OFT strategy in the selective play environment, we hosted the second computer tournament. In the second tournament, each pair played a unique PD matrix so that

[4] See Yamagishi & Yamagishi (1994) for the measurement of subjects' trust levels. Subjects in this experiment interacted with a partner of the same level (high or low) of trust.
[5] van Lange, Camac, Visser & Marsman (1995) also reports similar results.

the payoff of mutual cooperation in one relation could be worse than the payoff of mutual cooperation in another. Furthermore, outcomes of mutual defection in some relations were better than mutual cooperation outcomes in some others. In this situation finding the "right partner" who has the greatest rewarding capability to the player was at least as important as finding cooperative partners. The winner of this second tournament was a strategy called DOG, submitted by Nobuhito Jin of Hokkaido University. DOG is a *nice* and *cool* actor. DOG is nice in the sense that he never betrays the partner. He cooperates with anyone whom he has chosen to play with. He is cool in the sense that only the outcome matters to him; he does not pay any attention to the intention of the partner. DOG never plays again with a partner who ever gave him a negative outcome[6] no matter how good an intention the partner had (i.e., even when the partner cooperated). These two features of DOG, however, were also shared with the other top performers.

The only difference that remains between DOG, by far the best performer, and the other top performers is its "trustfulness." In estimating the payoff to be obtained from interacting with a "stranger," with whom the player had never interacted with, only DOG had a "positive bias." All the top performers including DOG placed preference order for partners according to the expectation of the payoff to be obtained from other players. The expectations of those payoffs were based on the average payoffs the player had obtained in the past in the case of the partners with whom the player had previously interacted. In the case of the partners whom the player had never interacted with, the other top players used the average of the payoffs they had earned in the past or simply assumed a payoff of zero. DOG was the only exception. DOG used the average of *only the positive payoffs* it had earned in the past; all negative payoffs DOG earned in the past were ignored in expecting the payoff from interacting with a stranger. This positive "cognitive bias" in estimating the payoff to be obtained from a stranger, according to Yamagishi & Yamagishi (1994), is the *general trust.*[7] Further simulation studies in

---

[6] The entries of the payoff matrices were constructed by combining the following three components which were randomly varied for each pair within the range specified by conditions: (1) cost of cooperation, *C*, (2) efficiency of cooperation, *E*, and (3) basic rewarding capability, *B*. The payoff a player received was determined by the following formula: $C_pE_pD_p + B_p - C_o$, where subscript p refers to partner and o refers to own. D_p=0 when partner defects and 1 when partner cooperates. The range of *C* and *E* had two conditions, 1~3, 3~5; and *B* had three conditions, -3~-1, -1~1, 1~3. The overall performance was obtained by averaging each player's performances in 12 cells created by factorially combining these ranges. It was thus possible for mutual cooperation to produce a negative payoff for one or the other partner. A negative payoff for a player resulted, for example, when the partner did not have enough rewarding capability to at least compensate for the player's cost of cooperation. An example of such a situation would be a collaborative relationship between a capable researcher and an incapable one; the incapable researcher does his best but contributes practically nothing, or sometimes is detrimental, to the progress of a joint research project, and yet the credit for the research product is shared by the two.

[7] They define general trust as a "default" expectation of the trustworthiness of anonymous

which neutral DOG, who acted exactly the same way as DOG except that the simple average replaced the positively biased average, was added to the existing players demonstrated that it is in fact the trustful nature of DOG that made it by far the best performer in the tournament. DOG was again the winner by a large margin, and the newly added "neutral DOG" occupied only the 7th place among 24 players. Thus, the winner of the second tournament, DOG, is shown to be nice, cool, and trustful.[8]

The importance of trust for a strategy to be successful in the selective play environment with opportunity costs was further demonstrated by another simulation study by Hayashi (1995b). Each player of a 100 player group in this simulation[9] was endowed with a randomly determined base line rewarding capability of 0, 1, or 2 points for each of the other players. For example, Player A's base line rewarding capability for B is 0, for C is 2, for D is 1, etc. This base line value was added to the common payoff matrix shown in Figure 1a. Players were either unconditional cooperators or unconditional defectors. The overall proportion of unconditional cooperators (20%, 40%, 60%, or 80%) in the group was used as a between-groups factor. Players were also randomly assigned to 11 levels of trustfulness ranging from 0 to 100 with intervals of 10, and the level of trust was used as a within-groups factor. The level of trustfulness was operationally defined as the expected percentage of cooperators in the group, such that the trustfulness level of 20 meant that the player expected the proportion of the cooperators in the group to be 20 percent. Players were all informed of the nature of the payoff matrix with each of their potential partners and used the estimated proportion of cooperators (i.e., trustfulness level) in calculating the payoff that was to be expected if they exited the current relationship and were randomly matched with a new partner. They made the exit decision when this expected payoff exceeded the payoff they were currently eraning. Results of this computer simulation indicated that trust was important for cooperators, but not for defectors, in determining their average payoffs. That is, trustful cooperators did better than distrustful cooperators[10] whereas the performance of trustful defectors was not different from that of distrustful defectors. Furthermore, the advantage of trustfulness for cooperators did not depend on the proportion of cooperators in the group. Less trustful cooperators tended to form a premature commitment with another cooperator who had only a

---

other people. High-trusters in this sense overestimate trustworthiness of others when they do not have enough evidence for such an expectation. Trust in this sense seems to imply gullibility, but they argue that this positive bias provides an advantage to high-trusters in a social environment that is characterized with high levels of social uncertainty and opportunity costs.

[8] See Hayashi (1995c) for details.

[9] This simulation used Schuessler's (1989) type non-forced environment rather than fully-fledged selective play environment such that the player who exited was randomly matched with another available player.

[10] Exactly speaking, the advantage of trustfulness for cooperators was not a linear function of trust; rather, it was quadratic and reached its peak at about the trust level of 83.

low level of rewarding capability.

6 One-shot Play with the Option for Not Playing

At about the same time as the above development of the selective play paradigm was taking place in the form of the prisoner's dilemma network, Orbell and Dawes (1991,1993) were also exploring theoretical implications of allowing players to choose between playing and not playing. While the above development focused on strategies such as CONCO (Schuessler,1989) or OFT (Yamagishi et al.,1994), Orbell and Dawes focused their analysis on non-strategic factors. The choice that players in the simulations mentioned above (Schuessler,1989; Vanberg & Congleton,1992; Hayashi et al.,1993; Yamagishi et al.,1994) faced was between staying in the current relationship and keep interacting with the same partner and leaving the current relationship, looking for a new partner. In contrast, players in Orbell & Dawes's mathematical analysis (1991) and experiment (1993) faced with a choice of interacting with strangers or not on a one-shot basis. No room for strategic considerations existed for the players.

With no room for strategic considerations in a one-shot dilemma, defection is the dominant choice. This standard description of the one-shot prisoner's dilemma is valid, however, only in the forced play paradigm in which players are forced to play with a particular partner. The addition of the option for not playing itself does not introduce a fundamental change to the game. Figure 2 shows the payoff-matrix in which an extra choice of N (not playing) is added to the original PD matrix shown in Figure 1a. No dominant choice exists in Figure 2 anymore. If Player A expects that the partner, Player B, to cooperate, D is the best choice for A. If A expects that B would defect, then N is the best choice. Despite these new features of the transformed matrix, however, it still remains true that there is no incentive-based reason for choosing C over D. In this sense, adding an option for not playing by itself does not make players in a one-shot PD game cooperate.[11]

Player A \ Player B	C	N	D
C	1 / 1	0 / 0	-3 / 3
N	0 / 0	0 / 0	0 / 0
D	3 / -3	0 / 0	-1 / -1

Figure 2 Payoff matrix in which the option for not playing to a prisoner's dilemma, N, has been added to the original payoff matrix shown in Figure 1a

The above analysis of the payoff-matrix does not fully appreciate the logic provided by the embeddedness of the

[11] This conclusion differs from the conclusion of Vanberg and Congleton (1992), since their simulation was not on-shot games. Their players had an additional choice of not playing, but the game was repeated until the exit option was chosen.

PD-relationship. The analysis was, in a sense, localized to the particular dyad, and macro implications of the players' choices were ignored. What Orbell & Dawes (1991,1993) demonstrated is the macro im plications of the option for not playing, the fact that the option for not playing changes the population composition of the players. They focused on the entire population composed of players endowed with the option for not playing instead of on a particular player or a particular relationship. The effect of adding the option for not playing at the individual player's or relationship's level is the transformation of the payoff-matrix mentioned above. At the global level, however, it changes the composition of the available population. With the option for not playing, the entire population of game players now consists of the ones who have chosen to play; the ones who have chosen not to play weed themselves out of the pool of "available" players. Orbell & Dawes (1991,1993) further argue that this new pool of available players who have chosen to play is different from the original population of players in their average level of cooperativeness due to the false consensus effect. False consensus is the tendency that people overestimate similarities between themselves and the others.[12] Orbell & Dawes (1991,1993) interpreted the correlation between own cooperation and expectation of the others' cooperation frequently observed in social dilemma research (e.g., Dawes, McTavish & Shaklee,1977; Marwell & Ames,1979; Yamagishi & Sato,1986; Tyszka & Grzelak,1976) to be mostly due to the effect of false consensus. Given this consensus, and the resulting correlation between own cooeprativeness and expectation of the others' cooperativeness, majority in the pool of players who have chosen to play would be trustful *and* cooperative players.[13] Only trustful players who expect that the other players are cooperative would choose to play, and, given the correlation resulting from the aforementioned false consensus, those are themselves cooperative players as well. The nature of the population has now been transformed, and the average cooperation level in the pool of self-selected players should be higher than the average in the original population. This further implies the possibility that cooperative people who have selected themselves into the pool of available players do better than non-cooperative players who have stayed out, since the chance is high that the former players enjoy the fruits of mutual cooperation with another cooperative player in the pool. Orbell & Dawes (1991) analytically demonstrated this possibility, and Orbell & Dawes (1993) demonstrated the same result with a laboratory experiment. In a more recent simulation work, Morikawa, Orbell & Runde (1995) further investigated cooperator's advantages in non-iterated games. In this simulation, they demonstrated that cooperating at about the same rate as the population average is most

---

[12] As a good illustration of this effect, Ross, Greene & House (1977) demonstrated that the subjects who had agreed to walk on campus wearing big sandwich boards expected 62% of the other subjects would do the same whereas those who had not agreed expected only 33% to agree.

[13] This argument assumes that the payoff a player receives when the partner defects is worse than the payoff of not playing.

adaptive.

7 One-shot Play with the Choice of Partners

While Orbell & Dawes (1991,1993) and Morikawa et al.(1995) demonstrated important theoretical implications of freeing players from the constraints of the forced play paradigm, and of analyzing the social context in which a particular relationship is embedded, their players were not allowed to choose partners.[14] The choice of partners (not the choice of whether or not to play but of with whom to play) that did not play any role in Orbell & Dawes (1991,1993), however, was the central concern of Frank, Gilovich & Regan (1993). The environment in which players voluntarily engage in one-shot prisoner's dilemma games *with partners of their choice* is the situation presumed in Frank et al.'s (1993) argument. According to our terminology, this is a fully-fledged one-shot selective play situation. Whether individual players' cooperative dispositions can be discerned by others is the issue Frank et al. (1993) addressed in their experiment. If people somehow discern cooperative players from non-cooperative ones, only cooperative players would be chosen for interaction. Even though non-cooperative players would invite cooperative players into a game, their invitations would not be accepted by cooperators (and by defectors either). Thus, if people somehow discern cooperative players from non-cooperative ones in the selective one-shot play environment, only cooperative players would play the game. In an experiment in which subjects had a group discussion for 30 minutes before playing one-shot prisoner's dilemma games, they demonstrated that subjects predicted the partner's choice (either C or D) more accurately than chance. However, their experiment did not examine whether cooperators would in fact be chosen more often than non-cooperators as interaction partners.

The advantage of choosing to play discussed by Orbell & Dawes (1991,1993) and the advantage of being chosen to play discussed by Frank et al.(1993) provide two independent bases for making cooperation (or having the cooperative disposition) more profitable than defection (or having the non-cooperative disposition) in the selective one-shot play situation. A series of experiments conducted by Yamagishi and his colleagues simultaneously examined these two potential advantages of cooperators using a selective one-shot play paradigm. Subjects in Watanabe & Yamagishi's (1995) experiment met briefly in a group of 9 to 12 members before playing prisoner's dilemma games. Subjects were scheduled such that each subject had a few acquaintances as fellow participants in the same group. Subjects were told that they would play dyadic prisoner's dilemma games with randomly matched participants. While each subject would be matched with a few of the other participants, he/she was able to make only one choice between C and D. That is, if the subject chose C (or D), he/she would cooperate (or defect) with all of his/her partners. The choice of C cost 20 yen (about 20 cents) to the subject and benefited the

---

[14] Players in those experiments and simulations made decisions between playing and not playing. However, they did not decide whom they wanted to interact with.

partner with 100 yen in each relationship. Thus, if a subject decided to choose C and was randomly matched with 4 partners, he/she was required to pay 20 times 4 or 80 yen. If two of the four partners cooperated, he/she would receive 100 yen from each of the two. Overall, the subject would earn 120 (200 minus 80) yen. After all the group members had made their decisions, they were given an unexpected option for declining to play with each of the other participants.[15] They were told that they would play a prisoner's dilemma game on the mutual choice basis. The game would not be played in a relationship in which either the subject or the partner declined to play. They were finally reminded that, although they could choose to play or not with each of the other participants, they could not change the decision of C or D they had made before. Thus, existence of a particularistic relationship between the subject and a particular other was not important for the subject in deciding whether to play or not with that particular partner; what mattered was whether that particular partner looked like one who would cooperate with anyone, not particularly with the subject.

The result of this experiment confirmed both types of advantage. First, cooperators predicted that 72% of the participants would cooperate whereas the average expected cooperation rate among defectors was 55%, and the difference was statistically significant. Furthermore, cooperators chose to interact with an average of 7.48 others and played the game on mutual choice with an average of 6.12 partners; the comparable figures for defectors were 6.24 and 3.24. These differences between cooperators and defectors were also statistically significant. Finally, as Orbell & Dawes (1991,1993) predicted, the average cooperation rate in the actually formed pairs was 86%, which was significantly higher than the overall average cooperation rate of 76%. These results provide additional empirical support for the advantage of choosing to play predicted by Orbell & Dawes (1991,1993). At the same time, results of this experiment provide a support for the advantage of being chosen to play predicted by Frank et al.(1993). As predicted by Frank et al.(1993), cooperators were chosen more frequently (by an average of 7.88 others) than were defectors (an average of 4.95 others), and the difference was statistically significant. A replication of this experiment with a few design changes[16] (Kikuchi, Watanabe & Yamagishi,1995) confirmed Orbell & Dawes's (1991,1993) prediction that cooperators would choose to play more often than defectors, but failed to confirm Frank et al.'s (1993) prediction that cooperators would be chosen more frequently than defectors.

---

[15] In another condition, subjects decided whom they would play with before making the decision between C and D. Watanabe & Yamagishi (1995) predicted that the cooperator's advantage would emerge only in the condition described in the main text. This prediction received a support by the experimental result. See Watanabe & Yamagishi (1995) for the reasoning behind this prediction.

[16] Subjects discussed in groups of 6 for 30 minutes on various problems related to garbage collection. After the discussion, subjects were randomly separated into two groups of three each. The rest of the procedures was similar to the previous experiment (Watanabe & Yamagishi,1995).

8 Downward OFT versus Downward TFT

With the introduction of the option for selecting interaction partners, the scope of the incentive basis for cooperation has been greatly expanded. It was shown that in the selective play environment cooperators can and often do better than defectors, and the requirement of a long-term future relationship for the emergence of cooperation is no longer needed. A similar expansion was explored recently by Takahashi & Yamagishi (in press) in the context of unilateral resource giving. The problem they pursued in their simulation was how to explain altruistic behavior in the situation where no direct return can be expected. A person who helps a driver stuck in the snow, for example, will have practically no chance of getting a help from the *same* driver when she needs one in a similar situation in the future. Such a situation is similar to the one-shot prisoner's dilemma situation in the sense that no room for reciprocity exists in either situation.

Approaching the same problem from biology, Boyd & Richerson (1989) demonstrated that a strategy called "downward TFT" is effective in promoting altruistic behavior in a unilateral resource giving situation. What is assumed in their study is a circle of unilateral resource giving, A→B→C→....→A, where a player cannot directly return a favor to the one who has provided a favor to him/her. Downward TFT is the strategy according to which a player, A, provides resources to the player next in line on the circle (A→B) insofar as the player had provided resources to his/her next neighbor (B→C). In contrast, their simulation results show that another strategy called the "upward TFT"—a player, B, provides resources to the player next in line on the circle (B→C) insofar as he/she has been provided resources by his/her upward neighbor (A→B)—is not effective in promoting altruistic behavior at all. The effectiveness of the downward TFT in promoting altruistic behavior or one-way resource giving is also reported by Yamagishi & Cook (1993) who studied four-person and eight-person chain of one-way resource giving in laboratory experiments. Many subjects in their experiments did use the downward TFT strategy and unilaterally provided resources at a high level.[17]

The effectiveness of the downward TFT, however, requires the existence of a fixed network structure, a requirement similar to the requirement of the fixed dyadic relationship for the effectiveness of TFT. In this sense, the "chain-generalized exchange system" (Ekeh, 1974; Yamagishi & Cook,1993) represents a forced play version of one-way resource giving. This forced play nature of the chain-generalized exchange system was removed in Takahashi & Yamagishi's (in press) simulation where players selected the target of their unilateral resource giving. The choice of targets of altruistic behavior in this simulation expanded the scope of the research from the forced play paradigm to the selective play paradigm. In this simulation, all players had the "downward OFT" strategy according to which a

[17] The level of unilateral resource giving was even higher (although the difference was not statistically significant) in 8-person chains than in 4-person chains.

player kept giving resources at a level reflecting the player's "altruism" to the same target insofar as the target had given her own resources to someone else at a "satisfactory" level. If the target's level of altruistic behavior did not reach the "satisfactory" level, the player stopped giving own resources to that target with a certain probability and instead gave resources to a randomly selected target. Some players were more "demanding" than the others and were "satisfied" only when the target was more altruistic than themselves (that is, when the target gave more resources than the player him/herself did). More lenient players were "satisfied" even when the target was less altruistic than themselves. What was examined in the simulation was whether players' level of "altruism" would evolve (that is, whether the amount of resource given out would increase) over "generations" if players have adopted the downward OFT strategy; the purpose of the simulation was *not* to examine whether the use of downward OFT would come to be widely accepted by the players.[18] Results of this computer simulation indicate the effectiveness of "fairness-minded downward OFT" in one-way resource giving in the absence of a fixed network structure. That is, the level of players' altruism increased over generations and stayed at a fairly high level when and only when players were neither too demanding nor too lenient. When players were too demanding, even highly altruistic players failed to receive enough resources from the other players and eventually died out. When players were too lenient, even "stingy" players received resources from the other players and became to dominate the population over generations. It was only when players were "satisfied" with the target who was at least equally altruistic as the players themselves that players' level of altruism increased to over generations.

In a recently completed experiment, Yamagishi and his colleagues experimentally examined whether one-way resource giving in fact would "evolve." Members of six-person groups decided how much and to whom they were to give money. They could give any amount between 0 and 10 yen (about 10 cents) per trial. The one who was given the money received twice the amount provided by the donor. The money they kept to themselves was to be accumulated and paid to them, together with money they received from the other participants, at the end of the experiment. It was practically impossible, however, to return the favor to the donor since information about who gave to whom was not revealed to them. The only information subjects had in deciding to whom and how much to give was the amount of donation each of the other participants provided in the previous trial. This information was displayed on the subject's computer display in descending order according to the amount of money the other players gave. Players were not marked with personal identification symbols, and thus the subject could not trace the history of a particular player. This experiment represents a unilateral resource giving situation without any fixed network structure. No direct reciprocity was possible in this situation, and thus no incentive for the "altruistic" behavior (giving up to 10 yen per trial to someone else whose identity the subject did not know)

---

[18] See Axelrod (1984,1986) for the logic behind this type of "evolutionary" simulation.

seemed to exist. Nonetheless, subjects of this experiment displayed a fairly high level of "altruism," providing an average of 6.74 yen of the total of 10 yen per trial. Most of the subjects in this experiment had adopted strategies broadly classified as downward OFT by the end of the experiment (the 45th trial). First, they were almost fully "cooperative," providing close to 10 yen each trial. Second, they gave to the participant who had given the most in the previous trial. It is interesting to note that subjects in this experiment have unknowingly created a situation in which full cooperation was a Nash equilibrium. They did so by "rewarding" the most "altruistic" player. Insofar as most players act in this manner, giving at least some money to the most "altruistic" player, acting altruistically becomes a "rational" choice. On the other hand, if most players had not rewarded "altruistic" players, this equilibrium would not have been reached; they would have reached another equilibrium where no one provided any money.

9 A Typology of Selective Play

The research presented above only partially represents the entire range potentially covered by the selective play paradigm. Table 1 presents a typology of research formats to be covered under the rubric of selective play. The typology presented there has been created by combining the three features discussed above—what options players have, whether or not the game is repeated, and whether or not direct reciprocity exists. A cursory look at the table reveals the existence of situations that have not been studied so far. In the row of "no exit option, choice of payoff size," three cells are empty. Cell 7 in the table represents a one-shot variant of the experiment by Yamagishi & Kakiuchi; players choose the size of their payoffs before playing a one-shot PD. The other two cells might provide interesting research environment. Cells 6 and 8 represent a chain-generalized exchange situation in which each player may unilaterally either reward or exploit another player. Unilaterally rewarding another player costs the player, say, a dollar, and the target receives two dollars. The player who unilaterally exploit another player earns a dollar while imposing a loss of two dollars on the target. You, as a target in this situation has a choice of multiplying these figures by a certain factor. Would you prefer the incentive structure mentioned above, or another incentive structure in which all figures are ten times as large as the current one so that you receive $20 instead of $2 or lose $20 instead of $2. In Cells 10 and 12 no fixed-network structure (or a chain) exists. Each player rewards or exploits another player, and the choice players face is whether they join in the situation or not. The action-expectation correlation based on false consensus may have the same effect here as in Cell 11, the situation studied by Orbell & Dawes's (1993). Cells 15 and 16 are logically untenable, and thus we do not discuss them here.[19] Finally, Cell 20 represents a one-shot version of Takahashi & Yamagishi's (1995) simulation. What theoretical issues are involved in this cell is not clear to us yet.

[19] In one-shot games the player who has chosen not to play does not play a game.

Table 1 Typology of selective play

	Repeated Play		One-shot Play	
Options	Direct Reciprocity	No Direct Reciprocity	Direct Reciprocity	No Direct Reciprocity
No Exit Option	[Cell 1] Standard Iterated Prisoner's Dilemma	[Cell 2] Chain-generalized exchange; Yamagishi & Cook's (1993) experiment; Boyd & Richarson's (1989) simulation	[Cell 3] Standard One-shot Prisoner's Dilemma	[Cell 4] Experiments of pure altruism; e.g., Orbell, van de Kragt & Dawes (1988), Yamagishi (1990), Kiyonari & Yamagishi (1995)
No Exit Option, Choice of Payoff Size	[Cell 5] Experiments by Yamagishi & Kakiuchi and by van Lange et al.(1995)	[Cell 6]	[Cell 7]	[Cell 8]
Exit Option with No Alternative Partner; Choice of playing or not playing*	[Cell 9] Simulation by Vanberg & Congleton (1992)	[Cell 10]	[Cell 11] Experijments by Orbell & Dawes's (1993); Simulation by Morikawa et al. (1995)	[Cell 12]
Exit Option with Random Assignment of a New Partner	[Cell 13] Simulations by Schuessler (1989) and by Hayashi (1995b)	[Cell 14] Simulation by Takahashi & Yamagishi (in press)	[Cell 15]	[Cell 16]
Choice of Partners	[Cell 17] Prisoner's Dilemma Network; Experiments by Jin et al. (1993), Yamagishi and Komiyama (1995); simulation by Hayashi (1993) and by Hayashi et al.(1993)	[Cell 18] Experiment by Yamagishi & his colleagues (unpublished)	[Cell 19] Experiments by Watanabe & Yamagishi (1995) and by Kikuchi et al.(1995)	[Cell 20]

*The option of not playing in a one-shot game implies that the player who has chosen not to play does not play at all (i.e., has no partner to play a game with).

10 Theoretical Implications

The overall image of the actor that has emerged from the research discussed in this paper as the most efficient player in the selective play environment is the one who is *nice*, *prudent* and *trustful*. Niceness plays a positive role in three contexts. First, in the repeated selective play situation involving direct reciprocity, players have to be nice in order to be selected by other players. Only the choice of a nice player may be reciprocated by another nice player. Second, niceness or cooperativeness is needed for a player to be chosen by other players even in the one-shot context insofar as players can discern cooperators from defectors in a brief interaction as demonstrated by Frank et al.(1993) and Kikuchi et al.(1995). If people are in fact endowed with such capability for identifying cooperators in a relatively brief encounter, niceness would play the same role in the one-shot environment as in the repeated play environment. Finally, given the correlation between niceness and trustfulness, nice players will have a larger chance of encountering another nice player, again even in the one-shot context. Nice players tend to overestimate the cooperative tendencies of other players and thus self-select themselves into a social dilemma situation, resulting in a higher cooperation rate among the actual players than among the entire population of players (Orbell & Dawes,1991,1993).

Prudence is another important feature for a player to be successful in the selective play environment. Prudence takes the form of retaliation in kind in the case of TFT. In the case of OFT, prudence takes the form of leaving the relationship. In either case, prudent players never continues exposing themself vulnerable to "predators." Although the combination of niceness and prudence is critical for a success of a player even in the forced play environment, as evidenced by the success of the TFT strategy in Axelrod's (1984) computer tournament, the same combination is even more important in the selective play environment because responding the partner's defection by leaving the relation never starts the vicious circle of conflict spiral (Deutsch & Krauss,1960; Lawler,1986). In fact, a preliminary analysis of the experiment by Yamagishi and Kakiuchi mentioned above suggest that subjects who responded to a defecting partner by reducing the payoff size while keeping cooperating performed better than those who responded in kind.

Finally, and most importantly, *trust* is the unique feature defining the successful player in the selective play environment. In the one-shot play context discussed by Orbell & Dawes (1991,1993), trust pulls players out of the security of isolation and thus sets them out to harvest the crop of mutual cooperation in a social dilemma situation. Although such a trustful person can be exploited by defectors, the correlation between trust and cooperativeness provides a safeguard at the macro level for the trustful against becoming a victim. In the repeated play context, trust prevents players from forming a commitment relationship prematurely and thus helps them to capitalize on potentially profitable relations and to reduce opportunity costs.[20] Here again, trustful players can become a target of exploitation by defectors, but the aforementioned *prudence* helps them from serious losses imposed by defecting partners. The advantage of trust in the selective play context, however, is limited only to nice (i.e., cooperative) players. "Nasty" players who are trustful may as well seek to capitalize on potentially profitable opportunities, but they will not be chosen by others and thus cannot exploit the opportunities. Only nice players enjoy the fruits of trust since they are the only ones whose invitation is likely to be responded. Thus, the correlation between trust and cooperativeness that is treated as an extraneous factor (i.e., extraneous to the social dilemma incentive structure) is likely to emerge internally in the repeated play context. In the context of repeated selective play with relatively high opportunity costs, cooperators

[20] This is the "emancipation function" of trust discussed by Yamagishi & Yamagishi (1994).

would be better off by trusting than not trusting since trust helps them to capitalize on outside opportunities. This would create the cooperativeness-trust correlation and make the combination of trustfulness and cooperativeness even more profitable through the self-selection process discussed by Orbell & Dawes (1991,1993).

The advantage of having a high level of trust in the high-opportunity cost situation constitutes the core of Yamagishi & Yamagishi's (1994) "emancipation theory" of trust. They argue that trust "emancipates" people from confines of "*Yakuza*-type commitment" (Yamagishi,1995a) and thus helps them capitalize on opportunities that exist outside the commitment relationship. *Yakuza*-type commitment is formed as a means to provide a "guarantee" of mutual cooperation, typically characterizing the relationship between a boss and his soldiers in *Yakuza* (Japanese equivalent of Mafia) organization. Such an advantage of trust as a tool for pulling people out of the security of commitment relationship should be greater when opportunity costs are generally high than low. Yamagishi & Yamagishi (1994) draws a hypothesis based on this theory of trust that the average level of general trust (trust in people in general) would be higher in American society than in Japanese society. This counter-intuitive hypothesis was confirmed by the result of their cross-societal questionnaire survey.[21] Their survey results also replicated the previous findings (Chun & Campbell,1974; Kaplan,1973; Yamagishi, 1988) that trust does not necessarily imply lack of prudence, and argued that prudent trusters are most advantaged in an uncertain world characterized with high opportunity costs (see also Yamagishi,1995a,b,c,d; Yamagishi & Komiyama,1995; Yamagishi, Watabe, Hayashi, Takahashi & Yamagishi, in Press; Yamagishi, Yamagishi, Takahashi, Hayashi & Watabe,1995, for more elaborate discussions on this issue). A series of follow-up studies (Kikuchi et al.,1995; Kiyonari & Yamagishi,1995; Kosugi & Yamagishi,1995) further provides evidence that high-trusters who are trustful of people in general are actually more capable of discerning cooperators from defectors and are more sensitive to information potentially revealing trustworthiness of a person. In these experiments high-trusters were more accurate in predicting other participants' behavior than low-trusters. For example, subjects in Kikuchi et al.'s (1995) experiment predicted whether two other randomly matched strangers with whom they had had a discussion on garbage collection issue for 20 minutes would cooperate or defect in a PD game. One point of accuracy score was given to a subject who correctly predicted the choice of both partners; the accuracy score of a subject who was correct on one but not correct on the other was 0.5; the accuracy score of a subject who failed on both was 0. The average accuracy score of high-trusters (n=23) was 0.57, which was significantly higher than the accuracy score, 0.42, of low-trusters (n=25). In an experiment by Kiyonari & Yamagishi (1995), high-trusters were able to discern "fair" players from "unfair" ones more accurately than were low-trusters in the context of unilateral resource distribution.

---

[21] Another questionnaire survey using representative national samples both in the U. S. and Japan (Hayashi, Suzuki, Suzuki & Murakami,1982) also found that Americans were more trustful than Japanese.

And, in a vignette experiment, Kosugi & Yamagishi (1995) showed that high-trusters responded more quickly to negative clues that could potentially reveal untrustworthiness of a target than did low-trusters. In the absense of such clues high-trusters expected that the target would act in a more trustworthy way than did low-trusters. However, when negative clues were provided, the high-trusters' expectation of the trustworthiness of the target became lower than that of low-trusters.

Based on these findings, Yamagishi (1995b) is proposing an "investment model" of trust development. According to this model, people who are raised in an environment characterized with a high level of opportunity costs invest a large amount of cognitive resources (attentions, etc.) in discerning cooperators from defectors. People who have made such "investment" can quickly detect signals of trustworthiness and untrustworthiness in others. For them it is relatively safe to maintain a high level of default expectation about trustworthiness of unknown person and expand relations with new partners since they can quickly pull out of the relations with an early sign of a danger. In contrast, people who are raised in a low-opportunity cost environment (e.g., in a traditionally isolated mountain village where people hardly meet outsiders) do not invest a large amount of cognitive resources in discerning cooperators from defectors and thus need to maintain trust in strangers at a very low level. In this sense, prudence, not lack of prudence, constitutes the foundation of general trust. Given a high level of opportunity costs in the environment, investment in such "cognitive capital" generates a dividend in the form of a higher level of trust that sets people out to capitalize on profitable opportunities outside the security of a commitment relationship.

The three factors that have been shown above to be critical for a success in the selective play environment, niceness, prudence and trust, are useless unless all three are simultaneously present. Niceness means vulnerability or even gullibility without being backed up by prudence (either TFT or OFT). The advantage of trust is limited to nice players; for nasty players trust is only a liability. Similarly, prudence is not needed unless the player is nice and/or trustful. Some of the combinations among these factors may be supplied by processes extraneous to the social dilemma incentive structure, as in the case of false consensus discussed by Orbell & Dawes (1991,1993). However, the incentive structure of social dilemmas may contain within itself bases for some of the combinations, as suggested by Yamagishi's (1995b) investment model of trust development. More of such internal processes may be discovered[22] as more social dilemma researchers start appre-

[22] Another very interesting theoretical development that has occurred in the past few years concerns the importance of the "multiple trait approach" (Yamagishi,1995e). According to this approach, cognitive traits or behavioral dispositions that are not effective in providing a solution to the social dilemma problem insofar as they vary independently of each other provide an effective solution to the problem if they vary together. A good example of this is the action-expectation correlation discussed by Orbell & Dawes (1991,1993). Another example is the consistency of actions in the first order dilemma and in the second order dilemma discussed by Yamagishi & Takahashi (1994).

ciating theoretical implications of the social embeddedness of social dilemmas.

References

Axelrod, R. (1984). *The evolution of cooperation.* New York: Basic Books.

Axelrod, R. (1986). An evolutionary approach to norms. *American Political Science Review, 80,* 1095-1111.

Boyd, R. & Richarson, P. J. (1989). The evolution of indirect reciprocity. *Social Networks, 11,* 213-236.

Chun, K. & Campbell, J. B. (1974). Dimensionality of the Rotter Interpersonal Trust Scale. *Psychological Report, 35,* 1059-1070.

Dawes, R. M., McTavish, J., & Shaklee, H. (1977). Behavior, communication and assumptions about other people's behavior in a commons dilemma situation. *Journal of Personality and Social Psychology, 35,* 1-11.

Deutsch, M. & Krauss, R. M. (1960). The effect of threat upon interpersonal bargaining. *Journal of Abnormal and Social Psychology,* 61, 181-189.

Ekeh, P. P. (1974). *Social exchange theory: The two traditions.* Cambridge: Harvard University Press.

Frank, R. H., Gilovich, T., & Regan, D. T. (1993). The evolution of one-shot cooperation: An experiment. *Ethology and Sociobiology, 14,* 247-256

Hayashi, C., Suzuki, T., Suzuki, G., & Murakami, M. (1982). *A study of Japanese national character, Volume 4.* Tokyo: Idemitsushoten. (In Japanese with an English summary)

Hayashi, N. (1993). From TIT-FOR-TAT to OUT-FOR-TAT. *Sociological Theory and Methods, 8,* 19-32. (In Japanese with an English abstract)

Hayashi, N. (1995a). Emergence of cooperation in one-shot prisoner's dilemmas and the role of trust. Paper presented at the 6th International Conference on Social Dilemmas. June 18-23, NIAS, Wassenaar, NL.

Hayashi, N. (1995b). Emergence of cooperation in one-shot prisoner's dilemmas and the role of trust. *Japanese Journal of Psychology, 66,* 184-190. (In Japanese with an English abstract)

Hayashi, N. (1995c). *Theoretical and empirical research on the socio-relational basis of "irrational" cooperation.* Doctoral dissertation submitted for review to Department of Behavioral Science, Hokkaido University, Sapporo, Japan. (In Japanese)

Hayashi, N., Jin, N. & Yamagishi, T. (1993). Prisoner's Dilemma network: A computer simulation of strategies. *Research in Social Psychology, 8,* 33-43. (In Japanese with an English abstract)

Hayashi, N. & Yamagishi, T. (1995). A socio-relational basis of "irrational" cooperation: An experimental study. Paper submitted for publication. (In Japanese with an English abstract)

Jin, N., Hayashi, N., & Shinotsuka, H. (1993). An experimental study of Prisoner's Dilemma network: The formation of commitment in selective dyads. *Japanese Journal of Experimental Social Psychology, 33,* 21-30. (In Japanese with an

English abstract)
Kaplan, R. M. (1973). Components of tust: Note on use of Rotter's scale. *Psychological Report, 33*, 13-14.
Kikuchi, M., Watanabe, Y. & Yamagishi, T. (1995). Trust and prediction of others' behavior: An experimental study. *Proceedings of the 43rd annual meetings of the Japanese Group Dynamics Association*, 164-165. (In Japanese)
Kiyonari, T. & Yamagishi, T. (1995). General trust and cautiousness: An experimental study. *Proceedings of the 43rd annual meetings of the Japanese Group Dynamics Association*, 152-153. (In Japanese)
Kosugi, M. & Yamagishi, T. (1995). Trust as a cognitive trait. *Proceedings of the 43rd annual meetings of the Japanese Group Dynamics Association*, 150-151. (In Japanese)
Lawler, E. J. (1986). Bilateral deterrence and conflict spiral: A theoretical analysis. Pp.107-130 in Lawler, E. J. (Ed.), *Advances in group processes, vol. 3*. Greenwich, CT: JAI Press.
Marwell, G. & Ames, R. E. (1979). Experiments on the provision of public goods, I: Resources, interest, group size, and the free-rider problem. *American Journal of Sociology, 84*, 1335-1360.
Marwell, G. & Schmitt, D. R. (1972). Cooperation in a three-person prisoner's dilemma. *Journal of Personality and Social Psychology, 21*, 376-383.
Morikawa, T., Orbell, J. M., & Runde, A. S. (1995). The advantage of being moderately cooperative. *American Political Science Review, 89*, 601-611.
Orbell, J., & Dawes, R. M. (1991). A cognitive miser theory of cooperators' advantage. *American Political Science Review, 85*, 515-528.
Orbell, J. & Dawes, R. M. (1993). Social welfare, cooperator's advantage, and the option of not playing the game. *American Sociological Review, 58*, 787-800.
Orbell, J., Schwartz-Shea, P., & Simmons, R. T. (1984). Do cooperators exit more readily than defectors? *American Political Science Review, 78*, 147-162.
Orbell, J., van de Kragt, A., & Dawes, R. M. (1988). Explaining discussion-induced cooperation. *Journal of Personality and Social Psychology, 54*, 811-819.
Ross, L., Greene, D. & House, P. (1977). The "false consensus effect": An egocentric bias in social perseption and attribution processes. *Journal of Experimental Social Psychology, 13*, 279-301.
Schuessler, R. (1989). Exit threats and cooperation under anonymity. *Journal of Conflict Resolution, 33*, 728-749.
Takahashi, N. & Yamagishi, T. In Press. Social relational foundations of altruistic behavior. *Japanese Journal of Experimental Social Psychology*. (In Japanese with an English abstract)
Tyszka, T. & Grzelak, J. L. (1976). Criteria of choice in nonconstant zero-sum games. *Journal of Conflict Resolution, 20*, 357-376.
Vanberg, V. & Congleton, R. (1992). Rationality, morality, and exit. *American Political Science Review, 86*, 418-431.
van Lange, P. A. M., Camac, C., Visser, K., & Marsman, G. (1995). Movement in social dilemmas. Paper presented at the 6th International Conference on Social Dilemmas. June 18-23, NIAS, Wassenaar, NL.

Watanabe, Y & Yamagishi, T. (1995). When "false consensus" turns out to be not false: An experimental study. *Proceedings of the 43rd annual meetings of the Japanese Group Dynamics Association*, 160-161. (In Japanese)

Yamagishi, T. (1988). The provision of a sanctioning system in the United States and Japan. *Social Psychology Quarterly, 51*, 265-271.

Yamagishi, T. (1990). Factors mediating residual effects of group size in social dilemmas. *Japanese Journal of Psychology, 61*, 162-169. (In Japanese with an English abstract)

Yamagishi, T. (1995a). Yakuzas, lovers, commitment, and trust. Paper presented at Workshop on Construction and Maintenance of Trust, Feb. 25-26, New York.

Yamagishi, T. (1995b). Trust, distrust and cautiousness. *Proceedings of the 43rd annual meetings of the Japanese Group Dynamics Association*, 3-33. (In Japanese)

Yamagishi, T. (1995c). Trust as cognition, trust as reflection. Paper presented at the Second Workshop on Construction and Maintenance of Trust. September 9-10, Seattle.

Yamagishi, T. (1995d). Have Americans really become distrustful? Paper presented at the American Sociological Association Annual Meetings. Washington, D.C., August 19-23, 1995.

Yamagishi, T. (1995e). Recent promising developments in the social dilemmas research. Paper presented at the Sixth International Conference of Social Dilemmas, Wassenaar, NL, June 18-23.

Yamagishi, T. & Cook, K. S. (1993). Generalized exchange and social dilemmas. *Social Psychology Quarterly, 56*, 235-249.

Yamagishi, T., Hayashi, N., & Jin, N. (1994). Prisoner's dilemma networks: Selection strategy versus action strategy. Pp.233-250 in Schulz, U., Albers, W. & Mueller, U. (Eds.) *Social dilemmas and cooperation*. Berlin: Springer-Verlag.

Yamagishi, T. & Komiyama, H. (1995). Significance and the structure of trust: Theoretical and empirical research on trust and commitment relations. *INSS Journal*, 2, 1-59. (In Japanese with an English abstract)

Yamagishi, T. & Sato, K. (1986). Motivational bases of the public good problem. *Journal of Personality and Social Psychology, 50*, 67-73.

Yamagishi, T. & Takahashi, N. (1994). Evolution of norms without metanorms. Pp.311-326 in Schulz, U., Albers, W. & Mueller, U. (Eds.) *Social dilemmas and cooperation*. Berlin: Springer-Verlag.

Yamagishi, T., Watabe, M., Hayashi, N., Takahashi, N. & Yamagishi, M. In Press. Trust and commitment under social uncertainty. *Research in Social Psychology*. (In Japanese with an English abstract)

Yamagishi, T. & Yamagishi, M. (1994). Trust and commitment in the United States and Japan. *Motivation and Emotion, 18*, 129-166.

Yamagishi, T., Yamagishi, M., Takahashi, N., Hayashi, N., & Watabe, M. (1995). Trust and commitment formation: An experimental study. *Japanese Journal of Experimental Social Psychology*, 35, 23-34. (In Japanese with an English abstract)

'Self-organizing' Friendship Networks

Frans N. Stokman and Evelien P.H. Zeggelink[1]

[1] University of Groningen, Interuniversity Center for Social Science Theory and Methodology (ICS), Groningen, The Netherlands

Abstract. We introduce principles of self-organization in a dynamic individual oriented model of the evolution of friendship networks. The main aim of the model is to explain the emergence of structure in a friendship network from an initial situation of mutual strangers.

In contrast to the individual behavioral rules in previously developed models, we explicitly deal with the interplay between network dynamics and changing characteristics of individuals as a result of their friendships. Moreover, learning mechanisms and 'bounded' rationality principles, due to limited information and restricted capabilities to foresee strategically, are more explicitly dealt with.

The incorporation of these elements is facilitated by the application of principles of self-organization known from the fields of cellular automata and neural networks.

Keywords. Evolution, simulation, social networks, friendship, rational choice models, backward learning, clustering

1. Introduction[1]

The question "How does social network structure emerge?" is difficult to answer, but the attempt to do so is necessary and certainly challenging. It is challenging because the emergence of structure involves a process between two different levels of analysis: the micro - and the macro level, individuals and structure. It is even more challenging because the process deals with causes at the local micro level and consequences at the more encompassing global macro level (Lin, 1994).

Social network analysis in general studies (the behavior of) the individual at the micro level, and the pattern of relationships (network structure) at the macro level. Almost all social network studies focus on a description of the

---

[1] Part of the research was carried out while the first author was research fellow at the Netherlands Institute for Advanced Studies in the Humanities and Social Sciences (NIAS) in Wassenaar (The Netherlands) and the second author a visiting postdoctoral fellow at the University of California, Irvine, USA. The latter stay was subsidized by the Netherlands Organization for Scientific Research (NWO, grant nr. S50-384). The research of the second author has also been made possible by a fellowship of the Royal Netherlands Academy of Arts and Sciences. We thank Henk Hangyi and the editors for their comments on an earlier draft.

static network structure (Sprenger & Stokman, 1989; Wasserman and Faust, 1994) and / or the effects of the network structure on the behavior and attributes of the network members. In other words, the network is considered given and constant, and it is examined how this network influences processes or individuals within the network, i.e. macro-micro phenomena are studied (e.g. Erickson, 1988; Hansel, 1985; Morris, 1991; Leenders, 1995). It is usually ignored that these networks are dynamic entities and change over time, let alone that it is taken into account how these networks came into existence from individual actions. An answer to this question can be extremely helpful in understanding processes that operate in the opposite direction: from the network to the individual. Therefore, in this paper we deal with the problem of the emergence of network structure as a result of individual actions and interactions. We investigate whether the emergence of network structure itself can be seen as a social dilemma where the network resulting from these individual actions is suboptimal for all members in the group. This gives a new perspective to the relationship between social networks and social dilemmas. In the past, in the field of social dilemmas, the emphasis was on the effect a given network structure on compliance (Homans, 1951; Hogg, 1992). Important exceptions are Glance and Huberman (1994), Flache and Macy (1996), and Flache (1996). The former focus on fluid structures in organizations and their effect on cooperation, the latter on compliance in social production groups. Flache and Macy dispute the often found relationship between density of affective relations and compliance in such groups. They emphasize that approval can be exchanged against approval (and thus be an aim in itself), whereas former studies solely emphasized the exchange of approval against compliance. We pursue that line of reasoning and focus on the emergence of affective relationships, independent of individual goals outside the relationships themselves (like compliance to group goals or cooperation in organizations). Our emphasis is on conditions under which friendship networks tend to result in highly clustered networks. Moreover, we investigate whether such clustering effects have negative consequences for the realization of the 'desired' number of friendships. How such a clustering is related to the attainment of external group goals is beyond the scope of this article, but it will be clear that highly clustered affective networks do not promote cooperation of the group as a whole and will influence the relationship between density and compliance. As we will see later, in our model, the clustering effect is stronger in sparse networks (where the number of 'desired' friendships of group members is relatively small) than in dense networks with larger numbers of 'desired' friendships. This raises the question whether the often reported relation between density and compliance cannot (partially) be attributed to these stronger clustering effects in less dense networks.

In our approach we assume that phenomena at the macro level can only be understood from individual actions at the micro level. However, network structure as it exists is seldom constructed consciously by its individuals. It is often the 'unintended' effect of individual actions and can as such be called a "spontaneous order" (see e.g. Hayek, 1973; Witt, 1994). This is especially true and interesting when relationships, such as friendships, emerge from individual choice: individuals initiate, construct, maintain, and break up friendships and thereby determine the global structure of the friendship network. The examination of this kind of phenomena is not simple: cause and consequence of network structure are difficult to separate because on the one hand, individuals actively construct the network, and on the other hand, they simultaneously react on it. The network provides and limits opportunities for choices of individuals. To explain network structure, both directions, from the individual to the network and from the network to the individual, need to be taken into account.

This is enabled by the construction of so-called individual oriented models. Such models take into account the differences in attributes and behavior of individuals and furthermore explicitly consider the influence of the network on the individual. Our individual oriented models start with a set of 'rational' individuals. Every individual has a goal function which he or she tries to optimize (utility maximization). Attempts to optimize take place by establishing and breaking up friendships. This behavior is formulated within a certain action space: a number of alternative actions from which the individual may choose. That alternative is chosen, that, according to the expectations of the individual, will lead to the largest increase of utility for him or her. The real increase of utility of individuals does not only depend on their own actions but also on the (unknown, possibly simultaneous) actions of the others. Thus, an essential subsequent step is how these individual behaviors interact and lead to a network structure. This aggregation of individual behaviors into a network structure is more than just the sum of individual actions because not all actions are successful. The formulation of the individual behavioral rules is the most important aspect of modelling. Interesting elements of this part of the modelling are that every individual has only limited capacity to foresee strategically and furthermore has only limited information: this concerns models of bounded rationality. With regard to these kind of cognitive elements, existing models of friendship network evolution constructed within this approach (among others: Zeggelink, 1993, 1995; Zeggelink et al., 1996) have been too limited.

The preliminary incorporation of some of such cognitive elements is one of the main goals of the present paper. While aiming at this goal, we think that much can be benefited by taking over a number of principles from theories of cellular automata and neural networks (Stokman and Doreian, 1996). In particular, we want to show how principles of self organization, known from these fields, can be implemented in dynamic models of friendship network evolution such that these models resemble reality more closely than they did previously.

In Section 2, we first summarize our existing models of friendship network evolution and present their main limitations. In Section 3 we summarize principles of self-organization that may prove to be useful in the application to social networks. Subsequently, we introduce self-organizing principles into the dynamic modelling of friendship network evolution in Section 4. In Section 5 we illustrate the workings of the new model by showing some simulation results. Section 6 contains some remarks on future developments.

2. Previous dynamic models of friendship network evolution and their limitations

The main goal of our previous individual oriented models of friendship network evolution is the prediction of global network structure based on simple individual behavioral rules of friendship formation (Zeggelink, 1993, 1994, 1995, 1996, Zeggelink et al., 1996). These behavioral rules take into account that individuals differ in their need for social contact, show a preference for similarity in one's friends, and tend to form subgroups. The number of friends in these models is always that important such that an individual never establishes more friendships than 'desired'.[2] The choices they make depend on their preferences with regard to similarity aspects and group membership. In each of these models, friendships cannot dissolve. Once a friendship choice is mutual, a friendship is assumed to be established and maintained. This is a relatively strong assumption because individuals may become or show to be less attractive than they were supposed to be initially. Also, other individuals may show or become more attractive over time. This assumption of maintenance will be relaxed in the model to be developed here. Moreover, in the previous models every individual is assumed to know the total number of individuals in the population, is informed about the relevant characteristics of all other individuals, and is able to discern subgroups of friends. An individual will never approach an other individual for friendship twice, once that individual has shown not to be interested in a friendship. It seems more plausible to assume that individuals learn about the behavior of others in a more subtle manner.

In order to extend the limitations described above, by incorporating more realistic assumptions, we distinguish two relevant elements of individual behavioral rules that refer to aspects of bounded rationality: the *capability of imagination* and the *amount of information*. The former represents that individuals can never fully foresee the end results of their own actions. In existing models it is usually assumed that individuals apply so-called myopic behavioral rules, meaning that they can imagine only what would happen at the next point in time as a result of their own actions. This capability of imagination is further limited because actions of the other individuals are not

---

[2]This is a strong assumption because the number of friendships an individual can or wants to establish or maintain depends on the strengths of these relationships and the boundaries of his or her available time and energy.

known. Moreover, all individuals act and interact simultaneously. As such, macro effects may emerge that were completely unanticipated by the initiative individuals (Weick, 1979).

As a consequence, in existing models, the individuals always assume that actions of others are such that their own actions will lead to optimal outcomes for themselves. These simplifying assumptions make the individuals relatively 'dumb' in their attempts to achieve their goals. It is seldom taken into consideration that every individual *learns from experience* and can anticipate actions of others (Stokman and Doreian, 1996).

Closely related to the previous aspect is the limited *amount of information* of individuals with regard to other individuals and the network to which they belong.[3] As a result they cannot make accurate calculations of expected utilities of behavioral alternatives. Although individuals can try to obtain more information actively and receive information passively, it remains difficult to possess exact knowledge on all relevant elements in the system to compute the exact utility of a friendship and the probability of success with regard to establishing a friendship. Especially with regard to the latter, individuals learn during the process of friendship formations. In order to 'perform' as good as possible, individuals rely on previous experiences to determine both the probabilities of success and the values of different relationships. Individuals evaluate their friendships with other individuals in order to strengthen those that have been useful and weaken those that have been less useful in the past. As such, individuals use the frequencies of success and failure of their actions in the past as a guideline for future actions.

Individuals do not only use information on their previous behavior and that of others (whether or not their choices were reciprocated) to approximate the probability of success in establishing a friendship. This estimation also involves, if present, knowledge of the others' 'position' in the network and other relevant 'status' attributes.

Another dominant simplifying assumption in existing versions of the friendship model is that individual attributes are non-varying. Differences in individual attributes that matter in the formation of friendship are taken into account but are not subject to change through realized friendships. To make this more realistic, principles of social influence will be incorporated.

The incorporation of mechanisms of social influence and other assumptions with regard to limited information also enables us to introduce the possibility of dissolving friendships. Over time, individuals may now become more or less attractive, not only as a result of their changing individual attributes, but also

[3] Relevant related questions are the following. Which information does an individual have? How does the quality and the quantity of this information depend on the position of the individual in the network? How does an individual cope with limited information? Does he or she try to obtain information more actively? If so, what are the benefits and costs of obtaining information?

as a result of varying probabilities of success with regard to establishing a friendship with the specific individual.

Another important limitation in existing models is that only the preference for similarity and group belongings is considered to be important in the choice of friends. Other, asymmetric, mechanisms, like the preference for those with higher 'status' also play an important role. We will take care of such mechanisms in the model to be developed by the introduction of so-called aspiration issues.

The introduction of learning processes and other connected cognitive elements, as elaborations of the bounded rationality of the individuals, and other more realistic mechanisms in the process of friendship choice will hopefully lead to improvement of the models. To summarize, the present model improves existing models in four respects: (1) individuals are given the opportunity to dissolve friendships; (2) they may retry to establish a friendship with a specific other once they were rebuffed by that individual; (3) they influence each other (changing individual characteristics); and (4) their friendship motives are not necessarily symmetric (differences in saliences of the individual characteristics and asymmetric status effects). In doing so, we apply principles of self-organization.

3. Self-organization

Self-organization is the process of the emergence of a global order in a system without any other system imposing that ordering on that system. There is no explicit internal or external goal that enforces a system initially in a state of disorganization to show patterned behavior. It emerges spontaneously (Prigogine, 1980). The ordering simply is the result of interactions of different subsystems of units with each other and with the environment.

In Section 2 we demonstrated that with our individual oriented models we attempt to explain the emergence of friendship network structure on the basis of interaction of individual behaviors in the process of friendship formation. If we consider an initial situation of a population of mutual strangers (no relationships between the individuals at all), it is easily seen that the dynamics that we model resemble self-organizing principles. Properties at the macro level (network structure) emerge from properties at the micro level (individuals) without any internal or external goal.

Self-organization is mainly applied in the biological, physical, and cognitive sciences. *Cellular automata* (*CA*) are used in these disciplines to represent dynamic *local* processes (for a classification and overview see Wolfram, 1984). CA are represented as cells on a checkerboard. The state of a cell at the next point in time depends on its own present state and the present states of all its surrounding cells (neighbors). The size of the neighborhood varies across applications. In the rare social science applications, CA represent individuals. The applications aim to model *social dynamics* due to contagion and migration. In CA contagion models automata (cells) cannot move. In these models, attitudes of individuals change through social influence processes between neighbors. In migration models automata can move to other cells if they are dissatisfied with their neighborhood.

In CA models, social structures typically emerge in thousands of iterations. Nowak *et al* (1990), Nowak and Latané (1994), Latané *et al* (1994) investigate the emergence of clusters and polarization through contagion. Starting with random distributions of attitudes among the cells on the checkerboard, they show how minorities can survive by the emergence of clusters of similarly thinking persons. Survival of minorities and polarization of attitudes and opinions can be explained by the transformation of individual attitudes and opinions into socially organized attitudes and opinions within a *social space*. Nowak *et al* (1996) give very convincing empirical evidence of this mechanism in post-communist Poland. Economically prosperous regions emerge as clusters and coincide with clusters with a strong preference for non-communist parties.

Hegselmann (1994; 1996) developed a CA migration model to explain the emergence of solidarity among selfish persons with different needs for help. If persons are not satisfied with the help they can expect from their neighbors, they move to a new neighborhood with better perspectives (if present). These better perspectives depend on the ability and willingness of neighbors to help. Starting from random distributions of persons in different help categories, he shows the emergence of spatial clusters of persons in the same or adjacent help categories. The most and least healthy persons experience most difficulties in finding help. The former because they are not willing to help others, the latter because they are unable to help others.

Our main objection against these types of CA models is the simple structure of relationships they assume. In most applications neighborhoods have equal size for each cell. In social networks the size of the neighborhood of individuals is equal to the number of their relationships and usually varies systematically over individuals. Similarly, the overlap in neighborhoods of two individuals (the number of their common neighbors) depends on the structure of the network and may vary more than in CA models. Finally, the strength of contagion can depend on the strength of (not necessarily symmetric) relations between individuals. We therefore advocate to integrate CA contagion principles with dynamic modelling aspects of social networks.

Also in the field of artificial neural networks, the principles of self-organization have been proven to be very useful to imitate the process by which biological nervous systems consisting of a large set of neurons and their interconnections learn complex tasks. Artificial neural network models are models of how the brain works and can be applied to a variety of research problems. They have a much smaller set of neurons than real neural systems, and the neurons are much simpler (Rumelhart and McLelland, 1988). The self-organizing principle in neural networks falls in the category of unsupervised learning of neural networks. In general, more practical forms of training or learning are used, such as supervised learning or reinforcement. Self-organization or unsupervised learning (no feedback of output to input) is generally considered to be meaningful only theoretically. As such, it will be used in developing our new model.

A number of researchers has recognized the large resemblance between neural and social networks (Ritschard, 1991; Artyushkin, 1990; Zoethout, 1994). Both social and neural networks exist of interacting elements and usually show complex behavior. Behavior that is in general impossible to derive directly from the properties of the individual elements, but should be seen as a consequence of the interactions between the elements, and is consequently often called an emerging property of the system. Social and neural networks are concerned with relationships (and interactions) between units. In social networks, the units are the actors (usually individuals), whereas in neural networks, the units are the neurons. Every neuron has a certain variable activity level or state. It is a little processor that receives one or more incoming signals over its connections with other neurons.[4] According to some activation function, the activity level of the neuron may change. Dependent on the new activity level of the neuron, it may send out an output signal to one or more other neurons. The strength or weight of the link between these two neurons determines the net effect of the signal incoming with the other neuron. This input is computed as the activation of the 'sending' neuron times the weight of the connection. These weights have evolved and are evolving continuously (the network's learning process) according to adaptation rules, also known as learning rules. As mentioned earlier, self-organization is a form of unsupervised learning, which means that the weights are adjusted without any comparison to some target output (as in supervised learning). Moreover, there is no teaching input signal to the network (Blum, 1992).[5] This shows the relevance for the application in *dynamic* social networks.

The similarities between these mechanisms within neural networks and dynamics in social networks are twofold. The first stage of changes in a neural network, the short term update of activity levels of neurons, is similar to updates in a social network when individual attributes change as a result of the individuals they are connected to (which also depends on the strengths of the connections). In particular we refer to the correspondence with social influence aspects in friendship networks. Individuals' variable attributes, like opinions and attitudes, are changed by their friendships. The size of change depends on how influential the friendship tie is relative to other friendship ties (among

---

[4] Possibly also from the environment as exogenous inputs

[5] This is in large contrast to more practical training methods such as supervised learning (using a teaching input and feedback that is based on error with respect to desired output) and reinforcement learning (each output gets an error value).

others depending on the status characteristics of the friend). The second stage of change, the long term memory updates of the strengths of the connections in a neural network, resembles the evolution of relationships in a social network: Friendships emerge, strengthen or weaken and may eventually disappear.

The major difference between neurons and individuals is the more complex structure of the latter. This results in four main points of deviation between behavior of neurons and social actors: (1) social actors have more alternative actions to choose from; (2) social actors can apply more learning strategies, in particular they cannot solely learn from past experience but also from observation of the success of other actors; (3) actors are only able to interact with a limited number of other actors, since they have limited resources (Macy & Flache, 1995); and (4) interactions between social actors are, in general, only effective when both sides agree on the interaction.[6] Due to these fundamental differences we do not seek a neural network representation of social network evolution, but attempt to include only some of the similarities between neural and social networks.

4. A new model of friendship network evolution

Based on the proposed adaptations of Section 2 and the correspondences with self-organization of Section 3, we present a new model of friendship network evolution. The model has the following characteristics. Individual evaluation functions are presented in utility functions. As a result of limited information and limited capability to foresee strategically, individuals use heuristics of these complex utility functions and evaluate them on the basis of past experiences. This is reflected in the more complicated learning mechanisms of individuals. Realized friendships have effects on characteristics of the individuals, the weights of relationships in the social influence process, and the network structure.

In developing the model, we use the decomposition of social processes in networks proposed by Stokman and Van Oosten (1994). They distinguish five fundamental steps. In the first step (actor issue analysis), actors evaluate the different alternatives, which involves the definition of individual preference functions. To connect these alternatives to actions, individuals need to collect information on the social system (second step: domain evaluation). The combined information from the first two steps leads to friendship proposals to

---

[6] A few other differences between neural and social networks may be mentioned. First, neural networks actually operate as black boxes. Consequently, it is often difficult to trace why and what relationships emerged and changed (Masters, 1993). In social networks we at least have some theoretical notion why some relationships strengthen and others weaken. Second, in neural networks the emphasis lies on the learning capabilities of the network as a whole, whereas in social networks the emphasis lies on the learning capabilities of individuals. Finally, inputs are essential in neural networks, whereas they seem to be less important for friendship evolution models.

others (third step: proposal utterance). In the fourth step (proposal effectuation), some of these offers lead to relationships based on evaluations of all proposals received and made. In the fifth step (transformation into "macro"-effects), the effects of the realized relations for the whole system are derived.

4.1 Actor issue analysis

Individuals 'determine' their preferences on the issues relevant to them in the formation of friendships.

Individuals differ in their need for social contact (Crocket, 1965, Duck, 1988, Milardo, 1986). Some individuals need many friends. Others need less. The number of friends desired depends on the strengths of the friendships under consideration and the amount of time and energy available.

The first issue in the overall utility function of an individual thus involves a comparison between the preferred number of friends and the actual number of friends, in other words a comparison between one's own preferred and actual position on the scale of number of friends. The loss of utility with respect to this first issue can be given by[7]:

$$U_i^{nf} = -s_{ib}^{nf} |x_i^{nf} - y_i^{nf}|^q \qquad (1)$$

The subscript i refers to individual i and the superscript ^{nf} refers to the issue *n*umber of *f*riends. s_i^{nf} is the importance of the number of friends for i. x_i^{nf} is i's desired number of friends and y_i^{nf} is the actual number of friends. The parameter ^{q} specifies the shape of the distance function between actual and desired numbers.

In choosing potential friends, or with respect to attractions to or preferences for friends, the following three dimensions seem to be generally important, but always apply with specific 'adaptations' in specific contexts (Davison and Jones, 1976): There seems to be a general attraction to higher status

Some of the elements in this function are time dependent. Our models primarily differ from one another in the specification of constant and time dependent elements. For that reason and to simplify notation we do not yet specify which elements are time dependent.

individuals.[8] The most important dimension is that of likeability or similarity: Individuals prefer to be friends with those who are similar to themselves (among others: Lazarsfeld and Merton, 1954; Duck, 1991). Although it depends on the context of concern, status heavily influences attraction, but similarity aspects are most important. As a consequence, we introduce comparison issues and aspiration issues.[9]

Comparison issues:
To incorporate the preference for similarity, comparison issues are introduced. Examples of comparison issues are variable attributes like opinions, attitudes, and behaviors, and non-variable characteristics like gender. Individuals compare their own value on the comparison issue with that of a potential friendship candidate or friend. Jones (1982) suggests to model the strength of a similarity-attraction relationship as an inverse function of distance between the implicit ideal point of an individual and the other's position on the relevant dimension. If similarity is relevant the ideal point of the other is the individual's perceived position of him or herself. The more similar two individuals are, the more satisfaction (utility) is obtained from the (potential) friendship relation between them.

Individuals evaluate their distances to others on a number of dimensions. It is crucial that differences exist among individuals in the number and meaning of dimensions, in the saliences attached to them, and in the positioning of self and others on these dimensions. It may even be so that dependent on the individual's position on a dimension he or she attaches more or less salience to that dimension or issue (Jones, 1982). It is for example found that individuals on the extreme of a dimension attach more importance to that dimension (Hirschberg, Jones & Haggerty, 1978). Moreover, saliences of dimensions may be related to positions within the social network structure (Jones and Young, 1972). Dimensions, and especially saliences of dimensions also change over time. Dependent on how long an individual has been in the population (or context), one or more dimensions may become more relevant, not only in general but also in specific friendships.

---

[8] It seems that this preference does not hold for those with very low status. These individuals probably see some kind of social barrier. It is not only the fact that higher status individuals do not accept or choose to be friends with those with lower status, but there actually is a feeling of uncomfortableness among those with lower status to attempt to become friends with higher status individuals. Nevertheless, we assume in our first specification (see Section 5) that the preference to be friends with higher status individuals is valid for all individuals, independent of their own status.

[9] Also, professional interest seems to be relevant. This certainly applies in specific contexts of friendship formation (organizations) and can refer to preferences for similarity but also to complementarity aspects of individual characteristics. We do not yet introduce complementarity in our models, however.

Thus the utility loss for deviation on comparison issues not only depends on the distance between the individual's own value and that of the (potential) friend, but also on the salience attached to that dimension by the individual. For now, we do not take into account that salience may depend on all the factors mentioned above. This results in a single-peaked preference function.[10] Values on the comparison issues are assumed to be on a unidimensional scale from 0 to 1. The closer *i*'s value on the comparison issue to *j*'s value, the more utility *i* can derive from a friendship with *j* (or the less utility *i* looses from a friendship with *j*). For now, we disregard the dependence with the issue number of friends. Suppose individual *i* has $y_i^{nf}=f_i$ actual friends. y_{ib}^c refers to the actual value of *i* on comparison issue (dimension) b^c, y_{jb}^c refers to the actual value of *j* on comparison issue b^c. s_{ib}^c is the salience attached to comparison issue b^c by individual *i*. The superscript ^{c} refers to the fact that this utility function represents comparison issues.[11]

Now suppose that m^c comparison issues exist. The overall utility function

$$U_{ib}^c = -s_{ib}^c \sum_{j=1}^{f^i} |y_{ib}^c - y_{jb}^c|^q \qquad (2)$$

then becomes:

$$U_i^c = \sum_{b=1}^{m^c} U_{ib}^c \qquad (3)$$

Aspiration issues:

Friendship choices are partly determined on the basis of status differences, where status can be defined on a number of different dimensions (e.g. social economic status, educational level). We represent this with so-called aspiration issues (Festinger, 1954; Schachter, 1959). Aspiration issues imply a comparison between one's own aspiration level or preferred value on the issue and the actual position of the (potential) friend on the issue. The utility functions reflect the fact that an individual aims at friends that are similar to his or her own aspiration level. Again the relevance of an aspiration issue varies among individuals, and is again represented by the salience of that issue for that individual. For now, we choose a utility function as general as possible. Again

[10] Actually we will formulate loss-functions where the loss is zero if the friend has the desired characteristics.

[11] Single-peaked preference functions imply that it is much more difficult for those at the extremes to find potential friends than for those in the middle of the dimension when individuals are unimodally or equally distributed on the comparison issue.

suppose individual i has f_i actual friends. x_{ib}^a refers to the preferred value of i on aspiration issue (dimension) b^a, y_{jb}^a refers to the actual value of j on aspiration issue b^a. s_{ib}^a is the salience attached to aspiration issue b^a by individual i. The superscript ^{a} refers to the fact that this utility function represents aspiration issues.

$$U_{ib}^a = -s_{ib}^a \sum_{j=1}^{f^i} |x_{ib}^a - y_{jb}^a|^q \qquad (4)$$

and:

$$U_i^a = \sum_{b=1}^{m^a} U_{ib}^a \qquad (5)$$

An overall utility function that incorporates all relevant issues, the number of friends, and the two dimensions of comparison and aspiration cannot be given without additional assumptions by the addition of the three separate utility components because they are interdependent (f_i in (4) and (5) equals y_i^{nf}). As a preliminary solution, to be incorporated in the individual heuristics (behavioral rules), we assume that utility increases when the actual number of friends gets closer to the desired number of friends.[12] The increase is faster when these actual friends' values on the comparison dimensions are closer to those of ego, and if the actual friends' values on the aspiration issues are closer to ego's aspiration value.

4.2 Domain evaluation

In order to translate the utility functions introduced above into expected utility values for potential and actual friendships, individuals attempt to obtain information as complete as possible to assess the values of different behavioral alternatives. These expected utilities consist of an approximation of the utility of a (potential) relationship and an estimation of the probability of success of realizing a relationship with the other actor.

---

[12] This implies that in the present model individuals base their friendship proposals (see Section 4.3) on a comparison over individuals, namely how much each individual contributes to his or her expected utility loss over comparison and aspiration issues.

Although we can benefit from research in the field of social cognition and social perception, we initially assume complete information about the other individual's values on all relevant comparison and aspiration issues.

4.3 Proposal utterance

In this step, individuals determine which interactions they want to initiate by making so-called friendship proposals to other individuals. Because of incomplete information, limited capability to foresee strategically, and simultaneous actions of others, individuals are not able to know exactly how to maximize the expected utility of friendship relations. Since no complete information ever exists, individuals make rough assumptions about the expected utilities of friendships and update these estimations on the basis of experiences. The expected utility of a (potential) friendship is the product of the estimated value of utility of that friendship and the estimated probability of actually establishing (or maintaining) that relationship. Subsequently, based on the best information available, individuals construct a so-called preference order over all possible alternatives, all possible friendship candidates.

The probability of success is a crucial element. Its value can only be guessed or estimated mainly based on an individual's experiences in the past. Since we assume that a mutual friendship choice means a friendship relation, and thus 'success', the likelihood of success p_{ij} of a friendship proposal from *i* to *j* is the likelihood that the other individual, *j*, will also make a friendship choice towards *i*.

The initial estimation of the probability of success, $p_{ij}(0)$, depends on the 'resources' (or status) *i* has with regard to *j*. We assume that the value of an individual's resources depends heavily on the individual who evaluates them. The closer *i*'s actual values on the aspiration issues to those aspired by *j*, the more weight *i* will eventually have on *j*'s opinions, attitudes, and behavior, in our terms the more resources *i* has relative to *j*. Resources as such differ for every pair of individuals, and are by definition not symmetric (direction dependent).[13] We define r_{ij} as the value of the resources of *i* with respect to *j* over all aspiration issues b^a, where m^a is the number of aspiration issues, $x_{jh}{}^a$ is *j*'s desired value on aspiration dimension b^a, $y_{ih}{}^a$ is *i*'s actual value on aspiration dimension b^a, $s_{jh}{}^a$ is *j*'s salience with regard to dimension b^a. The smaller the differences between *i*'s actual values and *j*'s preferred values on the aspiration issues, the larger the resources of *i* with regard to *j*.

---

[13] In a related dynamic network model for policy domains, the authors assume that resources of actors are attributes of actors and not pair-dependent (Stokman and Zeggelink, 1996). There, resources are related to the capability of actors to influence outcomes of political decisions. Consequently, they have a more objective character, whereas in the friendship networks here the value of resources depends heavily on the importance the individual attaches to the aspiration issues.

$$r_{ij} = \frac{1}{m^a} \sum_{b=1}^{m^a} s_{jb}^a (1 - |x_{jb}^a - y_{ib}^a|^q) \qquad (6)$$

In order to obtain initial estimations of probability of success of *i* establishing a relationship with *j*, $p_{ij}(0)$, we assume:

$$\begin{array}{lll} \text{If } r_{ij} \geq 0.9 & \Rightarrow p_{ij}(0) = 0.9 & \\ \text{If } 0.1 \leq r_{ij} \leq 0.9 & \Rightarrow p_{ij}(0) = r_{ij} & \qquad (7) \\ \text{If } r_{ij} \leq 0.1 & \Rightarrow p_{ij}(0) = 0.1 & \end{array}$$

From all possible friendship proposals, a person will select those with the highest estimated expected utility (utility * probability of success) up to a number close to his ideal number of friends (dependent on the saliences attached to the different issues).

4.4 Proposal effectuation

Proposals are evaluated and result in friendships when choice is mutual. Probabilities of success with all other individuals are updated in this step, dependent on the existence of incoming proposals, and reciprocation of choices. If *i* makes a friendship choice to *j*, and *j* also chooses *i*, the probability of success for the next step is estimated to be 0.9. Individuals learn that non-responding individuals will not suddenly have different motives to respond at later points in time. If *i* chooses *j* but *j* does not choose *i*, *i* lowers the previous probability of success with 0.1. If *i* does not choose *j*, but *j* chooses *i*, the probability of success is equal to that in the previous round plus 0.1. If *j* does not choose *i*, the probability of success is equal to that in the previous round. As such, we do not enforce full reciprocity (among others: Hallinan, 1979, Wasserman, 1980a; 1980b).

4.5 Transformation into "macro" - effects

The friendships that become established in this process continuously have their effects at three different levels: the individual level, the relational level and the network level. At the individual level, individual characteristics change as a result of their friendships. Friendships are not only formed on the basis of preferences for similarity, but friends also tend to become more similar. Friends tend to influence each other, such that there opinions, attitudes, behaviors and so on, become more similar. This is a social influence process. According to Hunter et al. (1984), different theories exist that try to explain how attitude change comes about. We assume that the strength with which individuals influence each other depends on the so-called amount of control they have over each other, which depends on their relative resources with regard to each other and the number of other friends and their 'resources' that try to influence the same individual. The amount of control $c_{ij}(t)$ of i over j is defined as follows[14] (see also Stokman and Van den Bos, 1992)

$$c_{ij}(t) = \frac{r_{ij}(t)\,a_{ij}(t)}{\sum_{k=1}^{n} r_{kj}(t)\,a_{kj}(t)} \tag{8}$$

where $a_{ij}(t) = 0$ if i and j are not friends at time t
1 if i and j are friends at time t.
Since we assumed a friendship to exist as soon as choice is mutual, $a_{ij}(t) = a_{ji}(t)$.

This definition of control implies that individuals have a certain buffer to resist control from others. This depends on their own resources over themselves (r_{ii}). According to equation (6), individuals' own resources with respect to themselves are equal to their saliences over all aspiration issues discounted for the difference between their own actual and ideal characteristics on the aspiration issues. Moreover, for each individual, by definition, all incoming control (including the control over him or herself) sums to unity.

We assume that social influence has its effects only on those dimensions that are variable (like behavior, opinions, or attitudes opposed to constant characteristics like gender or age), and (in some models) on the saliences of all issues. When saliences are subject to social influence, the salience of individual i for issue b at time $(t+1)$, $s_{ib}(t+1)$, is the median of i's own and i's friends' saliences at time t where each $s_{jb}(t)$ is weighted by $c_{ji}(t)$.

Social influence on actual values of individuals on variable issues depends not only on the amount of control, but also on the saliences individuals attach to the dimensions. The amount of control of individual j on i at time t is seen as the *potential* influence of j on i. Whether j is *willing* to mobilize his or her potential control to affect i's value on a variable issue, depends on how salient the issue is for j. An individual's salience on an issue is seen as the fraction of control he or she is willing to mobilize in influence relations (Stokman and Van den Bos, 1992). The actual value of individual i on variable issue b at

---

[14] As c_{ij} and the next concepts are directly related to the social influence process in each iteration, we explicitly formulate in the coming equations which elements are time-dependent or not. The pair-dependent resources r_{ij} are only time dependent when the individual' values on one or more aspiration issues are time-dependent (subject to social influence).

time $(t + 1)$, $y_{ib}(t+1)$, is obtained by taking the median of i's own and i's friends' values at time t where each $y_{jb}(t)$ is weighted by $w_{ji}(t)$:[15]

By introducing a measure of control that is resource dependent, and

$$w_{ji}(t) = \frac{s_{jb}(t)\,c_{ji}(t)}{\sum_{j=1}^{n} s_{jb}(t)\,c_{ji}(t)} \qquad (9)$$

dependent on the number of other friendships, we have already shown how the process has its effects on the relational level.

The effects at the network level are trivial. Friendships emerge, are maintained, or disappear, and as such network structure changes.

4.6 Verbal summary of the dynamic friendship model

Let us finally briefly summarize the dynamics of the model and specify some of the assumptions in more detail:

We consider a closed set of individuals, a number of comparison and aspiration issues that are relevant in the process of friendship formation. Every individual has a certain position on every issue and attaches a certain salience to the issue. All values of the positions and saliences are between 0 and 1. With this information, every individual can determine his or her resources over every other individual in the population (dyad dependent resources). Individual i's resources with regard to j are larger the closer i's actual value on an aspiration issue is to j's desired value. This is the more so, the more salience j attaches to that aspiration issue. On the basis of the other individuals' values on the comparison and aspiration issues, every individual computes a preference order over all individuals. The utility for individual i of a (potential) friendship with an individual j is higher, the closer j's values on aspiration issues are to i's desired values, and the closer i and j's values on comparison issues are to each other. The weight of the distance on each issue depends on how salient that issue is for individual i.

Every individual also computes the probability of success of establishing (or maintaining) a friendship with every other individual. In general this depends on a number of aspects. If i already makes a friendship choice to j, and j also chooses i, the probability of success is estimated to be 0.9. If i chooses j but j

[15] Stokman and Van den Bos (1992) and Stokman and Zeggelink (1996) take the weighted mean. The disadvantage of the mean is that groups quickly become homogeneous in their values. We prefer the median in our present models to increase the likelihood that minorities will be able to uphold their values on variable issues within a larger group.

does not choose *i*, *i* lowers the probability (of the previous round) of success with 0.1. If *i* does not choose *j*, but *j* chooses *i*, the probability of success is equal to that in the previous round plus 0.1. If *j* does not choose *i*, the probability of success is equal to that in the previous round. If no previous round exists, the probability of success is equal to *i*'s relative resources with regard to *j*, with a maximum of 0.9 and a minimum of 0.1.

By multiplying utility with probability of success a preference order is constructed. Subsequently individuals choose as many candidates for friendship as their desired number of friends in the order of their constructed preference order. We assume that the number of friends is so important that individuals will always try to establish as many friendships as their desired number, never more than that.

After having made offers (friendship choices) to other individuals, individuals update their information with regard to the probabilities of success of establishing friendships with the others. A friendship is assumed to exist once a friendship choice is mutual.

For established friendships, control values are computed and the consequent influence process of individual attributes takes place. Since individuals' values and saliences on issues change as a result of their friendships, their and others' preference orders change accordingly. Consequently, friendships may well disappear again if one (or both) of the friends removes his or her choice to the other as a result of more attractive alternatives. The process repeats itself until equilibrium emerges or after a predetermined maximal number of iterations.

5. An illustration: some simulation results

We present some preliminary simulation results that show the processes of self-organization. We examine situations of a set of ten individuals who take into consideration two comparison issues or dimensions, and one aspiration issue. We assume the comparison issue to be dichotomous: the only possible values on the comparison issues are 0 and 1. The possible aspiration issue values are 0.2, 0.4, 0.6, 0.8, and 1.0. We assume that every individual prefers to be friends with other individuals that have a higher value on the aspiration dimension (the aspired value is 1.0 for all). Salience with regard to the aspiration issue is 0.5 for every individual. Saliences with respect to the two comparison issues are either moderately high (0.75) or moderately low (0.25). We randomly distribute these possible salience values and values on the comparison and aspiration issues over all individuals to obtain 10 different initial situations. Three of the randomly obtained initial distributions are presented in the upper-left corner (a) of Fig. 5.1, Fig. 5.2, and Fig. 5.3 (the initial distributions in Fig. 5.3.1 and 5.3.2 are identical). Every individual either has value 1 (black) or value 0 (white) on the two comparison issues. The value on the aspiration dimension is denoted next to the node. Moderately high and low saliences are represented by an 'h' and an 'l' respectively.

In all simulations we assume the individual values on the aspiration issue to be constant and the values on the two comparison issues to be variable (subject to social influence). In our simulations we systematically vary conditions along two dimensions. The first dimension is related to the number of 'desired' friends (*df*). We compare 'equilibrium networks' for different numbers of friendship needs and examine the situations in which all individuals want to establish either three ($df = 3$), four ($df = 4$) or five ($df = 5$) friends. The second dimension ('salience influence') aims to compare the effect of constant versus variable saliences on the comparison issues.

With respect to the resulting networks, three different parameters describing the network structure, are relevant as dependent variables. First, it is important to know to what degree the individuals actually succeed in establishing their desired number of friendships. Two parameters describe this aspect: the mean number of friends per individual *(nf)* in the population and the variance in this number *(vnf)*. The lower the mean number of friends in the network compared to the 'desired' one, the more difficulties the individuals have in establishing friendships under the given conditions. If the variance of the number of friends within a network is high, some individuals have fewer problems fulfilling their need, and others have more problems. So, the variance is a measure of the extent to which the restrictions are equally or unequally distributed over the individuals. Partly, these restrictions result from their own actions through the network they construct. Since we are especially interested in the effects on clustering within the network (see Section 1), a strict measure of clustering is desirable. Baerveldt and Snijders (1994) propose the segmentation index S_3 that is defined as the number of pairs within the network at distances three or larger as a fraction of the number of pairs at distances two or larger. S_3 is an index for the fraction of individuals that are distant from each other among those who are not friends (friends are at distance 1). This index allows for comparisons between networks with different densities. The higher the value of S_3, the more segmented (clustered) the network is. $S_3 = 1$ if the network is completely segmented: there are relatively few indirect connections and the network is divided into a number of disjoint clusters in which density is high.

We expect that segmentation or the clustering effect will be higher in the model with changing saliences of the comparison issues than in the model with constant saliences. Within a population of ten individuals, the clustering effect will always be smaller when the need for friendship, and thus the resulting number of realized relationships, is higher. However, the degree of segmentation will be high in comparison to models where individual characteristics do not play a role. We expect that this clustering effect is particularly high in sparse networks (*i.e.* the deviation from the random model decreases from three to five 'desired' friendships).

We run fifty simulations with every single initial situation. Every simulation consists of maximally ten iterations in which every individual attempts to establish friendships according to the rules of Section 4. In each iteration, friendships form, expectations are adapted, and variable comparison issue values (and saliences) change through mutual influence processes. If equilibrium is established before the tenth iteration, the process comes to a halt. We chose a maximum of ten because generally not many changes occur at later stages in the process. However, future experiments will run the simulation until 'real' equilibrium. In the following we will speak of equilibrium networks, also when the process ran ten iterations.

To give a first impression of the combined effects of individual choices and social influence, we first illustrate some results under different conditions for the three initial distributions in Figures 5.1 to 5.3. The first observation to be made is that some initial situations result in at least twenty-five different equilibrium networks due to random choices at certain times in the process. Other initial situations result, however, in one and only one equilibrium network. Figure 5.1. illustrates the latter for the initial distribution presented in (a). In (b) we see the network that results with the process without salience change and a general desire for three friends ($df = 3$). The average number of friends in this equilibrium network is $nf = 2.8$, the variance in number of friends $vnf = .36$, and the degree of segmentation $S_3 = .77$. The latter are explained by the presence of two subgroups in the equilibrium network: one subgroup of size four and one subgroup of size six. Within the larger group, values on the comparison issues are not homogeneously distributed as a result of the presence of two high-status individuals with deviant values. For the individual with complete opposite values this coincides with a smaller number of friendships than desired. With the same model and $df = 4$, the network in (c) emerges. Now we see complete segmentation in two clusters of size five. At the end, all individuals have the same value on the second comparison issue. Each cluster is also homogeneous on the first comparison issue, but individuals in different clusters have opposite values. The average number of friends in this network is $nf = 4.0$, the variance in number of friends is $vnf = 0$, and the degree of segmentation is maximal, $S_3 = 1.0$. When saliences are subject to change, the same network structure arises, but now also with a homogeneous distribution of salience values within the clusters (d).

In Fig. 5.2. we see that the given initial distribution can lead to the maximal possible degree of segmentation when the need for friends is $df = 3$ and salience can change in the process (b). The network presented is one of the possible equilibrium results, but it is the most frequently resulting network. The network consists of three different subgroups within which the values of the comparison issues and the values of the saliences are homogeneously distributed. For this network, the average number of friends is $nf = 2.6$, the variance in number of friends is $vnf = .64$, and the degree of segmentation is $S_3 = 1.0$. The relatively high variance in the number of friends and the smaller mean number of realized friends than 'desired' ones are entirely due to the subgroup of two individuals with a deviant combination of values on the comparison issues. In sharp contrast with this result, the same initial

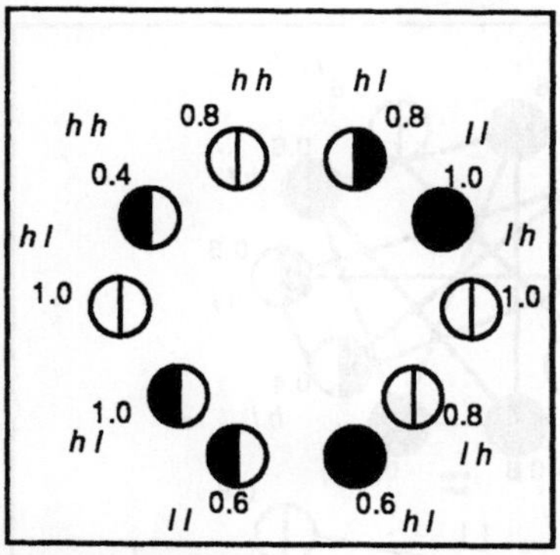

a: initial distribution

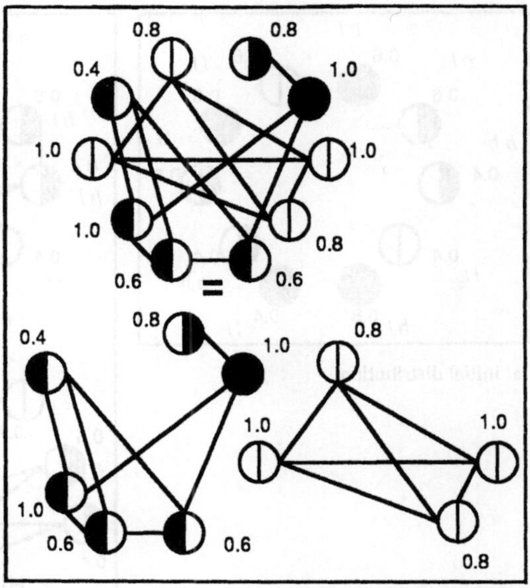

b: the equilibrium distribution for nf = 3 *without* salience influence (S_3 = .77)

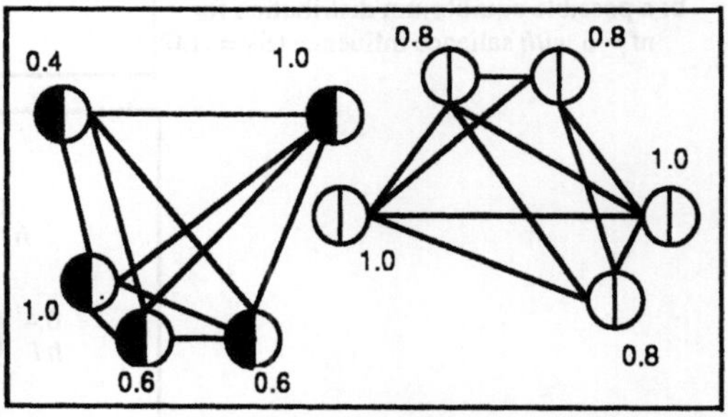

c: the equilibrium distribution for nf = 4 *without* salience influence (S_3 = 1.0)

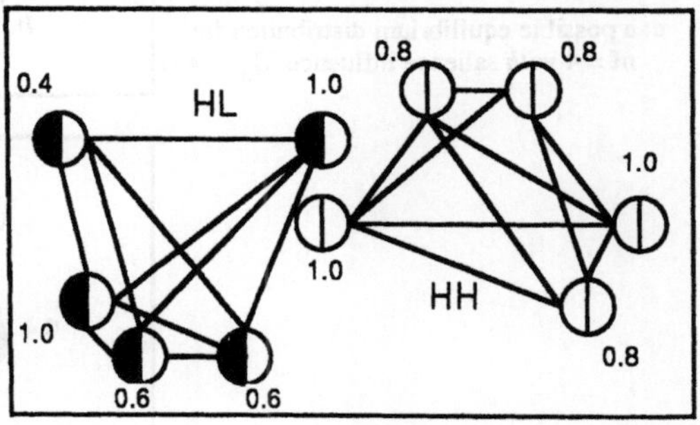

d: the equilibrium distribution for nf = 4 *with* salience influence (S_3 = 1.0)

Fig 5.1. Equilibrium distributions for one initial distribution with different model parameters

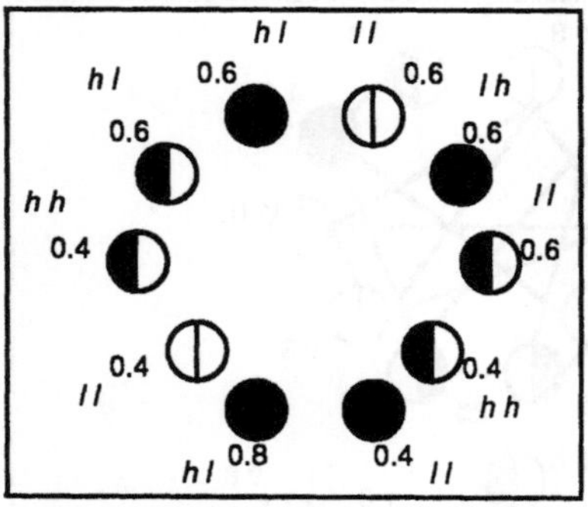

a: initial distribution

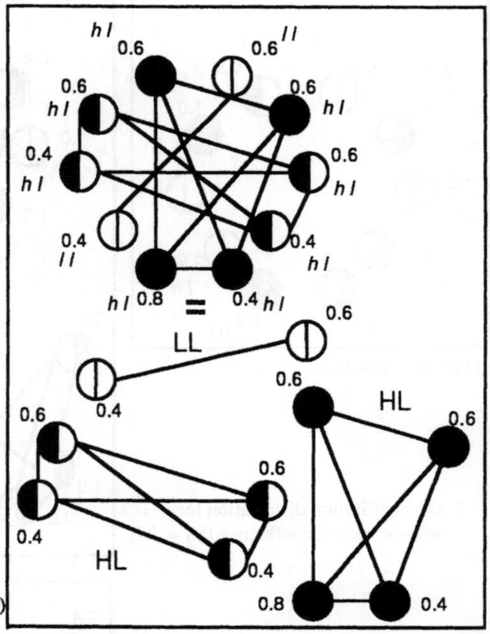

b: a possible equilibrium distribution for nf = 3 *with* salience influence (S_3 = .1.0)

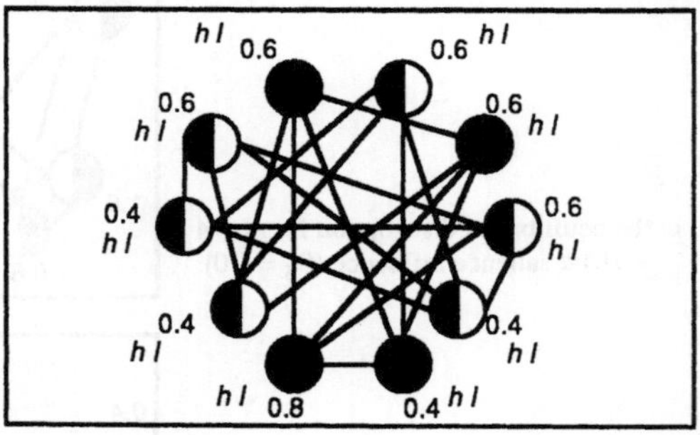

c: a possible equilibrium distribution for nf = 4 *with* salience influence (S_3 = .43)

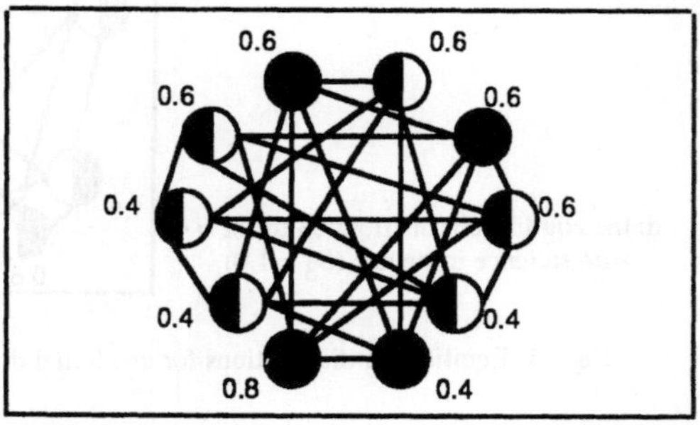

d: a possible equilibrium distribution for nf = 5 *without* salience influence (S_3 = .00)

Fig 5.2. Equilibrium distributions for one initial distribution with different model parameters

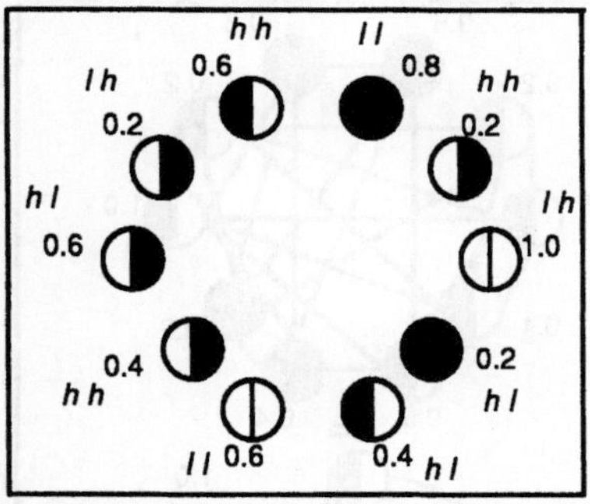

a: initial distribution

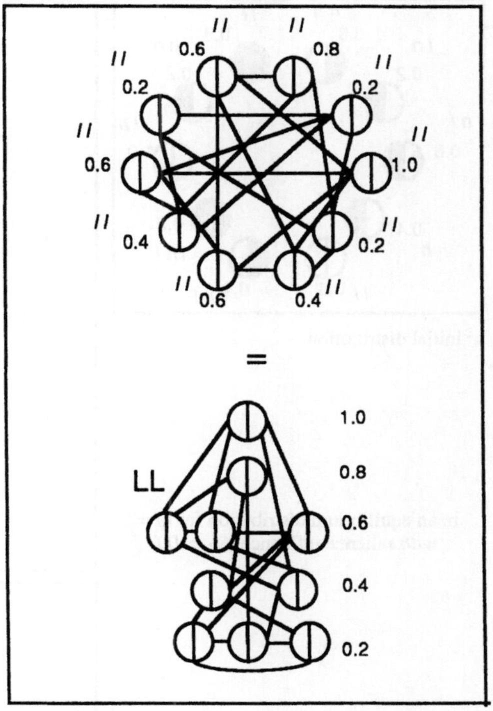

b: an equilibrium distribution for nf = 4 *with* salience influence (S_3 = .19)

Fig 5.3.1. Equilibrium distributions for one initial distribution with different model parameters

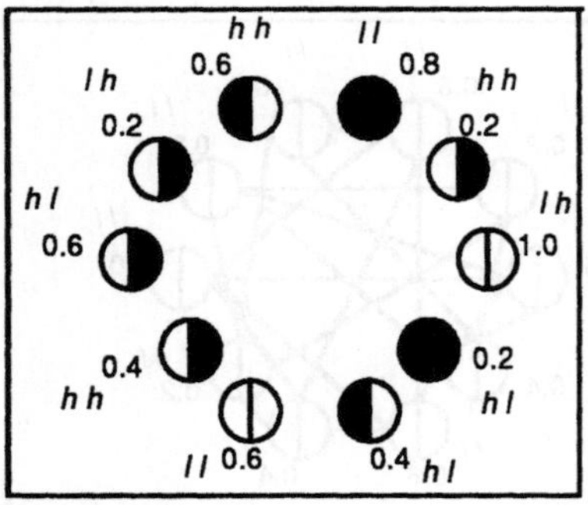

a: initial distribution

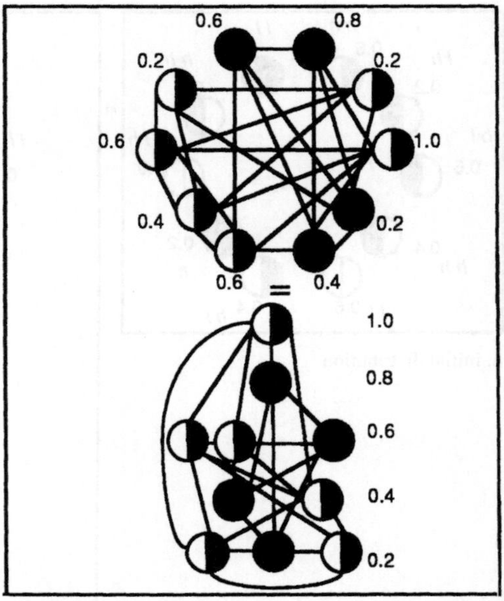

b: an equilibrium distribution for nf = 5 *with* salience influence (S_3 = .00)

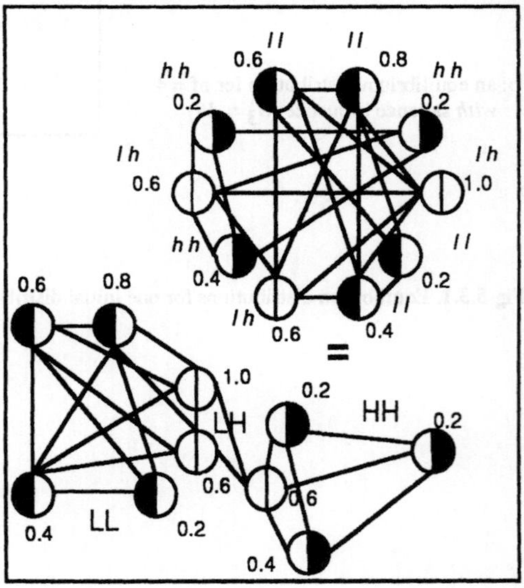

c: an equilibrium distribution for nf = 5 *with* salience influence (S_3 = .54)

Fig 5.3.2. Equilibrium distributions for initial distribution of Fig 5.3.1.

distribution leads to the smallest or one but smallest average degree of segmentation when the desired number of friends is four or five. In (c) we show the most frequently resulting network for $df = 4$ with changing saliences. The average number of friends in this network is $nf = 3.4$, the variance in number of friends is $vnf = .84$, and the degree of segmentation is $S_3 = .43$. The two individuals that initially have a deviant value on the first comparison issue (the two completely 'white' individuals in Fig. 5.2 (a)), change this value, resulting in unanimity on the first comparison issue. All individuals maintain their original value on the second issue, resulting in a divided population on that issue. Nevertheless, the established friendships do not result in two clusters. This implies that all individuals are able to keep their initial value on the second issue while maintaining friendship relations with individuals with opposite values. The same holds for the network presented in (c) when $df = 5$ where the average number of friends is $nf = 5.0$, the variance in number of friends is $vnf = .00$, and the degree of segmentation is $S_3 = .00$.

The initial distribution, given both in Fig. 5.3.1 (a) and Fig. 5.3.2 (a), always leads to small average values of degree of segmentation for four and five 'desired' friends. Fig. 5.3.1 (b) shows one of the possible completely unsegmented networks in which all individuals have the same values and saliences on both comparison issues. The network is strongly structured according to the values on the aspiration issue. The few friendships that cross one or more 'status' levels (levels at the aspiration issue) result from initial similarity on the comparison issues. The sole link between a 0.2-status individual and a 0.8-status one is established between the only two completely 'black' individuals. Also the sole 0.2 - 0.6 link is due to the original similarity of the two individuals on the comparison issues. For this network, the average number of friends is $nf = 3.8$, the variance in number of friends is $vnf = .16$, and the degree of segmentation is $S_3 = .19$. In Fig. 5.3.2 (b) and Fig. 5.3.2 (c) we present the least and most segmented network respectively that emerge under the model with salience influence and $df = 5$. In the least segmented network all individuals become unanimous on the second issue, but remain divided on the first. In the most segmented network three combinations of comparison values keep alive. The 'completely white' individuals link the two subgroups within which complete homogeneity exists but that are mirrored to one another. The linking individuals are thus similar with the one subgroup on one issue and with the other subgroup on the other issue. The saliences of these linking individuals are also 'in the middle' of those in the two subgroups: on each issue the linking individuals have the same salience as the subgroup with which they disagree on that issue. It is more difficult to establish friendships in the more segmented group: the average number of friends is $nf = 4.6$ in (c) and $nf = 4.2$ in (b). Also the variances in number of friends are larger in the more segmented network ($vnf = .96$ against $vnf = .24$).

Table 1: Overview simulation results

df	process	*nf*	*vnf*	S_3
	variable salience	2.66 (.20)	.40 (.26)	.81 (.10)
3	constant salience	2.63 (.22)	.38 (.21)	.75 (.10)
	no salient issues	1.46 (.27)	.33 (.20)	.98 (.03)
	base model Zeggelink	2.94 (.09)	.07 (.13)	.37 (.13)
	variable salience	3.70 (.32)	.34 (.44)	.68 (.27)
4	constant salience	3.75 (.22)	.22 (.24)	.66 (.26)
	no salient issues	1.98 (.30)	.66 (.29)	.91 (.06)
	base model Zeggelink	3.91 (.11)	.10 (.14)	.07 (.06)
	variable salience	4.45 (.22)	.57 (.50)	.27 (.19)
5	constant salience	4.44 (.21)	.66 (.62)	.28 (.27)
	no salient issues	3.06 (.35)	.95 (.47)	.63 (.10)
	base model Zeggelink	4.89 (.11)	.13 (.15)	.00 (.01)

Statistical results over all fifty simulations and all ten initial configurations for each experimental set of conditions are shown in Table 1. Column (1) denotes whether it concerns the process with a desired number of friends being three, four, or five. Column (2) indicates whether it concerns the process with variable or constant saliences for the comparison issues or one of the two null models to be introduced later. In columns (3), (4), and (5), we present the averages of the mean number of friends per individual (*nf*), the variance in the mean number of friends (*vnf*), and the degree of segmentation (S_3) respectively.

The degree of segmentation strongly depends on the number of 'desired' friends. Segmentation is especially high when three or four friends are desired. As expected, for needs of three and four friends, segmentation increases when, next to comparison values, saliences are also subject to social influence. For a need of five friendships, the differences in segmentation between the processes with and without salience influence are in the opposite direction. This unexpected decrease is small and explained by one single initial situation with an average degree of segmentation of S_3 = 1.0 without salience change and an average S_3 = .57 with salience change. Whether the decrease is in fact opposite to our expectations, needs to be examined in more detail on the basis of more initial situations. The number of 'desired' friends and salience influence explain 50 percent of the variation in segmentation across simulations.

From the perspective of social dilemmas, it is an important question whether it is more difficult to realize the number of 'desired' friends in segmented networks and whether segmentation coincides with a larger variance in the number of realized friends. In addition, on the basis of inspection of some final configurations like the ones in Figures 5.1 to 5.3, we suspect that the degree of segmentation is smaller when friendships are established mainly along small status differences rather than according to similarity of comparison issues. Our aspiration issue represents a status dimension on which every individual aims at becoming friends with somebody with higher values on the dimension. Moreover, differences in values on the aspiration dimension determine probabilities of success of actually establishing a friendship. As a result, if similarity of comparison issues is less or not relevant, the aspiration dimension determines which friendships are going to be established. Our status dimension is interval-scaled whereas the comparison dimensions are dichotomous. Interval-scaled issues more easily lead to layered network structures in which most friendships are within the same category or in adjacent categories. Networks with disjoint subgroups will consequently not emerge. When many individuals have low saliences on the comparison issues or when individuals initially are or gradually become more homogeneous on the comparison issues, similarity on these issues is likely to be a less important factor that determines the final network structure.

Controlling for the number of 'desired' friends and salience influence, none of the correlations with segmentation hypothesized above is present. It seems not to be more difficult to realize the number of desired friends in more segmented networks, nor is the variance in realized friends larger in more segmented networks. Also, the correlation between segmentation and the number of initially low saliences for comparison issues is absent. The partial correlations are all in the range of r = -.02 to r =.02. However, the correlations between segmentation and the other variables are suppressed by the special case of four 'desired' friends in a group of ten individuals. The specific combination of four 'desired' friends within a group of ten individuals enables all individuals to realize the desired number of friendships when the group is divided in two clusters of equal size. This specific combination may well result in a positive correlation of segmentation with the number of realized friends and a negative one with its variance. Moreover, it may well be easier to realize a split in two clusters through the process of social influence if many individuals attach low saliences to comparison issues. Individuals with low salience change their values on the comparison issues more easily, which might result in the quick formation of homogeneous clusters. The specific combination of df = 4 and a population size of ten would consequently result in a positive correlation between segmentation and the number of low saliences on comparison issues.

The results of df = 3 and df =5 indeed show that part of the remaining variation in segmentation is explained by the number of low saliences for comparison issues. Controlling for the number of desired friends and salience influence, the partial correlation between number of low salience comparison issues and segmentation is r = -.09. In accordance with our earlier expectations, it is indeed more difficult to realize the 'desired' number of friends in more segmented networks, in particular for some individuals. The partial correlation between segmentation and the mean number of realized friends is strongly negative (r = -.58), whereas the partial correlation between segmentation and the variance of realized friends across individuals is moderately positive (r = .34). The comparatively small negative partial correlation between segmentation and the number of low saliences might well be due to the fact that, also in these populations, low saliences for comparison issues lead to opposite forces. On the one hand, low saliences for comparison issues increase the likelihood of friendship choices along status lines. On the other, they enlarge social influence effects on the comparison issues, thereby promoting quick formation of homogeneous clusters. Further research on the dynamics of the process is needed here. We also need a clearer picture of the actual dynamics of the process to explain why some initial configurations result in one and only one equilibrium network, whereas others lead to a distribution of possible networks.

When df = 4, all correlations are indeed in opposite directions. Controlling for salience influence, the partial correlation between segmentation and the number of low saliences is slightly positive (r = .07). Individuals indeed realize the 'desired' number of friends more easily in more segmented networks (r = .35). Finally, segmentation is negatively correlated with the variance in the mean number of realized friends (r = -.26).

In order to see whether differences in individual characteristics and social influence increase segmentation in friendship networks, we compare the generated networks with networks resulting from a model in which friendships emerge without similarity or status effects. Such a model simply is the model presented here with all saliences equal to zero. All individuals attach no importance to comparison and aspiration issues and randomly seek to establish their desired number of friendships. Characteristics of their friends are irrelevant and no social influence takes place. The statistical results for this model are presented under 'no salient issues' in every third row of the specific 'desired' number of friends in Table 1. Results are again based on a maximum of ten iterations and fifty replications with a single initial distribution. Relatively small mean numbers of friends result: individuals have much more difficulties establishing friendships. This occurs for different reasons. First, since all individuals choose randomly, the likelihood of reciprocated choices by chance is much smaller with this model, especially for low desired numbers of friends. Second, an individual lowers the probability of success with another individual once that individual does not reciprocate his or her choice. Consequently, since all individuals are equally attractive, the choice is withdrawn before it can even be reciprocated. Thus a major conclusion is that our models in which individual characteristics do play a role, generate not that few but so many friendships. Since only few friendships are established in the model without any saliences, segmentation is very high. This model consequently is not an adequate null model to test whether friendship formation based on individual characteristics and social influence leads to more segmented networks. For this purpose we introduce a slightly different model in which individual characteristics do neither play any role in friendship choice. This model is the base model presented in Zeggelink (1993). Results are presented under 'base model Zeggelink' in every fourth row corresponding with the relevant 'desired' number of friends. Within this model, individuals keep choices towards potential friendship candidates extended until such a candidate reacts 'negatively' as a result of the actual realization of his or her desired number of friendships. Moreover, this model runs until 'real' equilibrium. As a consequence, much more friendships are established, also more than with the models introduced here. With these latter models, the mean actual number of friends is smaller and the variance in this number is higher. Most interesting is that, corresponding with our expectations, the degree of segmentation obtained with the present models is much higher. This is in particular true for small values of 'desired' numbers of friends relative to the size of the population.

6. Discussion

We have presented a new dynamic individual oriented model of friendship network evolution. Individuals in the population make friendship choices to other individuals on the basis of preference for similarity and preferences for those with higher status. The preference for similarity is encompassed in comparison issues. The preference for higher status individuals is modelled on the basis of aspiration issues. Individuals attach different saliences to different issues. Individuals also take into account the probability of success with regard to establishing a friendship with another individual. This probability initially depends on the status difference between the two individuals, and is updated during the process of friendship formation on the basis of behavior of the other individual (whether he or she does or does not reciprocate choices). This update mechanism is a learning process of the individual. Moreover, we include the fact that individuals are influenced by their friendships. Those with higher status have more control over others with lower status and as such influence their friends, at least if they have interest in the issues.

These mechanisms correspond to a large extent with self-organizing principles: network structures emerge from individual actions and interactions without any 'supervisor' imposing that structure on the population of individuals. We compared models of processes in which salience of issues is or is not subject to social influence. In both models we systematically varied the number of friendships that every individual would like to establish. Preliminary results indicate that the same initial distribution of saliences and values on comparison and aspiration issues may result in a variety of network structures, just a few network structures, or one and only one network structure. The degree of segmentation in these networks increases with a decrease in the desired number of friends. For small numbers of desired friendships, segmentation is higher when salience is subject to social influence than when salience is constant. When individual characteristics do not play a role at all (when salience is zero for all individuals on all issues), individuals have extremely high difficulties in establishing the 'desired' number of friendships. Notwithstanding this effect, segmentation is always higher when comparison and aspiration issues play a role. Thus, our simulation results mirror the emergence of subgroups and transitivity of choices, often reported in empirical friendship network studies, without explicitly introducing these network characteristics in our models. They simply emerge from more fundamental choice and influence processes. As such, they are a result, not a cause. We also presented preliminary evidence that segmentation is smaller if networks are formed along interval scaled dimensions, like status. Such an issue makes it possible to form layered networks where friendships are established mainly within and between adjacent status categories, whereas dichotomous issues have stronger tendencies to result in completely segmented networks unless the influence process results in unanimity. Finally, except for the very specific case of four 'desired' friends in a group of ten individuals, individuals face more difficulties to realize the desired number of friendships in more segmented groups. Such difficulties are larger for the one than for the other, resulting in larger variances in the number of realized friends in more segmented networks. This implies that friendship formation based on individual characteristics and social influence create social dilemmas.

In several respects, the models presented here improve earlier models of friendship evolution (see the end of Section 2). We believe that the most important improvement still to be made is weakening the dominant role of the number of 'desired' friends. In the present models, individuals try to realize this 'desired' number, even if this implies the choice of friends with characteristics that are seen as highly undesirable. We aim to include in our future models the number of 'desired' friends as one of the individual characteristics that can be of more or less importance to them. Individuals may then prefer a smaller number of 'good' friends above their 'desired' number if that would imply many compromises in terms of their characteristics.

Apart from this elaboration of the present models, the first results presented here show that the final configuration of friendships and the effects of social influence depend on complex interactions between initial configurations of saliences, values on comparison and aspiration issues, and the process in which friendship is formed and social influence is materialized. Why do certain initial configurations result in so many final configurations, while others result in unique ones? More variation in population size, more initial configurations, and more systematic examinations of the dynamics of the process are required and are on our research agenda.

References

Artyushkin, V.F, Belyayev, A.V., Sandler, Y.M. & Sergeyev, V.M. (1990). Neural network ensembles as models of interdependence in collective behavior. *Mathematical Behavioral Sciences, 19*, 167-177.

Baerveldt , C. & Snijders, T.A.B. (1994). Influences on and from the segmentation of networks: hypotheses and tests. *Social Networks 16*, 213-232.

Blum, A. (1992). *Neural networks in C++: an object-oriented framework for building connectionist systems.* New York: Wiley.

Crockett, W.H. (1965). Cognitive complexity and impression formation. In B.A. Maher (Ed.), *Progress in experimental personality research, vol 2.* New York: Academic Press.

Davison, M.L. & Jones, L. E. (1976). A similarity-attraction model for predicting sociometric choice from perceived group structure. *Journal of Personality and Social Psychology, 33*, 601- 612.

Duck, S.W. (1988). *Handbook of personal relationships: theory, research, and interventions.* Chichester, Wiley.

Duck, S.W. (1991). *Friends, for life: the psychology of personal relationships. Second (revised) Edition.* New York: Harvester.

Erickson, B.H. (1988). The relational basis of attitudes. In B.Wellman & S.D. Berkowitz (eds.), *Social structures: a network approach.* Cambridge: Cambridge University Press.

Festinger, L. (1954). A theory of social comparsion processes. *Human relations, 7*, 117-140.

Flache, A. & Macy, M.W. (1996). The weakness of strong ties: Collective action failure in a highly cohesive group, *Journal of Mathematical Sociology, 21,* (forthcoming)

Flache, A. (1996). *The double edge of approval. An analysis of the effect of informal networks on cooperation in social dilemmas.* Amsterdam: Thesis Publ.

Glance, N.S. & Huberman, B.A. (1994). Social dilemmas and fluid organizations. In K.M. Carley & M.J. Prietula (eds.), *Computational Organization Theory.* Hillsdale, N.J.: Lawrence Erlbaum Associates

Hallinan, M.T. (1979). The process of friendship formation. *Social Networks,1*, 193-210.

Hansell, S. (1985). Adolescent friendship networks and distress in school. *Social Forces, 63*, 698-715.

Hayek, F.A. (1973). *Law, Legislation and Liberty*. Chicago: Univeristy of Chicago Press

Hegselmann, R. (1994). Zur Selbstorganisation von Solidarnetzwerken unter Ungleichen. Ein Simulationsmodell. In V. Arnold *et al* (eds) *Wirtschaftsethische Perspektiven I: Theorie, Ordnungsfrage, Internationale Institutionen.* Berlin: Duncker&Humblot

Hegselmann, R. (1996). Modeling Social Dynamics by Cellular Automata. In W.B.G. Liebrand, A. Nowak, R. Hegselmann (eds) *Computer modeling of network dynamics.* (forthcoming)

Hirschberg, N., Jones, L.E. & Haggerty, M. (1978). Individual differences in face perception. *Journal of Research in Personality, 12*, 488-499.

Hogg, M.A. (1992). *The social psychology of group cohesiveness.* New York: Harvester

Homans, G.C. (1951). *The Human Group*. New York: Harcourt Brace

Hunter, J.E., Danes, J.E., Cohen, S.H. (1984). *Mathematical Models of Attitude Change; Volume 1: Change in Single Attitudes and Cognitive Structures.* Orlando: Academic Press.

Jones, L.E. (1982). Construal of social environments: multidimensional models of interpersonal perception and attraction. In N. Hirschberg & L.G. Humphreys (Eds.), *Multivariate Applications in the Social Sciences.* Hillsdale, NJ: Erlbaum.

Jones, L.E. & Young, F.W. (1972). Structure of a social environment: longitudinal individual differences scaling of an intact group. *Journal of personality and social psychology, 24*, 108-121.

Latané, B., Nowak, A. & Liu, J.L. (1994). Dynamism, polarization, and clustering as order parameters of social systems. *Behavioural Science, 39*, 1-24

Lazarsfeld, P.F. & Merton, R.K. (1954). Friendship as social process: a substantive and methodological analysis. In M. Berger, T. Abel & C.H. Page (eds.), *Freedom and Control in Modern Society*. Toronto: Nostrand.

Leenders, R.Th.A.J. (1995). *Structure and Influence. Statistical Models for the Dynamics of Actor Attributes, Network Structure and their Interdependence*. Amsterdam: Thesis Publishers

Lin, N. (1994). Action, social resources, and the emergence of social structure: a rational choice theory. *Advances in group processes, 11*, 67-85.

Macy, M.W. & Flache, A. (1995). Beyond rationality in models of choice. *Annual Review of Sociology, 21*, 73-91

Masters, T. (1993). *Practical Neural Network Recipes in C++*. San Diego, CA: Academic Press.

Milardo, R.M. (1986). Personal choice and social constraint in close relationships: appplicaions of network analysis. In V.D. Derlega & B.A. Winstead (Eds.), *Friendship and Social Interaction.* New York: Springer Verlag.

Morris, M. (1991). A log-linear modeling framework for selective mixing. *Mathematical Biosciences, 107*, 349-377.

Nowak, A., Szamrej, J. & Latané, B. (1990). From private attitude to public opinion: A dynamic theory of social impact. *Psychological Review, 97*, 362-376

Nowak, A. & Latané, B. (1994). Simulating the emergence of social order from individual behavior. In N. Gilbert and J. Doran (eds), *Simulating Societies: The Computer simulation of Social Phenomena.* London: University College London Press

Nowak, A., Lewenstein, M. & Szamrej, J. (1996). Bubbles - A model of social transition. *Scientific American* (forthcoming)

Prigogine, I. (1980). *From Being to Becoming: Time and Complexity in the Physical Sciences.* San Francisco: Freeman.

Ritschard, G. (1991). *On the Use of Neural Principles in Social Networks.* Paper presened at the Second European Conference on Social Network Analysis, Paris, June 1991.

Rumelhart, D.E. & McLelland, J.L. (1988). *Explorations in Parallel Distributed Processing: A Handbook of Models, Programs, and Exercises.* Cambridge, MA: MIT Press.

Schachter, S. (1959). *The Psychology of Affiliation.* Stanford: Stanford University Press.

Sprenger, C.J.A. & Stokman, F.N. (1989). *Gradap User's Manual.* Groningen: iec ProGamma.

Stokman, F.N. & Van den Bos, J.M.M. (1992). A two-stage model of policy making with an empirical test in the U.S. energy-policy domain. In G. Moore and J. A. Whitt (eds), *The Political Consequences of Social Networks. Volume 4 of Research and Society.* Greenwich, Conn.: JAI Press

Stokman, F.N. & Van Oosten, R. (1994). *Generic Steps in Collective Decision Making.* Paper presented at the Sunbelt XIV International Social Network Conference, New Orleans, Louisiana, USA, February 17-20.

Stokman, F.N. & Zeggelink, E.P.H. (1996). Is politics power or policy oriented? A comparative analysis of dynamic access models in policy networks. *Journal of Mathematical Sociology, 21* (forthcoming)

Stokman, F.N. & Doreian, P. (1996). Evolution of social networks: Principles and processes. In P. Doreian & F.N. Stokman (eds), *Evolution of Social Networks.* Langhorne, PA: Gordon and Breach (forthcoming)

Wasserman, S.S. (1980a). Analyzing social networks as stochastic processes. *Journal of American Statistical Association, 75,* 280-294.

Wasserman, S.S. (1980b). A stochastic model for directed graphs with transition rates determined by reciprocity. In K. Schuessler (ed.), *Sociological Methodology.* San Fransisco: Jossey Bass.

Wasserman, S.S. & Faust, K. (1994). *Social Network Analysis. Methods and Applications.* Cambridge: Cambridge University Press

Weick, K.E. (1979). *The Social Psychology of Organizing.* Reading, Massachusetts: Addison Wesley.

Witt, U. (1994). The theory of societal evolution: Hayek's unfinished legacy. In J. Birner & R. van Zijp (eds.). *Hayek, Co-ordination and Evolution; His Legacy in Philosophy, Politics, Economics and the History of Ideas.* London: Routledge.

Wolfram, St. (1984). *Universality and Complexity in Cellular Automata*, Physica

Zeggelink, E.P.H. (1993). *Strangers into Friends; The Evolution of Friendship Networks Using an Individual Oriented Approach*. Amsterdam: Thesis Publishers

Zeggelink, E.P.H. (1994). Dynamics of structure: an individual oriented approach. *Social Networks, 16*, 295-333.

Zeggelink, E.P.H. (1995). Evolving friendship networks: an individual oriented approach implementing similarity. *Social Networks, 17*, 83-110.

Zeggelink, E.P.H. (1996). Group formation in friendship networks. *Journal of Mathematical Sociology, 21* (forthcoming)

Zeggelink, E.P.H., Stokman, F.N. & Van de Bunt, G.G. (1996). The emergence of groups in the evolution of friendship networks. *Journal of Mathematical Sociology, 21* (forthcoming)

Zoethout, K. (1994). *Groepsvorming als Mechanisme van Zelforganisatie*. Student report, Psychologisch Instituut Heymans, University of Groningen.

The Evolution of Cooperation in a Simulated Inter-Group Conflict

Ramzi Suleiman[1] and Ilan Fischer[2]

[1] Department of Psychology, University of Haifa, Haifa, 31905, Israel
[2] Department of Psychology, University College London, London, UK

Abstract

The present study simulates an enduring intergroup conflict in which each one of two interacting groups is represented by a unitary representative elected for a given constituency period. We assume that the conflict between the two groups can be modeled as an iterated Prisoner's Dilemma game played by the groups' representatives. In addition, we assume that the performance of each representative influences her constituents and that this, in turn, affects her prospects to be reelected. At the end of a constituency period, new elections are called for, and their results determine whether she remains in her position or is replaced by another representative. Our main objectives are: (1) to investigate the effect of this common democratic procedure, namely, the periodic election of group representatives, on the evolution of cooperation between the groups; and (2) to investigate the effect of the frequency of elections in the two groups on the evolving intergroup relations. Results of 150 simulations yield the following main results: (1) the dynamics of the intergroup conflict evolve into phases of well-defined patterns. (2) when mutual cooperation emerged, it was more enduring for high than for low rates of cooperation between the groups' representatives; and (3) the prospects for reaching phases of mutual cooperation along the evolutionary path were considerably better for longer election periods, than for shorter ones.

Key terms: Computer simulations, evolution of cooperation, intergroup conflict.

1 Introduction

The study of competition and cooperation has long been the focus of attention for many researchers in the social sciences. Although we make no claim here in favor of any single approach, we nevertheless argue that laboratory and simulation studies using the Prisoner's Dilemma (PD) game have proven beneficial for understanding competitive and cooperative behaviors in dyadic and group settings. Of special interest here is the body of theoretical and simulation research using the iterative two-person PD game to study the evolution of cooperation (c.f. Axelrod, 1981, 1984; Axelrod & Hamilton, 1981, Nowak & May, 1992, Marinoff, 1992, Messick & Liebrand, 1995) and the extension of Axelrod's work to account for evolutionary games with heterogeneous populations (c.f. Mueller, 1987; Lomborg, 1992; Hegselmann, in press), and social dilemmas (Schuessler, 1990; Macy, 1990, 1991a, 1991b).

Compared to the extensive research using the PD game to study competition and cooperation in dyads and groups, very little has been done to investigate these important aspects in intergroup settings. All the relevant literature that uses the PD game to model enduring intergroup conflicts assumes that the situation is reducible to a two-person game in which each group is represented by a unitary player. Such modeling is characteristic of several analyses of international conflicts and deterrence between superpowers (Schelling, 1960; Brahms, 1975), and of competition between firms (Dixit and Nalebuff, 1992). The representation of an intergroup conflict by a dyadic game can be justified if we assume that all members of each group agree on the same strategy in every interaction with the outgroup. Another justification is to assume that each group selects one person, an appointed delegate or group leader, who represents the entire group. Apparently, the second justification has greater validity, since it captures many real-life situations in which groups' representatives negotiate on behalf of their groups. Notwithstanding its plausibility, the last interpretation raises non-trivial questions concerning the rules that govern the selection of group representatives and the duration of their representation.

To illustrate, consider the role of a state president as the representative of her country in an international dispute. To achieve her position, she must first win her party's nomination, and later the general elections. In countries with a parliamentary system, prime ministers and cabinet members attain their positions after being elected by their parties, and after their parties win elections or succeed in forming a winning coalition with other parties. Regardless of the specific electoral system, leaders of democratic countries serve in positions for a given constituency period, after which new elections are called for and new representatives may be elected in their place. The same applies to leaders of political parties, corporations, universities, and many other groups whose representatives are selected for a fixed duration, after which new elections determine whether they resume their positions or are replaced by new candidates.

The present study simulates an enduring intergroup conflict in which each one of two interacting groups is represented by a unitary representative elected for a given constituency period. We assume that the conflict can be modeled by an iterated PD game played by the two groups' representatives. In addition, we assume that the performance of each representative influences her constituents (in a manner to be detailed later) and that this, in turn, affects her prospects to be reelected. At the end of a constituency period, new elections are called for, and their results determine whether she remains in her position or is replaced by another representative. Our main objectives are (1) to investigate the effect of this common democratic procedure, namely, the periodic election of group representatives, on the relations between the two conflicting groups, and the prospects of the evolution of cooperation between the groups; and (2) to investigate the effect of the frequency of elections in the groups on the evolving intergroup relations. Based on anecdotal evidence from international politics, we hypothesize that in protracted conflicts, more frequent elections may act in two ways: in some instances it might regulate retaliatory actions taken against the outgroup and in others it might escalate them.

The following section provides a detailed description of the intergroup simulation. Section 3 summarizes the main results of this study. Section 4 ends with a brief discussion.

2 The Simulation

The basic features of the simulation can be described as follows:

(1) The intergroup conflict is modeled by an iterated two-person PD game played by elected delegates of the two groups. The specific PD payoff matrix in each step of the game is shown in Table 1.

Table 1 Prisoner's Dilemma Payoff Matrix

		Delegate B: C	Delegate B: D
Delegate A	C	5 , 5	-10 , 10
	D	10 , -10	-5 , -5

(2) The simulation begins by defining two group sizes, n and m. Each group member is characterized by an initial propensity, or probability p, that she will cooperate in a PD game with an outgroup member. Group members with p=0 are those who will never cooperate, while those with p=1 will always cooperate. To obtain a reasonable degree of flexibility in defining the distributions of cooperation in the two groups, we used a beta function for defining these distributions. This function is sufficiently rich to describe most random variables having a restricted range (Derman et al., 1973). It can assume a wide variety of shapes, including uniform, symmetric, positively skewed, negatively skewed, and U-shaped functions. In formal notation, the beta density function for the probability of cooperation, p, can be written as:

$$f(p) = \begin{cases} p^u (1-p)^v / B(u,v) & \text{if } 0 \leq p \leq 1 \\ 0 & \text{Otherwise} \end{cases} \quad (1)$$

where u and v are the parameters of the beta distribution ($u \geq 0$, $v \geq 0$), and B(u,v) is the Beta function (see e.g. Johnson & Kotz, 1969).

The results reported here were obtained for symmetrical distributions with u = v = 5 for the two groups. For these values, the distribution is bell-shaped, and resembles a normal distribution in the range (0, 1). In all the simulations, continuous beta functions were approximated by discrete functions with equal intervals of Δ=0.05.

(3) Following the construction of each group, the simulation finds the "minimal winning coalition" that contains 51% or more group members. The simulation was designed to search only coalitions defined over a continuous (i.e., non-fragmented) segment of the cooperativeness range. The mean of the "minimal winning coalition" was then chosen to represent the entire group in the PD game played against the second group representative. To illustrate this procedure, consider a population with the cooperation distribution portrayed in Figure 1.

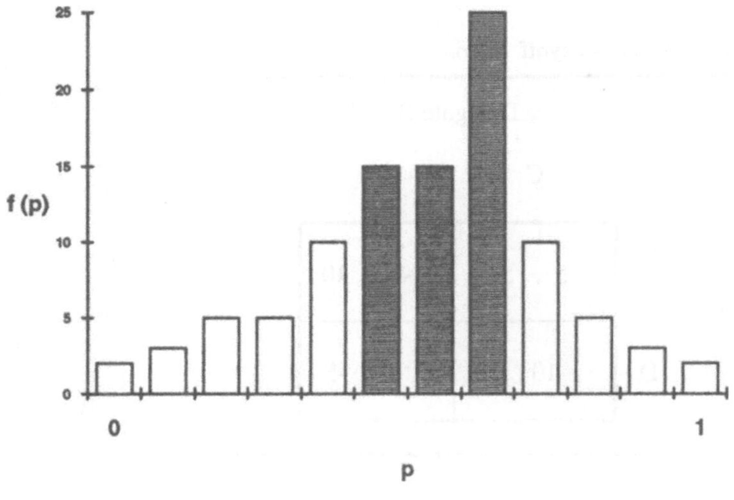

Fig.1 The minimal winning coalition and its representative for a hypothetical distribution of cooperation.

To locate the group delegate, the simulation starts by finding all possible non-fragmented subgroups containing 51% or more of the population. Of all the possible subgroups satisfying this condition, the simulation selects the most compact one (i.e., the one with the minimal range on the p continuum). This is the dark shaded subgroup in Figure 1. This subgroup is sought as the minimal winning coalition in democratic elections held in this population, and its mean is sought as the elected group delegate. This delegate represents the entire group for the duration of a constituency period. After this period, new "elections" are held according to the procedure described above and a new delegate is "elected".

(4) The time intervals between successive elections (viewed as a measure of democracy) are defined separately for each group.

(5) After being elected, the delegates engage in an iterative PD game with each other. At every stage of the game, the strategy of each delegate is probabilistic and

is defined by her probability to cooperate. Following each interaction, the simulation records each delegate's payoffs, as well as her cumulative gain.

(6) Following each interaction, each group delegate influences the propensities for cooperation of all her group members. This process can be considered as an ongoing social learning process (Axelrod, 1984) in which group members learn and adapt their strategies depending on their delegate's performance. We assume that the social influence of a delegate d on any group member i is inversely proportional to the social distance (measured on the cooperation continuum) between d and i. Moreover, we assume that this influence is proportional to the delegate's payoff. To express this relationship in formal notation, denote the probabilities that an individual i and the delegate d will cooperate at period t by $p_i(t)$ and $p_d(t)$, respectively. Also denote the outcome for delegate d at period t by $O_d(t)$. The social influence of d on i can be expressed by:

$$p_i(t + 1) = p_i(t) + K\, O_d(t)/(p_d(t)-p_i(t)) \qquad (2)$$

where $p_i(t + 1)$ is the probability that the individual i will cooperate at period t+1, and K is a constant. In the reported simulations, the values for the outcome $O_d(t)$ are given by the matrix in Table 1. Accordingly, a delegate d can either win 10 or 5 units, or lose 10 or 5 units. The numerical value for K in the reported simulations was $K = 0.1$.

In essence, the social influence function in Equation 2 resembles recent formulations of Latane's "social impact function" (Latane, 1981; Nowak, et al., 1992). Nevertheless, it has a number of unique properties that differentiate it from Latane's function in several important ways: (1) Distances here are social and not spatial, because they are defined on the continuum which maps the individuals' propensities to cooperate, (2) Group members are influenced by the outcomes of their delegate (the source), not by the strength of his or her attitude. (3) The type of social learning defined in Equation 2 is probabilistic and not deterministic as in Latane's model. (4) Social influence is sought as a continuous or an incremental process in which delegates gradually affect their constituents' cooperativeness, whereas in Latane's theory the change of attitudes is a binary, all-or-none process.

Note that Equation 2 has a singular point when $p_d(t) - p_i(t) = 0$, which means that the delegate's social influence on a group member with $p_i(t) = p_d(t)$ is not defined. To account for such cases, the probability $p_i(t + 1)$ at the singular point is defined as:

$$\begin{aligned} &\text{if } O_d(t) \geq 0 \text{ then } && p_i(t + 1) = p_i(t) \\ &\text{if } O_d(t) < 0 \text{ then } && p_i(t + 1) = p_i(t) + m\, K\, O_d(t) \qquad (3) \end{aligned}$$

Where m is a random parameter which assumes the values $\pm$ 1 with equal probabilities.

According to this definition, for a nonnegative delegate outcome ($O_d(t) \geq 0$), the initial propensity of group member i to cooperate is not changed (i.e., it remains equal to the probability of cooperation of the delegate). On the other hand, if delegate d loses ($O_d(t) < 0$), then the probability that i will cooperate at period t+1

will either increase or decrease, depending on the realization of the random parameter m.
To illustrate the dynamics of social influence generated by the model, consider the distribution in Figure 2 which shows a hypothetical population at some period t.

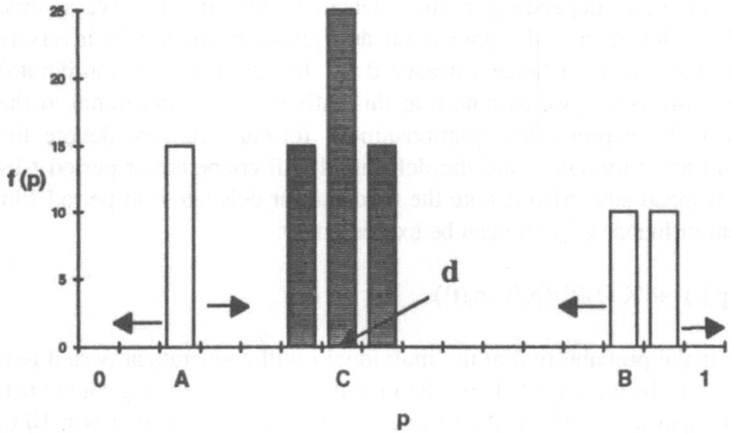

Fig. 2 The Social influence process in a hypothetical population.

If the delegate d of the winning coalition C wins at period t, then she will "pull" all other group members toward her position (i.e. closer to her probability to cooperate). The "pull" force will be strongest on members in cluster C. In addition, it will be stronger on members in cluster A, whose positions are closer to the position of the delegate, than on members in cluster B whose positions are more distant from the delegate's position. Conversely, if the delegate loses, then all group members will be "pushed" away from her position, and the "push" force will be inversely proportional to the proximity between their positions and the delegate's position.

Following each interaction between the delegates, the simulation updates the cooperation propensities of all other group members according to the social influence function described above. Each delegate remains in position until the next elections, regardless of the changes in the distribution of cooperation that take place in her group. When elections are due, the most recent distribution of cooperation determines who becomes the new group's delegate for the next constituency period.

While Equation 2 describes the form of social influence in almost all cases, special treatment was needed for the two boundary situations in which group members shift toward all-cooperate or all-defect, while their delegate lags behind them and incurs losses. Suppose that members in group A shift to the right and concentrate very close to the p=1 point, while their delegate, who is still in position, is located somewhere very close, but still to the left (having lower p value). In the case in which the delegate of group B is much less cooperative, group A's delegate will lose continuously, and all group members having higher p

values will be "pushed" away from her towards the far right end (i.e., toward the all-cooperate position). When the next elections are due, the new delegate will be an all-cooperate one and will lose continuously. Still, a majority of her group members will have have higher p values , and thus will continue to be “pushed” to the right end of the p continuum. Because these members can not be “pushed” to the right further, they may be "stuck" at the right end of the p continuum. The same situation, though less frequently, might occur at the all-defect end. To avoid such counter-intuitive situations, we modified the social influence rule for these extreme situations, such that group members "pushed" away from a losing delegate will move inward, towards the center of the p range.
Operationally, the extreme boundaries were defined as the 2.5% ends on both sides of the p continuum. The simulation treatment of the upper boundary condition can be formalized as follows:

for $p_i(t) \geq .975$, $p_d(t) \geq .975$, and $O_d(t) < 0$:

If $p_i(t) > p_d(t)$ then $p_i(t+1) = p_d(t) + K\, O_d(t)$ (4-a)

Similarly, the lower boundary condition can be formalized as follows:

for $p_i(t) \leq .025$, $p_d(t) \leq .025$, and $O_d(t) < 0$:

If $p_i(t) < p_d(t)$ then $p_i(t+1) = p_d(t) - K\, O_d(t)$ (4-b)

For all other situations $p_i(t + 1)$ is determined according to one of the influence functions stated before (i.e., Equations 2 or 3).

3 Results

As stated earlier, the main objectives of the reported simulations were: (1) to investigate the effects of a common democratic procedure (i.e., the periodic election of group representatives) on the evolution of intergroup relations between two conflicting groups; and (2) to investigate the effect of the frequency of elections in the two groups on the evolution of cooperation between the two groups. The simulations were run on a PC. The results reported here were obtained for two equal groups with size n = m = 300. The initial propensities for cooperation in both groups were identical, with symmetrical beta distributions with parameters u = v = 5. To test the effect of the election period on the evolution of intergroup conflict, we ran thirty simulations under each one of five election conditions. These conditions were: (1, 1), (10, 10), (1000, 1000), (5000, 5000), and (10000, 10000), where each pair indicates the number of iterations between successive elections in the first and second groups. Each one of the 150 simulations was run for 80,000 iterations. For every iteration, the computer program generated (and displayed) the distributions of cooperation for the two groups, their delegates' probabilities of cooperation, and their commutative payoffs. In reporting the results, however, we focus on the first two variables and omit the reporting of the payoffs, which is of no value for understanding the evolution of cooperation between the two groups.

To study the emerging patterns of intergroup dynamics, we plotted the probabilities of cooperation of the groups' delegates as functions of the number of iterations. The investigation of these graphs revealed that for some simulations, the intergroup dynamics followed certain well defined "pure" patterns. In most other simulations, the emerging patterns exhibited some alternating mixes of these "pure" patterns. Typically, a certain "pure" pattern prevailed for a relatively long period (counted in iterations), after which the dynamics shifted to another "pure" pattern, and so on. The emerging pattern was chaotic only for very few simulations. Before we present the results obtained for each election period, it is useful to demonstrate the main "pure" patterns using some representative examples.

(a) A Defection vs. Oscillation (D-O) pattern: A typical example of this pattern obtained under the (10,10) elections condition is shown in Figure 3.1.

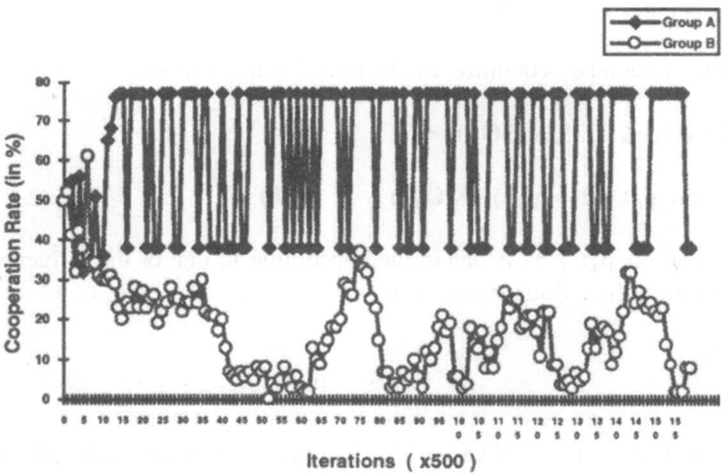

Fig. 3.1 The delegates rates of cooperation for a typical Defection vs. Oscillation pattern.

This figure depicts the delegates' probabilities for cooperation as a function of iteration. It clearly shows that after some transitional phase, a relatively stable steady state emerges in which group A's delegate continuously oscillates between high and low levels of cooperation, while group B's delegate converges slowly toward a very low level of cooperation. A better understanding of this pattern can be achieved by looking at the evolution of cooperation within each of the two interacting groups. Figure 3.2 depicts the distributions of cooperation in groups A and B for the same run sampled at various periods between 0 and 80,000. The vertical axis for each graph shows the respective frequency distribution, and the horizontal axis shows the probability to cooperate, given in equal intervals of 0.05 (denoted by 0, 1, ..., 19).

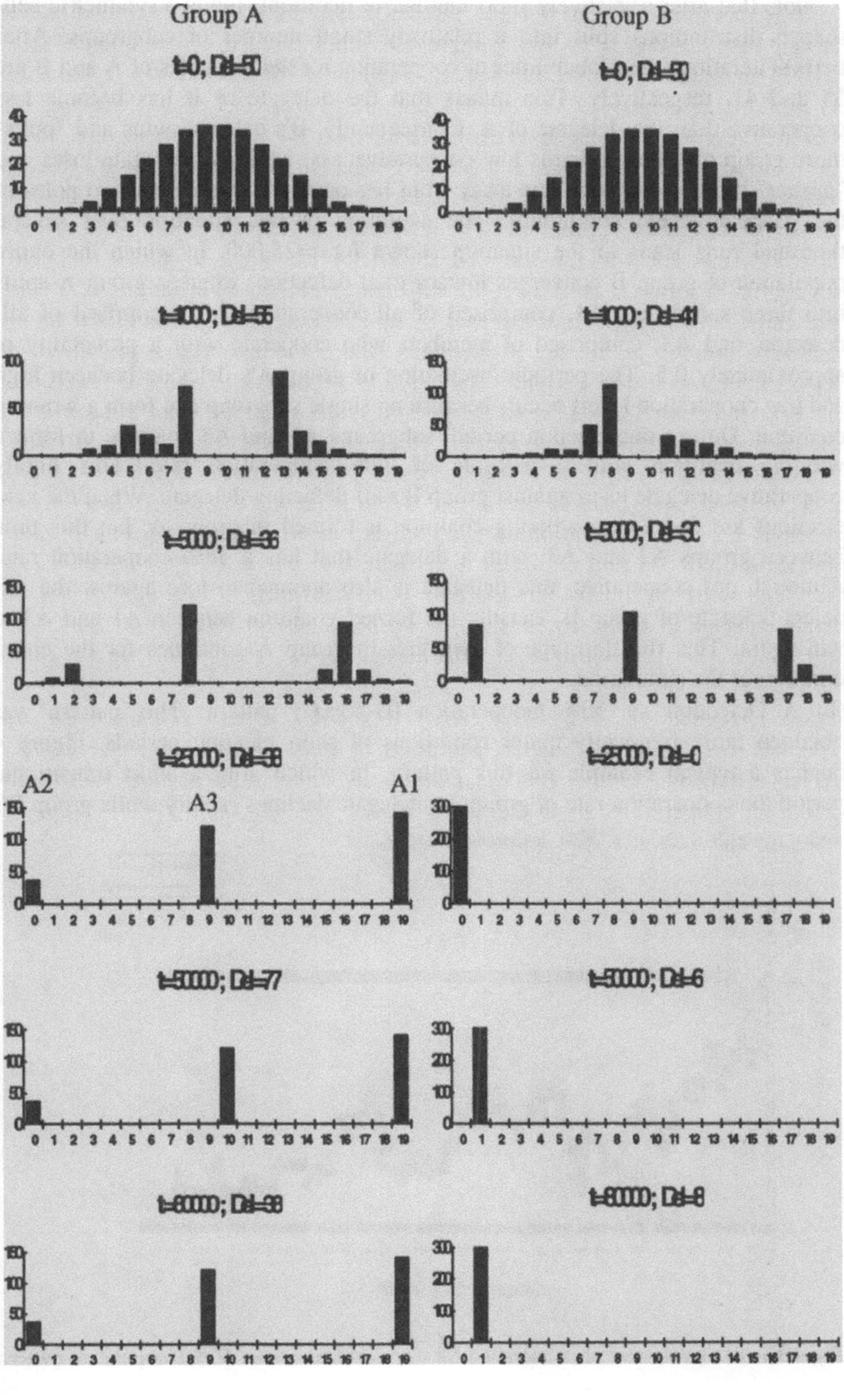

Fig. 3.2 The intragroup processes for a typical Defection - Oscillation pattern.

Note that after a relatively short number of iterations, the two symmetric bell-shaped distributions split into a relatively small number of subgroups. After t=1000 iterations the probabilities of cooperation for the delegates of A and B are 55 and 41, respectively. This means that the delegate of B has become less cooperative than the delegate of A. Consequently, B's delegate wins and "pulls" more group members towards low cooperativeness, while B's delegate loses and "pushes" more group members away from her position towards the two poles of the cooperativeness continuum. The evolution of this situation over several thousand runs leads to the situation shown for t=25,000, in which the entire population of group B converges toward total defection, whereas group A splits into three subgroups: A1, comprised of all-cooperators; A2, comprised of all-defectors and A3, comprised of members who cooperate with a probability of approximately 0.5. The periodic oscillation of group A's delegate between high and low cooperation levels occurs because no single subgroup can form a winning coalition. During one election period, subgroups A1 and A3 coalesce to form a winning coalition with a delegate of 77% cooperation rate. This highly cooperative delegate loses against group B's all-defecting delegate. When the next elections are due a new winning coalition is formed in group A, but this time between groups A2 and A3, with a delegate that has a 38% cooperation rate. Although not cooperative, this delegate is also doomed to lose against the all-defect delegate of group B, causing the former coalition between A1 and A3 to win again. This flip-flop type of dynamics in group A continues for the entire duration of the simulation.

(b) A Defection vs. 50% Cooperation (D-50%C) pattern: This pattern was obtained more frequently under conditions of short election periods. Figure 4 depicts a typical example for this pattern, in which after a short transitional period the cooperation rate of group A's delegate declines rapidly while group B's delegate stabilizes at a 50% cooperation rate.

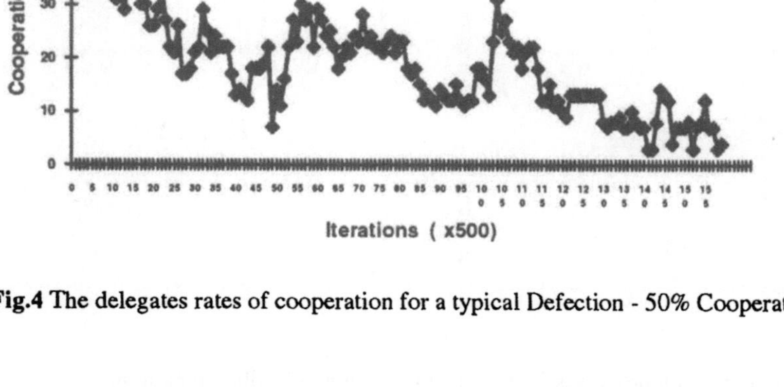

Fig.4 The delegates rates of cooperation for a typical Defection - 50% Cooperation pattern.

The evolution of the intragroup process in this pattern is qualitatively similar to the one explained earlier for the Oscillation vs. Defection pattern (see Fig. 3.2). The only difference here is that group B evolves into two subgroups: all-cooperators and all-defectors, each containing exactly 50% of the population which is less than the minimum 51% needed to form a winning coalition. In this situation, no single group can form a winning coalition. The only possible coalition is one that encompasses the entire group, with a delegate of 50% cooperation rate.

(c) A Cooperation - Cooperation (C-C) pattern : In this pattern, the two groups converge to mutual cooperation as shown in the result portrayed in Figure 5.1.

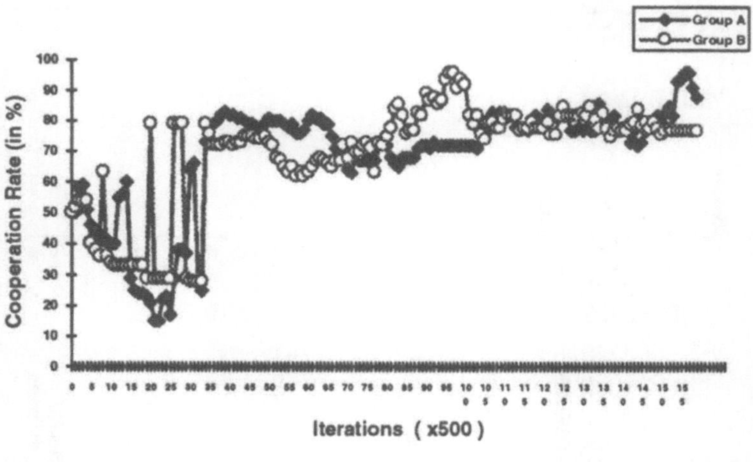

Fig. 5.1 The delegates rates of cooperation for a Cooperation-Cooperation pattern.

The maximum level of mutual cooperation obtained in this result is quite impressive (about 80% for both delegates). In most other results the delegates' rates of cooperation were lower. For classification purposes, we decided to classify a pattern as a C-C pattern if it exhibited a clear and enduring pattern of mutual cooperation, and if the rate of cooperation of both delegates did not drop below the 51% threshold. For the reported simulations (each of which consisted of 80,000 periods), an "enduring" pattern was defined as one that stabilizes for at least 5000 iterations.

The corresponding intragroup dynamics for the result in Figure 5.1 is depicted in Figure 5.2. As in Figure 3.2, The vertical axis shows the frequency distributions, and the horizontal axis shows the probabilities to cooperate given in equal intervals of 0.05 (denoted in the graphs by 0, 1, ..., 19).

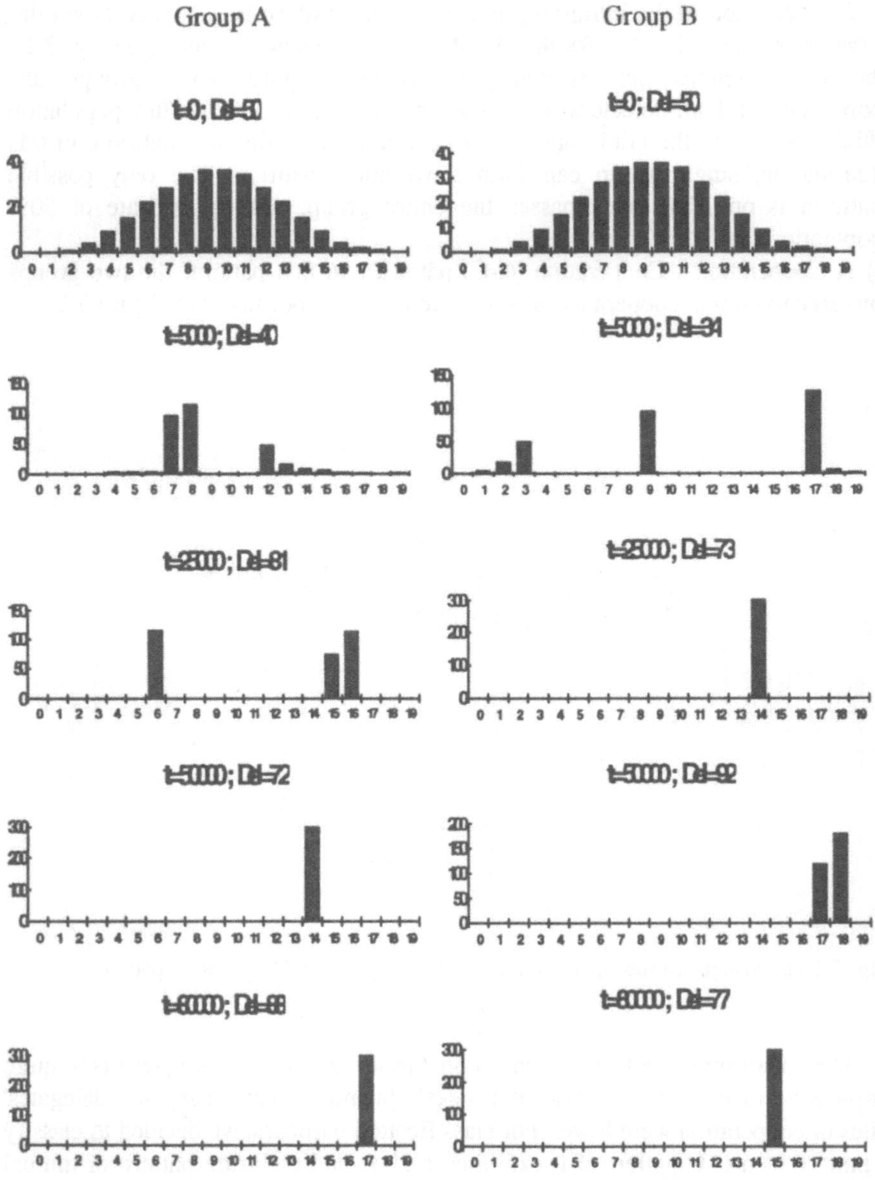

Fig. 5.2 The intragroup processes for a typical Cooperation - Cooperation pattern.

The figure shows that after some transitional period the two groups move towards high cooperation rates. When such a situation is reached, both delegates win (in expected values) and mutual cooperation is maintained.

As noted earlier, some simulation results were predominantly comprised of one of the "pure" patterns described above, but most others exhibited an alternating mix of "pure" patterns, as well as other, less frequent patterns. Figures 6.1 and 6.2 demonstrate two typical mixed patterns results.

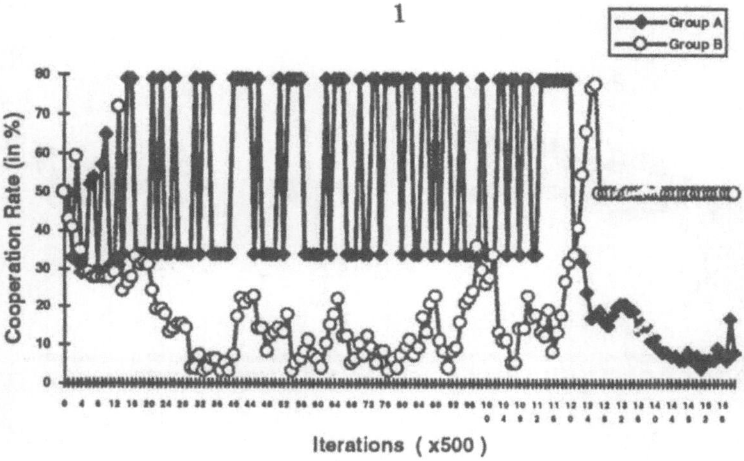

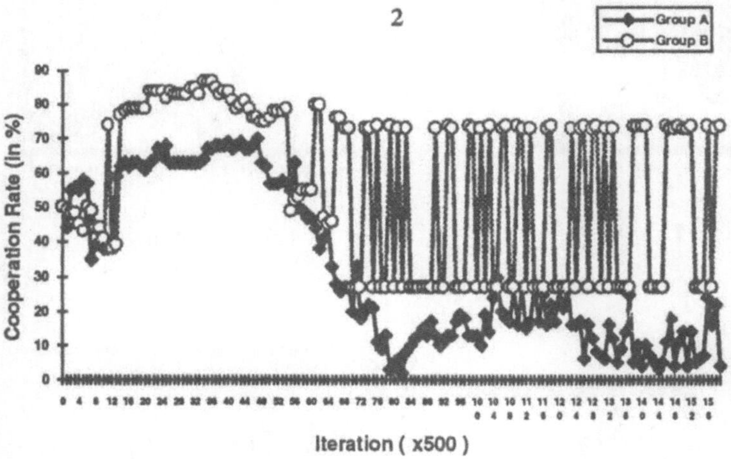

Figures 6.1 & 6.2 Examples for two typical mixed patterns.

Figure 6.1 depicts a result obtained under the (1,1) election condition. It demonstrates that after a short transitional period, the dynamics evolve into a Defection vs. Oscillation pattern for about 60 thousand iterations, and then shift to a Defection vs. 50% cooperation pattern for the next 20 thousand iterations. The result shown in Figure 6.2 was obtained under the (10,10) election condition.

It shows that after a transitional period, both delegates shift to a Cooperation - Cooperation mode that lasts about 20 thousand iterations. After this phase the dynamics shift to a Defection-Oscillation pattern for the remainder of the evolutionary path.

Figure 7 depicts three typical results for each elections condition.

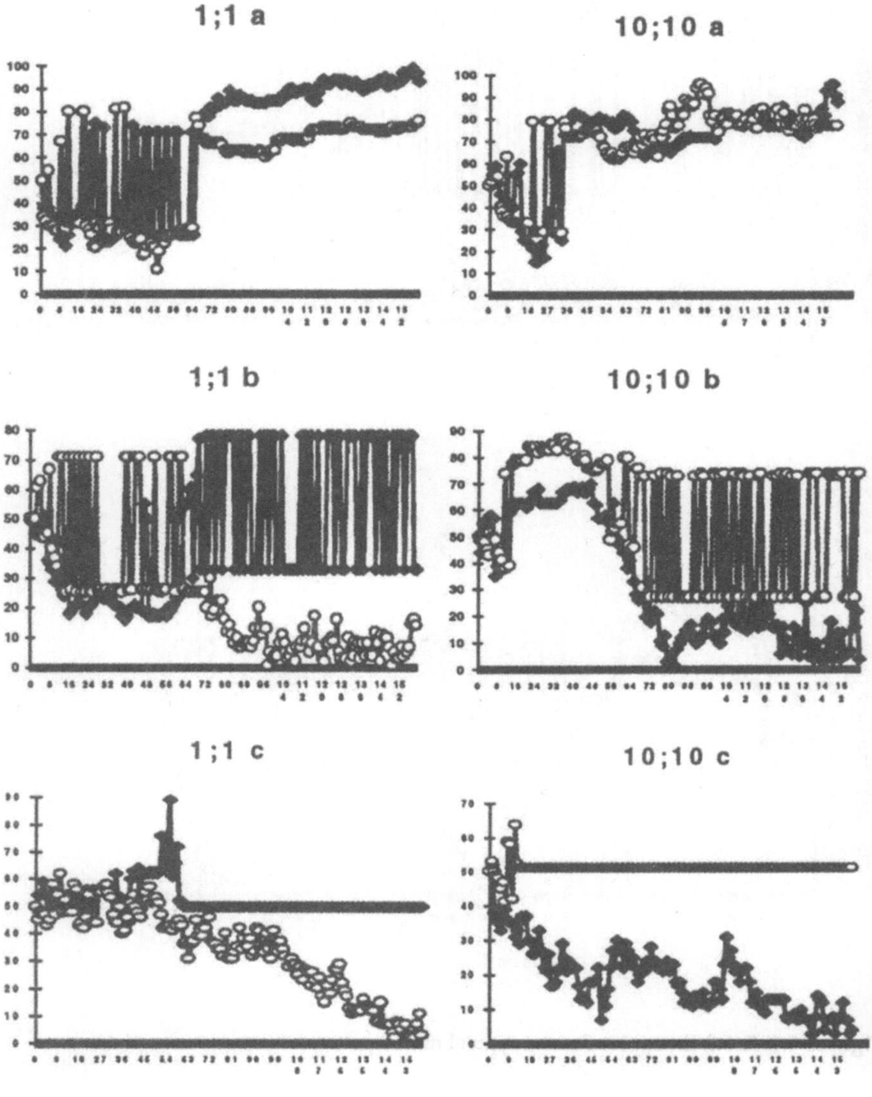

Fig. 7 Three typical simulation results for each election condition.

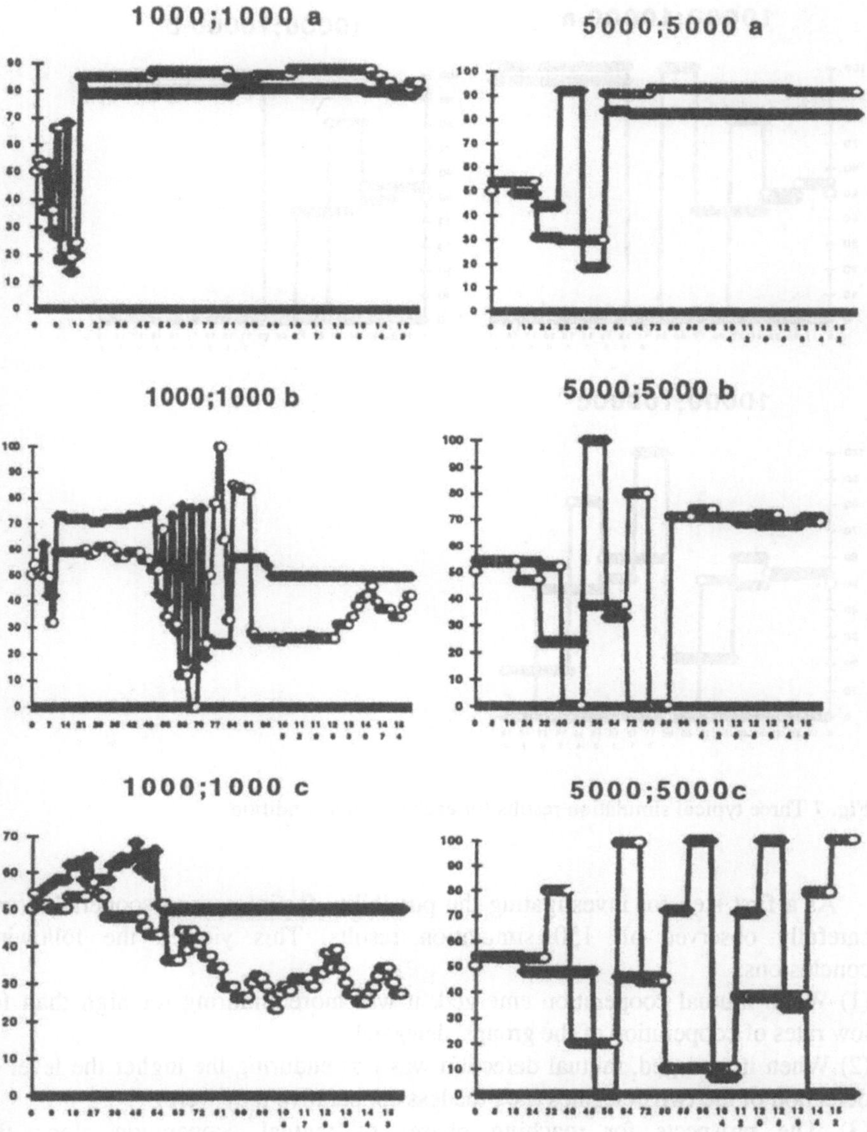

Fig. 7 Three typical simulation results for each election condition.

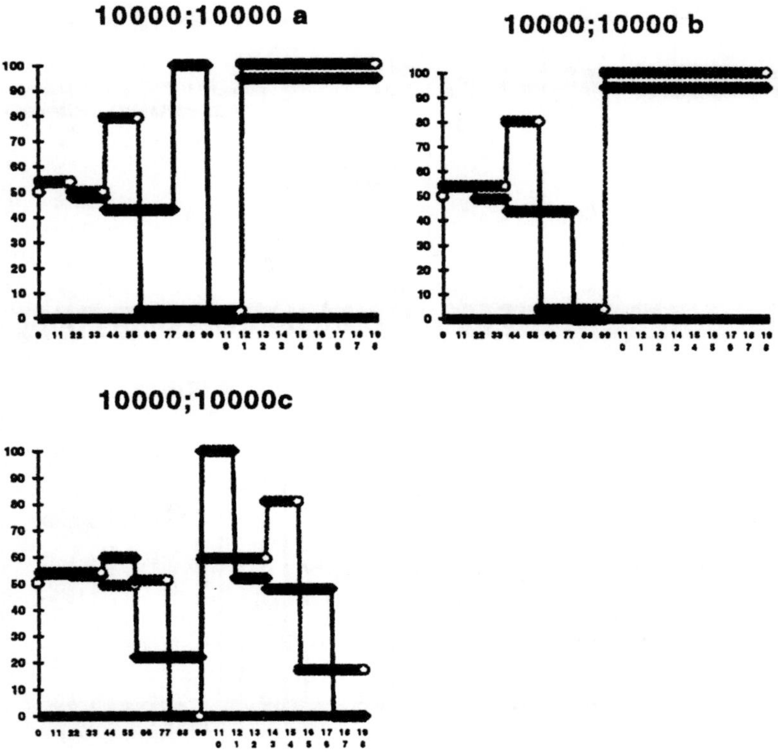

Fig. 7 Three typical simulation results for each election condition.

As a first step for investigating the possibility for intergroup cooperation, we carefully observed all 150 simulation results. This yielded the following conclusions:

(1) When mutual cooperation emerged, it was more enduring for high than for low rates of cooperation of the groups' delegates.

(2) When it emerged, mutual defection was less enduring the higher the level of defection of the two delegates (i.e., the less cooperative they were).

(3) The prospects for reaching phases of mutual cooperation along the evolutionary path were considerably better for longer election periods (5000, 10,000), than for shorter periods (1, 10).

To further investigate the effect of election frequency on the prospects of mutual cooperation, we sampled each one of the 150 simulation results at eight sampling points separated by equal intervals of 10 thousand iterations. The sampling points were 10, 20, ... 70, 80 thousand iterations. At each sampling point, we calculated the relative frequency of "hitting" a Cooperation-Cooperation (C-C) pattern under each of the five election conditions. Consistent with our earlier definition of an "enduring" C-C pattern, a pattern was classified as a C-C pattern only if mutual cooperation was stable for at least 2500 iterations on each side of the sampling point.

Figure 8 depicts the relative frequencies of mutual cooperation (in %) at each sampling point, for each one of the five elections conditions.

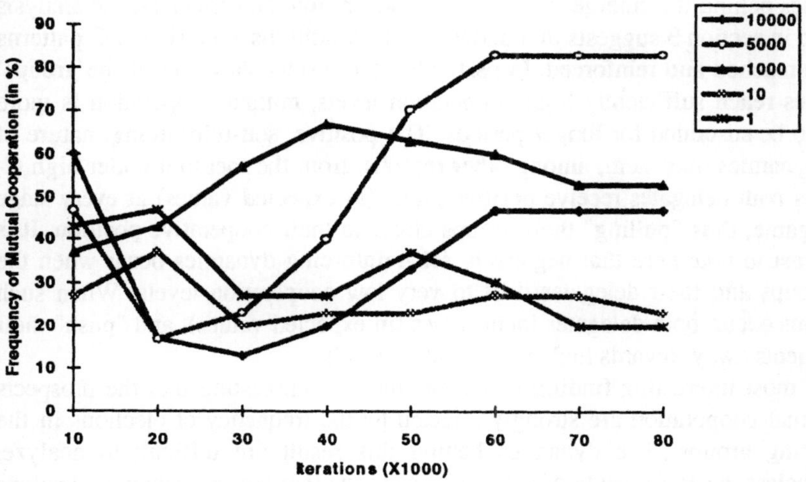

Fig.8 The relative frequencies of mutual cooperation (in %) for each one of the five election conditions.

A qualitative inspection of the five graphs in Figure 8 (corresponding to the five election conditions) reveals some interesting results that can be summarized as follows: (1) The two graphs corresponding to the shorter election periods (1 and 10) exhibit similar patterns. Except for the first two sampling periods, the graphs are more or less flat, indicating very little change in C-C rates along the evolutionary path. For all sampling points between 30 and 80 thousand iterations the C-C rates for both conditions fall between 20-30%. (2) The graphs corresponding to the longer election periods (5000 and 10,000) exhibit similar patterns. Both graphs are s-shaped, with a monotonic increase in C-C rates for sampling points between 30 - 60 thousand iterations. After the 60 thousand point the C-C rates for both conditions stabilize. (3) Interestingly, the highest rate of C-C under the 10,000 election period was only 47%, while under the 5,000 period condition, the C-C rate reaches an impressive maximum of 83%. (4) The second best condition in terms of the C-C rate is the 1000 period condition, with a maximum of 67%. Figure 8 shows that the graph for this condition is somewhat convex, with a peak around the 40 thousand sampling point. Beyond this point, the C-C rate drops monotonically reaching 53% for points near the end of the observed evolution path.

4 Concluding Remarks

The results indicate that for the conditions tested in the present study, the dynamics of the intergroup conflict evolve into phases of well-defined patterns. Of all the patterns of intergroup dynamics described earlier, our main interest was in the emergence of mutual cooperation. Given the considerable complexity of the simulation, it is extremely difficult to achieve a complete understanding of the dynamics behind the emergence of mutual cooperation. Nevertheless, the analysis detailed in section 3 suggests that under certain conditions, enduring C-C patterns may be reached and reinforced. In particular, the results show that if the groups' delegates reach sufficiently high cooperation levels, mutual cooperation is more likely to be sustained for longer periods. The positive, self-reinforcing, nature of these dynamics may stem, among other reasons, from the fact that under high C-C levels both delegates receive positive gains (in expected values) at every stage of the game, thus "pulling" their groups closer to their cooperative position. It is of interest to note here that negatively self-reinforcing dynamics occur when the two groups and their delegates drift to very low cooperation levels. When such situations occur, both delegates incur losses (in expected values), and "push" their constituents away towards higher cooperation levels.

The most interesting finding is perhaps the one suggesting that the prospects for mutual cooperation are strongly affected by the frequency of elections in the interacting groups. The dynamics behind this result are difficult to analyze. Nevertheless, a careful study of the results suggests that the frequency of elections can enhance mutual cooperation through at least two possible effects: (1) Longer periods between elections allow the delegates to exercise a more systematic and directional influence on their constituents. The build-up of such an influence can result in a coherent and directional shift of group members in one defined direction. In contrast, frequent changes of delegates can result in an incoherent, "random-walk" type of movement caused by the frequent changes in the delegate's position. This results in frequent non-orderly "pulls" and "pushes" in alternating directions. (2) The positive effect of longer election periods is dramatically pronounced when the two groups drift to very low cooperation levels and their delegates engage in a lose-lose D-D interaction. In such situations, long election periods have a positive effect in that they provide a sufficient period for "pushing" the populations of both groups towards high cooperation levels.

The above analysis is consistent with the results, which showed that the rates of C-C patterns were higher under long election periods (i.e., 1000, 5000, 10,000) than under short periods (i.e.; 1, 10). The fact that mutual cooperation was higher under 5000 (and 1000) election periods than under the 10,0000 period is hard to interpret. Nevertheless, it suggests that an optimal election frequency exists, for which mutual cooperation occurs with highest probability. Our results indicate that under the tested conditions, the optimal point is close to the 5000 election period point. More simulations are needed, however, to locate the optimal point precisely.

The present study constitutes a pioneering effort in an ongoing project to simulate the evolution of enduring intergroup conflicts. The result regarding the nonlinear effect of election frequency on the evolution of mutual cooperation is intriguing. Its robustness, as well as the robustness of other findings reported here, remain to be tested for other parameter values and conditions. As a first step, we plan to rerun the simulation for: (a) groups with unequal election periods, (b) groups with different initial distributions of cooperation, (c) other (especially asymmetric) distributions of initial propensities, and (d) other influence functions. We also plan to pursue more ambitious objectives, such as substitution of the probabilistic strategies by cellular automata with reactive strategies and inclusion of physical space in the model.

A major motivation behind the present study lies in the authors' interest in real group conflicts. In particular, we were challenged by the protracted Arab-Israeli conflict and the emerging prospects for its resolution. We contend that the effort taken here is too limited to allow any speculations, let alone predictions, regarding the evolution of the Arab-Israeli, or any other real-life conflict. While the future extensions outlined above can prove helpful for testing the robustness of the obtained results, ecological validity can be significantly enhanced if some of the simulation parameters (e.g., the initial propensities for cooperation) can be based on empirical data. Notwithstanding, we believe that the obtained results bear an educational value. The result showing that under optimal election frequency, conflicts between democratic groups are likely to evolve into mutual cooperation bears a nice historical lesson. If taken seriously, this lesson means that conflicting groups, and their representatives, can "cut short" towards mutual cooperation, and avoid unnecessary losses of precious lives, time, and scarce resources.

References

Axelrod, R. (1981). The emergence Of cooperation among egoists *The American Political Science Review, 75*, 306-318.

Axelrod, R. (1984). *The Evolution of Cooperation*. New York: Basic Books.

Axelrod, R., & Hamilton, W. D. (1981). The evolution of cooperation. *Science, 211*, 1390-1396.

Brahms, S. (1975). *Game Theory and Politics*. New York: Free Press.

Derman, C., Gleser, L. J., & Olkin, I. (1973). *A Guide to Probability Theory and Application*. New York: Holt, Rinehart, and Winston.

Dixit, A. K., & Nalibuff, B. J. (1992). *Thinking Strategically*. Norton and Company, New York.

Hegselmann, R. (in press). Modeling social dynamics by cellular automata. In W. B. G. Liebrand, R. Hegselmann, & A. Nowak (Eds.). (in press). *Computer Modeling and the Study of Dynamic Processes*. Sage Series on Social Science Computing.

Johnson, N. L., & Kotz, S. (1969). *Distributions in Statistics*. Boston, MA: Houghton Mifflin.

Latane, B. (1981). The psychology of social impact. *American Psychologist, 36*, 343-365.

Lomborg, B. (1992). Game theory vs. multiple agents: Thc iterated prisoner's dilemma. In C. Castelfranchi & E. Werner (Eds.) *Artificial Social Systems*. (pp. 69-93). Springer -Verlag.

Macy, M. W. (1990). Learning theory and the logic of critical mass. *American Sociological Review, 55*, 809-826.

Macy, M. W. (1991a). Chains of cooperation: Threshold effects in collective action. *American Sociological Review, 56*, 730-747.

Macy, M. W. (1991b). Learning to cooperate: Stochastic and tacit collusion in social exchange. *American Journal of Sociology, 97* (3), 808-843.

Marinoff, L. (1992). Maximizing expected utilities in the Prisoner's Dilemma. *Journal of Conflict Resolution, 36* (1), 183-216.

Messick, D. M., & Liebrand, W. B. G. (1995). Individual heuristics and the dynamics of cooperation in large groups. *Psychological Review, 102* (1), 131-145.

Mueller, U. (1987). Optimal retaliation for optimal cooperation. *Journal of Conflict Resolution, 31* (4), 692-724.

Nowak, A., Szamrej, J., & Latan'e, B. (1990). From private attitude to public opinion: A dynamic theory of social impact. *Psychological Review, 97* (3), 362-374.

Nowak, M. A., & May, R. M. (1992). Evolutionary games and spatial chaos. *Nature, 395*, 826-829.

Schelling, T. (1960). *The Strategy of Conflict*. Cambridge, MA: Harvard University Press.

Schuessler, R. (1990). Threshold effects and the decline of cooperation. *Journal of Conflict Resolution, 34* (3), 476-494.

Acknowledgments:

This research was supported by a fund from the the Harry S. Truman Research Institute for the Advancement of Peace at the Hebrew University, Jerusalem. We wish to thank Rainer Hegselmann and Nigel Harvey for very helpful remarks on an earlier draft, and Smadar Alon for her help in preparing the simulation graphs.

Springer-Verlag and the Environment

We at Springer-Verlag firmly believe that an international science publisher has a special obligation to the environment, and our corporate policies consistently reflect this conviction.

We also expect our business partners – paper mills, printers, packaging manufacturers, etc. – to commit themselves to using environmentally friendly materials and production processes.

The paper in this book is made from low- or no-chlorine pulp and is acid free, in conformance with international standards for paper permanency.

MIX
Papier aus verantwortungsvollen Quellen
Paper from responsible sources
FSC® C105338

If you have any concerns about our products,
you can contact us on
ProductSafety@springernature.com

In case Publisher is established outside the EU,
the EU authorized representative is:
Springer Nature Customer Service Center GmbH
Europaplatz 3, 69115 Heidelberg, Germany

Printed by Libri Plureos GmbH
in Hamburg, Germany